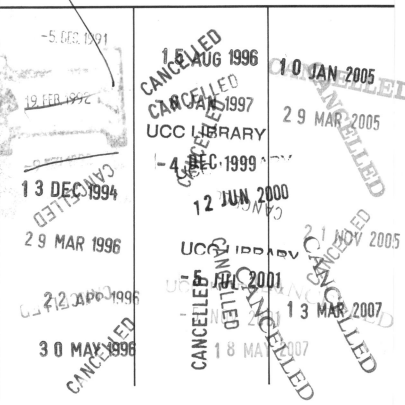

Uniform with this volume:
The Study of Anglicanism
Edited by Stephen Sykes and John Booty
(SPCK/Fortress Press 1988)

THE
ANGLICAN TRADITION

A Handbook of Sources

Edited by

G.R. Evans and J. Robert Wright

SPCK / FORTRESS PRESS

First published in Great Britain 1991
SPCK
Holy Trinity Church
Marylebone Road
London NW1 4DU

First published in the USA 1991
Fortress Press
426 S. Fifth St., Box 1209
Minneapolis, MN 55440

British Library Cataloguing in Publication Data

The Anglican Tradition: a handbook of sources.
    1. Church of England, history
    I. Evans, G. R. (Gillian Rosemary) *1944*– II. Wright, J.
Robert (John Robert) *1936*–
283.42

ISBN 0-281-04496-1

Library of Congress Cataloging in Publication Data

The Anglican tradition: a collection of Anglican documents
edited by G. R. Evans & J. Robert Wright.
    p.   cm.
    Includes bibliographical references and index.
    ISBN 0-8006-2483-1
1. Anglican Communion–History–Sources. 2. Anglican Communion-
-Doctrines. 3. Anglican Communion–Liturgy–Texts. I. Evans, G.
R. (Gillian Rosemary) II. Wright, J. Robert (John Robert), 1936–

BX500B.AB4 1991
283'.09–dc20
                                     90-27180
                                       CIP

Typeset by the Literary and Linguistic Computing Centre,
University of Cambridge
Printed and bound in Great Britain by Biddles Ltd, Guildford
and King's Lynn

This Conference encourages the publication of the proposed Handbook of Anglican Sources, which will reflect the catholicity of our tradition from the beginning and the concerns of the worldwide Anglican Communion today.

Lambeth Conference, 1988, Resolution 66

CONTENTS

FOREWORD
ARCHBISHOP OF CANTERBURY, 1980–91

The comprehensiveness of Anglicanism used to be cited with confidence as a virtue by those explaining the character of our tradition. Yet it does not provide a very satisfying answer to those seeking a coherent account of what Anglicans believe. This handbook provides a more convincing reply. It is not a catechism, but it reflects the integrity and coherence of Anglican belief and practice. Like the Lambeth Conference itself, which encouraged its publication, this book reflects the continuity and identity of our tradition.

I am glad to commend this scholarly yet accessible collection as a rich source for all Anglicans – and others — to draw upon in their understanding of the nature of our Church, in their search for Christian unity and in their service of God's Kingdom.

✠ Robert Cantuar.

Robert Runcie
Archbishop of Canterbury, 1980–91
June 1990

Acknowledgements

Consultative Editorial Board:

The Venerable K.N. Booth	The Church of the Province of New Zealand
The Most Rev. Peter Carnley	The Church of England in Australia
The Rev. Professor Henry Chadwick, KBE	Church of England
The Rev. Canon Simon Chiwanga	The Church of the Province of Tanzania
The Rt. Rev. J.J. Gnanapragasam	The Church in Sri Lanka
Ueda Jintaro	Nippon Sei Ko Kai
The Rt. Rev. Samir Kafity	The Episcopal Church in Jerusalem and the Middle East
The Rev. Peter Lee	The Church of the Province of Southern Africa
The Rev. Dr Leslie Lett	The Church in the Province of the West Indies
The Rev. Aeneas Mackintosh	Scottish Episcopal Church
The Rev. Trevor Mwamba	The Church of the Province of Central Africa
The Rt. Rev. Michael Nazir-Ali	Anglican Consultative Council
The Rt. Rev. J.R.W. Neill	Church of Ireland
The Rev. Canon Jubal P. Neves	Igreja Episcopal do Brasil (Anglicana)
The Rev. D.T.W. Price	The Church in Wales

The Editors gratefully acknowledge the help of:

J. Olu Arufela, Nigeria; Miss Deidre Hoban, Anglican Consultative Council; Miss Elizabeth Hyde, British Columbia, Canada; Professor Robert Bruce Mullin, U.S.A.; The Rt. Rev. Crispus D. Nzano, Mombasa, Kenya; Susan Waymarck, Inglesia Anglicana del Cono sur de América.

The text was prepared and typeset by Beatrix Bown of the Literary and Linguistic Computing Centre of the University of Cambridge, to whose skill, accuracy and inexhaustible patience the editors are deeply indebted. We are grateful to the Centre's Manager, Dr John Dawson, and to the Computing Service of the University of Cambridge (Director: Dr D.F. Hartley), for their willingness to undertake the project.

INTRODUCTION

In this collection of Anglican documents[1] the editors have sought to show the continuity of the history of the Anglican Communion with that of the whole Church throughout the ages. This catholicity of Anglicanism, which is a strong theme of sixteenth and seventeenth century authors, is important for our further purpose of providing a convenient reference book for both Anglicans, and others engaged with Anglicans in ecumenical conversations. The Anglican Church has always understood itself to be a catholic as well as a reformed Church, continuous in faith and worship, and in its common life, with the community of the Apostles. We begin with a series of texts chosen to illustrate the unfolding of Christian understanding of the Faith from the beginning, in writings which did not find their way into the Canon of Holy Scripture, but which reflect the concerns of the faithful in the ancient and medieval centuries. These extracts are included here to show something of that continuity, and to provide a background against which to set the specifically Anglican materials of the sixteenth century and since.[2]

Such a collection must be selective, but we have striven, in consultation with advisers in the Anglican Provinces worldwide, to present a balanced and representative picture of those themes which have, in each generation, seemed important to Anglicans; and to do so against the fuller background of the perennial Christian concerns of faith and order. We have kept to a chronological arrangement as the most generally satisfactory, and provided topical and doctrinal indexes. For historical reasons, the bulk of the material from the sixteenth to the nineteenth centuries derives from the Church of England. But the other Anglican Provinces have contributed material which reflects their own particular concerns and which tells an essential part of the story.

We take Scripture as the primary and normative witness and the basis of the faith of Anglicans, as of all Christians. Everything included here is to be tested against that supreme authority. We begin with a series of extracts which represent the developing

---

[1] See Lambeth Conference of 1988, Resolution 66.

[2] A series of brief comments preceding the texts relates them in many cases directly to the later 'Anglican' extracts.

understanding of Christian faith and order in the universal and catholic Church of the first millennium and a half, among them a number which relate especially to England. These are included because Anglicans share this heritage and it is impossible to make sense either of the sixteenth century Anglican documents, or of our subsequent history, without laying this common foundation.

The unfolding of the story age by age makes it plain not only that certain topics have been of perennial concern, and have regularly needed to be restated or insisted upon; but also that from time to time particular controversies have made an issue especially pressing — one might almost say, fashionable. In the seventeenth century, for example, the debate with the Presbyterians made the question of episcopacy especially urgent; in the same period several thinkers were concerned with 'fundamentals'. In the nineteenth century Lambeth Conferences speak of mission in quite different language, and with quite different assumptions from those which would be appropriate today, when the West is beginning to learn that it does not have a superior 'culture' to offer with its Christian Faith, and indeed has a house of its own to set in order. Similarly, we should not now speak of moral 'purity' in the same language or with the same preconceptions as did the early Lambeth Conferences, because we live in a different climate of thought. The interplay of Christian concern with themes of perennial importance, and of ideas and anxieties peculiarly of their time, is visible throughout the collection. It is a necessary tension because it is here that the duty of the community to maintain the faith entrusted to it meets its equally compelling obligation to preach the Faith to every creature — that is, to the human condition as it finds it. We have given a perhaps disproportionate amount of space to what may be called classic theological matters, and some may feel that we have not left enough room for 'life', for liturgy, or for the issues of peace and justice. We have chosen this balance in the expectation that readers in some parts of the world may find it more difficult to get access to copies of some earlier source-materials than of modern documents on the burning social problems which confront us; and that theological colleges or seminaries in particular may be glad to have these texts in a convenient form.

The editorial process

We must say something of the process by which this collection of sources has been brought together. After the Lambeth Conference of 1988 the Editors discussed the project as widely as possible with many who had special knowledge of particular Provinces. Letters of invitation to name a representative willing to act as a member of the Consultative Editorial Board were then sent out worldwide. Not all Provinces were able to respond with a name, although support for the project was everywhere warmly expressed. Where a local consultant was not, for practical reasons, possible, we have drawn upon the generous help of the Anglican Consultative Council in supplying material. Despite our best efforts the result in this first edition must inevitably be imperfect in its representativeness of the concerns of the whole Anglican Communion. If those within any particular Province would like to see further, or different, texts from their own history, the editors will welcome suggestions to be incorporated in future editions.

We have selected the extracts in consultation with members of the Consultative Editorial Board for each Province, with the intention of providing as comprehensive a coverage as possible of catholic and reformed Anglican tradition. It has not been possible for reasons of space and balance to include everything submitted by those who have helped us in the various Provinces, but a copy of the text at an advanced stage was submitted to the Provinces for comment and approval, and the editors have endeavoured to reflect the mind of the Church faithfully. We have striven to represent the spirit of the Anglicanism of earlier ages, although a few texts written in a polemical mood in earlier centuries have been omitted because it would have required lengthy commentary to set them in context so that they might now serve an eirenic purpose. This has meant some sacrifice of historical exhaustiveness. But we have taken theological consistency to be of higher importance in bringing together materials which portray what we humbly and tentatively trust to be the cumulative common mind of Anglicanism.

Some readers may regret the omission of particular texts, or prefer a rather different balance of items representing the various styles of 'Churchmanship' to be found in Anglicanism. The editors will be glad to receive comments on these lines, again with a view to achieving a more widely acceptable balance in later editions.

Each entry has been given a title to indicate its main theme, although in almost every case other topics are also touched on which may be of equal importance to the reader. As far as possible, every major topic and key term in each entry is covered in the indexes, where complex matters (such as 'episcopacy') will be found to be further indexed under sub-headings, and the reader is referred there to the text by its number. In this way the book may be used either by reading through its contents in sequence in search of material on particular issues, or by beginning with the index.

The entries are dated. Where a text (such as the Thirty-Nine Articles, the Book of Common Prayer, the Ordinal) was issued with revisions on a number of occasions, it appears or is noted under the date of first issue with cross-reference to the later dates.

A source-reference is given for each entry, to facilitate further research. The most commonly cited sources appear in the Abbreviations and are referred to in the text by their standard abbreviation. Where two dates are given, the first refers to the date of first publication, the second to the edition actually used here, where that differs. A very brief indication of date and career is normally given in order to 'place' an author. Many of the texts are prefaced by short comments. In some cases it has been necessary to establish the historical context in which the text was produced, in others to explain a phrase or an emphasis as it affects the purpose or intention of the piece.

For reasons of accessibility, in the case of patristic or medieval documents, we have usually given the text in English where the original language was Latin or Greek. For the sixteenth and seventeenth centuries we have included some documents in their original spelling as examples, but for the most part we have modernized the spelling. In a few cases, texts have been included with English versions. We have retained American spelling for documents of United States origin. Some Provinces have sent documents in languages other than English, and we have printed these with an English translation. Original punctuation has been retained for nineteenth century and earlier documents which give a capital H to the pronoun 'he' and its variants when speaking of the Deity, and which otherwise use capitals where a modern text would not do so. We have not altered the originals so as to make the language 'inclusive' of the feminine gender, because it would be impossible to do so without distorting the historical picture; it is commonly the case that 'he' includes 'she' in the original.

Authoritativeness

We have included both *acta*, or 'official' documents; and *exempla*, or texts which illustrate the concerns of Anglican authors age by age. We have done so in the interests of the fullest possible representativeness, and also because no collection of Anglican sources can be 'authoritative' in any sense which can make it fully 'official'.

It is instructive to consider why this is so. An example may be helpful. William Goode, writing in 1862 (see no. 314), draws a distinction between 'the mere work of an individual', and a text 'set forth with the consent of the Bishops' and with 'the concurrence of the whole English clergy'. He was writing about John Jewel's *Apology* of 1562 in defence of the Church of England, which, he says, was made still more authoritative by the fact that three successive monarchs and four successive Archbishops of Canterbury ordered it 'to be read and chained up in all parish churches throughout England and Wales'. The *Apology*, Goode adds, is also 'recognised in our present Code of Canons, agreed to by the Convocations of Canterbury and York, as "the Apology of the Church of England".' It has been 'always understood to speak the sense of the whole Church, in whose name it is written', and it was always 'publicly received and allowed'. 'Moreover,' Goode concludes, 'Bishop Jewel himself was a man of such weight among the authorities of the Church in his day, that at the revision of the Thirty-Nine Articles in 1571, they were left in his hands for final correction and publication.' William Goode gives many reasons here for regarding a text as carrying some authority for Anglicans: that the author is respected; that it carries the endorsement of those who themselves have authority as ordained ministers, especially of the Bishops (and Jewel himself was a .Bishop); that it was recommended for public reading by Archbishops of Canterbury or by the monarch as exercising a royal supremacy; that it has the backing of Canon Law; that it is publicly 'received'; that it has the consent of the faithful; that it has the synodical or conciliar backing of Convocations. Yet there would be no need to give so many reasons if one were sufficient in itself. The present collection includes documents and extracts which have, in differing degrees, some or all of these kinds of 'authority for Anglicans'.

Some documents may seem to stand out among them as having a better claim than others to be 'official': notably perhaps the Thirty-Nine Articles themselves, the Book of Common Prayer and the Ordinal, or the Resolutions of Lambeth Conferences. The Thirty-Nine Articles, for example, could be seen in the nineteenth century as the 'official document of a public body'.[3] Yet the Lambeth Conference of 1888 resolved that the new Anglican Churches in other parts of the world could not reasonably be expected to accept in their entirety a set of Articles in sixteenth century language and directed towards the calming of, in some cases, peculiarly sixteenth century disquiets (Resolution 19). Similarly, there was no sense in the early Lambeth Conferences that their own Resolutions could carry any 'official' status which would make them binding on all Anglican Provinces. They were simply to be formally communicated 'to the various National Churches, Provinces and extra-Provincial Dioceses for their consideration' (1897, Resolution 3).

It is in this light that we must read the discussions of the 1888 Lambeth Conference on 'authoritative standards of doctrine and worship' (Encyclical Letter). The Conference was profoundly concerned both with 'Home Reunion', that is, with unity among Anglicans, and (as all Lambeth Conferences have been), with the unity of the Church as a whole. In 1888 the assembled bishops put unity in matters of faith first. There must be, they insisted, 'substantially the same form of doctrine' among Christians who share eucharistic Communion (Resolution 19). They underlined the fundamental ecumenical principle that unity is not a matter of compromise, but of truly reaching a common mind (Encyclical Letter). They made an attempt, prompted by the work of the Bishops who had met earlier in Chicago in 1886, to draft a list of the minimum basis on which Churches might come together. This 'Lambeth Quadrilateral' of 1888 proposed four things as essential: Scripture (accepted as containing all things necessary to salvation and as being the rule and ultimate standard of faith); the Creeds as

---

[3]   W.J.E. Bennett, introduction to T.I. Ball on the Thirty-Nine Articles (1877).

a 'sufficient statement of the Christian faith'; the sacraments of Baptism and Holy Communion which Christ himself instituted, 'ministered with unfailing use of Christ's words of Institution, and of the elements ordained by Him'; the 'historic episcopate',[4] 'locally adapted in the methods of its administration' to the varying needs and conditions of Christians in different parts of the world (see no. 355). These are 'standards' in a special sense. They are not propositions to which Christians must assent, but the stuff of Christian life and worship.

It has not been an Anglican concern to seek to create a body of documents deemed to carry an automatic and binding authority for all Anglicans, but to take Holy Scripture as the foundation and to discover as consonant with it 'those truths and institutions which we can trace back to the first age of the Church, and on which all its after life is based' (John Wordsworth, 1902, see no. 373). That is to say, 'There is not... a system of distinctively Anglican Theology. The Anglican Churches have received and hold the Faith of Catholic Christendom'.[5]

---

[4]   On the historic and present position of the episcopal ministry in the Church at large, see *Episcopal Ministry: Report of the Archbishops' Group on the Episcopate* (Church of England), (London, 1990).

[5]   (1922 Doctrine Commission of the Church of England, 1938, p. 25, see no. 412).

Abbreviations

Alberigo

Conciliorum Oecumenicorum Decreta, ed. J. Alberigo et al., 3rd edition (Bologna, 1973).

Becon, *Catechism*

Thomas Becon, *Catechism*, ed. J. Ayre, in *Works*, PS (Cambridge, 1843–4), 3 vols.

Buchanan

The Latest Anglican Liturgies, ed. C. Buchanan (London, 1985).

Cardwell, *Synodalia*

Edward Cardwell, *Synodalia* (London, 1842), 2 vols.

CCSL

Corpus Christianorum Series Latina.

A Communion of Communions

A Communion of Communions: One Eucharistic Fellowship, ed. J. Robert Wright (New York, 1979).

CSEL

Corpus Scriptorum Ecclesiasticorum Latinorum.

Doctrinal Documents

The Christian Faith: Doctrinal Documents of the Catholic Church, ed. J. Neuner and J. Dupuis (New York, 1982), revised edition in translation of *Der Glaube der Kirche*, ed. J. Neuner and H. Roos, 1938, later edns. ed. K. Rahner. The first English translation was published in 1967 as *The Teaching of the Catholic Church*. This collection depends substantially upon the *Enchiridion Symbolorum, Definitionum et Declarationum de Rebus Fidei et Morum* (see DS below). Where the English translation given in *Doctrinal Documents* has been used, the number in the 1982 edn. is given.

DS

Enchiridion Symbolorum, definitionum et declarationum de rebus fidei et morum, ed. H. Denzinger, A Schönmetzer (1854–), (edition of 1965).

Episcopacy Asserted	Jeremy Taylor, *Episcopacy Asserted, Works*, ed. C.P. Eden (London, 1847–54), vol. 5.
Funk	F.X. Funk, *Patres Apostolici* (Tübingen, 1901), 2 vols.
Gee and Hardy	*Documents Illustrative of English Church History*, ed. H. Gee and W.J. Hardy (London, 1896).
Growth	*Growth in Agreement*, ed. H. Meyer and L. Vischer (New York–Geneva, 1984).
Homilies	*Sermons and Homilies appointed to be read in Churches* (London, 1833, repr. 1986 in facsimile).
Hooker, *Ecclesiastical Polity*	Hooker, *Ecclesiastical Polity*, ed. G. Edelen, W. Speed Hill and P.G. Stanwood (Cambridge, Mass., 1977–81).
Johnson	John Johnson, *A Collection of the Laws and Canons of the Church of England* (1720) (Oxford, 1850–1), 2 vols.
Lambeth Conference	The texts and resolutions of the Lambeth Conferences are taken in each case from the official publication.
More and Cross	*Anglicanism: the thought and practice of the Church of England, illustrated from the religious literature of the seventeenth century*, ed. P.E. More and F.L. Cross (London, 1935, repr. 1951).
PG	*Patrologia Graeca.*
PL	*Patrologia Latina*
Prayer Book Spirituality	*Prayer Book Spirituality: A Devotional Companion to the Book of Common Prayer Compiled from Classical Anglican Sources*, ed. J. Robert Wright (New York, 1989).
PS	Parker Society Series (Cambridge, 1840ff).

SC   *Sources chrétiennes.*

Source Book of
  Scottish History   *A Source Book of Scottish History*, ed. W.C.
                           Dickinson, G. Donaldson, I.A. Milne, 2nd edn.
                           (repr. 1963), vols 2 and 3.

Wilkins, *Concilia*   D. Wilkins, *Concilia Magnæ Britanniæ et
                           Hiberniæ* (London, 1737), 4 vols.

Wright and Kelly   *Handbook of American Orthodoxy*, ed. J. Robert
                           Wright and C.P. Kelly (Cincinnati, 1972).

Yarnold   *The Study of Spirituality*, ed. C. Jones, G.
                           Wainwright, E.J. Yarnold (London and New
                           York, 1986).

1
CHRISTIAN BEGINNINGS
96–451

1

c.96
Order in the Church

*Clement I, Bishop of Rome, c.96. Letter to the Corinthians,
Doctrinal Documents, 1701, translation revised.*

Clement, Bishop of Rome, wrote in the name of the Church in Rome to the
Church at Corinth, where there was fierce dissension, and some of the
presbyters had been deposed. Clement reminds the Corinthian Christians that
there needs to be order in the life of the Church and in its ministry, and
describes for them the way in which the ordained ministry is derived from
the apostles. He emphasises the interdependence of mission and order in the
Church. Cf. 8, 20, 40, 43, 94, 115 on 'sacrifice'. See, too, Article xxxi of the
Thirty-Nine Articles.

Exploring the depths of the divine knowledge, we must
methodically carry out all that the Lord has commanded us to
perform at stated times: namely, he has enjoined the offerings and
the services to be performed, not at random or without order, but
at fixed times and seasons. He himself, by his sovereign will, has
determined where and by whom he wants them to be performed.
Then everything being religiously accomplished with his approval
will be acceptable to his will... To the High Priest special functions
have been attributed; to the priest a special place has been assigned
and special services fall to the Levite.[1] The layman is bound by the
precepts laid down for the laity. The apostles received the gospel
for us from the Lord Jesus Christ; Jesus Christ was God's
ambassador. Thus Christ [is sent] from God and the apostles from
Christ; both these dispositions originated in an orderly way from
God's will. Having thus received their mandate and fully convinced
by the resurrection of [our] Lord Jesus Christ, and committed to

---

[1]   It became customary in the early Church to see the threefold ministry
    of bishop, presbyter and deacon as having been foreshadowed in the
    'high priest', 'priest' and 'Levite' of the Old Testament.

the Word of God, they went forth with the full assurance of the Holy Spirit, announcing the good news that the Kingdom of God was close at hand. Preaching from country to country and from city to city, they established some of their first followers as '*episkopoi*' and '*diakonoi*' of the future believers, after having tested them by the Spirit... Our apostles were also given to know by Jesus Christ our Lord that the name [office] of '*episkopos*' would give rise to rivalries. This is why, endowed as they were with a perfect foreknowledge, they established the men mentioned above and for the future laid down the rule that, after their death, other approved men should succeed them in their office. Therefore,... we judge it an injustice to deprive of their office.... those who were established by them, or later by other eminent men, with the consent of the whole Church, and have served Christ's flock faultlessly and humbly.

2

Before *c*.115
A theology of Holy Orders

Ignatius, Bishop of Antioch and Martyr, d. c.115, Letter to the Trallians 1, 1–8, 1: Funk 1, pp. 203–9, also SC 2 (2nd ed, 1951). Tr. The Office of Readings according to the Roman Rite (Slough, 1983), pp. 1131–2, translation revised.

Ignatius' account of the relationship in which the community's pastoral leaders stand to their people, written as it was very early in the Church's history, has been an important influence on the theology of ordained ministry and in particular upon the view that there are properly three 'orders' of ordained ministry. Ignatius' main point is that the community is able to act as one with its minister, that is, that the minister's distinctive function is to unite the Body of Christ. He also emphasises the importance of humility in the Church's leaders.

Ignatius, also called Theophorus, to the holy church at Tralles in the Province of Asia, dear to God the Father of Jesus Christ, elect and worthy of God, enjoying peace in body and in the Spirit through the passion of Jesus Christ, who is our hope through our resurrection when we rise to him. In the manner of the apostles, I too send greetings to you with the fullness of grace and extend my every best wish. Reports of your splendid character have reached me: how you are beyond reproach and ever unshaken in your patient endurance — qualities that you have not acquired, but are yours by nature. My informant was your own bishop Polybius, who by the will of God and Jesus Christ visited me here in Smyrna. He so fully entered into my joy at being in chains for Christ that I came to see your whole community embodied in him. Moreover, when I learned from him of your God-given kindliness towards me, I broke out in words of praise for God. It is on him, I discovered, that you model your lives. Your submission to your bishop, who is in the place of Jesus Christ, shows me that you are not living as men usually do but in the manner of Jesus himself, who died for us that you might escape death... Thus one thing is necessary, and you already observe it, that you do nothing without your bishop; indeed, be subject to the clergy as well, seeing in them the apostles of Jesus Christ our hope, for if we live in him we shall be found in him. deacons, too, who are ministers of the mysteries of Jesus, should in all things be pleasing to all men. For they are not mere servants with food and drink, but emissaries of God's Church; hence they should guard themselves against anything deserving reproach as they would against fire....

All should respect the deacons as Jesus Christ, just as all should regard the bishop as the image of the Father, and the clergy as God's senate and the college of the apostles. Without these three orders you cannot begin to speak of a Church.

I am confident that you share my feelings in this matter, for I have had an example of your love in the person of your bishop who is with me now. His whole bearing is a great lesson, and his very gentleness wields a mighty influence. By God's grace there are many things I understand, but I keep well within my limitations for fear that boasting should be my undoing. At the moment, then, I must be more apprehensive than ever and pay no attention at all to those who flatter me; their praise is a scourge. For though I have a fierce desire to suffer martyrdom, I do not know whether I am worthy of it. Most people are unaware of my passionate longing, but it assails me with increasing intensity. My present need, then, is for that humility by which the prince of this world is overthrown. And so I strongly urge you, not I so much as the love of Jesus Christ, to be nourished exclusively on Christian fare, abstaining from all the alien food that is heresy. And this you will do if you are neither arrogant nor cut off from God, from Jesus

Christ, and from the bishop and the teachings of the apostles. Whoever is within the sanctuary is pure; but whoever is not is unclean. That is to say, whoever acts apart from the bishop and the clergy and the deacons is not pure in his conscience. In writing this, it is not that I am aware of anything of the sort among you; I only wish to forewarn you, for you are my dearest children.

3

*c.*124
Early Christian lifestyle

Letter to Diognetus, c.124, chapters 5–6: Funk 1, pp. 397–401. Tr. The Office of Readings according to the Roman Rite (Slough, 1983), pp. 591–2, translation revised.

The author of this letter seems likely to have been Quadratus of Asia Minor, and 'Diognetus', to whom this piece of Christian apologetic is addressed, perhaps the Emperor Hadrian. See *The Early Christian Fathers*, ed. and tr. C.C. Richardson (London, 1953), pp. 205ff., for a discussion of the evidence.

Christians are indistinguishable from other men either by nationality, language or customs. They do not inhabit separate cities of their own, or speak a strange dialect, or follow some outlandish way of life.... Unlike some other people, they champion no purely human doctrine. With regard to dress, food and manner of life in general, they follow the customs of whatever city they happen to live in, whether it is Greek or foreign. And yet there is something extraordinary about their lives. They live in their own countries as though they were only passing through. They play their full role as citizens, but labour under all the disabilities of aliens. Any country can be their homeland, but for them their homeland, wherever it may be, is a foreign country. Like others, they marry and have children, but they do not expose them.[1] They share their meals, but not their wives. They live in the flesh, but they are not governed by the desires of the flesh. They pass their days upon earth, but they are citizens of heaven. Obedient to the laws, they yet live on a level that transcends the law. Christians

---

[1]   That is, 'expose' unwanted children to death, as was done in some contemporary societies.

love all men, but all men persecute them. Condemned because they are not understood, they are put to death, but raised to life again. They live in poverty, but enrich many; they are totally destitute, but possess an abundance of everything. They suffer dishonour. but that is their glory. They are defamed, but vindicated. A blessing is their answer to abuse; deference is their response to insult. For the good they do they receive the punishment of malefactors, but even then they rejoice, as though receiving the gift of life. They are attacked by the Jews as aliens; they are persecuted by the Greeks; yet no one can explain the reason for this hatred.

To speak in general terms, we may say that the Christian is to the world what the soul is to the body. As the soul is present in every part of the body, while remaining distinct from it, so Christians are found in all the cities of the world, but cannot be identified with the world. As the visible body contains the invisible soul, so Christians are seen living in the world, but their religious life remains unseen. The body hates the soul and wars against it, not because of any injury the soul has done it, but because of the restriction the soul places on its pleasures. Similarly, the world hates the Christians, not because they have done it any wrong, but because they are opposed to its enjoyments. Christians love those who hate them just as the soul loves the body and all its members despite the body's hatred. It is by the soul, enclosed within the body, that the body is held together, and similarly, it is by the Christians, detained in the world as in a prison, that the world is held together. The soul, though immortal, has a mortal dwelling place; and Christians also live for a time amidst perishable things, while awaiting the freedom from change and decay that will be theirs in heaven. As the soul benefits from the deprivation of food and drink, so Christians flourish under persecution. Such is the Christian's lofty and divinely appointed function, from which he is not permitted to excuse himself.

4

177
An early Christian woman as an image of Christ in her martyrdom

The Letter of the Churches of Lyons and Vienne, 177, Eusebius, Ecclesiastical History 5, 1, 17ff.: SC 41 (1955), pp. 10ff. *Eusebius,*

The History of the Church from Christ to Constantine, tr. G.A. Williamson (Penguin, 1965), pp. 196–202.

The heroism of those who were martyred during periods of persecution in the Church is celebrated here so as to hold them up as examples of Christian faith and fortitude.

The whole fury of crowd, governor, and soldiers fell with crushing force on... the deacon from Vienne; on Maturus, very recently baptized but heroic in facing his ordeal; on Attalus, who had always been a pillar and support of the church in his native Pergamum; and on Blandina, through whom Christ proved that things which men regard as mean, unlovely, and contemptible are by God deemed worthy of great glory, because of her love for him shown in power and not vaunted in appearance. When we were all afraid, and her earthly mistress, who was herself facing the ordeal of martyrdom, was in agony lest she should be unable to make a bold confession of Christ because of bodily weakness, Blandina was filled with such power that those who took it in turns to subject her to every kind of torture from morning to night were exhausted by their efforts and confessed themselves beaten — they could think of nothing else to do to her. They were amazed that she was still breathing, for her whole body was mangled and her wounds gaped; they declared that torment of any one kind was enough to part soul and body, let alone a succession of torments of such extreme severity. But the blessed woman, wrestling magnificently, grew in strength as she proclaimed her faith, and found refreshment, rest, and insensibility to her sufferings in uttering the words: 'I am a Christian: we do nothing to be ashamed of.'

Blandina was hung on a post and exposed as food for the wild beasts let loose in the arena. She looked as if she was hanging in the form of a cross, and through her ardent prayers she stimulated great enthusiasm in those undergoing their ordeal, who in their agony saw with their outward eyes in the person of their sister the One who was crucified for them, that he might convince those who believe in him that any man who has suffered for the glory of Christ has fellowship for ever with the living God. To crown all this, on the last day of the sports Blandina was again brought in, and with her Ponticus, a lad of about fifteen. Day after day they had been taken in to watch the rest being punished, and attempts

were made to make them swear by the heathen idols. When they
stood firm and treated these efforts with contempt, the mob was
infuriated with them, so that the boy's tender age called forth no
pity and the woman no respect. They subjected them to every
horror and inflicted every punishment in turn, attempting again and
again to make them swear, but to no purpose. Ponticus was
encouraged by his sister in Christ, so that the heathen saw that she
was urging him on and stiffening his resistance, and he bravely
endured every punishment till he gave back his spirit to God. Last
of all, like a noble mother who had encouraged her children and
sent them before her in triumph to the King, blessed Blandina
herself passed through all the ordeals of her children and hastened
to rejoin them, rejoicing and exulting at her departure as if invited
to a wedding supper, not thrown to the beasts. After the whips,
after the beasts, after the griddle, she was finally dropped into a
basket and thrown to a bull. Time after time the animal tossed her,
but she was indifferent now to all that happened to her, because of
her hope and sure hold on all that faith meant, and of her
communing with Christ. Then she, too, was sacrificed, while the
heathen themselves admitted that never yet had they known a
woman suffer so much or so long.

5

before *c*.189
An Easter homily

*Melito, Bishop of Sardis, d. c.190, Easter Homily 65–71: SC 123,
pp. 95–101.*

This homily, thoroughly scriptural as it is, employs a device of great antiquity
in exegesis. It compares Old Testament figures and events with those of the
New Testament, seeing in them prophetic images or 'types' of what was to
come.

Much was proclaimed by the Prophets about the mystery of the
Passover. That mystery is Christ, and to him be glory for ever and
ever. Amen. For the sake of suffering humanity he came down
from heaven to earth, clothed himself in that humanity in the
Virgin's womb, and was born a man. Having then a body capable
of suffering, he took the pain of fallen man upon himself. He

triumphed over the diseases of soul and body that were its cause, and by his Spirit, which was incapable of dying, he dealt man's destroyer, death, a fatal blow. He was led forth like a lamb; he was slaughtered like a sheep. He ransomed us from our servitude to the world, as he had ransomed Israel from the hand of Egypt; he freed us from our slavery to the devil, as he had freed Israel from the hand of Pharaoh. He sealed our souls with his own Spirit, and the members of our body with his own blood. He is the One who covered death with shame and cast the devil into mourning, as Moses cast Pharaoh into mourning. He is the One who smote sin and robbed iniquity of offspring, as Moses robbed the Egyptians of their offspring. He is the One who brought us out of slavery into freedom, out of darkness into light, out of death into life, out of tyranny into an eternal kingdom; who made us a new priesthood, a people chosen to be his own for ever. He is the Passover that is our salvation. It is he who endured every kind of suffering in all those who foreshadowed him. In Abel he was slain, in Isaac bound, in Jacob exiled, in Joseph sold, in Moses exposed to die. He was sacrificed in the Passover lamb, persecuted in David, dishonoured in the Prophets. It is he who was made man of the Virgin, he who was hung on the tree; it is he who was buried in the earth, raised from the dead, and taken up to the heights of heaven. He is the mute lamb, the slain lamb, the lamb born of Mary, the fair ewe. He was seized from the flock, dragged off to be slaughtered, sacrificed in the evening, and buried at night. On the tree no bone of his was broken; in the earth his body knew no decay. He is the One who rose from the dead, and who raised man from the depths of the tomb. We should understand, beloved, that the paschal mystery is at once old and new, transitory and eternal, corruptible and incorruptible, mortal and immortal. In terms of the Law it is old; in terms of the Word it is new. In its figure it is passing; in its grace it is eternal. It is corruptible in the sacrifice of the lamb, incorruptible in the eternal life of the Lord. It is mortal in his burial in the earth, immortal in his resurrection from the dead. The Law indeed is old, but the Word is new. The type[1] is transitory, but grace is eternal. The lamb was corruptible, but the Lord is incorruptible. He was slain as a lamb; he rose again as

---

[1]   The terms 'figure' and 'type' refer to things and events which are the outward and visible tokens of the eternal and spiritual realities.

God. 'He was led like a sheep to the slaughter',[2] yet he was not a sheep. He was silent as a lamb, yet he was not a lamb. The type has passed away; the reality has come. The lamb gives place to God, the sheep gives place to a man, and the man is Christ, who fills the whole of creation. The sacrifice of the lamb, the celebration of the Passover, and the prescriptions of the Law have been fulfilled in Jesus Christ. Under the old Law, and still more under the new dispensation, everything pointed toward him. Both the Law and the Word came forth from Zion and Jerusalem, but now the Law has given place to the Word, the old to the new. The commandment has become grace, the type a reality. The Lamb has become a Son, the Son man, and man, God.... Come, then, all you nations of men, receive forgiveness for the sins that defile you. I am your forgiveness. I am the Passover that brings salvation. I am the Lamb who was immolated for you. I am your ransom, your life, your resurrection, your light, I am your salvation and your king. I will bring you to the heights of heaven. With my own right hand will I raise you up, and I will show you the eternal Father.

6

c.190
Baptism in the name of the Trinity

Irenaeus, Bishop of Lyons, d. c.202, Demonstration of Apostolic Preaching 6–8: SC 62, pp. 39–44. Tr. Christian Readings, ed. John E. Rotelle (Catholic Book Publishing, New York), IV, p. 7.

Irenaeus explains here why baptism must be administered in the name of the Trinity.

This is the rule of our faith, the foundation of our building, and the consolidation of our way of life. God, the Father, uncreated, unlimited, invisible, one God, the creator of the universe — this is the first article of our faith. The second article is the Word of God, the Son of God, Jesus Christ our Lord, who was revealed by the Prophets in accord with the genre of their prophecies and in accord with the plan of the Father; through him all things have been made. At the end of times, in order to recapitulate all things, he has become a man among men, visible and palpable, so as to

---

2   Isaiah 53.7

destroy death, bring life to light, and effect the reconciliation of God and man. And the third article is the Holy Spirit; through him the Prophets prophesied, our fathers were taught the things of God, and the just were led along the path of righteousness. At the end of times, he has been poured forth in a new manner upon all men, in order to renew them for God over the whole earth. Therefore, the baptism of our new birth is placed under the sign of these three articles. God the Father grants it to us in view of our new birth in his Son through the Holy Spirit. For those who are bearers of the Holy Spirit are led to the Word who is the Son, and the Son leads them to the Father, and the Father confers incorruptibility on us. Without the Spirit it is impossible to see the Word of God, and without the Son one cannot approach the Father. For the Son is the knowledge of the Father, and the knowledge of the Son is had through the Holy Spirit; and the Son gives the Spirit according to the Father's good pleasure. Through the Spirit, the Father is called Most High, Almighty, and Lord of Hosts. Thus, we come to the knowledge of God: we know that God exists, that he is the creator of heaven and earth and all things, the maker of angels and men, the Lord, through whom all things come into existence, and from whom all things proceed, rich in mercy, grace, compassion, goodness, and justice.

7

c.190
The vision of God

Irenaeus, Bishop of Lyons, d. c.202, Against Heresies 4, 5–7: SC 100, pp. 641–9. Tr. Christian Readings, ed. John E. Rotelle (Catholic Book Publishing, New York), I, p. 193, translation revised.

Those who see God will partake of life, for the splendour of God is life-giving. It is for this reason that he who is indiscernible, incomprehensible, and invisible offers himself to be seen, comprehended, and discerned by men: that he may give life to those who discern him and see him. For, if his greatness is inscrutable, his kindness also is inexpressible, and it is out of his kindness that he reveals himself and gives life to those who see him. It is impossible to live without life, and there is no life except by... a partaking which consists of seeing God and enjoying his kindness. In this way, then, men will see God in order to live, becoming immortal through this vision and attaining to God. This is what the Prophets proclaimed, in figurative speech, that God would be seen by those who hear his spirit within them and ceaselessly look to his coming, as Moses said in Deuteronomy: 'We have found out today that a man can still live after God has spoken with him.'[1] He who brings about all things in everyone is invisible and inexpressible, in so far as his power and grandeur are concerned, to all those he has made; however, he is not entirely unknown to them, for all come to know through his Word that there is only one God the Father, who contains all things and gives existence to all things, in accordance with our Lord's words: 'No one has ever seen God. It is God the only Son, ever at the Father's side, who has revealed him.' Thus from the beginning the Son is the Revealer of the Father, since from the beginning he was with the Father. The Prophetic visions, the diversity of spiritual gifts, his ministries, the glorifying of the Father, all that, like a well-composed and harmonious melody he unfolded before the eyes of men at the appointed time, for their benefit...

That is why the Word made himself the dispenser of the Father's grace, for the benefit of men, for whom he accomplished such great mysteries. He revealed God to men and presented man to God, safeguarding the invisibility of the Father... At the same time he made God visible to man through numerous mysteries lest, if he were to be totally deprived of God, man should lose everything, even his very existence... If the revelation of God through creation gives life to all who live on earth, how much more does the manifestation of the Father through the Word give life to those who see God.

8

before 199
The Eucharist

'The Teaching of the Twelve Apostles' (Didache), Didache 9, 1–10, 6; 14, 1–3: Funk 2, pp. 19–22, 26. Tr. The Office of Readings

---

[1]   Deuteronomy 4.33

according to the Roman Rite *(Slough, 1983), pp. 864–5, translation revised.*

The exact date and origin of the *Didache*, or *Teaching*, is not certain, but it undoubtedly preserves early teaching in the Church. It is a code of Christian behaviour, with a manual of Church order. See *Early Christian Fathers*, ed. and tr. C.C. Richardson (London, 1953), pp. 161ff. for discussion of the text. Several familiar elements of the eucharistic liturgy are already established here, together with the emphasis on the importance of coming to Holy Communion with a pure heart and in love and charity with one's neighbours. For early reference to the Eucharist as a sacrifice, cf. nos. 1, 20, 40, 43.

Celebrate the Eucharist as follows: Say over the cup: 'We give you thanks, Father, for the holy vine of David, your servant, which you made known to us through Jesus your servant. To you be glory for ever.' Over the broken bread say: 'We give you thanks, Father, for the life and the knowledge which you have revealed to us through Jesus your servant. To you be glory for ever. As this broken bread scattered on the mountains was gathered and became one, so too, may your Church be gathered together from the ends of the earth into our Kingdom. For glory and power are yours through Jesus Christ for ever.' Do not let anyone eat or drink of your Eucharist except those who have been baptized in the name of the Lord. For the statement of the Lord applies here also: 'Do not give to dogs what is holy.'[1]

When you finish the meal, offer thanks in this manner: 'We thank you, Holy Father, for your name which you enshrined in our hearts. We thank you for the knowledge and faith and immortality which you revealed to us through your servant Jesus. To you be glory for ever. Almighty Ruler, you created all things for the sake of your name; you gave men food and drink to enjoy so that they might give you thanks. Now you have favoured us through Jesus your servant with spiritual food and drink as well as with eternal life. Above all we thank you because you are mighty. To you be glory for ever.' 'Remember your Church, Lord, and deliver her from all evil. Perfect her in your love; and, once she has been sanctified, gather her together from the four winds into the Kingdom which you have prepared for her. For power and glory are yours for ever.' 'May grace come and this world pass away! Hosanna to the God of David. If anyone is holy, let him come. If

---

[1]   Matthew 7.6

anyone is not, let him repent. Maranatha. Amen.' On the Lord's day, when you have gathered together, break bread and celebrate the Eucharist. But first confess your sins so that your offering may be pure. If anyone has a quarrel with his neighbour, that person should not join you until he has been reconciled. Your sacrifice must not be defiled. In this regard, the Lord has said: 'In every place and time offer me a pure sacrifice. I am a great king, says the Lord, and my name is great among the nations.'[2]

9

before *c.*215
A reason to pray standing facing the East

Clement of Alexandria, Priest, d. c.215, *Stromata 7, 7, 39–40: ed. F.J.A. Hort and J.B. Mayor (London, 1903). Tr.* Alexandrian Christianity, *ed. J.E.L. Oulton and H. Chadwick (Library of Christian Classics, 1954), II, pp. 117, 120, translation revised.*

Prayer,... to speak somewhat boldly, is converse with God. Even if we address him in a whisper, without opening our lips or uttering a sound, still we cry to him in our heart. For God never ceases to listen to the inward converse of the heart. For this reason also we raise our head and lift the hands towards heaven, and stand on tiptoe as we join in the closing outburst of prayer, following the eager flight of the spirit into the intelligible world.[1] And while we thus endeavour to detach the body from the earth by lifting it upwards along with the uttered words, we spurn the fetters of the flesh and constrain the soul, winged with desire of better things, to ascend into the holy place. And since the East symbolizes the day of birth, and it is from thence that the light spreads after it has first 'shone forth out of darkness'..., and indeed from thence that the day of the knowledge of the truth dawned like the sun upon those who were lying in ignorance ..., therefore our prayers are directed towards the place where the sun rises. It was for this reason that the most ancient temples looked towards the West in order that

---

2 Malachi 1.11

1 That is, the world open in this life only to the understanding and not accessible to our bodies.

they who stood facing the images might be taught to turn eastwards. 'Let my prayer ascend up as incense before thee, the lifting up of my hands be an evening sacrifice'[2] is the language of the Psalms.

10

before *c*.215
God the teacher

From the Macmillan Book of Earliest Christian Prayers, *ed. J. Forrester Church and Terrence J. Murphy (London, 1988).*

The earliest Christian school prayer, from the adult catechetical school at Alexandria *c.* A.D. 200 , from the *Paedagogus* of Clement of Alexandria.

O Educator, be gracious to thy children, O Educator, Father, Guide of Israel, Son and Father, both one Lord. Grant that we, who follow thy command, may fulfil the likeness of thy image, and that we may see, as far as we may be able, the God who is both a good God and a merciful Judge. Do thou thyself bestow all things on us who dwell in thy peace, who have been placed in thy city, who sail the sea of sin unruffled, that we may be made tranquil and be supported by the Holy Spirit, the unutterable Wisdom, by night and day, unto the perfect day, to sing eternal thanksgiving to the one, only Father and Son, Son and Father, Educator and Teacher, with the Holy Spirit... To him be glory now and forever. Amen.

11

c.215–217
The eucharistic rite of Hippolytus

The Apostolic Tradition of saint Hippolytus, *ed. G. Dix and H. Chadwick (1968), and* Prayers of the Eucharist: early and reformed, *ed. R.C.D. Jasper and G.J. Cuming (London, 1975), pp. 22–3, translation revised.*

---

[2]   Psalm 141.2

This is probably the earliest surviving text of a liturgy of Holy Communion after the New Testament.

The Great Prayer of Thanksgiving

The Lord be with you.	*And with your spirit.*
Lift up your hearts.	*We lift them to the Lord.*
Let us give thanks to the Lord.	*It is meet and right.*

We give you thanks, O God, through your beloved Son Jesus Christ;
whom in the last times you sent to us as Saviour and Redeemer and Messenger of your will;
who is your Word, inseparable from you;
through whom you made all things, and whom in your good pleasure you sent from heaven into the womb of a virgin;
who was conceived and was made flesh and was manifested as your Son, born of the Holy Spirit and the Virgin;
who fulfilling your will and winning for you a holy people, stretched out his hands when he suffered, that by his suffering he might set free those who believe in you;
who, when he was given over to his voluntary suffering, that he might destroy death and break the bonds of the devil, and tread hell under foot, and enlighten the righteous, and establish the limit of hell, and manifest the resurrection,
took bread and gave thanks to you and said,
'Take, eat, this is my body which is broken for you.'
In the same manner also the cup, saying,
'This is my blood which is shed for you. When you do this, do it in remembrance of me.'

Remembering therefore his death and resurrection, we offer you this bread and cup, giving thanks to you because you have counted us worthy to stand before you and minister to you as priests.

And we pray you to send your Holy Spirit upon the offering of the holy Church, gathering into one all who receive these holy things, that we may be filled with Holy Spirit for the confirmation of faith in truth, that we may praise and glorify you, through your Son Jesus Christ, through whom be glory and honour to you, with the Holy Spirit in the holy Church, both now and world without end.

Amen

12

c.215–217(?)
Creeds and professions of Faith

The Apostolic Tradition of Hippolytus (c.170–c.236), theologian of the Church in Rome, Doctrinal Documents, 2. Cf. B. Bottle, La Tradition Apostolique de saint Hippolyte. Essai de reconstitution (Munster, 1963), pp. 48–50.

Written at Rome in the early third century, probably by a Syrian priest, the *Apostolic Tradition* contains a baptismal liturgy.

Do you believe in God, the Father almighty? Do you believe in Jesus Christ, the Son of God, who was born of the Virgin Mary by the Holy Spirit, has been crucified under Pontius Pilate, died [and was buried], who, on the third day rose again, alive, from the dead, ascended into heaven and took his seat at the right hand of the Father, and shall come to judge the living and the dead? Do you believe in the Holy Church and the resurrection of the body in the Holy Spirit?

13

c.251
The unity of the episcopal ministry in the unity of the Church

Cyprian, Bishop and Martyr of Carthage, d. 258, On the Unity of the Catholic Church 5: CSEL 3. pp. 213ff. Tr. Early Latin Theology, ed. S.L. Greenslade (Library of Christian Classics), V, 1956, pp. 126–7.

It is particularly incumbent upon those of us who preside over the Church as bishops to uphold this unity firmly and to be its champions, so that we may prove the episcopate also to be itself one and undivided. Let no one deceive the brotherhood with lies or corrupt the true faith with faithless treachery. The episcopate is a single whole, in which each bishop's share gives him a... responsibility for the whole. So is the Church a single whole, though she spreads far and wide into a multitude of churches as her fertility increases. We may compare the sun, many rays but one light; or a tree, many branches but one firmly rooted trunk. When many streams flow from one spring, although the bountiful supply of water welling out has the appearance of plurality, unity is preserved in the source. Pluck a ray from the body of the sun, and its unity allows no division of the light. Break a branch from the tree, and when it is broken off it will not bud. Cut a stream off from its spring, and when it is cut off it dries up. In the same way the Church, bathed in the light of the Lord, spreads her rays throughout the world, yet the light everywhere diffused is one light and the unity of the body is not broken. In the abundance of her plenty she stretches her branches over the whole earth. Far and wide she pours her generous flowing streams. Yet there is one head, one source, one mother boundlessly fruitful. Of her womb are we born; by her milk we are nourished; by her breath we are quickened.

14

before *c*.254
'Prayer without ceasing'

Origen, Priest and Theologian, d. c.254, Treatise on Prayer *12, 2–13, 1:* Werke, ed. P. Koetschau (Leipzig, 1899–), vol. 7. Tr. Alexandrian Christianity, *ed. J.E.L. Oulton and H. Chadwick (Library of Christian Classics, 1954), vol. II, pp. 261–2, translation revised.*

That man 'prays without ceasing' (virtuous deeds or commandments fulfilled being included as part of prayer) who combines with prayer the deeds he ought to do; and the prayer with fitting actions. For only in this way can we accept 'pray without ceasing' as a saying which can be put into practice, if we speak of the whole life of the saints as one great unbroken prayer; of this prayer that which is commonly called 'prayer' is a part. ... Now if Jesus prays, and does not pray in vain, obtaining through prayer what he asks for (and perhaps he would not have received it without prayer), which of us may neglect prayer?

15

before *c*.254
Your God is too small

Origen, Priest and Theologian, d. c.254, Treatise on Prayer 23,
1–3: Werke, ed. P. Koetschau (Leipzig, 1899–), vol. 7. Tr.
Alexandrian Christianity, *ed. J.E.L. Oulton and H. Chadwick*
(Library of Christian Classics, 1954), vol. II, pp. 283–4.

This is a significant patristic witness to the importance of recognising that the language of Scripture has to use human analogies to express divine realities, and that we must be careful not to let our idea of God be limited by such comparisons.

When 'the Father' of the saints is said to be 'in heaven', we are not to suppose that he is circumscribed in bodily fashion and dwells 'in heaven'; otherwise, if the heaven contained him, God would be found less than, because contained by, the heaven; but we must believe that by the ineffable power of his Godhead all things are contained and held together by him. And, speaking generally, sayings which taken literally are supposed by simple folk to assert that God is in a place, must instead be understood in a manner that befits grand and spiritual conceptions of God....

I think it necessary to consider these sayings carefully in connection with the words 'Our Father which art in heaven,' in order to remove a mean conception of God held by those who consider that he is locally 'in heaven'; and to prevent anyone from saying that God is in a place after the manner of a body (from which it would follow that he is a body) — a tenet which leads to most impious opinions, namely, to supposing that he is divisible, material, corruptible.

16

before *c*.254
Attitudes in prayer

Origen, Priest and Theologian, d. c.254, Treatise on Prayer 31,
2–3: Werke, ed. P. Koetschau (Leipzig, 1899–), vol. 7. Tr.
Alexandrian Christianity, *ed. J.E.L. Oulton and H. Chadwick*
(Library of Christian Classics), vol. II, pp. 323–4, translation
revised.

It seems to me... that he who is about to come to prayer... should put aside every kind of distraction and disturbance of mind, and recollect as far as possible the greatness of him to whom he comes, and that it is a sacrilege to approach him lightly and carelessly and as if with disdain; and he should cast off all alien thoughts. Thus ought he to come to prayer, as it were stretching out the soul before the hands, and directing the mind to God before the eyes; and... raising up the reason from the ground and making it look up towards the Lord of all. All malice towards anyone who appears to have wronged him he should cast aside in so far as he wishes God to bear no malice towards himself, since he has injured and sinned against many a neighbour, or else is conscious of deeds of various kinds that he has committed contrary to right reason. Neither ought he to doubt that, as there are countless attitudes of the body, that attitude in which the hands are stretched out and eyes lifted up is to be preferred to all others, since the body brings to prayer the image, as it were, of the qualities suitable to the soul. We mean, however, that these attitudes should be given preference unless an obstacle opposes. For where there is an obstacle it is permissible... to pray... in a sitting position, or even lying down (because of fever or some such sickness). And also, on account of circumstances, if we are sailing, let us say, or if our business does not allow us to withdraw and offer the prayer that is due, it is permitted to pray without even seeming to do so. And as for kneeling, it ought to be known that it is a symbol of the man who is abject and submissive, and that it is necessary when one is about to accuse oneself of one's sins before God, supplicating him for healing therefrom and for forgiveness thereof. Paul says, 'For this cause I bow my knees unto the Father, from whom every family in heaven and on earth is named.'[1] Spiritual kneeling, so named because every creature falls down before God 'in the name of Jesus' and humbles himself before him, appear to me to be indicated in the words: 'That in the name of Jesus every knee should bow, of things in heaven and things on earth and things under the earth.'[2]

---

[1]   Ephesians 3.15

[2]   Philippians 2.10

17

before *c.*254
Black is beautiful

Origen, Priest and Theologian, d.c.254, Commentary on the Song of Songs 2, 1: Werke, *ed. P. Koetschau (Leipzig, 1899–), vol. 33, pp. 113–14.*

A classic Christian discussion of class and racial difference.

'I am dark and beautiful, o ye daughters of Jerusalem, as the tents of Cedar, as the curtains of Solomon.'[1] In some copies we read: 'I am black and beautiful.' Here again the person of the Bride is introduced as speaking, but she speaks now not to those maidens who are wont to run with her, but to the daughters of Jerusalem. To these, since they have spoken slightingly about her as being ugly, she now makes answer, saying; 'I am indeed dark — or black — as far as my complexion goes, O daughters of Jerusalem; but, should a person scrutinize the features of my inward parts, then I am beautiful. For the tents of Cedar, which is a great nation,' she says, 'also are black, and their very name of Cedar means blackness or darkness. The curtains of Solomon likewise are black; but that blackness of his curtains is not considered unbecoming for so great a king in all his glory. Do not reproach me for my colour, then, O daughters of Jerusalem, seeing that my body lacks neither natural beauty, nor that which is acquired by practice.'... This Bride who speaks represents the Church gathered from among the Gentiles; but the daughters of Jerusalem to whom she addresses herself are the souls who are described as being 'most dear because of the election of the fathers, but enemies because of the gospel.'[2] Those are, therefore, the daughters of this earthly Jerusalem who, seeing the Church of the Gentiles, despise and vilify her for her ignoble birth; for she is baseborn in their eyes, because she cannot count as hers the noble blood of Abraham and Isaac and Jacob, for all that she forgets her own people and her father's house and comes to Christ. The Bride knows that the daughters of the former people impute this to her, and that because of it they call her black, as one who has not been enlightened by the patriarchs' teaching. She answers their objections thus: 'I am

---

[1]   Song of Songs 1.5
[2]   Romans 11.28

indeed black, O daughters of Jerusalem, in that I cannot claim descent from famous men; neither have I received the enlightenment of Moses' Law. But I have my own beauty, all the same. For in me too there is that primal thing, the Image of God wherein I was created; and, coming now to the Word of God, I have received my beauty. Because of my dark colouring you may compare me to the tents of Cedar and the curtains of Solomon; but even Cedar was descended from Ismael, being born his second son; and Ismael was not without a share in the divine blessing. You liken me even to the curtains of Solomon, which are none other than the curtains of the tabernacle of God — indeed I am surprised, O daughters of Jerusalem, that you should want to reproach me with the blackness of my hue. How have you come to forget what is written in your Law, as to what Miriam suffered who spoke against Moses because he had taken a black Ethiopian to wife?[3] How is it that you do not recognize the true fulfilment of that type in me? I am that Ethiopian. I am black indeed by reason of my lowly origin; but I am beautiful through penitence and faith. For I have taken to myself the Son of God, I have received "the Word made flesh";[4] I have come to him "who is the Image of God, the Firstborn of every creature " and who is "the brightness of the glory and the express Image of the substance of God";[5] and I have been made fair. What are you doing, then, reproaching one who turns away from sin, which reproach the Law entirely forbids? How do you come to glory in the Law, and yet to violate it?'

18

256
Rebaptism condemned

*Stephen I, Letter to Cyprian, d. 258, Bishop of Carthage, * Doctrinal Documents, *1401.*

Stephen I, Bishop of Rome (254–7) writes to Cyprian about the opinion he and others hold that baptism by heretics is not valid. The understanding which eventually emerged from this debate is of importance in later centuries

---

[3]   Numbers 12.1–4
[4]   John 1.14
[5]   Colossians 1.15

in connection with the general question of 'unworthy ministers'. (See Article xxvi of the Thirty-Nine Articles.) The sacraments are effective by God's action, not that of the human minister. So, provided that the individual has been baptized with water, and in the name of the Father, Son and Holy Spirit, there has been true baptism; and since baptism cannot be repeated, there should be no second ceremony of baptism.

If, therefore, some come to you from any heresy whatsoever,... let an imposition of hands be made on them by way of penance;[1] for the heretics themselves are right in not baptizing other heretics who come over to them but simply receiving them into their communion.

19

before 258

At one in prayer in one Church

Cyprian, Bishop and Martyr of Carthage, d. 258, On the Lord's Prayer 8–9, 11: CSEL 3, pp. 271–2, 274. Tr. Christian Readings, ed. John E. Rotelle (Catholic Book Publishing, New York), III, p. 221, translation revised.

The Master of peace and unity would not have all men pray singly and severally. For when anyone prays he is not to pray only for himself. For we neither say, 'My Father, who art in heaven' nor 'Give me this day my bread'; nor does each individual pray for his own debt to be forgiven; nor does he ask that he himself alone should not be led into temptation; nor that he only should be delivered from evil.

Our prayer is general and for all; and when we pray, we pray not for one person but for us all, because we are all one. God, the Master of peace and concord, so willed that one should pray for all,... The three youths in the fiery furnace[1] kept this rule of prayer, being in unison in prayer and agreeing in spirit. The authority of the Scriptures tells us this; and in teaching how they prayed gives an example which we ought to imitate in our prayers, so that we

---

[1]   That is, in token that they have repented of their errors and returned to orthodox faith.

[1]   Daniel 3.8–30

might become like them. 'Then these three,' it says, 'with one voice sang, glorifying and blessing God.' They sang with one voice although Christ had not yet taught them to pray. Hence their words in prayer were effectual, because the Lord was gained by simple, peaceful, and spiritual praying. We find that the apostles too prayed in this way after the Lord's ascension: 'Together', we are told, 'they devoted themselves [with one accord] to constant prayers.'[2]

20

before 258
The bishop or priest as icon of Christ

Cyprian, Bishop and Martyr of Carthage, d. 258, Letter 63, 14: CSEL 33, pp. 712ff. 106. Fathers of the Church, tr. S.B. Donna (Washington, 1964), 51, pp. 212–13. See, too, nos, 1, 43, 95, 116 and Article xxi of the Thirty-Nine Articles.

This is an early witness to the tradition that the Eucharist is the offering of a true and complete sacrifice in the Church to the Father. That sacrifice is the Passion of the Lord, the president acting as Christ's representative as he imitates what Christ did in the institution of the Supper. See *The Priesthood of the Ordained Ministry*, Board for Mission and Unity of the General Synod of the Church of England (London, 1986), p. 33, and nos. 1, 8, 40, 43.

If Christ alone is to be heard, we ought not to attend to what anyone else before us thought ought to be done, but what Christ, who is before all, first did. Neither ought we to follow the custom of men, but the truth of God... But if it is not allowed to break the least of the commandments of the Lord, how much more important is it not... in any way to change for human tradition what has been divinely instituted? If Christ Jesus, our Lord and God, is himself the High Priest of God the Father and first offered himself as a sacrifice to his Father, and commanded this to be done in commemoration of himself, certainly the priest who imitates that which Christ did and offers the true and full sacrifice in the Church of God the Father, if he begins to offer according to what he sees Christ himself offered, truly acts in the person of Christ.[1]

---

2   Acts 1.14

1   Latin: *Vice Christi*

21

300–*c*.303
The bishop the normal minister of baptism

The Council of Elvira in Spain, Doctrinal Documents, *1402.*

The Council of Elvira was held at a period when it was felt that discipline and order in the life of the Church needed to be clarified and enforced, after a period of distress under persecution. This text should be read in conjunction with the extract from Innocent I on confirmation (no. 46) and with the service of confirmation in the Book of Common Prayer. The principle which is being underlined here is that the bishop is, as head of the local eucharistic community, the normal officer of baptism, and a Christian baptized by a priest (or in emergency by a lay person), is to be brought to him in due course, not so that his baptism may be in any sense 'completed', but so that the bishop may lay hands on him in token of the gift of the Holy Spirit and as a sign of his belonging to the local as well as the universal Christian community. The usual pattern envisaged by the Book of Common Prayer is of infant baptism, followed by confirmation when the child is old enough to make a profession of faith for himself. The Council of Elvira is concerned with cases of adults baptized by someone other than their bishop, (and in particular by a baptized lay person at a time when they seemed in danger of death), but who will already have made their personal profession of faith.

Canon 38:... A member of the faithful who has been fully baptized... may in case of need arising from sickness baptize a catechumen, so that, if he survives, he will bring him to the bishop that he may be perfected by the imposition of hand.

22

325
The Christian Faith

The Creed of Eusebius, Bishop of Caesarea, Doctrinal Documents, *6.*

In a letter addressed to his diocese (in 325), Eusebius, Bishop of Caesarea, refers to the profession of faith with which he had been baptized. This testifies to the use of this Creed around the middle of the third century. Its historical importance consists chiefly in the influence it exercised on the composition of the Creed of Nicaea.

We believe in one God, the Father almighty, the maker of all things visible and invisible. And in one Lord Jesus Christ, the

Word of God, God from God, Light from Light, Life from Life, the only-begotten Son, first born of all creation, begotten from the Father before all ages, through whom all things were made. For our salvation he became flesh and lived as a man; he suffered and rose again on the third day and ascended to the Father. He shall come again in glory to judge the living and the dead. We believe also in one Holy Spirit.

23

325
The Christian Faith

The First General Council of Nicaea, Creed of Nicaea (325), Doctrinal Documents, 7.

Convened by the Emperor Constantine to affirm the faith in the Arian crisis, the Council of '318 Fathers', from East and West, was held at Nicaea from 16 June to 25 August, 325; a representative sent from Rome by Pope Sylvester attended the Council. Arius, a priest in Alexandria (d. 336), denied the equality of the Son with the Father. The Son was understood by him to have been created in time by the Father and to have been used by him as his instrument for the creation of the world. In its Creed the Council solemnly proclaimed the oneness in being ('consubstantiality') of the Son with the Father; a clear condemnation of the Arian errors is appended. Cf. I. Oritz de Urbina, *Nicée et Constantinople* (Paris, 1963), pp. 69–92. Cf. no. 233.

We believe in one God, the Father almighty, maker of all things, visible and invisible. And in one Lord Jesus Christ, the Son of God, the only-begotten generated from the Father, that is, from the being[1] of the Father, God from God, Light from Light, true God from true God, begotten, not made, one in being[2] with the Father, through whom all things were made, those in heaven and those on earth. For us men and for our salvation he came down, and became flesh, was made man, suffered, and rose again on the third day. He ascended to the heavens and shall come again to judge the living and the dead. And in the Holy Spirit.

---

[1]   Greek: *ousia*
[2]   Greek: *homoousios*

24

c.347
Baptism and the gift of the Spirit

Cyril, Bishop of Jerusalem, d. 386, Mystagogical Catechesis 3, 1–3: SC 126, pp. 120–5. Tr. Christian Readings, ed. John E. Rotelle (Catholic Book Publishing, New York), vol. I, p. 13, translation revised.

Cyril's instruction of those preparing for their baptism on the Saturday before Easter Sunday includes descriptions of the practices in use in mid-fourth century Palestine.

Having been 'baptized into Christ',[1] and 'put on Christ'[2] you have been made conformable to the Son of God; for God having 'predestined us to the adoption of sons',[3] made us 'share the fashion of Christ's glorious body'.[4] Being therefore made 'partakers of Christ',[5] you are properly called Christs, and of you God said, 'Touch not my Christ', or 'anointed'.[6] Now you were made Christs, by receiving the emblem of the Holy Spirit, and all things were in a figure[7] wrought in you, because you are figures of Christ. He also bathed himself in the River Jordan, and having imparted of the fragrance of his Godhead to the waters, he came up from them; and the Holy Spirit in substance lighted on him, like resting upon like. In the same manner to you also, after you had come up from the pool of the sacred streams, was given the unction, the emblem of that wherewith Christ was anointed; and this is the Holy Spirit; of whom also the blessed Isaiah, in his prophecy respecting him, says in the person of the Lord, 'The Spirit of the Lord is upon me, because he has anointed me to preach glad tidings to the poor.'[8] For Christ was not anointed by men with oil or material ointment, but the Father having appointed him to be the Saviour of the whole world, anointed him with the Holy Spirit, as Peter says, 'Jesus of

---

[1]   Romans 6.3

[2]   Romans 13.14

[3]   Ephesians 1.5

[4]   Philippians 3.21

[5]   Hebrews 3.14

[6]   I Chronicles 16.22 Psalm 105.15

[7]   that is, symbolically

[8]   Isaiah 61.1

Nazareth, whom God anointed with the Holy Spirit.'[9] And David the Prophet cried, saying, 'Your throne, O God, is for ever and ever; a sceptre of righteousness is the sceptre of your kingdom; you have loved righteousness and hated iniquity; therefore God, even your God, has anointed you with the oil of gladness above your fellows.'[10] And as Christ was in truth crucified, and buried, and raised; and you in likeness are in baptism accounted worthy of being crucified, buried, and raised together with him; so is it with the unction also. As he was anointed with the spiritual oil of gladness, the Holy Spirit (who is so called, because he is the author of spiritual gladness), so you were anointed with ointment, having been made partakers and 'fellows' of Christ. But beware of supposing this to be plain ointment. For as the Bread of the Eucharist, after the invocation of the Holy Spirit, is mere bread no longer, but the Body of Christ, so also this body ointment, after the invocation, is no more simple ointment, nor (so to say) common, but the gift of Christ; and by the presence of his Godhead, it causes in us the Holy Spirit. It is symbolically applied to your forehead and your other senses; and while your body is anointed with visible ointment, your soul is sanctified by the Holy and lifegiving Spirit.

25

c.347

What it means to call the Church 'catholic'

The Catechetical Instructions of Cyril, Bishop of Jerusalem, d. 386, Catechesis *18, 23–5: PG 33, 1043–50. Tr.* The Office of Readings according to the Roman Rite *(Slough, 1983), p. 926.*

The early Anglicans stressed that the Church in England remained catholic.

The Church is called 'catholic' or 'universal' because it has spread throughout the entire world, from one end of the earth to the other. Again, it is called catholic because it teaches fully and unfailingly all the doctrines which ought to be brought to men's knowledge, whether concerned with visible or invisible things, with the realities

---

[9]   Acts 10.38
[10]   Psalm 45.6

of heaven or the things of earth. Another reason for the name 'catholic' is that the Church brings under religious obedience all classes of men, rulers and subjects, learned and unlettered. Finally, it deserves the title 'catholic' because it heals and cures without restriction every type of sin that can be committed in soul or in body, and because it possesses within itself every kind of virtue that can be named, whether exercised in actions or in words or in some kind of spiritual charism.

26

374–5

The Holy Spirit

Basil the Great, Bishop of Caesarea, d. 379, On the Holy Spirit *9, 22–3: SC 17, pp. 145ff. Tr.* The Office of Readings according to the Roman Rite *(Slough, 1983), pp. 631–2.*

The phrase 'become God' is used by Augustine, too, when he speaks of it as happening in a time of recollection (*deificari in otio*) (Letter 10). It means growing more like God, entering fully into that 'image and likeness of God' in which we were made (Genesis 1.28), not literally 'becoming' God himself.

The titles given to the Holy Spirit must surely stir the soul of anyone who hears them, and make him realize that they speak of nothing less than the supreme Being. Is he not called the Spirit of God, the Spirit of truth who proceeds from the Father, the steadfast Spirit, the guiding Spirit? But his principal and most personal title is the 'Holy Spirit'. To the Spirit all creatures turn in their need for sanctification; all living things seek him according to their ability. His breath empowers each to achieve its own natural end. The Spirit is the source of holiness, a spiritual light; and he offers his own light to every mind to help it in its search for truth. By nature the Spirit is beyond the reach of our mind, but we can know him by his goodness. The power of the Spirit fills the whole universe, but he gives himself only to those who are worthy, acting in each according to the measure of his faith. Simple in himself, the Spirit is manifold in his mighty works. The whole of his being is present to each individual; the whole of his being is preserved everywhere. Though shared in by many, he remains unchanged; his self-giving is no loss to himself. Like the sunshine, which permeates all the atmosphere, spreading over land and sea, and yet is enjoyed by each person as though it were for him alone, so the Spirit pours forth his grace in full measure, sufficient for all; and yet is present as though exclusively to everyone who can receive him. To all creatures that share in him he gives a delight limited only by their own nature, not by his ability to give. The Spirit raises our hearts to heaven, guides the steps of the weak, and brings to perfection those who are making progress. He enlightens those who have been cleansed from every stain of sin and makes them spiritual by communion with himself. As clear, transparent substances become very bright when sunlight falls on them and shine with a new radiance, so also souls in whom the Spirit dwells, and who are enlightened by the Spirit, become spiritual themselves and a source of grace for others.

From the Spirit comes foreknowledge of the future, understanding of the mysteries of faith, insight into the hidden meaning of Scripture, and other special gifts. Through the Spirit we become citizens of heaven; we are admitted to the company of the angels; we enter into eternal happiness, and abide in God. Through the Spirit we acquire a likeness to God; indeed, we attain what is beyond our most sublime aspirations — we 'become' God.

27

381
The Christian Faith

The First General Council of Constantinople, Creed of Constantinople (381), Doctrinal Documents, *12.*

The Council was convened by Emperor Theodosius I to 'confirm the Faith of Nicaea' and to reaffirm it against the Arian current of opinion which had not entirely died out; more particularly the intention was to determine the doctrine of the Holy Spirit — about which Nicaea had remained silent — against various heretical tendencies, notably that of Eunomius and the Macedonians, also called 'Pneumatomachs', who denied his divinity. The Council was held from May to July 381. It was composed of '150 Fathers', all from the East. Pope Damasus was not represented. See the extract from the 'Tome of Damasus' (no. 33) for his endorsement of the Creed.

We believe in one God, the Father almighty, maker of heaven and earth, of all things visible and invisible. And in one Lord Jesus

Christ, the only-begotten Son of God, generated from the Father before all ages, Light from Light, true God from true God, begotten not made, one in being[1] with the Father, through whom all things were made. For us men and for our salvation he came down from the heavens, and became flesh from the Holy Spirit and the Virgin Mary and was made man. For our sake too he was crucified under Pontius Pilate, suffered and was buried. On the third day he rose again according to the Scriptures. He ascended to the heavens and is seated at the right hand of the Father. He shall come again in glory to judge the living and the dead; to his Kingdom there will be no end. And in the Holy Spirit, the Lord[2] and Giver of life, who proceeds[3] from the Father,[4] who together with the Father and the Son is worshipped and glorified, who has spoken through the Prophets. [And] in one Holy Catholic and apostolic Church. We acknowledge one baptism for the forgiveness of sins. We expect the resurrection of the dead and the life of the world to come. Amen.

28

*c.*381–4
The Lenten Fast

The Journey of Egeria, Abbess and pilgrim to Jerusalem, late fourth century, Pilgrimage *27–8: SC 296, 256–8, 264–6.*

---

[1]   Greek: *homoousios*

[2]   Greek: *to Kurion*

[3]   Greek: *ekporeuomenon*

[4]   The Latin translation adds 'and the Son' (*filioque*). This addition was first introduced in Spain in the sixth century; it is found in the profession of faith of the Third Council of Toledo (589). From Spain, it spread to Gaul and Germany. Under the Carolingian Empire, a Synod at Aachen (809) requested Pope Leo III to have it introduced in the entire Latin Church; the Pope, however, did not acquiesce to this request for fear of imposing a clause in addition to the traditional text of the Creed. It was introduced in the Roman liturgy of the Mass by Pope Benedict VIII (d. 1024). The Greeks ignored the *filioque* and denied every right to make any addition to the Creed. The question was later to be discussed between Latins and Greeks at the two union Councils: Lyons II (1274) and Florence (1439). It is still a matter of importance in ecumenical conversations between Orthodox and Western Christians. The Western Churches are now beginning to omit the additional clause.

Egeria: Diary of a Pilgrimage, *tr. George E. Gringras (Ancient Christian Writers, 1979), pp. 97–101.*

This and the following passages, nos. 29–32, describe the passionate devotion of Christians in the Holy Land in the fourth century, and some of the rites and ceremonies they used.

When the season of Lent is at hand, it is observed in the following manner. Now whereas with us the forty days preceding Easter are observed, here they observe the eight weeks before Easter. This is the reason why they observe eight weeks: on Sundays and Saturdays they do not fast, except on the one Saturday which is the vigil of Easter, when it is necessary to fast. Except on that day, there is absolutely no fasting here on Saturdays at any time during the year. And so, when eight Sundays and seven Saturdays have been deducted from the eight weeks — for it is necessary, as I have just said, to fast on one Saturday — there remain forty-one days which are spent in fasting, which are called here... 'Lent'. This is a summary of the fasting practices here during Lent. There are some who, having eaten on Sunday after the dismissal, that is, at the fifth or the sixth hour, do not eat again for the whole week until Saturday, following the dismissal from the Anastasis. These are the ones who observe the full week's fast. Having eaten once in the morning on Saturday, they do not eat again in the evening, but only the following day, on Sunday, that is, they eat after the dismissal from the church at the fifth hour or later. Afterwards, they do not eat again until the following Saturday, as I have already said.

29

*c.*381–4
Catechism before Easter baptism

The Journey of Egeria, Abbess and pilgrim to Jerusalem, late fourth century, Pilgrimage 45–6: SC 296, 304–12, Egeria: Diary of a Pilgrimage, tr. Gringras, pp. 122–5.

At baptism the candidate makes his profession of faith, and must therefore be given careful instruction in the faith beforehand. It was, however, the practice in some early churches to reserve more advanced teaching until after baptism. The bishop is seen here in his role as teacher.

I must also describe how those who are baptized at Easter are instructed. Whoever gives his name does so the day before Lent, and the priest notes down all their names; and this is before those eight weeks during which, as I have said, Lent is observed here. When the priest has noted down everyone's name, then on the following day, the first day of Lent, on which the eight weeks begin, a throne is set up for the bishop in the centre of the major church, the martyrium. The priests sit on stools on both sides, and all the clergy stand around. One by one the candidates are led forward, in such a way that the men come with their godfathers and the women with their godmothers. Then the bishop questions individually the neighbours of the one who has come up, inquiring: 'Does he lead a good life? Does he obey his parents? Is he a drunkard or a liar?' And he seeks out in the man other vices which are more serious. If the person proves to be guiltless in all these matters concerning which the bishop has questioned the witnesses who are present, he notes down the man's name with his own hand. If, however, he is accused of anything, the bishop orders him to go out and says: 'Let him amend his life, and when he has done so, let him then approach the baptismal font.' He makes the same inquiry of both men and women. If, however, someone is a stranger, he cannot easily receive baptism, unless he has witnesses who know him....

[Each day], as soon as the dismissal from the morning service has been given at the Anastasis, immediately a throne is placed for the bishop in the major church, the martyrium. All those who are to be baptized, both men and women, sit closely around the bishop, while the godmothers and godfathers stand there; and indeed all of the people who wish to listen may enter and sit down, provided they are of the faithful.... Beginning with Genesis he goes through the whole of Scripture during these forty days, expounding first its literal meaning and then explaining the spiritual meaning. In the course of these days everything is taught, not only about the resurrection, but concerning the body of faith. This is called catechetics. When five weeks of instruction have been completed, they then receive the Creed. He explains the meaning of each of the clauses of the Creed in the same way he explained Holy Scripture, expounding first the literal and then the spiritual sense. In this fashion the Creed is taught. And thus it is that in these places all the faithful are able to follow the Scriptures when they are read in the churches, because all are taught through those forty days, that is, from the first to the third hours, for during the three hours instruction is given... The dismissal from catechetics is given at the third hour, and immediately, singing hymns, they lead the bishop to the Anastasis, and the office of the third hour takes place. And thus they are taught for three hours a day for seven weeks. ...

Now when seven weeks have gone by and there remains only Holy Week, which is here called the Great Week, then the bishop comes in the morning to the major church, the martyrium. To the rear, at the apse behind the altar, a throne is placed for the bishop, and one by one they come forth, the men with their godfathers, the women with their godmothers. And each one recites the Creed back to the bishop. After the Creed has been recited back to the bishop, he delivers a homily to them all, and says: 'During these seven weeks you have been instructed in the whole law of the Scriptures, and you have heard about the faith. You have also heard of the resurrection of the flesh. But as for the whole explanation of the Creed, you have heard only that which you are able to know while you are still catechumens. Because you are still catechumens, you are not able to know those things which belong to a still higher mystery, that of baptism. But that you may not think that anything would be done without explanation, once you have been baptized in the name of God, you will hear of those things during the eight days of Easter in the Anastasis following the dismissal from church. Because you are still catechumens, the most secret of the divine mysteries cannot be told to you.'

30

*c.*381–4
Palm Sunday celebrations

The Journey of Egeria, Abbess and pilgrim to Jerusalem, late fourth century, Pilgrimage *30–1: SC 296, pp. 270–4,* Egeria: Diary of a Pilgrimage, *tr. Gringras, pp. 103–5.*

The following day, Sunday, marks the beginning of Holy Week, which they call here the Great Week. On this Sunday morning... everyone assembles for the liturgy according to custom in the major church, called the martyrium. It is called the martyrium because it is on Golgotha, behind the cross, where the Lord suffered his Passion, and is therefore a shrine of martyrdom. As soon as everything has been celebrated in the major church as usual, but before the dismissal is given, the Archdeacon raises his voice and first says: 'Throughout this whole week, beginning tomorrow at the ninth hour, let us gather in the martyrium, in the major church.' Then he raises his voice a second time, saying: 'Today let us all be ready to assemble at the seventh hour at the Eleona.' When the dismissal has been given in the martyrium or major church, the bishop is led, to the accompaniment of hymns, to the Anastasis, and there all ceremonies are accomplished which customarily take place every Sunday at the Anastasis following the dismissal from the martyrium. Then everyone retires to his home for a quick meal, so that at the beginning of the seventh hour everyone will be ready to assemble in the church on the Eleona, by which I mean the Mount of Olives, where the grotto in which the Lord taught is located. At the seventh hour all the people go up to the church on the Mount of Olives.... The bishop sits down, hymns and antiphons appropriate to the day and place are sung, and there are likewise readings from the Scriptures. As the ninth hour approaches, they move up, chanting hymns, to the Imbomon, that is, to the place from which the Lord ascended into heaven; and everyone sits down there. When the bishop is present, the people are always commanded to be seated, so that only the deacons remain standing. And there hymns and antiphons proper to the day and place are sung, interspersed with appropriate readings from the Scriptures and prayers.

As the eleventh hour draws near, that particular passage from Scripture is read in which the children bearing palms and branches came forth to meet the Lord, saying: 'Blessed is he who comes in the name of the Lord.'[1] The bishop and all the people rise immediately, and then everyone walks down from the top of the Mount of Olives, with the people preceding the bishop and responding continually with 'Blessed is he who comes in the name of the Lord'[2] to the hymns and antiphons. All the children who are present here, including those who are not yet able to walk because

---

[1]   Matthew 23.39

[2]   *ibid.*

they are too young and therefore are carried on their parents' shoulders; all of them bear branches, some carrying palms, others, olive branches. And the bishop is led in the same manner as the Lord once was led. From the top of the mountain as far as the city, and from there through the entire city as far as the Anastasis, everyone accompanies the bishop... the whole way on foot, and this includes distinguished ladies and men of consequence,[3] reciting the responses all the while; and they move very slowly so that the people will not tire. By the time they arrive at the Anastasis, it is already evening. Once they have arrived there, even though it is evening, vespers is celebrated; then a prayer is said at the cross and the people are dismissed.

31

*c.*381–4
Liturgy for Good Friday

The Journey of Egeria, Abbess and pilgrim to Jerusalem, late fourth century, Pilgrimage *37: SC 296, pp. 284–90,* Egeria: Diary of a Pilgrimage, *tr. Gringras, pp. 110-3.*

Egeria's description shows how objects with sacred associations, and holy places, have helped to bring alive for Christians the historical events of Christ's life and Passion from an early period of the Church's life. As the Scriptures are read, the people, standing at the very place where Christ died, are deeply moved.

[On Good Friday,] following the dismissal from the cross, which occurs before sunrise, everyone... goes immediately to Sion to pray at the pillar where the Lord was whipped. Returning from there, everyone rests for a short time in his own house, and soon all are ready. A chair is set up for the bishop on Golgotha behind the cross, which now stands there. The bishop sits on his chair, a table covered with a linen cloth is set before him, and the deacons stand around the table. The gilded silver casket containing the sacred wood of the Cross is brought in and opened. Both the wood of the Cross and the inscription are taken out and placed on the table. As

---

[3]   That is to say, everyone walks humbly together. The rich and powerful do not ride and are not carried, so that they enjoy no special privileges.

soon as they have been placed on the table, the bishop, remaining seated, grips the ends of the sacred wood with his hands, while the deacons, who are standing about, keep watch over it. There is a reason why it is guarded in this manner. It is the practice here for all the people to come forth one by one, the faithful as well as the catechumens, to bow down before the table, kiss the holy wood, and then move on. It is said that someone (I do not know when) took a bite and stole a piece of the holy cross. Therefore, it is now guarded by the deacons standing around, lest there be anyone who would dare come and do that again.

All the people pass through one by one; all of them bow down, touching the cross and the inscription, first with their foreheads, then with their eyes; and, after kissing the cross, they move on. No one, however, puts out his hand to touch the cross. As soon as they have kissed the cross and passed on through, a deacon, who is standing, holds out the ring of Solomon and the phial with which the kings were anointed. They kiss the phial and venerate the ring from more or less the second hour; and thus until the sixth hour all the people pass through, entering through one door, going out through another. All this occurs in the place where the day before, on Thursday, the Eucharist was offered. When the sixth hour is at hand, everyone goes before the cross, whether it is raining or whether it is hot. This place has no roof, for it is a sort of very large and beautiful courtyard lying between the Cross and the Anastasis. The people are so clustered together there that it is impossible for anything to be opened.

A chair is placed for the bishop before the cross, and from the sixth to the ninth hour nothing else is done except the reading of passages from Scripture. First, whichever Psalms speak of the Passion are read. Next, there are readings from the apostles, either from the Epistles of the apostles or the Acts, wherever they speak of the Passion of the Lord. Next, the texts of the Passion from the gospels are read. Then there are readings from the Prophets, where they said that the Lord would suffer; and then they read from the gospels, where the Passion is foretold. And so, from the sixth to the ninth hour, passages from Scripture are continuously read and hymns are sung, to show the people that whatever the Prophets had said would come to pass concerning the Passion of the Lord can be shown, both through the gospels and the writings of the apostles, to have taken place. And so, during those three hours, all the people are taught that nothing happened which was not first prophesied, and that nothing was prophesied which was not completely fulfilled. Prayers are continually interspersed, and the prayers themselves are proper to the day. At each reading and at every prayer, it is astonishing how much emotion and groaning there is from all the people. There is no one, young or old, who on this day does not sob more than can be imagined for the whole three hours, because the Lord suffered all this for us.

After this, when the ninth hour is at hand, the passage is read from the gospel according to St John where Christ gave up his spirit. After this reading, a prayer is said and the dismissal is given. As soon as the dismissal has been given from before the cross, everyone gathers together in the major church, the martyrium, and there everything which they have been doing regularly throughout this week from the ninth hour when they came together at the martyrium, until evening, is then done. After the dismissal from the martyrium, everyone comes to the Anastasis, and, after they have arrived there, the passage from the gospel is read where Joseph seeks from Pilate the body of the Lord and places it in a new tomb. After this reading a prayer is said, the catechumens are blessed, and the faithful as well; then the dismissal is given. On this day no one raises his voice to say the vigil will be continued at the Anastasis, because it is known that the people are tired. However, it is the custom that the vigil be held there. And so, those among the people who wish, or rather those who are able, to keep the vigil, do so until dawn; whereas those who are not able to do so, do not keep watch there. But those of the clergy who are either strong enough or young enough, keep watch there, and hymns and antiphons are sung there all through the night until morning. The greater part of the people keep watch, some from evening on, others from midnight, each one doing what he can.

32

*c.*381–4
Liturgy for the Ascension

The Journey of Egeria, Abbess and pilgrim to Jerusalem, late fourth century, Pilgrimage 43: SC 296, pp. 298–302, Egeria: Diary of a Pilgrimage, tr. Gringras, pp. 119-20.

Immediately after lunch, everyone, in so far as possible, goes up to the Mount of Olives,... with the result that not a single Christian remains in the city.... As soon as they have climbed the Mount of Olives,... they go first of all ... to the place from which the Lord ascended into heaven. The bishop sits down there, and the priests and all the people, too. Passages from Scripture are read, hymns are interspersed and sung, and also antiphons proper to the day itself and the place are sung. The prayers which are interspersed are said in such a manner that they fit both the day and the place. Then the passage from the gospel is read which speaks of the Ascension of the Lord; then there is the reading from the Acts of the apostles which speaks of the Ascension of the Lord into Heaven after the resurrection. When this has been done, the catechumens are blessed and then the faithful. Then at the ninth hour everyone comes down from there and goes, singing hymns, to the church... in that grotto where the Lord sat teaching the apostles. By the time they arrive there it is already past the tenth hour. Vespers is held there, a prayer is said, the catechumens and then the faithful are blessed.

33

382
The Christian Faith

The Council of Rome 'Tome of Damasus' (382), Doctrinal Documents *(1976 edition), 306.*

Shortly after the General Council of Constantinople (see no. 27), Pope Damasus (366–84) called a Council at Rome to renew the condemnation of errors of the time. Those regarding the Trinity are mainly concerned with the divinity of the Son and of the Holy Spirit, which had been questioned by those who said that only the Father is supreme God, and his Son and the Holy Spirit lesser beings.

We anathematize those who do not with full freedom proclaim that the Holy Spirit is of one power and substance with the Father and the Son. We likewise anathematize those who follow the error of Sabellius in saying that the Father and the Son are one and the same. We anathematize Arius and Eunomius who, with equal impiety in different words, assert that the Son and the Holy Spirit are creatures. Anyone who denies that the Father is always, the Son is always, and the Holy Spirit is always, is a heretic. Anyone who denies that the Son is born of the Father, that is of his divine substance, is a heretic. Anyone who denies that the Son of God is true God, as the Father is true God, that he can do all things, knows all things, and is equal to the Father, is a heretic. Anyone who says that the Son, while incarnate on earth, was not in heaven with the Father, is a heretic. Anyone who denies that the Holy Spirit, like the Son, is really and truly from the Father, of the divine substance, and true God, is a heretic. Anyone who denies that the Holy Spirit can do all things, knows all things and is everywhere present, just like the Father and the Son, is a heretic. Anyone who says that the Holy Spirit is a creature, or made by the Son, is a heretic. Anyone who denies that the Father made all things, that is, things visible and invisible, through the Son and the Holy Spirit, is a heretic. Anyone who denies that the Father, the Son and the Holy Spirit have one Godhead, one Might, one Majesty, one Power, one Glory, one Lordship, one Kingdom, one Will and Truth, is a heretic. Anyone who denies that there are three true Persons, the Father, the Son and the Holy Spirit, equal, living eternally, containing all things visible and invisible, all-powerful, judging, creating and saving all things, is a heretic. Anyone who denies that the Holy Spirit is to be adored by all creatures just as the Son and the Father is, is a heretic. Anyone who has a correct idea about Father and Son, but not about the Holy Spirit, is a heretic, because all heretics who do not think correctly about the Son and the Spirit share in the unbelief of the Jews and pagans. We condemn those who affirm two Sons, one who is before the ages, the other after the assumption of the flesh from the Virgin. We condemn those who say that the Word of God dwelling in human flesh took the place of the rational and spiritual soul, since the Son and the Word of God did not replace the rational and spiritual soul in his body, but rather assumed our soul[1] without sin and saved it. If anyone says that in the passion of the cross it is God himself who felt the pain and not the flesh and the soul which Christ, the Son of God, had taken to himself — the form of servant which he had accepted as Scripture says[2] — he is mistaken.

---

[1]   i.e. a rational and spiritual one

[2]   Philippians 2.7

34

c.386–98
The mission of the Church to society's needs

John Chrysostom, Bishop of Constantinople, d. 407, Homily 50 on Matthew 3–4, ed. F. Field (Cambridge, 1839). Tr. The Office of Readings according to the Roman Rite (Slough, 1983), pp. 1019–20.

Do you want to honour Christ's body? Then do not scorn him in his nakedness, nor honour him here in the church with silken garments while neglecting him outside where he is cold and naked. For he who said: 'This is my body',[1] and made it so by his words, also said: 'You saw me hungry and did not feed me', and 'inasmuch as you did not do it for one of these, the least of my brothers, you did not do it for me'.[2] What we do here in the church requires a pure heart, not special garments; what we do outside requires great dedication. Let us learn, therefore, to be men of wisdom and to honour Christ as he desires. For a person being honoured finds greatest pleasure in the honour he desires, not in the honour we think best. Peter thought he was honouring Christ when he refused to let him wash his feet; but what Peter wanted was not truly an honour, quite the opposite! Give him the honour prescribed in his law by giving your riches to the poor. For God does not want golden vessels but golden hearts. Now, in saying this I am not forbidding you to make such gifts; I am only demanding that along with such gifts and before them you give alms. He accepts the former, but he is much more pleased with the latter. In the former, only the giver profits; in the latter, the recipient benefits too. A gift to the church may be taken as a form of ostentation, but alms is pure kindness.

Of what use is it to weigh down Christ's table with golden cups, when he himself is dying of hunger? First, fill him when he is hungry; then use the means you have left to adorn his table. Will you have a golden cup made but not give a cup of water? What is the use of providing the table with cloths woven of gold thread, and not providing Christ himself with the clothes he needs? What profit is there in that? Tell me: If you were to see him lacking the

---

[1] . Matthew 26.26
[2] Matthew 25.42,44

necessary food but were to leave him in that state and merely surround his table with gold, would he be grateful to you or would he not rather be angry? What if you were to see him clad in worn-out rags and stiff from the cold, and were to forget about clothing him and instead were to set up golden columns for him, saying that you were doing it in his honour? Would he not think he was being mocked and greatly insulted? Apply this also to Christ when he comes along the roads as a pilgrim, looking for shelter. You do not take him in as your guest, but you decorate floor and walls and the capitals of the pillars. You provide silver chains for the lamps, but you cannot bear even to look at him as he lies chained in prison. Once again, I am not forbidding you to supply these adornments; I am urging you to provide these other things as well, and indeed to provide them first. No one has ever been accused for not providing ornaments, but for those who neglect their neighbour a hell awaits with an inextinguishable fire and torment in the company of the demons. Do not, therefore, adorn the church and ignore your afflicted brother, for he is the most precious temple of all.

35

386–401
Conversion

The Confessions *of Augustine, Bishop of Hippo, d. 430, Confessions 8, 12, 28–9: CSEL 33, pp. 194–5. Tr. H. Chadwick (Oxford, 1991), pp. 152–3.*

Augustine's conversion displays characteristic elements of the classic conversion experience: a growing sense of sin, resistance to change, then the sudden release and joy of a 'change of heart' which persists and proves to be a permanent commitment. The year 386 is the date of Augustine's conversion, 401 is the year of the completion of the *Confessions*.

Rivers streamed from my eyes, a sacrifice acceptable to you,[1] and (though not in these words, yet in this sense) I repeatedly said to you: 'How long, O Lord? How long, Lord, will you be angry to the uttermost? Do not be mindful of our old iniquities.'[2] For I felt

---

[1]   Psalm 50.19
[2]   Psalm 6.4

my past to have a grip on me. It uttered wretched cries: 'How long, how long is it to be?' 'Tomorrow, tomorrow.' 'Why not now? Why not an end to my impure life in this very hour?'

As I was saying this and weeping in the bitter agony of my heart, suddenly I heard a voice from the nearby house chanting as if it might be a boy or a girl (I do not know which), saying and repeating over and over again, 'Pick up and read, pick up and read.' At once my countenance changed, and I began to think intently, whether there might be some sort of children's game in which such a chant is used. But I could not remember having heard of one. I checked the flood of tears and stood up. I interpreted it solely as a divine command to me to open the book and read the first chapter I might find. For I had heard how Antony happened to be present at the gospel reading, and took it as an admonition addressed to himself when the words were read: 'Go, sell all you have, give to the poor, and you shall have treasure in heaven; and come, follow me.'[3] By such an inspired utterance he was immediately 'converted to you.'[4] So I hurried back to the place where Alypius was sitting. There I had put down the book of the Apostle when I got up. I seized it, opened it and in silence read the first passage on which my eyes lit: 'Not in riots and drunken parties, not in eroticism and indecencies, not in strife and rivalry, but put on the Lord Jesus Christ and make no provision for the flesh in its lusts'.[5]

I neither wished nor needed to read further. At once, with the last words of this sentence, it was as if a light of relief from all anxiety flooded into my heart. All the shadows of doubt were dispelled.

36

386–401
The eternal Sabbath

Augustine, Bishop of Hippo, d. 430, Confessions 13, 35–8: CSEL 33, pp. 386–8. Tr. H. Chadwick (Oxford, 1991), pp. 304-5.

---

[3]   Matthew 19.21
[4]   Psalm 50.15
[5]   Romans 13.13–4

Lord God, grant us peace; for you have given us all things,[1] the peace of quietness, the peace of the sabbath, a peace with no evening.[2] This entire most beautiful order of very good things will complete its course and then pass away; for in them by creation there is both morning and evening.

The seventh day has no evening and has no ending. You sanctified it to abide everlastingly. After your 'very good' works, which you made while remaining yourself in repose, you 'rested the seventh day'.[3] This utterance in your book foretells for us that after our works which, because they are your gift to us, are very good, we also may rest in you for the sabbath of eternal life.

There also you will rest in us, just as now you work in us. Your rest will be through us, just as now your works are done through us. But you, Lord, are always working and always at rest. Your seeing is not in time, your movement is not in time, and your rest is not in time. Yet your acting causes us to see things in time, time itself, and the repose which is outside time.

As for ourselves, we see the things you have made because they are. But they are because you see them. We see outwardly that they are, and inwardly that they are good. But you saw them made when you saw that it was right to make them. At one time we were moved to do what is good, after our heart conceived through your Spirit. But at an earlier time we were moved to do wrong and to forsake you. But you, God, one and good, have never ceased to do good. Of your gift we have some good works, though not everlasting. After them we hope to rest in your great sanctification. But you, the Good, in need of no other good, are ever at rest since you yourself are your own rest.

37

before *c.*394
There is neither male nor female in God

A reading from A Commentary on the Song of Songs *by Gregory, Bishop of Nyssa, c.394. Homily 7 on the Song of Songs, Jaeger 6, pp. 212–3; PG 44, p. 916, tr. J.R. Wright.*

---

[1]   Isaiah 26.12
[2]   2 Thessalonians 3.16
[3]   Genesis 2.2–3

No one who has given thought to the way we talk about God can adequately grasp the terms pertaining to God. [Where] 'Mother', for example, is mentioned[1] instead of 'Father', both terms mean the same, because there is neither male nor female in God. How, after all, could anything transitory like this be attributed to the Deity, when this is not permanent even for us human beings? For when we all become one in Christ we are divested of the signs of this difference along with the whole of our old humanity. Therefore every name we invent is of the same [limited] adequacy for indicating God's ineffable nature, since neither 'male' nor 'female' can defile the meaning of God's pure nature.

38

before 397
The Christian Faith

The Creed of St Ambrose, Bishop of Milan, d. 397, Doctrinal Documents, *3.*

Ambrose, Bishop of Milan, seems to have been one of the first to speak of an 'apostles' Creed'. He gives a text which he believes to be substantially the same as that in early use in Rome.

I believe in God, the Father almighty, and in Jesus Christ, his only Son, our Lord,
who was born of the Virgin Mary by the Holy Spirit, who suffered under Pontius Pilate, died and was buried.
On the third day he rose again from the dead.
He ascended into heaven, and is seated at the right hand of the Father, wherefrom he shall come to judge the living and the dead.
And in the Holy Spirit, the Holy Church, the forgiveness of sins and the resurrection of the body.

---

[1]   Song of Songs 3.11

39

*c.*404
The Christian Faith

The Creed of Rufinus of Aquilaea c.*404*, Doctrinal Documents, *4.*

Rufinus described the small differences between the text of the Creed used in Aquilaea and that in use at Rome, and, like Ambrose, he speaks of an 'apostles' Creed'. He was a widely travelled Christian scholar and author of the first full commentary on the Creed.

I believe in God, the Father almighty, invisible and impassible, and in Jesus Christ, his only Son, our Lord, who was born of the Virgin Mary by the Holy Spirit, was crucified under Pontius Pilate and was buried.
He went down to the dead.[1] On the third day he rose again from the dead. He ascended into heaven, and is seated at the right hand of the Father. From there he shall come to judge the living and the dead.
And in the Holy Spirit, the Holy Church, the forgiveness of sins and the resurrection of the body.

40

before 407
Priesthood

John Chrysostom, Bishop of Constantinople, d. 407, On the Priesthood *3, 4: ed. J.A. Nairn (Cambridge, 1906); tr. Graham Neville (SPCK, 1964), pp. 70–1.*

For early references to the Eucharist as a sacrifice, cf. nos. 1, 8, 20, 43.

The work of the priesthood is done on earth, but it is ranked among heavenly ordinances. And this is only right, for no man, no angel, no archangel, no other created power, but the Paraclete himself ordained this succession, and persuaded men, while still remaining in the flesh, to represent the ministry of angels. The priest, therefore, must be as pure as if he were standing in heaven itself, in the midst of those powers. When you see the Lord

---

[1]   Latin: *ad inferna*

sacrificed and lying before you, and the High priest standing over the sacrifice and praying, and all who partake being tinctured with that precious blood, can you think that you are still among men and still standing on earth? Are you not at once transported to heaven, and, having driven out of your soul every carnal thought, do you not with soul naked and mind pure look round upon heavenly things? Oh, the wonder of it! Oh, the loving-kindness of God to men! He who sits above with the Father is at that moment held in our hands, and gives himself to those who wish to clasp and embrace him — which they do, all of them, with their eyes. Do you think this could be despised? Or that it is the kind of thing anyone can be superior about?

41

before 407
An Easter Homily

The Easter Homily of John Chrysostom, Bishop of Constantinople, d. 407: PG 52, 765–72. Tr. Wright and Kelly.

The theme of this homily is the triumphant joy of the resurrection and Christ's victory over death.

If anyone be devout and a lover of God, let him enjoy this beautiful and radiant Feast of Feasts! If anyone is a wise servant, let him rejoice and enter into the joy of his Lord. If anyone has wearied himself in fasting, let him now receive his recompense. If anyone has laboured from the first hour, let him today receive his just reward,... If anyone has come at the third hour, with thanksgiving let him keep the feast. If anyone has arrived at the sixth hour, let him have no misgivings; for he shall suffer no loss. If anyone has delayed until the ninth hour, let him draw near without hesitation. If anyone has arrived even at the eleventh hour, let him not fear on account of his delay. For the Lord is gracious, and receives the last even as the first. He gives rest to him that comes at the eleventh hour, just as to him who has laboured from the first. He has mercy upon the last, and cares for the first; to the one he gives, and to the other he is gracious.[1] He honours both the

---

[1]   Cf. Matthew 20.1–16

work and... the intention. Enter all of you, therefore, into the joy of our Lord, and whether first or last, receive your reward. O rich and poor, one with another, dance for joy! O you ascetics and you negligent, celebrate the Day! You that have fasted and you that have disregarded the fast, rejoice today! The table is richly-laden; feast royally, all of you! The calf is fatted; let no one go forth hungry! Let all partake of the Feast of Faith! Let all receive the riches of goodness! Let no one lament his poverty, for the Universal Kingdom has been revealed! Let no one mourn his transgressions, for pardon has dawned from the tomb! Let no one fear death, for the Saviour's death has set us free!

'He that was taken by Death has annihilated it!
He descended into Hell, and took Hell captive!...'[2]
'O Death, where is thy sting? O Hell, where is thy victory?'...[3]
Christ is risen, and you are overthrown!
Christ is risen, and the demons are fallen!
Christ is risen, and the Angels rejoice!
Christ is risen, and Life reigns!
Christ is risen, and not one dead remains in the tombs!
For Christ, being raised from the dead, has become the first-fruits of them that slept,[4] ...To Him be glory and dominion through all the ages of ages!

42

413–27
Good Government

Augustine, Bishop of Hippo, d. 430, The City of God V, 24: CCSL 47, p. 160. Tr. H. Bettenson (Harmondsworth, 1972), p. 220.

We Christians call rulers happy, if they rule with justice; if amid the voices of exalted praise and the reverent salutations of excessive humility, they are not inflated with pride, but remember that they are but men; if they put their power at the service of God's majesty, to extend his worship far and wide; if they fear

---

[2]   Psalm 68.18
[3]   I Corinthians 15.55
[4]   I Corinthians 15.20

God, love him and worship him; if, more than their earthly kingdom, they love that realm where they do not fear to share the kingship; if they are slow to punish, but ready to pardon; if they take vengeance on wrong because of the necessity to direct and protect the state, and not to satisfy their personal animosity; if they grant pardon not to allow impunity to wrong-doing but in the hope of amendment of the wrong-doer; if, when they are obliged to take severe decisions, as must often happen, they compensate this with the gentleness of their mercy and the generosity of their benefits; if they restrain their self-indulgent appetites all the more because they are more free to gratify them, and prefer to have command over their lower desires rather than over any number of subject peoples; and if they do all this not for a burning desire for empty glory, but for the love of eternal blessedness; and if they do not fail to offer to their true God, as a sacrifice for their sins, the oblation of humility, compassion, and prayer. It is Christian rulers of this kind whom we call happy.

43

413–27
Sacrifice

Augustine, Bishop of Hippo, d. 430, The City of God X, 6, 20; XIX, 23: CCSL 47, pp. 278–9, 294; CCSL 48, p. 695. Tr. The Office of Readings according to the Roman Rite (Slough, 1983), pp. 1162–3 and H. Bettenson (Harmondsworth, 1972), pp. 400–1, 889, translation revised.

Cf. nos. 1, 20, 40, 94, 108ff., 116 and Article xxxi of the Thirty-Nine Articles.

Every work that effects our union with God in a holy fellowship is a true sacrifice; every work, that is, which has as its purpose that final end, that ultimate good, by which we are able to be in the true sense happy. As a consequence even that mercy by which aid is given to man is not a sacrifice unless it is shown for the sake of God. Sacrifice, though performed or offered by man, is something divine; that is why the ancient Latin authors gave it this name of 'sacrifice', because it is sacred. Man himself, consecrated in the name of God and vowed to God, is therefore a sacrifice in so far as he dies to the world in order to live for God. This too is part of mercy, the mercy that each one shows to himself. Scripture tells us: 'Have mercy on your soul by pleasing God.'[1] Works of mercy, then, done either to ourselves, or to our neighbour before... God, are true sacrifices. Works of mercy, however, are performed for no other reason than to free us from wretchedness and by this means to make us happy (and we cannot be happy except through that good of which Scripture speaks: 'It is good for me to cling to God.')[2] It clearly follows that the whole redeemed city, that is, the assembly and fellowship of the saints, is offered to God as a universal sacrifice through the great High Priest, who in the nature of a slave offered his very self for us in his Passion, in order that we might be the body of so great a Head. He offered this nature of a slave; he was offered in that nature, because in that nature he is the Mediator, in that nature he is the High Priest, in that nature he is the sacrifice. The apostle urges us to present our bodies 'as a living sacrifice, holy and pleasing to God, and as our spiritual worship',[3] and not to follow the pattern of this world but to be transformed by the renewal of our minds and hearts, so that we may discern what is the will of God, what is good and pleasing and perfect, the total sacrifice that is ourselves. 'By the grace of God that has been given me', he says, 'I say to all who are among you: Do not think more highly of yourselves than you should, but judge yourselves with moderation according to the measure of faith God has given to each of you. As we have in the same body many members, yet all the members do not have the same functions, so we are many, but are one body in Christ; we are each of us members of one another, having different gifts according to the grace that has been given us.'[4] This is the sacrifice of Christians, the many who are one body in Christ. This is the sacrifice which the Church celebrates in the sacrament of the altar, the sacrament known to the faithful; in that sacrament it is made clear to the Church that in the sacrifice she offers, she herself is offered. Hence it is that the true Mediator ... receives the sacrifice 'in the form of God', in union with the Father, with whom he is one God. And yet

---

[1] Ecclesiasticus 30.24

[2] Psalm 73.28

[3] Romans 12.1

[4] Romans 12.3–6

'in the form of a servant' he preferred to be himself the sacrifice rather than to receive it, to prevent anyone from supposing that sacrifice, even in this circumstance, should be offered to any created being. Thus he is both the priest, himself making the offering, and the oblation. This is the reality, and he intended the daily sacrifice of the Church to be the sacramental symbol of this; for the Church, being the body of which he is the head, learns to offer itself through him. This is the true sacrifice; and the sacrifices of the saints in earlier times were many different symbols of it. This one sacrifice was prefigured by many rites, just as many words are used to refer to one thing, to emphasize a point without inducing boredom. This was the supreme sacrifice, and the true sacrifice, and all the false sacrifices yielded place to it. And yet it is we ourselves — we, his City — who are his best, his most glorious sacrifice.

44

413–27
The two cities

Augustine, Bishop of Hippo, d. 430. The City of God, XIV, 28; XVIII, 54: CCSL 48, pp. 451–2, p. 656. Tr. H. Bettenson (Harmondsworth, 1972), pp. 593–4, 842, translation revised.

The two cities were created by two kinds of love: the earthly city was created by self-love which goes as far as contempt for God; the Heavenly City by the love of God carried as far as contempt of itself. In fact, the earthly city glories in itself; the Heavenly City glories in the Lord. The former looks for glory from men; the latter finds its highest glory in God, the witness of a good conscience. The earthly lifts up its head in its own glory; the Heavenly City says to its God: 'My glory; you lift up my head'.[1] In the former, the lust for domination lords it over its princes as over the nations it subjugates; in the other both those put in authority and those subject to them serve one another in love, the rulers by their counsel, the subjects by obedience. The one city loves its own strength shown in its powerful leaders; the other says to its God, 'I

---

[1] Psalm 3.3

will love you, my Lord, my strength.'[2] Consequently in the earthly
city... men who live by men's standards have pursued the goods of
the body or of their own mind, or of both. Or those of them who
were able to know God 'did not honour him as God, nor did they
give thanks to him, but they dwindled into futility in their thoughts,
and their senseless heart was darkened'.[3] In asserting their
'wisdom' — that is, exalting themselves in their wisdom, under the
domination of pride — 'they became foolish, and changed the
glory of the imperishable God into an image representing a
perishable man, or birds or beasts or reptiles' — for in the
adoration of idols of this kind they were either leaders or followers
of the general public — 'and they worshipped and served created
things instead of the Creator, who is blessed forever'.[4] In the
Heavenly City, on the other hand, man's only wisdom is the
devotion which rightly worships the true God, and looks for its
reward in the fellowship of saints; not only holy men but also holy
angels, 'so that God may be all in all'.[5] One of these cities has
created for herself such false gods as she wanted, from any source
she chose — even creating them out of men — in order to worship
them with sacrifices. The other city, the Heavenly City on
pilgrimage in this world, does not create false gods. She herself is
the creation of the true God, and she herself is to be his true
sacrifice. Nevertheless, both cities alike enjoy the good things, or
are afflicted with the adversities of this temporal state, but with
different faiths, different expectations, different loves, until they are
separated by the final judgement, and each receives her own end,
of which there is no end.

45

413–27
Honouring saints and martyrs

*Augustine, Bishop of Hippo, d. 430, The City of God XXII, 10:
CCSL 48, 828. Tr. H. Bettenson (Harmondsworth, 1972), pp.
1048–9, translation revised.*

---

2   Psalm 18.1

3   Romans 1.21

4   Romans 1.25

5   I Corinthians 15.28

It was necessary in the early Christian world, where polytheism was widespread, to guard carefully against any tendency to popular confusion which might lead to idolatry among Christians.

Christian miracles are the work... of God, with the co-operation of the martyrs or in response to their prayers; and the purpose of those miracles is the advancement of that faith by which we believe, not that the martyrs are our gods, but that we and they have the same God. It comes to this: the pagans have built temples for their gods, they have set up altars, established priesthoods and offered sacrifices, whereas we Christians construct, in honour of our martyrs, not temples, as if to gods, but memorial shrines, as to men who are dead but whose spirits are living with God. We do not in those shrines raise altars on which to sacrifice to the martyrs, but to the one God, who is the martyrs' God and ours; and at this sacrifice the martyrs are named, in their own place and in the appointed order, as men of God who have overcome the world in the confession of his name. They are not invoked by the priest who offers the sacrifice. For, of course, he is offering the sacrifice to God, not to the martyrs (although he offers it at their shrine) because he is God's priest, not theirs. Indeed, the sacrifice itself is the Body of Christ, which is not offered to them, because they themselves are that Body... And among all the truths they speak this is the most important: that Christ rose from the dead and first displayed the immortality of the resurrection in his own body, and promised that we should experience it at the beginning of the new age or (which is the same) at the end of this world.

46

416
Chrism, confirmation and the anointing of the sick

Innocent I, Bishop of Rome, Letter to Decentius, Bishop of Gubbio, Doctrinal Documents, *1406 and 1603.*

Several early Fathers speak of the use of oil mixed with balsam for anointing in baptism and confirmation. In ancient practice only bishops may consecrate the chrism (Second Council of Carthage, 390, Canon 3). 'Chrism' is used in some Anglican Churches today, in baptism, confirmation and ordination, and it may be used at the consecration of Churches and the blessing of water for baptism, or of church bells. It is one of the usages which fall under the heading of 'rites and ceremonies' which a Church has 'power to decree' but not to 'enforce' (Article xx and xxxiv of the Thirty-Nine Articles). Oil consecrated for the anointing of the sick differed from chrism from the early Middle Ages in that it did not have balsam added to it, as was usual for chrism from at least the sixth century. In the Anglican Prayer Book of 1549 there was provision for the unction of the sick, but that was omitted in 1552 and subsequently. Recently there has been a series of moves to restore anointing of the sick, with a prayer for the healing of both body and mind, for forgiveness, and for spiritual strengthening. In the Scottish and American revised Prayer Books of 1929; and in the Alternative Book of Occasional Offices and the Prayer Book of 1989 authorized for the Province of South Africa, there is provision for the anointing of the sick. A Form of Unction and the Laying on of Hands was available for English use, in dioceses which approved it, from 1935.

As for the signing of infants [with chrism][1] it is clear that it may only be done by the bishop. For, though the presbyters are priests of the second order, yet they do not have the fullness of the pontificate.[2] That this pontifical authority of confirming[3] or of conferring the Spirit, the Paraclete, is proper only to the bishops is clearly shown, not only by the Church's custom, but by the passage of the Acts of the apostles which affirms that Peter and John were directed to confer the Holy Spirit on those who were already baptized[4] For it is allowed to presbyters when they baptize either in the absence of the bishop or in his presence, to anoint with chrism those who are being baptized, though only with chrism consecrated by the bishop; but not to sign their forehead with the same oil, which is reserved to the bishops when they confer the Spirit, the Paraclete.

...[Your next question] concerns the text from the epistle of the blessed apostle James: 'Is any among you sick? Let him call for the elders of the Church, and let them pray over him, anointing him with oil in the name of the Lord; and the prayer of faith will save the sick man, and the Lord will raise him up; and if he has committed sins, he will be forgiven'.[5] This must undoubtedly be

---

[1] Latin: *De consignandis infantibus*
[2] This is a reference to the question whether the priesthood and the episcopate are two distinct orders in addition to the Diaconate.
[3] Latin: *Ut consignent*
[4] Cf. Acts 8.14–17
[5] James 5.14ff.

accepted and understood as referring to the faithful who are sick and can be anointed with the holy oil of chrism, prepared by the bishop, which can be used for anointing not only by priests but also by all Christians whenever they themselves or their people are in need of it. The question whether the bishop can do what undoubtedly can be done by priests seems superfluous, for priests are mentioned simply because the bishops are prevented by other occupations and cannot visit all the sick. But if a bishop is in a position to do so and thinks it proper, he, to whom it belongs to prepare the chrism, can himself without hesitation visit the sick to bless them and anoint them with chrism.

47

418

Our need for Grace

The Sixteenth Council of Carthage, Doctrinal Documents, *1901–6.*

This contribution to contemporary debate between Augustine of Hippo and Pelagius belongs to a long series of discussions about the way in which grace works in the Christian, not only for the forgiveness of sin, but also to make it possible for the believer to resist sin and to live a good life. At issue were questions still controversial in the sixteenth century about whether 'good works' matter or count in the sight of God, or whether human actions, even when they are made possible by grace, can be good at all. (Compare no. 61 and Articles xii, xiii, xiv of the Thirty-Nine Articles.)

3. Likewise it has been decided: Whoever says that the grace of God by which man is justified through Jesus Christ our Lord serves only for the remission of sins already committed, and is not also a help not to commit them, *anathema sit.*[1]
4. Again: Whoever says that the same grace of God through our Lord Jesus Christ helps us not to sin solely because through it an understanding of the commandments is revealed and opened to us that we may know what we should seek and what we should avoid; but not because through it is given to us the love and the strength to do what we have recognised to be our duty, *anathema sit.* For, since the Apostle says: 'Knowledge puffs up, but love

---

[1]   'Let him be anathema'

builds up',[2] it would be very wrong to believe that we have the grace of Christ for knowledge which puffs up and not for love which builds up; for both are the gift of God: the knowledge of what we should do and the love to do it, so that built up by love we may not be puffed up by knowledge. Just as it is written of God: 'He teaches men knowledge',[3] so too is written: 'love is of God'.[4]

5. Likewise it has been decided: Whoever says that the grace of justification is given to us so that we may do more easily with grace what we are ordered to do by our free will, as if even without grace we are able, though not easily, to fulfil the divine commandments, *anathema sit*. For when the Lord spoke of the fruits of the commandments, he did not say that apart from him we could do things with greater difficulty, but rather: 'Apart from me you can do nothing'.[5]

6. Likewise it has been decided: When St John the apostle says: 'If we say we have no sin we deceive ourselves, and the truth is not in us',[6] whoever takes this to mean that we must say we have sin out of humility, not because it is true, *anathema sit*. For the apostle continues: 'If we confess our sins, he is faithful and just, and will forgive our sins and cleanse us from all unrighteousness'.[7] From this passage it is quite clear that that is not said only out of humility, but also in truth. For the apostle could have said: 'If we say that we have no sin, we are boasting and humility is not in us.' But since he says: 'We deceive ourselves and the truth is not in us,' he clearly shows that anyone who says he has no sin is not speaking truly but falsely.

7. Likewise it has been decided: Whoever says that the reason why the saints say in the Lord's prayer: 'Forgive us our debts'[8] is not that they are saying this for themselves — for such a petition is no longer necessary for them — but for others among their people who are sinners, and that this is why none of the saints says

---

[2]   I Corinthians 8.1
[3]   Psalm 94 (93).10
[4]   I John 4.7
[5]   John 15.5
[6]   John 1.8
[7]   1 John 1.9
[8]   Matthew 6.12

'Forgive me my debts', so that the just man is understood to pray for others rather than for himself, *anathema sit*. For the apostle James was a holy man when he said: 'We all offend in many things.'[9] Why was the word 'all' added, if not to bring the expression into agreement with the Psalm where we read: 'Enter not into judgement with thy servant, for no man living is righteous before thee'?[10] And in the prayer of Solomon, the wise man, [we read]: 'There is no man who does not sin';[11] and in the book of the holy man Job: 'He seals up the hand of every man, that every man may know his weakness'[12] Even the holy and just Daniel used the plural form in his prayer, when he said: 'We have sinned, we have done wickedly'[13] and other things which he there truly and humbly confesses. And lest anyone should think, as some do, that he was not speaking of his own sins, but of those of his people, he said further: 'While I was... praying and confessing my sin and the sin of my people'[14] to the Lord my God. He would not say 'our sins', but he spoke of the sins of his people and of his own sins, for as a Prophet he foresaw that in the future there would be some who would badly misunderstand him.

8. Likewise it has been decided: Whoever holds that the words of the Lord's prayer where we say: 'Forgive us our debts'[15] are said by the saints out of humility but not truthfully, *anathema sit*. For who could tolerate that a man who prays be lying not to men but to the Lord himself, by saying with his lips that he wishes to be forgiven while in his heart he denies that he has any debts to be forgiven?

---

9   James 3.2. Vulgate version
10   Psalm 143 (142). 2
11   1 Kings 8.46
12   Cf. Job 37.7, ancient mistranslation
13   Daniel 9.5, 15
14   Daniel 9.20
15   Matthew 6.12

48

before 428
The kiss of peace

Theodore, Bishop of Mopsuestia, d. 428, Baptismal Homily *4, 33–40, Yarnold, pp. 233–4, translation revised.*

When the bishop and the congregation have exchanged blessings, the bishop begins to give the kiss of peace, and the church herald, that is to say, the deacon, in a loud voice tells all the people to exchange the kiss of peace, following the bishop's example. This kiss, which all present exchange, constitutes a kind of profession of the unity and charity that exists among them. Each of us gives the kiss of peace to the person next to him, and so in effect gives it to the whole assembly, because this act is an acknowledgement that we have all become the single body of Christ our Lord, and so must preserve with one another that harmony that exists among the limbs of a body, loving one another equally, supporting and helping one another, regarding the individual's needs as concerns of the community, sympathizing with one another's sorrows and sharing in one another's joys. The new birth that we underwent at baptism... joins us into a natural unity; and so we all share the same food when we partake of the same body and the same blood, for we have been linked in the unity of baptism. St Paul says: 'Because there is one loaf, we who are many are one body, for we all partake of the same loaf.'[1] This is why before we approach the sacrament of the liturgy we are required to observe the custom of giving the kiss of peace, as a profession of unity and mutual charity. It would certainly not be right for those who form a single body, the body of the Church, to entertain hatred towards a brother in the faith, who has shared the same birth so as to become a member of the same body, and whom we believe to be a member of Christ our Lord, just as we are, and to share the same food at the spiritual table. Our Lord said: 'Every one who is angry with his brother without cause shall be liable to judgement.'[2] This ceremony, then, is not only a profession of charity, but a reminder to us to lay aside all unholy enmity, if we feel that our cause of complaint against one of our brothers in the Faith is not just. After

---

[1]   I Corinthians 10.17

[2]   Matthew 5.22

our Lord had forbidden any unjust anger, he offered the following remedy to sinners of every kind: 'If you are offering your gift at the altar, and there remember that your brother has something against you, leave your gift there before the altar and go; first be reconciled to your brother, and then come and offer your gift.'[3] He tells the sinner to seek immediately every means of reconciliation with the man he has offended, and not to presume to make his offering[4] until he has made amends to the one he has wronged and done all in his power to make peace with him; for we all make the offering by the agency of the bishop.

49

before 430
We have no merit but that
which is the gift of God

Augustine of Hippo, Letter 194, 5, 19: CSEL 44. Tr. W. Parsons *(Catholic University Press, Washington), IV, p. 313.*

What merit, then, do we have before grace which could make it possible for us to receive grace, when nothing but grace produces good merit in us? When God crowns our merits, it is his own gifts that he crowns. For, just as in the beginning we obtained the mercy of faith, not because we were faithful but that we might become so, in like manner God will crown us at the end with eternal life, as the Psalm says, 'with mercy and compassion'.[1] Not in vain, therefore, do we sing to God: 'His mercy shall go before me' and 'His mercy shall follow me'.[2] Consequently, eternal life itself, which will certainly be possessed at the end without end, is in a sense awarded to antecedent merits, yet, because the same merits for which it is awarded are not effected by us through our sufficiency, but are effected in us by grace, even this very grace is so called for no other reason than that it is given freely; not, indeed, that it is not given for merit, but because the merits

---

[3]   Matthew 5.23–4

[4]   That is, not to presume to take part in the Eucharist.

[1]   Psalm 103.8

[2]   Psalm 23.6; Psalm 59.10

themselves are given for which it is given. And when we find eternal life itself called grace, we have in the same apostle Paul a magnificent defender of grace: 'The wages of sin', he says, 'is death. But [God's free gift of grace] is life everlasting in Christ Jesus our Lord.'[3]

50

before 430
The responsibilities of a bishop

Augustine, Bishop of Hippo, d. 430, Sermon 430, on the Anniversary of his Episcopal Consecration, PL 38, 1482–4. Tr. Christian Readings, ed. John E. Rotelle (Catholic Book Publishing, New York) vol. IV, p. 99, translation revised.

Solicitude about my office as bishop has engrossed me since the time this burden was placed upon my shoulders, for I shall have to give a strict account. But what ought we to fear after receiving this grace of the episcopacy? We must fear the danger of being led astray by the honour it brings to us, instead of using that office in a fruitful ministry. Help me, therefore, by your prayers, that he who has deigned to give me this charge may also deign to help me to bear my burden. When you pray in this way for me, it is really for yourselves that you are praying. For what is the burden of which I am speaking, but you? Pray that I may be strong, as I myself pray that you may not be burdensome. For, indeed, our Lord Jesus Christ would never have said that his burden was light if he did not himself bear it along with the one who is charged with it. And you, too, support me. In that way, according to the commandment of the apostle, we shall bear one another's burdens,[1] thus fulfilling the law of Christ. If he does not bear the burden with us, we succumb. If he does not carry us, we fall. If what I am *for* you frightens me, what I am *with* you reassures me. For you, I am the bishop; with you, I am a Christian. 'Bishop', this is the title of an office one has accepted to discharge; 'Christian', that is the name of the grace one receives. Dangerous title! Salutary name!

---

3   Romans 6.23

1   Galatians 6.2

We are tossed around in the whirlpool of that activity as in an immense sea. But, reminding ourselves of the blood with which we were ransomed, and calmed by this thought, we enter, as it were, into a safe harbor. Labouring in a personal task, we find rest in the blessing that is common to all. If I am more pleased to have been redeemed with you, than to be your head, I shall more fully be your servant, and this is what the Lord commands. May I thus not be accountable for the price in virtue of which I have received the favour of being your companion in serving. For I must love my Redeemer and I know what he said to Peter: 'Simon, son of John, do you love me?' 'Feed my sheep.'[2] He said that once, twice, three times. He questioned him about love; he commanded the labour, for the greater the love, the lighter the burden. How shall I make a return to the Lord for all the good he has done for me? Should I dare to say that I reimburse him because I lead his flock to pasture? I am doing that, of course, yet not I, but the grace of God with me.[3] Where then can I discover what is due to me if he goes before me everywhere? For one cannot ask any salary from him whom he loves gratuitously unless the salary is the very one who is loved!

51

before 430
Peter and Paul

Augustine, Bishop of Hippo, d. 430, Sermon 295, 1–2, 4, 7–8: PL 38, 1348–1352. Tr. The Office of Reading according to the Roman Rite (Slough, 1983), pp. 1458–9, translation revised.

This day has been made holy by the passion of the blessed apostles Peter and Paul. We are, therefore, not talking about some obscure martyrs. 'For their voice has gone forth to all the world, and to the ends of the earth their message'.[1] These martyrs realized what they taught: they pursued justice; they confessed the truth; they died for it.

---

2   John 21.15–17
3   I Corinthians 15.10
1   Psalm 18.5

St Peter, the first of the apostles and a fervent lover of Christ, deserved to hear these words: 'I say to you that you are Peter', for he had said: 'You are the Christ, the Son of the living God'. Then Christ said: 'And I say to you that you are Peter, and on this rock I will build my Church'.[2] On this rock I will build the Faith that you now confess, and on your words: 'You are the Christ, the Son of the living God',[3] I will build my Church. For you are Peter, and the name Peter comes from *petra*, the word for 'rock', and not vice versa. 'Peter' comes, therefore, from *petra*, just as 'Christian' comes from Christ. As you are aware, Jesus chose his disciples before his Passion and called them apostles; and among these... Peter alone deserved to represent the entire Church. And because of that role which he alone had, he deserved to hear the words: 'To you I shall give the keys of the Kingdom of heaven'.[4] For it was not one man who received the keys, but the entire Church considered as one. Now in so far as he represented the unity and universality of the Church, Peter's pre-eminence is clear from the words: *To you I give*, for what was given was given to all. For the fact that it was the Church that received the keys of the Kingdom of God is clear from what the Lord says elsewhere to all the apostles: 'Receive the Holy Spirit', adding immediately, 'whose sins you forgive, they are forgiven, and whose sins you retain, they are retained'.[5] Rightly then did the Lord, after his resurrection, entrust Peter with the feeding of his sheep. Yet he was not the only disciple to merit the feeding of the Lord's sheep; but Christ in speaking only to one suggests the unity of all; and so he speaks to Peter, because Peter is first among the apostles. Therefore do not be disheartened, Peter: reply once, reply twice, reply a third time.[6] The triple confession of your love is to regain what was lost three times by your fear. You must loose three times what you bound three times; untie by love that which your fear bound. Once, and again, and a third time did the Lord entrust his sheep to Peter. Both apostles share the same feast day, for these two were one; and even though they suffered on different days, they were as one.

---

2   Matthew 16.18
3   Matthew 16.16
4   Matthew 16.19
5   John 20.23
6   Cf. John 21.15–17

Peter went first, and Paul followed. And so we celebrate this day made holy for us by the apostles' blood. Let us embrace what they believed, their life, their labours, their sufferings, their preaching and their confession of faith.

52

c.430
Mary, Mother of God, and the Incarnation

Cyril, Bishop of Alexandria, d. 444, Letter 1: PG 77, 14–18, 27–30. Tr. The Office of Readings according to the Roman Rite (Slough, 1983), pp. 1453–4.

Cyril wrote this letter during the controversy of the 430s as to whether Mary bore the incarnate Son or merely the 'humanity' of Christ. His letter to the heretic Nestorius with decrees from a Council held at Rome in 430, and another at Alexandria, was approved by the Ecumenical Councils of Ephesus in 431 and Chalcedon in 451.

That anyone could doubt the right of the holy Virgin to be called the Mother of God fills me with astonishment. Surely she must be the Mother of God if our Lord Jesus Christ is God, and she gave birth to him? Our Lord's disciples may not have used those exact words, but they delivered to us the belief those words enshrine, and this has also been taught us by the holy Fathers. In the third book of his work on the holy and consubstantial Trinity, our father Athanasius, of glorious memory, several times refers to the holy Virgin as 'Mother of God.' I cannot resist quoting his own words: 'As I have often told you, the distinctive mark of holy Scripture is that it was written to make a twofold declaration concerning our Saviour; namely, that he is and has always been God, since he is the Word, Radiance and Wisdom of the Father; and that for our sake in these latter days he took flesh from the Virgin Mary, Mother of God, and became man.'... It is held, therefore, that there are in Emmanuel two entities, divinity and humanity. Yet our Lord Jesus Christ is none the less one, the one true Son, both God and man; not a deified man on the same footing as those who share the divine nature by grace, but true God who for our sake appeared in human form. We are assured of this by St Paul's declaration: 'When the fullness of time came, God sent his Son, born of a woman, born under the law, to redeem those who were under the law and to enable us to be adopted as sons'.[1]

53

435-42
The Fall and our rescue by Grace through Christ

The Indiculus, Doctrinal Documents, *503.*

Compare Articles ix and x of the Thirty-Nine Articles. The Indiculus was composed in the course of the controversy over the Semi-Pelagians, probably by Prosper of Aquitaine. (This group, led by the monastic scholar Cassian, held that all men receive an equal measure of grace from God and differences in their reception of it depend on their own response.) The teaching of the Indiculus received the support of the Church very widely in later centuries and was based on papal pronouncements, the decree of African Councils and the doctrine implied in the liturgy. It stresses the helplessness of men and women as a result of the original sin of Adam, the consequences of which all have inherited.

In Adam's sin all men lost their natural power for good and their innocence. No one can of his own free will rise out of the depth of this Fall if he is not lifted up by the grace of the merciful God. This is the pronouncement of Pope Innocent of blessed memory in his letter to the Council of Carthage: 'He [Adam] acted of his own free will when he used his gifts thoughtlessly; he fell into the abyss of sin and sank and found no means to rise again. Betrayed by his freedom for ever, he would have remained weighed down by his fall had not the advent of Christ later raised him up by his grace when through the cleansing of a new regeneration he washed away all previous guilt in the bath of baptism'.

---

[1]   Galatians 4.4

54

before 450
The test of true Faith

The first instruction by Vincent of Lérins, before 450,
Commonitorium 2, 1–3: ed. R.S. Moxon (Cambridge, 1915), 7–11.

This famous 'dictum' describes the consensus of the faithful as the most
reliable test of orthodoxy. Vincent, monk of Lérins, formulated the
'Vincentian canon' which says that the truths of faith are to be tested by
whether they have been accepted by the *consensus fidelium*, the consent of
the faithful, 'always, everywhere and by everyone'. He also asked whether
understanding of the Faith can develop in the Church. In all this he saw
Scripture as the bedrock. See no. 55.

I have... continually given the greatest pains and diligence to
inquiring, from the greatest possible number of men outstanding in
holiness and in doctrine, how I can secure a kind of fixed and, as
it were, general and guiding principle for distinguishing the true
catholic Faith from the degraded falsehoods of heresy. And the
answer that I receive is always to this effect: that if I wish, or
indeed if anyone wishes, to detect the deceits of heretics that arise,
and to avoid the snares and to keep healthy and sound in a healthy
faith, we ought, with the Lord's help, to fortify our faith in a
twofold manner: firstly, that is, by the authority of God's Law;
then by the tradition of the Catholic Church. Here, it may be,
someone will ask, since the canon of Scripture is complete, and is
in itself abundantly sufficient, what need is there to join to it the
interpretation of the Church? The answer is that because of the
very depth of Scripture all men do not place one identical
interpretation upon it. The statements of the same writer are
explained by different men in different ways, so much so that it
seems almost possible to extract from it as many opinions as there
are men.... Therefore, because of the intricacies of error, which is
so multiform, there is great need for the laying down of a rule for
the exposition of Prophets and apostles in accordance with the
standard of the interpretation of the Church Catholic. Now in that
Catholic Church itself was taken the greatest care to hold THAT
WHICH HAS BEEN BELIEVED EVERYWHERE, ALWAYS AND BY ALL. That is
truly and properly 'catholic', as is shown by the very force and
meaning of the word, which comprehends everything almost
universally. We shall hold to this rule if we follow universality [i.e.

oecumenicity], antiquity, and consent. We shall follow universality if we acknowledge that one Faith to be true which the whole Church throughout the world confesses; antiquity, if we in no wise depart from those interpretations which it is clear that our ancestors and fathers proclaimed; consent, if in antiquity itself we keep following the definitions and opinions of all.

55

before c.450
Development and the 'test' of catholicity

Vincent of Lérins, d. c.450, Commonitorium *23, pp. 28–30: ed. R.S. Moxon (Cambridge, 1915), pp. 88–92. Tr.* The Office of Readings according to the Roman Rite *(Slough, 1983), pp. 1140–1.*

Is there to be no development of religion in the Church of Christ? Certainly, there is to be development and on the largest scale. Who can be so grudging to men, so full of hate for God, as to try to prevent it? But it must truly be development of the Faith, not alteration of the Faith. Development means that each thing expands to be itself, while alteration means that a thing is changed from one thing into another. The understanding, knowledge and wisdom of one and all, of individuals as well as of the whole Church, ought then to make great and vigorous progress with the passing of the ages and the centuries, but only along its own line of development, that is, with the same doctrine, the same meaning and the same import. The religion of souls should follow the law of development of bodies. Though bodies develop and unfold their component parts with the passing of the years, they always remain what they were. There is a great difference between the flower of childhood and the maturity of age, but those who become old are the very same people who were once young. Though the condition and appearance of one and the same individual may change, it is one and the same nature, one and the same person... If, however, the human form were to turn into some shape that did not belong to its own nature, or even if something were added to the sum of its members or subtracted from it, the whole body would necessarily perish or become grotesque or at least be enfeebled. In the same way, the doctrine of the Christian religion should properly follow these laws of development, that is, by becoming firmer over the years, more ample in the course of time, more exalted as it advances in age. In ancient times our ancestors sowed the good seed in the harvest field of the Church. It would be very wrong and unfitting if we, their descendants, were to reap, not the genuine wheat of truth but the intrusive growth of error. On the contrary, what is right and fitting is this: there should be no inconsistency between first and last, but we should reap true doctrine from the growth of true teaching, so that when, in the course of time, those first sowings yield an increase it may flourish and be tended in our day also.

2

ONE CHURCH

451–1054

56

451
The incarnate Son

The General Council of Chalcedon, Creed of Chalcedon, Doctrinal Documents, *613–16.*

The Council of Chalcedon repudiated the heresies of Nestorius (who taught that Mary did not 'bear God', but that there were two Persons in Christ, a divine and a human), and Eutyches (who taught Monophysitism, that, on the contrary, there was not only a single Person, but also a single nature). The Chalcedonian Definition was accepted by all Churches in the East and West, except the Monophysites, whose modern descendants are the Coptic Churches, the Syrian Jacobites and the Armenians. Compare the Third General Council of Constantinople, 681. On the ecumenical position today, see extract on Oriental Orthodox relations no. 589. In giving the title 'One Church' to Part II we have not intended to exclude these heirs of the non-Chalcedonian Churches, but merely to reflect the understanding of later centuries that the Church had now entered a period of unity in faith and order.

(Prologue)
[The Council] opposes those who attempt to divide the mystery of the incarnation into two 'sons'. It excludes from the sacred assembly those who dare to declare subject to suffering the divinity of the only-begotten. It withstands those who imagine a mixture or confusion of Christ's two natures.[1] It rejects those who fancy that the form of servant assumed by him among us is of a heavenly nature and foreign to ours in essence.[2] It condemns those who invent the myth of two natures of the Lord before the union and of one nature after the union.

(Definition)
Therefore, following the holy Fathers, we unanimously teach to

---

[1]   Greek: *physis*

[2]   Greek: *ousia*

confess one and the same Son, our Lord Jesus Christ, the same perfect in divinity and perfect in humanity, the same truly God and truly man composed of rational soul and body, the same one in being[3] with the Father as to the divinity and one in being with us as to the humanity, like unto us in all things but sin.[4] The same was begotten from the Father before the ages as to the divinity and in the latter days for us and our salvation was born as to his humanity from Mary the Virgin Mother of God. We confess that one and the same Lord Jesus Christ, the only-begotten Son, must be acknowledged in two natures, without confusion or change, without division or separation. The distinction between the natures was never abolished by their union but rather the character proper to each of the two natures was preserved as they came together in one Person[5] and one hypostasis. He is not split or divided into two persons, but he is one and the same only-begotten, God in the Word, the Lord Jesus Christ, as formerly the Prophets and later Jesus Christ himself have taught us about him and as has been handed down to us by the Creed of the Fathers. As these points have been determined by us with all possible precision and care, the holy ecumenical Council has ordained that no one may propose, put into writing, devise, hold or teach to others any other faith than this.

57

after 451?

The Christian Faith

The Pseudo-Athanasian Symbol, Quicumque, *Doctrinal Documents, 16–17.*

This Creed has, since the seventh century, been wrongly attributed to Athanasius of Alexandria (d. 373), who had attended the Council of Nicaea as a deacon and had later become the champion of the Nicene faith in the East. In reality, it is an original Latin composition belonging to the end of the fifth century, the author of which remains unknown. It has enjoyed great authority in the Latin Church; its rhythmic character has contributed to its

---

[3]   Greek: *homoousios*

[4]   Cf. Hebrews 4.15

[5]   Greek: *prosopon*

widespread diffusion among various Western Liturgies. Cf. J.N.D. Kelly, *The Athanasian Creed* (London, 1964).

Whoever wishes to be saved must, first of all, hold the catholic Faith, for, unless he keeps it whole and inviolate, he will undoubtedly perish for ever. Now this is the catholic Faith: We worship one God in the Trinity and the Trinity in unity, without either confusing the persons or dividing the substance; for the person of the Father is one, the Son's is another, the Holy Spirit's another; but the Godhead of Father, Son and Holy Spirit is one, their glory equal, their majesty equally eternal. Such as the Father is, such is the Son, such also the Holy Spirit; uncreated is the Father, uncreated the Son, uncreated the Holy Spirit; infinite[1] is the Father, infinite the Son, infinite the Holy Spirit; eternal is the Father, eternal the Son, eternal the Holy Spirit; yet, they are not three eternal beings but one eternal, just as they are not three uncreated beings or three infinite beings but one uncreated and one infinite. In the same way, almighty is the Father, almighty the Son, almighty the Holy Spirit; yet, they are not three almighty beings but one almighty. Thus, the Father is God, the Son is God, the Holy Spirit is God; yet, they are not three gods but one God. Thus, the Father is Lord, the Son is Lord, the Holy Spirit is Lord; yet, they are not three lords but one Lord. For, as Christian truth compels us to acknowledge each person distinctly as God and Lord, so too the catholic religion forbids us to speak of three gods or lords. The Father has neither been made by anyone, nor is he created or begotten; the Son is from the Father alone, not made nor created but begotten; the Holy Spirit is from the Father and the Son, not made nor created nor begotten, but proceeding. So there is one Father, not three Fathers; one Son, not three Sons; one Holy Spirit, not three Holy Spirits. And in this Trinity there is no before or after, no greater or lesser, but all three persons are equally eternal with each other and fully equal. Thus, in all things, as has already been stated above, both unity in the Trinity and Trinity in the unity must be worshipped. Let him therefore who wishes to be saved think this of the Trinity. For his eternal salvation it is necessary, however that he should also faithfully believe in the incarnation of our Lord Jesus Christ.

---

[1]   Latin: *immensus*

Here then is the right faith: We believe and confess that our Lord Jesus Christ, the Son of God, is both and equally God and man. He is God from the substance of the Father, begotten before the ages, and he is man from the substance of a mother, born in time; perfect God and perfect man, composed of a rational soul and a human body; equal to the Father as to his divinity, less than the Father as to his humanity. Although he is God and man, he is nevertheless one Christ, not two; however, not one because the divinity has been changed into a human body, but because the humanity has been assumed into God; entirely one, not by a confusion of substance but by the unity of personhood. For, as a rational soul and a body are a single man, so God and man are one Christ. He suffered for our salvation, went down to the underworld,[2] rose again from the dead on the third day, ascended to the heavens, is seated at the right hand of the Father, wherefrom he shall come to judge the living and the dead. At his coming all men are to rise again with their bodies and to render an account of their own deeds; those who have done good will go to eternal life, but those who have done evil to eternal fire. This is the catholic Faith. Unless one believes it faithfully and firmly, he cannot be saved.

58

452
Reconciliation

Leo I, Bishop of Rome (440–461), Letter to Theodore, Bishop of Frejus, Doctrinal Documents, *1605, translation revised.*

We see here an affirmation of the principle that there is forgiveness for those who fall into sin after baptism, a hope which some early Christian communities denied, on the grounds that those who set their hands to the plough and then look back are not fit for the Kingdom of Heaven. It was required in early Christian communities that the penitent should demonstrate the sincerity of their repentance through acts of penance, so that they and the community could know that they had tried to make up for their wrongdoing. Article xvi of the Thirty-Nine Articles declares that 'grant of repentance is not to be denied to such as fall into sin after baptism'. It is also affirmed that bishops have authority in the Church to declare God's forgiveness to those

---

[2]   Latin: *ad infernos*

who repent, and show the sincerity of their repentance in newness of life, and to welcome them back to the sacramental life of the community. Anglican practice, like that of the whole Church in the West in the Middle Ages, allows priests as well as bishops to declare God's forgiveness. The 'warning for the celebration of Holy Communion' in the Book of Common Prayer invites those whose consciences are troubled to come to a minister 'that by the ministry of God's holy Word they may receive the benefit of absolution', and it is expected that repentant sinners will show 'amendment of life'. Matins and Evensong, as well as Holy Communion, include a General Confession and an Absolution. Cf. no. 234.

God's manifold mercy comes to the aid of men who have fallen so that the hope of eternal life may be restored not only through the grace of baptism but also through the remedy of penance. Thus, those who have violated the gifts of their new birth can come to the forgiveness of their crimes by a judgement in which they condemn themselves... For 'the mediator between God and men, the man Jesus Christ'[1] gave to those who hold authority in the Church the power to grant the discipline of penance to those who confess and, after they have been purified by making salutary satisfaction, to admit them to the communion of the sacraments through the door of reconciliation.

59

459
Private Confession

Leo I, Bishop of Rome, (440–461), Letter to the bishops of Roman Rural Districts, Doctrinal Documents *1606, translation revised.*

This extract illustrates a general change of penitential practice, especially in the West, from the 'public penance' of the early Church to the 'private penance' of the Middle Ages. The early practice laid stress on public excommunication of those who had fallen into serious sin (apostasy, murder, adultery). But here we see a preference for regular private confession of all one's sins to a priest, because it began to be thought that in that way the pastoral needs of penitents might be met more effectively. The Anglican practice of General Confession does not involve the mention of the specific sins of named individuals in public, and there is provision for private confession in the 'warning for the celebration of Holy Communion' in the

---

[1]   I Timothy 2.5

Book of Common Prayer. The priest's role is seen here as one of intercession on behalf of the sinner. It is emphasized that it is the priest's duty to respect the secrecy of the confessional. This tradition is spoken of as apostolic. It should be emphasised that what is rejected here is not General Confession in which the whole congregation acknowledges its sinfulness together, but individual confession of specific sins in public.

I order that all measures be taken to eradicate the presumptuous deviation from the apostolic rule through an illicit abuse of which I have learned of late. In the procedure of penance, for which the faithful ask, there should be no public confession of sins in kind and number read from a written list, since it is enough that the guilt of conscience be revealed to the priests alone in secret confession. Though such fullness of faith as out of the fear of God is not afraid of shame before men seems praiseworthy, yet some sins are such that those who ask for penance would fear them to become publicly known. Hence this objectionable practice must be removed lest many be kept away from the remedies of penance, either out of shame or for fear that their enemies may come to know of facts which could bring harm to them through legal procedures. For that confession is sufficient which is first offered to God, then also to the priest whose role is that of an intercessor for the sins of the penitents. Lastly, a greater number will be induced to penance only if the conscience of the penitent is not made public for all to hear.

60

before 461
The mission of the Church to society's needs

Leo the Great, Bishop of Rome, 461, Sermon on the Beatitudes, *2–3: SC 22, Sermon 96.*

It cannot be doubted that the poor can more easily attain the blessing of humility than those who are rich. In the case of the poor, the lack of worldly goods is often accompanied by a quiet gentleness, whereas the rich are more prone to arrogance. Nevertheless, many wealthy people are disposed to use their abundance not to swell their own pride but to perform works of benevolence. They consider their greatest gain what they spend to alleviate the distress of others. This virtue is open to all men, no matter what their class or condition, because all can be equal in their willingness to give, however unequal they may be in earthly fortune. Indeed, their inequality in regard to worldly means is unimportant, provided they are found equal in spiritual possessions. Blessed, therefore, is that poverty which is not trapped by the love of temporal things and does not seek to be enriched by worldly wealth, but desires rather to grow rich in heavenly goods. The apostles were the first after the Lord himself to provide us with an example of this generous poverty, when they all equally left their belongings at the call of the heavenly Master. By an immediate conversion they were turned from the catching of fish to become fishers of men, and by their own example they won many others to the imitation of their own faith. In these first sons of the Church there was but one heart and one soul among all who believed. Abandoning all their worldly property and possessions in their dedicated poverty, they were enriched with eternal goods, and in accordance with the apostolic preaching they rejoiced to have nothing of this world and to possess all things with Christ.

61

529
Our need for Grace

The Second Council of Orange, Doctrinal Documents, *1915–21.*

See *Our need for grace*, extract from the sixteenth Council of Carthage, 418, (no. 47). A particular point is made here of the importance of denying 'double predestination', that is, the view that God not only predestines some to glory but also predestines others to hell; for such a view would seem to make God the author of evil. Here, as in the earlier extract, the Council has striven to rest its conclusions solidly on Scripture.

Canons of Grace

3. If anyone says that the grace of God can be conferred because of a human prayer, and not rather that it is grace itself that prompts us to pray, he contradicts the Prophet Isaiah, or the apostle who says the same thing: 'I have been found by those who did not

seek me; I have shown myself to those who did not ask for me.'[1]

4. If anyone contends that God awaits our will before cleansing us from sin, but does not confess that even the desire to be cleansed is aroused in us by the infusion and action of the Holy Spirit, he opposes the Holy Spirit himself speaking through Solomon: 'The will is prepared by the Lord',[2] and the apostle's salutary message: 'God is at work in you, both to will and to work for his good pleasure'.[3]

5. If anyone says that the increase as well as the beginning of faith, and the very desire of faith — by which we believe in him who justifies the sinner and by which we come to the regeneration of holy baptism — proceeds from our own nature and not from the gift of grace, namely from an inspiration of the Holy Spirit changing our will from unbelief to belief and from godlessness to piety, such a man reveals himself to be in contradiction with the apostolic doctrine, since Paul says: 'I am sure that he who began a good work in you will bring it to completion at the day of Christ Jesus';[4] and again: 'It has been granted to you that for the sake of Christ you should not only believe in him but also suffer for his sake';[5] and also: 'By grace you have been saved, through faith; and this is not your own doing, it is the gift of God.'[6] For those who say that the faith by which we believe in God is natural, declare that all those who are strangers to the Church of Christ are, in some way, believers.

6. If anyone says that mercy is divinely conferred upon us when, without God's grace, we believe, will, desire, strive, labour, pray, keep watch, endeavour, request, seek, knock, but does not confess that it is through the infusion and inspiration of the Holy Spirit that we believe, will or are able to do all these things as is required; or if anyone subordinates the help of grace to humility or human obedience, and does not admit that it is the very gift of grace that makes us obedient and humble, he contradicts the apostle who

---

[1]   Romans 10.20; cf. Isaiah 65.1
[2]   Proverbs 8.35, Septuagint
[3]   Philippians 2.13
[4]   Philippians 1.6
[5]   Philippians 1.29
[6]   Ephesians 2.8

says: 'What have you that you did not receive?';[7] and also: 'By the grace of God I am what I am.'[8]

7. If anyone asserts that by his natural strength he is able to think as is required or choose anything good pertaining to his eternal salvation, or to assent to the saving message of the gospel without the illumination and inspiration of the Holy Spirit, who gives to all ease and joy in assenting to the truth and believing it, he is deceived by the heretical spirit and does not understand the word said by God in the gospel: 'Apart from me you can do nothing',[9] nor the word of the apostle: 'Not that we are sufficient of ourselves to claim anything as coming from us; our sufficiency is from God.'[10] If anyone maintains that some are able to come to the grace of baptism through [God's] mercy, but others through their own free will — which, it is clear, is wounded in all those who are born from the transgression of the first man — he shows that he has departed from the orthodox faith. For he does not acknowledge that free will has been weakened in all by the sin of the first man, or at least he holds that free will has been wounded only in such a way that some are still able to attain to the mystery of eternal salvation by themselves without divine revelation. Yet that the opposite is true is proved by the Lord himself, who does not testify that some can come to him, but that nobody can, unless he is drawn by the Father,[11] as he also says to Peter: 'Blessed are you, Simon Bar Jona! For flesh and blood has not revealed this to you, but my Father who is in heaven.'[12] And the apostle too says: 'No one can say: "Jesus is the Lord", except by the Holy Spirit.'[13]

---

[7]   I Corinthians 4.7

[8]   I Corinthians 15.10

[9]   John 15.5

[10] II Corinthians 3.5

[11] Cf. John 6.55

[12] Matthew 16.17

[13] I Corinthians 12.3

62

530–40
The monastic ideals of Christian love and obedience

The Rule of St Benedict, *Chapters 53 and 68 ed. and tr. J. McCann (London, 1972).*

Benedict's *Rule* of monastic life became the standard pattern in the West throughout most of the Middle Ages.

Chapter 53

Let all guests that come be received like Christ, for he will say: 'I was a stranger and ye took me in'.[1] And let fitting honour be shown to all, but especially to... pilgrims. As soon, therefore, as a guest is announced, let the superior or some brethren meet him with all charitable service. And first of all let them pray together, and let them unite in the kiss of peace. This kiss of peace shall not be offered until after the prayers have been said, on account of the delusions of the Devil.[2] In the greeting of all guests, whether they be arriving or departing, let the greatest humility be shown. Let the head be bowed or the whole body prostrated on the ground, and so let Christ be worshipped in them, for indeed he is received in their persons....

Chapter 68

If it happens that something hard or impossible be laid upon any brother, let him receive the command of his superior with all docility and obedience. But if he see that the weight of the burden altogether exceeds the measure of his strength, let him explain the reasons for his incapacity to his superiors calmly and in due season, without pride, obstinacy, or contentiousness. If after his representations the superior still persists in his decision and command, let the subject know that it is expedient for him, and let him obey out of love, trusting in God's help.

---

[1] Matthew 25.35

[2] That is, in case the visitor is Satan in disguise. No evil spirit could join in the prayer, and so praying together is a test.

63

534
The Incarnate Son

John II, Bishop of Rome, Letter to the Senate of Constantinople, Doctrinal Documents, 617.

This extract summarizes several of the rulings the Church had by now arrived at, on questions raised in connection with the Incarnation during preceding centuries. Compare Article ii of the Thirty-Nine Articles.

[The Emperor Justinian] has pointed out, as you have learned from the contents of his letter, that disputes have arisen over the following three questions:
[1] can one say that Christ our God is 'one of the Trinity', that is, one holy Person among the three Persons of the Holy Trinity?
[2] Did Christ our God who in his divinity is impassible suffer in the flesh?
[3] Must Mary, the ever Virgin Mother of our Lord and God Jesus Christ, be called truly and properly Mother of God and Mother of God the Word incarnate from her?...
Christ is one of the Holy Trinity, that is, one holy person or subsistence[1] – one 'hypostasis' as the Greeks say – among the three persons of the Holy Trinity.[2] The fact that God did truly suffer in the flesh we confirm likewise by the following witnesses...[3] We teach that it is right for catholic Christians to confess that the glorious and holy Mary, ever Virgin, is truly and properly the Mother of God... the Word, incarnate from her. For it is he himself who truly and properly became incarnate in these latter days and deigned to be born of the holy and glorious Virgin Mother. Hence, since the Son of God became incarnate and was born from her truly and properly, we confess her to be truly and properly the Mother of God incarnate and born from her.

---

[1]   Latin: *subsistentia*

[2]   There follow among other quotations: Genesis 3.22; I Corinthians 8.6; The Nicene Creed.

[3]   Deuteronomy 28.66; John 14.6; Malachi 3.8; Acts 3.15, 20.28; I Corinthians 2.8; Cyril of Alexandria, *Anathematism* 12; Leo I, Tome to Flavian, etc.

64

543
The Incarnate Son

The Council of Constantinople, Anathematism Against the Origenists, Doctrinal Documents, *618–19*.

Among the errors attributed to the disciples of Origen (*c*.185–*c*.254) as regards the relation between soul and body, some touched on the doctrine of the Incarnation of the Word. The two errors described here would make Christ less fully human in his Incarnation.

If anyone says or holds that the soul of the Lord has existed first and has been united to God the Word before the incarnation and the birth from the Virgin, let him be anathema. If anyone says or holds that the body of our Lord Jesus Christ was first formed in the womb of the holy Virgin and that God the Word and the soul already in existence were later united with it, let him be anathema.

65

590–604
Missionary practice

Gregory the Great, Bishop of Rome 590–604, Letter to Abbot Mellitus, Doctrinal Documents, *1102*.

There had been Christians in Britain in Roman times, and Christianity continued to flourish in Ireland after the Roman occupation. In the sixth century Irish missionaries went to Scotland and the Continent, establishing a 'Celtic' Church. In 596, Pope Gregory I sent Augustine, then prior of St Andrew's monastery in Rome, to revive Christianity in England. Here we see the Bishop of Rome advising his missionary to England on the best way to help his new converts to leave behind their pagan superstitions without stripping them of all that is familiar and dear to them in their own culture. Elsewhere he expresses rather different views of the best way to help new converts over this difficulty, which remains a delicate one in all missionary situations even in the different circumstances of our own time. Cf. no. 97.

Tell Augustine [of Canterbury] that he should by no means destroy the temples of the gods but rather the idols within those temples. Let him, after he has purified them with holy water, place altars and relics of the saints in them. For, if those temples are well built,[1] they should be converted from the worship of demons to the service of the true God. Thus, seeing that their places of worship are not destroyed, the people will banish error from their hearts and come to places familiar and dear to them in acknowledgement and worship of the true God. Further, since it has been their custom to slaughter oxen in sacrifice to the demons, they should receive some solemnity in exchange. Let them, therefore, on the day of the dedication of their churches, or on the feast of the martyrs whose relics are preserved in them, build themselves huts around their one-time temples and celebrate the occasion with religious feasting. They will sacrifice and eat the animals not any more as an offering to the Devil, but for the glory of God, to whom, as the giver of all things, they will give thanks for having been satisfied. Thus, if they are not deprived of all the exterior joys, they will more easily taste the interior ones. For surely it is impossible to efface everything all at once from their... minds, just as, when someone wishes to reach the top of a mountain, he must climb by stages and step by step, not by leaps and bounds... Mention this then to our brother the bishop, that he may dispose of the matter as he sees fit according to the conditions of time and place.

66

604
Angels

Gregory the Great, Bishop of Rome, 604, Homily 34 *on the gospels 8–9: PL 76, pp. 1250–1. Tr.* The Office of Readings according to the Roman Rite *(Slough, 1983), pp. 1575–6.*

Cf. nos. 156, 157. Gregory the Great followed the fifth century author then thought to be Dionysius the Areopagite in developing the implications of the biblical references to angels. The Homilies on the Gospels are one of Gregory's earlier works, preached in the Roman basilica.

You should be aware that the word 'angel' denotes a function rather than a nature. Those Holy Spirits of heaven have indeed

---

[1] That is, if they are strong and serviceable buildings, they should not be wasted.

always been spirits. They can only be called angels when they deliver some message.[1] Moreover, those who deliver messages of lesser importance are called angels; and those who proclaim messages of supreme importance are called archangels. And so it was not merely an angel but the archangel Gabriel who was sent to the Virgin Mary. It was only fitting that the highest angel should come to announce the greatest of all messages. Some angels are given proper names to denote the service they are empowered to perform. In that holy city, where perfect knowledge flows from the vision of almighty God, those who have no names may easily be known. But personal names are assigned to some, not because they could not be known without them, but rather to denote their ministry when they come among us. Thus, Michael means 'Who is like God?'; Gabriel is 'The Strength of God'; and Raphael is 'God's Remedy'. Whenever some act of wondrous power must be performed, Michael is sent, so that his action and his name may make it clear that no-one can do what God does by his superior power. So also our ancient foe desired in his pride to be like God, saying; 'I will ascend into heaven; I will exalt my throne above the stars of heaven; I will be like the Most High.'[2] He will be allowed to remain in power until the end of the world, when he will be destroyed in the final punishment. Then, he will fight with the archangel Michael, as we are told by John: 'A battle was fought with Michael the archangel'.[3] So too Gabriel, who is called God's strength, was sent to Mary. He came to announce the One who appeared as a humble man to quell the cosmic powers. Thus God's strength announced the coming of the Lord of the heavenly powers, mighty in battle. Raphael means, as I have said, God's remedy, for when he touched Tobit's eyes in order to cure him, he banished the darkness of his blindness. Thus, since it is his task to heal, he is rightly called God's remedy.

---

[1]   *Angelos* means 'messenger' in Greek
[2]   Isaiah 14.13–14
[3]   Revelation 12.7

67

673
Councils as ratifiers of past expressions of the mind of the Church

Council of Hertford, 673, described by Bede, Historia Ecclesiastica, *iv, 5, Gee and Hardy, pp. 10–11.*

This 'provincial' or 'national' synod of the Anglo-Saxon bishops met in collegiality to reaffirm their unanimous consent to a number of decrees of earlier Councils. The conciliar theology which lies behind their action emerges clearly in the text in the references to the brotherhood of bishops and their responsibility for maintaining the Faith down the ages, and for love and unity in the Church. The Council had the further purpose of settling the organisation of the Church in England. Christians of the Celtic and Roman traditions had been celebrating Easter at different times, and there had been disagreement about diocesan boundaries. These issues were now being resolved. Compare no. 70.

In the name of our Lord God and Saviour Jesus Christ, in the perpetual reign and government of our Lord Jesus Christ. It seemed good that we should come together according to the prescription of the venerable canons, to treat of the necessary affairs of the Church. We are met together on this the 24th day of September, in a place called Hertford. I, Theodore, Bishop of the Church of Canterbury, appointed thereto, unworthy as I am, by the Apostolic See, and our most reverend brother Bisi, Bishop of the East-Angles, together with our brother and fellow-bishop Wilfrid, bishop of the nation of the Northumbrians, who was present by his proper legates, as also our brethren and fellow-bishops, Putta, Bishop of the Castle of the Kentishmen, called Rochester, Leutherius, Bishop of the West Saxons, and Winfrid, Bishop of the Province of the Mercians were present; and when we were assembled and had taken our proper places, I said: 'I beseech you, beloved brethren, for the fear and love of our Redeemer, that we may faithfully enter into a common treaty for the sincere observance of whatsoever has been decreed and determined by the holy and approved Fathers.' I enlarged upon these and many other things tending unto charity, and the preservation of the unity of the Church. And when I had finished my speech I asked them singly and in order whether they consented to observe all things which had been of old canonically decreed by the Fathers? To which all... answered: we are all well agreed readily and cheerfully to keep whatever the canons of the holy Fathers have prescribed.

68

675

Resurrection of the body, judgement and the life to come

The Eleventh Council of Toledo, Symbol of Faith, Doctrinal Documents, *2302.*

Thus, according to the example of our Head, we confess that there is a true resurrection of the body for all the dead. And we do not believe that we shall rise in an ethereal body or in any other body, as some foolishly imagine, but in this very body in which we live and are and move. After having given an example of this holy resurrection, our Lord and Saviour by his ascension returned to the throne of his Father from which in his divine nature he had never departed. There, seated at the right hand of the Father, he is awaited till the end of time as judge of all the living and the dead. From there he shall come... to pass judgement and to render to each one the reward due to him, according to what each one has done while he was in the body, whether good or evil.[1] We believe that the holy Catholic Church, which he purchased at the price of his own blood, will reign with him for ever. Taken up into her bosom, we believe in and profess one baptism for the remission of all sins. By this faith we truly believe in the resurrection of the dead and look forward to the joys of the world to come. This only must we pray and beg for, that when the Son, having completed the judgement, will have delivered the Kingdom to God the Father,[2] he may make us sharers in his kingdom, so that through this faith by which we have adhered to him, we may reign with him for ever.

---

[1]   Cf. II Corinthians 5.10
[2]   Cf. I Corinthians 15.24

69

675
The Incarnation

The Eleventh Council of Toledo, Symbol of Faith, Doctrinal Documents, *628.*

A pronouncement on a seventh-century controversy about the Virgin Birth.

Of these three persons we believe that only the person of the Son has assumed a true human nature, without sin, from the holy and immaculate Virgin Mary, for the liberation of the human race. He was begotten from her in a new order and by a new birth: in a new order, because, invisible in his divinity, he is shown visible in the flesh; by a new birth, because an inviolate virginity, without knowing the contact of man, supplied the matter of his body, being made fruitful by the Holy Spirit. This Virgin-Birth is neither grasped by reason nor illustrated by example. Were it grasped by reason, it would not be wonderful; were it illustrated by example, it would not be unique. Yet, we must not believe that the Holy Spirit is the Father of the Son because Mary conceived by the overshadowing of the same Holy Spirit, lest we should seem to affirm that the Son has two fathers – which it is certainly impious to say.

70

680
Declaration of Faith and
acceptance of the Ecumenical Councils

Council of Hatfield, described by Bede, Historia Ecclesiastica, *iv, 17, 18, Gee and Hardy, pp. 13–15, translation revised.*

Here we see an English Council, with the Archbishop of Canterbury acting as President, endorsing and recognizing the decrees of the great Ecumenical Councils, and giving a clear statement of orthodoxy against the heretical opinions they had condemned on the subject of the divine and human natures and the person of Christ. Compare the emphasis at the Council of Hertford (673) on unanimous consent (no. 67).

At this time Theodore, hearing that the Faith of the Church at Constantinople had been much disturbed by heresy..., and being desirous that the Churches of the English, over which he ruled, should contrive to be free from such a stain, collected an assemblage of venerable priests and very many learned men. He diligently inquired what belief they each held, and found an unanimous agreement of all in the catholic Faith; and this he took care to commit to a synodal letter for the instruction and remembrance of posterity. This is the beginning of the letter: 'In the name of our Lord and Saviour Jesus Christ, in the reign of our most pious lords, Egfrid, king of the Humbrians, in the tenth year of his reign, on the fifteenth day before the Kalends of October; and Ethelred, king of the Mercians, in the sixth year of his reign; and Aldwulf, king of the East Angles, in the seventeenth year of his reign; and Hlothair, king of the Kentishmen, in the seventh year of his reign. Theodore being president, by the grace of God, Archbishop of this island of Britain and of the city of Canterbury, and other venerable men sitting with him, bishops of the island of Britain, with the holy Gospels laid before them, in the place which is called by the Saxon name of Hatfield; we, discussing everything together, have made an exposition of the right and orthodox faith, even as our Incarnate Lord Jesus Christ delivered it to his disciples, who saw him present, and heard his discourses, and as the Creed of the holy Fathers has delivered, and generally all the assembly of approved doctors of the Catholic Church — we therefore, piously following them in orthodoxy, and making our profession according to their divinely inspired teaching, believe in unison with it, and confess according to the holy Fathers, that the Father and Son and Holy Ghost are properly and truly a consubstantial Trinity in Unity and Unity in Trinity; that is, one God in three consubstantial subsistencies,[1] or persons of equal glory and honour.' And after many things of this kind that pertained to the confession of the right faith, the holy synod also adds this to its letter: — 'We have received, as holy and universal, five synods of the fathers blessed and acceptable to God, that is of the 318 who were assembled at Nicaea against the most impious Arius and the tenets of the same; and of 150 at Constantinople against the madness of Macedonius and Eudoxius and their dogmas; and of 200 in the first Council of Ephesus against the most wicked Nestorius, and the dogmas of the same; and of 630 at

---

[1]   Latin: *subsistentiis*

Chalcedon against Eutyches and Nestorius and their dogmas; and again of those who were assembled in a fifth Council at Constantinople, in the time of the younger Justinian, against Theodore and the epistles of Theodoret and Ibas and their dogmas, against Cyril.' And a little after: 'also we have received the synod that was held in the city of Rome in the time of the blessed Pope Martin in the eighth indiction in the ninth year of the reign of the most pious Constantine.[2] And we glorify our Lord Jesus Christ as they glorified him, neither adding nor subtracting anything; and we anathematize with heart and mouth those whom they anathematize; and those whom they receive we receive, glorifying God the Father without beginning, and his only-begotten Son, begotten of the Father before the world began, and the Holy Ghost proceeding ineffably from the Father and the Son, as those holy apostles and Prophets and doctors have declared of whom we have spoken above. And all we who have with Theodore made an exposition of the catholic Faith have subscribed hereto.'

71

681
On the two wills and ¨actions in Christ

The Third General Council of Constantinople (680–1), Doctrinal Documents, *635.*

The 'Monothelite' heresy arose in the seventh century out of an attempt to find an understanding of the Incarnation on which the Chalcedonian and Monophysite Christians could agree. The suggestion was made that there was only one will or 'energy' in Christ. After some decades of debate a Roman Synod in 679 and then the Council of Constantinople in 680–1 expressed the view that Christ had both a divine and a human will, working together without conflict.

We say that [Christ's] two natures shine forth in his one Person.[1] In it, throughout his entire human existence in the flesh, he made manifest his miracles and his sufferings, not in mere appearance but in reality. The difference of natures in that same and unique

---

[2] See nos. 23,27,56. The Councils of Ephesus in 431 and Constantinople in 553 make up the five. The Council at Rome was in 649.

[1] Greek: *hypostasis*

hypostasis is recognized by the fact that each of the two natures wills and performs what is proper to it in communion with the other. Thus, we glory in proclaiming two natural wills and actions concurring together for the salvation of the human race.

72

725
Respect for the sacred

Wilkins, I, 62; Johnson, I, 156, from Anglo-Saxon Laws of 725.

This passage from an early English law-code stresses the importance of respect for what is holy and consecrated to God, especially in an age of violence against persons and property.

For whatever is consecrated, orders, and God's hallowed house, ought diligently to be honoured, for the fear of God.

73

726–30
A defence of the veneration of images

The Exposition of the Orthodox Faith by John of Damascus, Priest, d. c.749, 'On the Orthodox Faith' 4, 16: PG 94, pp. 1169–73, and tr. S.D.F. Salmond (Oxford, 1899), and F.H. Chase (Washington, 1958), translation revised.

John of Damascus is writing in the period of the iconoclast controversy in the Orthodox Church in the East. He explains the way an image reminds us of its original. He distinguishes this process of recall from 'worship' of the image itself. When we venerate an image, he argues, we honour him whose image it is. Cf. nos. 74 and 75 and Article xxii of the Thirty-Nine Articles.

Let them remember that in the beginning God created man after his own image. On what grounds, then, do we show reverence to each other unless because we are made after God's image? For... the honour given to the image passes over to the prototype. Now a prototype is that which is imaged, from which the derivative is obtained. In the Old Testament the use of images was not common. But after God in his bowels of pity became in truth man for our salvation (not as he was seen by Abraham in the semblance of man, nor as he was seen by the Prophets, but in being truly man); and after he lived upon the earth and dwelt among men, worked miracles, suffered, was crucified, rose again and was taken back to Heaven; all these things which actually took place and were seen by men, were written for the remembrance and instruction of those of us who were not alive at that time in order that though we saw not, we may still, hearing and believing, obtain the blessing of the Lord. But seeing that not every one has a knowledge of letters nor time for reading, the Fathers gave their sanction to depicting these events in images ... Often, certainly, when we have not the Lord's Passion in mind and see the image of Christ's crucifixion, his saving Passion is brought back to remembrance, and we fall down and worship not the material but that which is imaged: just as we do not worship the material of which the gospels are made, nor the material of the cross, but that which these typify.... It is just the same also in the case of the Mother of the Lord. For the honour which we give to her is for the sake of him who was made Incarnate of her. And similarly also the brave acts of holy men stir us up to be brave and to emulate and imitate their valour and to glorify God.

74

726–30
A right reverence for created matter

The First Apology in Defence of Divine Images by John of Damascus, Priest, d. c.749. Apology 1, 16: PG 94, p. 1245, tr. St John of Damascus, On the Divine Images, D. Anderson (St Vladimir's Press, 1980), pp. 23–4, translation revised.

See comment on no. 73 above. John of Damascus here adds remarks on the goodness of matter. In his day the issue was whether the dualists (Gnostics, or Manichees) were right in saying that the spiritual alone is good and all matter evil. But his defence of matter's power to bring us to thoughts of God has relevance for today's concern with ecology.

In former times God, who is without form or body, could never be depicted. But now when God is seen in the flesh conversing with men, I make an image of the God whom I see. I do not worship matter; I worship the Creator of matter who became matter for my sake; who willed to make his abode in matter; who worked out my salvation through matter. Never will I cease honouring the matter which wrought my salvation! I honour it, but not as God. How could God be born out of things which have no existence in themselves? God's body is God because it is joined to his person by a union which shall never pass away. The divine nature remains the same; the flesh created in time is quickened by a soul endowed with reason. Because of this I salute all the rest of matter with reverence, because God has filled it with his grace and power. Through it my salvation has come to me. Was not the thrice-happy and thrice-blessed wood of the cross matter? Was not the holy and exalted mountain of Calvary matter? What of the life-bearing rock, the holy and life-giving tomb, the fountain of our resurrection, was it not matter? Is not the ink in the most holy Gospel-book matter? Is not the life-giving altar made of matter? From it we receive the bread of life! Are not gold and silver matter? From them we make crosses, patens, chalices! And over and above all these things, is not the Body and Blood of our Lord matter? Either do away with the honour and veneration these things deserve, or accept the tradition of the Church and the veneration of images. Reverence God and his friends; follow the inspiration of the Holy Spirit. Do not despise matter, for it is not despicable. Nothing God has made is despicable. To think such things is Manichaeism. Only that which does not have its source in God is despicable — that which is our own invention, our wilful choice to disregard the law of God — namely, sin.

75

787
Showing Respect for holy things

The Second General Council of Nicaea, Doctrinal Documents, *1251–2.*

The iconoclast controversy divided Eastern Christendom in the eighth century. The iconoclasts argued that there was a danger of idolatry in the veneration of images. The settlement of the Council of Nicaea stressed the difference between respect and worship and insisted that while worship is for God alone, pious contemplation of images can be a help to Christians seeking God.

We define that... the representations of the precious and life-giving cross, and the venerable and holy images as well... must be kept in the holy Church of God..., in houses and on the roads, whether they be images of God our Lord and Saviour Jesus Christ or of our immaculate Lady the Mother of God, or of the holy angels and of all the saints and just. For, the more frequently one contemplates these pictorial representations, the more gladly will he be led to remember the original subject whom they represent, the more too will he be drawn to it and inclined to give it... a respectful veneration,[1] which, however, is not the true adoration[2] which, according to our faith, is due to God alone. But, as is done for the image of the revered and life-giving cross and the holy Gospels and other sacred objects and monuments, let an oblation of incense and light be made to give honour to those images according to the pious custom of the ancients. For 'the honour given to an image goes to the original model';[3] and he who venerates an image, venerates in it the person represented by it.

76

796–7

The Incarnate Son

The Council of Friuli, Profession of Faith, Doctrinal Documents, *639.*

In eighth century Spain it was suggested that Christ was 'adopted' in his humanity by the Father and was therefore not truly his Son. The teaching seems to have arisen partly in a missionary endeavour to Muslims, who occupied Toledo at this time and who were resistant to the orthodox doctrine of the Incarnation. This profession of faith expresses the Church's view. This heresy is an early version of the familiar modern notion that Jesus was 'only a man'.

The human and temporal birth did not interfere with the divine timeless birth, but in the one Person of Jesus Christ are the true Son of God and the true son of man. There is not one who is son

---

[1]   Greek: *prosekunêsis*

[2]   Greek: *latria, latreia*

[3]   St Basil, *De Spiritu Sancto*, 18.45

of man and another who is Son of God, but one and the same Son of God and son of man, in two natures, the divine and the human, true God and true man. He is not the putative Son of God, but the true Son; not the adoptive Son but the real Son, for he was never estranged from the Father because of the man (human nature) which he assumed... And, therefore, we confess him to be in each of the two natures the real, not the adoptive, Son of God, because, having assumed the human nature,[1] one and the same is Son of God and son of man without confusion and without separation. He is naturally Son of the Father as to his divinity, naturally son of his Mother as to his humanity, but he is properly Son of the Father in both [natures].

77

Before the ninth century
The Christian Faith

The Creed of the Roman Order of Baptism, Doctrinal Documents, *5.*

This is the form of the 'Symbol of the Apostles' accepted in Rome during the tenth century, but already previously recognized throughout the Western Church, although not in the East. Ninth-century manuscripts witness to its being used in Gaul in the local language. Except for accidental variants, this text of the 'Symbol of the Apostles' thereafter remained traditional in the West, and is used in Anglican worship. The twelve 'clauses' numbered here were for a long time believed to have been contributed individually by the twelve apostles.

I believe in God, the Father almighty,
  creator of heaven and earth (1).
And in Jesus Christ, His only Son, our Lord (2),
who was conceived by the Holy Spirit,
  born of the Virgin Mary (3),
suffered under Pontius Pilate, was crucified, died and was buried;
  he went down to the dead (4).[1]
On the third day he rose again from the dead (5).

---

[1] Latin: *assumpto homine*
[1] Latin: *ad inferna*

He ascended to the heavens, and is seated at the right hand of God,
the Father almighty (6),
wherefrom he shall come again to judge
the living and the dead (7).
I believe in the Holy Spirit (8),
the Holy Catholic Church, the communion of saints (9),
the forgiveness of sins (10),
the resurrection of the body (11),
and the life everlasting (12).

78

c.850

Consent and unity

Hincmar of Rheims, De Praedestinatione *38.1, PL 125.419B.*

The Carolingian abbot Hincmar here expresses the importance of unity of
faith in unity of life in the communion of the Church.

If one communion is not a sign of a single consent, what reason
will there be to celebrate as a mystery our faith in the harmony of
the whole Church?

79

960

Discipline of the clergy

*Canons of the reign of King Edgar, 960, Wilkins I, 225, Johnson,
I, 412–13, translation revised.*

These Anglo-Saxon laws encourage both civil obedience and a sense of the
importance of canonical obedience in the Church. It proved impracticable to
implement the provision for an annual synod of the clergy.

1. We charge that God's servants diligently perform their service
and ministry to God, and intercede for all Christian folk, and that
they be all faithful and obedient to their superiors, and all of one
mind for their common benefit, and that they all be helpful to each
other in relation both to God and to the world; and that they be
faithful and true to their worldly lords.

2. And that they all honour each other, and that the inferiors obey the superiors with diligence, and that the superiors love, and diligently instruct their inferiors.

3. And that at every synod every year they have their books, and vestments for divine ministration, as also ink, and parchment for [writing down] their instructions, and three days' provision...

5. And that every priest give information in synod, if any thing aggrieve him, and if any man hath highly abused him.

80

960
Ecclesiastical Courts

Canons of the reign of King Edgar, Johnson, I, 413.

The principle that the Church had jurisdiction in her own courts over members of the clergy who committed any offence was clear in early English laws.

Let no suit between priests be commended before secular men, but let their equals be arbitrators and umpires; or let them lay their cause before a bishop, if there be a necessity.

81

963
Confession of sins

Penitential canons, 963, Wilkins, I, 229, Johnson, I, 426.

When any one will confess his sins, let him act like a man, and not be ashamed to acknowledge his wickedness and crimes by accusing himself; because that brings pardon; and because without confession there is no forgiveness; for confession cures, confession justifies, confession brings forgiveness of sins.[1]

We begin the next section at 1054, because that was the date of formal separation of the Western and Eastern (Orthodox) Churches. From about the sixth century the West had begun to add 'and the Son' to the clause of the Nicene Creed 'the Holy Spirit who proceeds from the Father'. The Greeks resisted this addition and by the mid-eleventh century communication had broken down over this and a number of differences of practice and rite. Article v of the Thirty-Nine Articles follows the Western tradition, but it is now increasingly accepted in the West that the clause should be omitted. Cf. no. 27, note 4 and no. 85.

---

[1] We give the Latin here because of the importance of the terms *indulgentia; justificare; venia: Quando aliquis voluerit confessionem facere peccatorum suorum, viriliter agat, et non erubescat confiteri scelera et facinora se accusando; quia inde venit indulgentia, et quia sine confessione nulla est venia, confessio sanat, confessio justificat, confessio veniam peccatis donat.*

3
THE MATURING OF FAITH AND ORDER
1054–1520

82

1070

An attempt to settle the question whether Canterbury or York should be regarded as the senior Archbishopric in England

William of Malmsbury, Gesta Pontificum, *ed. N.E.S.A. Hamilton, Rolls Series (1870), pp. 63–5, tr. by Gee and Hardy, pp. 52–4, translation revised.*

Irish missionaries had been converting the north of England to Christianity before the mission of St Augustine arrived from Rome. For that reason the Archbishopric of York did not accept the seniority of Canterbury, and the relationship between the two metropolitans remained a somewhat vexed question until the late eleventh century. The question was settled in favour of Canterbury by the twelfth century. Here it is argued that it was the date, not of the first conversions, but of the settlement of the local Church with its bishop which should be the determining factor; and that that was done through the Canterbury mission.

Whilst [Thomas, Archbishop of York] was proceeding with these and similar arguments, as the necessity of proving his case and his own ignorance of antiquity supplied weapons to his eloquence, Lanfranc [Archbishop of Canterbury] put an end to the discussion, meeting him with this most circumspect answer: ... The blessed Paulinus, the first prelate of the same city [York], was sent there, not in the days of Augustine, the first Archbishop [of Canterbury], but of Justus, the fourth Archbishop of Canterbury. English history will prove what I say. Knowing this, the supreme Pontiffs have confirmed to the successors of Augustine the submission of all the bishops of England, as the privileges recited show.... Now they hold that all the Churches of the English should borrow the discipline of life from that place from whose fire they caught the flame of faith. For who knows not that the Faith of Christ flowed from Kent to York and all the other Churches of England? As for your assertion that St Gregory could have confirmed to Augustine's successors by word what he had granted to Augustine, had he wished, it is quite true and beyond denial. But, pray, what prejudice does this give to the See of Canterbury? I will put a parallel case: for when our Lord and Saviour said to St Peter 'Thou art Peter', etc,[1] he could have added, had he wished, 'and this same power I grant to thy successors'. As it is, the omission detracts nothing from the reverence due to St Peter's successors.

83

1075
Regional Councils

The Council of London, Johnson, II, 12–13.

The holding of provincial or national councils, though recognized to be desirable, was sometimes irregular in early medieval centuries. Lanfranc, Archbishop of Canterbury (1070–89), tried to institute a more regular system.

A council of the whole English nation, viz., of bishops, abbots, and many persons of religious order, Lanfranc the arch-prelate of the holy church of Canterbury, primate of the whole isle of Britain, calling and presiding in the same ... Many things were renewed, which are known to have been defined by old canons, because councils had been disused in the kingdom of England for many years past.

84

1076
Inter-faith relations

Gregory VII, Bishop of Rome (1073–85), Letter to Anzir, Muslim King of Mauritania, Doctrinal Documents, *1002, translation revised.*

God, the Creator of all, without whom we cannot do or even think anything that is good, has inspired your heart to this act of

---

[1]   Matthew 16.18

kindness. He who enlightens all men coming into this world[1] has enlightened your mind for this purpose. Almighty God, who desires all people to be saved[2] and that none should perish, is well pleased to approve in us most of all that besides loving God, people should love one another, and do not do to others anything they do not want to be done unto themselves.[3] We and you must show an example of this charity in a special way to the other nations, for we believe and confess one God, although in different ways; and praise and worship him daily as the Creator of all ages and the Ruler of this world. For as the apostle says: 'He is our peace who has made us both one'.[4] Many among the Roman nobility, informed by us of this grace granted to you by God, greatly admire and praise your goodness and virtues... God knows that we love you purely for his honour and that we desire your salvation and glory, both in the present and the future life. And we pray in our hearts and with our lips that God may lead you to the abode of happiness, to the bosom of the holy patriarch Abraham, after long years of life here on earth.

85

c.1077–8

A proof of God's existence

Anselm, Archbishop of Canterbury 1093–1109, Proslogion, 2, tr. M.J. Charlesworth (Oxford, 1965), p. 117.

Anselm's ontological argument was designed, he says, not only to prove that God exists, but also what his attributes are. Anselm explores God's goodness, omnipotence, truth, justice and mercy, for example. He wrote the *Proslogion* before he became Archbishop of Canterbury, but as Archbishop he continued to be a leading theologian, and Pope Urban II gave him the ecumenical responsibility of trying to reconcile Greek and Latin Christians on the question of the Procession of the Holy Spirit.

Well then, Lord, you who give understanding to faith, grant me that I may understand, as much as you see fit, that you exist as we

---

[1]   John 1.9

[2]   I Timothy 2.4

[3]·   Cf. Matthew 7.14

[4]   Ephesians 2.14

believe you exist, and that you are what we believe you to be. Now we believe that you are something than which nothing greater can be thought. Or can it be that a thing of such a nature does not exist, since 'the Fool has said in his heart, there is no God'?[1] But surely, when this same Fool hears what I am speaking about, namely, 'something-than-which-nothing-greater-can-be-thought', he understands what he hears, and what he understands is in his mind, even if he does not understand that it actually exists. For it is one thing for an object to exist in the mind, and another thing to understand that an object actually exists. Thus, when a painter plans beforehand what he is going to execute, he has the picture in his mind, but he does not yet think that it actually exists because he has not yet executed it. However, when he has actually painted it, then he both has it in his mind and understands that it exists because he has now made it. Even the Fool, then, is forced to agree that something-than-which-nothing-greater-can-be-thought exists in the mind, since he understands this when he hears it, and whatever is understood is in the mind. And surely that-than-which-a-greater-cannot-be-thought cannot exist in the mind alone. For if it exists solely in the mind even, it can be thought to exist in reality also, which is greater. If then that-than-which-a-greater-cannot-be-thought exists in the mind alone, this same that-than-which-a-greater-*cannot*-be-thought is also that-than-which-a-greater-*can*-be-thought. But this is obviously impossible. Therefore there is absolutely no doubt that something-than-which-a-greater-cannot-be-thought exists both in the mind and in reality.

86

1079
The eucharistic presence of Christ

Oath of Berengar of Tours, Doctrinal Documents, *1501.*

The Council of Rome required this oath of recantation from Berengar of Tours at the end of thirty years of controversy. He had argued that the bread and wine consecrated at Holy Communion do not change, but are merely 'signs'. In response, the Church's apologists developed an increasingly technical explanation of the way in which the bread and wine 'become'

---

[1]   Psalms 13.1; 51.1

Christ's 'true' body and blood. They taught that the actual historical body, in which Christ lived and died, replaces the substance of the bread and wine, and that only their appearance and taste are unchanged. This doctrine, called 'transubstantiation' from the late twelfth century, and included in a credal formula in the first canon of the Fourth Lateran Council in 1215, is condemned by Article xxviii of the Thirty-Nine Articles. Roman Catholics today do not generally want to insist on the exact manner of the change in this way, but rather to affirm (as Anglicans do) the real presence of Christ. See the *First Report* of ARCIC, Eucharist, 6 and footnote 2.

I, Berengar, believe in my heart and confess with my lips that the bread and wine which are placed on the altar are, by the mystery of the sacred prayer and the words of the Redeemer, substantially changed into the true and proper and life-giving body and blood of Jesus Christ our Lord; and that, after consecration, they are Christ's true body, which was born of the Virgin and hung on the cross, being offered for the salvation of the world, and which sits at the right hand of the Father; and Christ's true blood, which was poured forth from His side; not only by way of sign and by the power of the sacrament, but in their true nature and in the reality of their substance.[1]

87

before 1090
Mary, Mother of the Lord

Prayer to St Mary by Anselm, Archbishop of Canterbury, d. 1109, Prayer to St Mary 3, Oratio 7: Opera Omnia, ed. Schmitt, 3, 18, 22, tr. Benedicta Ward (London, 1973).

Mary, great Mary, most blessed of all martyrs,
greatest among all women, great Lady, great beyond measure,
I long to love you with all my heart,
I want to praise you with my lips,
I desire to venerate you in my understanding,
I love to pray to you from my deepest being,
I commit myself wholly to your protection.
All nature is created by God and God is born of Mary.

---

[1]   Latin: *in proprietate naturae et veritate substantiae*

God created all things, and Mary gave birth to God.
God who made all things made himself of Mary,
and thus he refashioned everything he had made.
He who was able to make all things out of nothing
refused to make it by force but first became the son of Mary.
So God is the Father of all created things,
and Mary is the mother of all re-created things.
God is the Father of all that is established,
and Mary is the mother of all that is re-established.
For God gave birth to him by whom all things were made
and Mary brought forth him by whom all are saved.
God brought forth him without whom nothing is,
Mary bore him without whom nothing is good.
O truly, 'the Lord is with you', to whom the Lord gave himself,
that all nature in you might be in him.

88

before 1090
The 'Motherhood' of Jesus and the apostles

Prayer to St Paul by Anselm, Archbishop of Canterbury, 1109,
Prayer to St Paul, Oratio 10: Opera Omnia, *ed. Schmitt, 3, 40–1,*
tr. Benedicta Ward (London, 1973).

And you, Jesus, are you not also a mother?
Are you not the mother who, like a hen,
gathers her chickens under her wings?
Truly, Lord, you are a mother;
for both they who are in labour
and they who are brought forth are accepted by you.
You have died more than they, that they may labour to bear.
It is by your death that they have been born,
for if you had not been in labour, you could not have borne death;
and if you had not died, you would not have brought forth.
For, longing to bear sons into life,
you tasted of death, and by dying you begot them.
You did this in your own self,
your servants by your commands and help,
You as the author, they as the ministers.

So you, Lord God, are the great mother.
Then both of you [Jesus and Paul] are mothers.
Even if you are fathers, you are also mothers.
For you have brought it about that those born to death
should be reborn to life —
you by your own act, you by his power.
Therefore you are fathers by your effect
and mothers by your affection.
Fathers by your authority, mothers by your kindness.
Fathers by your teaching, mothers by your mercy.
Then you, Lord, are a mother, and you, Paul, are a mother too.
If in quantity of affection you are unequal,
yet in quality you are not unalike.
Though in the greatness of your kindness you are not co-equal,
yet in will you are of one heart.
Although you have not equal fullness of mercy,
yet in intention you are not unequal.
And you, my soul, dead in yourself,
run under the wings of Jesus your mother
and lament your griefs under his feathers.
Ask that your wounds may be healed and that,
comforted, you may live again.
Christ, my mother, you gather your chickens under your wings;
this dead chicken of yours puts himself under those wings.
For by your gentleness the badly frightened are comforted,...
your warmth gives life to the dead, your touch justifies sinners.
Mother, know again your dead son,
both by the sign of your cross and the voice of his confession.
Arm your chicken, give life to your dead man, justify your sinner.
Let your terrified one be consoled by you;
and in your whole and unceasing grace
let him be refashioned by you.
For from you flows consolation for sinners;
to you be blessing for ages and ages.   Amen

89

1130–1143
Baptism of desire

Innocent II, Bishop of Rome (1130–43), Letter to the Bishop of Cremona, Doctrinal Documents, *1408.*

In this letter Pope Innocent II explains that 'baptism of desire', that is, the desire for baptism where actual baptism has not been possible, can be a means of grace for the remission of original sin and lead to salvation. The same doctrine is taught by Pope Innocent III, Bishop of Rome (1198–1216), in a letter to Bertolius, Bishop of Metz (1206) (*cf. DS 788*).

We affirm without hesitation that the old man who, according to information received from you, died without having received the baptism of water, has been relieved of original sin and granted the joy of the heavenly home, because he has persevered in the Faith of holy Mother the Church and in the confession of Christ's name. Read on this the eighth book of Augustine's *The City of God*[1] where among other things we read the following: 'baptism is invisibly administered which has been impeded, not by contempt for religion, but by unavoidable death.' And read over again the book of St Ambrose *On the Death of Valentianus*[2] which affirms the same doctrine.

90

1200
Baptism in emergency

Hubert Walter, Archbishop of Canterbury (1193–1205), Canons at Westminster, 1200; Wilkins I, 505; Johnson II, 85–6.

This English canon makes provision for baptism in emergency and when there is no way of knowing whether the individual has already been baptized. It preserves the rule that baptism cannot be repeated, while acknowledging the importance of baptism.

If there be any doubt whether one may have been baptized or confirmed, we charge according to the holy canons, that the

---

[1]   The correct reference is to St Augustine's *De baptismo contra Donatistas*, IV, 22, 29.

[2]   St Ambrose, *De obitu Valentiani*, 51

sacrament of which there is a doubt, be conferred. Let foundlings be baptized ... A deacon may not baptize, or give penance, except when the priest cannot, or will not, and yet death threatens the child or the sick man. If a layman baptize a child in case of necessity (and even a father or mother may do it...), let all that follows after the immersion be performed by the priest [at a later date].

91

1200
Reverent and careful celebration of Holy Communion

Hubert Walter, Archbishop of Canterbury (1193–1205), Canons at Westminster, 1200; Wilkins I, 505; Johnson, II, 85.

These provisions are designed to ensure that Holy Communion is celebrated with due reverence and a sense of its seriousness. The practice of reservation of the consecrated bread for the sick is intended to make it possible for them to share in the Communion. The same purpose is served by the service for the Communion of the Sick in the Book of Common Prayer, but there the minister is instructed to hold a fresh service, with two or three present, so that there is no need to 'reserve' what has been consecrated on another occasion. The doctrine of transubstantiation had led to the practice of 'reserving' the consecrated bread for veneration as the Body of Christ, and the English reformers were anxious to avoid any risk of idolatry arising from confusion in the minds of the simple faithful. It has, however, been a common Anglican practice where no such danger arises, to reserve the sacrament for the sick and housebound, and for it to be taken to them as soon as possible after the celebration of the Eucharist.

1. Whereas an error in divine offices endangers both the souls and bodies of men, it is wholesomely provided by this Council, that the words of the canon be roundly and distinctly pronounced by every priest in celebrating mass;
2. A priest may not celebrate twice a day, unless the necessity be urgent. When he does, let nothing be poured into the chalice after the receiving of the blood at the first celebration; but let the least drops be diligently supped out of the chalice, and the fingers sucked or licked with the tongue, and washed, and the washings kept in a clean vessel to be had for this purpose; which washings

are to be drunk after the second celebration; except a deacon or some other considerable minister be present to drink the washings at the first celebration. Further, let the Eucharist be reserved in a clean decent pyx, and so carried to the sick with a clean cloth laid over it, and a candle and cross before it, unless the sick man dwell at too great a distance. Let the host be renewed every Lord's day.

92

1201
Baptism and consent

Innocent III, Bishop of Rome (1198–1216), Letter to Humbert, Archbishop of Arles, Doctrinal Documents, *1410.*

Innocent III raises here the question of the efficacy of baptism where the person baptized has no faith. This arose in the circumstances of both crusades, and missions to unbelievers, when there were sometimes attempts to make converts by force. Baptism is seen here as indelible (that is, conferring a 'character') except where the candidate is baptized against his will.

It is contrary to the Christian religion to force someone into accepting and practising Christianity if he is consistently unwilling and totally opposed. Wherefore, some, not without reason, distinguish between willing and unwilling, unforced and forced. For whoever is violently drawn by fear of punishment and receives the sacrament of baptism to avoid harm to himself, such a one, just like the one who comes to baptism in bad faith, receives the imprint of the Christian character; and, since he gave his consent conditionally though not absolutely, he is to be held to the observance of the Christian faith... But one who never consents and is absolutely unwilling receives neither the reality nor the character of the sacrament, because to express dissent is something more than the absence of any consent.

93

1208
Infant baptism and the effect of baptism in general

Innocent III, Bishop of Rome (1198–1216), Profession of Faith prescribed to the Waldensians, Doctrinal Documents, *1411.*

The Waldensians, or 'Poor Men of Lyons', were a group of dissenters of the later twelfth century who challenged the worldliness and wealth of the clergy and questioned the sacramental theology of the day. They believed that they themselves were living the Christian life as the apostles had taught. Pope Innocent III prescribed a Creed for those who were willing to return to the Church's fold, which they were to affirm to show that they had abandoned their heretical beliefs. Similar professions of the true faith were required in other centuries from repentant heretics or schismatics. Here they are required to acknowledge the effectiveness of baptism and to approve the baptism of infants. Compare Articles xxv, xxvii of the Thirty-Nine Articles.

We therefore approve the baptism of infants. We profess and believe that they are saved if they die after baptism before having committed any sins. And we believe that all sins are remitted in baptism, the original sin which has been contracted as well as those committed voluntarily.

94

1208
Only an ordained priest may be
the celebrant at the Eucharist

Innocent III, Bishop of Rome (1198–1216), Profession of Faith prescribed to the Waldensians, Doctrinal Documents, *1703.*

Here the Waldensians, who had been ordaining their own ministers, are required to accept that the minister of the Eucharist must be ordained within the due order of the Church by a bishop. This is an important statement of the rule that a lay person may not act as president at the celebration of Holy Communion. On the Waldensians, see previous document.

Hence we firmly believe and confess that nobody, however honest, religious, holy and prudent he may be, either can or should consecrate the Eucharist... if he is not a priest regularly ordained by a bishop, visible and tangible.[1] According to our faith, three things are necessary for this office [of presidency at the Eucharist], namely: a definite person, i.e., a priest who, as we have said above, has been properly constituted in that office by a bishop; those solemn words which have been expressed in the canon by the holy

---

[1]   That is to say, not by God alone, 'invisibly', as some of the Waldensians claimed was possible.

Fathers; the faithful intention of the one who pronounces them. And, therefore, we firmly believe and confess that anyone who believes and contends that he can perform the sacrifice of the Eucharist without having first been ordained by a bishop as mentioned above, is a heretic.

95

1208
The Eucharist and the true body and blood of Christ

Innocent III, Bishop of Rome (1198–1216), Profession of Faith prescribed to the Waldensians, Doctrinal Documents, *1504.*

Here the Waldensians are asked to accept that the bread and wine consecrated in the Eucharist become in some way really, and not just symbolically, the body and blood of Christ. This doctrine was first clearly set out as a result of the 'Berengarian' controversy at the end of the eleventh century. It remained controversial during the Middle Ages and the Reformation periods. Cf. nos. 1, 20, 40, 43, 86, 111 and Article xxviii of the Thirty-Nine Articles.

With sincere hearts, we firmly and unhesitatingly believe and loyally affirm that after consecration the... bread and the wine, are the true body and the true blood of our Lord Jesus Christ.

96

1208
Unworthy ministers and the validity of the sacraments

Innocent III, Bishop of Rome (1198–1216), Profession of Faith Prescribed to the Waldensians, Doctrinal Documents, *1301.*

The Waldensians had raised again the question with which Augustine of Hippo and others dealt: whether the unworthiness of the minister affects the value of the sacraments or their validity. Here they are required to concede that the community of the Church provides the context within which grace works in the sacraments, and that the unworthiness of individual ministers does not invalidate them. Compare Article xxvi of the Thirty-Nine Articles.

Furthermore, we do not reject the sacraments which are conferred in the Church, in co-operation with the inestimable and invisible power of the Holy Spirit, even though these sacraments be administered by a sinful priest, as long as he is recognized by the Church. And we do not disparage ecclesiastical duties and blessings performed by such a one; but we accept them with benevolence, as we would those performed by the most just man. For the evil life of a bishop or a priest has no harmful effect on either the baptism of an infant, or the consecration of the Eucharist, or other ecclesiastical duties performed for the faithful... And we believe that in the sacrifice a good priest effects nothing more than a bad priest; because it is not by the merit of the one consecrating that the sacrifice is accomplished, but by the word of the Creator and by the power of the Holy Spirit.

97

1215
Converts to the Faith must be wholehearted

The Fourth Lateran Council, Doctrinal Documents, *1103.*

Compare the advice of Gregory I (590–604) to Augustine of Canterbury on missionary practice (no. 65). The converts envisaged here are from the Jewish faith.

There are some, as has been reported to us, who after having freely approached the sacred bath of baptism do not put off the old man fully in order the better to put on the new one;[1] they retain elements of their former rites and thus by a sort of mixture introduce confusion in the splendour of the Christian religion. Since it is written: 'woe to the man who walks along two ways',[2] and that one must not wear a mingled dress, wool and linen together,[3] we decide that such converts must be forced by those who preside over the Churches to abandon altogether the observance of their ancient rites, so that after having given to the Christian religion the assent of their free will they may be preserved in its observance by the pressure of salutary compulsion. For it is a lesser evil not to recognize the way of the Lord than to step back after having recognized it.

---

[1]   Cf. Colossians 3.9
[2]   Cf. Ecclesiasticus 2.12
[3]   Cf. Deuteronomy 22.11

98

1215
The diversity of rites in the unity of Faith

The Fourth Lateran Council, Doctrinal Documents, *1201.*

On the freedom of the Churches in different places to vary rites and ceremonies, see Article xxxiv of the Thirty-Nine Articles. A second difficulty with modern relevance is also addressed here. When people from different nations and cultures live in the same place, their special needs must be met as far as possible. But they must see themselves as belonging first and foremost to the local Church, whose unity in that place is focussed in the person of its one bishop. On the principles involved here, see *Episcopal Ministry: the Report of the Archbishops' Group on the Episcopate* (London, 1990).

Because in many regions people of different languages live in the same city or diocese, keeping different rites and customs in the unity of faith, we clearly prescribe that the bishops of such cities or dioceses must provide men capable of celebrating the divine liturgy for them and of administering to them the sacraments of the Church as the variety of rites and languages will require, and who will instruct them by word and example. But we altogether forbid one and the same city or diocese to have several bishops, like one body having several heads, which is a monstrous thing. If for the reasons mentioned above, it is found urgent and necessary, let the Bishop of the place after due consideration appoint a catholic prelate[1] from those nations to be his vicar in these matters; he will be subject and obedient to the bishop in all things.

99

1215
Providing preachers

The Fourth Lateran Council, Doctrinal Documents, *1202, translation revised.*

This text underlines the bishop's special responsibility for the ministry of the Word, and for the provision of preachers in his diocese. Compare Anglican Canons of 1604, 34ff., 43ff., 49ff., nos. 175, 177, 179 in this collection.

---

[1]   Latin: *praesul.* The provision envisaged is for a suffragan 'ethnic bishop'.

Among other things pertaining to the salvation of the Christian people, it is known that the food of the Word of God is of the utmost necessity; for, as the body is nourished by material food, so the soul is by spiritual food; for 'man shall not live by bread alone, but by every word that proceeds from the mouth of God'.[1] Hence, since it often happens that bishops because of many occupations or ill-health or hostilities or other reasons ... cannot by themselves suffice to administer the Word of God to their people, especially in vastly spread-out dioceses; in order that the sacred duty of preaching be duly fulfilled, we ordain by this general Constitution that bishops must enrol for it capable men, mighty in deed and in word.[2] When the bishops are not able to do so themselves, these men will visit the people entrusted to the bishops, in their name and with due solicitude, and will edify them by word and example. When the preachers are in need, the bishops will provide them with what is reasonable and necessary, lest they be compelled, because of want, to give up the ministry they have undertaken.

100

1215
The rule of annual confession

The Fourth Lateran Council, Doctrinal Documents, *1608–9, translation revised.*

This rule of annual confession is linked to the requirement that every Christian must receive Holy Communion at least once a year, at Easter (compare the exhortation at the warning for the celebration of Holy Communion in the Book of Common Prayer. The emphasis in both is upon coming to Communion 'with a quiet conscience'). The pastoral responsibility of the priest for his own people is stressed here, although, as in the exhortation, it is allowable for the sinner to go to any ordained minister for the help he needs. The secrecy of the confession is sacrosanct. Cf. 186, 234, 268, 487.

Every faithful person of either sex who has reached the age of discretion should at least once a year faithfully confess all his sins

---

[1]   Matthew 4.4

[2]   Cf. Luke 24.19

in secret to his own priest. He [or she] should strive as far as possible to carry out the penance imposed on him, and receive with reverence the sacrament of the Eucharist at least during Easter time.... But if anyone wishes for good reasons to confess his sins to another priest, he must first ask and obtain permission from his own priest because otherwise that priest has no power to bind or loose him.

Let [the confessor] take absolute care not to betray the sinner through word or sign, or in any other way whatsoever. If he needs expert advice he may seek it, but without in any way identifying the person. For we decree that he who presumes to reveal a sin which has been manifested to him in the tribunal of penance is not only to be deposed from his priestly office, but also to be consigned to a closed monastery for perpetual penance.

101

1222
Careful and devout performance of Divine Office

Langton's Constitutions, Stephen Langton, Archbishop of Canterbury (1207–28), 1222; Wilkins, I, 585, Concilium Oxoniense, British Library, MS. Cotton Otho A XV; Johnson, II, 105–7.

Compare the emphasis of later Anglican texts upon the reverent performance of the words and actions of the minister and congregation alike, in all the Church's worship. (See nos. 144, 168.)

We decree with the General Council, that both the nocturnal and day office be celebrated with diligence and devotion, as God gives ability; and that all the sacraments, those of baptism and of the altar especially, be performed with such devotion as God inspires; that the words of the canon, especially of the consecration of Christ's body, be perfectly pronounced.

102

1311–1312
Learning languages for missionary work

The Council of Vienna, Doctrinal Documents, *1104.*

Therefore, unworthy as we are of the commission which Christ has entrusted to us in the world, following his own example when he wished that the apostles who were to go to evangelise the whole world should be well versed in all languages,[1] we desire that the holy Church should have an abundant number of catholics well versed in the languages,... so as to be able to instruct in the sacred doctrine and to join [converts] to the Christian community by the acceptance of the Christian faith and the reception of holy baptism.

103

1373 and after
A vision of the universe

The Revelations of Divine Love by Dame Julian of Norwich, c.1342 — after 1413, chapters 5, 42, 86: E. Colledge and J. Walsh (Toronto, 1978), 2, pp. 299–300, 471, 732–3.

Julian of Norwich was a mystic who seems to have lived as a hermit beside the walls of the church of St Julian in Norwich in the East of England. She wrote her *Sixteen Revelations of Divine Love* after twenty years of meditation upon visions given to her in 1373. She appears to have had some access to neoplatonic ideas through the English mystical tradition.

And he showed me more, a little thing, the size of a hazelnut, on the palm of my hand, round like a ball. I looked at it thoughtfully and wondered, 'What is this?' And the answer came, 'It is all that is made.' I marvelled that it continued to exist and did not suddenly disintegrate; it was so small. And again my mind supplied the answer. 'It exists, both now and forever, because God loves it.' In short, everything owes its existence to the love of God. This is the meaning, as if to say, 'See, I have done all this long before your prayers; and now you exist and pray to me.' He means that we ought to know that the greatest deeds are already done, as Holy Church teaches.

---

[1]　Cf. Acts 2.4; I Corinthians 12.30

From the time these things were first revealed I had often wanted to know what was our Lord's meaning. It was more than fifteen years after that I was answered in my spirit's understanding. 'You would know our Lord's meaning in this thing? Know it well. Love was his meaning.' So it was that I learned that love was our Lord's meaning. And I saw for certain, both here and elsewhere, that before ever he made us, God loved us.

104

1373 and after
The motherhood and fatherhood of God

The Revelations of Divine Love by Dame Julian of Norwich, c.1342 — after 1413, chapter 59: E. Colledge and J. Walsh (Toronto, 1978), 2, pp. 589–600.

Here Julian of Norwich (see no. 103) explores the work of Christ for us not only on the Cross, but also in his continuing care in the life of the Church.

It is the way of God to set good against evil. So Jesus Christ who sets good against evil is our real Mother. We owe our being to him — and this is the essence of motherhood! — and all the delightful, loving protection which ever follows. God is as really our Mother as he is our Father. He showed this in everything, and particularly when he said that sweet word, 'It is I.' In other words, 'It is I who am the strength and goodness of Fatherhood; I who am the wisdom of Motherhood; I who am light and grace and blessed love; I who am Trinity; I who am Unity; I who am the sovereign goodness of every single thing; I who enable you to love; I who enable you to long. It is I who am the eternal satisfaction of every genuine desire.' For the soul is at its best, its most noble and honourable, when it is most lowly, and humble, and gentle. Springing from this fundamental source and as part of our natural endowment, are all the virtues of our sensual nature, aided and abetted as they are by mercy and grace. Without such assistance we should be in a poor way! Our great Father, God almighty, who is being, knew and loved us from eternity. Through his knowledge, and in the marvellous depth of his charity, together with the foresight and wisdom of the whole blessed Trinity, he willed that the Second person should become our Mother, Brother, and Saviour. Hence it follows that God is as truly our Mother as he is our Father. Our Father decides, our Mother works, our good Lord, the Holy Spirit, strengthens. So we ought to love our God in whom we have our own being, reverently thanking him, and praising him for creating us, earnestly beseeching our Mother for mercy and pity, and our Lord, the Spirit, for help and grace.

For in these three is contained our life: nature, mercy, grace. From these we get our humility, gentleness, patience and pity. From them too we get our hatred of sin and wickedness (it is the function of virtue to hate these). So we see that Jesus is the true Mother of our nature, for he made us. He is our Mother, too, by grace, because he took our created nature upon himself. All the lovely deeds and tender services that beloved motherhood implies are appropriate to the Second person. In him the godly will is always safe and sound, both in nature and grace, because of his own fundamental goodness.

I came to realize that there were three ways of looking at God's motherhood: the first is based on the fact that our nature is 'made'; the second is found in the assumption of the nature (there begins the motherhood of grace); the third is the motherhood of work which flows out over all by that same grace. The length and breadth and height and depth of it is everlasting, and so is his love.... Our Mother by nature and grace (for he would become our Mother in everything) laid the foundation of his work in the Virgin's womb with great and gentle condescension. (This was shown in the first revelation when I received a mental picture of the Virgin's true simplicity at the time she conceived.) In other words, it was in this lowly place that God most high, the supreme wisdom of all, adorned and arrayed himself with our poor flesh, ready to function and serve as Mother in all things.

A mother's is the most intimate, willing, and dependable of all services, because it is the truest of all. None has been able to fulfil it properly but Christ, and he alone can. We know that our own mother's bearing of us was a bearing to pain and death, but what does Jesus, our true Mother, do? Why, he, All-love, bears us to joy and eternal life! Blessings on him! Thus he carries us within himself in love. And he is in labour until the time has fully come for him to suffer the sharpest pangs and most appalling pain possible — and in the end he dies. And not even when this is over, and we ourselves have been born to eternal bliss, is his marvellous love completely satisfied. This he shows in that overwhelming word of love, 'If I could possibly have suffered more, indeed I would have done so.' He can die no more, but that does not stop him working, for he needs to feed us... It is an obligation of his dear, motherly, love. The human mother will suckle her child with her own milk, but our beloved Mother, Jesus, feeds us with himself, and, with the most tender courtesy, does it by means of the Blessed Sacrament, the precious food of all true life. And he sustains us through his mercy and grace by all the sacraments. ...

The human mother may put her child tenderly to her breast, but our tender Mother Jesus simply leads us into his blessed breast through his open side, and there gives us a glimpse of the Godhead and heavenly joy — the inner certainty of eternal bliss. The tenth revelation showed this, and said as much with that word, 'See how I love you', as looking into his side he rejoiced. This fine and lovely word 'Mother' is so sweet and so much its own that it cannot properly be used of any but him, and of her who is his own true Mother — and ours. In essence 'motherhood' means love and kindness, wisdom, knowledge, goodness. Though in comparison with our spiritual birth our physical birth is a small, unimportant, straightforward sort of thing, it still remains that it is only through his working that it can be done at all by his creatures. A kind, loving mother who understands and knows the needs of her child will look after it tenderly just because it is the nature of a mother to do so. As the child grows older she changes her methods — but not her love. When it is older still, she allows the child to be punished so that its faults are corrected and its virtues and graces developed. This way of doing things, with much else that is right and good, is our Lord at work in those who are doing them. Thus he is our Mother in nature, working by his grace in our lower part, for the sake of the higher. It is his will that we should know this, for he wants all our love to be fastened on himself. In this way I could see that our indebtedness, under God, to fatherhood and motherhood – whether it be human or divine — is fully met in truly loving God. And this blessed love Christ himself produces in us. This was shown in all the revelations, and especially in those splendid words that he uttered, 'It is I whom you love'.

105

1373 and after
The working of the Trinity in our salvation

The Revelations of Divine Love by Dame Julian of Norwich, c.1342
— after 1413, chapter 58: E. Colledge and J. Walsh (Toronto,
1978), 2, pp. 582–8.

On Julian, see 103. Images of the Trinity in which three aspects of God's
relation to humanity are discussed are common in medieval preaching and
devotional writing.

So when he made us, God almighty was our kindly Father, and
God all-wise[1] our kindly Mother, and the Holy Spirit their love and
goodness; all one God, one Lord. In this uniting together he is our
real, true husband, and we his loved wife and sweetheart. He is
never displeased with his wife! 'I love you and you love me,' he
says, 'and our love will never be broken.' I saw the blessed Trinity
working. I saw that there were these three attributes: fatherhood,
motherhood, and lordship — all in one God. In the almighty Father
we have been sustained and blessed with regard to our created
natural being from before all time. By the skill and wisdom of the
second person we are sustained, restored, and saved with regard to
our sensual nature, for he is our Mother, Brother, and Saviour. In
our good Lord the Holy Spirit we have, after our life and hardship
is over, that reward and rest which surpasses for ever any and
everything we can possibly desire — such is his abounding grace
and magnificent courtesy.

Our life too is threefold. In the first stage we have our being, in
the second our growth, and in the third our perfection. The first is
nature, the second mercy, and the third grace. For the first I
realized that the great power of the Trinity is our Father, the deep
wisdom, our Mother, and the great love, our Lord. All this we
have by nature and in our created and essential being. Moreover I
saw the second person who is our Mother with regard to our
essential nature; that same dear person has become our Mother in
the matter of our sensual nature. We are God's creation twice:
essential being and sensual nature. Our being is that higher part
which we have in our Father, God almighty; and the second person
of the Trinity is Mother of this basic nature, providing the

---

[1]   that is, the Son as Wisdom

substance in which we are rooted and grounded. But he is our Mother also in mercy, since he has taken our sensual nature upon himself. Thus 'our Mother' describes the different ways in which he works, ways which are separate to us, but held together in him. In our Mother, Christ, we grow and develop; in his mercy he reforms and restores us; through his passion, death, and resurrection he has united us to our being. So does our Mother work in mercy for all his children who respond to him and obey him. Grace works with mercy too, and especially in two ways. The work is that of the third person, the Holy Spirit, who works by 'rewarding' and 'giving'. Rewarding is the generous gift of truth that the Lord makes to him who has suffered. Giving is a magnanimous gesture which he makes freely by his grace: perfect, and far beyond the deserts of any of his creatures. Thus in our Father, God almighty, we have our being. In our merciful Mother we have reformation and renewal, and our separate parts are integrated into perfect man. In yielding to the gracious impulse of the Holy Spirit we are made perfect. Our essence is in our Father, God almighty, and in our Mother, God all-wise, and in our Lord the Holy Spirit, God all-good. Our essential nature is entire in each person of the Trinity, who is one God. Our sensual nature is in the Second person alone, Jesus Christ. In him is the Father too, and the Holy Spirit. In and by him have we been taken out of hell with a strong arm, and out of earth's wretchedness have been wonderfully raised to heaven, and united, most blessedly, to him who is our true being. And we have developed in spiritual wealth and character through all Christ's virtues, and by the gracious work of the Holy Spirit.

106

1373 and after
God cares for us like a mother for an erring child

The Revelations of Divine Love by Dame Julian of Norwich, c.1342 — after 1413, chapter 61: E. Colledge and J. Walsh (Toronto, 1978), 2, pp. 604–9.

On Julian, see no. 103. The indefectibility of the Church is also stressed here.

A mother may allow her child sometimes to fall, and to learn the hard way, for its own good. But because she loves the child she will never allow the situation to become dangerous. Admittedly earthly mothers have been known to let their children die, but our heavenly Mother Jesus will never let us, his children, die. He, and none but he, is almighty, all wisdom, all love. Blessings on him! But often when we are shown the extent of our fall and wretchedness we are so scared and dreadfully ashamed that we scarcely know where to look. Yet our patient Mother does not want us to run away; nothing would be more displeasing to him. His desire is that we should do what a child does; for when a child is in trouble or is scared it runs to mother for help as fast as it can. That is what he wants us to do, saying with the humility of a child, 'Kind, thoughtful, dearest Mother, do be sorry for me. I have got myself into a filthy mess, and am not a bit like you. I cannot begin to put it right without your special and willing help.' Even if we do not feel immediate relief we can still be sure that he behaves like a wise mother. If he sees it is better for us to mourn and weep he lets us do so — with pity and sympathy, of course, and for the right length of time — because he loves us. And he wants us to copy the child who always and naturally trusts mother's love through thick and thin.

Moreover he wills that we should hold tight to the Faith of Holy Church, and find there in that Communion of Saints our dearest Mother, who comforts us because she really understands. Individuals may often break down — or so it seems to them — but the whole body of Holy Church is unbreakable, whether in the past, present, or future. So it is a good, sound, grace-bringing thing to resolve, humbly but firmly, to be fastened and united to Holy Church our Mother — in other words, to Jesus Christ. For the merciful ample flood of his precious blood and water[1] suffices to make us sweet and clean; the Saviour's blessed wounds are open, and rejoice to heal us; the dear, gracious hands of our Mother are ever about us, and eager to help. In all this work he functions as a kindly nurse who has no other business than to care for the well-being of her charge. It is his business to save us; it is his glory to do this for us; and it is his will that we should know it. For it is also his will that we should love him dearly, and trust him humbly and wholeheartedly. All this he showed in those gracious words, 'I will keep you safe and sound.'

---

[1]   that is, baptism and the Eucharist

107

1393
Church and State

The Second Statute of Praemunire, *16 Richard II, cap. 5, Gee and Hardy, p. 123, translation revised.*

This text is included to illustrate the entrenched character of the dispute of the Middle Ages between the Kings of England and the Papacy as to the respective limits of royal and papal jurisdiction in England. The grounds here are clearly not doctrinal. This long-standing rivalry also underlies the events of Henry VIII's reign, and accounts in part for his actions.

And also it is said, and a common clamour is made, that the said holy Father the Pope has ordained and purposed to translate some prelates of the same realm, some out of the realm, and some from one bishopric to another within the same realm, without the King's assent and knowledge, and without the assent of the prelates, which so shall be translated; which prelates be much profitable and necessary to our said lord the King, and to all his realm; by which translations, if they should be allowed, the statutes of the realm would be defeated and made void; and his said liege wise men of his council, without his assent, and against his will, carried away and gotten out of his realm, and the substance and treasure of the realm shall be carried away, and so the realm be destitute as well of council as of substance, to the final destruction of the same realm; and so the crown of England, which has been so free at all times, that it has been in no earthly subjection, but immediately subject to God in all things touching the royalty of the same crown, and to none other, should be submitted to the Pope, and the laws and statutes of the realm by him defeated and avoided at his will, to the perpetual destruction of the sovereignty of our lord the King, his crown, and his royalty, and of all his realm, which God defend.

108

1415
Communion in both kinds

The Council of Constance, Decree on Communion under the species of bread alone, Doctrinal Documents, *1506.*

The practice of giving only the bread and not the wine to the laity at Holy Communion is acknowledged here to have arisen as a matter of convenience, but it is pointed out that the laity do not thus receive anything less than the whole Christ. The matter became highly controversial in fifteenth-century Bohemia, and the Thirty-Nine Articles insist on the laity's receiving both bread and wine. Present-day Roman Catholic practice normally gives both elements to all. Compare Article xxx of the Thirty-Nine Articles and no. 437.

The present custom has been introduced for good reasons to avoid some dangers and scandals and thus it has been legitimate to maintain and observe it for similar or even greater reasons. It is true that in the early Church this sacrament was received by the faithful under both kinds, but later it came to be received under both kinds by those who consecrate it and under the species of bread alone by the laity. [This custom is legitimate] for it must be firmly believed and can in no way be doubted that the body and the blood of Christ are truly and integrally contained under the species of bread as well as under that of wine.

109

1439
Baptism and Confirmation

The Council of Florence, Decree for the Armenians, Doctrinal Documents, *1412–18.*

This decree of the Council of Florence has an ecumenical purpose, as have those which follow, and we include a good deal of material from this Council to illustrate the thrust of ecumenism at this date. The present text is an attempt to state, in terms of the contemporary fashion for identifying the 'matter' and 'form' of sacraments, their principal (or 'final') cause and the instrumental cause (or 'instrument') through which the divine power works, that understanding of the nature and value of the sacraments which we have seen developing in earlier texts. Compare 110–116 and Article xxv of the Thirty-Nine Articles. The Armenians were a non-Chalcedonian Church.

Among the sacraments holy baptism holds the first place because it is the gateway to the spiritual life; by it we are made members of Christ and belong to his body, the Church. And since through the first man death has entered into all,[1] unless we are born again of water and the Spirit, we cannot, as Truth said, enter into the Kingdom of heaven.[2] The (matter' of this sacrament is true natural water; it is of no importance whether it is cold or warm. The form is: 'I baptize you in the name of the Father and of the Son and of the Holy Spirit.' We do not deny, however, that true baptism is also effected by these words: 'May the servant of Christ, N., be baptized in the name of the Father and of the Son and of the Holy Spirit', or: 'By my hands N. is baptized in the name of the Father and of the Son and of the Holy Spirit.' For as the principal cause from which baptism derives its virtue is the Holy Trinity, while the instrumental cause is the minister who confers the sacrament externally, the sacrament is performed whenever the act carried out by the minister is expressed along with the invocation of the Holy Trinity. The minister of this sacrament is the priest, to whom by reason of his office it belongs to baptize. But in case of necessity not only a priest or deacon, but also a layman, or a woman, or even a pagan and a heretic may baptize, provided he observes the Church's form and intends to do what the Church does.

The effect of this sacrament is the remission of all guilt, original and actual, and also of all punishment due to the guilt itself. For this reason, no satisfaction is to be enjoined on the baptized for their past sins; and if they die before committing any fault, they immediately gain access to the Kingdom of heaven and the beatific vision.

The second sacrament is confirmation.[3] Its matter is chrism made from oil, signifying the purity of conscience, and balsam, signifying the fragrance of a good reputation; it is blessed by the bishop. The form is: 'I sign you with the sign of the Cross and I confirm you with the chrism of salvation, in the name of the Father

---

[1]   Cf. Romans 5.12.

[2]   Cf. John 3.5.

[3]   It was not controversial at this date to speak of confirmation as a sacrament. It became so for a time during the sixteenth century. See Article xxv of the Thirty-Nine Articles on the distinction between baptism and Holy Communion as sacraments 'ordained of Christ' and the other five 'commonly called sacraments'.

and of the Son and of the Holy Spirit.' The ordinary minister is the bishop. Whereas other anointings may be performed by a simple priest, this one must be conferred only by the bishop. For we read that only the apostles, whose place the bishops hold, imparted the Holy Spirit by the laying on of hands. Reading the Acts of the apostles makes it clear, for it is said: 'Now when the apostles at Jerusalem heard that Samaria had received the word of God, they sent to Peter and John, who came down and prayed for them that they might receive the Holy Spirit: for it had not yet fallen on any of them, but they had only been baptized in the name of the Lord Jesus. Then they laid their hands on them and they received the Holy Spirit'.[4] Confirmation given by the Church takes the place of that imposition of hand. Nevertheless, we read that sometimes through a dispensation of the Apostolic See, for a reasonable and very urgent cause, a simple priest has administered the sacrament of confirmation with chrism prepared by the bishop. The effect of this sacrament is that in it the Holy Spirit is given for strength, as he was given to the apostles on the day of the Pentecost, in order that the Christian may courageously confess the name of Christ. And, therefore, the one to be confirmed is anointed on the forehead which is the seat of shame, so that he may not be ashamed to confess the name of Christ, and chiefly his Cross, which according to the apostle, is a stumbling block for the Jews and foolishness for the Gentiles.[5] This is why he is signed with the sign of the Cross.

110

1439
Why wine in the Eucharist is mixed with water

The Council of Florence, Decree for the Armenians, Doctrinal Documents, *1509.*

Compare no. 109 for this series of texts.

The third sacrament is the Eucharist. The matter of this sacrament is wheat-bread and grape-wine with a small amount of water to be mixed in before the consecration. Water is mixed in because,

---

4 Acts 8.14–17
5 Cf. I Corinthians 1.23

according to the testimony of the holy Fathers and Doctors of the Church mentioned in the preceding discussions, it is believed that our Lord himself instituted this sacrament with wine mixed with water. Furthermore, this is a fitting representation of our Lord's passion. For, as Blessed Alexander, the fifth Pope after St Peter, says: 'In the oblation of the mysteries which are offered to the Lord during the solemnities of the Mass, let only bread and wine mixed with water be offered in sacrifice. Not wine only nor water only should be offered in the chalice of the Lord, but a mixture of both. For we read that both, that is, blood and water, flowed from the side of Christ'.[1] Finally, this is a fitting way to signify the effect of this sacrament, that is, the union of the Christian people with Christ. For, water represents the people, as the Apocalypse says: 'many waters... many peoples'. And Julius, the second Pope after Blessed Sylvester, says: 'According to the prescription of the canons, the Lord's chalice should be offered with wine mixed with water. For we see that the water represents the people and the wine manifests the blood of Christ. Thus, when wine and water are mixed in the chalice, the people are united with Christ, and the faithful people are closely joined to him in whom they believe.'[2]

111

1439

The Eucharist

The Council of Florence, Decree for the Armenians, Doctrinal Documents, *1510.*

The emphasis here is on the principle that the prayer of consecration is said *in persona Christi*, 'in the person [or name] of Christ'.[1] The 'effect' of the Eucharist is of a fuller incorporation into the Body of Christ by grace for those who receive it worthily (compare Article xxviii of the Thirty-Nine Articles).

---

[1] John 19.34 Revelation 17.15 Pseudo-Alexander I. *Epistola ad omnes orthodoxos,* 9.

[2] Pseudo-Julius I, *Epistola ad episcopos Aegypti.*
    These texts, now known not to be the work of the Popes in question, were believed in the fifteenth century to be authentic.

[1] The usual rendering at this date of II Corinthians 2.10

The form of this sacrament is the words of the Saviour with which he effected this sacrament; for the priest effects this sacrament by speaking in the person of Christ. It is by the power of these words that the substance of bread is changed into the body of Christ, and the substance of wine into his blood; in such a way, however, that the whole Christ is contained under the species of bread and the whole Christ under the species of wine. Further, the whole Christ is present under any part of the consecrated host or the consecrated wine when separated from the rest...

The effect which this sacrament produces in the soul of a person who receives it worthily, is to unite him with Christ. For, since it is by grace that a man is incorporated into Christ and united to his members, it follows that those who receive this sacrament worthily receive an increase of grace. And all the effects which material food and drink have on the life of the body — maintaining and increasing life, restoring health and giving joy — all these effects this sacrament produces for the spiritual life. As Pope Urban says,[2] in this sacrament we celebrate in thanksgiving the memory of our Saviour, we are drawn away from evil, we are strengthened in what is good, and we advance and increase in virtue and grace.

112

1439
Leavened or unleavened bread

The Council of Florence, Decree for the Greeks, Doctrinal Documents, *1508.*

Again there is an ecumenical purpose here. One of the differences over which the Greek Christians had divided from the Latin in 1054 had been the use of leavened or unleavened bread in Holy Communion. Anselm of Canterbury had argued that 'substantial' agreement remained, for whether leavened or unleavened, it was bread that both Greeks and Latins used.

Likewise we define that the body of Christ is truly effected with either unleavened or leavened wheaten bread; and that priests must consecrate the body of the Lord in one way or the other, namely, each following the custom of their Church, either the Western or the Oriental Church.

---

[2]   Cf. *DS* 846

113

1439
Penance

The Council of Florence, Decree for the Armenians, Doctrinal Documents, *1612.*

During the Middle Ages penance had come to involve three elements: contrition for one's sins, confessing them to a priest, and carrying out some action to show that one's repentance was sincere, usually an act of prayer, fasting or almsgiving. The priest declares God's forgiveness to the penitent in the absolution. Compare 109, and texts following, and Article xxv of the Thirty-Nine Articles on the use of the word 'sacrament' here.

The fourth sacrament is penance. Its quasi-matter consists in the actions of the penitent which are divided into three parts. The first of these is contrition of the heart, which requires that he be sorry for the sin committed, with the resolve not to sin in the future. The second is oral confession which requires the sinner to confess to his priest fully all the sins he remembers. The third is satisfaction for the sins according to the judgement of the priest, which is mainly achieved by prayer, fasting and almsgiving. The form of this sacrament is the words of absolution spoken by the priest when he says: 'I absolve you'. The minister of this sacrament is the priest who has authority to absolve... The effect of this sacrament is absolution from sins.

114

1439
'Extreme Unction'

The Council of Florence, Decree for the Armenians, Doctrinal Documents, *1613.*

Compare 109 and texts following, and Article xxv of the Thirty-Nine Articles on the use of the word 'sacrament' here.

The fifth sacrament is extreme unction. Its matter is olive oil blessed by the bishop. This sacrament may not be given except to a sick person whose life is feared for. He is to be anointed on the following parts: on the eyes on account of sight, on the ears on account of hearing, on the nostrils on account of smelling, on the mouth on account of taste and speech, on the hands on account of touch, on the feet on account of movement, on the loins on account of the lust seated there. The minister of this sacrament is the priest. The effect is the healing of the mind and, as far as it is good for the soul, of the body as well. Of this sacrament blessed James the apostle says: 'Is any among you sick?'[1]

115

1439
Ordination

The Council of Florence, Decree for the Armenians, Doctrinal Documents, *1705, translation revised.*

The discussion of ordination here lays stress on 'matter' and 'form'. The Book of Common Prayer preserves the 'matter' by giving a New Testament to the deacon and a Bible to the priest at ordination. It also preserves the 'form' (see the Preface to the Ordinal). See 1, 20, 43, 95 on the usage of the word 'sacrifice' here and 109 and texts following, and Article xxv of the Thirty-Nine Articles on 'sacrament'.

The sixth sacrament is that of Order. Its matter is... that handing over[1] by which the Order is conferred: thus the presbyterate is conferred by handing over[2] the chalice with wine and the paten with the bread; the diaconate by giving the book of the gospels; the subdiaconate by handing over the empty chalice covered with an empty paten; and similarly the other Orders by assigning the things pertaining to their office. The form of the presbyterate is this: 'Receive the power of offering the Sacrifice in the Church for the living and the dead, in the name of the Father and of the Son and of the Holy Spirit.' And similarly for the forms of the other Orders, as is contained in detail in the Roman Pontifical. The ordinary minister of this sacrament is the bishop. The effect is an increase of grace so that one may be a fitting minister of Christ.

---

[1]　　James 5.14ff.

[1]　　Latin: *traditio*

[2]　　Latin: *porrectio*

116

1439
Matrimony

The Council of Florence, Decree for the Armenians, Doctrinal Documents, *1803.*

See 109 and texts following, and Article xxv of the Thirty-Nine Articles.

The seventh is the sacrament of matrimony, which is the sign of the union of Christ and the Church according to the saying of the apostle: 'This is a great mystery, and I mean in reference to Christ and the Church'.[1] The efficient cause of matrimony is the mutual consent duly expressed in words relating to the present. A triple good is found in matrimony. The first is the begetting of children and their education to the worship of God. The second is the faithfulness which each spouse owes to the other. Third is the indissolubility of marriage, inasmuch as it represents the indissoluble union of Christ and the Church. But, although it is permitted to separate on account of adultery, nevertheless it is not permitted to contract another marriage since the bond of marriage legitimately contracted is perpetual.

117

1439
Life after death

The Council of Florence, Decree for the Greeks, Doctrinal Documents, *2308.*

The doctrine of purgatory had been developing since patristic times, but it was only in the twelfth century that it became clearly established in the West. Here an attempt is made to state the doctrine in a form acceptable to Greek Christians. Souls in purgatory are seen as sure of heaven but as in need of final transforming change. This was thought of as a 'purification', and it was described in concrete terms as an opportunity to discharge the debts of this life's sins. It was recognized that God gives free forgiveness to those who repent, but it seemed important that the sinner should discharge the 'penalties' due for his sins, to show the sincerity of his repentance. These 'penalties' could be commuted into a different form in the ancient penitential

---

[1]   Ephesians 5.32

system, or a fellow-Christian could, it was held, bear them on behalf of the sinner, even after his or her death. Compare Article xxii of the Thirty-Nine Articles, which condemns belief in purgatory and the indulgences ('pardons') which remitted the penalties due. This Article needs to be read in the light of the sixteenth century controversy over the abuse of the system of indulgences. Luther complained that instead of remitting, as an act of loving mercy, the penalties she had imposed, the Church was selling pardons for money, and the simple faithful believed that they had to buy their way to heaven. The present text is included because it states the real doctrine of the late medieval Church. The corruptions were a matter of practice, not of doctrine. It should be noted that the sale of indulgences continued for a time in the post-Henrician sixteenth century Church of England, because it remained a valuable source of ecclesiastical revenue.

And, if they are truly penitent and die in God's love before having satisfied by worthy fruits of penance for their sins of commission and omission, their souls are cleansed after death by purgatorial penalties. In order that they be relieved from such penalties, the acts of intercession[1] of the living faithful benefit them, namely the sacrifices of the Mass, prayers, alms, and other works of piety which the faithful are wont to do for the other faithful according to the Church's practice.

The souls of those who, after having received baptism, have incurred no stain of sin whatever, and those souls who, after having contracted the stain of sin, have been cleansed, either while in their bodies or after having been divested of them as stated above, are received immediately[2] into heaven, and see clearly God himself, one and three, as he is.

118

1442
All things are lawful but not all things are helpful

The Council of Florence, Decree for the [Monophysite] *Jacobites, Doctrinal Documents, 1004.*

[The Holy Roman Church] firmly believes, professes and preaches that 'everything created by God is good and nothing is to be

---

[1]   Latin: *suffragia*

[2]   Latin: *mox*

rejected if it is received with thanksgiving';[1] because, according to the word of the Lord it is 'not what goes into the mouth that defiles a man'.[2] She asserts that the distinction of clean and unclean food in the Mosaic Law belongs to religious observances which have passed away with the rise of the gospel and have ceased to be efficacious. She also asserts that the command of the apostles to 'abstain from what has been sacrificed to idols and from blood and from what is strangled'[3] was fitting in those times when the one Church was emerging from the Jews and the Gentiles, who previously had observed different religious customs and moral habits. For in this way the Gentiles should share some observances in common with the Jews, and, the causes of dissent being removed, it would be possible to come to a common worship and profession of faith. For to the Jews, because of their ancient traditions, blood and what is strangled is abhorrent; thus, if they saw the Gentiles eat what was sacrificed to idols they might suspect them of returning to idolatry. But, once the Christian religion had been so widely spread that no Jew according to the flesh is found in it but all who enter the Church agree on the same rites of the gospel and modes of worship, believing that 'to the pure all things are pure',[4] the reason for the apostolic prohibition had ceased to exist and, therefore, the prohibition itself has also ceased. The Church declares, therefore, that none among the kinds of food which human civilization admits must be condemned; and that no distinction must be made between animals, whoever be the person, man or woman, by whom they are killed, and whatever be the way in which they are killed. However, for the sake of bodily health, for the exercise of virtue, for the observance of monastic and ecclesiastical discipline, a man may and must refrain from many things which are not condemned. For, as the Apostle says: 'All things are lawful but not all things are helpful'.[5]

---

[1] I Timothy 4.4

[2] Matthew 15.11

[3] Acts 15.29

[4] Titus 1.15

[5] I Corinthians 6.12; 10.22

119

1442
Christ the Redeemer

The Council of Florence, Decree for the [Monophysite] *Jacobites,*
Doctrinal Documents, *644, translation revised.*

The Church firmly believes, professes and preaches that one Person
of the Trinity, true God, Son of God begotten from the Father, one
in being with the Father and equally eternal with him, has, in the
fullness of time designed by the divine counsel in its inscrutable
majesty, assumed fom the immaculate womb of the Virgin Mary
for the salvation of the human race a true and complete human
nature and united it to himself in the unity of person.[1] This unity is
so intimate that neither is anything which in him belongs to God
separated from the man, nor is anything belonging to the man
divided from the divinity; one and the same is undivided, each of
the two natures persisting with its own properties. He is God and
man, Son of God and son of man, equal to the Father, as to the
divinity, inferior to the Father as to the humanity; immortal and
eternal by his divine nature, subject to suffering and to time by the
human condition which he has assumed. She firmly believes,
professes and preaches that the Son of God was truly born of the
Virgin in the humanity which he assumed, that he truly suffered,
truly died and was buried, truly rose from the dead, ascended to
heaven and is seated at the right hand of the Father, and that he
will come at the end of times to judge the living and the dead. She
firmly believes, professes and preaches that no one ever conceived
from man and woman has been freed from the domination of the
devil, except through faith in Jesus Christ our Lord, the Mediator
between God and men, who, conceived without sin, having been
born and having died, alone crushed the enemy of the human race
by his death which destroyed our sins, and secured again entry into
the Kingdom of heaven which the first man had lost by his sin and
all his descendants with him.

---

[1]   Latin: *in unitatem personae*

120

1442
Salvation and the Church

The Council of Florence, Decree for the [Monophysite] *Jacobites, Doctrinal Documents, 1005.*

The teaching that 'outside the Church none can be saved' needs to be understood in relation to a number of ecclesiological developments of the later Middle Ages. The Church is here understood to be the visible and institutional Church only, whose members can be identified by baptism, and whose definitions of faith make it plain where heresy lies. Some reformers were to argue that only God himself can know who his people are, and that the true Church is therefore 'invisible'. Compare Thirty-Nine Articles xviii and xix, and the opening of Article vi on 'necessary for salvation'.

[The Holy Roman Church]... firmly believes, professes and preaches that no one remaining outside the Catholic Church, not only pagans, but also Jews, heretics or schismatics, can become partakers of eternal life; but they will go to the 'eternal fire prepared for the devil and his angels',[1] unless before the end of their life they are received into it. For union with the body of the Church is of so great importance that the sacraments of the Church are helpful to salvation only for those remaining in it; and fasts, almsgiving, other works of piety, and the exercises of a militant Christian life bear eternal rewards for them alone. 'And no one can be saved, no matter how much alms he has given, even if he sheds his blood for the name of Christ, unless he remains in the bosom and unity of the Catholic Church.'[2]

---

[1]   Matthew 25.41

[2]   Cf. Fulgentius of Ruspa, *De fide liber ad Petrum*, 38, 79, and 39, 80

4

THE SIXTEENTH CENTURY EMERGENCY
1520–1604

121

1527–47

Henry VIII

J.R.H. Moorman, Bishop of Ripon, A History of the Church in England *(3rd edn, London, 1973), pp. 163 ff., quoted and summarized.*

This material is included by way of a brief account of the events surrounding the break of the English Church with Rome.

'Early in the 1520s Lutheran teaching was being discussed at Cambridge... Similar discussions were also held in other parts of the country. But... the king much disliked what he had heard of Luther and replied to his attack on the Sacraments by a counter-attack which earned for him the Pope's gratitude and that title of "Defender of the Faith" which the English sovereign still bears.'[1] [Henry VIII had decided in 1527 that his wife Katherine of Aragon would not now bear him a male heir because she was getting past the age of childbearing. He asked the Pope for a decree of nullity, on the grounds that Katherine had been the widow of his brother Arthur and he had married her within prohibited degrees. The Pope played for time because he did not want to offend Katherine's nephew, the Emperor Charles V. Henry became sufficiently angry, after several years' delay, to take matters into his own hands. In 1530 he indicted Wolsey, the Pope's legate in England, for having taken orders from a foreign power. He died under arrest for high treason. In 1531, Henry accused the whole body of the clergy of having accepted Wolsey as legate, and thus of having themselves been guilty of treason. He pardoned them only on payment of a large fine and acknowledgement that Henry was 'Singular Protector, only and supreme Lord, and, as far as the law of Christ allows, even Supreme Head' of the Church in England.] 'Between

---

[1]   p. 163

1532 and 1534 seven bills were passed through Parliament, each carefully designed to cut one of the threads which bound England to Rome.'[2] [These cut off the payment of taxes and the making of appeals to Rome, provided for the election of bishops, and transferred the power of granting dispensations and licences from the Pope to the Archbishop of Canterbury.] 'The Supreme Head Act' not only gave the king the title which he had always sought (and that without any saving clause about the 'Law of Christ'); it also gave him the power to define doctrine and to punish heresy. The final act, the Succession Act, gave parliamentary sanction to the divorce, and made it possible for the king to demand an oath from any subject in favour of the new régime. Refusal to take the oath was regarded as ... high treason. It was under this act that More and Fisher went to their deaths...

For almost a thousand years the Church in England had been directly under the jurisdiction of Rome. Now... that ancient allegiance had been severed and all the powers which the papacy had exerted had been transferred to the king and the Archbishop of Canterbury. In carrying through this revolution the Church in England had played little part... The English Reformation, at any rate in its earlier stages, was 'a parliamentary transaction', or an 'act of state'.[3] [In 1533 Thomas Cranmer had become Archbishop of Canterbury. With Hugh Latimer, who became Bishop of Worcester in 1535, and Nicholas Ridley, he now took a lead in matters of doctrine and worship. An English translation of the Bible was published in 1535, mainly the work of Miles Coverdale; and the Great Bible in 1538 (Tyndale and Coverdale). From now onwards people might read the Bible freely in English without breaking the law. There was destruction, too, of statues and images, and of the monasteries, whose wealth the king took into his own hands. Henry took an interest in doctrine and supervised the composition of the Ten Articles of 1536 (passed by Convocation and issued by the king with his own preface), and the Six Articles of 1539.]

---

[2]   p. 167

[3]   pp. 167–9

122

1531
Faith and love

William Tyndale (1494?–1536), translator of the Bible, Exposition of I John 4.16–18, *ed. H. Walter, PS (1848), p. 202.*

Tyndale is commenting here on the contemporary debate about justification by faith. Some of the reformers were anxious to insist that neither good works ('the outward deed'), nor love could count in the sight of God, but only faith. On Anglican thinking, see further nos. 123, 214.

But yet how shall I see my faith? I must come down to love again, and thence to the works of love, ere I can see my faith. Not always, but sometimes, thou shalt feel thy faith without the outward deed; as in great adversity and persecution, when the devil assaulteth thee with desperation, and layeth thy sins before thee, and would bear thee in hand that God had cast thee away, and left thee succourless, for thy sins' sake: then cometh faith forth with her shield, and turneth back again the darts of the devil, and answereth: 'Nay; for Jesus is the Son of God, yea, and my very God and my very Lord, and hath taken away my sins and all damnation.'

123

*c.*1532
Faith and works

William Tyndale (1494?–1536), translator of the Bible, Prologue *to the* Exposition of Matthew v, vi, vii, *PS, pp. 13–14.*

Cf. nos. 122, 214, and Articles xii, xiii, xiv of the Thirty-Nine Articles.

For if thou wilt be sure that thy faith be perfect, then examine thyself whether thou love the law. And in like manner, if thou wilt know whether thou love the law aright, then examine thyself whether thou believe in Christ only for the remission of sin, and obtaining the promises made in the Scripture.

124

c.1532
The indefectibility of the Church

William Tyndale (1494?–1536), translator of the Bible, Prologue *to the* Exposition of Matthew v, vi, vii, *PS, p. 12.*

The Church of Christ, then, is the multitude of all them that believe in Christ for the remission of sin; and, of a thankfulness for that mercy, love the law of God purely... and, of hate they have to the sin of this world, long for the life to come. This is the church that cannot err damnably; nor any long time; nor all of them: but as soon as any question ariseth, the truth of God's promise stirreth up one or the other to teach them the truth of everything needful to salvation out of God's word; and lighteneth the hearts of the other true members, to see the same, and to consent thereto.

125

1532
Articles to which Mr Latimer was required to subscribe, 11 March 1532

Latimer, Remains, *PS, pp. 218–19, and British Library, Harl. MS. 435, Art. 7.*

Hugh Latimer (c. 1485–1555) was one of the leading reformers of Henry VIII's reign. His preaching challenged ecclesiastical authority and in the years before the king's break with Rome he was frequently in trouble with the authorities. He was censured by the Convocation of Canterbury in 1532, and made to subscribe to these 'articles'. They should be read as representing the reverse of what he was believed to have been teaching and as a summary of pre-Reformation positions; they should be compared with the Thirty-Nine Articles, especially xxii, xxv, xxxii.

The eleventh day of March, 1532, Master Hugh Latimer, Bachelor of Divinity, of Cambridge, noted and suspected of his faith and erroneous preachings,... called before the Archbishop of Canterbury, the Bishop of London, and other prelates and clerks of the Province of Canterbury, in their Convocation holden at Westminster, did confess as followeth:[1]

1. Inprimis,[2] that there is a place of purgation for souls after this life.
2. That souls in purgatory are holpen by masses, prayer, and alms-deed.
3. That the holy apostles and martyrs of Christ, being dead, are in heaven.
4. That the same saints, as mediators, pray for us in heaven.
5. That the said saints are to be honoured in heaven. That pilgrimages and oblations are meritorious for the sepulchres and relics of saints.
6. That whosoever hath vowed chastity may not marry, nor break their vow, without dispensation of the high bishop.[3]
7. That the keys of binding and loosing, given unto Peter, doth remain to his successors bishops, although they live evil; and they were never given for any cause to laymen.
8. That it is profitable for Christian men to invocate saints, that they, as mediators, may pray unto God for us.
9. That men by alms-deed, prayer, and other good works, may merit at God's hands.
10. That men forbidden of the bishops, by reason of suspicion, ought not to preach till such time as they had purged themselves to them or their superiors, and be lawfully restored.
11. That the Lent, and their fasting-days, commanded by the canons, and used with the Christians, are to be kept, except necessity require otherwise.
12. That God, by the merits of Christ's passion, doth give his grace in all the whole seven sacraments to the lawful receiver.
13. That the consecrations, sanctifications, and benedictions, received in the christian church, are laudable and profitable.

---

[1] That is, he declared his belief in these articles and thus denied what he had been teaching.

[2] 'First'.

[3] That is, priests, monks, friars and nuns. The reference here is to the monastic orders, against which many of the reformers spoke out, in particular.

14. That [it] is laudable and profitable, that the images of the crucifix and saints are to be had in the church, in memory, honour, and worship of Jesus Christ and his saints.
15. That it is laudable and profitable for the saints to be decked and trimmed; and to set candles burning before them, in the honour of the said saints.

126

1532
Church and State:
The submission of the English clergy to Henry VIII

Convocation, 15 May, 1532, Gee and Hardy, pp. 176–8.

See no. 121 above.

We your most humble subjects, daily orators and bedesmen of your clergy of England, having our special trust and confidence in your most excellent wisdom, your princely goodness and fervent zeal to the promotion of God's honour and Christian religion, and also in your learning, far exceeding, in our judgement, the learning of all other kings and princes that we have read of, and doubting nothing but that the same shall still continue and daily increase in your majesty — First, do offer and promise, *in verbo sacerdotii*,[1] here unto your highness, submitting ourselves most humbly to the same, that we will never from henceforth [enact]... any [new canons or constitutions provincial, or any other new ordinance, provincial or synodical], in our Convocation [or synod] in time coming, which Convocation is, always has been, and must be, assembled only by your highness' commandment of writ, unless your highness by your royal assent shall license us to [assemble our Convocation, and] to make, promulge, and execute [such constitutions and ordinances as shall be made in] the same; and thereto give your royal assent and authority. Secondly, that whereas divers [of the] constitutions, [ordinances] and canons, provincial [or synodal] which have been heretofore enacted, be thought to be not only much prejudicial to your prerogative royal, but also overmuch onerous to your highness' subjects, [your clergy aforesaid is

---

[1] 'The word of a priest'

contented, if it may stand so with your highness' pleasure, that] it be committed to the examination and judgement [of your grace, and] of thirty-two persons, whereof sixteen to be of the upper and nether house of the temporalty,[2] and other sixteen of the clergy, all to be chosen and appointed by your [most noble grace]. So that, finally, whichsoever of the said constitutions, [ordinances, or canons, provincial or synodal] shall be thought and determined by [your grace and by] the most part of the said thirty-two persons [not to stand with God's laws and the laws of your realm, the same] to be abrogated and [taken away by your grace and the clergy; and such of them as shall be seen by your grace, and by the most part of the said thirty-two persons, to stand with God's laws and the laws of your realm, to stand in full strength and power, your grace's most royal assent and authority] once impetrate and fully given to the same.

127

1534
Royal Supremacy

The Supremacy Act, 26, Henry VIII, cap. 1, Gee and Hardy, pp. 243-4.

See no. 121 above.

Albeit the king's majesty justly and rightfully is and ought to be the supreme head of the Church of England, and so is recognized by the clergy of this realm in their Convocations, yet nevertheless for corroboration and confirmation thereof, and for increase of virtue in Christ's religion within this realm of England, and to repress and extirp all errors, heresies, and other enormities and abuses heretofore used in the same; be it enacted by authority of this present Parliament, that the king our sovereign lord, his heirs and successors, kings of this realm, shall be taken, accepted, and reputed the only supreme head on earth of the Church of England, called *Anglicana Ecclesia*; and shall have and enjoy, annexed and united to the imperial crown of this realm, as well the title and style thereof, as all honours, dignities, pre-eminences, jurisdictions,

---

[2]   i.e. Parliament

privileges, authorities, immunities, profits, and commodities to the said dignity of supreme head of the same Church belonging and appertaining; and that our said sovereign lord, his heirs and successors, kings of this realm, shall have full power and authority from time to time to visit, repress, redress, reform, order, correct, restrain, and amend all such errors, heresies, abuses, offences, contempts, and enormities, whatsoever they be, which by any manner [of] spiritual authority or jurisdiction ought or may lawfully be reformed, repressed, ordered, redressed, corrected, restrained, or amended, most to the pleasure of Almighty God, the increase of virtue in Christ's religion, and for the conservation of the peace, unity, and tranquillity of this realm; any usage, custom, foreign law, foreign authority, prescription, or any other thing or things to the contrary hereof notwithstanding.

128

1537
The Church of Ireland becomes separated from Rome

Who are the Anglicans?, ed. *Charles Long, prepared for the Lambeth Conference, 1988 (Ohio, 1988), p. 57.*

Christianity in Ireland traces its origin to St Patrick and his companions in the fifth century and from the beginning until now, Irish churches have been marked by a strong missionary zeal. In 1537 the English king was declared head of the Church of Ireland and submission to Roman authority was forbidden. While Anglicanism thus received state support, most Irish Christians identified patriotism with continued loyalty to Rome. In 1867 the Anglican Church in Ireland was dis-established and continued as an independent Province, centred mainly in the north. It is governed by a General Synod with a House of Bishops and a House of Representatives (clergy and laity). The Primate, the Archbishop of Armagh, is elected by the House of Bishops from their own number.

129

1539
The Six Articles of Henry VIII

The Six Articles Act, 31 Henry VIII, cap. 14, Gee and Hardy, pp. 305–6.

See nos. 121, 125 above. These very conservative Articles go against a number of views of continental and English reformers, notably on transubstantiation; communion in both kinds, clerical celibacy; monastic vows; 'private', as distinct from parish, Eucharists; individual confession to a priest. See Thirty-Nine Articles xxviii, xxx, xxxii. Henry VIII supported them, but he had his small son, Edward, born in 1537, educated by men of reforming opinions. It is not always easy to know exactly where he himself stood on the points which were in dispute at the end of his reign. These Articles are included to illustrate something of the lengthy process of arriving at the formulation of the Thirty-Nine Articles. (See no. 151.)

First, that the most blessed Sacrament of the altar, by the strength and efficacy of Christ's mighty word[1] (it being spoken by the priest), is present really, under the form of bread and wine, the natural body and blood of our Saviour Jesus Christ, conceived of the Virgin Mary; and that after the consecration there remaineth no substance of bread or wine, nor any other substance, but the substance of Christ, God and man. Secondly, that communion in both kinds is not necessary *ad salutem*,[2] by the law of God, to all persons; and that it is to be believed, and not doubted of, but that in the flesh, under the form of bread, is the very blood; and with the blood, under the form of wine, is the very flesh; as well apart, as though they were both together. Thirdly, that priests after the order of priesthood received, as afore, may not marry, by the law of God. Fourthly, that vows of chastity or widowhood, by man or woman made to God advisedly, ought to be observed by the law of God; and that it exempts them from other liberties of Christian people, which without that they might enjoy. Fifthly, that it is meet and necessary that private masses be continued and admitted in this the king's English Church and congregation, as whereby good

---

[1]   References to *vis verborum*, the power of words, are common in the Middle Ages, with the implication that something is brought about by grace when they are uttered by a duly commissioned minister with a right intention, and within the sacramental life of the Church.

[2]   'For salvation'

Christian people, ordering themselves accordingly, do receive both godly and goodly consolations and benefits; and it is agreeable also to God's law. Sixthly, that auricular confession is expedient and necessary to be retained and continued, used and frequented in the Church of God.

130

1542–3
Act authorising Scripture in the vernacular in Scotland

Source Book of Scottish History, *II. pp. 127–8.*

This and nos. 136, 137 are printed here in sixteenth century Scottish English. Here permission is given by civil law for the use of an approved translation of Scripture in the vernacular, and for everyone to be free to read it.

It is statute and ordanit that it salbe lefull to all our souirane ladyis lieges to haif the haly write baith the new testament and the auld in the vulgar toung in Inglis or Scottis of ane gude and trew translatioun.

It is decreed and ordained that it shall be lawful to all our Lady's subjects to have the Holy Writ both the New Testament and the old in the vulgar tongue in English or Scottish of a good and true translation.

131

1547–8
Edward VI and the Protector Somerset

J.R.H. Moorman, A History of the Church in England *(3rd edn, London, 1973), pp. 180ff.*

Henry VIII was succeeded by Edward VI (his son by his third queen, Jane Seymour), who was nine years old. 'Henry had given so much power over the Church to the State that everything now depended on the personnel of the Councils which was to govern for the next seven years... Edward Seymour, shortly to become Duke of Somerset, an uncle of the king and a convinced reformer, soon got power into his own hands. It immediately became clear that reforms... would now be put in hand'.[1] Cranmer and Somerset together went ahead with changes 'using the extensive powers which Henry VIII had usurped for the crown. In these reforms the Church played only a small part. Convocation was seldom consulted and the bishops were too much divided to offer any united front... Conservative bishops like Gardiner and Bonner who showed any opposition were immediately imprisoned, while the policy of the government went inexorably forward, using the machinery of commissions, injunctions and statutes'.[2] In 1547 the first set of royal injunctions required each parish Church to have a copy of the Book of Homilies. '... Cranmer... was busy with his liturgical schemes and his plans for the supersession of the Roman service books by an English Prayer Book. By 1549 such a book was ready, and was imposed on the country as a schedule to an Act of Uniformity which demanded that... from now onwards all clergy must use the new book on pain of imprisonment'[3] ... 'In 1552 an attempt had been made to define the doctrine of the Church of England in a series of Articles. Cranmer had drawn up forty-five, but these were reduced to forty-two, before receiving the royal assent in 1553'.[4]

132

1547
'Exhortation to the reading and knowledge of Holy Scripture, as containing everything necessary to salvation'

Homilies, *Book I, p. 1.*

Compare Thirty-Nine Articles, vi. In 1542 Convocation agreed to the publication of a book of Homilies which could be used by clergy whose education did not fit them to be preachers. The first Book, of twelve Homilies, was issued in 1547, early in Edward VI's reign. A second Book, begun in Elizabeth I's reign, and probably ready by 1553, was revised until 1571 before it was published. Article xxxv of the Thirty-Nine Articles refers

---

[1]   p. 180
[2]   p. 181
[3]   p. 184
[4]   p. 186

to the two books of Homilies as suitable to be read in churches. Cranmer was the author of most of the first collection, Jewel of most of the second, with the help of Grindal and Parker.

There can be nothing either more necessary or profitable, than the knowledge of Holy Scripture.... And there is no truth nor doctrine, necessary for our justification and everlasting salvation, but that is, or may be, drawn out of that fountain and well of truth.

133

1547
'A short declaration of the
true, lively, and Christian Faith'

Homilies, *Book I, p. 22.*

The distinction made here was a sixteenth century commonplace, between faith which merely assents to Christian truth, and a real commitment which shows itself in growing holiness and a life of love, and is a sign of those who are justified in God's eyes. Cf. nos. 122, 123. On the Homilies, see no. 132.

Faith is taken in the Scripture two manner of ways. There is one faith, which in Scripture is called a dead faith; which bringeth forth no good works, but is idle, barren, and unfruitful. And this faith, by the holy apostle St James, is compared to the faith of devils; which believe God to be true and just, and tremble for fear, yet they do nothing well, but all evil. And such a manner of faith have the wicked and naughty Christian people; which confess God, as St Paul saith, in their mouths, but deny him in their deeds.... Another faith there is in Scripture, which... worketh by charity, as St Paul declareth, which as the other vain faith is called a dead faith, so this may be called a quick or lively faith.

134

1547
'An exhortation concerning
good order, and obedience to Rulers and Magistrates'

Homilies, *Book I, p. 72.*

This Homily outlines a hierarchical and medieval conception of order,
drawing parallels between the order of creation, civil order and order in the
Church; its main thrust, however, is the idea that 'right order' is a divinely
instituted means of maintaining peace and of binding together members of the
Christian community in mutual care. It was of particular importance to
Protestant reformers in England and in Europe that the 'civil magistrate', or
secular authority, should be obeyed. In England the monarch took over much
of the jurisdiction the Pope had previously exercised in the Church. On the
Homilies, see no. 132.

Almighty God hath created and appointed all things in heaven,
earth and waters, in a most excellent and perfect order.... Every
degree of people in their vocation, calling, and office, hath
appointed to them their duty and order... and every one hath need
of other: so that in all things is to be lauded and praised the
goodly order of God: without the which no house, no city, no
commonwealth, can continue and endure, or last. For, where there
is no right order, there... must needs follow all mischief and utter
destruction both of souls, bodies, goods, and commonwealths.

135

1549
Clerical marriage

Statute of 2–3 Edward VI, cap. 21, Gee and Hardy, pp. 366–7.

Clerical celibacy had been enforced in the West from the end of the eleventh
century. This change allows clergy to marry, but still sees marriage for the
clergy as less desirable than celibacy.

Although it were not only better for the estimation of priests, and
other ministers in the Church of God, to live chaste, sole, and
separate from the company of women and the bond of marriage,
but also thereby they might the better intend to the administration
of the gospel, and be less intricated and troubled with the charge of

household, being free and unburdened from the care and cost of finding wife and children, and that it were most to be wished that they would willingly and of their selves endeavour themselves to a perpetual chastity and abstinence from the use of women:

Yet forasmuch as the contrary has rather been seen, and such uncleanness of living, and other great inconveniences, not meet to be rehearsed, have followed of compelled chastity, and of such laws as have prohibited those (such persons) the godly use of marriage; it were better and rather to be suffered in the commonwealth, that those which could not contain, should, after the counsel of Scripture, live in holy marriage, than feignedly abuse with worse enormity outward chastity or single life.

136

1552
Archbishop Hamilton's Catechism
on Justification by Faith (Scotland)

Source Book of Scottish History *II, p. 150.*

Cf. nos. 122, 123, 150 on justification by faith.

To commit ourselves haiely to God, to put our hail traist and confidence in his help, defence, gudness and gracious provisioun in all our necessiteis, perellis, dangeris,... infirmiteis, in all forsakand our awin will, and with obediens commit all to the gracious will of God. Siclyk faith had Daniel, quhen he was put in the cave amang the lyonis.... This is the special faith of ane trew christin man, quhilk standis in the general faith afore rehersit and in sure confidence and hoip of Goddis mercy. This faith obtenis to us the abundant grace of the haly spret, quhilk pouris into our hartis the trew lufe of God and of our nychtbour.... This is the Faith that justifeis a christin man.

To commit ourselves wholly to God, to put our whole trust and confidence in his help, defence, goodness and gracious provision in all our necessities, perils, dangers,... infirmities, in all forsaking our own will and with obedience committing all to the gracious will of God. Such faith had Daniel, when he was put in the cave among the lions... This is the special faith of a true Christian man, which stands in the general faith beforementioned and in sure confidence and hope of God's mercy. This faith obtains to us the abundant grace of the Holy Spirit, which pours into our hearts the true love of God and of our neighbour... This is the Faith that justifies a Christian man.

137

1552
Archbishop Hamilton's Catechism
on the Eucharist (Scotland)

Source Book of Scottish History *II, pp. 149–50.*

The provincial council of the Scottish Church of 1552 agreed that a catechism should be provided for the instruction of the laity, while steps were being taken to provide a better-trained clergy who could teach the laity in future generations. The catechism was issued by Archbishop Hamilton's authority, although it may not be his own work.

First it is callit the Eucharist, that is to say, gud grace, because it contenis him really and essentially, quhilk is the well and giffar of grace,... It is callit the Communioun, for be worthi ressaving of this sacrament al trew Christin men and wemen are joynit al togidder amang thame self as spiritual memberis of ane body, and also ar joynit all togidder to our salviour Christ, heid of the same mistik bodye. It is callit the sacrifice of the altar, because it is ane quick and special remembrance of the passioun of Christ,... Quhen we ressave this sacrament in remembrance of his passioun, in deid we confess and grant that he deit for us, that be hes dede we mycht get remissioun of our syns and eternal lyfe.

First, it is called the 'Eucharist', that is to say, 'good grace', because it contains him really and essentially, who is the well and giver of grace... It is called the 'Communion', for by worthy receiving of this sacrament all true Christian men and women are joined together among themselves as spiritual members of one body, and are also joined all together to our Saviour Christ, head of the same mystic body. It is called the 'sacrifice of the altar', because it is a living and particular remembrance of the Passion of Christ... When we receive this sacrament in remembrance of his Passion, indeed we confess and grant that he died for us, that by his death we might get remission of our sins and eternal life.

1552

The Book of Common Prayer, see 1662 for extracts in modern English spelling.

1552

The Ordinal, see 1662 for extracts in modern English spelling.

1559

The Book of Common Prayer, see 1662 for extracts in modern English spelling.

1559

The Ordinal, see 1662 for extracts in modern English spelling.

138

1560
The Scottish Episcopal Church

Who are the Anglicans?, ed. *Charles Long, prepared for the Lambeth Conference, 1988 (Ohio, 1988), p. 59.*

The roots of Christianity in Scotland go back to Ninian in the fourth century and Columba in the sixth century. After the Reformation, between 1560 and 1689, sometimes the Episcopal Church, sometimes the Presbyterian Church, was 'established'. Following 1689 until the early nineteenth century, the Episcopal Church was weakened by penal statutes and disestablishment. It grew rapidly in the nineteenth century, influenced by the Tractarian Movement. There has been a slow decline of numbers in the twentieth century. The Church is numerically stronger in the East than in the West. In 1982 the Church adopted a system of government by General Synod which meets annually. The seven bishops elect one of their number as Primus, who is recognized as spokesman for the Church.

139

1560
The First Book of Discipline, Scotland

Source Book of Scottish History *II, pp. 171 ff.*

The Book of Discipline is the report and recommendations drawn up by the clergy of the provincial council at Edinburgh in 1559.

[Family Allowances]
Difficult it is to appoint a several stipend to every Minister, by reason that the charges and necessity of all will not be like; for some will be continuers in one place, [and] some will be compelled to travel, and oft to change dwelling place (if they shall have charge of divers kirks).[1] Amongst these, some will be burdened with wife and children, and one with more than another; and some perchance will be single men. If equal stipends should be appointed to all those that in charge are so unequal, either should the one suffer penury, or else should the other have superfluity and too much (288).

[The Care of the Poor]
Every several kirk must provide for the poor... We are not patrons for stubborn and idle beggars who, running from place to place, make a craft of their begging, whom the Civil Magistrate ought to punish; but for the widow and fatherless, the aged, impotent, or lamed, who neither can nor may travail for their sustentation, we say that God commandeth his people to be careful. And therefore, for such, as also for persons of honesty fallen in[to] decay and penury, ought such provision be made that of our abundance should their indigence be relieved. How this most conveniently and most easily may be done in every city and other parts of this Realm, God shall show you wisdom and the means, so that your minds be godly thereto inclined. All must not be suffered to beg that gladly so would do; neither yet must beggars remain where they choose; but the stout and strong beggar must be compelled to work, and every person that may not work, must be compelled to repair to the place where he or she was born (unless of long continuance they have remained in one place), and there reasonable provision must be made for their sustentation, as the church shall appoint (290–1).

---

[1] Churches

[Public and Family Worship]
baptism may be ministered whensoever the Word is preached; but we think it more expedient, that it be ministered upon the Sunday, or upon the day of prayers, only after the sermon... Four times in the year we think sufficient to the administration of the Lord's Table... the first Sunday of March... the first Sunday of June... the first Sunday of September... and the first Sunday of December...; we study to suppress superstition... We think that none are apt to be admitted to the Mystery who cannot formally say the Lord's Prayer, the Articles of the Belief, and declare the Sum of the Law. Further, we think it a thing most expedient and necessary, that every Church have a Bible in English, and that the people be commanded to convene to hear the plain reading or interpretation of the Scripture... We think it most expedient that the Scriptures be read in order ... For this skipping and divagation from place to place of the Scripture, be it in reading, or be it in preaching, we judge not so profitable to edify the Church, as the continual following of one text. Every Master of household must be commanded either to instruct, or else cause [to] be instructed, his children, servants, and family, in the principles of the Christian religion... Men, women and children would be exhorted to exercise themselves in the Psalms, that when the Church conveneth, and docs sing, they may be the more able together with common heart and voice to praise God. In private houses we think it expedient, that the most grave and discreet person use the Common Prayers at morn and at night, for the comfort and instruction of others (313–14).

140

1562
Binding and loosing

John Jewel (1522–71), Bishop of Salisbury, An Apology of the Church of England *(1564), PS. Works, vol, 3, pp. 351, 354, 361.*

Moreover, we say that Christ hath given to his ministers power to bind, to loose, to open, to shut;... and that the office of loosing consisteth in this point, that the minister either by the preaching of the gospel offers the merits of Christ and full pardon to such as have lowly and contrite hearts and do unfeignedly repent them, pronouncing unto the same a sure and undoubted forgiveness of their sins and hope of everlasting salvation; or else the same minister, when any have offended their brothers' minds with some great offense or notable and open crime, whereby they have, as it were, banished and made themselves strangers from the common fellowship and from the body of Christ, then, after perfect amendment of such persons, doth reconcile them, and bring them home again, and restore them to the company and unity of the faithful... We say also that the minister doth execute the authority of binding and shutting as often as he shutteth up the gate of the kingdom of heaven against the unbelieving and stubborn persons, denouncing unto them God's vengeance and everlasting punishment, or else, when he doth quite shut them out from the bosom of the church by open excommunication. Out of doubt, what sentence soever the minister of God shall give in this sort, God himself doth so well allow of it that whatsoever here in earth by their means is loosed and bound God himself will loose and bind the same in heaven.

141

1562
The Eucharist

John Jewel (1522–71), Bishop of Salisbury, An Apology of the Church of England *(1564), PS. Works, vol. 3, pp. 465, 472.*

We say that *eucharistia*, the supper of the Lord, is a sacrament, that is, an evident representation of the body and blood of Christ, wherein is set as it were before our eyes the death of Christ and his resurrection, and what act soever he did whilst he was in his mortal body; to that end we may give him thanks for his death and for our deliverance; and that, by the often receiving of this sacrament, we may daily renew the remembrance thereof, to the intent we, being fed with the body and blood of Christ, may be brought into the hope of the resurrection and of everlasting life and may most assuredly believe, that... as our bodies be fed with bread and wine, so our souls be fed with the body and blood of Christ... To this banquet we think the people of God ought to be earnestly bidden, that they may all communicate among themselves, and openly declare and testify both the godly society which is among them, and also the hope which they have in Christ Jesus.

1563
The Thirty-Nine Articles

see 1571 and 1662 for text.

142

1563–71
The efficacy of prayer

Homilies, *Book II, p. 219. On the Homilies, see no. 132.*

There is nothing in all man's life, well-beloved in our Saviour Christ, so needful to be spoken of, and daily to be called upon, as a hearty, zealous, and devout prayer; the necessity whereof is so great, that without it nothing may be well obtained at God's hand. For, as the Apostle James saith,[1] Every good and perfect gift cometh from above, and proceedeth from the Father of lights: who is also said to be rich and liberal towards all them that call upon him; not because he either will not or cannot give without asking, but because he hath appointed prayer as an ordinary means between him and us.

143

1563–71
Three kinds of prayer

Homilies, *Book II, p. 243. On the Homilies, see no. 132.*

The first... is the devout lifting up of the mind to God, without the uttering of the heart's grief or desire by open voice.... The second sort of Prayer is... vocal, that is to say, the secret uttering of the

---

[1]   James 1.17

griefs and desires of the heart with words, but yet in a secret closet or some solitary place. The third sort of Prayer is public or common. Of this prayer speaketh our Saviour Christ, when he saith, If two of you shall agree upon earth upon any thing, whatsoever ye shall ask, my Father which is in heaven shall do it for you: for wheresoever two or three be gathered together in my name, there am I in the midst of them.

144

1563–71
The importance of coming to the Lord's Supper

Homilies, *Book II, p. 306. On the Homilies, see no. 132. Cf., too, nos. 101, 168.*

Our Lord and Saviour thought it not sufficient to purchase for us his Father's favour again — which is that deep fountain of all goodness and eternal life — but also invented the ways most wisely, whereby they might redound to our commodity and profit. Amongst the which means, is the public celebration of the memory of his precious death at the Lord's table... To this his commandment forceth us, saying, Do ye this, drink ye all of this. To this his promise enticeth us: This is my body, which is given for you; this is my blood, which is shed for you. So then, of necessity, we must be ourselves partakers of this table, and not beholders of others: so we must address ourselves to frequent the same in reverent and due manner.

145

before 1564
Repentance

Becon, Catechism, *PS, p. 10.*

Thomas Becon (c. 1513–67) was a pupil of Hugh Latimer. At the beginning of Edward VI's reign he was made Chaplain to the Lord Protector. After a period of exile in Mary's reign he became more extreme in his views.

Father. What is repentance?

Son. Repentance is an inward and true sorrow of the heart, unfeignedly conceived in the mind by earnest consideration of our sins and wickednesses, which heretofore most unkindly we have committed against the Lord our God, of whom we have freely received so many, so great, and so noble benefits, with a perfect detestation and abhorring of our former wicked life; whereunto is added a fervent and inward desire from henceforth to live godly and virtuously, and to frame our life in all points according to the holy will of God expressed in the divine scriptures.

146

before 1564
Faith is the gift of God

Becon, Catechism, *PS, p. 14.*

Father. Cometh not faith then of ourselves, but it is rather the gift of God?

Son. Of ourself? What cometh of ourselves that good is, which are not able of ourselves once to think a good thought? Our destruction cometh of ourselves, but our salvation cometh only of God.

147

before 1564
The Church

Becon, Catechism, *PS p. 41.*

Becon here refers to the notion of the visible 'gathered church' or local worshipping community. Article xix of the Thirty-Nine Articles describes the visible Church as a 'congregation' of the faithful, but without any implication that the visible Church is not also a larger body which includes many local congregations.

Father. What meanest thou by this word 'church'?

Son. Nothing else than a company of people gathered together, or a congregation.

148

before 1564
The Ordained ministry

Becon, Catechism, *PS, pp. 317–19.*

Becon is here describing the difference between 'ordinary' and 'extraordinary' ministry; in the order of the Church 'ordinary' ordained ministry involves the calling of the Holy Spirit and also of the people among whom the pastoral ministry is to be exercised; the 'extraordinary' charismatic ministry Becon sees as belonging to an earlier age, when miracles attested the genuineness of the calling of the Holy Spirit. But in fact there has always been a charismatic and prophetic ministry in the Church, alongside the ordained ministry, sometimes in tension with it, but fundamentally complementary to it. Cf. nos. 189, 200, 259.

Father. First of all, tell me what a bishop or spiritual pastor is.
Son. He is the minister of Christ, and the dispensator of the mysteries of God.
Father. Why is he called 'the minister of Christ'?
Son. Because he is Christ's servant and ambassador to speak and to do those things which he hath received in commission of his Master Christ....
Father. Why is a spiritual pastor called 'a dispensator of the mysteries of God'?
Son. For as the steward of a nobleman hath the treasures and riches of his master and lord, to bestow and distribute them where his master's good will and pleasure is; so likewise he that is a spiritual pastor and overseer of the Lord's flock hath the heavenly riches and most blessed treasures of God... not to hide them under a bushel, nor to couch them in the ground, but to communicate them to other, even to such as the Lord hath committed to his spiritual charge....
Father. Shew me by the word of God, that the spiritual minister ruleth in the Church of Christ at God's appointment.
Son. A little before our Lord and Saviour Christ ascended with his body into the kingdom of his Father, he said to his apostles, and also to all their successors, which are all spiritual ministers that labour in word and doctrine: 'Teach all nations, baptizing them in the name of the Father, and of the Son, and of the Holy Ghost, teaching them to keep all things that I have commanded you. And

University of Chester, Seaborne Library

Title: An introduction to Christianity / Linda
Woodhead
ID: 36031872
Due: 26-02-13

Title: The study of Anglicanism [Book]
ID: 90410201
Due: 12-03-13

Title: Gays and the future of anglicanism :
responses to the windsor report / edited by
Andrew Linzey and R
ID: 36109107
Due: 12-03-13

Title: Celebrating the Anglican Way / edited
by Ian Bunting.
ID: 01041425
Due: 12-03-13

Title: The Anglican tradition: a handbook of
sources
ID: 90725801
Due: 12-03-13

Total items: 5
9/02/2013 15:09

Thank you for using Self Check

behold I am with you continually unto the world's end.'[1] Again: 'Go ye throughout the world, and preach the Gospel to every creature. He that believeth and is baptized shall be saved: but he that believes not shall be condemned.'[2] Once again: 'As my Father sent me, so send I you. Take the Holy Ghost. Whose sins ye shall forgive are forgiven them: whose sins ye to retain are retained.'[3] Item 'Feed my lambs.' 'Feed my sheep.'[4] And St Paul saith: 'God hath ordained in the church, first apostles, secondarily prophets, thirdly teachers,' etc....[5]

Father: How many ways may the ministers be called unto the ministry?

Son. Two. One is, when they be called immediately of God, as the Prophets and apostles were, which were raised up of God to prophesy and to teach without any vocation or calling of man. And this kind of vocation God useth customably outwardly to approve and confirm with wonderful testimonies and signs, as we may... see in Moses, Helias, etc. But this calling is now ceased. The other is, when the ministers be called mediately, as they say, and in order of men, that is to say, of the magistrate and people....

Father. May not a man offer himself to the church, and desire to be admitted unto the ministry?

Son. Yes, verily, so that it rise not of ambition and of the desire of ease and worldly lucre: again, so that he submit himself to the judgement of the congregation, either to be admitted, or to be refused.

149

1570

The place of the Fathers of the early centuries

John Jewel (1522–71), Bishop of Salisbury, A Treatise of the Holy Scriptures, *PS (1845–50), vol. 4, pp. 1173-4.*

---

[1]   Matthew 28.19

[2]   Mark 16. 15–16

[3]   John 20. 22-23

[4]   John 21. 15–17

[5]   I Corinthians 12.28

The reformers' dislike of much medieval theology did not extend to the writers of the first Christian centuries. In fact, there was a rediscovery of some Greek patristic authors to set alongside those familiar in both Greek and Latin traditions who continued to be read and used. The essential point made here is that they do not carry an authority comparable with that of Scripture.

They were learned men, and learned fathers; the instruments of the mercy of God, and vessels full of grace. We despise them not, we read them, we reverence them, and give thanks unto God for them. They were witnesses unto the truth, they were worthy pillars and ornaments in the Church of God. Yet may they not be compared with the word of God. We may not build up on them: we may not make them the foundation and warrant of our conscience: we may not put our trust in them. Our trust is in the name of the Lord. And thus we are taught to esteem of the learned fathers of the church by their own judgement... St Augustine says... 'Neither weigh we the writings of all men, be they never so worthy and catholic, as we weigh the canonical scriptures'... I could shew many the like speeches of the ancient fathers, wherein they reverence the holy scriptures; as to which only they give consent without gainsaying.

150

1570
Justifying faith

Alexander Nowell (c.1507–1602), Dean of St Paul's, A Catechism, *ed. G.E. Corrie, PS (1853), pp. 143–4.*

Nowell's *Catechism* was approved by both Upper and Lower Houses of Convocation in 1562 'for the bringing up of the youth in godliness, in the schools of the whole realm'. The text published in 1570 contains a number of changes made by Nowell himself in accordance with suggestions made to him by 'lerned men' whom Sir William Cecil had consulted. Nowell's, like other *Catechisms* of the period, covers the Creed, the Lord's Prayer and the Ten Commandments, and he draws upon contemporary work, particularly that of Calvin. The text here is Norton's translation of the Latin text into English, also published in 1570. Cf. nos. 122, 123, 136.

The general faith is that which crediteth the word of God; that is, which believeth all those things to be true that are contained in the scriptures concerning God... and likewise all other things taught in the scriptures... but the true faith goeth further... For thus far not only ungodly men, but also the very devils, do believe... But the true faith... doth... also embrace the promises made concerning the mercy of God the Father, and the forgiveness of sins to the faithful through Jesus Christ... For they know that Christ (whom they trust upon), appeasing the wrath of his Father, their sins shall never be imputed any more to them, than if the same had never been committed. And though themselves have not satisfied the law... yet believe they that Christ, with his most full observing of the law, hath abundantly satisfied God for them, and by this his righteousness and observing of the law of God, themselves are accounted in the number and state of the righteous... And this is the justification that the holy scriptures do declare that we obtain by faith.

151

1571
The Thirty-Nine Articles

The Latin and Sixteenth Century English texts are given here from Cardwell's Synodalia. *For the 1662 text in modern English spelling, and for comments on individual Articles, see no. 225.*

Elizabeth succeeded her half-sister Mary, Katharine of Aragon's daughter, in 1558. Mary's ecclesiastical legislators had revoked all the ecclesiastical legislation of Henry VIII and Edward VI. Elizabeth's first Parliament revived Henry's and Edward's legislation in the Act of Supremacy and the Act of Uniformity (1559), with Elizabeth acknowledged not as 'Supreme Head' but as 'Supreme Governor' of Church and State. The Prayer Book of 1552 was restored, with a few small alterations. In 1571 Canon Law was revised and the Latin Thirty-Nine Articles (adopted by Convocation in 1563, and ratified by the Crown), were now approved by Convocation in 1571 with an English translation, and promulgated with the authority of Parliament. These Articles, marked in places by the preoccupations of contemporary controversy, have their parallels in 'Articles' or 'Commonplaces' in most reforming Churches of the sixteenth century.

Articles whereupon it was agreed by the Archbyshops and Byshops of both prouinces and the whole cleargie, in the Conuocation holden at London in the yere of our Lorde God. 1562. accordyng to the computation of the Churche of Englande, for the auoyding of the diuersities of opinions, and for the stablishyng of consent touching true religion. Put foorth by the Queenes aucthoritie.

Articuli de quibus convenit inter Archiepiscopos et Episcopos utriusque provinciæ et Clerum universum in Synodo Londini an. Dom. 1562. secundum computationem ecclesiæ Anglicanæ, et consensum in vera religione firmandum. Æditi authoritate serenissimæ Reginæ. ... An. Domini. 1571.

i. Of faith in the holy Trinitie.

There is but one lyuyng and true God, euerlasting, without body, partes, or passions, of infinite power, wysdome, and goodnesse, the maker and preseruer of al things both visible and inuisible. And in vnitie of this Godhead there be three persons, of one substaunce, power, and eternitie, the father, the sonne, and the holy ghost.

i. De fide in Sacrosanctam Trinitatem. Vnus est viuus, et verus deus, æternus, incorporeus, impartibilis, impassibilis, immensæ potentiæ, sapientiæ, ac bonitatis, creator, et conseruator omnium, tum visibilium, tum inuisibilium. Et in vnitate hujus diuinæ naturæ, tres sunt personæ, eiusdem essentiæ, potentiæ ac æternitatis, pater, filius, et Spiritus sanctus.

ii. Of the wirde or sonne of God which was made very man.

The Sonne, which is the worde of the Father, begotten from euerlasting of the Father, the very and eternall GOD, of one substaunce with the father, toke mans nature in the wombe of the blessed Virgin, of her substaunce: so that two whole and perfect natures, that is to say, the Godhead and manhood, were ioyned together in one person, neuer to be diuided, whereof is one Christe, very GOD and very man, who truely suffered, was crucified, dead, and buried, to reconcile his father to vs, and to be a sacrifice, not onely for originall gylt, but also for all actuall sinnes of men.

ii. De Verbo, siue filio dei, qui verus homo factus est. Filius, qui est verbum partis, ab æterno a patre genitus, verus et æternus Deus, ac patri consubstantialis, in vtero beatæ virginis, ex illius substantia naturam humanam assumpsit: ita vt duæ naturæ, diuina et humana, integrè atque perfectè in vnitate personæ fuerint inseparabiliter.[1] coniunctæ, ex quibus est vnus Christus, verus Deus, et verus homo, qui verè passus est, crucifixus, mortuus, et sepultus, vt patrem nobis reconciliaret, essetque hostia, non tantum pro culpa originis, verumetiam pro omnibus actualibus hominum peccatis.

---

[1]   Inseparabiliter *is not exactly rendered by* 'never to be divided'.

iii. *Of the goyng downe of Christe into hell.*
As Christe dyed for vs, and was buryed: so also it is to be beleued
that he went downe into hell.
*iii. De descensu Christi ad Inferos. Qvemadmodum Christus pro nobis
mortuus est, et sepultus, ita est etiam credendus ad inferos descendisse.*

iv. *Of the resurrection of Christe.*
Chryste dyd truely aryse agayne from death, and toke ·agayne his
body, with flesh, bones, and all things apparteyning to the
perfection of mans nature, wherewith he ascended into heauen, and
there sitteth, vntyll he returne to iudge all men at the last day.
*iv. De resurrectione Christi. Christus verè a mortuis resurrexit, suumque
corpus cum carne, ossibus, omnibusque ad integritatem humanæ naturæ,
pertinentibus, recepit: cum quibus in cœlum ascendit, ibique residet, quòad,
extremo die, ad iudicandos homines reuersurus sit.*

v. *Of the holy ghost.*
The holy ghost, proceedyng from the father and the sonne, is of
one substaunce, maiestie, and glorie, with the father and the sonne,
very and eternall God.
*v. De Spiritu sancto. Spiritus sanctus a patre, et filio procedens, eiusdem est
cum patre, et filio essentiæ, maiestatis, et gloriæ, verus, ac æternus, Deus.*

vi. *Of the sufficiencie of the holy Scriptures for saluation.*
Holye Scripture conteyneth all thinges necessarie to saluation: so
that whatsoeuer is not read therein, nor may be proued thereby, is
not to be required of anye man, that it shoulde be beleued as an
article of the fayth, or be thought requisite necessarie to saluation.
In the name of holy Scripture, we do vnderstande those Canonicall
bookes of the olde and newe Testament, of whose aucthoritie was
neuer any doubt in the Churche.

Of the names and number of the Canonicall Bookes
Genesis. Exodus. Leuiticus. Numerie. Deuteronomium. Josue.
Judges. Ruth. The .1. boke of Samuel. The .2. boke of Samuel.
The .1. booke of Kinges. The .2. booke of Kinges. The .1. booke
of Chroni. The .2. booke of Chroni. The .1. booke of Esdras. The
.2. booke of Esdras. The booke of Hester. The booke of Job. The
Psalmes. The Prouerbes. Ecclesia, or preacher. Cantica, or songes
of Sa. 4. Prophetes the greater. 12. Prophetes the lesse.
And the other bookes (as Hierome sayth) the Church doth reade for
example of lyfe and instruction of maners: but yet doth it not
applie them to establishe any doctrine. Such are these folowyng.
The third boke of Esdras. The fourth boke of Esdras. The booke of

Tobias. The booke of Judith. The rest of the booke of Hester. The boke of Wisdome. Jesus the sonne of Sirach. Baruch, the Prophet. The song of the 3 children. The storie of Susanna. Of Bel and the Dragon. The prayer of Manasses. The .1. boke of Machab. The .2. booke of Macha.

All the bookes of the new Testament, as they are commonly receaued we do receaue and accompt them for Canonicall.

vi. De diuinis Scripturis, quod sufficiant ad salutem. *Scriptura sacra continet omnia, quæ ad salutem sunt necessaria, ita, vt quicquid in ea nec legitur, neque inde probari potest, non sit a quoquam exigendum, vt tanquam articulus fidei credatur, aut ad salutis necessitatem requiri putetur. Sacræ Scripturæ nomine, eos Canonicos libros veteris, et noui Testamenti intelligimus, de quorum authoritate, in Ecclesia nunquam dubitatum est.*

De nominibus, et numero librorum sacræ canonicæ Scripturæ veteris Testamenti. *Genesis. Exodus. Leuiticus. Numeri. Deuteron. Iosuæ. Iudicum. Ruth. Prior liber Samuelis. Secundus lib. Samuelis. Prior liber Regum. Secundus liber Regum. Prior liber Paralipom. Secundus liber Paralipomen. Primus liber Esdræ. Secundus liber Esdræ. Liber Hester. Liber Iob. Psalmi. Prouerbia. Ecclesiastes, vel concionator. Cantica Salomonis. 4. Prophetæ maiores. 12. Prophetæ minores.*

Alios autem libros (vt ait Hieronimus) legit quidem Ecclesia, ad exempla vitæ, et formandos mores:[2] *illos tamen ad dogmata confirmanda non adhibet, vt sunt.*

Tertius liber Esdræ. Quartus liber Esdræ. Liber Tobiæ. Liber Iudith. Reliquum libri Hester. Liber sapientiæ. Liber Iesu filij Sirach. Baruch Propheta. Canticum trium puerorum. Historia Susannæ. De Bel et Dracone. Oratio Manasses. Prior lib. Machabeorum. Secundus liber Machabeorum.

Noui Testamenti omnes libros, (vt vulgo recepti sunt) recipimus, et habemus pro Canonicis.

vii. *Of the olde Testament.*

The olde Testament is not contrary to the newe, for both in the olde and newe Testament euerlastyng lyfe is offered to mankynde by Christe, who is the onlye mediatour betweene God and man, being both God and man. Wherefore they are not to be hearde which faigne that the olde fathers dyd looke onlye for transitorie promises. Although the lawe geuen from God by Moyses, as touchyng ceremonies and rites, do not bynde Christian men, nor the ciuile preceptes thereof, ought of necessitie to be receaued in any common wealth: yet nothwithstandyng, no Christian man whatsoeuer, is free from the obedience of the commaundementes, whiche are called morall.

---

[2]   Latin: 'forming behaviour' rather than 'instruction of manners'.

vii. De veteri Testamento. *Testamentum vetus, nouo contrarium non est, quandoquidem tam in veteri, quam in nouo, per Christum, qui vnicus est mediator Dei, et hominum, Deus et homo, æterna vita, humano generi est proposita. Quare male sentiunt, qui veteres tantum in promissiones temporarias sperasse confingunt. Quamquam lex a deo data per Mosen (quoad ceremonias et ritus) Christianos non astringat, neque ciuilia eius præcepta in aliqua republica necessariò recipi debeant, nihilominus tamen ab obedientia mandatorum (quæ moralia vocantur) (nullus quantumuis Christianus) est solutus.*

viii. *Of the three Credes.*

The three Credes, Nicene Crede, Athanasius Crede, and that which is commonlye called the apostles Crede, ought throughlye to be receaued and beleued: for they may be proued by moste certayne warrauntes of holye scripture.

viii. De tribus Symbolis. *Symbola tria, Nycœnum, Athanasij, et quod vulgo Apostolorum appellatur, omnio recipienda sunt, et credenda, nam firmissimis Scripturarum testimonijs probari possunt.*

ix. *Of originall or birth sinne.*

Originall sinne standeth not in the folowing of Adam (as the Pelagians do vainely talke) but it is the fault and corruption of the nature of euery man, that naturally is engendred of the ofspring of Adam, whereby man is very farre gone from originall ryghteousnes, and is of hys owne nature enclined to euyll, so that the fleshe lusteth alwayes contrary to the spirite, and therefore in euery person borne into this worlde, it deserueth Gods wrath and damnation. And this infection of nature doth remayne, yea in them that are regenerated, whereby the luste of the fleshe, called in Greke φρόνημα σαρκός, which some do expounde the wisdome, some sensualitie, some the affection, some the desyre of the fleshe, is not subiect to the lawe of God. And although there is no condemnation for them that beleue and are baptized: yet the apostle doth confesse that concupiscence and luste hath of itselfe the nature of synne.

ix. De peccato originali. *Peccatum originis non est (vt fabulantur Pelagiani) in imitatione Adami situm, sed est vitium, et deprauatio naturæ, cuiuslibet hominis, ex Adamo naturaliter propagati: qua fit, vt ab originali iusticia quam longissime distet, ad malum sua natura propendeat, et caro semper aduersus spiritum concupiscat, vnde in vnoquoque nascentium, iram dei, atque damnationem meretur. Manet etiam in renatis hæc naturæ deprauatio. Qua fit, vt affectus carnis Greci* Φρόνημα σαρκός, *(quod alij sapientiam, alij sensum, alij affectum, alij studium carnis interpretantur,) legi dei non subijciatur. Et quanquam renatis et credentibus, nulla propter Christum est condemnatio, peccati tamen in sese rationem habere concupiscentiam, fatetur apostolus.*

x. *Of free wyll.*

The condition of man after the fall of Adam is suche, that he can not turne and prepare hym selfe by his owne naturall strength and good workes, to fayth and calling vpon God: Wherefore we haue no power to do good workes pleasaunt and acceptable to God, without the grace of God by Christe preuentyng vs, that we may haue a good wyll, and workyng with vs, when we haue that good wyll.

x. De libero arbitrio. *Ea est hominis post lapsum Adæ conditio, vt sese naturalibus suis viribus, et bonis operibus, ad fidem, et inuocationem Dei conuertere, ac præparare non possit. Quare absque gratia Dei (quæ per Christum est) nos præueniente, vt velimus, et cooperante, dum volumus, ad pietatis opera facienda, quæ Deo grata sunt, et accepta, nihil valemus.*

xi. *Of the iustification of man.*

We are accompted righteous before God, only for the merite of our Lord and sauior Jesus Christ, by faith, and not for our owne workes or deseruynges. Wherefore, that we are iustified by fayth onely, is a most wholesome doctrine, and very full of comfort, as more largely is expressed in the Homilie of iustification.

xi. De hominis iustificatione. *Tantum propter meritum Domini, ac Seruatoris nostri Iesu Christi, per fidem, non propter opera, et merita nostra, iusti coram Deo reputamur. Quare sola fide nos iustificari, doctrina est saluberrima, ac consolationis plenissima, vt in homilia de iustificatione hominis, fusius explicatur.*

xii. *Of good workes.*

Albeit that good workes, whiche are the fruites of fayth, and folowe after iustification, can not put away our sinnes, and endure the seueritie of Gods iudgement: yet are they pleasing and acceptable to God in Christe, and do spring out necessarily of a true and liuely fayth, in so muche that by them, a lyuely fayth may be as euidently known, as a tree discerned by the fruit.

xii. De bonis operibus. *Bona opera, quæ sunt fructus fidei, et iustificatos* [translation does not match the Latin here] *sequuntur, quanquàm peccata nostra expiare, et diuini iudicij seueritatem ferre non possunt: Deo tamen grata sunt, et accepta in Christo, atque ex vera et viua fide, necessario profluunt, vt planè ex illis, æquè fides viua cognosci possit, atque arbor ex fructu iudicari.*

xiii. *Of workes before iustification.*

Workes done before the grace of Christe, and the inspiration of his spirite, are not pleasaunt to God, forasmuche as they spring not of fayth in Jesus Christ, neither do they make men meete to receaue grace, or (as the schole aucthors saye) derserue grace of congruitie [That is, a grace which matches the works done]: yea rather for that they are not done as GOD hath wylled and commaunded them to be done, we doubt not but they haue the nature of sinne.

xiii. De operibus ante iustificationem. *Opera quæ fiunt, ante gratiam Christi, et spiritus eius afflatum, cum ex fide Jesu Christi non prodeant, minime Deo grata sunt, neque gratiam (vt multi vocant) de congruò merentur. Immo cum non sint facta, vt Deus illa fieri voluit, et præcepit, peccati rationem habere non dubitamus.*

xiv. *Of workes of supererogation.*

Voluntarie workes, besydes, ouer and aboue Gods commaundementes, which they call workes of supererogation, can not be taught without arrogancie and impietie. For by them men do declare that they do not onely render vnto God as muche as they are bounde to do, but that they do more for his sake then of bounden duetie is required: Whereas Christe sayth playnely, When ye haue done al that are commaunded to you, say, We be vnprofitable seruauntes.

xiv. De operis supererogationis. *Opera quæ supererogationis appellant, non possunt sine arrogantia, et impietate prædicari. Nam illis declarant homines, non tantum se Deo reddere, quæ tenentur, sed plus in eius gratiam facere, quàm deberent, cum apertè Christus dicat: Cum feceritis omnia quæcunque præcepta sunt vobis, dicite, serui inutiles sumus.*

xv. *Of Christe alone without sinne.*

Christe in the trueth of our nature, was made like vnto vs in al thinges (sinne only except) from which he was clearly voyde, both in his fleshe, and in his spirite. He came to be the lambe without spot, who by sacrifice of hym selfe once made, shoulde take away the sinnes of the worlde: and sinne (as S. John sayeth) was not in him. But al we the rest (although baptized, and borne agayne in Christe) yet offende in many thinges: and if we say we haue no sinne, we deceaue our selues, and the trueth is not in vs.

xv. De Christo, qui solus est sine peccato. *Christus, in nostræ naturæ veritate, per omnia similis factus est nobis, excepto peccato, a quo prorsus erat immunis, tum in carne, tum in spiritu. Venit vt agnus, absque macula, qui mundi peccata per immolationem sui semel factam, tolleret, et peccatum (vt inquit Iohannes) in eo non erat: sed nos reliqui etiam baptizati, et in Christo regenerati, in multis tamen offendimus omnes. Et si dixerimus, quia peccatum non habemus, nos ipsos seducimus, et veritas in nobis non est.*

xvi. *Of sinne after baptisme.*

Not euery deadly sinne willingly committed after baptisme, is sinne agaynst the holy ghost, and vnpardonable. Wherefore, the graunt of repentaunce is not to be denyed to such as fal into sinne after baptisme. After we haue receaued the holy ghost, we may depart from grace geuen, and fall into sinne, and by the grace of god (we may) aryse agayne and amende our lyues. And therefore, they are to be condemned, whiche say they can no more sinne as long as they lyue here, or denie the place of forgeuenesse to suche as truely repent.

xvi. De peccato post baptismum. Non omne peccatum mortale post baptismum voluntariè perpetratum, est peccatum in Spiritum sanctum, et irremissibile. Proinde lapsis a baptismo in peccata, locus pœnitentiæ non est negandus, post acceptum spiritum sanctum possumus a gratia data recedere, atque peccare: denuoque per gratiam Dei resurgere, ac resipiscere: ideoque illi damnandi sunt, qui se quàmdiu hic viuant, amplius non posse peccare affirmant, aut verè resipiscentibus, veniæ locum denegant.

xvii. Of predestination and election.

Predestination to lyfe, is the euerlastyng purpose of God, whereby (before the foundations of the world were layd) he hath constantly decreed by his councell secrete to vs, to deliuer from curse and damnation, those whom he hath chosen in Christe out of mankynde, and to bryng them by Christe to euerlastyng saluation, as vessels made to honour. Wherefore they which be indued with so excellent a benefite of God, be called accordyng to Gods purpose by his spirit workyng in due season: they through grace obey the callyng: they be iustified freely: they be made sonnes of God by adoption: they be made lyke the image of his onelye begotten sonne Jesus Christe: they walke religiously in good workes, and at length by gods mercy, they attaine to euerlastyng felicitie.

As the godly consyderation of predestination, and our election in Christe, is full of sweete, pleasaunt, and vnspeakeable comfort to godly persons, and such as feele in them selues the working of the spirite of Christe, mortifying the workes of the fleshe, and theyr earthly members, and drawyng vp theyr mynde to hygh and heauenly thinges, aswell because it doth greatly establyshe and confirme theyr fayth of eternall saluation to be enioyed through Christ, as because it doth feruently kindle their loue towardes God: So, for curious and carnal persons, lacking the spirite of Christe, to haue continually before theyr eyes the sentence of Gods predestination, is a most daungerous downefall, whereby the deuyll doth thrust them either into desperation, or into rechlesnesse of most vncleane liuing, no lesse perilous than desperation.

Furthermore, we must receaue Gods promises in such wyse, as they be generally set foorth to vs in holy scripture: and in our doynges, that wyl of God is to be folowed, which we haue expreslye declared vnto vs in the worde of God.

xvii. De prædestinatione, et electione. *Prædestinatio ad vitam, est æternum Dei propositum, quo ante iacta mundi fundamenta, suo consilio, nobis quidem occultò constanter decreuit, eos quos in Christo elegit ex hominum genere, e maledicto et exitio liberare, atque (vt vasa in honorem efficta) per Christum, ad æternam salutem adducere. Vnde qui tam præclaro Dei beneficio sunt donati, illi spiritu eius, oportuno tempore operante, secundum propositum eius, vocantur, vocationi per gratiam parent, iustificantur gratis, adoptantur in filios Dei vnigeniti eius Iesu Christi imagini efficiuntur conformes, in bonis operibus sanctè ambulant, et demum ex dei misericordia pertingunt ad sempiternam fœlicitatem. Quemadmodum prædestinationis, et electionis nostræ in Christo pia consideratio, dulcis, suauis, et ineffabilis consolationis plena est, verè pijs, et hijs qui sentiunt in se vim spiritus Christi, facta carnis, et membra, quæ adhuc sunt super terram, mortificantem, animumque ad cœlestia, et superna rapientem. Tum quia fidem nostram de æterna salute consequenda per Christum plurimum stabilit, atque confirmat, tum quia amorem nostrum in deum vehementer accendit. Ita hominibus curiosis, carnalibus, et Spiritu Christi destituis, ob oculos perpetuò versari, predestinationis Dei sententiam, pernitiosissimum est præcipitium, vnde illos diabolus protrudit, vel in desperationem, vel in æque pernitiosam impurissimæ vitæ securitatem, deinde promissiones diuinas sic amplecti oportet, vt nobis in sacris literis generaliter propositæ sunt, et Dei voluntas in nostris actionibus ea sequenda est, quam in verbo Dei habemus, desertè reuelatam.*

xviii. Of obtaynyng eternall saluation, only by the name of Christe. They also are to be had accursed, that presume to say, that euery man shalbe saued by the lawe or sect which he professeth, so that he be diligent to frame his lyfe according to that lawe, and the lyght of nature. For holye scripture doth set out vnto vs onlye the name of Jesus Christe, whereby men must be saued.

xviii. De speranda æterna salute tantum in nomine Christi. *Svnt et illi Anathematizandi, qui dicere audent vnumquemque in lege, aut secta quam profitetur esse seruandum, modo iuxta illam, et lumen naturæ accuratè vixerit, cum sacræ literæ tantum Iesu Christi nomen prædicent, in quo saluos fieri homines oporteat.*

xix. Of the Church.
The visible Church of Christe, is a congregation of faythfull men, in the which the pure worde of God is preached, and the Sacramentes be duely ministred, accordyng to Christes ordinaunce in all those thynges that of necessitie are requisite to the same. As

the Church of Hierusalem, Alexandria, and Antioche haue erred: so also the Church of Rome hath erred, not only in their lyuing and maner of ceremonies, but also in matters of fayth.

xix. De Ecclesia. Ecclesia Christi visibilis est cœtus fidelium, in quo verbum dei purum prædicatur, vt sacramenta, quod ea que necessario exigantur, iuxta Christi institutum rectè administrantur. Sicut errauit Ecclesia Hierosolimitana, Alexandrina, et Antiochena: ita et errauit ecclesia Romana, non solum quoàd agenda, et ceremonarium ritus, verum in hijs etiam quœ credenda sunt.

xx. Of the aucthoritie of the Church.

The Church hath power to decree Rites or Ceremonies, and aucthoritie in controversies of fayth: And yet it is not lawfull for the Church to ordayne any thyng that is contrarie to Gods word written, neyther may it so expounde one place of scripture, that it be repugnaunt to another. Wherefore, although the Church be a witnesse and a keper of holy writ: yet, as it ought not to decree any thyng agaynst the same, so besides the same, ought it not to enforce any thing to be beleued for necessitie of saluation.

xx. De Ecclesiæ authoritate. Habet Ecclesia ritus statuendi ius, et in fidei controversiis auctoritatem; quamvis Ecclesiæ non licet quicquam instituere, quod verbo Dei aduersetur, neque vnum Scripturæ locum sic exponere potest, vt alteri contradicat. Quare licet Ecclesia sit diuinorum librorum testis, et conseruatrix, attamen vt aduersus eos nihil decernere, ita præter illos, nihil credendum de necessitate salutis debet obtrudere.

xxi. Of the aucthoritie of generall Counselles.

Generall Counsels may not be gathered together without the commaundement and wyll of princes. And when they be gathered together (forasmuche as they be an assemblie of men, whereof all be not gouerned with the spirite and word of God) they mey erre, and sometyme haue erred, euen in thinges parteynyng vnto God. Wherfore, thinges ordayned by them as necessary to saluation, haue neyther strength nor aucthoritie, vnlesse it may be declared that they be taken out of holy scripture.

xxi. De authoritate Conciliorum generalium. Generalia concilia, sine iussu, et voluntate principum congregari non possunt, et vbi conuenerint, quia ex hominibus constant, qui non omnes spiritu, et verbo Dei reguntur, et errare possunt, et interdum errarunt etiam in his quœ ad normam pietatis pertinent: ideoque quœ ab illis constituuntur, vt ad salutem necessaria, neque robur habent, neque authoritatem, nisi ostendi possint è sacris literis esse desumpta.

xxii. Of Purgatorie.

The Romishe doctrine concernyng purgatorie, pardons, worshipping and adoration aswell of images, as of reliques, and also inuocation of saintes, is a fonde thing, vainly inuented, and grounded vpon no warrantie of Scripture, but rather repugnaunt to the worde of God.

*xxii.*De purgatorio. *Doctrina Romanensium de purgatorio, de indulgentijs, de veneratione, et adoratione, tum imaginum, tum reliquiarum, nec non de inuocatione sanctorum, res est futilis, inanitèr conficta, et nullis Scriptarum testimonijs, inititur: immo verbo Dei contradicit.*

xxiii. *Of ministryng in the congregation.*

It is not lawful for any man to take vpon hym the office of publique preachyng, or ministring the Sacramentes in the congregation, before he be lawfully called and sent to execute the same. And those we ought to iudge lawfully called and sent, whiche be chosen and called to this worke by men who haue publique aucthoritie geuen vnto them in the congregation, to call and sende ministers into the Lordes vineyarde.

xxiii. De vocatione ministrorum. Non licet cuiquam sumere sibi munus publicè prædicandi, aut administrandi sacramenta in ecclesia, nisi prius fuerit ad hæc obeunda legitimè vocatus, et missus. Atque illos legitimè vocatos et missos existimare debemus, qui per homines, quibus potestas vocandi ministros, atque mittendi in vineam Domini, publicè concessa est in ecclesia, coaptati fuerint, et asciti in hoc opus.

xxiv. *Of speakyng in the congregation, in such tongue as the people vnderstandeth.*

It is a thing playnely repugnaunt to the worde of God, and the custome of the primitiue Churche, to haue publique prayer in the Churche, or to minister the Sacramentes, in a tongue not vnderstanded of the people.

xxiv. De precibus publicis dicendis in lingua vulgari. Lingua populo non intellecta, publicas in ecclesia preces peragere, aut sacramenta administrare, verbo Dei et primitiuæ ecclesiæ consuetudini planè repugnat.

xxv. *Of the Sacramentes.*

Sacramentes ordayned of Christe, be not only badges or tokens of Christian mens profession: but rather they be certaine sure witnesses and effectuall signes of grace and Gods good wyll towardes vs, by the which he doth worke inuisiblie in vs, and doth not only quicken, but also strengthen and confirme our fayth in hym. There are two Sacramentes ordayned of Christe our Lorde in the Gospell, that is to say, baptisme, and the Supper of the Lorde. Those fyue, commonly called Sacramentes, that is to say, Confirmation, Penaunce, Orders, Matrimonie, and extreme Unction, are not to be compted for Sacramentes [of] the Gospel, being such as haue growen partly of the corrupt folowing of the apostles, partly are states of life alowed in the scriptures: but yet haue not lyke nature of Sacramentes with baptisme and the Lords Supper, for thet they haue not any visible signe or ceremonie ordayned of God. The Sacramentes were not ordayned of Christ to be gased vpon, or to be carryed about: but that we shoulde duely vse them. And in such only, as worthyly receaue the same, they haue a wholesome effect or operation: But they that receaue them vnworthyly, purchase to them selues damnation, as S. Paul sayth.

xxv. De Sacramentis. Sacramenta à Christo instituta, non tantum sunt notæ professionis Christianorum, sed certa quædam potius testimonia, et efficatia signa gratiæ, atque bonæ in nos voluntatis Dei, per quæ inuisibiliter ipse in nos operatur, nostramque fidem in se non solum excitat, verumetiam confirmat. Duo a Christo domino nostro in euangelio instituta sunt sacramenta, scilicet, baptismus, et cœna Domini. Quinque illa vulgo nominata sacramenta: scilicet, confirmatio, pœnitentia, ordo, matrimonium, et extrema vnctio, pro sacramentis euangelicis habenda non sunt, vt quæ, partim, a praua Apostolorum imitatione profluxerunt, partim vitæ status sunt in scripturis quidem probati: sed sacramentorum eandem cum baptismo, et cœna Domini rationem non habentes, vt quæ signum aliquod visibile, seu cæremoniam à Deo institutum, non habeant. Sacramenta non in hoc instituta sunt a Christo vt specarentur, aut circumferrentur, sed vt ritè illis vteremur, et in hijs duntaxat qui dignè percipiunt salutarem habent effectum: Qui verò indignè percipiunt, damnationem (vt inquit Paulus) sibi ipsis acquirunt.

xxvi. *Of the vnworthynesse of the ministers, which hinder not the effect of the Sacramentes.*

Although in the visible Churche the euyl be euer myngled with the good, and sometime the euyll haue cheefe aucthoritie in the ministration of the worde and Sacramentes: yet forasmuch as they do not the same in their own name, but in Christes, and do minister by his commission and aucthoritie, we may vse their ministerie, both in hearing the word of God, and in the receauing of the Sacramentes. Neither is the effecte of Christes ordinaunce taken away by their wickednesse, nor the grace of Gods gyftes diminished from such as by fayth and ryghtly do receaue the Sacramentes ministered vnto them, which be effectuall, because Christes institution and promise, although they be ministred by euyll men. Neuerthelesse, it apparteyneth to the discipline of the Churche, that enquirie be made of euyl ministers, and that they be accused by those that haue knowledge of their offences: and finally, beying founde gyltie by iust iudgement, be deposed.

xxvi. De vi institutionum diuinarum, quod eam non tollat malitia Ministrorum. Qvamuis in ecclesia visibili, bonis mali semper sunt admixti, atque interdum ministerio verbi, et sacramentorum administrationi præsint, tamen cum non suo, sed Christi nomine agant, eiusquè mandato, et authoritate ministrent, illorum ministerio vti licet, cum in verbo Dei audiendo, tum in sacramentis precipiendis. Nequè per illorum malitiam, effectus institutorum Christi tollitur, aut gratia donorum Dei minuitur, quoad eos qui fide, et ritè sibi oblata percipiunt, quæ propter institutionem Christi, et promissionem efficata sunt, licet per malos administrentur. Ad ecclesiæ tamen disciplinam pertinet, vt in malos ministros inquiratur, accusenturque ab his, qui eorum flagitia nouerint, atque tandem iusto conuicti iudicio deponantur.

xxvii. *Of baptisme.*

baptisme is not only a signe of profession, and marke of difference, whereby Christian men are discerned from other that be not christend: but is also a signe of regeneration or newe byrth, whereby, as by an instrument, they that receaue baptisme rightly, are grafted into the Church: the promises of the forgeuenesse of sinne, and of our adoption to be the sonnes of God, by the holy ghost, are visibly signed and sealed: fayth is confyrmed: and grace increased by vertue of prayer vnto God. The baptisme of young children, is in any wyse to be retayned in the Churche, as most agreable with the institution of Christe.

xxvii. De baptismo. baptismus non est tantum professionis signum, ac discriminis nota, qua Christiani a non Christianis discernantur, sed etiam est signum regenerationis, per quod, tanquam per instrumentum, rectè baptismum suscipientes, ecclesiæ inseruntur, promissiones de remissione peccatorum, atque adoptione nostra in filios Dei per Spiritum sanctum visibiliter obsignantur, fides confirmatur, et vi diuinæ inuocationis gratia augetur. baptismus paruulorum omnio in ecclesia retinendus est, vt qui cum Christi institutionè optimè congruat.

xxviii. *Of the Lordes supper.*

The Supper of the Lord, is not only a signe of the loue that Christians ought to haue among them selues one to another: but rather it is a Sacrament of our redemption by Christes death. Insomuch that to suche as ryghtlie, worthyly, and with fayth receaue the same, the bread whiche we breake is a parttakyng of the body of Christe, and likewyse the cuppe of blessing, is a parttakyng of the blood of Christe. Transubstantiation (or the chaunge of the substaunce of bread and wine) in the Supper of the Lorde, can not be proued by holye writ: but is repugnaunt to the playne wordes of scripture, ouerthroweth the nature of a Sacrament, and hath geuen occasion to many superstitions. The body of Christe is geuen, taken, and eaten in the Supper, only after an heauenly and spirituall maner: And the meane whereby the body of

Christe is receaued and eaten in the Supper, is fayth. The Sacrament of the Lordes Supper, was not by Christes ordinaunce reserued, caryed about, lyfted vp, or worshipped.

xxviii. De Cœna Domini. *Cœna Domini non est tantum signum mutuœ beneuolentiœ Christianorum inter sese, verum potius est Sacramentum nostrœ per mortem Christi redemptionis. Atque adeo, ritè, dignè, et cum fide sumentibus, panis quem frangimus est communicatio corporis Christi: similiter poculum benedictionis, est communicatio sanguinis Christi. Panis, et Vini transubstantiatio in Eucharistia, ex sacris literis probari non potest. Sed apertis Scripturœ verbis aduersatur, Sacramenti naturam euertit, et multarum superstitionum dedit occasionem. Corpus Christi datur, accipitur, et manducatur in Cœna, tantum cœlesti, et spirituali ratione. Medium autem quo corpus Christi accipitur, et manducatur in Cœna, fides est. Sacramentum Eucharistiœ, ex institutione Christi non seruabatur, circumferebatur, eleuebatur, nec adorabatur.*

xxix. *Of the wicked which do not eate the body of Christe in the vse of the Lordes Supper.*

The wicked, and suche as be voyde of a liuelye fayth, although they do carnally and visibly presse with theyr teeth (as saint Augustine sayth) the Sacrament of the bodye ad blood of Christ: yet in no wyse are they partakers of Christe, but rather to theyr condemnation, do eate and drinke the signe or Sacrament of so great a thing.

xxix. De manducatione corporis Christi, et impios illud non manducare. *Impij, et fide viua destituti, licet carnaliter, et visibilitèr (vt Augustinus loquitur) corporis, et sanguinis Christi sacramentum, dentibus premant, nullo tamen modo Christi participes efficiuntur. Sed potius tantœ rei sacramentum, seu symbolum, ad iudicium sibi manducant, et bibunt.*

xxx. *Of both kindes.*

The cuppe of the Lorde is not to be denyed to the laye people. For both the partes of the Lordes Sacrament, by Christes ordinance and commaundement, ought to be ministred to all Christian men alyke.

xxx. De vtraque specie. *Calix Domini laicis non est denegandus, vtraquè enim pars Dominici sacramenti, ex Christi institutione, et prœcepto, omnibus Christianis, ex œquo administrari debet.*

xxxi. *Of the one oblation of Christe finished vppon the crosse.*

The offering of Christ once made, is the perfect redemption, propiciation, and satisfaction for all the sinnes of the whole worlde, both originall and actuall, and there is none other satisfaction for sinne, but that alone. Wherefore the sacrifices of Masses, in the which it was commonly said that the priestes did offer Christe for the quicke and the dead, to haue remission of paine or gylt, were blasphemous fables and daungerous deceites.

xxxi. De vnica Christi oblatione in cruce perfecta. *Oblatio Christi semel facta, perfecta est redemptio, propitiatio, et satisfactio pro omnibus peccatis totius mundi, tàm originalibus, quàm actualibus. Nequè præter illam vnicam, est vlla alia pro peccatis expiatio, vnde missarum sacrificia, quibus, vulgò dicebatur, sacerdotem offerre Christum, in remissionem pœnæ, aut culpæ, pro viuis et defunctis, blasphema figmenta sunt, et perniciosæ imposturæ.*

xxxii. *Of the mariage of priestes.*

Byshops, priestes, and deacons, are not commaunded by Gods lawe eyther to vowe the estate of single lyfe, or to abstayne from mariage. Therefore it is lawfull also for them, as for all other Christian men, to mary at their own discretion, as they shall iudge the same to serue better to godlynesse.

xxxii. De coniugio sacerdotum. *Episcopis, Præsbiteris, et Diaconis nullo mandato diuino præceptum est, vt aut cœlibatum voueant, aut a matrimonio abstineant. Licet igitur etiam illis, vt cæteris omnibus Christianis, vbi hoc ad pietatem magis facere iudicauerint, pro suo arbitratu matrimonium contrahere.*

xxxiii. *Of excommunicate persons, howe they are to be auoyded.*

That person whiche by open denuntiation of the Churche, is ryghtly cut of from the vnitie of the Churche, and excommunicated, ought to be taken of the whole multitude of the faythfull as an Heathen and Publicane, vntyll he be openly reconciled by penaunce, and receaued into the Churche by a iudge that hath aucthoritie thereto.

xxxiii. De excommunicatis vitandis. *Qvi per publicam ecclesiæ denunciationem ritè ab vnitate ecclesiæ præcisus est, et excommunicatus, is ab vniuersa fidelium multitudine (donec per pœnitentiam publicè reconciliatus fuerit arbitrio Iudicis competentis) habendus est tanquam Ethnicus et publicanus.*

xxxiv. *Of the traditions of the Churche.*

It is not necessarie that traditions and ceremonies be in all places one, or vtterly like, for at all times they hauc ben diuerse, and may be chaunged accordyng to the diuersitie of countreys, times, and mens maners, so that nothing be ordeyned against Gods worde. Whosoeuer through his priuate iudgement, wyllyngly and purposely doth openly breake the traditions and ceremonies of the Church, which be not repugnaunt to the worde of God, and be ordayned and approued by common aucthoritie: ought to be rebuked openly, (that other may feare to do the lyke) as he that offendeth agaynst the Common order of the Churche, and hurteth the aucthoritie of the Magistrate, and woundeth the consciences of the weake brethren. Euery particuler or nationall Churche, hath aucthoritie to ordaine, chaunge, and abolishe ceremonies or rites of the Churche ordeyned onlye by mans aucthoritie, so that all thinges be done to edifying.

xxxiv. De traditionibus Ecclesiasticis. *Traditiones atquè ceremonias easdem, non omnio necessarium est esse vbiquè, aut prorsus consimiles. Nam et variæ semper fuerunt, et mutari possunt, pro Regionum, temporum, et morum diuersitate, modò nihil contra verbum Dei instituatur. Traditiones, et ceremonias ecclesiasticas quæ cum uerbo Dei non pugnant, et sunt authoritate publica institutæ, atquè probatæ, quisquis priuato consilio volens, et data opera, publicè violauerit, is, vt qui peccat in publicum ordinem Ecclesiæ, quiquè lædit authoritatem magistratus, et qui infirmorum fratrum conscientias vulnerat, publicè vt cæteri timeant, arguendus est. Quælibet ecclesia particularis, siuè Nationalis, authoritatem habet instituendi, mutandi, aut abrogandi Ceremonias, aut ritus ecclesiasticos, humana tantum authoritate institutos, modo omnia ad ædificationem fiant.*

xxxv. Of Homilies.

The seconde booke of Homilies, the seuerall titles whereof we haue ioyned vnder this article, doth conteyne a godly and wholesome doctrine, and necessarie for these tymes, as doth the former booke of Homilies, whiche were set foorth in the time of Edwarde the sixt: and therefore we iudge them to be read in Churches by the Ministers diligently, and distinctly, that they may be vnderstanded of the people.

Of the names of the Homilies.

1   Of the right vse of the Churche.
2   Agaynst perill of Idolatrie.
3   Of repayring and keping cleane of Churches.
4   Of good workes, first of fastyng.
5   Agaynst gluttony and drunkennesse.
6   Against excesse of apparell.
7   Of prayer.
8   Of the place and time of prayer.
9   That common prayers and Sacramentes
     ought to be ministred in a knowne tongue.
10 Of the reuerente estimation of Gods worde.
11 Of almes doing.
12 Of the Natiuitie of Christe.
13 Of the passion of Christe.
14 Of the resurrection of Christe.
·15 Of the worthie receauing of the Sacrament of
     the body and blood of Christe.

16 Of the gyftes of the holy ghost.
17 For the Rogation dayes.
18 Of the state of Matrimonie.
19 Of repentaunce.
20 Agaynst Idlenesse.
21 Agaynst rebellion.

xxxv. De Homiliis. *Tomus secundus Homiliarum, quarum singulos titulos huic articulo subiunximus, continet piam et salutarem doctrinam, et hijs temporibus necessariam, non minus quàm prior tomus Homiliarum, quæ editæ sunt, tempore Edwardi sexti: Itaque eas in ecclesiis per ministros diligenter, et clarè, vt a populo intelligi possint, recitandas esse iudicauimus.*
De nominibus Homiliarum.

> *Of the right vse of the Churche.*
> *Of the reuerent estimation of Gods word.*
> *Agaynst perill of Idolatrie.*
> *Of repayring and keping cleane of Churches.*
> *Of good workes, first of fastyng.*
> *Agaynst gluttony and drunkennes.*
> *Agaynst excesse of apparell.*
> *Of prayer.*
> *Of the place and time of prayer.*
> *That common prayers and Sacraments*
> > *ought to be ministred in a knowne tongue.*
> *Of the reuerente estimation of Gods worde.*
> *Of almes doing.*
> *Of the Natiuitie of Christ.*
> *Of the passion of Christ.*
> *Of the resurrection of Christe.*
> *Of the worthie receauing of the Sacrament of*
> > *the body and bloude of Christe.*
> *Of the giftes of the holy ghost.*
> *For the Rogation dayes.*
> *Of the state of Matrimonie.*
> *Of Repentaunce.*
> *Agaiynst Idlenesse.*
> *Agaynst rebellion.*

xxxvi. Of consecration of bishops and ministers.
The booke of Consecration of Archbyshops, and Byshops, and orderyng of priestes and deacons, lately set foorth in the tyme of Edwarde the sixt, and confyrmed at the same tyme by aucthoritie of Parliament, doth conteyne all thinges necessary to suche consecration and orderyng: neyther hath it any thyng, that of it selfe is superstitious or vngodly. And therefore, whosoeuer are consecrate or ordered accordyng to the rites of that booke, sence

the seconde yere of the aforenamed king Edwarde, vnto this time, or hereafter shalbe consecrated or ordered accordyng to the same rites, we decree all suche to be ryghtly, orderly, and lawfully consecrated and ordered.

xxxvi. De Episcoporum et Ministrorum consecratione. *Libellus de consecratione Archiepiscoporum, et Episcoporum, et de ordinatione præsbyterorum, et Diaconorum, editus nuper temporibus Edwardi vj. et authoritate Parliamenti illis ipsis temporibus confirmatus, omnia ad eiusmodi consecrationem, et ordinationem necessaria continet, et nihil habet, quod ex se sit, aut superstitiosum, aut impium: itaque quicunque iuxta ritus illius libri consecrati, aut ordinati sunt, ab anno secundo prædicti regis Edwardi, vsque ad hoc tempus, aut imposterum iuxta eosdem ritus consecrabuntur, aut ordinabuntur, ritè, atque ordine, atque legitimè statuimus esse, et fore consecratos, et ordinatos.*

xxxvii. *Of the Ciuill Magistrates.*

The Queenes Maiestie hath the cheefe power in this Realme of Englande, and other her dominions, vnto whom the cheefe gouernment of all estates of this Realme, whether they be Ecclesiasticall or Ciuile, in all causes doth apparteyne, and is not, nor ought to be subiect to any foraigne iurisdiction. Where we attribute to the Queenes Maiestie the cheefe gouernment, by whiche titles we vnderstande the mindes of some slaunderous folkes to be offended: we geue not to our princes the ministring either of Gods word, or of Sacramentes, the which thing the Iniunctions also lately set forth by Elizabeth our Queene, doth most plainly testifie: But that only prerogatiue whiche we se to haue ben geuen alwayes to all godly Princes in holy Scriptures by God him selfe, that is, that they should rule all estates and degrees committed to their charge by God, whether they be Ecclesiasticall or Temporall, and restraine with the civill sworde the stubberne and euyll doers. The Byshop of Rome hath no iurisdiction in this Realme of Englande. The lawes of the Realme may punishe Christian men with death, for heynous and greeuous offences.

It is lawfull for Christian men, at the commaundement of the Magistrate, to weare weapons, and serue in the warres.

xxxvii. De civilibus magistratibus. *Regia maiestas in hoc angliæ regno, ac cæteris eius dominijs, summam habet potestatem, ad quam, omnium statuum huius regni, siuè illi ecclesiastici sint, siuè ciuiles, in omnibus causis, suprema gubernatio pertinet, et nulli externæ iurisdictioni est subiecta, nec esse debet. Cum Regiæ Maiestati summam gubernationem tribuimus, quibus titulis intelligimus, animos quorundam calumniatorum offendi, non damus Regibus nostris, aut verbi Dei, aut Sacramentorum administrationem, quod etiam iniunctiones ab Elizabetha Regina nostra, nuper editæ, apertissimè testantur. Sed eam tantum prærogatiuam, quam in sacris scripturis a Deo ipso, omnibus pijs Principibus, videmus semper fuisse attributam, hoc est, vt omnes status, atque ordines fidei suæ a Deo commissos, siuè illi eclesiastici sint, siue ciuiles, in officio contineant, et contumaces ac delinquentes, gladio ciuili coerceant. Romanus pontifex nullam habet iurisdictionem in hoc regno Angliæ.*

Leges Regni possunt Christianos propter capitalia, et grauia crimina, morte punire. Christianis licet, ex mandato magistratus, arma portare, et iusta bella administrare.

xxxviii. *Of Christian mens goodes, which are not common.*

The ryches and goodes of Christians are not common, as touching the ryght, title, and possession of the same, as certayne Anabaptistes do falsely boast. Notwithstandyng euery man ought of suche thinges as he possesseth, liberallye to geue almes to the poore, accordyng to his habilitie.

xxxviii. De illicita bonorum communicatione. *Facultates et bona Christianorum non sunt communia, quoad ius et possessionem (vt quidam Anabaptistæ falso iactant) debet tamen quisque de his quæ possidet, pro facultatum ratione, pauperibus elemosynas benignè distribuere.*

xxxix. *Of a Christian mans othe.*

As we confesse that vayne and rashe swearing is forbidden Christian men by our lord Jesus Christe, and James his apostle: So we iudge that Christian religion doth not prohibite, but that a man may sweare when the Magistrate requireth, in a cause of faith and charitie, so it be done accordyng to the Prophetes teaching, in iustice, iudgement, and trueth.

xxxix. De iureiurando. *Qvemadmodum iuramentum vanum, et temerarium Domino nostro Iesu Christo, et Apostolo eius Jacobo, Christianis hominibus interdictum esse, fatemur: ita Christianorum religionem minimè prohibere censemus, quin iubente magistratu in causa fidei, et charitatis iurare liceat, modò id fiat iuxta Prophetæ doctrinam, in iustitia, in iudicio et veritate.*

xl. *The Ratification.*

This Booke of Articles before rehearsed, is agayne approued, and allowed to be holden and executed within the Realme, by the assent and consent of our Soueraigne Ladye Elizabeth, by the grace of GOD, of Englande, Fraunce, and Irelande Queene, defender of the fayth.

Which Articles were deliberately read, and confirmed agayne by the subscription of the handes of the Archbyshop and Byshoppes of the vpper house, and by the subscription of the whole Cleargie in the neather house in their Conuocation, in the yere of our Lorde GOD. 1571.

40. Confirmatio Articulorum *Hic liber antedictorum Articulorum iam denuo approbatus est, per assensum, et consensum Serenissimæ Reginæ Elizabethæ Dominæ nostræ, Dei gratia Angliæ, Franciæ, et Hiberniæ Reginæ defensoris fidei &c. retinendus, et per totum Regnum Angliæ exequendus. Qui Articuli, et lecti sunt, et denuò confirmati, subscriptione D. archiepiscopi, et Episcoporum superioris domus, et totius Cleri inferioris domus in Conuocatione Anno Domini. 1571.*

The Table.

  i Of fayth in the Trinitie.
  ii Of Christe the sonne of GOD.
  iii Of his goyng downe into hell.
  iv Of his resurrection.
  v Of the holy ghost.
  vi Of the sufficiencie of the Scripture.
  vii Of the olde Testament.
  viii Of the three Credes.
  ix Of originall sinne.
  x Of free wyll.
  xi Of Iustification.
  xii Of good workes.
  xiii Of workes before iustification.
  xiv Of workes of supererogation.
  xv Of Christ alone without sinne.
  xvi Of sinne after baptisme.
  xvii Of predestination and election.
  xviii Of obtayning saluation by Christe.
  xix Of the Churche.
  xx Of the aucthoritie of the Churche.
  xxi Of the aucthoritie of generall Counsels.
  xxii Of Purgatorie.
  xxiii Of ministring in the congregation.
  xxiv Of speakyng in the congregation.
  xxv Of Sacramentes.
  xxvi Of the vnworthynesse of ministers.
  xxvii Of baptisme.
  xxviii Of the Lords supper.
  xxix Of the wicked whiche eate not the body of Christe.
  xxx Of both kyndes.
  xxxi Of Christes one oblation.
  xxxii Of the mariage of priestes.

xxxiii Of excommunicate persons.
xxxiv Of traditions of the Churche.
xxxv Of Homilies.
xxxvi Of consecration of Ministers.
xxxvii Of Ciuill Magistrates.
xxxviii Of christian mens goods.
xxxix Of a christian mans othe.
xl Of the ratification.

152

1575
Ordained Ministry

Canons of 1575, Cardwell, Synodalia, *I. pp. 132–5.*

The points stressed here are the importance of ensuring the intellectual and educational suitability of a candidate for ordination (the Latin test was a reasonable one in its time); the requirements that he shall be of sufficient maturity, at least in age; proof of his orthodoxy; the importance of the use of the proper form of ordination; the linking of ordination with a 'title', that is, responsibility for the pastoral care of a community. All these have longstanding patristic and medieval precedent.

First, That none shall be made a deacon or minister hereafter, but only such as shall first bring to the bishop of that diocese from men known to the same bishop to be sound of religion, a testimonial both of his honest life, and of his professing the doctrine expressed in the 'Articles of religion which concern the confession of the true christian faith, and the doctrine of the sacraments' comprised in a book imprinted, entituled 'Articles whereupon it was agreed by the Archbishops and bishops, etc. anno 1562 put forth by the queen's authority'; and which also shall then be able to answer and render to the same bishop an account of his faith in Latin, agreeable and consonant to the said articles, and shall first subscribe to the said articles. And that every such deacon shall be of the age of twenty-three years, and shall continue in that office the space of a whole year at the least, before he be admitted to the order of priesthood: and every such minister shall be of the full age of twenty-four years. And that neither of those orders shall be given but only upon a Sunday or holy day, and in the face of the church, and in such manner and form, and with all such other circumstances as are appointed by the book entituled 'The form and manner of making and consecrating bishops, priests, and deacons.'

... Item, That from henceforth none shall be admitted to any orders ecclesiastical, unless he do presently shew to the bishops a true presentation of himself to a benefice then void within the diocese or jurisdiction of the said bishop; or unless he likewise shew to the said bishop a true certificate, where presently he may be placed to serve some cure within the same diocese or jurisdiction; or unless he be placed in some cathedral or collegiate church or college; or unless the bishop shall forthwith place him in some vacant benefice or cure; or unless he be known to have sufficient patrimony or livelihood of his own.

153

1575
Provision for preaching and instruction

Canons of 1575, Cardwell, Synodalia, *I. p. 137.*

This stresses the bishop's responsibility for teaching and maintenance of the faith, and especially for ensuring that ordained ministers and people alike know and study Holy Scripture.

Item, That every bishop take order, that able preachers within his diocese do earnestly and with diligence teach their auditors sound doctrine of faith and true religion, and continually exhort them to repentance and amendment of life, that they may bring forth the fruits of faith and charity, and be liberal in alms and other good deeds commanded by God's word. And that none be admitted to be a preacher, unless he be first a deacon at the least.

... Item, That every bishop in his diocese shall with all expedition take order, that the catechism allowed be diligently taught to the youth in every parish church, and that the homilies, (where no sermons be had,) be duly read in order, as they be prescribed, every Sunday and holy day.

... Item, That every bishop shall likewise take order within his diocese, that every parson, vicar, curate and stipendiary priest being under the degree of a master of art, and being no preacher, shall provide and have of his own, within two months after warning given to him or them, the New Testament both in Latin and English or Welch,[1] and shall confer daily one chapter of the same, the Latin and English or Welch together.

154

1586
Rites and ceremonies

Thomas Rogers, The Catholic Doctrine of the Church of England: An Exposition of the Thirty-Nine Articles, *ed. J.J.S. Perowne, PS (1848), pp. 321–2.*

The distinction between those matters of life and worship which may properly vary to reflect the needs of local diversity, and those which must be common to all Christians, was of importance to many sixteenth-century reformers. The emphasis on civil order is also characteristic of the period. (Cf. Article xx, xxxvii.)

(On Article xxxiv). It hath pleased our most merciful Lord and Saviour Christ, for the maintenance of his church militant, that two sorts of rites and ceremonies should be used, whereof some, God... hath himself ordained, as the ceremony of baptism and the Lord's Supper: which are till the end of the world, without all addition, diminution and alteration, with all zeal and religion to be observed.

Others be ordained by the authority of each provincial or national church, and that partly for comeliness, that is to say, that by these helps the people of God the better may be inflamed with a godly zeal; and that soberness and gravity may appear in the well-handling of ecclesiastical matters; and partly for order sake, even that governors may have rules and directions how to govern by... and a joyful peace may be continued, by the well-ordering of church-affairs.

---

[1] Welsh. The study of Scripture in the vernacular is to involve comparison with the Latin.

155

1597
Decision-making

Richard Hooker (c.1554–1600), Ecclesiastical Polity, *Preface, vi, 2–3.*

Richard Hooker, c. 1554–1600 wrote his *Laws of Ecclesiastical Polity* to support the Anglican retention of episcopacy and demonstrate the continuity of the Church of England in the sixteenth century with that of previous generations. On 'decision-making', cf. nos. 67, 70, 207.

When there grew in the Church of Christ a question, Whether the Gentiles believing might be saved, although they were not circumcised after the manner of Moses, nor did observe the rest of those legal rites and ceremonies whereunto the Jews were bound; after great dissension and disputation about it, their conclusion in the end was to have it determined by sentence at Jerusalem; which was accordingly done in a council there assembled for the same purpose.[1] Are ye able to allege any just and sufficient cause wherefore absolutely ye should not condescend in this controversy to have your judgements overruled by some such definitive sentence, whether it fall out to be given with or against you; that so these tedious contentions may cease?

Ye will perhaps make answer, that being persuaded already as touching the truth of your cause, ye are not to hearken unto any sentence, no not though Angels should define otherwise, as the blessed apostle's own example teacheth: again, that men, yea councils, may err; and that, unless the judgement given to satisfy your minds, unless it be such as ye can by no further argument oppugn, in a word, unless you perceive and acknowledge it yourselves consonant with God's word; to stand unto it not allowing it were to sin against your own consciences. But consider I beseech you first as touching the apostle, how that wherein he was so resolute and peremptory, our Lord Jesus Christ made manifest unto him even by intuitive revelation, wherein there was no possibility of error. That which you are persuaded of, ye have it no otherwise than by your own only probable collection, and therefore such bold asseverations as in him were admirable, should in your mouths but argue rashness. God was not ignorant that the

---

[1]   Acts 15

priests and judges, whose sentence in matters of controversy he ordained should stand, both might and oftentimes would be deceived in their judgement. Howbeit, better it was in the eye of His understanding, that sometime an erroneous sentence definitive should prevail, till the same authority perceiving such oversight, might afterwards correct or reverse it, than that strifes should have respite to grow, and not come speedily unto some end.

156

1597
Angels

Richard Hooker (c.1554–1600), Ecclesiastical Polity, *Book I, iv, 2.*

Cf. no. 66.

Of angels, we are not to consider only what they are and do in regard to their own being, but that also which concerneth them as they are linked into a kind of corporation amongst themselves, and of society or fellowship with men. Consider angels each of them severally in himself, and their law is that which the Prophet David mentioneth, 'All ye his angels praise him.' Consider the angels of God associated, and their law is that which disposeth them as an army, one in order and degree above another. Consider finally the angels as having with us that communion which the apostle to the Hebrews noteth, and in regard whereof angels have not disdained to profess themselves our 'fellow-servants;' from hence there springeth up a third law, which bindeth them to works of ministerial employment. Every of which their several functions are by them performed with joy.

157

1597
Fallen angels

Richard Hooker (c.1554–1600), Ecclesiastical Polity, *Book I, iv, 3.*

The mystery of the way in which it could be possible for spiritual beings, living in the sight of God, and created by him to love him, to fall into sin and become demons, has been discussed in every generation.

A part of the angels of God notwithstanding (we know) have fallen, and that their fall hath been through the voluntary breach of that law, which did require at their hands continuance in the exercise of their high and admirable virtue. Impossible it was that ever their will should change or incline to remit any part of their duty, without some object having force to avert their conceit from God, and to draw it another way; and that before they attained that high perfection of bliss, wherein now the elect angels are without possibility of falling. Of any thing more than of God they could not by any means like, as long as whatsoever they knew besides God they apprehended it not in itself without dependency upon God; because so long God must needs seem infinitely better than any thing which they so could apprehend. Things beneath them could not in such sort be presented unto their eyes, but that therein they must needs see always how those things did depend on God. It seemeth therefore that there was no other way for angels to sin, but by reflex of their understanding upon themselves; when being held with admiration of their own sublimity and honour, the memory of their subordination unto God and their dependency on him was drowned in this conceit; whereupon their adoration, love, and imitation of God could not choose but be also interrupted. The fall of angels therefore was pride. Since their fall, their practices have been the clean contrary unto those before mentioned.

158

1597
Sacraments

Richard Hooker (c.1554–1600), Ecclesiastical Polity, *Book V, i, 3.*

The use of Sacraments is but only in this life, yet so that here they concern a far better life than this and are for that cause accompanied with 'grace which worketh salvation'.[1] Sacraments are the powerful instruments of God to eternal life.

---

[1]   Cf. Titus 2. 11

159

1597
The Church's witness to Scripture

Richard Hooker (c.1554–1600), Ecclesiastical Polity, *Book V, xix, 2.*

The Church by her public reading of the book of God preacheth only as a witness. Now the principal thing required in a witness is fidelity. Wherefore... we cannot excuse that Church, which either through corrupt translations of the Scripture delivereth instead of divine speeches any thing repugnant unto that which God speaketh, or, through falsified additions, proposeth that to the people of God as scripture which is in truth no scripture.

160

1597
The ministry of the Word

Richard Hooker (c.1554–1600), Ecclesiastical Polity, *Book V, xxii, 1.*

Hooker is anxious here to ensure that the reformers' enthusiasm for preaching is not allowed to crowd out the straightforward reading of Holy Scripture in worship.

So worthy a part of divine service we should greatly wrong, if we did not esteem Preaching as the blessed ordinance of God, sermons as keys to the kingdom of heaven, as wings to the soul, as spurs to the good affections of man ... but our desire is to uphold... our custom of bare reading the word of God.

161

1597
Prayer

Richard Hooker (c.1554–1600), Ecclesiastical Polity, *Book V, xxiii, 1 and xxiv, 2.*

Here Hooker argues that if the Church in heaven ('triumphant') prays, then the Church on earth ('militant') certainly ought to do so.

The knowledge is small which we have on earth concerning things that are done in heaven. Notwithstanding thus much we know even of saints in heaven, that they pray.[1] And therefore prayer being a work common to the Church as well triumphant as militant, a work common unto men with angels, what should we think but that so much of our lives is celestial and divine as we spend in the exercise of prayer?... When we publicly make our prayers... the things we ask publicly are approved as needful and good in the judgement of all, we hear them sought for and desired with common consent.

162

1597
Christology: a summary

Richard Hooker (c.1554–1600), Ecclesiastical Polity, *Book V, liv, 10.*

Hooker here summarizes the Christological controversies of the first Christian centuries. Cf. no. 419.

[10.] To gather therefore into one sum all that hitherto hath been spoken touching this point, there are but four things which concur to make complete the whole state of our Lord Jesus Christ: his Deity, his manhood, the conjunction of both, and the distinction of the one from the other being joined in one. Four principal heresies there are which have in those things withstood the truth: Arians by bending themselves against the Deity of Christ; Apollinarians by maiming and misinterpreting that which belongeth to his human nature; Nestorians by rending Christ asunder, and dividing him into two persons; the followers of Eutyches by confounding in his person those natures which they should distinguish. Against these there have been four most famous ancient general councils: the council of Nice to define against Arians, against Apollinarians the council of Constantinople, the council of Ephesus against Nestorians, against Eutychians the Chalcedon council. In four words ἀληθῶς, τελέως, ἀδιαιρέτως, ἀσυγχύτως, *truly, perfectly, indivisibly, distinctly*; the first applied to his being God, and the

---

[1]   Revelation 6. 9

second to his being Man, the third to his being of both One, and the fourth to his still continuing in that one Both: we may fully by way of abridgment comprise whatsoever antiquity hath at large handled either in declaration of Christian belief, or in refutation of the foresaid heresies. Within the compass of which four heads, I may truly affirm that all heresies which touch but the person of Jesus Christ, whether they have risen in these later days, or in any age heretofore, may be with great facility brought to confine themselves.

We conclude therefore that to save the world it was of necessity the Son of God should be thus incarnate, and that God should so be in Christ as hath been declared.

163

1597
The indelibility of ordination

Richard Hooker (c.1554–1600), Ecclesiastical Polity, Book V, lxxvii, 1–3.

The ministry of things divine is a function which as God did himself institute, so neither may men undertake the same but by authority and power given them in lawful manner. That God which is no way deficient or wanting unto man in necessaries, and hath therefore given us the light of his heavenly truth, because without that inestimable benefit we must needs have wandered in darkness to our endless perdition and woe, hath in the like abundance of mercies ordained certain to attend upon the due execution of requisite parts and offices therein prescribed for the good of the whole world, which men thereunto assigned do hold their authority from him, whether they be such as himself immediately or as the Church in his name investeth, it being neither possible for all nor for every man without distinction convenient to take upon him a charge of so great importance. They are therefore ministers of God, not only by the way of subordination as princes and civil magistrates whose execution of judgement and justice the supreme hand of divine providence doth uphold, but ministers of God as from whom their authority is derived, and not from men. For in that they are Christ's ambassadors and his labourers, who should give them their commission but he whose most inward affairs they manage?

...To whom Christ hath imparted power both over that mystical body which is the society of souls, and over that natural which is himself for the knitting of both in one; (a work which antiquity doth call the making of Christ's body): the same power is in such not amiss termed a kind of mark or character and acknowledged to be indelible. Ministerial power is a mark of separation, because it severeth them that have it from other men, and maketh them a special *order* consecrated unto the service of the Most High in things wherewith others may not meddle. Their difference therefore from other men is in that they are a distinct *order*. So Tertullian calleth them.

... They which have once received this power may not think to put it off and on like a cloak as the weather serveth, to take it reject and resume it as oft as themselves list, of which profane and impious contempt these later times have yielded as of all other kinds of iniquity and apostasy strange examples; but let them know which put their hands unto this plough, that once consecrated unto God they are made his peculiar inheritance for ever. Suspension may stop, and degradations utterly cut off the use or exercise of power before given: but voluntarily it is not in the power of man to separate and pull asunder what God by his authority coupleth. So that although there may be through misdesert degradation as there may be cause of just separation after matrimony, yet if (as sometime it doth) restitution to former dignity or reconciliation after breach doth happen, neither doth the one nor the other ever iterate the first knot.

164

1600
Salvation

James Usher, 'The Seal of Salvation', Sermon I,[1] *Works, vol. xiii, p. 299.*

'The apostle sets down in this epistle a platform of Christian doctrine, whereupon all persons and churches might safely build

---

[1]   On Romans 8. 15–16

themselves; showing therein a sure way, how those might come to the Lord Jesus Christ who are to obtain salvation by him, which he delivers in three heads, showing,

1. First, how God will convince the world of sin.

2. Secondly, how he discovereth to them what that righteousness is, which without themselves is imputed to them.

3. Thirdly, he setteth forth that righteousness inherent, and created in us by sanctification of the Spirit with the effects thereof, and motives, and helps thereunto.'

5
HARMONY FROM DISSONANCE
1604–88

165

1604
The Royal Supremacy

Canons of 1604, I, Cardwell, Synodalia, *p. 248.*

These Canons, passed by the Convocation of Canterbury in 1604 and by that of York in 1606, bring together medieval canons and the principles of the sixteenth century Anglican formularies. This Canon upholds the principle of the authority of the civil magistrate (in England the monarch, in parts of Germany a prince), which most of the reformers had insisted upon.

As our duty to the king's most excellent majesty requireth, we first decree and ordain, that the Archbishop of Canterbury (from time to time), all bishops of this Province, all deans, archdeacons, parsons, vicars, and all other ecclesiastical persons, shall faithfully keep and observe, and (as much as in them lieth) shall cause to be observed and kept of others, all and singular laws and statutes, made for restoring to the crown of this kingdom the ancient jurisdiction over the state ecclesiastical, and abolishing of all foreign power repugnant to the same. Furthermore, all ecclesiastical persons having cure of souls, and all other preachers, and readers of divinity lectures, shall, to the uttermost of their wit, knowledge, and learning, purely and sincerely (without any colour or dissimulation), teach, manifest, open, and declare, four times every year (at the least), in their sermons and other collations and lectures, that all usurped and foreign power (forasmuch as the same hath no establishment nor ground by the law of God) is for most just causes taken away and abolished: and that therefore no manner of obedience, or subjection, within his majesty's realms and dominions, is due unto any such foreign power, but that the king's power, within his realms of England, Scotland, and Ireland, and all other his dominions and countries, is the highest power under God; to whom all men, as well inhabitants, as born within the same, do by God's laws owe most loyalty and obedience, afore and above all other powers and potentates in earth.

166

1604
Anglican Orders

Canons of 1604, VIII, Cardwell, Synodalia, *p. 251.*

Whosoever shall hereafter affirm or teach, that the form and manner of making and consecrating bishops, priests, or deacons, containeth any thing in it that is repugnant to the word of God, or that they who are made bishops, priests, or deacons, in that form, are not lawfully made, nor ought to be accounted, either by themselves or by others, to be truly either bishops, priests, or deacons, until they have some other calling to those divine offices; let him be excommunicated *ipso facto*, not to be restored until he repent, and publicly revoke such his wicked errors.

167

1604
Schismatics

Canons of 1604, IX, Cardwell, Synodalia, *pp. 251-2.*

Schism was regarded by Augustine of Hippo as itself a heresy, indeed the worst of heresies, because it divides the body of Christ. A similar line is taken by this Canon.

Whosoever shall hereafter separate themselves from the communion of saints, as it is approved by the apostles' rules, in the Church of England, and combine themselves together in a new brotherhood, accounting the Christians, who are conformable to the doctrine, government, rites and ceremonies of the Church of England, to be profane, and unmeet for them to join with in Christian profession; let them be excommunicated *ipso facto*, and not restored, but by the Archbishop, after their repentance, and public revocation of such their wicked errors.

168

1604
Reverence in worship

Canons of 1604, XVIII, Cardwell, Synodalia, *pp. 255-6.*

What constitutes 'due reverence' will vary in some of its details in different cultures. Here is an early seventeenth century English picture. Cf. nos. 101, 144.

In the time of divine service, and of every part thereof, all due reverence is to be used; for it is according to the apostle's rule, 'Let all things be done decently and according to order';[1] answerable to which decency and order, we judge these our directions following: No man shall cover his head in the church or chapel in the time of divine service, except he have some infirmity; in which case let him wear a nightcap or coif. All manner of persons then present shall reverently kneel upon their knees, when the general Confession, Litany, and other prayers are read; and shall stand up at the saying of the Belief, according to the rules in that behalf prescribed in the Book of Common Prayer: and likewise when in time of divine service the Lord Jesus shall be mentioned, due and lowly reverence shall be done by all persons present, as it hath been accustomed; testifying by these outward ceremonies and gestures, their inward humility, Christian resolution, and due acknowledgment that the Lord Jesus Christ, the true and eternal Son of God, is the only Saviour of the world, in whom alone all the mercies, graces, and promises of God to mankind, for this life and the life to come, are fully and wholly comprised. None, either man, woman, or child, of what calling soever, shall be otherwise at such times busied in the church, than in quiet attendance to hear, mark, and understand that which is read, preached, or ministered; saying in their due places audibly with the minister, the Confession, the Lord's Prayer, and the Creed; and making such other answers to the public prayers, as are appointed in the Book of Common Prayer: neither shall they disturb the service or sermon, by walking or talking, or any other way; nor depart out of the church during the time of service and sermon, without some urgent or reasonable cause.

---

[1]   I Corinthians 14.40

169

1604

The importance of receiving Holy Communion three times a year at least

Canons of 1604, XXI, Cardwell, Synodalia, *pp. 256-7.*

The question of 'frequency of communion' has been much disputed. The Fourth Lateran Council of 1215 insisted that everyone should receive communion at least once a year. In some communities it has been usual to do so daily.

In every parish-church and chapel, where sacraments are to be administered within this realm, the holy communion shall be ministered by the parson, vicar, or minister, so often, and at such times, as every parishioner may communicate at least thrice in the year, (whereof the feast of Easter to be one,) according as they are appointed by the Book of Common Prayer. Provided, That every minister, as often as he administereth the communion, shall first receive the sacrament himself.

170

1604

Grounds for excommunication or suspension from the fellowship

Canons of 1604, XXV, XXVI, XXVII, Cardwell, Synodalia, *p. 250.*

These three Canons are addressed to the problems of unorthodoxy of faith, grave and public moral fault and offences against 'order' in the Church.

XXV Whosoever shall hereafter affirm, That any of the nine and thirty Articles agreed upon by the Archbishops and bishops of both provinces, and the whole clergy, in the convocation holden at London, in the year of our Lord God one thousand five hundred sixty-two, for avoiding diversities of opinions, and for the establishing of consent touching true religion, are in any part superstitious or erroneous, or such as he may not with a good conscience subscribe unto; let him be excommunicated *ipso facto,* and not restored, but only by the Archbishop, after his repentance, and public revocation of such his wicked errors.

XXVI No minister shall in any wise admit to the receiving of the Holy Communion, any of his cure or flock, which be openly known to live in sin notorious, without repentance; nor any who have maliciously and openly contended with their neighbours, until they shall be reconciled; nor any church-wardens or side-men, who having taken their oaths to present to their ordinaries all such public offences as they are particularly charged to inquire of in their several parishes, shall... wittingly and willingly, desperately and irreligiously, incur the horrible crime of perjury, either in neglecting or in refusing to present such of the said enormities and public offences, as they know themselves to be committed in their said parishes, or are notoriously offensive to the congregation there.

XXVII No minister, when he celebrateth the communion, shall wittingly administer the same to any but to such as kneel, under pain of suspension, nor under the like pain to any that refuse to be present at public prayers, according to the orders of the Church of England; nor to any that are common and notorious depravers of the Book of Common Prayer and Administration of the Sacraments, and of the orders, rites, and ceremonies therein prescribed, or of any thing that is contained in any of the articles agreed upon in the convocation, one thousand five hundred sixty and two, or of any thing contained in the book of ordering priests and bishops; or to any that have spoken against and depraved his majesty's sovereign authority in causes ecclesiastical.

171

1604
The importance of worshipping in the local church

Canons of 1604, XXVIII, Cardwell, Synodalia, *p. 263.*

The society of England at this time placed great emphasis on local community responsibility for local people, and there were laws against vagrancy to discourage wandering. For this reason this canon states the general principle of the importance of the local worshipping community in particularly strong terms. Compare canon LVII. The rule of sending strangers home was appropriate in the special circumstances of a society in which ordinary people rarely travelled and strange faces in church were likely to be from a nearby parish and merely looking for novelty. Cf. nos. 180, 184.

The church-wardens..., and their assistants, shall mark, as well as the minister, whether all and every of the parishioners come so often every year to the holy communion, as the laws and our Constitutions do require; and whether any strangers come often and commonly from other parishes to their church; and shall shew their minister of them, lest perhaps they be admitted to the Lord's table amongst others, which they shall forbid; and remit such home to their own parish-churches and ministers, there' to receive the communion with the rest of their own neighbours.

172

1604
The use of the sign of the cross in baptism

Canons of 1604, XXX, Cardwell, Synodalia, *p. 264.*

The use of the sign of the cross in baptism is here insisted upon as being the custom of the early Church. Some reformers had wanted to dispense with it along with the habit of crossing oneself, which is seen as 'indifferent', that is, a matter for individual preference.

The use of the sign of the cross in baptism... being reduced in the Church of England to the primary institution of it, upon those true rules of doctrine concerning things indifferent, which are consonant to the word of God, and the judgements of all the ancient fathers, we hold it the part of every private man, both minister and other, reverently to retain the true use of it prescribed by public authority; considering that things of themselves indifferent do in some sort alter their natures, when they are either commanded or forbidden by a lawful magistrate; and may not be omitted at every man's pleasure, contrary to the law, when they be commanded, nor used when they are prohibited.

173

1604
Appropriate seasons for ordination

Canons of 1604, XXXI, XXXII, Cardwell, Synodalia, *pp. 264-5.*

Canon XXXII assumes that the threefold ministry was from ancient times regarded as a series of steps, with the diaconate a stepping-stone to the priesthood. There is in fact an equally or possibly even more ancient tradition of a 'distinctive diaconate', an order in which the deacon remained for life, and in which he acted as servant and administrator of the community in practical matters, in the manner of the deacons of the Acts. See *Deacons in the ministry of the Church: A Report Commissioned by the House of Bishops* (Church of England) (London, 1988).

XXXI Forasmuch as the ancient fathers of the Church, led by example of the apostles, appointed prayers and fasts to be used at the solemn ordering of ministers, and to that purpose allotted certain times, in which only sacred orders might be given or conferred; we, following their holy and religious example, do constitute and decree, that no deacons or ministers be made and ordained, but only upon the Sundays immediately following *Jejunia quatuor temporum*, commonly called 'Ember weeks', appointed in ancient time for prayer and fasting (purposely for this cause at their first institution), and so continued at this day in the Church of England; and that this be done in the cathedral or parish-church where the bishop resideth, and in the time of divine service, in the presence not only of the archdeacon, but of the dean and two prebendaries at the least, or (if they shall happen by any lawful cause to be let or hindered) in the presence of four other grave persons, being masters of arts at the least, and allowed for public preachers.

XXXII The office of deacon being a step or degree to the ministry, according to the judgement of the ancient fathers, and the practice of the primitive church; we do ordain and appoint, that hereafter no bishop shall make any person, of what qualities or gifts soever, a deacon and a minister[1] both together upon one day; but that the order in that behalf prescribed in the book of making and consecrating bishops, priests, and deacons, be strictly observed. Not that always every deacon should be kept from the ministry for a whole year, when the bishop shall find good cause to the contrary; but that there being now four times appointed in every year for the ordination of deacons and ministers, there may ever be some time of trial of their behaviour in the office of deacon, before they be admitted to the order of priesthood.

---

[1] i.e., a priest

174

1604
Title

Canons of 1604, XXXIII, Cardwell, Synodalia, *pp. 265-6.*

This canon stresses the pastoral purpose of ordination. By ancient tradition every person ordained must have a 'title', or place where he may serve the people of a local church. Since the Middle Ages scholars teaching at the universities of Oxford or Cambridge had been considered to be discharging a pastoral task and were allowed to be ordained.

It hath been long since provided by many decrees of the ancient fathers, that none should be admitted either deacon or priest, who had not first some certain place where he might use his function. According to which examples we do ordain, that henceforth no person shall be admitted into sacred orders, except he shall at that time exhibit to the bishop, of whom he desireth imposition of hands, a presentation of himself to some ecclesiastical preferment then void in that diocese; or shall bring to the said bishop a true and undoubted certificate, that either he is provided of some church within the said diocese, where he may attend the cure of souls, or of some minister's place vacant, either in the cathedral church of that diocese, or in some other collegiate church therein also situate, where he may execute his ministry; or that he is a fellow, or in right as a fellow, or to be a conduct or chaplain in some college in Cambridge or Oxford; or except he be a master of arts of five years' standing, that liveth of his own charge in either of the universities; or except by the bishop himself, that doth ordain him minister, he be shortly after to be admitted either to some benefice or curateship then void. And if any bishop shall admit any person into the ministry, that hath none of these titles as is aforesaid, then he shall keep and maintain him with all things necessary, till he do prefer him to some ecclesiastical living. And if the said bishop shall refuse so to do, he shall be suspended by the Archbishop, being assisted with another bishop, from giving of orders by the space of a year.

175

1604
Suitability for the ministry;
the responsibility of the ordaining bishop

Canons of 1604, XXXIV-V, Cardwell, Synodalia, *p. 266-7.*

XXXIV No bishop shall henceforth admit any person into sacred orders, which is not of his own diocese, except he be either of one of the universities of this realm, or except he shall bring letters dismissory (so termed) from the Bishop of whose diocese he is; and desiring to be a deacon, is three and twenty years old; and to be a priest, four and twenty years complete; and hath taken some degree of school in either of the said universities; or at the least, except he be able to yield an account of his faith in Latin, according to the *articles of religion* approved in the synod of the bishops and clergy of this realm, one thousand five hundred sixty and two, and to confirm the same by sufficient testimonies out of the holy scriptures; and except moreover he shall then exhibit letters testimonial of his good life and conversation under the seal of some college in Cambridge or Oxford, where before he remained, or of three or four grave ministers, together with the subscription and testimony of other credible persons, who have known his life and behaviour by the space of three years next before.

XXXV The bishop, before he admit any person to holy orders, shall diligently examine him in the presence of those ministers that shall assist him at the imposition of hands: and if the said bishop have any lawful impediment, he shall cause the said ministers carefully to examine every such person so to be ordered. Provided, that they who shall assist the bishop in examining and laying on of hands, shall be of his cathedral church, if they may conveniently be had, or other sufficient preachers of the same diocese, to the number of three at the least: and if any bishop or suffragan shall admit any to sacred orders who is not qualified and examined, as before we have ordained, the Archbishop of this Province, having notice thereof, and being assisted therein by one bishop, shall suspend the said bishop or suffragan so offending, from making either deacons or priests for the space of two years.

176

1604
Subscription to the Thirty-Nine Articles, etc.

Canons of 1604, XXXVI, XXXVII, Cardwell, Synodalia, *pp. 267-8.*

From the beginning, Subscription to the Articles has been required only of the clergy, and since 1865 they have been required to affirm only that the doctrine of the Church of England as set forth in the Book of Common Prayer and the Articles is agreeable to the Word of God. Cf. no. 346.

XXXVI No person shall hereafter be received into the ministry, nor either by institution or collation admitted to any ecclesiastical living, nor suffered to preach, to catechize, or to be a lecturer or reader of divinity in either university, or in any cathedral or collegiate church, city, or market-town, parish-church, chapel, or in any other place within this realm, except he be licensed either by the Archbishop, or by the Bishop of the diocese, where he is to be placed, under their hands and seals, or by one of the two universities under their seal likewise; and except he shall first subscribe to these three articles following, in such manner and sort as we have here appointed.

i. That the king's majesty, under God, is the only supreme governor of this realm, and of all other his highness's dominions and countries, as well in all spiritual or ecclesiastical things or causes, as temporal; and that no foreign prince, person, prelate, state, or potentate hath, or ought to have, any jurisdiction, power, superiority, pre-eminence, or authority, ecclesiastical or spiritual, within his majesty's said realms, dominions, and countries.

ii. That the Book of Common Prayer, and of ordering of bishops, priests, and deacons, containeth in it nothing contrary to the word of God, and that it may lawfully so be used; and that he himself will use the form in the said book prescribed, in public prayer, and administration of the sacraments, and none other.

iii. That he alloweth the Book of Articles of Religion agreed upon by the Archbishops and bishops of both provinces, and the whole clergy in the convocation holden at London in the year of our Lord God one thousand five hundred sixty and two; and that he acknowledgeth all and every the articles therein contained, being in number nine and thirty, besides the ratification, to be agreeable to the word of God.

XXXVII None licensed, as is aforesaid, to preach, read, lecture, or catechize, coming to reside in any diocese, shall be permitted there to preach, read, lecture, catechize, or minister the sacraments, or to execute any other ecclesiastical function, (by what authority soever he be thereunto admitted,) unless he first consent and subscribe to the three articles before mentioned, in the presence of the Bishop of the diocese, wherein he is to preach, read, lecture, catechize, or administer the sacraments, as aforesaid.

177

1604
Provision of preachers

Canons of 1604, XLIII, XLV, XLVI, XLVII, Cardwell, Synodalia, *p. 273.*

This series of canons is designed to ensure that those who have the cure of souls take seriously the duty to provide a regular ministry of the Word by preaching themselves, or arranging for preachers.

XLIII The dean, master, warden, or chief governor, prebendaries, and canons in every cathedral and collegiate church, shall not only preach there in their own persons so often as they are bound by law, statute, ordinance, or custom, but shall likewise preach in other churches of the šame diocese where they are resident.... And in case they themselves be sick, or lawfully absent, they shall substitute such licensed preachers to supply their turns, as by the Bishop of the diocese shall be thought meet to preach in cathedral churches....

XLV Every beneficed man allowed to be a preacher, and residing on his benefice, having no lawful impediment, shall in his own cure, or in some other church or chapel, where he may conveniently, near adjoining, (where no preacher is,) preach one sermon every Sunday of the year; wherein he shall soberly and sincerely divide the word of truth, to the glory of God, and to the best edification of the people.

XLVI Every beneficed man, not allowed to be a preacher, shall procure sermons to be preached in his cure once in every month at the. least, by preachers lawfully licensed, if his living, in the judgement of the ordinary, will be able to bear it. And upon every

Sunday, when there shall not be a sermon preached in his cure, he or his curate shall read some one of the homilies prescribed or to be prescribed by authority, to the intents aforesaid.

XLVII Every beneficed man, licensed by the laws of this realm, upon urgent occasions of other service, not to reside upon his benefice, shall cause his cure to be supplied by a curate that is a sufficient and licensed preacher, if the worth of the benefice will bear it. But whosoever hath two benefices, shall maintain a preacher licensed in the benefice where he doth not reside, except he preach himself at both of them usually.

178

1604
Responsibility for a local or 'parish' church entrusted at the discretion of the bishop

Canons of 1604, XLVIII, Cardwell, Synodalia, *p. 274.*

The principle endorsed here is that the bishop is pastor of the whole diocese, and that he shares his pastorate with priests given 'cure of souls' in the parishes.

No curate or minister shall be permitted to serve in any place, without examination and admission of the Bishop of the diocese, or ordinary of the place, having episcopal jurisdiction, in writing under his hand and seal, having respect to the greatness of the cure, and meetness of the party. And the said curates and ministers, if they remove from one diocese to another, shall not be by any means admitted to serve without testimony of the Bishop of the diocese, or ordinary of the place, as aforesaid, whence they came, in writing, of their honesty, ability, and conformity to the ecclesiastical laws of the Church of England. Nor any shall serve more than one church or chapel upon one day, except that chapel be a member of the parish-church, or united thereunto; and unless the said church or chapel, where such a minister shall serve in two places, be not able in the judgement of the bishop or ordinary, as aforesaid, to maintain a curate.

179

1604
Licensing of preachers

Canons of 1604, XLIX-LII, Cardwell, Synodalia, *pp. 274-76.*

This canon continues the medieval practice of licensing to preach only those whose faith and learning are known to their bishop. The medieval privilege of universities to authorize their scholars to preach is retained.

XLIX No person whatsoever not examined and approved by the Bishop of the diocese, or not licensed... for a sufficient or convenient preacher, shall take upon him to expound in his own cure, or elsewhere, any scripture or matter of doctrine; but shall only study to read plainly and aptly (without glossing or adding) the homilies already set forth, or hereafter to be published by lawful authority, for the confirmation of the true faith, and for the good instruction and edification of the people.

L Neither the minister, church-wardens, nor any other officers of the church, shall suffer any man to preach within their churches or chapels, but such as, by shewing their licence to preach, shall appear unto them to be sufficiently authorized thereunto, as is aforesaid.

LI The deans, presidents, and residentiaries of any cathedral or collegiate church, shall suffer no stranger to preach unto the people in their churches, except they be allowed by the Archbishop of the Province, or by the Bishop of the same diocese, or by either of the universities. And if any in his sermon shall publish any doctrine, either strange, or disagreeing from the word of God, or from any of the Articles of Religion agreed upon in the convocation-house, anno 1562, or from the Book of Common Prayers; the dean or the residents shall, by their letters subscribed with some of their hands that heard him, so soon as may be, give notice of the same to the Bishop of the diocese, that he may determine the matter, and take such order therein, as he shall think convenient.

LII That the bishop may understand (if occasion so require) what sermons are made in every church of his diocese, and who presume to preach without licence, the church-wardens and side-men shall see that the names of all preachers, which come to their church from any other place, be noted in a book, which they shall have ready for that purpose; wherein every preacher shall subscribe his name, the day when he preached, and the name of the Bishop of whom he had licence to preach.

180

1604
Ministry of the sacraments valid
where the ordained minister is not a preacher

Canons of 1604, LVII, Cardwell, Synodalia, *p. 279.*

This canon was designed to correct a tendency in reforming thinking which encouraged some to place the ministry of the Word above that of the Sacraments, instead of seeing the two as inseparable. It also reinforces the principle that Christians should worship in their own local church rather than go elsewhere, to worship where they feel their 'special requirements' are met. Compare Canons XXVIII and LXXI (nos. 171 and 184).

Whereas divers persons, seduced by false teachers, refuse to have their children baptized by a minister that is no preacher,[1] and to receive the holy communion at his hands in the same respect, as though the virtue of those sacraments did depend upon his ability to preach; forasmuch as the doctrine both of baptism and of the Lord's supper is sufficiently set down in the Book of Common Prayer to be used at the administration of the said sacraments, as nothing can be added unto it that is material and necessary ...; both the said sacraments being equally effectual, whether they be ministered by a minister that is no preacher, or by one that is a preacher. And if any hereafter shall offend herein, or leave their own parish-churches in that respect, and communicate, or cause their children to be baptized, in other parishes abroad, and will not be moved thereby to reform that their error and unlawful course; let them be presented to the ordinary of the place by the minister, church-wardens,... of the parishes where they dwell, and there receive such punishment by ecclesiastical censures, as such obstinacy doth worthily deserve; that is, let them (persisting in their wilfulness) be suspended, and then, after a month's further obstinacy, excommunicated.

---

[1] At this date not all priests were sufficiently well educated to be licensed to preach.

181

1604
Instruction in the Faith

Canons of 1604, LIX, LXI, Synodalia, *Cardwell, p. 281.*

LIX Every parson, vicar, or curate, upon every Sunday and holy-day, before evening prayer, shall, for half an hour or more, examine and instruct the youth and ignorant persons of his parish, in the Ten Commandments, the Articles of the Belief, and in the Lord's Prayer; and shall diligently hear, instruct, and teach them the Catechism set forth in the Book of Common Prayer. And all fathers, mothers, masters, and mistresses, shall cause their children, servants, and apprentices, which have not learned the Catechism, to come to the church at the time appointed, obediently to hear, and to be ordered by the minister, until they have learned the same.

LXI Every minister, that hath cure and charge of souls, for the better accomplishing of the orders prescribed in the Book of Common Prayer concerning confirmation, shall take such especial care as that none may be presented to the bishop for him to lay his hands upon, but such as can render an account of their faith according to the Catechism in the said book contained.

182

1604
Confirmation

Canons of 1604, LX, Cardwell, Synodalia, *p. 281.*

Cf. nos. 21, 46.

Forasmuch as it hath been a solemn, ancient, and laudable custom in the Church of God, continued from the apostles' times, that all bishops should lay their hands upon children baptized and instructed in the Catechism of Christian Religion, praying over them, and blessing them, which we commonly call *Confirmation*... we will and appoint, That every bishop or his suffragan, in his accustomed visitation, do in his own person carefully observe the said custom.

183

1604
The importance of baptism

Canons of 1604, LXIX, Cardwell, Synodalia, *pp. 285-6.*

If any minister, being duly... informed of the weakness and danger of death of any infant unbaptized in his parish, and thereupon desired to go or come... to baptize the same, shall either wilfully refuse so to do, or of purpose, or of gross negligence shall so defer the time, as, when he might conveniently have resorted to the place, and have baptized the said infant, it dieth... unbaptized; the said minister shall be suspended for three months.... Provided, that where there is a curate, or a substitute, this constitution shall not extend to the parson or vicar himself, but to the curate or substitute present.

184

1604
Avoidance of private preaching or ministry of sacraments, except in emergency

Canons of 1604, LXXI, Cardwell, Synodalia, *p. 287.*

This Canon also instructs the households of great houses in which private chapels existed to use them only 'very seldom upon Sundays and holy-days; so that both the... masters of the said houses, and their families, shall at other times resort to their own parish-churches.' The intention is to underline the importance of the local worshipping community or parish. Cf. nos. 171, 180.

No minister shall preach, or administer the holy communion, in any private house, except it be in times of necessity, when any being either so impotent as he cannot go to the church, or very dangerously sick, are desirous to be partakers of that holy sacrament, under pain of suspension for the first offence, and excommunication for the second.

185

1604
Equipping places of worship
for the ministry of prayer and sacrament

Canons of 1604, LXXX-LXXXIII, Cardwell, Synodalia, *pp. 292-3.*

LXXX The church-wardens... of every church and chapel shall, at the charge of the parish, provide the Book of Common Prayer.... And if any parishes be yet unfurnished of the Bible of the largest volume, or of the books of Homilies allowed by authority, the said church-wardens shall within convenient time provide the same at the like charge of the parish.

LXXXI... There shall be a font of stone in every church and chapel where baptism is to be ministered; the same to be set in the ancient usual places: in which only font the minister shall baptize publicly.

LXXXII Whereas we have no doubt, but that in all churches within the realm of England, convenient and decent tables are provided and placed for the celebration of the holy communion, we appoint, that the same tables shall from time to time be kept and repaired in sufficient and seemly manner, and covered, in time of divine service, with a carpet of silk or other decent stuff, thought meet by the ordinary of the place, if any question be made of it, and with a fair linen cloth at the time of ministration, as becometh that table, and so stand, saving when the said holy communion is to be administered: at which time the same shall be placed in so good sort within the church or chancel, as thereby the minister may be more conveniently heard of the communicants in his prayer and ministration, and the communicants also more conveniently, and in more number, may communicate with the said minister; and that the Ten Commandments be set upon the east end of every church and chapel where the people may best see and read the same, and other chosen sentences written upon the walls of the said churches and chapels, in places convenient; and likewise that a convenient seat be made for the minister to read service in. All these to be done at the charge of the parish.

LXXXIII A pulpit to be provided in every church....

186

1604
What is confessed to a minister
must be respected and kept secret

Canons of 1604, CIX, Cardwell, Synodalia, *p. 310.*

Cf. nos. 58, 59, 234.

If any man confess his secret and hidden sins to the minister, for the unburdening of his conscience, and to receive spiritual consolation and ease of mind from him; we do not any way bind the said minister by this our Constitution, but do straitly charge and admonish him, that he do not at any time reveal and make known to any person whatsoever any crime or offence so committed to his trust and secrecy, (except they be such crimes as by the laws of this realm his own life may be called into question for concealing the same,) under pain of irregularity.

187

1604
The authority of Synods

Canons of 1604, CXXXIX-CXLI, Cardwell, Synodalia *pp. 327-8.*

A council, synod or convocation of a Province or national Church is here identified as representing that Church in such a way that it may be said to 'be' that Church. This ruling has important implications for the authority of such a synod to 'bind' by its decisions the members of the Church who are not present at the meeting. Cf. nos. 67, 70, 155, 207, 208, 329.

CXXXIX... The sacred synod of this nation, in the name of Christ and by the king's authority assembled, is... the true Church of England by representation.

188

1606
The marks of the true Church

Richard Field, Of the Church, Ecclesiastical History Society
(Cambridge, 1847), I, 65, More and Cross, p. 45.

Compare 'one, holy, catholic and apostolic'; the 'notes of the Church' in
Article xix of the Thirty-Nine Articles (which were the 'marks' recognized by
most reforming communities); the four points in the Lambeth Quadrilateral
(no. 343). Field stresses the importance of 'lawful pastors' although he does
not mention the historic episcopate.

The Notes of the latter sort,... which perpetually distinguish the
true Catholic Church from all other societies of men and
professions of religions in the world, are three: First, the entire
profession of those supernatural verities, which God hath revealed
in Christ His Son; Secondly, the use of such holy ceremonies and
Sacraments as He hath instituted and appointed to serve as
provocations to godliness, preservations from sin, memorials of the
benefits of Christ, warrants for the greater security of our belief,
and marks of distinction to separate His Own from strangers;
Thirdly, a union or connexion of men in this profession and use of
these Sacraments under lawful pastors and guides, appointed,
authorized, and sanctified, to direct and lead them in the happy
ways of eternal salvation.

189

1606
Prophetic ministry

Bishop Overall's Convocation Book of 1606 on The Government of
God's Holy Catholic Church and the Kingdoms of the Whole
World *(Oxford, 1844), p. 38.*

John Overall (1560–1619), Bishop of Norwich, compiled this collection of
Canons on the government of the Church and its relations to the State in
1606; but there was controversy because he seemed to allow for the
possibility of legitimate rebellion, and it was not published until 1690. Here
he speaks of the place of 'extraordinary' charismatic ministry with authority
to challenge the existing order where it is defective (cf. nos. 148, 200, 259).

Almighty God, forseeing what defects there would be sometimes in kings and civil magistrates, and sometimes not only in the inferior priests, but likewise in the High-priests themselves; did still (as occasion required, and for the benefit of his Church) raise up and send unto them his Prophets, men endued by his Holy Spirit, with extraordinary authority, knowledge, zeal and courage; who neither feared king nor priest, but told them plainly of their thoughts, denounced the judgement of God against them for their sins, and executed without respect of persons such other parts of their duties as God himself immediately gave them.

190

c.1606

Marks of the true Church

Richard Field, Of the Church (1606), Dedicatory Letter to the Archbishop of Canterbury, pp. xix–xxi, and Book I, vii, p. 26.

Richard Field (1561–1616), friend of Richard Hooker, argues here that the Church cannot be fully herself in division.

The consideration of the unhappy divisions of the Christian world, and the infinite distractions of men's minds, not knowing, in so great variety of options, what to think, or to whom to join themselves, (every faction boasting of the pure and sincere profession of heavenly truth, challenging to itself alone the name of the Church, and fastening upon all that dissent, or are otherwise minded, the hateful note of schism and heresy,) hath made me ever think, that there is no part of heavenly knowledge more necessary, than that which concerneth the Church... that all men may know that we have not departed from the ancient faith, or forsaken the fellowship of the Catholic Church... Thus then, the Church having her being and name, from the calling of grace, all they must needs be of the Church, whom the grace of God in any sort calleth out from the profane and wicked of the world, to the participation of eternal . happiness, by the excellent knowledge of divine, supernatural, and revealed verity, and use of the good, happy, and precious means of salvation: but they only perfectly and fully in respect of outward being, which profess the whole truth in unity.

191

1609
A King's declaration of Faith

From A Premonition to All Most Mighty Monarchs, Kings, Free Princes, and States of Christendom. *James I,* Works, *ed. by James Montague, Bishop of Winchester (1616), pp. 301–8.* More and Cross, *p. 23.*

This was the first collected edition of James I's *Works.* In 1619 a Latin translation of them was issued, also by Montague. The *Premonition* itself was sent in the first place to the Emperor Rudolf II. It was published in Latin at Basle in 1609.

I will never be ashamed to render an accompt of my profession and of that hope that is in me, as the apostle prescribeth. I am such a Catholic Christian as believeth the three Creeds, that of the Apostles, that of the Council of Nice,[1] and that of Athanasius, the two latter being paraphrases of the former.[2] And I believe them in that sense as the ancient Fathers and Councils that made them did understand them, to which three Creeds all ministers of England do subscribe at their ordination. And I also acknowledge for Orthodox all those other forms of Creeds that either were devised by Councils or particular Fathers, against such particular heresies as most reigned in their times. I reverence and admit the Four First General Councils as Catholic and Orthodox. And the said Four General Councils are acknowledged by our Acts of Parliament, and received for orthodox by our Church. As for the Fathers, I reverence them... For whatever the Fathers for the first five hundred years did with an unanime consent agree upon, to be believed as a necessary point of salvation, I either will believe it also, or at least will be humbly silent, not taking upon me to condemn the same. But for every private Father's opinion, it binds not my conscience..., every one of the Fathers usually contradicting others. I will therefore in that case follow St Augustine's rule in judging of their opinions as I find them agree with the Scriptures. What I find agreeable thereto I will gladly embrace. What is otherwise I will (with their reverence) reject. As for the Scriptures,

---

[1]   Nicaea

[2]   This of course is not the case, but the history of the Creeds was not clearly understood at this date.

no man doubteth I will believe them. But even for the Apocrypha, I hold them in the same accompt that the Ancients did. They are still printed and bound with our Bibles, and publicly read in our Churches.

192

1609
Restoration of the bishop's consistorial jurisdiction, Scotland

Source Book of Scottish History, *III, pp. 58–9*.

The Presbyterian movement in Scotland had created a non-episcopal system of Church government. This was restored to an episcopal system after the union of England and Scotland under James VI and I in 1603. From 1639–53 Scottish Law provided for a presbyteral system again. See 1662 for the Act which restored the episcopate once more (no. 228).

Oure soverane lord, undirstanding that in all weill governed republictis the jurisdictioun civill and ecclesiastik ar severall, distinct and divers jurisdictiounes, whiche ocht to be administrat by the persones to quhome the samin propirlie belongis, and according to his hignes most loving and princelie affectioun borne alwayes to the Christiane reformed church within this realme... hes with express advyse and consent of the estaitis restored... the archibischoppis and bischoppis of this realme to thair former authoritie, dignitie, prerogative, privileges and jurisdictiounes lauchfullie pertening and shall be knawin to pertene to thame.

Our sovereign Lord, understanding that in all well governed republics civil and ecclesiastical jurisdiction are several, distinct and different jurisdictions, which ought to be administered by the persons to whom the same properly belongs; and according to his Highness's most loving and princely affection borne always to the Christian reformed Church within this realm,... has with express advice and consent of the Estates restored... the Archbishops and bishops of this realm to their former authority, dignity, prerogative, privileges and jurisdictions lawfully pertaining and shall be known to pertain to them.

193

1612
The atheist and the existence of God

Francis Bacon (1561–1626), philosopher and essayist, 'Of Atheism', Essays, More and Cross, p. 225.

Bacon comments here on the point made in Romans 1.19–20, that the created world is itself a revelation and evidence of God's existence; there is no need of miracles to prove it. This is a contribution to the 'science and religion' debate, which has arisen in every century. Cf. nos. 193, 211, 244, 246, 280, 374.

I had rather believe all the fables in the Legend and the Talmud and the Alcoran, than that this universal frame[1] is without a mind; and, therefore, God never wrought miracle to convince Atheism, because His ordinary works convince it. It is true, that a little philosophy inclineth man's mind to Atheism; but depth in philosophy bringeth men's minds about to religion.

194

1619–1638
The catholicity of the Anglican Church

John Cosin (1594–1672), Bishop of Durham, Notes and Collections on the Book of Common Prayer, Works (Oxford, 1855), V. p. 13.

John Cosin, Master of Peterhouse, Cambridge 1635–42 and Bishop of Durham from 1660, stresses here the catholicity of the Anglican Church and her continuity with the Church of earlier ages.

Those which make so perilous a matter of our retaining these ceremonies, common to us with the Church of Rome, do seem to imagine that we have of late erected a frame of some new religion, the furniture whereof we should not have borrowed from our enemies...; whereas in truth we have continued the old religion, and the ceremonies which we have taken from them that were before us are not things which belong to this or that sect, but they are the ancient rites and customs of the Church of Christ, whereof

---

[1]   that is, the universe

ourselves being a part, we have the self-same interest in them which our fathers before us had, from whom the same descended unto us.

195

1622
Councils of bishops for mutual correction

William Laud, Archbishop of Canterbury, Conference *with Fisher (1622), ed. C.H. Simkinson (London, 1901), IX, ix, p. 26, p. 231.*

Laud explains here that bishops, like other clergy, must be subject to discipline. He gives ancient conciliar precedent for the view that bishops should be judged by their fellow-bishops, under the presidency of their Primate.

The Council of Antioch submits ecclesiastical causes to the bishops. And what was done amiss by a bishop, was corrigible by a synod of bishops, but this with the metropolitan.

196

1637
The Preface to the Scottish Prayer Book

Source Book of Scottish History, *III, 91.*

The question of the extent of legitimate diversity in forms of worship has always been a vexed one. Early Anglicanism was strict in enforcing the use of a single Prayer Book, and upon that common liturgy rested a good deal of theology.

The Church of Christ hath in all ages had a prescript Form of Common Prayer, or Divine Service, as appeareth by the ancient Liturgies of the Greek and Latin Churches. This was done, as for other great causes, so likewise for retaining a uniformity in God's worship: a thing most beseeming them that are of one and the same profession. For by the Form that is kept in the outward worship of God, men commonly judge of Religion. If in that there be a diversity, straight they are apt to conceive the religion to be diverse. Wherefore it were to be wished, that the whole Church of Christ were one as well in form of Public Worship, as in doctrine.

197

1638
Fundamentals and infallibility

William Chillingworth (1602–44), Anglican divine, Works, vol. I,
(Oxford, 1838 ff.), p. 350, Answer to Charity Maintained, part I,
chapter III.

Chillingworth was one of the key figures in the seventeenth century debate
about fundamentals. Here he argues that the Church (that is, the true and
universal Church) cannot ever go astray in the fundamentals of faith, for then
it would cease to be the Church. On the other hand, in a divided
Christendom, it cannot be possible to point to any one 'Church' as infallible.

Good sir, you must... be so acute as to distinguish between being
'infallible in fundamentals', and being 'an infallible guide in
fundamentals'. That there shall be always 'a church infallible in
fundamentals', we easily grant; for it comes to no more but this,
'that there shall be always a church'. But that there shall be always
such a church, which is an infallible guide in fundamentals, this we
deny. For this cannot be without settling a known infallibility in
some one known society of Christians.

198

1642
Heaven and Hell

Thomas Browne (1605–82), physician, Religio Medici, part I, More
and Cross, p. 338.

I thank God, and with joy I mention it, I was never afraid of Hell,
nor ever grew pale at the description of that place. I have so fixed
my contemplations on Heaven, that I have almost forgot the idea
of Hell, and am afraid rather to lose the joys of the one, than
endure the misery of the other: to be deprived of them is a perfect
Hell, and needs, methinks, no addition to complete our afflictions.
That terrible term hath never detained me from sin, nor do I owe
any good action to the name thereof. I fear God, yet am not afraid
of Him: His mercies make me ashamed of my sins, before His
judgements afraid thereof. These are the forced and secondary
method of His wisdom,which He useth but as the last remedy, and

upon provocation; a course rather to deter the wicked, than incite the virtuous to His worship. I can hardly think there was ever any scared into Heaven; they go the fairest way to Heaven that would serve God without a Hell; other mercenaries, that crouch into Him in fear of Hell, though they term themselves the servants, are indeed but the slaves, of the Almighty.

199

1642
The mystery of Faith

Thomas Browne (1605–82), physician, Religio Medici, *part I, More and Cross, pp. 216–17.*

Thomas Browne comments here on the contemporary fashion for demanding proofs acceptable to reason for all the mysteries of faith. He rejoices in the faith which places its trust in Christ without the evidence of the senses.

As for those wingy Mysteries in Divinity and airy subtleties in Religion, which have unhinged the brains of better heads, they never stretched the *Pia Mater*[1] of mine. Methinks there be not impossibilities enough in Religion for an active faith; the deepest Mysteries ours contains have not only been illustrated, but maintained, by syllogism and the rule of reason. I love to lose myself in a mystery, to pursue my reason to an *O altitudo!*[2]

'Tis my solitary recreation to pose my apprehension with those involved enigmas and riddles of the Trinity, with Incarnation, and resurrection. I can answer all the objections of Satan and my rebellious reason with that odd resolution I learned of Tertullian, *Certum est, quia impossibile est.*[3] I desire to exercise my faith in the difficultest point; for to credit ordinary and visible objects is not faith, but persuasion. Some believe the better for seeing Christ's Sepulchre; and, when they have seen the Red Sea, doubt not of the Miracle. Now, contrarily, I bless my self and am thankful that I loved not in the days of Miracles, that I never saw Christ nor His Disciples. I would not have been one of those

---

[1]   An anatomical term for the membrane which covers the brain.

[2]   'To the limit'.

[3]   'It is certain because it is impossible'.

Israelites that passed the Red Sea, nor one of Christ's patients on whom He wrought His wonders; then had my faith been thrust upon me, nor should I enjoy that greater blessing pronounced to all that believe and saw not. It is an easy and necessary belief to credit what our eye and sense hath examined. I believe He was dead, and buried and rose again; and desire to see Him in His glory, rather than to contemplate Him in His Cenotaph or Sepulchre.

200

1642
The ordinary authority of bishops

Jeremy Taylor, Bishop of Down and Connor, (1613–67), Episcopacy Asserted, *Works, ed. C.P. Eden (London 1849) V, pp. 19–20.*

This text was written in the context of the debate with the Presbyterians of the day, who argued that the only 'ordinary' or permanent order was that of presbyters, and the apostles were an 'extraordinary' ministry which died out with their generation and were not succeeded, as episcopal Churches believed, by an episcopate. Cf. nos. 148, 189, 259.

That the apostolate might be successive and perpetual gave them a power of ordination, that by imposing hands on others they might impart that power which they received from Christ. For in the apostles there was something extraordinary, something ordinary. Whatsoever was extraordinary, as immediate mission, unlimited jurisdiction, and miraculous operations, that was not necessary to the perpetual regiment of the church, for then the church should fail when these privileges extraordinary did cease. It was therefore not in extraordinary powers and privileges that Christ promised his perpetual assistance.... It follows then that in all the ordinary parts of power and office, Christ did promise to be with them to the end of the world, and therefore there must remain a power of giving faculty and capacity to persons successively, for the execution of that in which Christ promised perpetual assistance.... Now what is this ordinary office?... Now in clear evidence of sense these offices and powers are preaching, baptizing, consecrating, ordaining and governing. For these were necessary for the perpetuation of a church.

201

1642
The relationship of the Orders of bishop, priest and deacon

Jeremy Taylor, Bishop of Down and Connor (1613–67), Episcopacy Asserted, Works, ed. C.P. Eden (London, 1849), V, p. 20.

Although deacons and priests have part of [the offices of the apostolate] and therefore, though in a very limited sense, they may be called *successores apostolorum*,[1] to wit, in the power of baptizing, consecrating the Eucharist,[2] and preaching, (an excellent example whereof, though we have none in Scripture, yet if I mistake him not we have in Ignatius, calling the college of presbyters... 'a combination of apostles');[3] yet the apostolate and episcopacy which did communicate in all the power and offices which were ordinary and perpetual, are in scripture clearly all one in ordinary ministration, and their names are often used in common to signify exactly the same ordinary function.

202

1642
Imposition of hands in ordination

Jeremy Taylor, Bishop of Down and Connor (1613–67), Episcopacy Asserted, Works, ed. C.P. Eden (London, 1849), V, p. 27.

Imposition of hands is a duty and office necessary for the perpetuating of a church... 'lest it expire in one age'. This power of imposition of hands for ordination is fixed upon the apostles and apostolic men, and not communicated to the seventy-two disciples or presbyters; for the apostles and apostolic men did so *de facto*, and were commanded to do so, and the seventy-two never did so.

---

[1]   'Successors of the apostles'
[2]   Which may be done by priests, but not by deacons.
[3]   *To the Trallians*, 3

Therefore this office and ministry of the apostolate is distinct and superior to that of presbyters; and this distinction must be so continued to all ages of the church; for the thing was not temporary, but productive of issue and succession, and therefore as perpetual as the clergy, as the church itself.

203

1642
The laying on of hands in Confirmation

Jeremy Taylor, Bishop of Down and Connor (1613–1667), Episcopacy Asserted, Works, ed. C.P. Eden (London, 1849), V, pp. 27–8.

It has been the normal practice in episcopal Churches for the ministry of Confirmation to be carried out by a bishop.

The apostles did impose hands for confirmation of baptized people, and this was a perpetual act of power to be succeeded to, and yet not communicated, nor executed... by any... presbyter.... This giving of the Holy Ghost by imposition of the apostle's hands, was not for a miraculous gift, but an ordinary grace. For St Philip[1] could do miracles enough; but this grace he could not give, the grace of... confirmation.

204

1642
Diocese and Parish

Jeremy Taylor, Bishop of Down and Connor (1613–67), Episcopacy Asserted, Works, ed. C.P. Eden (London, 1849), V, pp. 178–9.

At issue here is whether the fundamental unit of the Church's life and organisation is the local worshipping community or the diocese. Taylor points out that the eucharistic community with the bishop at its head was originally a single local church, and he suggests that the Presbyterians make a false distinction in rejecting the diocesan unit and the bishop as its pastor.

---

[1]   Acts 8

Which was first, a private congregation or a diocese? If a private congregation, then a bishop was at first fixed in a private congregation, and so was a parochial bishop; if a diocese was first, then the question will be how a diocese could be without parishes, for what is a diocese but a jurisdiction over many parishes? I answer, it is true that diocese and parish are words used now in contradistinction, ... *sed non fuit sic ab initio*,[1] for at first a diocese was the city and the... 'neighbouring towns', in which there was no distinction of parishes.

205

1642
The priest the bishop's deputy

Jeremy Taylor, Bishop of Down and Connor (1613–67), Episcopacy Asserted, *Works, ed. C.P. Eden (London, 1849), V, p. 152.*

The principle involved here is that the bishop has pastoral charge of the diocese, and that it is he who gives permission to ministers ordained to the priesthood to exercise their ministry in his diocese as his assistants. See also no. 206.

The whole power of ministration both of the word and sacraments was in the bishop by prime authority, and in the presbyters by commission and delegation, insomuch that they might not exercise any ordinary ministration without licence from the bishop. They had power and capacity by their order to preach, to minister, to offer, to reconcile, and to baptize; they were indeed acts of order: but they might not by the law of the church exercise any of these acts without license from the bishop, that is an act or issue of jurisdiction, and shews the superiority of the bishop over his presbyters by the practice of Christendom.

---

[1]   'But it was not so from the beginning'.

206

1642
Episcopacy cannot be delegated

Jeremy Taylor, Bishop of Down and Connor (1613–67), Episcopacy Asserted, *Works, ed. C.P. Eden (London, 1849), V, p. 156.*

The whole cure of the diocese is in the bishop[;] he cannot exonerate himself of it, for it is a burden of Christ's imposing, or it is not imposed at all; therefore this taking of presbyters into part of the regiment and care does not divest him of his own power or any part of it, nor yet ease him of his care, but that as he must still episkopein, 'visit' and 'see to' his diocese, so he hath authority still in all parts of his diocese.... When the bishop came to any place, there the *vicaria*[1] of the presbyters did cease... and... he being present might do any office, because it was in his own charge....; and therefore *praesente episcopo*[2] (saith the council of Carthage and St Leo) 'if the bishop be present', the presbyter without leave might not officiate.

207

1642
Legislative powers in Provincial Councils and Synods

Jeremy Taylor, Bishop of Down and Connor (1613–67), Episcopacy Asserted, *Works, ed. C.P. Eden (London, 1849), V, p. 169.*

See nos. 67, 70, 155, 187, 207, 208, 329.

I have shewn that the Bishop of every diocese did give laws to his own church for particulars, so it is evident that the law of provinces and of the catholic church were made by conventions of bishops... the instances of this are just so many as there are councils.

---

[1]   'Deputed office'
[2]   'When the bishop was present'.

208

1642
Decision-Making: the role of bishops in council

Jeremy Taylor, Bishop of Down and Connor (1613–67), Episcopacy Asserted, Works, ed. C.P. Eden (London, 1849), V, p. 172–3.

The principle that the Church is present as a whole in her representatives in a council or synod is stated here, with emphasis on the special responsibility of bishops. Cf. no. 207 and nos. 67, 70, 155, 187.

If it be objected... 'that which is of general concernment must also be of general scrutiny'; I answer, it is true, unless where God himself hath intrusted the care of others in a body, as he hath in the bishops, and will require the souls of others at his hand, and commanded us to require the law at their mouths, and to follow their faith, whom he hath set over us. And therefore the determination of councils pertains to all, and is handled by all, not in diffusion but in representation; for... saith St Cyprian, 'the church is in the bishop', viz., by representment, 'and the bishop is in the church', viz., as a pilot in a ship or a master in a family, or rather as a steward and guardian to rule in his master's absence.

209

1647
The Communion of Saints

Joseph Hall (1574–1656), Bishop of Norwich, A Treatise of Christ Mystical (published 1647), Works, ed. P. Hall (1837) VII, pp. 261f., More and Cross, p. 334.

As there is a perfect union betwixt the glorious saints in heaven, and an union, though imperfect, between the saints on earth, so there is an union, partly perfect and partly imperfect, between the saints in heaven and the saints below upon earth, perfect in respect of those glorified saints above, imperfect in respect of the weak returns we are able to make to them again. Let no man think that because those blessed souls are out of sight far distant in another world, and we are here toiling in a vale of tears, we have therefore lost all mutual regard to each other.

210

1650–51
Ministry to the sick

Jeremy Taylor, Bishop of Down and Connor (1613–67), Holy
Living and Holy Dying, Works, *ed. C.P. Eden (London, 1847), III,
p. 404.*

The intercourses of the minister with the sick man have so much
variety in them, that they are not to be transacted at once; and
therefore they do not well that send once to see the good man with
sorrow, and hear him pray, and thank him, and dismiss him civilly,
and desire to see his face no more. To dress a soul for funeral, is
not a work to be despatched at one meeting; at first he needs a
comfort, and anon something to make him willing to die; and by-
and-by he is tempted to impatience, and that needs a special cure;
and it is a great work to make his confessions well, and with
advantages; and it may be the man is careless and indifferent, and
then he needs to understand the evil of his sin, and the danger of
his person; and his cases of conscience may be so many and so
intricate, that he is not quickly to be reduced to peace, and one
time the holy man must pray, and another he must exhort, a third
time administer the holy sacrament; and he, that ought to watch all
the periods and little portions of his life, lest he should be
surprised and overcome, had need be watched when he is sick, and
assisted, and called on, and reminded of the several parts of his
duty in every instant of his temptation.

211

*c.*1650
The use of reason

Henry Hammond (1605–60), Oxford divine, Of the Reasonableness
of the Christian Religion *(c. 1650), Works, (3rd edn., ed. N.
Pocock, Oxford, 1849), I. pp. 29–30.*

The value of human reasoning in judging Christian truth had been
controversial throughout the Middle Ages. By the seventeenth century it was
common for Anglicans to speak of Scripture, Tradition and Reason as three
tests, with Scripture holding supreme place among them. This passage
foreshadows another phase in the debate, which was to arrive with the
eighteenth century 'Age of Reason'. Cf. nos. 193, 244, 246.

[In answer to the question] whether right reason be appointed the judge of controversies... Whether all doubts of all sorts be to be determined by the dictates of nature, in the heart of every man which hath the use of reason... Men are naturally able to judge only of those things which by some sure connection depend on those attributes of God which are communicated to, and particularly by, men, and are the like... for kind, though not degree, in man as in God... All controversies, i.e. all things subject to judgement, are reducible to two heads, goodness or truth; so that the question now is, whether right reason can infallibly judge what is good or bad, true or false... For a thing to be good morally (for metaphysical goodness is all one with truth) depends, by sure connections, from that eternal justice which is primarily in God... For a thing to be true ... depends partly on God's power, partly on his will.

212

1651
Conscience

Joseph Hall (1574–1656), Bishop of Norwich, Susurrium cum Deo,[1] *Soliloqui, 51,* Works, *ed. P. Hall (1837), VIII, p. 274, More and Cross, p. 645.*

It is a true word of the apostle, God is greater than our conscience,[2] and surely none but He. Under that great God, the supreme power on earth is the conscience. Every man is a little world within himself, and, in this little world, there is a court of judicature erected, wherein, next under God, the conscience sits as the supreme judge from whom there is no appeal; that passeth sentence upon us, upon all our actions, upon all our intentions; for our persons, absolving one, condemning another; for our actions, allowing one, forbidding another. If that condemn us, in vain shall all the world beside us acquit us; and, if that clear us, the doom which the world passeth upon us is frivolous and ineffectual.

---

[1]   'An intimate talk with God'.
[2]   Cf. Romans 13.5; II Timothy 1.3

213

1653–4
Fundamentals

Henry Hammond, Chaplain to Charles I, 1605–69, Of Fundamentals, Works, *(3rd edn., ed. N. Pocock, Oxford, 1849), II, pp. 76, 82, 98.*

Henry Hammond (1605–60) was one of the pioneers of biblical criticism in English and a contributor to the seventeenth century debate about what constitute the 'fundamentals' of the faith. Cf. nos. 197, 373.

The general way of defining what... fundamentals are, must in all reason be taken from the practice of the apostles, as the interpreter of God's appointment and judgement in this matter.... Jesus Christ is the one only foundation... The larger and fuller view of this foundation... is set down in the Creeds of the Church.

214

before 1654
Faith and works

John Selden (1584–1654), scholar, Table Talk, *recorded by his secretary Richard Milward, ed. S.H. Reynolds (Oxford, 1892), p. 69, More and Cross, p. 301.*

See Articles x–xviii of the Thirty-Nine Articles, and cf. nos. 122, 123.

It was an unhappy division that has been made betwixt faith and works, — though in my intellect I may divide them, just as in the candle I know there is both heat and light. But yet put out the candle, and they are both gone; one remains not without the other. So it is betwixt faith and works. Nay, in a right conception, *fides est opus*;[1] if I believe a thing because I am commanded, that is *opus*.[2]

---

[1]   'Faith is a work'

[2]   'A work'

215

1654
The catholicity and continuity of the Anglican Church

John Bramhall (1594–1663), Bishop of Derry (1634–61), then Archbishop of Armagh , A Just Vindication of the Church of England from the Unjust Aspersions of Criminal Schism, (London, 1654), Works, ed. A.W. Haddan, (Oxford, 1842), vol. I, p. 113.

The Church of England before the Reformation and the Church of England after the Reformation are as much the same Church as a garden before it is weeded and after it is weeded, is the same garden... By the Church of England we understand that Church, which was derived by lineal[1] succession from the British, English and Scottish bishops.

216

1654
The ascension and the resurrection of the body

Peter Heylin (b. 1600), controversialist and historian, Theologia Veterum (1654), p. 270, More and Cross, p. 273.

It was then in His natural Body that Christ ascended into Heaven; in it He hath acquired for it all those high pre-eminences which have been formerly expressed, — not altering thereby the nature which before it had, but adding a perfection of that glory which before it had not, and making it, though a natural Body still, yet a Body glorified. And this is generally agreed upon by all the Fathers, affirming with a joint consent this most Catholic truth, that notwithstanding the accessions of immortality and glory to the Body of Christ, yet it reserved still all the properties of a natural Body.

---

[1]   The succession of bishops should always be understood as a succession of communities with their pastors. See *Episcopal ministry: Report of the Archbishops' Group on the Episcopate* (London, 1990), 87.

217

1655–7
The burial of the dead

Anthony Sparrow, Bishop of Norwich, A Rationale upon the Book of Common Prayer of the Church of England *(1655–7).*

When the unlearned or unbeliever hears us sing triumphant songs to God for our victory over death, when he hears holy Lessons and discourses of the resurrection, when he hears us pray for a happy and joyful resurrection to Glory: by all these he must be convinced, that we do believe the resurrection, which is a principal Article of Christian faith, and the same may be the means to convince him also, and make him believe the same, and so fall down and worship God. And this is according to S. Paul's rule, I Corinthians 14.23–5, who thence concludes, that all our publick religious services ought to be done, that the unlearned or unbeliever may be convinced, and brought to worship God. For the due performance of these holy publick services, a priest, ordained for men in things pertaining to God, Hebrews 5.1, is required by the Church, as it ought to be, and as it was of old. It was an ancient custom, after Burial to go to the Holy Communion.

218

1655–7
The Litany

Anthony Sparrow, Bishop of Norwich, A Rationale upon the Book of Common Prayer of the Church of England *(1655–7).*

Concerning the Litany of our Church, we may boldly say, and easily maintain it, that there is not extant anywhere;
1. A more particular excellent enumeration of all the Christian's either private or common wants; Nor
2. A more innocent, blameless form, against which there lies no just exception; Nor
3. A more Artificial[1] Composure for the raising of our devotion, and keeping it up throughout, than this part of our Liturgy.

---

[1]   that is, skilfully framed

In the beginning it directs our *prayers* to the right object, the Glorious TRINITY. For necessary it is, that we should know whom we worship. Then it proceeds to *Deprecations*, or prayers against evil; lastly, to *Petitions* for good. In the *Deprecations*, as right method requires, we first pray against sin, then against punishment; because sin is the greatest evil. From all which we pray to be delivered by the holy actions and passions of CHRIST, the only merits of all our goods. The like good order is observed in our *Petitions* for good. First, we pray for the *Church Catholick*, the common mother of all Christians; then for *our own Church*, to which, next the Church Catholick, we owe the greatest observance and duty. And therein, in the first place for the principal members of it, in whose welfare the Churches peace chiefly consists. After this we pray particularly for those sorts of men that most especially need our prayers, such amongst others, as those whom the Law calls *miserable persons*. The Litany is not one long continued prayer, but broken into many short and pithy Ejaculations: that the intention and devotion which is most necessary in prayer, may not be dull'd and vanish, as in a long prayer it is apt to do; but be quickened and intended, by so many new and quick petitions; and the nearer to the end, the shorter and livelier it is, strengthening our devotions by raising in us an apprehension of our misery and distress, ready, as it were to sink and perish; and if therefore crying out as the Disciples did, 'Master, save us, we perish: O Lamb of God hear us, O Christ hear us, Lord have mercy upon us'.[2]

219

1655–7
Holy days

Anthony Sparrow, Bishop of Norwich, A Rationale upon the Book of Common Prayer of the Church of England *(1655–7).*

Holy in Scripture phrase is all one with separate or set apart to God, and is opposed to common. 'What God hath clean'd, that call

---

[2]   Matthew 8.25

not thou common',[1] Holy daies then are those which are taken out of common daies, and separated to Gods holy service and worship, either by Gods own appointment, or by holy Churches dedication. And these are either Fasting and Penitential daies (for there is a holy Fast,[2] as well as a holy Feast,[3] such as are *Ash-Wednesday, Good-Friday*, and the whole week before *Easter* commonly called the *Holy-week*, which daies holy Church hath dedicated to Gods solemn worship, in religious fasting and prayers. Or else holy Festivals which are set apart to the solemn and religious commemoration of some eminent mercies and blessings of God. And amongst those Holy-daies, some are higher daies than others, in regard of the greatness of the blessing commemorated, and of the solemnity of the Service appointed to them... This sanctification or setting apart of *Festival-daies*, is a token of that thankfulness, and a part of that publick honour which we owe to God for admirable benefits; and these dayes or Feasts so set apart are of excellent use, being, as learned *Hooker* observes, the
1. Splendor and outward dignity of our Religion.
2. Forcible Witnesses of ancient truth.
3. Provocations to the exercise of all Piety.
4. Shadows of our endless felicity in heaven.
5. On earth, everlasting records teaching by the eye in a manner, whatsoever we believe.

220

1658
The validity of Anglican Orders

John Bramhall (1594–1663), Bishop of Derry (1634–61), then Archbishop of Armagh. The Consecration of Protestant Bishops Vindicated, Works (Oxford, 1844) III, pp. 25 and 40–1 and 57–8.

The story of the 'consecration' at the Nag's Head tavern is without foundation, but was put about by those who wanted to argue that a break in succession had made Anglican Orders invalid from the time of Archbishop Parker.

---

[1]   Acts 10.15
[2]   Joel 2
[3]   Nehemiah 8.10

In the beginning of the late Parliament, some Presbyterian Lords presented to the Upper House a certain book, proving, that the Protestant bishops had no succession or consecration, and therefore were no bishops... They say, that Archbishop Parker and the rest of the Protestant bishops in the beginning of Queen Elizabeth's reign, or at least sundry of them, were consecrated at the Nag's Head in Cheapside together, by bishop Scory alone, or by him and bishop Barlow jointly, without sermon, without sacrament, without any solemnity, in the year 1559... by a new fantastic form... We say, Archbishop Parker was consecrated alone, at Lambeth, in the Church by four bishops, authorized thereunto by commission under the Great Seal of England, with sermon, with sacrament, with all due solemnities, upon the 17th day of Dec; anno 1559, before four of the most eminent public notaries in England. It was not we who made a discrimination between our bishops and their bishops, as to the point of ordination, but the Marian bishops themselves. The question in Queen Mary's days was not about the validity or invalidity of our orders, but about the legality or illegality of them; not whether they were conformable to the institution of Christ, but whether they were conformable to the laws of England.

221

1659
Confirmation

Anon., Aqua Genitalis: A Discourse Concerning Baptism *(1659).*

Confirmation.... is a word full, and significant of the thing that I would express, and consists of two parts. First, That a Person do undertake in his own name every part of the vow made by others for him in baptism, and so personally consent unto Christ to be wholly his, according to that Agreement. And so it is an act of *Confirmation* on our part; because we do hereby further ratify and establish that Contract which is between God and us, and by confessing of it to be valid and good, bind our selves faster still to him, whose we were before. The second part of it is, A receiving of God's Blessing and Grace by the Hands and holy Prayers of him that ministers, to strengthen us to perform our Engagement, and make good our Word and Faith which we have plighted unto

God; which many have taken to be the meaning of that place.[1] Where after baptism, follows laying on of Hands, which the *Jews* used in their Blessings. And so it is an *Act of Confirmation* of the Person on the part of God, who confers a new Grace to strengthen, and confirm in him these holy Principles, and that good Resolution, of which he hath made a faithful Profession, and to enable him to keep and persist in it. As in baptism, the Holy Ghost was conveyed as a Sanctifier, so herein as a Comforter and Strengthener, now that the Person is entering upon a great Contest and Conflict with himself, the World, and Principalities, and Powers, and spiritual wickedness in high places.

222

1659
Our common baptism

Anon., Aqua Genitalis: A discourse concerning Baptism *(1659).*

Let me beseech all the People of God to live in Love and Peace together. Let us not quarrel about every little Thing, nor make every petty Difference a cause of Trouble and Contention. For as the apostle saith,[1] 'By one Spirit we are all baptized into one Body'. We are all by this made of the same Corporation, and taken by baptism into the same Brotherhood, and therefore should not make them the Waters of strife, and so provoke the Lord to Anger against us. We are not baptized into this or that particular Opinion, nor received into a particular Church, but into the Belief of the Gospel, and into the Church of God in general, and therefore should love all the Disciples and Followers of our Lord, and embrace all of every Persuasion that live godlily in Christ Jesus. You were not baptized (saith the apostle) into the name of *Paul*; therefore do not say, I am of *Paul*, I adhere to this Man, or that: for whosoever did baptize you, it was not into the particular Love of him a and his Opinions, but into the Communion of the whole Church of Christ, who hold the Catholick Faith. Though an *Heretick* in ancient Times had baptized any Man, yet die not the

---

[1] Hebrew 6.4
[1] I Corinthians 12, 13

Christians therefore baptize him over again when he left those
Mens Company; because being baptized into the Name of the
Father, Son and Holy Ghost, he was not received into the
Profession of their particular Opinion, but of the Truth of Christ
universally believed by all good Christians. And therefore let us
live with them all as our Confederates, as those that are tied
together in the same Bonds, and united in the same Covenant, and
engaged in the same Cause against the common Enemies, the devil,
the World, and the Flesh; and let us never give these Enemies so
much cause to rejoice, as an unhandsome word against any sincere
Christian might administer. But let us endeavour to keep the Unity
of the Spirit in the Bond of Peace; for as the apostle speaks,
'There is one Lord, one Faith, one baptism, one God and Father of
All, who is above all, and through all, and in you all'.[2]

223

1659
One Church

John Pearson (1612–86), Bishop of Chester, An Exposition of the
Creed, *ed. E. Burton (Oxford, 1864), More and Cross, p. 26.*

When the Scripture speaketh of any country where the Gospel had
been preached, it nameth always by way of plurality the Churches
of that country, as the Churches of Judaea, of Samaria, and Galilee,
the Churches of Syria and of Cilicia, the Churches of Galatia, the
Churches of Asia, the Churches of Macedonia. But notwithstanding
there were several such Churches or congregations of believers in
great and populous cities, yet the Scriptures always speak of such
congregations in the notion of one Church; as when St Paul wrote
to the Corinthians, 'Let your women keep silence in the
Churches';[1] yet the dedication of his Epistle is 'Unto the Church of
God which is at Corinth'.[2] So we read not of the Churches, but the
Church at Jerusalem, the Church at Antioch, the Church at
Caesarea, the Church at Ephesus, the Church of the Thessalonians,

---

[2]   Ephesians 4.5
[1]   I Corinthians 14.34,35
[2]   I Corinthians 1.2

the Church of Laodicea, the Church of Smyrna, the Church of Pergamus, the Church of Thyatira, the Church of Sardis, the Church of Philadelphia. From whence it appeareth that a collection of several congregations, every one of which is in some sense a Church, and may be called so, is properly one Church by virtue of the subordination of them all in one government under one ruler. For thus in those great and populous cities where Christians were very numerous, not only all the several Churches within the cities, but those also in the adjacent parts, were united under the care and inspection of one bishop, and therefore was accounted one Church.

224

1660
The Real Presence

Simon Patrick (1625–1707), Bishop of Ely, Mensa Mystica, or a Discourse concerning the Sacrament of the Lord's Supper *(1660).*

I cannot pretend to have conversed much with barefac'd Truth, yet having been drawn to publish a few Thoughts concerning baptism, I shall now further endeavour to unfold those Mysteries that lie hid under the Coverings of Bread broken and Wine poured out in the Sacrament of the Lord's Supper, that Men may not... embrace a meer Cloud instead of God himself. My Sight is not so sharp as to discern the very Flesh and Blood of Christ in those Forms and Shapes of Bread and Wine... Yet I am so far from thinking that they are meer Signs of what Christ did for us, or only Representations of the Benefits we receive by him, that I am persuaded they exhibit our Lord himself unto believing Minds, and put them into a surer Possession of him. The Truth commonly lies between Two Extremes, and being a peaceable Thing, cannot join it self with either of the directly opposite Parties. And therefore I shall seek for her in a middle Path, not bidding such a Defiance to the Corporeal Presence as to deny the real, nor so subverting the Fancy of a miraculous Change into a Celestial Substance, as to level these Things into meer Shadows. We must further consider this Action *as a Rite whereby we enter into Covenant with him.* This is included in our *taking* the Bread and Wine, as well as in our *eating* and *drinking* of them, and was expressed before, when I said, we must offer our selves to God as the greatest Act of our Thanksgiving. That offering of our selves is such a thing, that it puts us out of our own Power; and besides we enter here into strict Engagements never to resume or draw back our selves again, never to challenge any right to have our selves in our own Disposal; we make a solemn Agreement with the Lord Jesus that he shall dwell in us, and possess himself of all our Faculties, as the sole Lord and Governor of our Souls. Tho' this hath been done once already when we were baptized, so that we cannot reverse the Deed, nor cancel the Bond that is between us, yet seeing the Matter of the Covenant is always to be perform'd, and more than one World depends upon it, God thinks fit to take new Security of us, and strengthen our Obligations, lest we think of letting the Debt run on unpaid one Day after another, till we be quite Bankrupts, and have nothing left whereby to discharge it....The next Festivity that we shall celebrate together, must be in Heaven. In the very Presence of God.

225

1662
The Thirty-Nine Articles

The Thirty-Nine Articles in the 1662 version may be found printed in the 1662 Book of Common Prayer. See, too, the text of 1571 in its earlier spelling and in Latin in the present volume, no. 152.

The first five Articles deal with matters covered in the Creeds, and largely non-controversial in the sixteenth century debate.

i. *Of Faith in the Holy Trinity*

There is but one living and true God, everlasting, without body, parts, or passions; of infinite power, wisdom, and goodness; the Maker and Preserver of all things both visible and invisible. And in unity of this Godhead there be three Persons, of one substance, power, and eternity; the Father, the Son, and the Holy Ghost.

ii. *Of the Word or Son of God, which was made very Man*

The Son, which is the Word of the Father, begotten from everlasting of the Father, the very and eternal God, and of one

substance with the Father, took
Man's nature in the womb of the blessed Virgin, of her substance:
so that two whole and perfect Natures, that is to say, the Godhead
and Manhood, were joined together in one Person, never to be
divided, whereof is one Christ, very God, and very Man; who truly
suffered, was crucified, dead, and buried, to reconcile his Father to
us, and to be a sacrifice, not only for original guilt, but also for all
actual sins of men.

iii. *Of the going down of Christ into Hell*

As Christ died for us, and was buried, so also is it to be believed,
that he went down into Hell.

iv. *Of the resurrection of Christ*

Christ did truly rise again from death, and took again his body,
with flesh, bones, and all things appertaining to the perfection of
Man's nature; wherewith he ascended into Heaven, and there
sitteth, until he return to judge all Men at the last day.

v. *Of the Holy Ghost*

The Holy Ghost, proceeding from the Father and the Son, is of one
substance, majesty, and glory, with the Father and the Son, very
and eternal God.

vi. *Of the Sufficiency of the holy Scriptures for salvation*

*Article vi attacks any attempt to add to (as distinct from drawing from) the
teaching of Scripture, and especially to require faith in any teaching not in
Scripture as a condition of salvation.*

Holy Scripture containeth all things necessary to salvation: so that
whatsoever is not read therein, nor may be proved thereby, is not
to be required of any man, that it should be believed as an article
of the Faith, or be thought requisite or necessary to salvation. In
the name of the Holy Scripture we do understand those Canonical
Books of the Old and New Testament, of whose authority was
never any doubt in the Church.

Of the Names and Number of the Canonical Books

*This Article was designed to clarify the Anglican position on the disputed
question of the canonical status of the 'apocryphal books' of the Old
Testament.*

Genesis, Exodus, Leviticus, Numbers, Deuteronomy, Joshua,
Judges, Ruth, The First Book of Samuel, The Second Book of
Samuel, The First Book of Kings, The Second Book of Kings,

The First Book of Chronicles, The Second Book of Chronicles, The First Book of Esdras, The Second Book of Esdras, The Book of Esther, The Book of Job, The Psalms, The Proverbs, Ecclesiastes or Preacher, Cantica or Songs of Solomon, Four Prophets the greater, Twelve Prophets the less. And the other Books (as *Hierome* saith) the Church doth read for example of life and instruction of manners; but yet doth it not apply them to establish any doctrine; such are these following:

The Third Book of Esdras, The Fourth Book of Esdras, The Book of Tobias, The Book of Judith, The rest of the Book of Esther, The Book of Wisdom, Jesus the Son of Sirach, Baruch the Prophet, The Song of the Three Children, The Story of Susanna, Of Bel and the Dragon, The Prayer of Manasses, The First Book of Maccabees, The Second Book of Maccabees,[1]

All the Books of the New Testament, as they are commonly received, we do receive, and account them Canonical.

vii. *Of the Old Testament*
Some reformers argued that the Old Testament, with its Laws, was wholly superseded by the New Covenant and indeed stood in opposition to it. There is a trace in this school of thought of the Gnostic or Manichee tradition of the early Christian centuries, which also sought to disjoin Old Testament and New.

The Old Testament is not contrary to the New: for both in the Old and New Testament everlasting life is offered to Mankind by Christ, who is the only Mediator between God and Man, being both God and Man. Wherefore they are not to be heard, which feign that the old Fathers did look only for transitory promises. Although the Law given from God by Moses, as touching Ceremonies and Rites, do not bind Christian men, nor the Civil precepts thereof ought of necessity to be received in any commonwealth; yet notwithstanding, no Christian man whatsoever is free from the obedience of the Commandments which are called Moral.

viii. *Of the Three Creeds*

The Three Creeds, *Nicene* Creed, *Athanasius's* Creed, and that which is commonly called the *apostle's* Creed, ought thoroughly to be received and believed: for they may be proved by most certain warrants of Holy Scripture.

---

[1]   Jewel added Tobias, Baruch, The Song of the Three Children, Susanna, Bel and Manasses.

ix. *Of Original or Birth-sin*

Original Sin standeth not in the following of *Adam*, (as the *Pelagians* do vainly talk);[2] but is the fault and corruption of the Nature of every man, that naturally is ingendered of the offspring of *Adam*; whereby man is very far gone from original righteousness, and is of his own nature inclined to evil, so that the flesh lusteth always contrary to the spirit; and therefore in every person born into this world, it deserveth God's wrath and damnation. And this infection of nature doth remain, yea in them that are regenerated; whereby the lust of the flesh, called in the Greek Ψρόνημα σαρκός,[3]

which some do expound the wisdom, some sensuality, some the affection, some the desire of the flesh, is not subject to the Law of God. And although there is no condemnation for them that believe and are baptized, yet the apostle doth confess, that concupiscence and lust hath of itself the nature of sin.

x. *Of Free-Will*

Articles x–xviii concern the contemporary debates on justification by faith; on growth in holiness and renewal of life (sanctification); on the place of good works; on what is needed for forgiveness when the believer sins after baptism. Cf. Cranmer's series of Homilies on Salvation, Faith, Good Works and Love, from which an extract is given above (no. 133), and the Second Anglican–Roman Catholic International Commission, Salvation and the Church (1986). (See nos. 122, 123, 214.)

The condition of Man after the fall of *Adam* is such, that he cannot turn and prepare himself, by his own natural strength and good works, to faith, and calling upon God: Wherefore we have no power to do good works pleasant and acceptable to God, without the grace of God by Christ preventing us, that we may have a good will, and working with us, when we have that good will.

xi. *Of the Justification of Man*

On justification by faith, cf. nos. 122, 123, 133, 214.

We are accounted righteous before God, only for the merit of our Lord and Saviour Jesus Christ by Faith, and not for our own works

---

2   The Pelagians of Augustine of Hippo's day at the beginning of the fifth century, denied the innate and irresistible power of original sin and taught that both vice and virtue are learned by imitation ('the following of Adam'), so that being good is just a question of trying.

3   *Phronema sarkos*

or deservings: Wherefore, that we are justified by Faith only is a most wholesome Doctrine, and very full of comfort, as more largely is expressed in the Homily of Justification.

xii. *Of Good Works*

Albeit that Good Works, which are the fruits of Faith, and follow after Justification, cannot put away our sins, and endure the severity of God's Judgement; yet are they pleasing and acceptable to God in Christ, and do spring out necessarily of a true and lively Faith; insomuch that by them a lively Faith may be as evidently known as a tree discerned by the fruit.

xiii. *Of Works before Justification*

Works done before the grace of Christ, and the Inspiration of his Spirit, are not pleasant to God, forasmuch as they spring not of faith in Jesus Christ, neither do they make men meet to receive grace, or (as the School-authors say) deserve grace of congruity: yea rather, for that they are not done as God hath willed and commanded them to be done, we doubt not but they have the nature of sin.

xiv. *Of Works of Supererogation*

Voluntary Works besides, over, and above, God's Commandments, which they call Works of Supererogation, cannot be taught without arrogancy and impiety: for by them men do declare, that they do not only render unto God as much as they are bound to do, but that they do more for his sake, than of bounden duty is required: whereas Christ saith plainly, When ye have done all that are commanded to you, say, We are unprofitable servants.

xv. *Of Christ alone without Sin*

Christ in the truth of our nature was made like unto us in all things, sin only except, from which he was clearly void, both in his flesh, and in his spirit. He came to be the Lamb without spot, who, by sacrifice of himself once made, should take away the sins of the world, and sin, as saint *John* saith, was not in him. But all we the rest, although baptized, and born again in Christ, yet offend in many things; and if we say we have no sin, we deceive ourselves, and the truth is not in us.

xvi. *Of Sin after baptism*

This Article touches on another debate of the first Christian centuries: that is, whether those who sin after baptism can ever be purged again of their sin. Cf. 58. Jewel changed the Latin to veniae *to agree with English 'forgiveness'.*

Not every deadly sin willingly committed after baptism is sin against the Holy Ghost, and unpardonable. Wherefore the grant of repentance is not to be denied to such as fall into sin after baptism. After we have received the Holy Ghost, we may depart from grace given, and fall into sin, and by the grace of God we may arise again, and amend our lives. And therefore they are to be condemned, which say, they can no more sin as long as they live here, or deny the place of forgiveness to such as truly repent.

xvii. *Of Predestination and Election*

Calvinist teaching placed great emphasis not only on predestination, but upon 'assurance', that is, the consciousness of being one of the elect. This Article stresses the pastoral danger of despair which this teaching brings to those who do not share this personal assurance, and encourages Christians to seek actively to do God's will.

Predestination to Life is the everlasting purpose of God, whereby (before the foundations of the world were laid) he hath constantly decreed by his counsel secret to us, to deliver from curse and damnation those whom he hath chosen in Christ out of mankind, and to bring them by Christ to everlasting salvation, as vessels made to honour. Wherefore, they which be endued with so excellent a benefit of God be called according to God's purpose by his Spirit working in due season: they through grace obey the calling: they be justified freely: they be made sons of God by adoption: they be made like the image of his only-begotten Son Jesus Christ: they walk religiously in good works, and at length, by God's mercy, they attain to everlasting felicity. As the godly consideration of Predestination, and our Election in Christ, is full of sweet, pleasant, and unspeakable comfort to godly persons, and such as feel in themselves the working of the Spirit of Christ, mortifying the works of the flesh, and their earthly members, and drawing up their mind to high and heavenly things, as well because it doth greatly establish and confirm their faith of eternal Salvation to be enjoyed through Christ, as because it doth fervently kindle their love towards God: So, for curious and carnal persons, lacking the ·Spirit of Christ, to have continually before their eyes the sentence of God's Predestination, is a most dangerous downfall, whereby the Devil doth thrust them either into desperation, or into wretchedness of most unclean living, no less perilous than desperation. Furthermore, we must receive God's promises in such wise, as they be generally set forth to us in holy Scripture: and, in our doings, that Will of God is to be followed, which we have expressly declared unto us in the Word of God.

xviii. *Of obtaining eternal Salvation only by the Name of Christ*

They also are to be had accursed that presume to say, That every man shall be saved by the Law or Sect which he professeth, so that he be diligent to frame his life according to that Law, and the light of Nature. For holy Scripture doth set out unto us only the Name of Jesus Christ, whereby men must be saved.

xix. *Of the Church*

These two 'notes of the Church' were stressed by most reformers of the sexteenth century as identifying the true Church.

The visible Church of Christ is a congregation of faithful men, in the which the pure Word of God is preached, and the Sacraments be duly ministered according to Christ's ordinance in all those things that of necessity are requisite to the same.

As the Church of *Jerusalem, Alexandria,* and *Antioch,* have erred; so also the Church of *Rome* hath erred, not only in their living and manner of Ceremonies, but also in matters of Faith.

xx. *Of the Authority of the Church*

This Article is of importance for questions of autonomy and of decision-making in matters of faith. Sixteenth century Anglican tradition did not define where the freedom to act independently in decreeing rites or ceremonies ends, or seek to determine when a point of order becomes a matter of faith. Cf. xxxiv. On the limits of conciliar authority in matters of faith, cf. xxi. The first clause was added after Convocation had approved the text in 1563, and remained controversial. The Latin lacks 'written', q. v.

The Church hath power to decree Rites or Ceremonies, and authority in Controversies of Faith: And yet it is not lawful for the Church to ordain any thing that is contrary to God's Word written, neither may it so expound one place of Scripture, that it be repugnant to another. Wherefore, although the Church be a witness and a keeper of the holy Writ, yet, as it ought not to decree any thing against the same, so besides the same ought it not to enforce any thing to be believed for necessity of Salvation.

xxi. *Of the Authority of General Councils*

The calling of Councils by secular rulers has patristic precedent. The immediate purpose of this Article is to deny the claim that no Council proper can be convened except by the authority of a Pope.

General Councils may not be gathered together without the commandment and will of Princes. And when they be gathered together, (forasmuch as they be an assembly of men, whereof all be not governed with the Spirit and Word of God,) they may err, and sometimes have erred, even in things pertaining unto God. Wherefore things ordained by them as necessary to salvation have neither strength nor authority, unless it may be declared that they be taken out of holy Scripture.

xxii. *Purgatory*

This Article expressed the Reformers' view that certain aspects of contemporary penitential practice had become misleading to popular understanding: particularly those which depended upon the belief in a 'treasury of merits' of Christ and the 'saints', from which the Church dispensed 'pardons' or 'indulgences', to shorten the time to be spent in purgatory by the soul after death before it was fit for heaven. The doctrine of the treasury of merits was relatively new. (It was first formally stated in the thirteenth century.) But it was an idea of great popular appeal which met a pastoral need. On the veneration of images cf. nos. 73, 74, 75.

The Romish Doctrine concerning Purgatory, Pardons, Worshipping, and Adoration, as well of Images as of Reliques, and also invocation of saints, is a fond thing vainly invented, and grounded upon no warranty of Scripture, but rather repugnant to the Word of God.

xxiii. *Of Ministering in the Congregation*

This Article stresses the need for order, and for calling by the Church, in the commissioning of the ordained ministry.

It is not lawful for any man to take upon him the office of publick preaching, or ministering the Sacraments in the Congregation, before he be lawfully called, and sent to execute the same. And those we ought to judge lawfully called and sent, which be chosen and called to this work by men who have publick authority given unto them in the Congregation, to call and send Ministers into the Lord's vineyard.

xxiv. *Of speaking in the Congregation in such a tongue as the people understandeth*

This Article attacks the practice of the use of Latin in services; this had remained normal in the West long after Latin could be understood by anyone but the clergy and some educated lay people.

It is a thing plainly repugnant to the Word of God, and the custom of the Primitive Church, to have publick Prayer in the Church, or to minister the Sacraments in a tongue not understanded of by the people.

xxv. *Of the Sacraments*

This Article stresses that sacraments are means of grace, that is, not only 'tokens' but 'effectual signs'. The two sacraments ordained by Christ himself are regarded as central, but Confirmation, Penance, ordination, Matrimony and Unction of the dying are allowed their due place in the life of the Church. Cf. 108ff.

Sacraments ordained of Christ be not only badges or tokens of Christian men's profession, but rather they be certain sure witnesses, and effectual signs of grace, and God's good will towards us, by the which he doth work invisibly in us, and doth not only quicken, but also strengthen and confirm our Faith in him.

There are two Sacraments ordained of Christ our Lord in the gospel, that is to say, baptism, and the Supper of the Lord. Those five commonly called Sacraments, that is to say, Confirmation, Penance, Orders, Matrimony, and extreme Unction, are not to be counted for Sacraments of the gospel, being such as have grown partly of the corrupt following of the apostles, partly are states of life allowed in the Scriptures; but yet have not like nature of Sacraments with baptism, and the Lord's Supper, for that they have not any visible sign or ceremony ordained of God. The Sacraments were not ordained of Christ to be gazed upon, or to be carried about, but that we should duly use them. And in such only as worthily receive the same they have a wholesome effect or operation: but they that receive them unworthily purchase to themselves damnation, as saint *Paul* saith.

xxvi. *Of the Unworthiness of the Ministers, which hinders not the effect of the Sacrament*

The principle that it is Christ, not the minister, who makes the Sacraments effectual had been of importance in the West since Augustine's day, when the question became urgent in relation to baptisms performed by schismatic ministers. The Article conforms with tradition here.

Although in the visible Church the evil be ever mingled with the good, and sometimes the evil have chief authority in the Ministration of the Word and Sacraments, yet forasmuch as they do not the same in their own name, but in Christ's, and do minister by his commission and authority, we may use their ministry, both in hearing the Word of God, and in receiving of the Sacraments. Neither is the effect of Christ's ordinance taken away by their wickedness, nor the grace of God's gift diminished from such as by faith and rightly do receive the Sacraments ministered unto them; which be effectual, because of Christ's institution and promise, although they be ministered by evil men. Nevertheless, it appertaineth to the discipline of the Church, that inquiry be made of evil Ministers, and that they be accused by those that have knowledge of their offences; and finally being found guilty, by just judgement be deposed.

xxvii. *Of baptism*

baptism is not only a sign of profession, and mark of difference, whereby Christian men are discerned from others that be not christened, but is also a sign of Regeneration or new Birth [not in the Latin], whereby, as by an instrument, they that receive baptism rightly are grafted into the Church; the promises of forgiveness of sin, and of our adoption to be the sons of God by the Holy Ghost, are visibly signed and sealed; Faith is confirmed, and Grace increased by virtue of prayer unto God. The baptism of young Children is in any wise to be retained in the Church, as most agreeable with the institution of Christ.

xxviii. *Of the Lord's Supper*
On transubstantiation, see no. 86.

The Supper of the Lord is not only a sign of the love that Christians ought to have among themselves one to another; but rather is a Sacrament of our Redemption by Christ's death: insomuch that to such as rightly, worthily, and with faith, receive the same, the Bread which we break is a partaking of the Body of Christ; and likewise the Cup of Blessing is a partaking of the Blood of Christ.

Transubstantiation (or the change of the substance of Bread and Wine) in the Supper of the Lord, cannot be proved by holy Writ; but is repugnant to the plain words of Scripture, overthroweth the nature of a Sacrament, and hath given occasion to many superstitions. The Body of Christ is given, taken, and eaten, in the Supper, only after an heavenly and spiritual manner. And the mean whereby the Body of Christ is received and eaten in the Supper is Faith.

The Sacrament of the Lord's Supper was not by Christ's ordinance reserved, carried about, lifted up, or worshipped.

xxix. *Of the Wicked which eat not the Body of Christ in the use of the Lord's Supper*

The Wicked, and such as be void of a lively faith, although they do carnally and visibly press with their teeth (as saint *Augustine* saith) the Sacrament of the Body and Blood of Christ, yet in no wise are they partakers of Christ; but rather, to their condemnation, do eat and drink the signs or Sacrament of so great a thing.

xxx. *Of both kinds*

The controversy to which this Article refers had been acute since the time of Hus, a Bohemian contemporary of Wyclif. The practice of giving the laity only the consecrated bread had become usual in the Western Church for practical reasons. It is not now the rule in the Roman Catholic Church. See no. 108.

The Cup of the Lord is not to be denied to the Lay-people: for both the parts of the Lord's Sacrament, by Christ's ordinance and commandment, ought to be ministered to all Christian men alike.

xxxi. *Of the one Oblation of Christ finished upon the cross*

This controversy turns on the question of the relationship of the Passion to the Eucharist. Reformers were anxious to make it quite clear that there could not be any repetition of Christ's once-and-for-all offering of himself on the cross, for that would imply that his offering had not been all-sufficient. For that reason the use of the term 'sacrifice' in connection with the Eucharist was deemed to be unacceptable. Modern ecumenical understanding is that there is no repetition but an 'entering into Christ's self-offering' which is made present and effective for us in the Eucharist. (Cf. ARCIC I, Final Report *on the Eucharist, 5. and nos. 1, 8, 20, 40, 43, 93, 111, 115.)*

The Offering of Christ once made is that perfect redemption, propitiation, and satisfaction, for all the sins of the whole world, both original and actual; and there is none other satisfaction for sin, but that alone. Wherefore the sacrifices of Masses, in which it was commonly said, that the priest did offer Christ for the quick and the dead, to have remission of pain and guilt, were blasphemous fables, and dangerous deceits.

xxxii. *Of the Marriage of priests*

bishops, priests, and deacons, are not commanded by God's Law, either to vow the estate of a single life, or to abstain from marriage: therefore it is lawful for them, as for all other Christian men, to marry at their own discretion, as they shall judge the same to serve better to godliness.

xxxiii. *Of Excommunicate Persons, how they are to be avoided*
This canon conforms with ancient disciplinary practice.

That person which by open denunciation of the Church is rightly cut off from the unity of the Church, and excommunicated, ought to be taken [out] of the whole multitude of the faithful, as an Heathen and Publican, until he be openly reconciled by penance, and received into the Church by a Judge that hath authority thereunto.

xxxiv. *Of the Traditions of the Church*
Cf. Article xx on rites and ceremonies and on diversity and uniformity. The crucial questions here are of ecclesial authority in relation to private judgement and about the competence of a given ecclesial body to decree local practice.

It is not necessary that Traditions and Ceremonies be in all places one, and utterly like; for at all times they have been divers, and may be changed according to the diversities of countries, times, and men's manners, so that nothing be ordained against God's Word. Whosoever through his private judgement, willingly, and purposely, doth openly break the traditions and ceremonies of the Church, which be not repugnant to the Word of God, and be ordained and approved by common authority, ought to be rebuked openly, (that others may fear to do the like,) as he that offendeth against the common order of the Church, and hurteth the authority of the Magistrate, and woundeth the consciences of the weak brethren. Every particular or national Church hath authority to ordain, change, and abolish, ceremonies or rites of the Church ordained only by man's authority, so that all things be done to edifying.

xxxv. *Of the Homilies*
See extracts from the Homilies, *nos. 132, 133, 134, 142, 143, 144.*

The second Book of Homilies, the several titles whereof we have joined under this Article, doth contain a godly and wholesome

Doctrine, and necessary for these times, as doth the former Book of Homilies, which were set forth in the time of *Edward* the Sixth; and therefore we judge them to be read in Churches by the Ministers, diligently and distinctly, that they may be understanded of the people.

Of the Names of the Homilies

1 Of the right Use of the Church.
2 Against peril of Idolatry.
3 Of repairing and keeping clean of Churches.
4 Of good Works: first of Fasting.
5 Against Gluttony and Drunkenness.
6 Against Excess of Apparel.
7 Of Prayer.
8 Of the Place and Time of Prayer.
9 That Common Prayers and Sacraments
   ought to be ministered in a known tongue.
10 Of the reverend estimation of God's Word.
11 Of Alms-doing.
12 Of the Nativity of Christ.
13 Of the Passion of Christ.
14 Of the resurrection of Christ.
15 Of the worthy receiving of the Sacrament
   of the Body and Blood of Christ.
16 Of the Gifts of the Holy Ghost.
17 For the Rogation-days.
18 Of the State of Matrimony.
19 Of Repentance.
20 Against Idleness.
21 Against Rebellion.

xxxvi. Of Consecration of Bishops and Ministers

The Book of Consecration of Archbishops and Bishops, and Ordering of Priests and Deacons, lately set forth in the time of *Edward* the Sixth, and confirmed at the same time by authority of Parliament, doth contain all things necessary to such Consecration and all Ordering: neither hath it any thing, that of itself is superstitious and ungodly. And therefore whosoever are consecrated or ordered according to the Rites of that Book, since the second year of the forenamed King *Edward* unto this time, or hereafter shall be consecrated or ordered according to the same Rites; we decree all such to be rightly, orderly, and lawfully consecrated and ordered.

xxxvii. *Of the Civil Magistrates*
This Article formally denies the jurisdiction of the Bishop of Rome in the Realm of England, replacing it with royal jurisdiction.

The King's Majesty hath the chief power in this Realm of *England*, and in other his Dominions, unto whom the chief Government of all Estates of this Realm, whether they be Ecclesiastical or Civil, in all causes doth appertain, and is not, nor ought to be, subject to any foreign Jurisdiction. Where we attribute to the King's Majesty the chief government, by which Titles we understand the minds of some slanderous folks to be offended; we give not to our Princes the ministering either of God's Word or of the Sacraments, the which thing the Injunctions also lately set forth by *Elizabeth* our Queen do most plainly testify; but that only prerogative, which we see to have been given always to all godly Princes in holy Scriptures by God himself; that is, that they should rule all estates and degrees committed to their charge by God, whether they be Ecclesiastical or Temporal, and restrain with the civil sword the stubborn and evildoers. The Bishop of *Rome* hath no jurisdiction in this Realm of *England*.

The Laws of the Realm may punish Christian men with death, for heinous and grievous offences.

It is lawful for Christian men, at the commandment of the Magistrate, to wear weapons, and serve in the wars.

xxxviii. *Of Christian men's Goods, which are not common*
Some radical reformers pressed for the abolition of private property and the holding of all things in common by Christians.

The Riches and Goods of Christians are not common, as touching the right, title, and possession of the same, as certain Anabaptists do falsely boast. Notwithstanding, every man ought, of such things as he possesseth, liberally to give alms to the poor, according to his ability.

xxxix. *Of a Christian man's Oath*

As we confess that vain and rash Swearing is forbidden Christian men by our Lord Jesus Christ, and *James* his apostle, so we judge, that Christian Religion doth not prohibit, but that a man may swear when the Magistrate requireth, in a cause of faith and charity, so it be done according to the Prophet's teaching, in justice, judgement, and truth.

226

1662
Insistence upon episcopal ordination

The Act of Uniformity

On the restoration of Charles II to the English throne a series of legislative measures was needed to restore the Church of England to its established position after the period of Cromwellian rule. This clause is directed against nonconformist ministers. Compare the Thirty-Nine Articles on the ordering of ministers, Article xxiii.

No person... shall be capable to be admitted to any... benefice or other ecclesiastical promotion... nor shall presume to consecrate and administer the holy sacrament of the Lords Supper before such time as he shall be ordained priest according to the form and manner by the said booke[1] prescribed, unless he have formerly beene made priest by episcopall ordination.

227

1662
The case for Uniformity

The Act of Uniformity

The Act argues that failure to keep consistently to the forms of service set out in the Book of Common Prayer has led to schism and also to apathy among the people about going to church. Cf. the Thirty-Nine-Articles, no. xxxiv.

A great number of people... do willfully and schismatically abstaine and refuse to come to theire parish churches... and by the great and scandalous neglect of ministers in using the said order or liturgy set forth and enjoyned... unhappy troubles have arisen and grown and many people have been led into factions and schismes... to the hazard of many souls... Be it enacted that... All ministers in any... place of public worship... shall be bound to say and use... such order and forme as mencioned in... The Book of Common Prayer.

---

[1] The Ordinal

228

1662
Act for the Restitution and Re-establishment of the ancient Government of the Church by Archbishops and bishops (Scotland)

Source Book of Scottish History, *III, p. 157.*

This text is part of the legislation of the Restoration Settlement. It was not certain at first that an episcopal system would be restored to Scotland when Charles II returned to the English and Scottish throne in 1662. From 1639–53 Scottish law had supported a presbyteral form of Church government. This Act restores government by bishops.

Forasmuch as the ordering and disposall of all externall government and policie of the church doth propperlie belong unto his majestie as ane inherent right of the croun, by vertew of his royal prerogative and supremacie in causes ecclesisticall; and in discharge of this trust his majestie and his estates of parliament takeing to their serious consideration that in the beginning of, and by, the late rebellion within this kingdome in the yeer 1637 the ancient and sacred order of bishops wes cast off, their persons and rights wer injured and overturned and a seeming paritie among the clergie factiously and violently brought in, to the great disturbance of the public peace, the reproach of the reformed religion and violation of the excellent lawes of the realme for preserveing ane orderlie subordination in the church; and therwithall considering what disorders and exorbitancies have been in the church, what encroachments upon the prerogative and rights of the croun, what usurpations upon the authoritie of parliaments, and what prejudice the libertie of the subject hath suffered by the invasions made upon the bishops and episcopall government, which they find to be the church government most agreeable to the Word of God, most convenient and effectuall for the preservation of treuth, order and unitie and most suteable to monarchie and the peace and quyet of the state: Thairfor his majestie, with advice and consent of his estates of parliament, hath thought it necessar and accordingly doth heirby redintegrat the state of bishops to their ancient places and undoubted priveledges in parliament, and to all their other accustomed dignities, priveledges and jurisdictions; and doth heirby restore them.

229

1662
The elements of the Anglican Liturgy

John Durel, Minister of the French Church in the Savoy, Dean of Windsor, The Liturgy of the Church of England Asserted *(1662).*

Our Liturgy is an admirable piece of Devotion and Instruction. It is the marrow and substance of all that the Piety and Experience of the first five Centuries of Christianity found most proper to Edification in the publick Assemblies. It is a Compound of Texts of Scripture, of Exhortations to repentance, of Prayers, Hymns, Psalmes, Doxologies, Lessons, Creeds, and of Thanksgiving: of Forms for the Administration of Sacraments, and for other publick duties of Christians in the Church. And of Comminations against impenitent sinners. And all this mixed and diversified with great care expressly to quicken devotion, and stir up attention.

230

1662
Baptism

The Book of Common Prayer, 1662.

Work on the Book of Common Prayer began in 1548. In 1549 the First Prayer Book of Edward VI was issued and Parliament passed an Act of Uniformity to ensure that it was used everywhere. In 1552 the Second Prayer Book of Edward VI was issued with some revisions. The Elizabethan Book of Common Prayer of 1559 reissued this with only slight modifications. In 1662, after further revision, the Book of Common Prayer was issued in the form in which it is still used in England (with some revisions issued in 1928). The text given here is taken from the 1662 version. The Church of England retained the practice of infant baptism, and expresses in its liturgy its theology of baptism.

Then the Priest shall take the Child into his hands, and shall say to the Godfathers and Godmothers,

Name this Child.

And then naming it after them (if they shall certify him that the Child may well endure it) he shall dip it in the Water discreetly and warily... But if they certify that the Child is weak, it shall suffice to pour Water upon it, saying the foresaid words.

I baptize thee in the Name of the Father, and of the Son, and of the Holy Ghost. Amen.

Then the Priest shall say,
WE receive this Child into the Congregation of Christ's flock,[1] and sign *him* with the sign of the cross, in token that hereafter *he* shall not be ashamed to confess the Faith of Christ crucified, and manfully to fight under his banner against sin, the world, and the devil, and to continue Christ's faithful soldier and servant unto *his* life's end. Amen.

Then shall the Priest say,
Seeing now, dearly beloved brethren, that *this Child* is regenerate and grafted into the body of Christ's Church, let us give thanks unto Almighty God for these benefits, and with one accord make our prayers unto him, that *this Child* may lead the rest of *his* life according to this beginning....

Then shall the Priest say,
We yield thee hearty thanks, most merciful Father, that it hath pleased thee to regenerate *this Infant* with the Holy Spirit, to receive *him* for thine own *Child* by adoption, and to incorporate *him* into thy holy Church. And humbly we beseech thee to grant that *he* being dead unto sin, and living unto righteousness, and being buried with Christ in his death, may crucify the old man, and utterly abolish the whole body of sin; and that, as *he* is made *partaker* of the death of thy Son, *he* may also be *partaker* of his resurrection; so that finally, with the residue of thy holy Church, *he* may be an *inheritor* of thine everlasting kingdom; through Christ our Lord. *Amen.* ...

Then shall he add and say,
Ye are to take care that *this Child* be brought to the bishop to be confirmed by him, so soon as *he* can say the Creed, the Lord's Prayer and the Ten Commandments in the vulgar tongue, and be further instructed in the Church Catechism set forth for that purpose.

---

[1]   *Here the Priest shall make a Cross upon the Child's forehead.*

231

1662
Confirmation

The Book of Common Prayer, 1662.

Cf. nos. 21, 46.

Do ye here, in the presence of God, and of this Congregation, renew the solemn promise and vow that was made in your name at your *baptism*; ratifying and confirming the same in your own persons, and acknowledging yourselves bound to believe and to do all those things, which your Godfathers and Godmothers then undertook for you?

And every one shall audibly answer,

I do. ...

Then all of them in order kneeling before the Bishop, he shall lay his hand upon the head of every one severally, saying,

DEFEND, O Lord, this thy Child [or *this thy servant*] with thy heavenly grace, that *he* may continue thine for ever; and daily increase in the Holy Spirit, more and more, until *he* come unto the everlasting kingdom. Amen.

232

1662
Marriage

The Book of Common Prayer, 1662.

Dearly beloved, we are gathered together here in the sight of God, and in the face of this Congregation, to join together this man and this woman in holy Matrimony; which is an honourable estate, instituted by God in the time of man's innocency, signifying unto us the mystical union that is betwixt Christ and his Church; which holy estate Christ adorned and beautified with his presence, and first miracle that he wrought, in Cana of Galilee; and is commended of saint Paul to be honourable among all men: and therefore is not by any to be enterprized, nor taken in hand, unadvisedly, lightly, or wantonly, to satisfy men's carnal lusts and appetites, like brute beasts that have no understanding; but reverently, discreetly, advisedly, soberly, and in the fear of God; duly considering the causes for which Matrimony was ordained. First, It was ordained for the procreation of children, to be brought up in the fear and nurture of the Lord, and to the praise of his holy Name. Secondly, It was ordained for the remedy against sin, and to avoid fornication; that such persons as have not the gift of continency might marry, and keep themselves undefiled members of Christ's body. Thirdly, It was ordained for the mutual society, help, and comfort, that the one ought to have of the other, both in prosperity and adversity.

233

1662

The Nicene Creed
as used in the service of Holy Communion

The Book of Common Prayer, 1662. Cf. no. 23.

I believe in one God the Father Almighty, Maker of heaven and earth, And of all things visible and invisible: And in one Lord Jesus Christ, the only-begotten Son, Begotten of his Father before all worlds, God of God, Light of Light, Very God of Very God, Begotten, not made, Being of one substance with the Father, By whom all things were made: Who for us men and for our salvation came down from heaven, And was incarnate by the Holy Ghost of the Virgin Mary, And was made man, And was crucified also for us under Pontius Pilate. He suffered and was buried, And the third day he rose again according to the Scriptures, And ascended into heaven, And sitteth on the right hand of the Father. And he shall come again with glory to judge both the quick and the dead: Whose kingdom shall have no end. And I believe in the Holy Ghost, The Lord and giver of life, Who proceedeth from the Father and the Son, Who with the Father and the Son together is worshipped and glorified, Who spake by the Prophets. And I believe one Catholick and Apostolick Church. I acknowledge one baptism for the remission of sins. And I look for the resurrection of the dead, And the life of the world to come. Amen.

234

1662
The General Confession and the Absolution
at Holy Communion

The Book of Common Prayer, 1662. Cf. nos. 58–9.

Then shall the Priest say to them that come to receive the holy Communion,

Ye that do truly and earnestly repent you of your sins, and are in love and charity with your neighbours, and intended to lead a new life, following the commandments of God, and walking from henceforth in his holy ways: Draw near with faith, and take this holy Sacrament to your comfort; and make your humble confession to Almighty God, meekly kneeling upon your knees.

Then shall this general Confession be made, in the name of all those that are minded to receive the holy Communion, by one of the Ministers: both he and all the people kneeling humbly upon their knees and saying,

ALMIGHTY God, Father of our Lord Jesus Christ, Maker of all things, Judge of all men: We acknowledge and bewail our manifold sins and wickedness, Which we from time to time most grievously have committed, By thought, word, and deed, Against thy Divine Majesty, Provoking most justly thy wrath and indignation against us. We do earnestly repent, And are heartily sorry for these our misdoings; The remembrance of them is grievous unto us; The burden of them is intolerable. Have mercy upon us, Have mercy upon us, most merciful Father; For thy Son our Lord Jesus Christ's sake, Forgive us all that is past; And grant that we may ever hereafter Serve and please thee In newness of life, To the honour and glory of thy Name; Through Jesus Christ our Lord. Amen.

Then shall the Priest (or the Bishop, being present,) stand up, and turning himself to the people, pronounce this Absolution,

ALMIGHTY God, our heavenly Father, who of his great mercy hath promised forgiveness of sins to all them that with hearty repentance and true faith turn unto him; Have mercy upon you; pardon and deliver you from all your sins; confirm and strengthen you in all goodness; and bring you to everlasting life; through Jesus Christ our Lord. *Amen.*

235

1662
The importance of receiving the Eucharist 'worthily'

Book of Common Prayer, 1662.

My duty is to exhort you to consider the dignity of that holy mystery, and the great peril of the unworthy receiving thereof; and so to search and examine your own consciences, and that not lightly, and after the manner of dissemblers with God: but so that ye may come holy and clean to such a heavenly Feast,... The way and means thereto is; First, to examine your lives and conversations by the rule of God's commandments; and whereinsoever ye shall perceive yourselves to have offended, either by will, word, or deed, there to bewail your own sinfulness, and to confess yourselves to Almighty God, with full purpose of amendment of life. And if ye shall perceive your offences to be such as are not only against God, but also against your neighbours; then ye shall reconcile yourselves unto them; being ready to make restitution and satisfaction, according to the uttermost of your powers, for all injuries and wrongs done by you to any other; and being likewise ready to forgive others that have offended you, as you would have forgiveness of your offences at God's hand; for otherwise the receiving of the holy Communion doth nothing else but increase your damnation.... And because it is requisite, that no man should come to the holy Communion, but with a full trust in God's mercy, and with a quiet conscience; therefore if there be any of you, who by this means cannot quiet his own conscience herein, but requireth further comfort or counsel, let him come to me, or to some other discreet and learned Minister of God's Word, and open his grief; that by the ministry of God's holy Word he may receive the benefit of absolution, together with ghostly counsel and advice to the quieting of his conscience, and avoiding of all scruple and doubtfulness.

236

1662
Ordination, and the threefold Order of Ministry

The Ordinal (1662).

The Ordinal, first published in 1550, was revised in 1552. There were few changes in 1559, but in 1662 an important alteration was made necessary by Roman Catholic querying of the validity of Anglican Orders, on the grounds that the words 'Receive the Holy Ghost' did not specify that priesthood was to be conferred if they stood alone. The new version added 'for the office of a priest'. The Ordinal is not strictly part of the Book of Common Prayer, although commonly published with it. In the passage which follows we find two important assertations: that the Church of England intends to maintain the ancient threefold pattern of ordained ministry; and that no-one may act as an ordained minister unless he has been called and ordained within the order of the Church. See, too, following extracts on the ordering of deacons, priests and bishops.

It is evident unto all men diligently reading holy Scripture and ancient Authors, that from the Apostles' time there have been these Orders of Ministers in Christ's Church: Bishops, Priests, and Deacons.[1] Which offices were evermore had in such reverend estimation, that no man might presume to execute any of them, except he were first called, tried, examined, and known to have such qualities as are required for the same; and also by publick Prayer, with Imposition of Hands, were approved and admitted thereunto by lawful authority. And therefore, to the intent that these Orders may be continued, and reverently used and esteemed, in the Church of England; No man shall be accounted or taken to Be a lawful bishop, Priest, or Deacon in the Church of England, or suffered to execute any of the said functions, except he be called, tried, examined, and admitted thereunto, according to the Form hereafter following, or hath had formerly Episcopal Consecration or Ordination.

---

[1] This assertion needs to be qualified now. The New Testament speaks of bishops, presbyters and deacons but not of a settled pattern of three-fold ministry. Such a pattern emerged, however, very soon after the New Testament period.

237

1662
The Ordering of Deacons

The Ordinal (1662).

Here the specific tasks of the deacon are listed with an emphasis upon the practical care which was the special task of the deacons of the New Testament. It is stressed that he, like other ordained ministers, is to set an example to the flock of Christ; and that he owes canonical obedience to those in whose pastoral charge he himself serves.

And before the Gospel, the Bishop, sitting in his Chair, shall examine every one of them that are to be ordered, in the presence of the people, after this manner following.

DO you trust that you are inwardly moved by the Holy Ghost to take upon you this office and ministration to serve God, for the promoting of his glory, and the edifying of his people?
Answer. I trust so.

The Bishop. DO you think that you are truly called, according to the will of our Lord Jesus Christ, and the due order of the Realm, to the ministry of the Church?
Answer. I think so.

The Bishop. DO you unfeignedly believe all the Canonical Scriptures of the Old and New Testament?
Answer. I do believe them.

The Bishop. WILL you diligently read the same unto the people assembled in the Church where you shall be appointed to serve?
Answer. I will.

The Bishop. IT appertaineth to the office of deacon, in the Church where he shall be appointed to serve, to assist the priest in Divine Service, and specially when he ministereth the holy Communion, and to help him in the distribution thereof, and to read the holy Scriptures and Homilies in the Church; and to instruct the youth in the Catechism; in the absence of the Priest to baptize infants; and to preach, if he be admitted thereto by the Bishop. And furthermore, it is his office, where provision is so made, to search for the sick, poor, and impotent people of the Parish, to intimate their estates, names, and places where they dwell, unto the Curate, that by his exhortation they may be relieved with the alms of the

Parishioners, or others. Will you do this gladly and willingly?
Answer. I will do so, by the help of God.

The Bishop. WILL you apply all your diligence to frame and fashion your own lives, and the lives of your families, according to the doctrine of Christ; and to make both yourselves and them, as much as in you lieth, wholesome examples of the flock of Christ?
Answer. I will do so, the Lord being my helper.

The Bishop. WILL you reverently obey your Ordinary, and other chief Ministers of the Church, and them to whom the charge and government over you is committed, following with a glad mind and will their godly admonitions?
Answer. I will endeavour myself, the Lord being my helper.

Then the Bishop laying his hands severally upon the head of every one of them, humbly kneeling before him, shall say,

TAKE you authority to execute the office of a Deacon in the Church of God committed unto thee; In the Name of the Father, and of the Son, and of the Holy Ghost. Amen.

Then shall the Bishop deliver to every one of them the New Testament, saying,

TAKE thou authority to read the Gospel in the Church of God, and to preach the same, if thou be thereto licensed by the Bishop himself.

238

1662
The Ordering of Priests

The Ordinal (1662).

And now, that this present Congregation of Christ here assembled may also understand your minds and wills in these things, and that this your promise may the more move you to do your duties, ye shall answer plainly to these things, which we, in the Name of God, and of his Church, shall demand of you touching the same. DO you think in your heart that you be truly called, according to the will of our Lord Jesus Christ, and the order of this Church of *England*, to the Order and Ministry of Priesthood?
Answer. I think it.

The Bishop. ARE you persuaded that the holy Scriptures contain sufficiently all doctrine required of necessity for eternal salvation through faith in Jesus Christ? And are you determined out of the said Scriptures to instruct the people committed to your charge, and to teach nothing (as required of necessity to eternal salvation) but that which you shall be persuaded may be concluded and proved by the Scripture?

Answer. I am so persuaded, and have so determined by God's grace.

The Bishop. WILL you then give your faithful diligence always so to minister the doctrine and sacraments, and the discipline of Christ, as the Lord hath commanded, and as this Church and Realm hath received the same, according to the commandments of God; so that you may teach the people committed to your cure and charge with all diligence to keep and observe the same?

Answer. I will do so, by the help of the Lord.

The Bishop. WILL you be ready, with all faithful diligence, to banish and drive away all erroneous and strange doctrines contrary to God's Word; and to use both publick and private monitions and exhortations, as well to the sick as to the whole, within your cures, as need shall require, and occasion shall be given?

Answer. I will, the Lord being my helper.

The Bishop. WILL you be diligent in prayers, and in reading of the holy Scriptures, and in such studies as help to the knowledge of the same, laying aside the study of the world and the flesh?

Answer. I will endeavour myself so to do, the Lord being my helper.

The Bishop. WILL you be diligent to frame and fashion your own selves, and your families, according to the doctrine of Christ; and to make both yourselves and them, as much as in you lieth, wholesome examples and patterns to the flock of Christ?

Answer. I will apply myself thereto, the Lord being my helper.

The Bishop. WILL you maintain and set forwards, as much as lieth in you, quietness, peace, and love, among all Christian people, and specially among them that are or shall be committed to your charge?

Answer. I will so do, the Lord being my helper.

The Bishop. WILL you reverently obey your Ordinary, and other chief Ministers, unto whom is committed the charge and government over you; following with a glad mind and will their godly admonitions, and submitting yourselves to their godly judgements?

Answer. I will so do, the Lord being my helper.

Then shall the Bishop, standing up, say,

ALMIGHTY GOD, who hath given you this will to do all these things; Grant also unto you strength and power to perform the same; that he may accomplish his work which he hath begun in you; through Jesus Christ our Lord. *Amen.*

...The Bishop with the Priests present shall lay their hands severally upon the head of every one that receiveth the Order of Priesthood; the receivers humbly kneeling upon their knees, and the Bishop saying,

RECEIVE the Holy Ghost for the office and work of a Priest in the Church of God, now committed unto thee by the imposition of our hands. Whose sins thou dost forgive, they are forgiven; and whose sins thou dost retain, they are retained. And be thou a faithful dispenser of the Word of God, and of his holy Sacraments; In the Name of the Father, and of the Son, and of the Holy Ghost. Amen.

Then the Bishop shall deliver to every one of them kneeling the Bible into his hand, saying,

TAKE thou authority to preach the Word of God, and to minister the holy Sacraments in the Congregation, where thou shalt be lawfully appointed thereunto.

239

1662
The Consecration of bishops

The Ordinal (1662).

After the gospel, and the Nicene Creed, and the Sermon are ended, the elected Bishop (vested with his Rochet) shall be presented by two Bishops unto the Archbishop of that Province, (or to some other Bishop appointed by lawful commission,) the Archbishop sitting in his Chair, near the holy Table, and the Bishops that present him saying,

MOST reverend Father in God, we present unto you this godly and well-learned man to be ordained and consecrated bishop.

Then shall the Archbishop demand the Queen's Mandate for the Consecration, and cause it to be read. And then shall be ministered unto them the Oath of due obedience to the Archbishop, as followeth.

The Oath of obedience to the Archbishop

IN the Name of God, Amen. I *N*. chosen Bishop of the Church and See of *N*. do profess and promise all due reverence and obedience to the Archbishop and to the Metropolitical Church of *N*. and to their Successors: So help me God, through Jesus Christ. ...

Then the Archbishop, sitting in his Chair, shall say to him that is to be consecrated,

BROTHER, forasmuch as the holy Scripture and the ancient Canons command we should not be hasty in laying on hands, and admitting any person to government in the Church of Christ, which he hath purchased with no less price than the effusion of his own blood: Before I admit you to this administration, I will examine you in certain articles, to the end that the Congregation present may have a trial, and bear witness, how you be minded to behave yourself in the Church of God.

ARE you persuaded that you be truly called to this ministration, according to the will of our Lord Jesus Christ, and the order of this Realm?

Answer. I am so persuaded.

The Archbishop. ARE you persuaded that the holy Scriptures contain sufficiently all doctrine required of necessity for eternal salvation through faith in Jesus Christ? And are you determined out of the same holy Scriptures to instruct the people committed to your charge, and to teach or maintain nothing as required of necessity to eternal salvation, but that which you shall be persuaded may be concluded and proved by the same?

Answer. I am so persuaded and determined, by God's grace.

The Archbishop. WILL you then faithfully exercise yourself in the same holy Scriptures, and call upon God by prayer, for the true understanding of the same; so as ye may be able by them to teach and exhort with wholesome doctrine, and to withstand and convince the gainsayers?

Answer. I will so do, by the help of God.

The Archbishop. BE you ready, with faithful diligence, to banish and drive away all erroneous and strange doctrine contrary to God's Word; and both privately and openly call upon and encourage others to the same?
Answer. I am ready, the Lord being my helper.

The Archbishop. WILL you deny all ungodliness and worldly lusts, and live soberly, righteously and godly in this present world; that you may shew yourself in all things an example of good works unto others, that the adversary may be ashamed, having nothing to say against you?
Answer. I will so do, the Lord being my helper.

The Archbishop. WILL you maintain and set forward (as much as shall lie in you) quietness, peace, and love among all men; and such as be unquiet, disobedient and criminous within your Diocese, correct and punish, according to such authority as ye have by God's Word, and as to you shall be committed by the Ordinance of this Realm?
Answer. I wil do so, by the help of God.

The Archbishop. WILL you be faithful in ordaining, sending, or laying hands upon others?
Answer. I will so be, by the help of God.

The Archbishop. WILL you shew yourself gentle, and be merciful for Christ's sake to poor and needy people, and to all strangers destitute of help?
Answer. I will so shew myself, by God's help.

Then the Archbishop, standing up, shall say,

ALMIGHTY GOD, our heavenly Father, who hath given you a good will to do all these things; Grant also unto you strength and power to perform the same; that he accomplishing in you the good work which he hath begun, ye may be found perfect and irreprehensible at the latter day; through Jesus Christ our Lord. *Amen....*

Then the Archbishop and Bishops present shall lay their hands upon the head of the elected Bishop kneeling before them upon his knees, the Archbishop saying,

RECEIVE the Holy Ghost for the office and work of a bishop in the Church of God, now committed unto thee by the imposition of our hands; in the Name of the Father, and of the Son, and of the Holy Ghost. Amen. And remember that thou stir up the grace of God which is given thee by this imposition of our hands: for God hath not given us the spirit of fear, but of power, and love, and soberness.

Then the Archbishop shall deliver him the Bible, saying,

GIVE heed unto reading, exhortation, and doctrine. Think upon the things contained in this Book. Be diligent in them, that the increase coming thereby may be manifest unto all men. Take heed unto thyself, and to doctrine, and be diligent in doing them: for by so doing thou shalt both save thyself and them that hear thee. Be to the flock of Christ a shepherd, not a wolf; feed them, devour them not. Hold up the weak, heal the sick, bind up the broken, bring again the outcasts, seek the lost. Be so merciful, that ye be not too remiss; so minister discipline, that you forget not mercy; that when the chief Shepherd shall appear ye may receive the never-fading crown of glory; through Jesus Christ our Lord. *Amen.*

240

1662
Royal ratification of the Thirty-Nine Articles

The Thirty-Nine Articles, Prefatory Declaration of Charles I (1625–49).

This Declaration is printed before the Articles in the 1662 Prayer Book. The text illustrates the complex character of the mutual authorisation by Church and State set up by the sixteenth century legislation. The monarch both subscribes to and ratifies the Thirty-Nine Articles; he also seeks to impose sanctions by secular authority to ensure an end to dispute, and orthodoxy in the Church of England.

HIS MAJESTY'S DECLARATION Being by God's Ordinance, according to Our just Title, Defender of the Faith, and Supreme Governor of the Church, within these Our Dominions, We hold it most agreeable to this Our Kingly Office, and Our own religious Zeal, to conserve and maintain the Church committed to Our Charge, in Unity of true Religion, and in the Bond of Peace; and not to suffer unnecessary Disputations, Altercations, or Questions to be raised, which may nourish Faction both in the Church and

Commonwealth. We have therefore, upon mature Deliberation, and with the Advice of so many of Our bishops as might conveniently be called together, thought fit to make this Declaration following: That the Articles of the Church of England (which have been allowed and authorized heretofore, and which Our Clergy generally have subscribed unto) do contain the true Doctrine of the Church of England agreeable to God's Word: which We do therefore ratify and confirm, requiring all Our loving Subjects to continue in the uniform Profession thereof, and prohibiting the least difference from the said Articles; which to that End We command to be new printed, and this Our Declaration to be published therewith. That We are Supreme Governor of the Church of England: And that if any difference arise about the external Policy, concerning the Injunctions, Canons, and other Constitutions whatsoever thereto belonging, the Clergy in their Convocation is to order and settle them, having first obtained leave under Our Broad Seal so to do: and We approving their said Ordinances and Constitutions; providing that none be made contrary to the Laws and Customs of the Land. That out of Our Princely Care that the Churchmen may do the Work which is proper unto them, the bishops and Clergy, from time to time in Convocation, upon their humble Desire, shall have Licence under Our Broad Seal to deliberate of, and to do all such Things, as, being made plain by them, and assented unto by Us, shall concern the settled Continuance of the Doctrine and Discipline of the Church of England now established; from which We will not endure any varying or departing in the least Degree. That for the present, though some differences have been ill raised, yet We take comfort in this, that all Clergymen within Our Realm have always most willingly subscribed to the Articles established; which is an argument to Us, that they all agree in the true, usual, literal meaning of the said Articles; and that even in those curious points, in which the present differences lie, men of all sorts take the Articles of the Church of England to be for them; which is an argument again, that none of them intend any desertion of the Articles established. That therefore in these both curious and unhappy differences, which have for so many hundred years, in different times and places, exercised the Church of Christ, We will, that all further curious search be laid aside, and these disputes shut up in God's promises, as they be generally set forth to us in the holy Scriptures, and the general meaning of the Articles of the

Church of England according to them. And that no man hereafter shall either print, or preach, to draw the Article aside any way, but shall submit to it in the plain and full meaning thereof: and shall not put his own sense or comment to be the meaning of the Article, but shall take it in the literal and grammatical sense. That if any publick Reader in either of Our Universities, or any Head or Master of a College, or any other person respectively in either of them, shall affix any new sense to any Article, or shall publickly read, determine, or hold any publick Disputation, or suffer any such to be held either way, in either the Universities or Colleges respectively; or if any Divine in the Universities shall preach or print any thing either way, other than is already established in Convocation with Our Royal Assent; he, or they the Offenders, shall be liable to Our displeasure, and the Church's censure in Our Commission Ecclesiastical, as well as any other: And We will see there shall be due Execution upon them.

241

1662
The visitation of the sick

The Book of Common Prayer, 1662.

A provision for anointing replaced the Sacrament of Extreme Unction of the medieval Church in the 1549 Prayer Book, but in the versions of 1552 and later it is omitted from the Order for the Visitation of the Sick. Cf. nos. 46, 377.

Here the Minister shall rehearse the Articles of the Faith, saying thus,

DOST thou believe in God the Father Almighty, Maker of heaven and earth? And in Jesus Christ his only begotten Son our Lord? And that he was conceived by the Holy Ghost, born of the Virgin Mary; that he suffered under Pontius Pilate, was crucified, dead, and buried; that he went down into hell, and also did rise again the third day; that he ascended into heaven, and sitteth at the right hand of God the Father Almighty; and from thence shall come again at the end of the world, to judge the quick and the dead? And dost thou believe in the Holy Ghost; the holy Catholick Church; The Communion of saints; the Remission of sins; the resurrection of the flesh; and everlasting life after death?

The sick person shall answer,

All this I steadfastly believe...

Here shall the sick person be moved to make a special confession of his sins, if he feel his conscience troubled with any weighty matter. After which confession, the priest shall absolve him (if he humbly and heartily desire it) after this sort.

OUR Lord Jesus Christ, who hath left power to his Church to absolve all sinners who truly repent and believe in him, of his great mercy forgive thee thine offences: And by his authority committed to me, I absolve thee from all thy sins, In the Name of the Father, and of the Son, and of the Holy Ghost. Amen.

And then the priest shall say the Collect following.

Let us pray.

O MOST merciful God, who, according to the multitude of thy mercies, dost so put away the sins of those who truly repent, that thou rememberest them no more: Open thine eye of mercy upon this thy servant, who most earnestly desireth pardon and forgiveness. Renew in *him*[1] (most loving Father) whatsoever hath been decayed by the fraud and malice of the devil, or by *his* own carnal will and frailness; preserve and continue this sick member in the unity of the Church; consider *his* contrition, accept *his* tears, asswage *his* pain, as shall seem to thee most expedient for *him*. And forasmuch as *he* putteth *his* full trust only in thy mercy, impute not unto *him his* former sins, but strengthen *him* with thy blessed Spirit; and, when thou art pleased to take *him* hence, take *him* unto thy favour, through the merits of thy most dearly beloved Son Jesus Christ our Lord. *Amen.*

242

1662
Our need for Grace

The Catechism.

The Catechism, printed before the rite of Confirmation in the Book of Common Prayer, was enlarged in 1604 to meet the request of the Puritans at the Hampton Court Conference for more detailed treatment, especially of the

---

[1]   or *her*

Sacraments. We quote here from the 1662 text. This extract stresses the sinner's helplessness and need for grace. Cf. nos. 47, 61.

Thou art not able to... walk in the commandmants of God, and to serve him, without his special grace; which thou must learn at all times to call for by diligent prayer.

243

1662
What is a Sacrament?

The Catechism. (See no. 242)

On the definition of a Sacrament, cf. nos. 108ff, p. 118, note 3 and Article xxv of the Thirty-Nine Articles

Question. What meanest thou by this word *Sacrament?*
Answer. I mean an outward and visible sign of an inward and spiritual grace given unto us, ordained by Christ himself, as a means whereby we receive the same, and a pledge to assure us thereof.
Question. How many parts are there in a Sacrament?
Answer. Two: the outward visible sign, and the inward spiritual grace.
Question. What is the outward visible sign or form in baptism?
Answer. Water: wherein the person is baptized, *In the Name of the Father, and of the Son, and of the Holy Ghost.*
Question. What is the inward and spiritual grace?
Answer. A death unto sin, and a new birth unto righteousness: for being by nature born in sin, and the children of wrath, we are hereby made the children of grace.
Question. What is required of persons to be baptized?
Answer. Repentance, whereby they forsake sin: and faith, whereby they steadfastly believe the promises of God, made to them in that Sacrament.
Question. Why then are infants baptized, when by reason of their tender age they cannot perform them?
Answer. Because they promise them both by their sureties: which promise, when they come to age, themselves are bound to perform.
Question. Why was the Sacrament of the Lord's Supper ordained?

Answer. For the continual remembrance of the sacrifice of the death of Christ, and of the benefits which we receive thereby.
Question. What is the outward part or sign of the Lord's Supper?
Answer. Bread and Wine, which the Lord hath commanded to be received.
Question. What is the inward part, or thing signified?
Answer. The Body and Blood of Christ, which are verily and indeed taken and received by the faithful in the Lord's Supper.
Question. What are the benefits whereof we are partakers thereby?
Answer. The strengthening and refreshing of our souls by the Body and Blood of Christ, as our bodies are by the Bread and Wine.
Question. What is required of them who come to the Lord's Supper?
Answer. To examine themselves, whether they repent them truly of their former sins, stedfastly purposing to lead a new life; have a lively faith in God's mercy through Christ, with a thankful remembrance of his death; and be in charity with all men.

244

1666
Judging the meaning of Scripture

Daniel Whitby (1638–1726), divine and advocate of reconciliation with the Nonconformists, possibly a Unitarian in his last years, An Answer to Sure Footing *(Oxford, 1666), pp. 28–30,* More and Cross, *pp. 116–17.*

Cf. nos. 193, 211, 246 on the use of reason.

Reason in judging of the sense of Scripture is regulated partly by principles of Faith, partly by Tradition, partly by Catholic maxims of her own. First, By principles of Faith. For Scripture is to be interpreted *secundum analogiam Fidei*; that is (say we) particular Texts of Scripture, when dubious, are so to be interpreted as not to contradict the Fundamentals of Faith, or any doctrine which evidently and fully stands asserted in the Word of God. And secondly since Scripture cannot contradict itself, when any paragraph of Scripture absolutely considered is ambiguous, that sense must necessarily obtain which is repugnant to no other paragraph, against what may be so; and thus may Scripture regulate me in the sense of Scripture, and what I know of it lead me to the sense of what I do not.

Secondly, By Tradition. For since Tradition is necessary to assure us that there were once such men as the apostles who delivered that Christianity and these Scriptures to us which we now embrace, to question the sufficiency of the like tradition, to assure me of the sense of Scripture is virtually to call in question the motives which induce us to believe in such... Note only that I speak here of a 'like tradition', to which two things are requisite. First, That it be as general[1] as that of Scripture. And Secondly, That it be such as evidenceth itself by reason to have been no forgery (as here it doth, it being morally impossible that the whole Church, in the delivery of Scripture to us, should deceive or be deceived). For the infallibility of Tradition doth not consist entirely in the delivery of such a doctrine, but in the assurance which it gives my reason that it could not possibly have been embraced upon other terms. The baptism of Infants is at present (as the Communicating of Infants was of old) the tradition of the Church, but this gives no unquestionable assurance of the truth or derivation of these customs from our Lord and His apostles, for haply the Church embraced them upon other motives, — the first from a conceived analogy therein to Circumcision, the second from a mistake of that of the Evangelist, *Except you eat my flesh, etc.*...

Thirdly, Reason is herein guided by her proper maxims and cannot rationally admit of anything as the sense of Scripture which is apparently repugnant to them. For seeing it is impossible to yield a rational assent without reason, it must be more impossible to do it against reason. Besides, right reason must be true; and therefore should a revelation be manifestly repugnant unto right reason, it must equally be opposed to truth.

245

1669–70

The harmony of Scripture

George Bull (1634–1710), Bishop of St David's, Harmonia Apostolica *(1669–70), (Oxford, 1842), p. 3.*

---

[1]   Compare Vincent of Lérins' *dictum*, no. 54.

George Bull (1634–1710) defended the catholicity of Anglicanism. Here he touches on the ancient and classic difficulty of the apparent contradictions in Scripture.

All, who are truly called Christians, fully allow both the infallible authority of Scripture, and the most perfect harmony of its parts; still, unhappily, it too often occurs that no few apparent contradictions and almost inextricable difficulties are found in that sacred volume.

246

1671
Faith and scientific proof

Daniel Whitby (1638–1726), divine and advocate of reconciliation with the Nonconformists, possibly a Unitarian in his last years, An Endeavour to evince the Certainty of the Christian Faith *(Oxford, 1671), Preface, Moore and Cross pp. 221-2.*

Cf. nos. 193, 211, 244.

If then you do reject a Providence because you are not able to conceive God's Omnipresence or any other attribute on which this Providence depends, if you renounce the Mysteries of Christian Faith because you cannot apprehend them, have you not equal reasons to reject the notions of infinite unbounded space, of an external flux of time, or an indivisible eternity, which yet your reason must acknowledge? Must you not question the existence of the souls of men and brutes, a being not sufficient to conceive that spirits, if confined to points, can perform any of those actions which are ascribed to them, or that they can diffuse themselves through bodies, receive impressions from them, or make impressions on them, or that mere matter should perceive, reflect, and reason, or have any sense of pain and pleasure? Lastly, must not this principle oblige you to question the existence of all material compounds? For who is able to conceive that indivisibles can be united? Or that a grain of sand can be for ever divisible and have as many parts as the whole world?

247

1672–84
Public prayer

Thomas Comber, Dean of Durham, A Companion to the Temple, or a Help to Devotion in the Use of the Common Prayer *(1672–6, 1684), Preface.*

There are two principal ends of the Worship of God, *The Glory of him that is Worshipped,* and *the Benefit of the Worshippers....* But whether we look on them single or conjoyned, no part of *Divine Worship* doth so much express and advance God's glory, nor so directly tend to Man's good as *Publick Prayer*; in which we make the most universal solemn acknowledgments of our Obligations unto, and Dependence upon, the Supreme Lord of all the World; and by which all the Servants of God in all times, places and circumstances, do with heart and voice, by common consent reveal their wants, and obtain supplies for them. So that we may call this the *Life and Soul of Religion,* the *Anima Mundi,* that universal Soul which quickens, unites and moves the whole Christian World. Nor is the case of a private Man more desperate, when he breathes no more in secret Prayer, than the condition of a Church is, where publick Devotions cease.

248

1686
Respect for the Virgin Mary

William Clagett, A Discourse Concerning the Worship of the Blessed Virgin and the Saints *(London, 1686), 3, 1, More and Cross, pp. 535–6.*

Cf. nos. 73, 75 on the veneration of saints.

As to the Virgin Mary in particular, we do with men and Angels acknowledge that she was 'blessed amongst women',[1] since she brought forth the Saviour of mankind and the Lord of Heaven and earth; since she was not the Mother only, but the Virgin Mother

---

[1]   Luke 1.42

also of Our Lord, and conceived Him by the power of the Holy Ghost. Which confession so honourable to her, being inseparable from a right belief concerning Our Lord Jesus, we do not only set it forth upon the anniversary of the Annunciation, but frequently also in our sermons and daily in the Creed.

6
THE CHURCH IN, AND
OUT OF, ENGLAND
1688–1784

249

1698
The wonder of the incarnation

Robert South (1634–1716), opponent of the Toleration Act of 1689, and defender of the orthodox doctrine of the Trinity. Twelve Sermons *(London, 1698), III, pp. 367f., More and Cross, p. 265.*

But now was there ever any wonder comparable to this! To behold Divinity thus clothed in Flesh! The Creator of all things humbled not only to the company, but also to the cognation of His creatures! It is as if we should imagine the whole world not only represented upon, but also contained in, one of our little artificial globes; or the body of the sun enveloped in a cloud as big as a man's hand, all which would be looked upon as astonishing impossibilities, — and yet as short of the other as the greatest finite is of an infinite, between which the disparity is immeasurable. For that God should thus in a manner transform Himself, and subdue and master all His glories to a possibility of human apprehension and converse, the best reason would have thought it such a thing as God could not do, had it not seen it actually done. It is as it were to cancel the essential distances of things, to remove the bounds of Nature, to bring Heaven and Earth, and (what is more) both ends of the contradiction, together.

250

1698
The individual's need of the ordinary means of grace

Robert Nelson, layman and philanthropist, The Practice of True Devotion, in Relation to the End, as well as the Means of Religion *(1698).*

There is another *Extream*, which I hope is the case of but few; but since it is incident to those who make the greatest *Pretences* to *Spirituality*, it ought to be taken Notice of; which is, from a Purpose of *greater Perfection*, to lay aside the *ordinary Means of Grace*, which God has established: They *frequent* not the *Instructions* of *God's Ambassadors*, because they find themselves more enlightned from their own Meditations: They approach not frequently the *Holy Communion*, to feed themselves with the *Bread of Life* there distributed, because they feel not those *Raptures*, which they are supplied with from their own *Contemplations*: They seem to have a *mean Opinion* of all the holy *Functions* of the *priesthood*, because the Men that exercise them are not *animated* with their *Spirit*. Now that this is a great *Delusion*, is apparent, because it contradicts that *Order* and *Method* that *God* has *revealed* for the attaining everlasting Happiness. He has set apart an *Order* of *Men* under the *Gospel*, on purpose to assist us in the great *Business* of our *Salvation*; He has given them *Power* to declare to us the *Terms* upon which it is to be obtained; they are the *deputed Ministers* of Reconciliation, and therefore we ought to attend their Instructions: He has farther *Authoriz'd* them to administer Sacraments, that we might be made *Members* of *Christ's Body*, and nourish'd with all *Goodness*; these holy Actions receive their *Efficacy* from the *divine* Institution, which we must keep close to, if we pretend to receive the *Influences* and *Assistances* of God's Holy *Spirit*. To enlighten our *Understandings* in the Knowledge of our Duty, to influence our *Wills* in the Practice of it, he has *revealed* to us the holy *Scripture*, which, as it lays down the best Method for attaining that *Perfection* we are capable of in this Life; so it furnishes us with the best *Arguments* for the Prosecution of it; and though I am satisfied, that the Spirit of God does farther *direct* and *excite* those that seriously and reverently apply themselves to the Use of this Rule of *Belief* and *Practice*; yet they that lay it aside, under Pretence of *Inspirations* of equal *Authority*, have reason to *doubt* their own *Inspirations*. For if they proceeded from the Spirit of God, they would put the greatest *Stress* and highest *Value* upon what has been *stamped* with his *Mark*, by being *confirmed* by the Testimony of Miracles, the Demonstration of the Spirit, and what has been received by the *Catholick Church*, as the undoubted Word of God: Besides, since it is agreed that we are *unable* of our selves to do any Thing that is good; and that the

Grace of God is necessary to strengthen our *Weakness*, and to assist us in the Performance of our *Duty*; how can we expect the Influences of his Holy Spirit, if we *neglect* the Use of those Means which are prescribed by *divine Institution*, to convey to us the Benefits and Advantages of it.

251

1701
The need for government in the Church

Thomas Brett (1667–1744), liturgical scholar, An Account of Church-Government and Governours *(London, 1701) pp. 1, 5.*

The New Testament does so plainly assert a Government in the Church, and so apparently distinguish the Members of Christ's Mystical Body into that one would think this Matter could not admit of a dispute... which power before his Ascension Christ delegated to certain persons whom he sent into all the world with the same Power and Authority, to Collect, Settle, and Govern the Church, which he himself had before received of the Father. The Power was by no means given to all the Faithful, for if it was, all Christians must be made Governours of the Church, and then where shall we find any to be governed?

252

1702
The authority to summon a Synod or Council

Edmund Gibson (1669–1748), Bishop of London, Synodus Anglicana *(1702, repr. 1967), pp. 15–17.*

Edmund Gibson (1669–1748) wrote his *Synodus Anglicana: or the Constitution and Proceedings of an English Convocation* in the course of his participation in the controversy over Convocation at the turn of the century. Cf. comment on Article xxi of the Thirty-Nine Articles (no. 225).

When his majesty, by the advice of his Council, resolves to Summon his Parliament, and with it a Convocation, he signifies his Royal Pleasure by Writ to the Archbishop... Upon the reception whereof, his Grace always proceeded to summon it in the fixt and Canonical Method, that he ever us'd in calling of Convocations upon his own Motion, without that Writ. For tho' the King, as having a Right to the Assistance of the clergy, had also a Right to be obey'd by the Archbishop, in calling them together for that end; yet in the dispatch of that business, he left them to proceed according to the known Rules of a Provincial Synod, viz. to be summon'd before their Metropolitan, and to the place he should think fit to appoint... For the Archbishop has a Right to call a Convocation at pleasure, till the Statute 25 H.8.c.19[1] absolutely refrained him from doing it, unless empower'd by the King's Writ: which effected this Alteration in the Summons, that... now he is restrained from the Exercise of that Authority, till he receive leave or direction from the Prince: the summons upon that intimation of the Royal Pleasure, being still issued in his Grace's Name, and under the Archiepiscopal Seal; that is, remaining as properly Authoritative as before.

253

1702
The continuity of practice in the holding of Anglican Synods

E. Gibson (1669–1748), Bishop of London, Synodus Anglicana *(1702, repr. 1967) p. vi.*

Gibson says, p. iv, that he had examined Registers of Convocation from 1356.

In response to those who have asked how far the Registers before the Reformation are to be regarded in the Methods of Holding an English Synod... after the Reformation, they continue the self-same Ways of acting, that were established before.

---

[1]   That is, of the twenty-fifth year of the reign of Henry VIII.

254

1703
The destructiveness of polemic

William Wake (1657–1737), Archbishop of Canterbury, The State of the Church and Clergy of England *(London, 1703), Preface, p. i.*

There is something in the Nature of Controversial Writing so corruptive of Morality, so apt to destroy some of the Noblest Graces of a Christian Life, that I look upon the case to be much the same in That, as it is in Other Wars, and that nothing less than an absolute Necessity ought to engage a Good Man in Either.... I would to God our Own Time had not given us too many Instances of it; to the scandal of our Religion.... But of all kinds of Controversies, as there are usually none more unseasonable, so neither are there any which a Man would less desire to be engaged in, than those which arise among such as are Members of the same Church, as well as of the same Civil Society; and have thereby the strictest Obligations lying upon them to Love and Unity with one another.

255

1706
The powers of bishops

George Hickes, The Dignity of the Episcopal Order *(1695–1707), finally published in answer to Tindal's* The Rights of the Christian Church Asserted *(1706),* Works *(Oxford 1847), II. p. 301.*

Hickes expresses here a strong 'aristocratic' doctrine of the 'governing' powers of bishops. Compare the series of extracts nos. 200-6.

As [bishops] had power [in New Testament times] to make laws and orders, and give directions for the regulation of the Church, and all orders of men in it, so had they power to coerce or compel their subjects of the clergy and laity, without distinction of persons, to obey them, by spiritual censures and punishments, particularly by excommunication, which in the most holy and pure times was ever accounted more dreadful than death itself. This power of spiritual coercion was promised by Christ to the apostles...[1] ... Sir, I have wrote all this to help you to a just idea of the episcopal office and power, and to show you what reason I had... to call the spiritual princes and their dioceses principalities.

256

1707
Excommunication

George Hickes, Two Treatises on the Christian Priesthood and the Dignity of the Episcopal Order *(1707) (Oxford, 1847), p. 159.*

It is plain that the Christians of the second century looked upon the censured sinner as precondemned by God; and that the sentence of excommunication, and by consequence of absolution, was not only declarative but judicial.

257

1708
Individual participation in public worship

William Beveridge (1637–1708), Bishop of St Asaph, The Great Necessity and Advantage of Public Prayer and Frequent Communion, designed to revive Primitive Piety, with Meditations, Ejaculations, and Prayers before, at, and after the Sacrament *(1708).*

Here then is the great Task we have to do in all our *publick Devotions*, even to keep our Spirits or Hearts in a right Posture all the While that we are before GOD, who sees them, and takes special Notice of their Motions: That we may *pray with the Spirit, and pray with the Understanding also*, as S. *Paul* did,[1] I call this a great Task, because I know it is the hardest Work we have to do. Our *Thoughts* being so very quick and nimble, so unconstant and

---

[1]   Matthew 16.19
[1]   I Corinthians 16.15

desultory, that it is difficult to keep them close to the Work we are about, so as to serve the Lord without Distraction. But it is a Thing that must be done, if we desire to receive any real *Benefit* and *Comfort* from our Devotions. And blessed be GOD, by his Assistance we may all do it, if we will but set ourselves in good earnest about it, and observe these few Rules, which may be very helpful unto us in it.

First. When you go to the House of GOD *at the Hour of Prayer*, be sure to leave all worldly Cares and Business behind you... And now set yourselves, in good Earnest; as in GOD's Sight, keeping your Eye only upon Him, looking upon Him as observing what you think, as well as what you say or do, all the while you are before Him.

While one or more of the *Sentences* out of GOD's Holy Word (wherewith we very properly begin our Devotions to Him) are *reading*, apprehend it as spoken by GOD Himself at first, and now repeated in your Ears, to put you in mind of something, which He would have you to believe or do upon this Occasion.

While the *Exhortation* is reading, hearken diligently to it, and take particular Notice of every Word and Expression in it, as contrived on purpose to prepare you for the Service of GOD, by possessing your Minds with a due Sense of His special Presence with you, and of the great Ends of your Coming before Him at this Time.

While you are *confessing* your Sins with your Mouth, be sure to do it also in your Hearts, calling to Mind every one, as many as he can, of those particular Sins which he hath committed, either by *doing what he ought not to do*, or *not doing what he ought*, so as to repent sincerely of them, and steadfastly resolve never to commit them any more.

While the Minister is pronouncing the *Absolution* in the Name of GOD, every one should lay hold upon it for himself, so as firmly to believe, that upon true Repentance, and Faith in Christ, he is now discharged and *absolved* from all his Sins, as certainly as if GOD Himself had declared it with His own Mouth, as He hath often done it before, and now, by His Ministers.

While you, together with the Minister, are repeating the *Psalms* or *Hymns*, to the Honour and Glory of GOD, observe the Minister's Part as well as your own; and lift up your Hearts, together with your Voices, to the highest Pitch you can, in acknowledging, magnifying and praising the Infinite Wisdom, and Power, and Goodness, and Glory of the most High GOD in all His Works, *the Wonders that He* hath done, and still *doth, for the Children of Men,* and for you among the rest.

While GOD's *Word* is *read* in either of the Chapters, whether of the *Old or New Testament, receive it not as the Word of Men, but (as it is in Truth) the Word of God, which effectually worketh in you that believe,*[2] And therefore *hearken* to it with the same Attention, Reverence and Faith, as you would have done, if you had stood by Mount *Sinai,* when GOD proclaimed the *Law,* and by our Saviour's Side, when He published the gospel.

While the *Prayers* or *Collects* are reading, although you ought not to repeat them aloud, to the Disturbance of other People; yet you must repeat them in your Hearts, your Minds accompanying the Minister from one Prayer to another, and from one Part of each Prayer to the other, all along with Affections suitable to the Matter sounding in your Ears, humbly adoring and admiring GOD according to the Names, Properties or Works, which are attributed to Him at the Beginning of each *Prayer,* earnestly desiring the good Things which are asked Him in the Body of it, for your selves or others; and steadfastly believing in *Jesus Christ* for His Granting of them, when He is named, as He is at the End of every Prayer, except that of S. *Chrysostom*; because that is directed immediately to Christ Himself, as promising, that *when Two or Three are gathered together in His Name, He will grant their Requests*; which is therefore very properly put at the End of all our daily Prayers, and also of the *Litany,* (most Part whereof is directed also to our Saviour) that when we have made all our *Common Supplications* unto Him, we may act our Faith in Him again for GOD's granting of them according to His said *Promise*; and so may be dismissed with, *The Grace of our Lord Jesus Christ, the Love of God the Father, and the Communion or Fellowship of the Holy Ghost*; under which are comprehended all the Blessings, that we have, or can desire, to make us completely happy, both now and forever.

After the *Blessing,* it may be expedient still to continue for some Time upon your *Knees,* humbly beseeching Almighty GOD to pardon what He hath seen amiss in you, since you came into His

---

[2]   I Thessalonians 2.13

presence; and that he would be graciously pleased to hear the Prayers, and to accept of the Praises, which you have now offered up unto Him, thro' the Merits of *Jesus Christ* our only Mediator and Advocate.

These few *Directions* I thought good to lay before you, a being of great Use towards the right Performance of your publick Devotions, so as that they may be both acceptable to GOD, and profitable to yourselves.

258

1637–1708
The catholicity of the Anglican Church and its grounding in Holy Scripture

William Beveridge, Bishop of St Asaph (1637–1708), Thesaurus Theologicus, Works *(Oxford, 1847), vol. 10, p. 604.*

The doctrine of our Church was so reformed that it agrees exactly with God's holy word, as understood and interpreted by his whole Catholic Church.

259

1712
The ordinariness of bishops

John Hughes of Jesus College, Cambridge, Preliminary Dissertation to the edition of St Chrysostom, De Sacerdotio, *George Hickes, Appendix 8 in Hickes,* Christian priesthood *(Oxford, 1848), vol. III, pp. 327–9.*

Here the issue is whether bishops are an 'ordinary' or an 'extraordinary' provision of the Holy Spirit in the ministry of the Church. Cf. nos. 148, 189, 200.

[Episcopacy has been] ordinary and convenient for the Church at all times ... Since therefore all the characters and indications contained in the Epistles themselves do apparently declare his ministry to have been ordinary, we are under an obligation to assert that St Timothy was an ordinary minister, and that he exercised no more than an ordinary authority, such as is very necessary in the Church at all times... I cannot but think that St Timothy afforded us a most clear example of episcopal government. The same may be said of Titus... The second reason for which I asserted that Timothy and Titus were ordinary ministers... is taken from the contant opinion of the primitive Church... This is also farther proved from the catalogues of bishops compiled by Eusebius Bishop of Caesarea, by which we perceive, at first sight, that the primitive Church acknowledged no other form of government but the episcopal.

260

before 1715
General Councils

Gilbert Burnet (1689–1715), An Exposition of the Thirty-Nine Articles (Oxford, 1845), p. 239.

For the four general councils, which this Church declares she receives, they are received only because we are persuaded from the Scriptures that their decisions were made according to them... we reverence those councils for the sake of their doctrine; but we do not believe the doctrine for the authority of the councils.

261

1637–1708
Notes of the Church

William Beveridge, Bishop of St Asaph (1637–1708), Ecclesia Anglicana Ecclesia Catholica, Works, ed. J. Bliss (Oxford, 1846), vol. 2, pp. 104–5.

William Beveridge (1637–1708), Bishop of St Asaph, contributed to the debate about the catholicity of the Anglican Church. Here he discusses the reformers' view that the 'Notes' of the true Church are the preaching of the Word and the administration of the sacraments. He stresses that there is also the need for order as manifested in the provision for an ordained ministry in the Church (cf. Thirty-Nine Articles, xix).

Though the Church be always a congregation of faithful men, yet every congregation of faithful men is not a Church... wherein the pure word of God is preached, and the sacraments be duly administered according to God's ordinance, in all those things that of necessity are requisite to the same....The Church cannot subsist without church-officers, such whose duty it is thus to preach the word and administer the sacraments.

262

1716
The beauty of holiness in common prayer

Thomas Bisse, Preacher at the Rolls Chapel, Chancellor of Hereford Cathedral, The Beauty of Holiness in the Common Prayer *(1716).*

(On 'Worship the Lord in the beauty of holiness'.)[1]

Since the Worship of God is the greatest and most honourable among all the acts and employments of the children of men, from which as the meanest are not excluded, so neither are the greatest exempted; since the highest among men, even they that sit on thrones, must bow down before the altars of the Most High, and do never appear in so true glory in the eyes of God and of men, as when, like those above, they fall down before the throne, and *cast their crowns before the throne*; surely this universal work or duty of man ought to be set off with the greatest order and magnificence, with *the beauty of holiness*. When king David left instructions to Solomon for building the temple, he gave in charge that it should be *exceeding magnifical*: and the reason afterwards given is itself exceeding awful as well as just: *for*, saith he, *the palace is not for man, but for the Lord God*. As the house of God, so the worship performed in it should in like manner be *exceeding magnifical*. For it is a work of a superior and incommunicable nature: it is not a respect paid to our superiors; it is not an offering made to our governors; it is not an homage done to our princes; no, — worship *is not for man, but for the Lord God*.

---

[1]   I Chronicles 26.29

263

1716
Scripture and the authority of the Church in controversies

William Beveridge (1637–1708), Bishop of St Asaph, Ecclesia
Anglicana Ecclesia Catholica, *published posthumously 1716, from
Library of Anglo-Catholic Theology, 7 (1846), p. 378, More and
Cross, pp. 95–6.*

Now that the Church hath authority in controversies is a truth
which, should it not be granted, it would be impossible for any
controversies to be ever ended. I know the Scripture is the rule of
faith and the supreme judge of all controversies whatsoever, so that
there is no controversy of faith ought to be determined but from
the Scriptures. But I know also, that as all controversies of faith
are to be determined by the Scripture, so there are no controversies
of faith but what are grounded on the Scriptures. What is not
grounded upon the Scriptures I cannot be bound to believe, and by
consequence it cannot be a controversy of faith. Hence it is, that as
there is scarce an article of our Christian religion but hath been
some time controverted, so there is no controversy that ever arose
about it but still both parties have pretended to Scripture. As for
example, that great controversy betwixt Arius and Athanasius,
whether Christ was very God of the same substance with the
Father. Arius, he pretended to Scripture in that controversy as well
as Athanasius: and so for all other controversies, both sides still
make as if the Scripture was for them. Now in such cases the
question is, how the question must be decided, whether the
Scripture is for the one or for the other side of the controversy.
The Scripture itself cannot decide the controversy, for the
controversy is concerning itself: the parties engaged in the
controversy cannot decide it, for either of them thinks his own
opinion to be grounded upon Scripture. Now how can this question
be decided better or otherways, than by the whole Church's
exposition of the Scripture, which side of the controversy it is for,
and which side it is against? That it is lawful for the Church thus
to expound the Scripture is plain. For it is lawful even for every
particular person to pass his judgement upon any place of
Scripture; otherwise the Bereans would not have been commended
for searching the Scriptures to see whether those things which the

apostles preached were so or no[1] And if the particular persons which the Church consisteth of may give the exposition of the Scripture, much more the Church itself that consisteth of those particular persons. And as the exposition that any particular person passeth upon the Scripture is binding to that person so that he is bound to believe and act according to it, so whatsoever exposition of Scripture is made by the Church in general, it is binding to the Church in general.

264

1716
Provincial government in the Church

T. Lathbury, A History of the Convocation of the Church of England *(2nd edn., London, 1853), p. 450, on the year 1716.*

This text refers to the process of making the crucial decision to provide Anglicans outside the British Isles with their own bishops with full local jurisdiction.

The Archbishop was charged with obstructing the business of convocation, and with declining to send bishops to our American colonies. But here... he is less to be blamed than some persons imagine. With respect to the former part of the charge, it may be replied that the minister of the crown usually decided whether the convocation should meet for business; and the codicil to his will disproves the latter. He leaves one thousand pounds to the Society for the Propagation of the gospel for the endowment of two bishops in America... Until such lawful appointment and consecrations are complete, I am very sensible that... there never will or can be any regular church-discipline in those parts, or any confirmations, or due ordinations, or any setting apart in ecclesiastical manner of any public places for the more decent worship of God; or any timely preventing or abation of factions or divisions, which have been, and are at present very rife; no ecclesiastically legal discipline or corrections of scandalous manners either in the clergy or laity; or synodical assemblies as may be a proper means to regulate ecclesiastical proceedings.

---

[1]　Acts 17.11

265

1717
The episcopal commission to ordain

Wright, Ordination Sermon, *'The Rights of Christian Priesthood'*
(London 1717), p. 4.

Cf. nos. 148, 189, 200, 259.

It will be granted that the Persons here immediately commissioned
by our Saviour to preach the gospel, and exercise the other parts of
the Apostolic Office, acted by a Divine Authority; it must be said
therefore that either they had Authority from Christ to commission
others successively to ordain to the same offices or else that the
Power of exercising that Authority dy'd with them.

266

1718–1725
Moral theology

Joseph Butler (1692–1752), Bishop of Durham, Sermons at the
Rolls Chapel, 1718–25 *Preface,* Works *(London, 1900), vol. I, p. 4.*

Joseph Butler writes here as a philosopher, in the philosophical terms of his
time, but the question he is addressing is the perennial one of moral theology:
on what basis can we be sure what is right?

There are two ways in which the subject of morals may be treated.
One begins from inquiring into the abstract relations of things: the
other from a matter of fact, namely, what the particular nature of
man is, its several parts, their economy or constitution; from thence
it proceeds to determine what course of life it is, which is
correspondent to this whole nature... they both lead us to the same
things, our obligations to the practice of virtue; and thus they
exceedingly strengthen and enforce each other.
The first seems the most direct formal proof, and in some respects
the least liable to cavil and dispute: the latter is in a peculiar
manner adapted to satisfy a fair mind: and is more easily
applicable to the several particular relations and circumstances in
life.

267

1723
Keeping the Faith

Daniel Westland, A Critical History of the Athanasian Creed, *ed. W. Van Mildert,* Works, *vol. 3 (Oxford, 1856), 10, pp. 230-3.*

The *Critical History* was written as a contribution to the Trinitarian controversy of the eighteenth century.

The Catholic Faith... is another name for the true and right faith as taught in Scripture; called Catholic, or universal, as being held by the universal Church of Christ, against which the gates of hell shall never prevail.... Every one is obliged, under pain of damnation, to preserve, as far as in him lies, the true and right faith, in opposition to those that endeavour to corrupt it, either by taking from it, or adding to it.

268

before 1737
Binding and loosing

John Hutchinson (1674–1737), The Image of God, or Layman's Book, Works *(3rd edn., 1748–9), p. 96.*

Cf. nos. 100, 273, 487.

As every private man forgiveth his brother, so much more the ministers of God's word have power to do the same, for to them belongeth forgiving and retaining, binding and loosing of the whole congregation. To them Christ gave the keys of the kingdom of heaven. How then doth God only forgive sin? Truly, they are only ministers of the forgiveness, and preachers of his mercy, or of his wrath. Their forgiving and loosing is to declare the sweet and comfortable promises that are made through Jesus Christ in God's book to such as be penitent; and their binding and retaining is to preach the law, which causeth anger to such as be impenitent. Or, their loosing is to declare before the congregation, that God forgiveth the believing: and their binding is to show, that God will not pardon the unbelieving, because they are without purpose to amend and reform their livings. The common sort suppose, that

God forgiveth them, as soon as the minister layeth his hands upon their heads, although they return to their old living. Be not deceived. Except thou repent, he hath no authority to forgive thee; for he is a minister of forgiveness only to such as repent and will amend. His commission stretcheth no further.

269

1747
The value of familiar forms of prayer

Anon. The New Whole Duty of Man *(1747)*.

Nor do I see any reason why Christians should be weary of a well-composed Liturgy (as I hold this to be) more than of all other things, wherein the constancy abates nothing of the excellency and usefulness. I could never see any reason why any Christian should abhor, or be forbidden to use, the same forms of prayer, since he prays to the same God, believes in the same Saviour, professeth the same Truths, reads the same Scriptures, hath the same duties upon him, and feels the same daily wants for the most part, both inward and outward, which are common to the whole Church.

Sure we may as well before-hand know what we pray as to Whom we pray; and in what words, as to what sense. When we desire the same things, what hinders we may not use the same words? Our appetite and digestion too may be good when we use, as we pray for, *our daily bread*. Some men, I hear, are so impatient not to use in all their devotions their own invention and gifts, that they not only disuse (as too many), but wholly cast away and contemn the Lord's Prayer; whose great guilt is, that it is the warrant and original pattern of all set Liturgies in the Christian Church.

270

1751
The importance of Christian example

M.K. Kuriakose, History of Christianity in India: Source Materials (Madras 1982), p. 65, from Hugh Pearsons, Memoirs of the Life and Correspondence of the Rev. Christian Schwartz, I (1751), pp. 89–94.

'You astonish me,' said he; 'for, from what we daily observe and experience, we cannot but think Europeans, with but few exceptions, to be self-interested, incontinent, proud, full of illiberal contempt and prejudice against us Hindoos [*sic*], and even against their own religion, especially the higher classes. So at least I have found it with majority of those with whom I have had any intercourse.' This is a reproach which has been but too justly thrown upon Europeans by the unenlightened natives of India, and has ever formed one of the most powerful obstacles to their conversion to Christianity.

271

1751
The right use of natural reason

Benjamin Whichcote (1609–83), one of the Cambridge Platonists, Several Discourses, Works (Aberdeen, 1751), I, pp. 370f., More and Cross, p. 213.

The reference in the last sentence is to the ancient and medieval theory of 'causes'. God is seen here as 'efficient cause' of the soul of man and its 'final cause' or end and purpose.

They are not to be blamed, or looked upon as neglecters of God's grace, or undervaluers of it, or to abate in the least, who vigorously and with all imaginable zeal call upon men to use, employ, and improve the principles of God's creation, and the telling men they shall meet with no discouragement from God forasmuch as He will not leave them, till they first leave Him. And indeed this is a very profitable work to call upon men, to answer the principles of their creation, to fulfil natural light, to answer natural conscience, to be throughout rational in what they do; for these things have a Divine foundation. *The spirit in man is the candle of the Lord, lighted by God, and lighting men to God.* It is from God by way of efficiency, and to God finally.

272

1781
What is a bishop?

Thomas Wilson (1663–1755) Sacra Privata *(published posthumously by C. Cruttwell, 1781),* Works *(Oxford, 1860), vol. V, pp. 61 and 520.*

A bishop is a pastor set over other pastors. They were to ordain elders. They might receive an accusation against an elder. They were to charge them to preach such and such doctrines; to stop the mouths of deceivers; to set in order the things that were wanting; and lastly, this was the form of Church government in all ages. So that to reject this, is to reject an ordinance of God.... Every true and lawful bishop is the representative of Christ in his own Diocese.

273

1783
Absolution

Anon., The Companion or Spiritual Guide at the Altar *(1783).*

[On the Absolution by the priest]
The priest is required to pronounce the absolution *standing,* because it is an act of his authority in declaring the will of God, whose Ambassador he is. But the people receive it *upon their knees,* in token of that humility and reverence, with which they ought to receive the joyful news of a pardon from *God.* Don't look upon this *absolution* as a *presumptive act* of the priest, or that it receives more or less efficacy from the *intention* of the priest, that pronounceth it: neither set so light by it, as to imagine it to be *merely declarative,* or *a matter of form,* that conveys no benefit to

the people upon whom it is pronounced: But consider it *sacramentally,* conveying pardon to such only, as come duly, or *worthily* prepared, to receive that absolution from their sins, which being freely forgiven by *God,* are, by *his authority,* ratified upon earth by his minister. Thus the *unworthy* petitioner partakes *not* of that blessing, which is promised to such as come prepared for absolution, no more than the *unworthy communicant* is entitled to the benefits of a holy communion. Proportionable to the *sincerity* of one's *repentance* is the forgiveness of his sins. If we with a true faith and hearty repentance turn to *God,* he will have mercy upon us; he will pardon and deliver us from all our sins; he will confirm and strengthen us in all goodness, and bring us to everlasting life. These are the *conditions* of our *salvation,* and of our *absolution.* So that, if we be just and sincere to ourselves, God will ratify the priest's absolution of our sins, and perform all the promises he has made to us in this sacrament.

274

1783
The Real Presence

Anon. The Companion or Spiritual Guide at the Altar *(1783).*

After the *bread* and *wine* are deputed by holy prayer to God, to be used for a commemoration of Christ's death, though they do not cease to be what they were before; yet, they become something, which they were not before consecration: They become visible signs or pledges of that inward and spiritual grace, which they are appointed by Christ himself, to represent; which grace is no less than the *body and blood of Christ, which are verily and indeed taken and received by the faithful in the Lord's Supper.* For they have a real feel and portion given them in the death and sufferings of the Lord Jesus; whose body was broken and blood shed for the remission of sins. They truly and indeed partake of the virtue of his bloody sacrifice, whereby he hath obtained an eternal redemption for mankind. And it is the nature and office of these sacramental pledges to assure us of the good will of God, and of his truth in fulfilling his gracious promises. He engages to be faithful to us in *giving* them, as we engage ourselves to be faithful to him in *receiving* them. God bids us believe that we shall *be accepted in his beloved*: and he does after put us in possession of all that, which the gospel promises, and the sacrifice of Christ upon the cross obtained for us: no less than mercy, grace, and peace; remission of sins; the power of the Holy Ghost, and eternal life. This sacrament is also a bond of union amongst Christians. They, who believe in one common Saviour, and partake of the same sacrifice, will never forget the duty of that lesson. *Beloved, if God so loved us*, as to give his only begotten Son, to die for our sins, *we ought also to love one another.* — The sacrifice here offered is declarative of Christian unanimity, knit together in a firm and inseparable charity.

7
MISSION UNLIMITED
1784–1867

275

1784

The Episcopal Church in the United States of America

Who are the Anglicans?, ed. *Charles Long, prepared for the the Lambeth Conference, 1988 (Ohio, 1988), p. 37.*

The Church of England was brought to the New World by early explorers and colonists and during the 18th century was especially assisted by the SPCK and SPG.[1] Anglicanism was the dominant Church in the southern colonies such as Virginia (first celebration of Holy Communion, Jamestown 1607) and strong in some parts of the north, but no resident bishop was provided for nearly 200 years and many of the clergy sided with the Crown during the American Revolution. After the Revolution, the Church was slowly reorganized and rebuilt by state conventions (later dioceses), a series of national meetings and the securing of the Episcopate from England, thus forming the first Anglican Province independent from the Church of England. In 1784, Seabury of Connecticut, the first American bishop, was consecrated in Scotland. In 1785, the first General Convention was held, and in 1787 two more bishops were consecrated in England. In 1821, the Domestic and Foreign Missionary Society was organized. The Episcopal Church is governed by a triennial General Convention consisting of a House of Bishops, including all diocesan, suffragan, assistant and retired bishops and a House of (Clerical and Lay) Deputies elected by their dioceses. Between General Conventions, affairs are in the hands of an Executive Council, whose members are elected in part by the two Houses and in part by the regional provinces, and which meets several times a year. of America)

---

[1]   Society for Promoting Christian Knowledge and Society for the Propagation of the Gospel.

276

1784
Ecclesiastical union

'Resolution for an Episcopal Church in the United States of America', New York, October, 1784, William White, Memoirs of the Protestant Episcopal Church in the United States of America *(2nd edn., New York, 1836), pp. 79–81.*

This meeting set out the plan for union of the American Episcopal Church, rules for its government, and so on. There is an awareness of difficulties arising in relation to the state, especially in Clause 4. See, too, no. 288 on Provincial autonomy.

The principles of ecclesiastical union, recommended at the meeting, September, 1784, are as follows: —

1st. That there shall be a general convention of the Episcopal Church in the United States of America.

2nd. That the Episcopal Church, in each state, send deputies to the convention, consisting of clergy and laity.

3rd. That associated congregations, in two or more states, may send deputies jointly.

4th. That the said Church shall maintain the doctrines of the gospel, as now held by the Church of England, and shall adhere to the liturgy of the said Church, as far as shall be consistent with the American revolution, and the constitutions of the respective states.

5th. That in every state where there shall be a bishop duly consecrated and settled, he shall be considered as a member of the convention *ex officio.*

6th. That the clergy and laity, assembled in convention, shall deliberate in one body, but shall vote separately; and the concurrence of both shall be necessary to give validity to every measure.

7th. That the first meeting of the convention shall be at Philadelphia, the Tuesday before the feast of St Michael next; to which it is hoped, and earnestly desired, that the Episcopal churches in the several states will send their clerical and lay deputies, duly instructed and authorized to proceed on the necessary business herein proposed for their deliberation.

The above resolves were, in substance, what had been determined on in Pennsylvania, in May; and after having been discussed and accommodated in a committee, were adopted by the assembly.

277

1786
Holy Communion

The Communion Office... Recommended to the Episcopal
Congregations in Connecticut, by the Right Reverend Bishop
Seabury *(1786).*

This document, based on the Scottish liturgy, not only served as an
inspiration for the American liturgy but also reflects a distinctive strain in
American theology.

The communion-office, or order for the administration of the holy
Eucharist or supper of the Lord. With private devotions.
Recommended to the episcopal congregations in Connecticut, by
the Right Reverend Bishop Seabury.

The Exhortation.
Dearly beloved in the Lord, ye that mind to come to the holy
Communion of the body and blood of our Saviour Christ, must
consider how St Paul exhorteth all persons diligently to try and
examine themselves, before they presume to eat of that bread, and
drink of that cup. For as the benefit is great, if with a true penitent
heart and lively faith we receive that holy sacrament, (for then we
spiritually eat the flesh of Christ and drink his blood; then we
dwell in Christ, and Christ in us; we are one with Christ, and
Christ with us;) so is the danger great, if we receive the same
unworthily, not considering the Lord's body; for then we are guilty
of the body and blood of Christ our Saviour; we kindle God's
wrath against us, and bring his judgments upon us. Judge therefore
yourselves, brethren, that ye be not judged of the Lord; repent you
truly for your sins past; have a lively and steadfast faith in Christ
our Saviour; amend your lives, and be in perfect charity with all
men; so shall ye be meet partakers of those holy mysteries. And
above all things, ye must give most humble and hearty thanks to
God the Father, the Son, and the Holy Ghost, for the redemption of
the world, by the death and passion of our Saviour Christ, both
God and man, who did humble himself even to the death upon the
cross for us miserable sinners, who lay in darkness and the shadow
of death, that he might make us the children of God, and exalt us
to everlasting life. And to the end that we should always remember
the exceeding great love of our Master and only Saviour Jesus

Christ thus dying for us, and the innumerable benefits which by his precious blood-shedding he hath obtained to us, he hath instituted and ordained holy mysteries, as pledges of his love, and for a continual remembrance of his death, to our great and endless comfort. To him, therefore, with the Father, and the Holy Ghost, let us give (as we are most bounden) continual thanks, submitting ourselves wholly to his holy will and pleasure, and studying to serve him in true holiness and righteousness all the days of our life. *Amen*

Private Devotions for the Altar.
Blessed Jesu! Saviour of the world! who hast called me to the participation of these thy holy mysteries, accept my humble approach to thy sacred table, increase my faith, settle my devotion, fix my contemplation on thy powerful mercy; and while with my mouth I receive the sacred symbols of the body and blood, may they be the means of heavenly nourishment to prepare my body and soul for that everlasting life which thou hast purchased by thy merits, and promised to bestow on all who believe in and depend on thee. *Amen*

Prayer to God
O Gracious and merciful God, Thou supreme Being, Father, Word and Holy Ghost, look down from heaven, the throne of thy essential glory, upon me thy unworthy creature, with the eyes of thy covenanted mercy and compassion: O Lord my God, I disclaim all merit, I renounce all righteousness of my own, either inherent in my nature, or acquired by my own industry: And I fly for refuge, for pardon and sanctification, to the righteousness of Christ: For his sake, for the sake of the blessed Jesus, the Son of thy covenanted love, whom Thou hast set forth to be a propitiation for fallen man, and in whom alone Thou art well pleased, have mercy upon me, receive my prayers, pardon my infirmities, strengthen my weak resolutions, guide my steps to the holy altar, and there feed me with the meat which perishes not, but endureth to everlasting life. *Amen*

After Receiving.
Blessed Jesus! Thou hast now blest me with the food of thy own merciful institution, and, in humble faith of thy gracious promise, I have bowed myself at thy table, to receive the precious pledges of thy dying love; O may thy presence go with me from this happy

participation of thy goodness, that when I return to the necessary labours and employments of this miserable world, I may be enabled by thy grace to obey thy commandments, and conducted by thy watchful care through all trials, till, according to thy divine wisdom, I have finished my course here with joy, that so I may depart out of this world in peace, and in a steadfast dependence on thy merits, O blessed Jesus, in whose prevailing words I shut up all my imperfect wishes, saying, *Our Father, &c. Amen.*

278

1787
The Anglican Church of Canada

Who are the Anglicans?, *ed. Charles Long, prepared for the Lambeth Conference, 1988 (Ohio, 1988), p. 41.*

The Anglican Church of Canada came into existence as the result of the work of British churches and missionary societies, particularly the United Society for the Propagation of the Gospel and Church Missionary Society, which sent missionaries and teachers to the new land in the eighteenth and nineteenth centuries. First regular services began in 1710 at Port Royal; first church building, St Paul's, Halifax 1750; first bishop, Charles Inglis, Bishop of Nova Scotia 1787. Provincial Synod dates from the 1860s and General Synod from 1893. The Church includes in its membership large numbers of the original inhabitants of Canada — Indian, Eskimo and Metis — and has been a strong advocate of their rights.

279

1789
The election of a Presiding Bishop

Constitution of the Episcopal Church in the United States of America, adopted in General Convention, in Philadelphia, October 1789, as amended in subsequent General Conventions.

This is important as illustrating the need for Anglican provinces to provide for a local primacy or metropolitan bishopric. Cf. nos. 369, 530.

ARTICLE I.

Section 1. There shall be a General Convention of this Church, consisting of the House of Bishops and the House of Deputies, which Houses shall sit and deliberate separately; and in all deliberations freedom of debate shall be allowed. Either House may originate and propose legislation, and all acts of the Convention shall be adopted and be authenticated by both Houses.

Section 2. Every bishop of this Church having jurisdiction, every Bishop Coadjutor, and every bishop who by reason of advanced age or bodily infirmity, or, who under an election to an office created by the General Convention has resigned his jurisdiction, shall have a seat and vote in the House of Bishops. A majority of all bishops entitled to vote, exclusive of foreign missionary bishops and of bishops who have resigned their jurisdictions, shall be necessary to constitute a quorum for the transaction of business.

Section 3. Upon the expiration of the term of office of the Presiding Bishop, the General Convention shall elect the Presiding Bishop of the Church. The House of Bishops shall choose one of the bishops having jurisdiction within the United States to be the Presiding Bishop of the Church by a vote of a majority of all the bishops entitled to vote in the House of Bishops, such choice to be subject to confirmation by the House of Deputies. His term and tenure of office and duties shall be prescribed by the Canons of the General Convention. But if the Presiding Bishop of the Church shall resign his office as such, or if he shall resign his episcopal jurisdiction, or if by reason of infirmity he shall become disabled, or in case of his death, the senior bishop of this Church in the order of consecration, having jurisdiction within the United States, shall thereupon become the Presiding Bishop of the Church until an election of Presiding Bishop be held by the General Convention....

CANON 17.

Of the Presiding Bishop.

§I. The Presiding Bishop, when elected according to the provisions of Article I., Section 3, of the Constitution, shall hold office for a term of six years.

§II. The Presiding Bishop shall preside over meetings of the House of Bishops, and shall take order for the consecration of bishops when duly elected. He shall also perform all other duties prescribed for him by other Canons of the General Convention.

§III. The stipend of the Presiding Bishop and his necessary expenses shall be provided for in the budget approved by the General Convention.

280

1794
Evidences of Christianity

William Paley (1743–1805), philosopher and theologian, A View of the Evidences of Christianity *(1794), Part I, Preface, and chapter X.*

The debate about the 'evidences' on which a reasonable man or woman ought to accept the truth of the Christian faith was at its height in the eighteenth and early nineteenth centuries. Here the issue is whether miracles constitute satisfactory evidence for the truth of Christian faith. Cf. nos. 193, 311.

'There is satisfactory evidence that many, professing to be original witnesses of the Christian miracles, passed their lives in labours, dangers, and sufferings, voluntarily undergone in attestation of the accounts which they delivered, and solely in consequence of their belief of those accounts; and that they also submitted, from the same motives, to new rules of conduct...'
'The next question is, what they did this FOR. That it was *for* a miraculous story of some kind or other, is to my apprehension extremely manifest; because, as to the fundamental article, the designation of the person, viz., that this particular person, Jesus of Nazareth, ought to be received as the Messiah,... they neither had, nor could have, anything but miracles to stand upon'.

281

1801
Christian education

Hannah More (1745–1833), philanthropist, Letters, *ed. R. Brimley Johnson (London, 1925), Letter to the Bishop of Bath and Wells, 1801, p. 183.*

Hannah More (1745–1833) was a philanthropist who established village schools in the English county of Somerset, to give the children of the poor both religious education, and training in the skills in spinning which could help them earn a living.

When I settled in this country thirteen years ago, I found the poor in many of the villages sunk in a deplorable state of ignorance and vice... Not one school there did I ever attempt to establish without the hearty concurrence of the clergyman of the parish. My plan of instruction is extremely simple and limited... I knew no way of teaching morals but by teaching principles; or of inculcating Christian principles without imparting a good knowledge of Scripture.... The Collect is learned every Sunday. They generally learn the Sermon on the Mount, with many other chapters and psalms... For many years I have given away annually, nearly two hundred Bibles, Common Prayer Books and Testaments.

282

1804
Hearing a sermon

John Henry Hobart, Bishop of New York, founder of the General Theological Seminary, A Companion for the Festivals and Fasts of the Protestant Episcopal Church *(1804).*

Q. *When a sermon is delivered, with what disposition ought we to hear it?*
A. However frail and unworthy the ministering servants of the sanctuary may be, yet, as they bear the commission of God, and are appointed by him to promulgate the terms of salvation, we should listen to their instructions with humble and earnest attention; and our prayers should be directed to God, that he would impress the truths which they may deliver, on our hearts, to our conviction, our consolation, and our growth in holiness and virtue.

283

1804
The advantages of a prescribed liturgy

John Henry Hobart, Bishop of New York, founder of the General Theological Seminary, A Companion for the Festivals and Fasts of the Protestant Episcopal Church *(1804).*

When a form of prayer is used, the people are previously acquainted with the prayers in which they are to join, and are thus enabled to render unto God a reasonable and enlightened service. In forms of prayer, the greatest dignity and propriety of sentiment and expression may be secured. They prevent the particular opinions and dispositions of the minister from influencing the devotions of the congregation; they serve as a standard of faith and practice; and they render the service more animating, by uniting the people with the minister in the performance of public worship.... In the Liturgy of our Church there is an admirable mixture of instruction and devotion. The Lessons, the Creeds, the Commandments, the Epistles and Gospels, contain the most important and impressive instruction on the doctrines and duties of religion; while the Confession, the Collects and Prayers, the Litany and Thanksgivings, lead the understanding and the heart through all the sublime and affecting exercises of devotion. In this truly evangelical and excellent Liturgy, the supreme Lord of the universe is invoked by the most appropriate, affecting, and sublime epithets; all the wants to which man, as a dependent and sinful being, is subject, are expressed in language at once simple, concise, and comprehensive; these wants are urged by confessions the most humble, and supplications the most reverential and ardent; the all-sufficient merits of Jesus Christ, the Saviour of the world, are uniformly urged as the only effectual plea, the only certain pledge of divine mercy and grace; and with the most instructive lessons from the sacred oracles, and the most profound confessions and supplications, is mingled the sublime chorus of praise, begun by the minister, and responded with one heart and one voice from the assembled congregation. The mind, continually passing from one exercise of worship to another, and, instead of one continued and uniform prayer, sending up its wishes and aspirations in short and varied collects and supplications, is never suffered to grow languid or weary. The affections of the worshipper ever kept alive by the tender and animating fervour which breathes through the service, he worships his God and Redeemer in spirit and in truth, with reverence and awe, with lively gratitude and love; the exalted joys of devotion are poured upon his soul; he feels that it is good for him to draw near unto God, and that a day spent in his courts, is better than a thousand passed in the tents of the ungodly.

284

1805–27
Daily worship

John Henry Hobart, Bishop of New York, founder of the General Theological Seminary, A Companion for the Book of Common Prayer *(1805–1827),* Of the Order for Daily Morning and Evening Prayer.

In the primitive ages of the Church it was customary to meet not only on Sundays, but *daily,* for the public worship of God. Our Church, hoping that the time will come when the devotion of the people will admit of the restoration of this pious and primitive custom, continues to style her service, the Order for *Daily* Morning and Evening Prayer. The service is performed daily in the Cathedrals, and in some of the parish churches in England. Many of our churches are opened for public worship on Wednesdays and Fridays, which are the days on which the litany is read, and also on the festivals and fasts. Every pious member of our Church should endeavour regularly to attend on those days; not only to enjoy the inestimable advantage and privilege of worshipping God 'in the beauty of holiness'; not only for the purpose of commemorating the great events of redemption set forth in the festivals and fasts, and of celebrating the memories of the apostles and first disciples of our Lord; but also with the view of contributing, by the force of example, to the revival of primitive piety, and to the more general attention to the solemn duty of public worship.

285

1808
The establishment of ecclesial identity in a new Province

A Pastoral Letter from the House of Bishops of the Protestant Episcopal Church in the United States of America to the members of the same (Baltimore, 1808), p. 352.

It is within the memory of many of you, that when these states, in the course of divine Providence, became elevated to a place among the nations of the earth; and when, in consequence, our congregations, planted under the jurisdiction of the Church of England, were withdrawn from it, they had no longer any common centre of union; being not only without an entire ministry, but severally in a state of separate independence, inconsistent with the catholic principles which they had inherited from their founders. Under these circumstances, there was required no small measure of faith, as well in the integrity of our system, as in the divine blessing on any endeavours which might be begun, to elevate us above those apprehensions which described the continuance of our communion as problematical, if not to be despaired of. From correspondence in some instances, and from personal communications in others, it soon appeared, that there was at least so much attachment to the religious principles of our church, as ought to prevent our considering of her cause as desperate. The correctness of this sentiment became confirmed, by connections speedily created of our churches until then detached from one another, on terms which contemplated the perpetuating of the communion, with all the distinguishing properties of the Church of England. And the unanimity with which this was accomplished, afforded a pleasing presage of whatever else we now gratefully remember.

286

1811
Primacy and Episcopal Succession in Scotland

The Protestant Episcopal Church in Scotland, Code of Canons *(Aberdeen, 1911), Canons 1, 2.*

CANON I. For preserving the episcopal succession.

The Episcopal Church in Scotland inviolably retaining in the sacred ministry, the three Orders of Bishops, Priests and Deacons, as of Divine Institution, requires, according to the Apostolic Canon, that a Bishop be ordained by two or three Bishops, not fewer than three in all ordinary cases; and Priests and Deacons, by one Bishop; the right of ordination belonging to the Order of Bishops only: And it is hereby decreed, that no Person shall be consecrated a Bishop of the Episcopal Church in Scotland, without the consent and approbation of the majority of the Bishops; and that, if any three, or more Bishops, not being a Majority, shall take upon them, without such consent, to consecrate any Person to that Office, both the Consecrators, and the Person so consecrated, shall be holden as Schismatics.

CANON II. Regulating the election and office of the Primus.

Before the Distinction of *Archbishop* was introduced into Scotland, one of the Bishops had precedency under the title of *Primus Scottiæ Episcopus*; and the Episcopal College having for a century past adopted the old form, it is hereby ordered, that the Bishop shall, without respect either to seniority of Consecration, or precedency of District, choose a *Primus* by majority of voices, who shall have no other privilege among the Bishops, but the right of convocating and presiding; and that expressly under the following restrictions:

1st, That he shall always be obliged to notify to the other Bishops the reason of his calling a Meeting, as well as the time and place for holding it; and if the majority shall dissent, as judging either the reasons insufficient, or the time and place improper, the proposal of such Meeting shall be either wholly set aside, or the time and place altered, as shall seem to them most expedient.

2ndly, That if the *Primus* shall at any time refuse to call a Meeting, when desired by a majority of the other Bishops, they shall in that case have power to meet, and act synodically without him: And,

3rdly, The *Primus* thus chosen by the majority, is to continue in that office only during their pleasure. That the Church, however, may suffer as little inconvenience as possible, by the death or resignation of the *Primus*, the senior Bishop shall instantly succeed to his powers, until a majority of the Bishops shall appoint one to the office, by a formal Deed of Election.

287

1813
Trade as a vehicle of mission

M.K. Kuriakose, History of Christianity in India: Source Materials *(Madras, 1982), pp. 89–90, The Charter of the East India Company, 52.*

Wilberforce had been working to make the East India Company take responsibility for education and 'religious improvement' in Indian territories in the early 1790s. The Company accepted such responsibilities in part in the revision of its Charter in 1813. At issue here was a special case of the question of the relation between ecclesiastical and civil authority.

And be further enacted, that it shall and may be lawful for His Majesty, from time to time, if he shall think fit, by His Letters Patent under the Great Seal of the United Kingdom, to grant to such Bishop so to be nominated and appointed as aforesaid, such ecclesiastical jurisdiction, and the exercise of such episcopal functions, within the East Indies and parts aforesaid, as His Majesty shall think necessary for the administering holy ceremonies, and for the superintendence and good government of the Ministers of the Church Establishment within the East Indies and parts aforesaid; any Law, Charter, or other matter or thing to the contrary notwithstanding.

288

1817
Provincial autonomy

Pastoral Letter to the Members of the Protestant Episcopal Church in the United States of America, House of Bishops, May 1817 (New York, 1817), p. 7.

When in the year 1785, a Convention of Clerical and Lay Deputies from seven States, assembled in the city of Philadelphia, addressed the English Bishops for the obtaining of the Episcopacy, there were stated by the former an independency in religious concerns, the result of a civil independency, brought about in the course of Divine Providence. When, subsequently, three Clergymen of this Church crossed the Atlantic for consecration; the executive authorities in the states from which they went did not hesitate to certify, that the object was consistent with the constitutions and the laws of the respective states, and of the Union. Since the accomplishment of the object, the proceedings of the Bishops, under the character with which they have been clothed, have been in public view; and there are no legitimate provisions by which their ministration can be governed... At the source from which the Episcopacy was derived, all the proceedings implied the independence of the American Church.

289

1818
The collection taken during a service

Anon. The Companion for the Altar *(contained within* The New Week's Preparation for a Worthy Receiving of the Lord's Supper as Recommended and Appointed by the Church of England*) (1818).*

This text stresses the link between the ancient practice of almsgiving and modern Christian giving.

When it comes to your turn to make your offering, do not let the basin pass by you without putting something into it: for this reason, among others, that you may join in that part of the prayer for the Church militant, wherein you beseech God to accept your alms; and you may depend upon it, he will accept them as given to himself, if they bear a proportion to your ability, and are done in obedience to his commands, and with an eye to his glory, as a grateful acknowledgment of his mercies to yourself, and as a testimony of your dependence upon him for the continuance of them. With such reflections your present offering, and all your other gifts to the services of religion and the uses of charity, ought to be accompanied. They that are poor and cannot give as they are disposed in their hearts, must remember that the alms, given on this occasion, are not matter of necessity, but a free gift; and that their small contribution will, like the poor widow's two mites, be preferred to the richest oblations of the wealthy. And even he that hath nothing at all to give, is invited freely to partake of these spiritual blessings without money, and without price.

290

1819
Ordination of ministers to serve outside England

The ordinations for Colonies Act, 1819, 59 George III, c. 60.

The problem with which this Act of Parliament is designed to deal is that the requirement that a person to be ordained shall have a local pastoral charge or 'title' where he is to serve, is difficult to implement when the service is to be in the mission field, or where there is as yet no settled pattern of local ministry.

It shall be lawful for the Archbishop of Canterbury, the Archbishop of York... or any Bishop specially authorized and empowered by any or either of them, to admit into the holy orders of Deacon or Priest any person whom he shall upon examination deem duly qualified, specially for the purpose of taking upon himself the cure of souls, or officiating in any spiritual capacity in his Majesty's colonies or foreign possessions and residing therein; and ... a ... declaration of such purpose and a written engagement to perform the same under the hand of such person, being deposited in the hands of such Archbishop or Bishop, shall be held to be a sufficient title with a view to such ordination; and... in every such case it shall be distinctly stated in the letters of ordination of every person so admitted to holy orders that he has been ordained for the cure of souls in his Majesty's foreign possessions.

291

1832
Episcopacy and mission

A Pastoral Letter to the Clergy and Members of the Protestant Episcopal Church in the United States, House of Bishops (1832), p. 4.

A very important addition to the Canons, is the authorizing of the consecration of missionary bishops for those portions of the United States, in which the Church has not yet been organized. To this has been added another provision, for the extending of the episcopacy to other countries, in which the Gospel is as yet unknown... In January, 1834, there took place the consecration of the Rev James

H. Otey, D.D., for the Diocese of Tennessee. In that State there was not a church, nor the vestige of a congregation, until the introduction of our liturgy into it by their present bishop, when he began his labours there in the character of a deacon. That it should so soon contain an Episcopal population, entitling to the choice of a bishop, is a remarkable fact, not to be noticed without the commendation due to the zeal and the labours which, under the blessing of GOD have accomplished so extensive a work.

292

1835
Equality in Christ

M.K. Kuriakose, History of Christianity in India: Source Materials *(Madras, 1982), p. 121,* Diary *of bishop Daniel Wilson of Calcutta, 27 January, 1835.*

At this celebration of the Eucharist the congregation took it into their own hands to show that there are no distinctions of class, rank or race in Christ.

I told the congregation that I aimed at no distinction of civil ranks; that the Europeans would naturally approach the altar first; that the respectable and educated natives, Soodras and Pariahs, would naturally come next; that servants and persons of the humblest stations would follow; but that there was to be no inseparable barrier, no heathen dread of defilement, only the natural gradations of society which prevailed in Christian churches at home.[1] However, the English gentry voluntarily mixed themselves, on purpose to show the natives there were no inseparable divisions in Christianity, but all were one body. Positively, a Pariah kneeled between the Collector (the chief personage of the station) and his lady, at the lady's request. Out of five hundred, ten or twelve only left the church, and would not submit to my demands. Such is God's goodness!

---

[1] He means, in England at that time.

293

1836
The Church of England in Australia

Who are the Anglicans?, *ed. Charles Long, prepared for the Lambeth Conference, 1988 (Ohio, 1988), p. 67.*

Anglicanism came to Australia with the 'First Fleet' of convicts and their guards in 1788 and it grew with the establishment of other settlements as a colonial extension of the Church of England, although with growing autonomy, until 1962 when it became an independent Anglican Province. In 1824 the whole continent was an archdeaconry of the Bishop of Calcutta. In 1836, Broughton was consecrated the first Bishop of Australia. The subsequent development of new dioceses led to the first General Synod in 1872. The twentieth century has been marked by continued growth of membership until recently; by the development of missionary work among aborigines and in adjacent Pacific islands and elsewhere; by the consolidation of regional provinces and the adoption of an Australian Prayer Book in 1978.

294

1840
Bishops and unity

J.H. Newman (1801–90), Tractarian, 'The Catholicity of the Anglican Church', Essays Critical and Historical (London, 1890), II, p. 20.

On Newman, see Ian Ker, *John Henry Newman* (Oxford, 1989).

Dodwell and Hickes... teach, agreeably with what has above been called the Anglican theory, that the Church is complete in one bishopric; that a number of bishoprics are but reiterations of one, and add nothing to the perfection of the system. As there is one Bishop invisible in heaven, so there is but one Bishop on earth; and the multitude of bishops are not acknowledged in the Gospel system *as* man, or as if (viewed *as* representatives of the Bishop invisible) they were *capable* of mutual relations one with another, but as being one and all shadows and organs of one and the same divine reality... It is true they can act with each other in Synods, but then they form a sort of board of presbyters, and are our Lord's Council, as Ignatius views them. Considered as bishops, each is the ultimate centre of unity, an independent channel of grace.

295

1840
Salvation and the Church

J.H. Newman (1801–90), Tractarian, 'The Catholicity of the Anglican Church', Essays Critical and Historical (London, 1890), II, p. 23.

Newman refers here to the third-century controversy over what was to be done for Christians who had abandoned their faith under persecution and later wanted to be reconciled with the Church. Cyprian (d. 258) had argued that it was important for this to take place not casually but seriously, with the pastor of the community acting on its behalf to welcome back the penitents. This was an early instance of discussion about whether there can be salvation 'outside the Church'. As Newman points out, it is important to be clear whether 'the Church' is understood to mean the 'local', 'universal' or 'invisible' community of God's people.

It is well known that St. Cyprian has written a treatise on the Unity of the Church, besides various Epistles on the same subject.... He insists... on there being but one Church... Now the question... is whether *the* Church spoken of, in which is salvation, is the particular and local Church everywhere (or, again, the abstract Church of which the local is its realisation under the bishop), or whether it is the literal and actual extended communion of all Christians everywhere viewed as one body.

296

1840
The Church in each place

J.H. Newman (1801–90), Tractarian, 'The Catholicity of the Anglican Church' Essays Critical and Historical *(London, 1890), II, p. 29.*

On 'the Church in each place', cf. no. 294.

Each diocese is a perfect independent Church, sufficient for itself; and the communion of Christians one with another, and the unity of them all together, lie... in what they are and what they have in common, in... Succession, their Episcopal form, their Apostolic faith, and the use of the Sacraments.

297

1840–1904
Unity in Christ

J.W. Chadwick (1840–1904) Eternal Ruler of the Ceaseless Round, The English Hymnal, *p. 384.*

> We are of thee, the children of thy love,
> The brothers of thy well-beloved Son;
> Descend, O Holy Spirit, like a dove,
> Into our hearts, that we may be as one:
> As one with thee, to whom we ever tend;
> As one with him, our Brother and our Friend.
> We would be one in hatred of all wrong,
> One in our love of all things sweet and fair,
> One with the joy that breaketh into song,
> One with the grief that trembleth into prayer,
> One in the power that makes the children free
> To follow truth and thus to follow thee.[1]

---

[1]   Cf. Philippians 4

298

1841
Bishops outside England

The Bishops in Foreign Countries Act, 1841, 5 Victoria c. 6.

This Act of Parliament is designed to get over the difficulty that a bishop consecrated to serve outside England by the Archbishop of Canterbury or York (acting of course with other bishops), and not necessarily a subject of the English monarch, could not reasonably be expected to take oaths of Homage. Cf. no. 305.

The Archbishop of Canterbury or the Archbishop of York ... together with such other bishops as they may call to their assistance [may] consecrate British subjects or the subjects or citizens of any foreign kingdom or state, to be bishops in any foreign country, whether such foreign subjects or citizens be or be not subjects or citizens of the country in which they are to act, and without the Queen's licence for their election, or the royal mandate under the great seal for their confirmation and consecration, and without requiring such of them as may be subjects or citizens of any foreign kingdom or state to take oaths of allegiance and supremacy, and the oath of due obedience to the Archbishop for the time being.

299

1842
Church and Diocese

Richard Whately (1787–1863), Archbishop of Dublin, The Kingdom of Christ *(London, 1842), Essay II, 20, p. 165.*

Whately is speaking here of the early Church's preference for a system of oversight in which a single pastor has personal responsibility for the care of his people; and of the ancient practice of regarding the local 'Church' of the diocese as the basic unit of Church organization.

It seems plainly to have been at least the general, if not the universal, practice of the apostles, to appoint over each separate Church a single individual as chief Governor, ... A Church and a Diocese seem to have been for a considerable time coextensive and identical.

300

1842
Holy Scripture the foundation

William Goode, The Divine Rule of Faith and Practice *(London, 1842), ed. A. Metcalfe (London, 1903), p. 367.*

Compare Article ix of the Thirty-Nine Articles.

The great principle of the Church of England we maintain to be, to require nothing to be believed as an Article of the Christian faith but what, in her judgement, has good and indubitable foundation for it in the Holy Scriptures, and to make the Scripture proof of it the ground upon which it is to be believed.

301

1842
The rights and liberties of the House of Clergy in Convocation

T. Lathbury, A History of the Convocation of the Church of England *(2nd edn., London, 1853), pp. 374 and 380 on the year 1701.*

The British Parliamentary model had a strong influence on the Church of England's synodical government from the beginning (cf. no. 252). In the disputes between the two Houses of Convocation at the beginning of the eighteenth century it was realized that deeper principles of ministerial authority and the role of bishops were involved.

And now a debate arose concerning the privileges of the lower house, where a majority of the members claimed to be on the same footing as to the upper house that the Commons in parliament are in regard to the House of Lords. Whereas they had been scandalously and maliciously represented as favourers of presbytery, in opposition to the episcopacy, they now declared, that they acknowledged the order of bishops as superior to presbyters, to be of divine apostolic institution, and that they claimed no rights but what they conceived necessary to the very being of the lower house of convocation.

302

1842
Primatial power to determine the continuance of a meeting in Convocation

T. Lathbury, A History of the Convocation of the Church of England (2nd edn., London, 1853), pp. 468–9.

The question of the power of the Archbishop presiding in Council to determine with his brother bishops, when to end the meeting, is an aspect of that of the power to summon and constitute a council. See no. 252. The most important point here is the insistence that primacy and collegiality are inseparable and that the bishops as a body carry a special responsibility in brotherhood.

In the reign of Queen Anne the question of the Archbishop's power, apart from his suffragans,[1] was only incidentally introduced... Whenever a prorogation took place, it was made with the consent of the suffragans, because the Archbishop and bishops acted in harmony; and the question of the president's sole power was not raised... Supposing the principle, that the Archbishop will not act against a majority of his brethren, to be sound, it follows, as a necessary consequence, that he would not prorogue the convocation, in case his suffragans should be opposed, and should wish to discuss matters pertaining to the Church. [No one]... denies the power... of the Archbishop in conjunction with his brethren.

303

1847
Church and State

The Letters of Thomas Hayton, Vicar of Long Crendon, Buckinghamshire, 1821–87, ed. Joyce Donald, The Bucks Advertiser, 17 July 1847; Buckinghamshire Record Society, 20 (1979).

This text is of interest as illustrating the persistence of a sophisticated anti-clericalism in Victorian England, alongside a serious popular interest in the maintenance of a due balance between the authority of the Church and that of the State.

---

[1] 'Suffragans' here means diocesan bishops regarded as the suffragans of their Metropolitan, not bishops acting as assistants to or vicars for a diocesan bishop.

DINNER AT THE SPREAD EAGLE HOTEL — UPROARIOUS PROCEEDINGS.
On Tuesday last, Mr Disraeli, as announced upon placards, met a number of the electors of Bucks around the dinner-table at the Spread Eagle Hotel, for the purpose of making an exposition of his sentiments. A large number sat down to a good dinner; and afterwards, the doors being thrown open, the room became excessively crowded in every corner. ...The loyal toasts came first in order, and were given and received without any commotion — Next came 'The bishop and Clergy'. The Revd. Mr Stevens rose to reply. He was glad to find that the public were ready to support the authority of the clergy, and none more so than the old nobility, gentry, and yeomanry of England. The clergy, he hoped, would maintain their sacred character by their good deeds. (A sarcastic voice — 'As they are accustomed'.) Many opinions prevailed in the present day respecting the position of the clergy with the state (*hear, hear*). It was true they were connected with the state; but they did not derive their power of authority from the state — they were the ambassadors of Him to whom all power was given in earth and heaven (loud cheers). They depended upon their commission from His authority, that commission which enabled the first preachers of Christianity to overthrow Paganism, even without the aid of the state. For three centuries Christianity was assailed by the Pagans. (A voice — 'And is now trampled down by the clergy'.) However, even a Pagan emperor was at last compelled to bow to its merits; to confess its merits, and to make it the religion of his empire (applause). In the time of Constantine the clergy were upheld by the state.

304

1848
The Lord's Prayer and our neighbours

F.D. Maurice, Professor of Theology at King's College, London, Professor of Moral Philosophy at Cambridge, The Prayer Book and the Lord's Prayer *(1848).*

Maurice here underlines the equality of all Christ's people in their Lord.

The Paternoster is not, as some fancy, the easiest, most natural, of all devout utterances. It may be committed to memory quickly, but it is slowly learnt by heart. Men may repeat it over ten times in an hour, but to use it when it is most needed, to know what it means, to believe it, yea, not to contradict it in the very act of praying it, not to construct our prayers upon a model the most unlike it possible, this is hard; this is one of the highest gifts which God can bestow upon us; nor can we look to receive it without others that we may wish for less — sharp suffering, a sense of wanting a home, a despair of ourselves.... Much of the practical difficulty of the prayer lies assuredly in the first word of it. How can we look round upon the people whom we habitually feel to be separated from us by almost impassable barriers; who are above us so that we cannot reach them, or so far beneath us, that the slightest recognition of them is an act of gracious condescension; upon the people of an opposite faction to our own, whom we denounce as utterly evil; upon men whom we have reason to despise; upon the actual wrong-doers of society, those who have made themselves vile, and are helping to make it vile – and then teach ourselves to think that in the very highest exercise of our lives these are associated with us; that when we pray, we are praying for them and with them; that we cannot speak for ourselves without speaking for them; that if we do not carry their sins to the throne of God's grace, we do not carry our own; that all the good we hope to obtain there, belongs to them just as much as to us, and that our claim to it is sure of being rejected, if it is not one which is valid for them also? Yet all this is included in the word 'Our'.

305

May 1850
Synodical government

Votes and Proceedings of the House of Commons, May 1850.

The inclusion of the laity in provisions for the setting up of synodical government outside England is of significance here. Cf. no. 298.

...Be it Enacted, That it shall be lawful for the bishop or bishops of any diocese, or dioceses... in any Colony... and the clergy and lay persons, being declared members of the Church of England, or being otherwise in communion with him or them respectively, to meet together from time to time, and, at such meeting, by mutual consent, or by a majority of voices of the said clergy and laity, severally and respectively, with the assent of the said bishop, or of a majority of the said bishops, if more than one, to make all such regulations as may be necessary for the better conduct of their ecclesiastical affairs, and for the holding of meetings for the said purpose thereafter....

306

1852
The Church and Province of New Zealand

Who are the Anglicans?, *ed. Charles Long, prepared for the Lambeth Conference, 1988 (Ohio, 1988), p. 71.*

Began with Church Missionary Society mission to the Maori people in early 19th century. Settler church began alongside the Maori church in 1852. Governed by General Synod — of three orders — meeting every two years. Current thrust: mission and evangelism as expressed by equal partnership and bi-cultural development, stemming from the terms of Treaty of Waitangi at the founding of the nation.

307

1852
The value of synodical government

The Chronicle of Convocations, *12 November, 1852, Representation from the Lower House of the Convocation of Canterbury, p. 21.*

The point made here is that if the Church does not make decisions as a 'body' and with 'universal intention' where that is appropriate; or if it leaves everything to civil legislation or individual conscience, Christian people may be left without a sense of direction in matters of common interest and importance.

They are persuaded that the silence of the corporate voice of the Church supplies to her members a powerful temptation, and sometimes imposes a necessity, to act upon their own individual opinion, in opposition to the letter of the law. They appeal to experience in proof of the inadequacy of a mere civil legislation to meet the ever-varying requirements of a religious system which... extends into every quarter of the globe.

308

1854
The doctrine of sacrifice, the doctrine of priesthood

F.D. Maurice (1805–72), Anglican divine, The Doctrine of Sacrifice Deduced from the Scriptures *(Cambridge, 1854), pp. 275, 280–1.*

The Sonship of Christ is the basis of all intercourse between God and man. The possibility of a priesthood — the fact of a priesthood — rests upon that relation.... Never for a moment let us think of the sacrifice apart from the priest; or the priest as separate from those for whom he prayed, that they might be one with Him... All who trusted God and gave up themselves, felt that there must be an obedience, and a sacrifice which was the ground of theirs; an obedience and a sacrifice which was essentially divine, and, therefore, essentially human.

309

1856
The Real Presence

William Goode, The Nature of Christ's Presence in the Eucharist *(London, 1856), I, p. viii.*

The reference here is to the teaching of some of the sixteenth century reformers that the Eucharist is merely an act of recollection of Christ's Passion. William Goode argues that there is a real and objective presence of Christ which is constitutive for Eucharistic Communion.

The whole difficulty that is felt in interpreting such phrases as 'real Presence'... arises from the carnal and earthly notions with which men come to the subject... If only they would put the body out of sight for the moment, and think merely of the soul and its acts, they would find no difficulty in understanding such language... the terms 'real, etc.' would be seen to be properly used for the purpose of discriminating a true and real union with Christ, and participation of the Spirit that dwells in him, and complete communion with his human nature, from a mere act of the reflective powers of the mind meditating upon the person of Christ, and remembering with gratitude his death and passion.

310

1857
The first Diocesan Synod at Cape Town

Closing address of Bishop Gray of Cape Town, South African Church Magazine, *1857 in* Historical Records of the Church of the Province of South Africa, *ed. C. Lewis and G.E. Edwards (London, 1934), pp. 74–6.*

This synod preceded the first English Diocesan Conference of clergy and laity in England, held at Lichfield in 1868.

We assembled with prayer to God that His Holy Spirit might be with us, to overrule our thoughts and words and guide us to sound conclusions. All of us must feel... that we have laid down sound and safe principles for the future guidance and government of the Church in this land..., because they are the principles of that Church from which we take our origin.... Our first duty was to settle what our *Constitution* as a diocesan synod was. I believe we have been very unanimous in all our conclusions; there was no important principle in doubt, as all the principles we had to settle were those which had been embodied in the Church at large, and had been drawn out very carefully both in the Bill of the Archbishop and in the constitutions of other diocesan synods in other parts of the world. The next subject was the *declaration of principles* which we found it necessary to make in the face of the whole world. I thank God that we have declared our perfect unity and identity with our own dear Mother Church,[1] that in doing so we have used no words which would have compromised our own position here as a Church, or the rights and privileges and

---

[1]   that is, the Church of England

supremacy of the Crown... I thank God also... that we all look on the Prayer Book as the true interpretation of what the word of God teaches, and that we have received the forms of worship used in the Church at home, and adopted for our use here the laws, canons, constitutions, and practices of our Mother Church as far as they are practicable in this land, reserving to ourselves the right of enacting such local constitutions on local matters as we deem to be necessary... One of the first works we grappled with was that of *parcelling out the country*, already divided into dioceses by the Crown and the Church at home, into parochial divisions... over each of which a clergyman shall be placed, and he will be responsible for the souls within that district... We have laid down *rules for parishes*, and declared who are parishioners, who have the right of electing churchwardens, and what the duties of churchwardens should be. They are to be elected in the same way and their duties are to be the same as at home... In all parishes where there is a church consecrated to God, a clergyman shall be inducted and instituted to the charge of that parish as our clergy are at home, and shall have the same rights and privileges as a rector has there. The next thing that came before us was to establish *courts for the trial of any clergy* who might be found to have committed any crime against morality or religion. This court will be different from any court which exists in England. We have for the first time declared that there shall sit in it as assessors to the bishop not less than three of the clergy – that of these three, two at least shall be taken out of a panel elected by the clergy in synod. I should, myself, have two or three years ago shrunk from the proposition, but the Lower House of Convocation has adopted this principle, and concluded that in future such should be the constitution of diocesan courts in England; and I think we are justified in adopting that principle here... the assessors are to be counsellors not co-ordinate judges.... Another important resolution on which we agree is that we shall *not apply to parliament for legislative* sanction to the conclusions we have come to. We send them forth as the resolutions of a voluntary and spiritual association, needing no support but their force.

311

1859
The grounds for believing what Scripture says

F.D. Maurice (1805–72), Anglican divine, Revelation *(Cambridge, 1859), pp. 455–6.*

The Bible pointed... our fathers... to a ground of certainty... beneath them, beneath itself. Its power rested on no arguments about the origin of documents. It proved itself in another way, — by the facts of life, by sore and blessed experiences. They could trust these proofs. They could trust God to show forth His mind and purpose... in their day as in other days, through common events, through the righteous or the foul doings of men, through mighty deliverances and mighty judgements. They felt that they understood the Bible very imperfectly, but it helped them to understand all that was passing around them.

312

1862
Music in worship

A. Morden Benet, Scripture Authority for Choral Worship *(London, 1862), p. 4.*

This defence of the use of music in worship is directed against a school of thought among some Puritans which had regarded it as distracting from worship of God, and even as a temptation to idolatry. Compare no. 316.

Sacred music is calculated to inspire the mind with devotional and reverential feelings. It raises, enlarges, and sustains spiritual desires and affections, which are apt to be stifled amidst the cares and pleasures of the world. Did we need an illustration of this great truth we might refer to the wonderful change which was wrought upon the mind of King Saul by the sweet Psalmist of Israel when he played before him on the harp, and expelled the evil spirit which troubled his repose by the charms of his sacred melody. From the Bible we also learn that the practice of singing praises has always been regarded as a suitable part of the homage which is due from man to his Heavenly Guardian.

313

1862
Scripture and tradition

William Goode, Holy Scripture the Sole Authoritative Expositor of the Faith *(London, 1862), p. 39.*

William Goode, writing as an Evangelical, insists here on the importance of respecting the early tradition of the Church.

The Church of England is far from admitting any discrepancy between her faith and that of the Primitive Church... Show us any vital doctrine established by even probable consent of the Primitive Church, which we do not receive, or any which we do receive, unsupported by the records of that Church. Our creed is precisely that of the Primitive Church, as far as it can be ascertained. True, we take it from the Scriptures, and rest it upon the authority of the Scriptures only; but we look with great respect to the records of the Primitive Church, and value highly their confirmation of our views; and we think it a good argument against various doctrines... that they are utterly destitute of support in the records of the Primitive Church.

314

1862
What supports the authority of an individual's writing

W. Goode, Holy Scripture the Sole Authoritative Expositor of the Faith *(London, 1862), p. 37.*

It has always been the case that a variety of factors contribute to make a text or document 'authoritative' for Anglicans. A number of such factors are listed here, including reception by bishops, by clergy, by the whole people of God, and 'official' publication by royal or archiepiscopal command (Cf. Introduction, where this text is quoted).

Bishop Jewel's Apology is not the mere work of an individual bishop, but was 'set forth with the consent of the bishops,' and had the concurrence of the whole English clergy... and by Queen Elizabeth, King James, King Charles, and four successive Archbishops, was ordered to be read and chained up in all parish churches throughout England and Wales; and is recognized in our present Code of Canons, agreed to by the Convocations of Canterbury and York, as 'the Apology of the Church of England.' (Canon 30.) Bishop Randolph says of it, that it was 'always understood to speak the sense of the whole Church, in whose name it is written,' and was 'publicly received and allowed.'... Moreover, Bishop Jewel himself was a man of such weight among the authorities of the Church in his day, that at the revision of the Thirty-Nine Articles in 1571, they were left in his hands for final correction and publication.

315

1862
The diaconate

A.J.Gilbert, Sermon preached at an ordination to the diaconate in Horsham Church (Lent, 1862), p. 11.

The diaconate developed in two directions from the early Church: as an administrative order (whose holders might be very senior members of a bishop's staff in the late Roman world); and as an order with liturgical duties, from which it became usual to proceed to the priesthood.

But the occasion reminds us that we must now confine our attention to one especial part of the ministry of the Church, of the ministry of the body of Christ, viz., the deacons. I trust you are all familiar with the origin of that order. You remember you will find the account of its first institution in the Christian Church in the early part of the sixth chapter of the Acts of the Apostles. I say in the Christian Church, because there is reason to believe that a similar office, as far at least as regarded the superintendence of the distribution of alms, existed already in the Jewish Church in the Apostle's time. And, if the record of the order of deacons had stopped with the reasons assigned for their first institution, we might possibly have concluded that their office was intended to be limited to temporal matters in the distribution of pecuniary alms. But, in the selection of those who were to be the first ordained to this office, the apostles enjoined that those should be chosen who were "full of the Holy Ghost and wisdom".[1]

---

[1]   Acts 6.3

316

1862
The place of Christian art

A.P. Forbes (1817–75), Bishop of Brechin, The Sanctity of Christian Art *(Edinburgh, 1862), p. 11.*

Compare no. 312 on *Music in worship.*

Lastly, if it be said that a worship which appeals to the senses and enlists the imagination in the service of religion is discordant to the purely spiritual nature of the religion of Jesus Christ, we answer by denying that the religion of Jesus Christ is, in this sense, purely spiritual. So far from this being a valid argument, we hesitate not to assert that the profoundest theological reasons may be adduced for a worship and adoration that appeals to every power of humanity. Had the divine Word in the Economy of Redemption condescended to be exhibited only inwardly and spiritually in the minds of individuals, a purely spiritual worship would be the fitting expression of Its adoration.

317

1862–3
A lay voice in the election of bishops (Scotland)

History of the Lay Claims Under the Scottish Bishops 1789–1905, G.T.S. Farquhar (Dumfries, 1911), p. 73.

1. *On the sixth day* of the Synod
   (a) the *Upper Chamber* frequently mentioned this point, and it appeared that the Primus, S. Andrews, Brechin, and Aberdeen were explicitly in favour of extending the privilege to the Laity. Argyll, while expressing himself generally in favour of the Lay Claims, did not happen to mention the point of the vote in Episcopal elections particularly. Edinburgh, being prevented by illness from attending, sent a letter, in which he explained that, while strongly in favour of Lay Claims in the abstract, he doubted the wisdom of granting them in the present state of public opinion; and Glasgow was evidently against them altogether.

(b) In the *Lower House* the Dean of Brechin (Thom) summed up the result of their first day's debate on this question thus: — He 'thought that the discussion, which had taken place on the subject, was of great importance, as it showed, generally speaking, that the feeling was... that there ought to be such a representation of the Laity, as would enable them to give a vote in the election of Bishops.'

318

1863
The framing of Ecclesiastical Canons (Scotland)

Code of Canons of the Episcopal Church in Scotland (1876), Introduction, pp. xiii–xiv.

The Revolution in 1688 set aside the legally established Episcopacy of Scotland; and for several years after the shock which our Church received by the termination of that national struggle, the bishops had enough to do in keeping up a pure Episcopal Succession, till it should be seen what, in the course of Providence, might be further effected towards the preservation, though not of an Established, yet of a purely primitive Episcopal Church, in this part of the Kingdom. For this purpose, a few Canons were drawn up, and sanctioned by the bishops, in the year 1743, which, though very well calculated to answer the purposes intended by them, while the Church was under legal restraint and threatened with persecution, still left room for considerable enlargement, and required to have embodied with them, or added to them, several regulations suited to the condition of the Episcopal Church in this country after the restrictions and penalties imposed by the State had been withdrawn. In accomplishing this good work, some aid was naturally to be looked for from the Canons appointed for the Church of England in the year 1603, for the Church of Ireland in 1634, and for the Church of Scotland in 1636. For the purpose of collecting from these, and other sources, a system of Ecclesiastical Discipline proper for the Church under their episcopal charge, the Protestant bishops of Scotland came to the resolution of holding a General Ecclesiastical Synod; and being duly convocated by the Primus, did accordingly meet in Aberdeen, on Wednesday the 19th day of June in the year of our Lord 1811, together with the Deans of their several Dioceses, and a Representative of the Clergy from each Diocese containing more than four Presbyters, when a Code of Canons for preserving and regulating Order and Discipline in the Protestant Episcopal Church in Scotland was adopted and sanctioned. A second General Synod met at Laurencekirk, in the county of Kincardine, on Wednesday the 18th day of June 1828, when the Canons of 1811 were revised and altered. A third was held at Edinburgh on Wednesday, 17th of June 1829, when some enactments in the Sixteenth Canon of 1828 were repealed. A fourth General Synod assembled in Edinburgh on Wednesday the 29th of August 1838, when the Canons were again revised and considerably altered. Subsequently, in the course of time, cases of difficulty having arisen, especially respecting Judicial Processes, for which the Canons appeared to contain no adequate provisions and regulations, it was deemed necessary and expedient, for this and other purposes, that the whole Code should be submitted to a careful revision, amendment, and extension. A Committee was consequently appointed by the College of bishops in the year 1859, composed of an equal number of Clergy and Laity, who were requested "to consider the state of the existing Code of Canons, and to draw up a Report, pointing out the particulars therein which should appear to them to require amendment, and specifying such amplifications and additions as they should think desirable." A General Synod was thereafter summoned to consider the Report of the Committee.

319

1864
Principles of study of Scripture

Brooke Foss Westcott (1825–1901), Bishop of Durham, The Bible in the Church *(London, 1864), Preface, p. x.*

The development of modern biblical scholarship was raising points of criticism in the study of Scripture at this date, which led some to reject the findings of scholarship. The controversy was a major reason for the calling of the first Lambeth Conference in 1867. Cf. *Faith and contemporary thought*, Lambeth Conference, 1908, no. 374.

If [the Bible] is, as we devoutly believe, the very source and measure of our religious faith, it seems impossible to insist too earnestly on the supreme importance of patience, candour and truthfulness in investigating every problem which it involves... And, unless all past experience is worthless, the difficulties of the Bible are the most fruitful guides to its divine depths. It was said long since that 'God was pleased to leave difficulties upon the surface of Scripture, that men might be forced to look below the surface'.

320

1864
The Bible in the Church

Brooke Foss Westcott (1825–1901), Bishop of Durham, The Bible in the Church *(London, 1864), Preface, pp. vii, x–xi.*

Westcott here stresses the impossibility of setting 'Scripture' over against the 'Church' as though their authority could be separated. He describes the process of formation and reception of the Canon of Scripture in the early Church. Compare *The First Report* of the Anglican-Roman Catholic International Commission (1982), *Authority in the Church*, I, 2.

The history of the Old Testament in the Christian Churches is intimately connected with the history of the New Testament... each illustrates the other in a remarkable degree, and when combined they show with the greatest clearness the principles by which the Church was guided in the ratification of the books of the Bible, and the power which she claimed to exercise in the work.... the formation of the collection of Holy Scriptures was... according to the natural laws;...slowly, and with an ever-deepening conviction, the Churches received, after that, and in some cases after doubt and contradictions, the books which we now receive;... the religious consciousness which was quickened by the words of prophets and apostles in turn ratified their writings.... The judgement which was, in this manner, the expression of the fullness of Christian life, was not confined in early times by rigid or uniform laws, but realized in ecclesiastical usage;... the Bible was not something distinct from, and independent of, the Christian body, but the vital law of its action;... the Church offered a living commentary on the Book, and the book an unchanging test of the Church.

321

1864
The nature of Scripture's witness to its own authority

Brooke Foss Westcott (1825–1901), Bishop of Durham, The Bible in the Church *(London, 1864), pp. 14–5.*

The Bible contains in itself the fullest witness to its Divine authority. If... a large collection of fragmentary records, written, with few exceptions, without any designed connexion, at most distant times and under the most varied circumstances, yet combine to form a definite whole, broadly separated from other books; if it further appear that these different parts, when interpreted historically, reveal a gradual progress of social spiritual life uniform at least in its general direction; if... they offer not only remarkable coincidences in minute details of facts... but also subtle harmonies of complementary doctrine; if... they are felt... to be instinct with a common spirit; then it will be readily acknowledged that, however they came into being first, however they were united afterwards into the sacred volume, they are yet legibly stamped with the Divine seal as 'inspired by God', in a sense in which no other writings are.

322

1865
The Colenso affair

Historical Records of the Church of the Province of South Africa, pp. 324–5.

See nos. 325ff. John Colenso (1814–83) was deposed from the bishopric of Natal in 1863 by the Archbishop of Cape Town, Robert Gray, who was his Metropolitan, on the grounds that he had been teaching heresy. He denied the Archbishop's authority to depose him and appealed to the Judicial Committee of the Privy Council in England. A crisis of jurisdiction resulted, which was one of the prompters of Canada's call for a world-wide Conference of Anglican bishops, and thus of the calling of the first Lambeth Conference.

In March, 1865, Dr. Colenso won his case before the Judicial Committee of the Privy Council. The judgement clearly showed that no more letters patent would be issued to bishops in the

Colonies, that the Church of South Africa was a voluntary society and must make its own rules. This cleared the way for the Metropolitan to seek for a new bishop without incurring the charge of breaking a law. Dr. Colenso, on the other hand, made a public statement on his return in November:

We have made our choice to be bound by the laws of the Church of England, to submit to the decision of her chief tribunals, to the interpretations that may be put upon her formularies by her Supreme Court of Appeal.

He had the support of influential laymen, amongst them his old friend, Sir Theophilus Shepstone.

In the meantime the clergy and laity of Natal held a conference and asked counsel from the South African bishops about the appointment of an orthodox bishop. Bishop Cotterill of Grahamstown, who had been at one time the supporter of Dr. Colenso, wrote very fully:

...It appears to me the following considerations are important:–

1. It is asked whether the acceptance of a new bishop would sever the clergy and laity from the Mother Church in England. I would reply that it seems to me that it would be a virtual act of separation from the Church for them to admit any episcopal authority of Bishop Colenso over them. For while his Letters Patent give him a certain titular status from which it appears he cannot be moved... yet if he were allowed still to have episcopal authority in Natal it would be in direct opposition to the conditions under which the Church of England sent him forth as bishop. That this view is recognized by the Church of England is apparent from the fact that in England itself he is inhibited from exercising any function of his office. Again, as he is no longer Bishop of Natal, though by law he retains the title, it is perfectly competent for those to whom the duty may belong to appoint a new bishop, whom, if appointed in accordance with principles sanctioned by the Church of England, it will be the manifest duty of the clergy and laity of the diocese of Natal to accept.

2. It is not so easy to answer the second question, What are the proper steps to take, to obtain a new bishop? because no principles universally applicable as to the appointment to vacant sees, have been recognized by the Church... If the majority of the clergy and representatives of the laity in the diocese will agree with the Metropolitan and majority of the bishops of the Province in selecting and nominating some one to be the new Bishop of Natal. he will be bishop, when consecrated, on principles sanctioned by the Church of England. (Signed) H. Grahamstown.

The other South African bishops replied in much the same way, and the Archbishop of Canterbury (Longley), to whom the same questions were sent, wrote a most important letter to the Dean of

Maritzburg in October, 1865, in which he says, among other things:

I do not see how you can accept Dr. Colenso as your bishop without identifying yourself with his errors. The bishops of the Church in England have, with scarcely an exception, either publicly prohibited Dr. Colenso from preaching in their dioceses, or intimated their unwillingness to allow him to do so. He has not preached in any diocese except on one occasion, so that the great majority of the English bishops have withdrawn from all communication with him. As to the appointment of a new bishop, the Privy Council has pronounced the Church of South Africa to be just as independent as any of the Nonconformist communities, and under this view, it is, I conclude, competent to elect its own bishop without reference to the authorities in England either civil or ecclesiastical; nor, as I conceive, will such an act separate you from communion with the Church of England. The Scotch Episcopal Church is in communion with us, but elects its own bishops, and is not obliged to submit to appeal to the Judicial Committee of the Privy Council. (Signed) C.T. Cantuar.

323

1865

The first Provincial Synod in South Africa —
a single Episcopate united in a common faith

Historical Records of the Church of the Province of South Africa, pp. 84–5.

Bishop Gray writes to Henry Cotterill, Bishop of Grahamstown, raising with him a number of constitutional points about the means by which a new Province might be formed.

All my letters from the Archbishop downwards, concurred with yours as to the next step being the election of a bishop by the Church in Natal and its organisation of itself as a voluntary religious association in communion with us and with the Church of England. I have therefore urged this course upon them... On your return, bishops, representatives of the clergy and laity from each diocese – St Helena, Free State, Natal, Grahamstown, and Capetown – meet here in conference with the understanding that the conference would probably end in a Provincial Synod. We agree in conference upon a line. Then the bishops meet in synod and lay down the principles, and agree to invite the clergy and laity. These form the mixed synod. This is the centre and basis of our voluntary association. The Church of England declares herself in communion with this body. *I* cannot call a Provincial Synod of clergy and laity. A future Privy Council would say that it was no synod at all... It seems to me that we bishops are the essential parts of this voluntary association, and that all steps towards organisation must *formally* proceed from us. I hope you will have many opportunities of talking over this scheme with those able to advise, and working out a plan that will stand the test of P.C.[1] enmity. One of the things that the Colonial Church wants more than ever is a basis of Ecclesiastical Law. As a branch of the Church we must adopt all the Canon Law which the Church of England has adopted according to our circumstances. But we want a code for our adoption deduced from the ancient canons.

324

1866
The first Anglican baptized member, Nippon Sei Ko Kai

Extract from A Hundred Year History of Nippon Sei Ko Kai, *Nippon Sei Ko Kai (Tokyo, 1959), p. 33.*

'The most thankful matter of Fr Channing Moore Williams[1] while he was stationed in Nagasaki would have been his giving baptism to a samurai from Higo called Suke-emon Sohmura. It was during a time when the trend of new learnings of Western culture was shifting from the use of Dutch towards that of English. Many youths came to Nagasaki from the various feudal states of Japan with a strong admiration of the new culture and they often became students under Mr Verbeck and Fr Williams, seeking out anyone from England and America. Sohmura was sent to Nagasaki by his feudal state to supervise those young people. As he himself was then already over 40 years old, full of insights, and very keen on absorbing the new Western knowledge, he also joined those students of Fr Williams. 'One samurai', referred to in a personal letter back home dated January, 1864, is judged to have been

---

[1]   Privy Council

[1]   First Anglican missionary to Japan, from the Episcopal Church in the USA.

Sohmura. According to this letter, the samurai visited Fr Williams carrying a volume of the Holy Bible which was said to have been given him by Verbeck, and from that day on, he came to William's home every evening for two weeks and read the Bible in Chinese translation. It is said that later, after this samurai returned to his home state and was promoted to a more responsible position, Williams was asked to obtain a book about military technique. In 1865 Sohmura was again sent to Nagasaki, and while he was engaged in studying military technique through this book, it is assumed that he often came to Williams and also learned more about Christianity. In February, 1866, as he learned that Fr. Williams was about to return to the USA,[2] Sohmura was determined to receive baptism, which was then a sacrament forbidden by law.'

---

[2]   To be consecrated Bishop of China and Japan.

8
ANGLICAN COMMUNION
1867–1967

325

1866[1]

The beginning of the Lambeth Conferences

Chronicle of Convocation, 1866.

There was a clear understanding from the outset that the Lambeth Conferences could not be 'councils' in the sense of being 'decision-making bodies'. At the Convocation of Canterbury in May 1866, the Lower House of Convocation expressed to the Archbishop of Canterbury:

'...an earnest desire that he would be pleased to issue an invitation to all the bishops in communion with the Church of England to assemble at such time and place, and accompanied by such persons as may be deemed fit, for the purpose of Christian sympathy and mutual counsel on matters affecting the welfare of the Church at home and abroad.' Archbishop Longley stated that 'It should be distinctly understood that at this meeting no declaration of faith shall be made, and no decision come to which shall affect generally the interests of the Church, but that we shall meet together for brotherly counsel and encouragement... I should refuse to convene any assembly which pretended to enact any canons or affected to make any decisions binding on the Church...'

326

1867

Church, State and the appointment of bishops

The Scottish Primus at the Lambeth Conference of 1867, in Historical Records of the Church of the Province of South Africa, pp. 84–5.

---

[1]   We include this text of 1866 as belonging to the Lambeth Conference story, although properly speaking this section begins in 1867.

[The Lambeth Conference] has for ever dissipated the erroneous Erastian notion that the Church of England could not recognize any man for a true bishop who was not made so by the authority of the Sovereign. One-third of the bishops present were not so made, nor was any distinction recognized between bishops of an established or an unestablished church. All were alike equal as parts of one Episcopate... The existence of different liturgies in churches is no bar to their intercommunion... Proved heresy separates a bishop from communion with the Anglican Church in every part of the world. One chair was vacant which should have been filled by a Bishop of the Church of South Africa. But that bishop had been deposed for heresy. That deposition was recognized by the bishops assembled at Lambeth, and no disapproval was heard from any quarter in that great assembly when the Archbishop informed us that he had sent no invitation to Dr. Colenso.

327

1867

The Archbishop of Canterbury's letter of invitation to the Lambeth Conference of 1867

The Synod of the Anglican Church in Canada, held in 1865, anxious about the implications of the Colenso Affair in South Africa (where appeal was made to the Privy Council in England over the heads of the provincial authorities), asked for the convening of a worldwide Conference of Anglican bishops to consider the principles of Church government at stake. Cf. no. 322.

Lambeth Palace,   *22 February 1867.*

'RIGHT REV. AND DEAR BROTHER,

'I request your presence at a meeting of the bishops in visible communion with the United Church of England and Ireland, purposed (God willing) to be holden at Lambeth, under my presidency, on the 24th of September next and the three following days.

'The circumstances under which I have resolved to issue the present invitation are these: — The Metropolitan and Bishops of Canada, last year, addressed to the two Houses of the Convocation of Canterbury the expression of their desire that I should be moved to invite the bishops of our Indian and Colonial Episcopate to meet myself and the Home Bishops for brotherly communion and conference.

'The consequence of that appeal has been that both Houses of the Convocation of my Province have addressed to me their dutiful request that I would invite the attendance, not only of our Home and Colonial Bishops, but of all who are avowedly in communion with our Church. The same request was unanimously preferred to me at a numerous gathering of English, Irish, and Colonial Archbishops and Bishops recently assembled at Lambeth; at which — I rejoice to record it — we had the counsel and concurrence of an eminent Bishop of the Church in the United States of America — the Bishop of Illinois.

'Moved by these requests, and by the expressed concurrence therein of other members both of the Home and Colonial Episcopate, who could not be present at our meeting, I have now resolved — not, I humbly trust, without the guidance of God the Holy Ghost — to grant this grave request, and call together the meeting thus earnestly desired. I greatly hope that you may be able to attend it, and to aid us with your presence and brotherly counsel thereat.

'I propose that, at our assembling, we should first solemnly seek the blessing of Almighty GOD on our gathering, by uniting together in the highest act of the Church's worship. After this, brotherly consultations will follow. In these we may consider together many practical questions, the settlement of which would tend to the advancement of the Kingdom of our Lord and Master Jesus Christ, and to the maintenance of greater union in our missionary work, and to increased intercommunion among ourselves.

'Such a meeting would not be competent to make declarations or lay down definitions on points of doctrine. But united worship and common counsels would greatly tend to maintain practically the unity of the faith: whilst they would bind us in straiter bonds of peace and brotherly charity.

'I shall gladly receive from you a list of any subjects you may wish to suggest to me for consideration and discussion....

328

1867
Inter-provincial and inter-diocesan communication with respect for local independence

Resolutions 1, 2, Lambeth Conference, 1867.

Resolution 1.–
That it appears to us expedient for the purpose of maintaining brotherly intercommunion, that all cases of establishment of new Sees, and appointment of new Bishops, be notified to all Archbishops and Metropolitans, and all Presiding Bishops of the Anglican Communion.
Resolution 2.–
That, having regard to the conditions under which intercommunion between members of the Church passing from one distant Diocese to another may be duly maintained, we hereby declare it desirable:–
(1) That forms of Letters Commendatory on behalf of Clergymen visiting other Dioceses be drawn up and agreed upon.
(2) That a form of Letters Commendatory for lay members of the Church be in like manner prepared.

329

1867
The higher authority of higher Synods

Resolution 4, Lambeth Conference, 1867.

The intention here is to make diocesan synods subordinate to provincial or national synods in their authority to make legislative decisions. (See also nos. 67, 70, 155, 187, 207, 208 and others.)

Resolution 4 –
That, in the opinion of this Conference, Unity in Faith and Discipline will be best maintained among our several branches of the Anglican Communion by due and canonical subordination of the Synods of the several branches to the higher authority of a Synod or Synods above them.

330

1867
The principles of synodical government

Committee Report 'A' of the Lambeth Conference of 1867, pp. 58-60.

This text stresses the centrality of the diocese with its bishop in the Church's order. It is also of significance in the process by which lay people came to be represented in synodical government at every level in the Anglican Communion.

I. In the organisation of Synodal order for the government of the Church, the Diocesan Synod appears to be the primary and simplest form of such organisation. By the Diocesan Synod the co-operation of all members of the body is obtained in Church action; and that acceptance of Church rules is secured, which, in the absence of other law, usage, or enactment, gives to these rules the force of laws 'binding on those who, expressly or by implication, have consented to them.' For this reason, wherever the Church is not established by law, it is, in the judgement of your Committee, essential to order and good government that the Diocese should be organised by a Synod. Your Committee consider that it is not at variance with the ancient principles of the Church, that both Clergy and Laity should attend the Diocesan Synod, and that it is expedient that the Synod should consist of the Bishop and Clergy of the Diocese, with Representatives of the Laity. The Constitution of the Diocesan Synod may be determined either by rules for that branch of the Church established by the Synod of the Province, or by general consent in the Diocese itself, its rules being sanctioned afterwards by the Provincial Synod. Your Committee, however, recommend that the following general rules should be adopted: viz., that the Bishop, Clergy, and Laity should sit together, the Bishop presiding; that votes should be taken by orders, whenever demanded; and that the concurrent assent of Bishop, Clergy, and Laity should be necessary to the validity of all acts of the Synod. They consider that the Clerical members of the Synod should be those Clergy who are recognized by the Bishop, according to the rules of the Church in that Diocese, as being under his jurisdiction. Whether in large Dioceses, when the Clergy are very numerous, they might appear by representation, is a difficult question, and one on which your Committee are not prepared to express an opinion.

The Lay Representatives in the Synod ought, in the judgement of your Committee, to be Male Communicants of at least one year's standing in the Diocese, and of the full age of twenty-one.[1] It should be required that the electors should be Members of the Church in that Diocese, and belong to the parish in which they claim to vote. It appears desirable that the regular meetings of the Synod should be fixed and periodical; but that the right of convening special meetings whenever they may be required should be reserved to the Bishop. The office of the Diocesan Synod is, generally, to make regulations, not repugnant to those of higher Synods, for the order and good government of the Church within the Diocese, and to promulgate the decisions of the Provincial Synod.

II. The Provincial Synod — or, as it is called in New Zealand, the General Synod, and in the United States the General Convention — is formed, whenever it does not exist already by law and usage, through the voluntary association of Dioceses for united legislation and common action. The Provincial Synod not only provides a method for securing unity amongst the Dioceses which are thus associated, but also forms the link between these Dioceses and other Churches of the Anglican Communion. Without questioning the right of the Bishops of any Province to meet in Synod by themselves, and without affirming that the presence of others is essential to a Provincial Synod, your Committee recommend that, whenever no law or usage to the contrary already exists, it should consist of the Bishops of the Province, and of Representatives both of the Clergy and of the Laity in each Diocese. Your Committee need not define the method in which a Provincial Synod may be first constituted, but they assume that its constitution and rules will be determined by the concurrence of the several Dioceses duly represented. Your Committee consider that it must be left to each Province to decide whether, and under what circumstances, the Bishops, Clergy, and Laity in a Provincial Synod should sit and discuss questions in the same chamber or separately; but, in the judgement of the Committee, the votes should in either case be taken by orders; and the concurrent assent of Bishops, Clergy, and Laity should be necessary for any legislative action, wherever the Clergy and Laity form part of the constitution of a Provincial

---

[1] A restriction of sex appeared appropriate in an age when women in Britain had no vote in parliamentary elections.

Synod; such powers and functions not involving legislation being reserved as belong to the Bishops by virtue of their office. The number, qualification, and mode of election of the Clerical and Lay Representatives from each Diocese must be determined by the Synods in the several Provinces. It is the office of the Provincial Synod, generally, to exercise, within the limits of the Province, powers in regard to Provincial questions similar to those which the Diocesan Synod exercises, within the Diocese, in regard to Diocesan questions. As to the relation between these two Synods, your Committee are of opinion, that the Diocese is bound to accept positive enactments of a Provincial Synod in which it is duly represented, and that no Diocesan regulations have force, if contrary to the decisions of a higher Synod; but that, in order to prevent any collision or misunderstanding, the spheres of action of the several Synods should be defined on the following principle, viz., That the Provincial Synod should deal with questions of common interest to the whole Province, and with those which affect the communion of the Dioceses with one another and with the rest of the Church; whilst the Diocesan Synod should be left free to dispose of matters of local interest, and to manage the affairs of the Diocese.

331

1867
The limits of local independence in fixing the rites and ceremonies of the liturgy

Resolution 8, Lambeth Conference, 1867.

This resolution is in the spirit of Article xxxiv of the Thirty-Nine Articles, where Churches are held to be free to make appropriate provision for local needs in decreeing 'rites and ceremonies' (cf. no. 485).

Resolution 8 –
That, in order to the binding of the Churches of our Colonial Empire and the Missionary Churches beyond them in the closest union with the Mother-Church, it is necessary that they receive and maintain without alteration the standards of Faith and Doctrine as now in use in that Church. That, nevertheless, each Province should have the right to make such adaptations and additions to the

services of the Church as its peculiar circumstances may require. *Provided*, that no change or addition be made inconsistent with the spirit and principles of the Book of Common Prayer, and that all such changes be liable to revision by any Synod of the Anglican Communion in which the said Province shall be represented.

332

1870
The Constitution of the Church of Ireland

First Schedule. Preamble and Declaration Adopted by the General Convention in the Year 1870.

This should be compared with the disestablishment of the Anglican Church in Wales, nos. 386, 407, 409.

In the Name of the Father, and of the Son, and of the Holy Ghost. Amen:
    Whereas it hath been determined by the Legislature that on and after the 1st day of January, 1871, the Church of Ireland shall cease to be established by law; and that the ecclesiastical law of Ireland shall cease to exist as law save as provided in the 'Irish Church Act, 1869', and it hath thus become necessary that the Church of Ireland should provide for its own regulation:
    We, the archbishops and bishops of this the Ancient Catholic and Apostolic Church of Ireland, together with the representatives of the clergy and laity of the same, in General Convention assembled in Dublin in the year of our Lord God one thousand eight hundred and seventy, before entering on this work, do solemnly declare as follows: –

I.
1. The Church of Ireland doth, as heretofore, accept and unfeignedly believe all the Canonical Scriptures of the Old and New Testament, as given by inspiration of God, and containing all things necessary to salvation; and doth continue to profess the faith of Christ as professed by the Primitive Church.
2. The Church of Ireland will continue to minister the doctrine, and sacraments, and the discipline of Christ, as the Lord hath commanded; and will maintain inviolate the three orders of

bishops, priests or presbyters, and deacons in the sacred ministry.

3. The Church of Ireland, as a reformed and Protestant Church, doth hereby reaffirm its constant witness against all those innovations in doctrine and worship, whereby the Primitive Faith hath been from time to time defaced or overlaid, and which at the Reformation this Church did disown and reject.

II.

The Church of Ireland doth receive and approve *The Book of the Articles of Religion*, commonly called the Thirty-Nine Articles, received and approved by the archbishops and bishops and the rest of the clergy of Ireland in the synod holden in Dublin. A.D. 1634; also, *The Book of Common Prayer and Administration of the Sacraments, and other Rites and Ceremonies of the Church, according to the use of the Church of Ireland; and the Form and Manner of Making, Ordaining, and Consecrating of Bishops, priests, and deacons*, as approved and adopted by the synod holden in Dublin, A.D. 1662, and hitherto in use in this Church. And this Church will continue to use the same, subject to such alterations only as may be made therein from time to time by the lawful authority of the Church.

III.

The Church of Ireland will maintain communion with the sister Church of England, and with all other Christian Churches agreeing in the principles of this Declaration; and will set forward, so far as in it lieth, quietness, peace, and love, among all Christian people.

IV.

The Church of Ireland, deriving its authority from Christ, Who is the Head over all things to the Church, doth declare that a General Synod of the Church of Ireland, consisting of the archbishops and bishops, and of representatives of the clergy and laity, shall have chief legislative power therein, and such administrative power as may be necessary for the Church, and consistent with its episcopal constitution.

333

1870
Church of the Province of South Africa

Who are the Anglicans?, *ed. Charles Long, prepared for the Lambeth Conference, 1988 (Ohio, 1988), p. 25.*

The Province is the oldest in Africa and formerly included parts of the Province of Central Africa. British Anglicans met regularly for worship in Cape Town after 1806. The first SPG[1] missionary arrived in 1821. Major growth began after the establishment of the first diocese, Cape Town, in 1847 and the appointment of the first bishop. In the same year that the Province was formed, in 1870, a dissident evangelical group separated to form another church known as the Church of England in South Africa. The work of the Province was extended to Lesotho in 1875, Mozambique in 1893, and in the 20th century to Namibia and Swaziland. Although Anglicanism is naturally strong among the descendants of British colonists and other English-speaking people, 75% of the church's membership is black. Many of its leaders, white and black, have been strong opponents of apartheid.

334

1870
The validity of Anglican Orders

T.J. Bailey, quoting the Bishop of Brechin, Ordinum Sacrorum in Ecclesia Anglicana Defensio *(London, 1870), p. 17.*

It is... objected... that the form of Anglican Orders is imperfect, inasmuch as the office of a bishop was not specified when hands were laid on Matthew Parker. The four consecrating bishops used... these words with imposition of hands, — 'Receive the Holy Ghost, and remember that thou stir up the grace of God, which is in thee by imposition of hands, for God hath not given us the spirit of fear, but of power and love and soberness'... It had been said that these do not determine the office, and would suit the case of a parish clerk as well as a bishop. To this it must be answered...

---

[1] Society for the Propagation of the Gospel

That the use of the words of St. Paul, in which he gives the charge to Timothy as Bishop of Ephesus, shows that it was in the minds of these consecrators to confer on the candidate the anointing of a primitive bishop;... That there were other prayers in the service which distinctly determined the meaning of the action; and... That the reformed bishops were in no worse case than their predecessors; for in none of the English Pontificals, except that of Exeter (which was never used...) is there any determining word at the time of the imposition of hands.

335

1873
The pastoral office

F.J.A. Hort (1828–92), New Testament Scholar, ordination Sermon, 15 June 1873, The Christian Ecclesia *(London, 1897), pp. 242–3.*

Two different kinds of service to the flock are hidden behind the one word "feed"... that core which consists in the providing fit pasture [and] that care... of which the shepherd's rod and staff in the twenty-third Psalm are the symbols, the care of government and guidance... It is [Christ's] own person, words, and acts that supply the ruling standard under which all this pastoral language has to be brought... He who speaks is the Shepherd of shepherds, the Good Shepherd, newly risen from the grave into which he had been brought by laying down his life to the uttermost for his sheep. The feeding and governing of the sheep are but parts of that wonder-working sacrifice.

336

1874
Mission and unity

A.H.Vinton, 'An Address to the First Church Congress' (1874). Authorized Report of the Proceedings of the First Congress of the Protestant Episcopal Church... *(New York, 1875), pp. 9–10.*

This address reflects the new intellectual currents flowing in the Episcopal Church in the United States of America at this time, and the concern to be open to the world.

There is one admitted and acknowledged way of expressing the unity of the Church, a method which both procures and denotes that unity, and that is what we call missionary work, the great work of labouring for Christ, when men get together with the heart of Christ, and labour side by side and hand in hand to do his work; when their zeal and their prayers and their wealth are gladly dedicated to his supreme service; when they labour side by side and stretch out hands alike to pluck souls from the burning; when they kneel by the bedside of the suffering poor, when they administer the Communion to the dying. But there is no distinctive action of the mind of the Church in this sort of work.

Now, is it possible that there can be a nearer approach to a perfect unity than this? Is it not conceivable that the mind of the Church may likewise be brought into an attitude in which it shall realize a unity of reason and of understanding, as truly as it realizes the unity of the spirit and of the heart?

This is the aim of the Church Congress. Its idea is this: in the common dogmatic, technical, traditional distinctions of thought which we find in the Church, which we must find in every assemblage of mankind, are there not underlying conditions recognized as more absolute truths? Is not there a broader platform, upon which our distinctive views have each an accredited and equally valid position?... May we not rise to a higher level than this, where the light is purer and brighter, and the blood cooler; where the simple intelligence can operate more freely, and we can take a bird's-eye view of the outspread field below, and mark the due position and relationship of each and all of the several dogmatic truths that men hold?

It is to this elevation that the Church Congress desires to lift up the Church's mind; to that state where prejudices and passions shall go to sleep, where sharp angles of differences shall be rubbed off by communion and contact; where the venom of prejudice shall be purged out, and where the reason sees by its own pure light.

337

1878
Liturgical revision

The Preface, Church of Ireland Prayer Book. Prefixed at the Revision of 1878.

This preface emphasizes the importance of liturgy as a vehicle of instruction in the faith; and of both continuity in the form of services and adjustmemt to the needs of each age. Cf. nos. 283, 378, 389, 517, 550 and others.

When this Church of *Ireland* ceased to be established by law, and thereupon some alteration in our Publick Liturgy became needful, it was earnestly desired by many that occasion should be taken for a new and full review thereof (such as had already more than once been made in former times), and for considering what other changes the lapse of years or exigency of our present times and circumstances might have rendered expedient. And though we were not unaware of many dangers attending on such an attempt, yet we were the more willing to make it, because we perceived to our comfort that all men, on all sides, professed their love and reverence for the Book of Common Prayer in its main substance and chief parts, and confessed that it contained the true doctrine of Christ, and a pure manner and order of Divine Service, according to the holy Scriptures and the practice of the Primitive Church; and that what was sought by those who desired such a review was not any change of the whole tenor or structure of the Book, but the more clear declaration of what they took to be its true meaning, and the removing of certain expressions here and there, which they judged open to mistake or perversion. And as this Church has already, in its Convention of 1870, received and approved the Book as it then stood and was in use, so we now declare that, in such changes as we have made on this review, we imply no censure upon the former Book, as containing anything contrary to the Scriptures, when it is rightly understood and equitably construed. The true reason of such changes will, for the most part, appear on a comparison of the two Books; but it has been thought good to add some further explanation why certain things have been altered and others retained.... And now, if some shall complain that these changes are not enough, and that we should have taken this opportunity of making this Book as perfect in all respects as they think it might be made, or if others shall say that these changes have been unnecessary or excessive, and that what was already excellent has been impaired by doing that which, in their opinion, might well have been left undone, let them, on the one side and the other, consider that men's judgements of perfection are very various, and that what is imperfect, with peace, is often better than what is otherwise more excellent, without it.

338

1878
Local independence within one Communion

Committee Report, Lambeth Conference, 1878.

Respect for the local jurisdiction of another bishop (and thus for the integrity of the Church in each place) is a sign of communion; where communion is broken or damaged, two bishops of different communions may find themselves acting as pastors in the same area.

Meanwhile, there are certain principles of Church order which, your Committee consider, ought to be distinctly recognized and set forth, as of great importance for the maintenance of union among the Churches of our Communion.

(1.) First, that the duly-certified action of every national or particular Church, and of each ecclesiastical Province (or Diocese not included in a Province), in the exercise of its own discipline, should be respected by all the other Churches, and by their individual members.

(2.) Secondly, that when a Diocese, or territorial sphere of administration, has been constituted by the authority of any Church or Province of this Communion within its own limits, no bishop or other clergyman of any other Church should exercise his functions within that Diocese without the consent of the bishop thereof.

(3.) Thirdly, that no bishop should authorise to officiate in his Diocese a clergyman coming from another Church or Province, unless such clergyman present letters testimonial, countersigned by the bishop of the Diocese from which he comes; such letters to be, as nearly as possible, in the form adopted by such Church or Province in the case of the transfer of a clergyman from one Diocese to another.

339

1878
Ecclesiastical Courts: the machinery for appeal

Committee Report, Lambeth Conference, 1878.

The difficulty addressed here is that the relation of Church and State in England, which made the Church of England the established Church, and created a certain relationship between ecclesiastical and civil jurisdiction, could not extend to other provinces; the principle of provincial autonomy is also relevant here.

There is no appeal from the Ecclesiastical Tribunals in the Colonial Churches to any of the ordinary Ecclesiastical Courts of England, or to the Judicial Committee of the Privy Council, when advising Her Majesty on appeals from Ecclesiastical Courts. No questions relating to the exercise of discipline in a Colonial Church[1] can come before the Judicial Committee of the Privy Council, except on appeal from civil courts in the colony, exercising jurisdiction in matters affecting property or civil rights. The subject, therefore, before your Committee is... whether there should be some external tribunals, or 'Voluntary Boards of Arbitration,' to which an appeal of reference ought to be made; how such Boards, when necessary, should be constituted; and under what circumstances they should be approached.

340

1878
Missionary bishops

Committee Report, Lambeth Conference, 1878.

The principle that a territorial diocese should have a single bishop is not easy to hold to in the early stages of mission. Here, practical rules are set out to try to provide for the various contingencies which may arise. Cf. no. 426.

II.

8. — Your Committee have considered the case of Missions in countries not under English or American rule, and they recommend as follows: —

---

[1]   The geographical areas under consideration here being at that time British 'colonies'.

9. — In cases where two bishops of the Anglican Communion are ministering in the same country, as in China, Japan, and Western Africa at the present time, your Committee are of opinion that under existing circumstances each bishop should have control of his own clergy, and their converts and congregations.

10. — The various bishops in the same country should endeavour, as members of the same Communion, to keep up brotherly intercourse with each other on the subject of their Missionary work.

11. — In countries not under English or American rule, the English or American Church would not ordinarily undertake to establish Dioceses with strictly-defined territorial limits; although either Church might indicate the district in which it was intended that the Missionary Bishop should labour.

12. — Bishops in the same country should take care not to interfere in any manner with the congregations or converts of each other.

13. — It is most undesirable that either Church should for the future send a Bishop or Missionaries to a town or district already occupied by a Bishop of another Branch of the Anglican Communion.

14. — When it is intended to send forth any new Missionary Bishop, notification of such an intention should be sent beforehand to the Archbishop of Canterbury, to the Presiding Bishop of the Protestant Episcopal Church in the United States of America, and to the Metropolitan of any Province near which the Missionary Bishop is to minister.

341

1878
Private Confession

Committee Report, Lambeth Conference, 1878.

The distinction drawn here is between a 'requirement' of full, detailed private confession to a priest on a regular basis and the provision of the option of such confession for those in need of 'relief' for 'troubled conscience'. Anglican tradition has always allowed a range of practice here for the faithful (see nos. 58, 59, 100, 186, 234, 268).

Your Committee desire to affirm that in the matter of Confession the Churches of the Anglican Communion hold fast those principles which are set forth in the Holy Scriptures, which were professed by the Primitive Church, and which were reaffirmed at the English Reformation; and it is their deliberate opinion that no minister of the Church is authorised to require from those who may resort to him to open their grief a particular or detailed enumeration of all their sins, or to require private confession previous to receiving Holy Communion, or to enjoin or even encourage the practice of habitual confession to a priest, or to teach that such practice of habitual confession, or the being subject to what has been termed the direction of a priest, is a condition of attaining to the highest spiritual life. At the same time your Committee are not to be understood as desiring to limit in any way the provision made in the Book of Common Prayer for the relief of troubled consciences.

342

1883
The Church in the Province of the West Indies

Who are the Anglicans?, *ed. Charles Long, prepared for the Lambeth Conference, 1988 (Ohio, 1988), p. 43.*

The Church of England established mission stations in various West Indies territories that became British colonies. In 1883 the Church in the Province of the West Indies was formally established, including a Provincial Synod. In 1897 the Most Rev. Enos Nuttall became the first Archbishop of the West Indies. In 1976 Trinidad hosted the third meeting of the Anglican Consultative Council.

343

1886
The Chicago Quadrilateral

General Convention of the Episcopal Church in the United States of America, A Communion of Communions *(1886).*

Cf. The Lambeth Quadrilateral, no. 355, which was based upon this text.

Whereas, many of the faithful in Christ Jesus among us are praying with renewed and increasing earnestness that some measures may be adopted at this time for the re-union of the sundered parts of Christendom... we Bishops of the Protestant Episcopal Church in the United States of America, in Council assembled as Bishops in the Church of God, do hereby solemnly declare to all whom it may concern, and especially to our fellow Christians of the different Communions in this land, who, in their several spheres, have contended for the religion of Christ:

1. Our earnest desire that the Saviour's prayer, 'That we all may be one', may, in its deepest and truest sense, be speedily fulfilled;
2. That we believe that all who have been duly baptized with water, in the name of the Father, and of the Son, and of the Holy Ghost, are members of the Holy Catholic Church;
3. That in all things of human ordering or human choice, relating to modes of worship and discipline, or to traditional customs, this Church is ready in the spirit of love and humility to forgo all preferences of her own;
4. That this Church does not seek to absorb other Communions, but rather, co-operating with them on the basis of a common Faith and Order, to discountenance schism, to heal the wounds of the Body of Christ, and to promote the charity which is the chief of Christian graces and the visible manifestation of Christ to the world;

But furthermore, we do hereby affirm that the Christian unity now so earnestly desired by the memorialists can be restored only by the return of all Christian communions to the principles of unity exemplified by the undivided Catholic Church during the first ages of its existence; which principle we believe to be the substantial deposit of Christian Faith and Order committed by Christ and his apostles to the Church unto the end of the world, and therefore incapable of compromise or surrender by those who have been ordained to be its stewards and trustees for the common and equal benefit of all men. As inherent parts of this sacred deposit, and therefore as essential to the restoration of unity among the divided branches of Christendom, we account the following, to wit:

1. The Holy Scriptures of the Old and New Testament as the revealed word of God.
2. The Nicene Creed as the sufficient statement of the Christian Faith.
3. The two Sacraments — Baptism and the Supper of the Lord — ministered with unfailing use of Christ's words of institution and the elements ordained by Him.
4. The Historic Episcopate, locally adapted in the methods of its administration to the varying needs of the nations and peoples called of God into unity of His Church.

Furthermore, Deeply grieved by the sad divisions which affect the Christian Church in our own land, we hereby declare our desire and readiness, so soon as there shall be any authorized response to this Declaration, to enter into brotherly conference with all or any Christian Bodies seeking the restoration of the organic unity of the Church, with a view to the earnest study of the conditions under which so priceless a blessing might happily be brought to pass.

344

1887
The Anglican Church in Japan

Who are the Anglicans?, ed. Charles Long, prepared for the Lambeth Conference, 1988 (Ohio, 1988), p. 53.

In 1859, the American Episcopal Church sent two missionaries from China to open new work in Japan. They were later joined by missionaries from England and Canada. A general Anglican Synod took place in 1887, adopted to constitution, canons and Prayer Book for the Province and unified the work of the various Anglican missionary societies. Its first Japanese bishops were consecrated in 1923. During World War II the church remained underground rather than comply with government decrees. After the war all responsibility for the life of the Church and its many educational and medical institutions was assumed by Japanese leadership and increasing assistance has been given from Japan to other parts of the Anglican Communion. The Province is governed by a triennial General Synod including a House of Bishops and a House of Clergy and Lay deputies. The Primate is elected from among the active bishops for a three year term.

345

1888
The Lambeth Conference is not a Council or Synod

Archbishop Benson, Diary (1888), in A.M.G. Stephenson, Anglicans and the Lambeth Conferences *(London, 1978), p. 79.*

Cf. nos. 67, 70, 155, 187, 207, 208, 329.

I opened the Conference by pointing out that the Conference was in no sense a Synod, and not adapted, or competent, or within its powers, if it should attempt to make binding decisions on doctrines or discipline.

346

1888
Authoritative standards of doctrine and worship and the needs of different cultures

Encyclical Letter, *Lambeth Conference, 1888.*

The Lambeth Conference is here wrestling with the problem of balancing the need for a common faith and order in a single Communion, with the proper pluriformity which respects differences between cultures, and from age to age.

The authoritative standards of doctrine and worship claim your careful attention.... It is of the utmost importance that our faith and practice should be represented, both to the ancient Churches and to the native and growing Churches in the mission-field, in a manner which shall neither give cause for offence; nor restrict due liberty, nor present any stumbling-blocks in the way of complete communion. We desire that these standards should be set before the foreign Churches in their purity and simplicity. A certain liberty of treatment must be extended to the cases of native and growing Churches, on which it would be unreasonable to impose, as conditions of communion, the whole of the Thirty-Nine Articles, coloured as they are in language and form by the peculiar circumstances under which they were originally drawn up. On the other hand it would be impossible for us to share with them in the matter of Holy Orders, as in complete intercommunion, without satisfactory evidence that they hold substantially the same form of doctrine as ourselves. It ought not to be difficult, much less impossible, to formulate articles, in accordance with our own standards of doctrine and worship, the acceptance of which should be required of all ordained in such Churches.

347

1888
Towards communion with other ecclesial communities
Encyclical Letter, *Lambeth Conference, 1888.*

Compare the tone of this passage, deeply desirous of Christian unity but fearful that some 'surrender' will be expected, with more recent ecumenical texts in this volume, where there is a new confidence that unity is not a matter of compromise but of discovering a common faith and order together.

The attitude of the Anglican Communion towards the religious bodies now separated from it by unhappy divisions would appear to be this: — We hold ourselves in readiness to enter into brotherly conference with any of those who may desire intercommunion with us in a more or less perfect form. We lay down conditions on which such intercommunion is, in our opinion, and according to our conviction, possible. For, however we may long to embrace those now alienated from us, so that the ideal of the one flock under the Shepherd may be realised, we must not be unfaithful stewards of the great deposit entrusted to us. We cannot desert our position either as to faith or discipline. That concord would, in our judgement, be neither true nor desirable which should be produced by such surrender. But we gladly and thankfully recognize the real religious work which is carried out by Christian bodies not of our Communion. We cannot close our eyes to the visible blessing which has been vouchsafed to their labours for Christ's sake. Let us not be misunderstood on this point. We are not insensible to the strong ties, the rooted convictions, which attach them to their present position. These we respect, as we wish that on our side our own principles and feelings may be respected. Competent observers, indeed, assert that not in England only, but in all parts of the Christian world, there is a real yearning for unity — that men's hearts are moved more than heretofore towards Christian fellowship. The Conference has shown in its discussions as well as its resolutions that it is deeply penetrated with this feeling. May the Spirit of Love move on the troubled waters of religious differences.

348

1888
Sunday Observance

Encyclical Letter, *Lambeth Conference 1888.*

The due observance of Sunday as a day of rest, of worship, and of religious teaching, has a direct bearing on the moral well-being of the Christian community.

349

1888
The teaching of the Faith

Encyclical Letter, *Lambeth Conference, 1888.*

This exhortation not only underlines the importance of the Church's perpetual duty to teach the faith; but also points to the special difficulties of doing so in the modern world.

Recognising thus the primary importance of maintaining the moral precepts and discipline of the Gospel in all the relations of life and society, we proceed to the consideration of the means, within the reach and contemplation of the Churches, for inculcating the definite truths of the Faith, which are the basis of such moral teaching. We cannot escape the conviction that this department of work requires great attention and much improvement. The religious teaching of the young is sadly deficient in depth and reality, especially in the matter of doctrine. This deficiency is not confined to any class of society, and the task of remedying the default is one which the Laity must be prepared to share with the Clergy. On parents it lies as a divine charge. Godfathers and Godmothers should be urged to fulfil the duty which they have undertaken for the children whose sponsors they have been, and to see that they are not left uninstructed, or inadequately prepared for Confirmation. The use of public catechising and regular preparation of candidates for Confirmation is capable of much development. The work done in Sunday Schools requires, as we believe, more constant supervision and more sustained interest than, in a great many cases, it receives from the Clergy. The instruction of Sunday-School teachers, and of the pupil-teachers in Elementary Schools, ought to be regarded as an indispensable part of the pastoral work of a Parish Priest; and the moral and practical lessons from the Bible ought to be enforced by constant reference to the sanctions, and to the illustrations of doctrine and discipline belonging to them, to be found in the same Holy Scripture. It would be possible, to a greater extent than is now done, to make sermons in church combine doctrinal and moral efficiency, and, by illustrating the rationale of divine service, lead on the congregation to the perception of the definite relations between worship, faith, and work — the lessons of the Prayer Book, the Catechism, and the Creeds. It is not, however, with reference to the young alone, or to the recognized members of their own flock, that the Clergy have need to look carefully to the security of definiteness in teaching the faith. The study of Holy Scripture is a great part of the mental discipline of the Christian, and the Bible itself is the main instrument in all teaching of religion. Unhappily, in the present day, there is a widespread system of propagandism hostile to the reception of the Bible as a treasury of Divine knowledge, and throughout society, in all its ranks, misgivings, doubts, hostile criticisms, and sceptical estimates of doctrinal truths as based on Revelations, are very common....We must recommend to the Clergy cautious and industrious treatment of these points of controversy, and most earnestly press upon them the importance of taking, as the central thought of their teaching, our Lord Jesus

Christ, as the sacrifice for our sins, as the healer of our sinfulness, the source of all our spiritual life, and the revelation to our consciences of the law and motive of all moral virtue. To Him and to His work all the teachings of the Old Testament converge, and from Him all the teachings of the New Testament flow, in spirit, in force, and in form. The work of the Church is the application and extension of the blessings of the Incarnation, and her teaching the development of its doctrinal issues as contained in the Creeds of the Church.

350

1888
Alcohol abuse

Encyclical Letter, *Lambeth Conference, 1888.*

The fear of alcohol abuse has led some Christian communities to advocate complete abstention. Compare no. 380 on drug-abuse, which raises further issues. The refusal to use wine in the Eucharist is firmly disapproved of here. Cf. no. 359.

Noble and self-denying efforts have been made for many years, within and without the Church, for the suppression of intemperance, and it is our earnest hope that these efforts will be increased manifold. The evil effects of this sin on the life of the Church and the nation can scarcely be exaggerated. But we are constrained to utter a caution against a false principle which threatens to creep in and vitiate much useful work. Highly valuable as we believe total abstinence to be as a means to an end, we desire to discountenance the language which condemns the use of wine as wrong in itself, independently of its effects on ourselves or on others, and we have expressed our disapproval of a reported practice (which seems to be due to some extent to the tacit assumption of this principle) of substituting some other liquid in the celebration of Holy Communion.

351

1888
The basis of acceptance of newly constituted Churches into the Anglican Communion

Resolution 19, Lambeth Conference, 1888.

19. That, as regards newly-constituted Churches, especially in non-Christian lands, it should be a condition of the recognition of them as in complete intercommunion with us, and especially of their receiving from us Episcopal Succession, that we should first receive from them satisfactory evidence that they hold substantially the same doctrine as our own, and that their Clergy subscribe Articles in accordance with the express statements of our own standards of doctrine and worship; but that they should not necessarily be bound to accept in their entirety the Thirty-Nine Articles of Religion.

352

1888
Christian marriage and polygamy

Encyclical Letter, Lambeth Conference, 1888.

Cf. no. 453. The pastoral problems raised by existing polygamous marriages in areas of mission were further discussed by the 1988 Lambeth Conference.

In vital connection with the promotion of purity is the maintenance of the sanctity of marriage, which is the centre of social morality. This is seriously compromised by facilities of divorce which have been increased in recent years by legislation in some countries. We have therefore held it our duty to reaffirm emphatically the precept of Christ relating thereto, and to offer some advice which may guide the Clergy of our Communion in their attitude towards any infringement of the Master's rule...
The sanctity of marriage as a Christian obligation implies the faithful union of one man with one woman until the union is severed by death... polygamous alliances... are allowed on all hands to be condemned by the law of Christ; but they present many difficult practical problems which have been solved in

various ways in the past. We have carefully considered this question in the different lights thrown upon it from various parts of the mission-field. While we have refrained from offering advice on minor points, leaving these to be settled by the local authorities of the Church, we have laid down some broad lines on which alone we consider that the missionary may safely act. Our first care has been to maintain and protect the Christian conception of marriage, believing that any immediate and rapid successes which might otherwise have been secured in the mission-field would be dearly purchased by any lowering or confusion of this idea.

353

1888
The needs of society

Encyclical Letter, *Lambeth Conference, 1888.*

Intimately connected with... moral questions is the attitude of the Christian Church towards the social problems of the day. Excessive inequality in the distribution of this world's goods; vast accumulation and desperate poverty side by side: these suggest many anxious considerations to any thoughtful person, who is penetrated with the mind of Christ. No more important problems can well occupy the attention — whether of the Clergy or Laity... To study schemes proposed for redressing the social balance, to welcome the good which may be found in the aims or operations of any, and to devise methods, whether by legislation or by social combinations, or in any other way, for a peaceful solution of the problem without violence or injustice, is one of the noblest pursuits which can engage the thoughts of those who strive to follow in the footsteps of Christ.

354

1888
Sunday Observance

Resolution 6, Lambeth Conference, 1888.

(a) That the principle of the religious observance of one day in seven, embodied in the Fourth Commandment, is of Divine obligation.

(b) That, from the time of our Lord's Resurrection, the first day of the week was observed by Christians as a day of worship and rest, and, under the name of 'The Lord's Day', gradually succeeded, as the great weekly festival of the Christian Church, to the sacred position of the Sabbath.

(c) That the observance of the Lord's Day as a day of rest, of worship, and of religious teaching, has been a priceless blessing in all Christian lands in which it has been maintained.

(d) That the growing laxity in its observance threatens a great change in its sacred and beneficent character.

(e) That especially the increasing practice, on the part of some of the wealthy and leisurely classes, of making Sunday a day of secular amusement is most strongly to be deprecated.

(f) That the most careful regard should be had to the danger of any encroachment upon the rest which, on this day, is the right of servants as well as their masters, and of the working classes as well as their employers.

355

1888
The Lambeth Quadrilateral

Resolution 11, Lambeth Conference, 1888.

Cf. no. 343, the Chicago Quadrilateral, upon which the Lambeth Quadrilateral was based.

That, in the opinion of this Conference, the following Articles supply a basis on which approach may be by God's blessing made towards Home Reunion: —

(a) The Holy Scriptures of the Old and New Testaments, as 'containing all things necessary to salvation', and as being the rule and ultimate standard of faith.

(b) The Apostles' Creed, as the Baptismal Symbol; and the Nicene Creed, as the sufficient statement of the Christian faith.

(c) The two Sacraments ordained by Christ Himself — Baptism and the Supper of the Lord — ministered with unfailing use of Christ's words of Institution, and of the elements ordained by Him.

(d) The Historic Episcopate, locally adapted in the methods of its administration to the varying needs of the nations and peoples called of God into the Unity of His Church.

356

1891
What is Christianity?

Charles Gore (1853–1932), Bishop of Oxford, The Incarnation of the Son of God *(London, 1891), p. 1.*

Christianity exists in the world as a distinctive religion; and if we are asked, 'What is the distinguishing characteristic of the religion?' we can hardly hesitate for an answer. Christianity is faith in a certain person Jesus Christ, and by faith in him is meant such unreserved self-committal as is only possible, because faith in Jesus is understood to be faith in God, and union with Jesus union with God.

357

1893
A Province's Solemn Declaration

The Book of Common Prayer of the Anglican Church of Canada.

In the Name of the Father, and of the Son, and of the Holy Ghost, Amen. WE, the Bishops, together with the Delegates from the Clergy and Laity of the Church of England in the Dominion of Canada, now assembled in the first General Synod, hereby make the following Solemn Declaration: ... in full communion with the Church of England throughout the world, as an integral portion of the One Body of Christ composed of Churches which, united under the One Divine Head and in the fellowship of the One Holy Catholic and Apostolic Church, hold the One Faith revealed in Holy Writ and defined in the Creeds as maintained in the undivided primitive Church in the undisputed Ecumenical Councils: receive the same Canonical Scriptures of the Old and New Testaments as containing all things necessary to Salvation; teach the same Word of God; partake of the same Divinely ordained Sacraments, through the ministry of the same Apostolic Orders; and worship One God and Father through the same Lord Jesus Christ, by the same Holy and Divine Spirit who is given to them that believe to guide them into all truth.

And we are determined by the help of God to hold and maintain the Doctrine, Sacraments, and Discipline of Christ as the Lord hath commanded in his Holy Word, and as the Church of England hath received and set forth the same in 'The Book of Common Prayer and Administration of the Sacraments and other Rites and Ceremonies of the Church, according to the use of the Church of England; together with the Psalter or Psalms of David, pointed as they are to be sung or said in Churches; and the Form and Manner of Making, Ordaining, and Consecrating of Bishops, Priests, and Deacons'; and in the Thirty-Nine Articles of Religion; and to transmit the same unimpaired to our posterity.

358

1895
Historical characteristics of 'Anglican theology'

Charles Gore (1853–1932), Bishop of Oxford, Dissertation on Subjects Connected with the Incarnation *(London, 1895), p. 196.*

Cf. no. 412.

The characteristic of the Anglican Church has been from the first that of combining steadfast adherence to the structure and chief formulae of the Church Catholic with the 'return to Scripture' which was the central religious motive of the Reformation. This has resulted in a theology ... which has been catholic, scriptural, rich in expression and application, but reserved and unscholastic in character.[1]

359

1897
Alcohol abuse

Encyclical Letter, *Lambeth Conference, 1897*.

Cf. nos. 350 and 380 on drug abuse.

Intemperance still continues to be one of the chief hindrances to religion in the great mass of our people. There are many excellent societies engaged in the conflict with it, but they need steady and resolute perseverance to effect any serious improvement. It is important to lay stress on the essential condition of permanent success in this work, namely, that it should be taken up in a religious spirit as part of Christian devotion to the Lord.

360

1897
Christian marriage

Encyclical Letter, *Lambeth Conference, 1897*.

The maintenance and the dignity and sanctity of marriage lies at the root of social purity, and therefore of the safety and sacredness of the family and the home. The foundation of its holy security and honour is the precept of our Lord, 'What therefore God hath joined together let not man put asunder.' We utter our most earnest words of warning against the lightness with which the lifelong vow of marriage is often taken; against the looseness with which those who enter into this holy estate often regard its obligations; and against the frequency and facility of recourse to the Courts of Law for the dissolution of this most solemn bond.

---

[1]   It is hard to know exactly what sense Gore would have attached to 'reserved and unscholastic', but he evidently intended the phrase to balance 'rich in expression and application'.

361

1897
The Church's responsibility to give a lead on moral questions

Encyclical Letter, *Lambeth Conference, 1897.*

We desire to repeat with the most earnest emphasis what was said on the subject of Purity by the last Conference, and we reprint herewith the Report which that Conference unanimously adopted. We know the deadly nature of the sin of impurity,[1] the fearful hold it has on those who have once yielded, and the fearful strength of the temptation. The need for calling attention to this is greatly increased at present by the difficulties that hamper all attempts to deal with the frightful diseases which everywhere attend it.

362

1897
The needs of society

Encyclical Letter, *Lambeth Conference, 1897.*

This extract reflects the changing nature of the Church's perception of her social responsibility.

The industrial problems of the present day present themselves under the double aspect of justice between man and man, and sympathy with human needs. It is widely thought in some classes that the present working of our industries is unjust to the employed and unduly favourable to the employer. It is obviously not possible for us to enter upon the consideration of such a question in detail. But we think it our duty to press the great principle of the Brotherhood of Man, and to urge the importance of bringing that principle to bear on all relations between those who are connected by the tie of a common cmployment.

---

[1]   i.e. sexual promiscuity

363

1897
Biblical criticism

Encyclical Letter, *Lambeth Conference, 1897.*

Compare nos. 319, 321.

We pass on to the consideration of the standards of all our teaching, the Bible and the Book of Common Prayer. The critical study of the Bible by competent scholars is essential to the maintenance in the Church of a healthy faith. That faith is already in serious danger which refuses to face questions that may be raised either on the authority or the genuineness of any part of the Scriptures that have come down to us. Such refusal creates painful suspicion in the minds of many whom we have to teach, and will weaken the strength of our own conviction of the truth that God has revealed to us. A faith which is always or often attended by a secret fear that we dare not inquire lest inquiry should lead us to results inconsistent with what we believe, is already infected with a disease which may soon destroy it. But all inquiry is attended with a danger on the other side unless it be protected by the guard of Reverence, Confidence, and Patience. It is quite true that there have been instances where inquiry has led to doubt and ultimately to infidelity. But the best safeguard against such a peril lies in that deep reverence which never fails to accompany real faith. The central object of Christian faith must always be the Lord Jesus Christ Himself. The test which St. Paul gives of the possession of the Holy Spirit is the being able to say that Jesus is the Lord. If a man can say with his whole heart and soul that Jesus is the Lord, he stands on a rock which nothing can shake. Read in the light of this conviction, the Bible, beginning with man made in the image of God, and rising with ever-increasing clearness of revelation to GOD taking on Him the form of man, and throughout it all showing in every page the sense of the Divine Presence inspiring what is said, will not fail to exert its power over the souls of men till the Lord comes again. This power will never really be affected by any critical study whatever.

364

1897
Mission and inter-faith questions

Encyclical Letter, *Lambeth Conference, 1897.*

This represents a cautious early attempt to settle a policy for inter-faith relations which recognizes that which is valuable in other world faiths. Cf. no. 473.

In preaching His Gospel to the world we have to deal with one great religious body, which holds the truth in part but not in its fullness, the Jews; with another which holds fragments of the truth embedded in a mass of falsehood, the Mohammedans; and with various races which hold inherited beliefs ranging down to the merest fetichism. In dealing with all these it is certainly right to recognize whatsoever good they may contain. But it is necessary to be cautious lest that good, such as it is, be so exaggerated as to lead us to allow that any purified form of any of them can ever be in any sense a substitute for the Gospel. The Gospel is not merely the revelation of the highest morality; it reveals also the wonderful love of God in Christ, and contains the promise of that grace given by Him by which alone the highest moral life is possible to man. And without the promise of that grace it would not be the Gospel at all.

365

1897
Monastic life

Encyclical Letter, *Lambeth Conference, 1897.*

Anglicans had little experience of the monastic life after the dissolution of the monasteries in England by Henry VIII until the revival of religious orders, partly as a result of the Oxford Movement of the 1830s and 1840s. A series of mainly active and teaching communities was founded in successive decades. Here the Lambeth Conference tries to give guidance for their reception in the work of the Church and for their spread outside England.

On the subject of Religious Communities we do not consider it to be yet possible to give advice which can be treated as final. We believe that such Communities are capable of rendering great services to the Church, and have indeed already done so... We express our strong sense of the care that ought to be taken in making sure that no one undertakes the obligations of Community life without having, as far as human judgement can ascertain it, a real vocation from God. Whether God means a particular person to live in this particular way is the preliminary question to be determined by the person who asks to be admitted into a Community and by the authority of the Community that admits that person.

366

1897
Provincial government and the unity of the Anglican Communion

Encyclical Letter, *Lambeth Conference, 1897.*

This and related themes have been a preoccupation of successive Lambeth Conferences and of individual Provinces as they have been formed. Their importance lies in their implications for the structural unity of the visible Church and for the role of the Episcopate as a ministry of unity. For this reason we have included a number of extracts bearing on the problem.

We desire to encourage the natural and spontaneous formation of Provinces, so that no Bishop may be left to act absolutely alone, and we think it desirable that, in accordance with the ancient custom of the Western Church, the Metropolitans of these Provinces should be known as Archbishops, recommending, however, that such titles should not be assumed without previous communication to the other Bishops of the Communion with a view to general recognition. We think it would be well for the further consolidation of all provincial action that every Bishop at his consecration should take the Oath of Canonical Obedience to his own Metropolitan, and that every Bishop consecrated in England under the Queen's Mandate for service abroad should make a solemn declaration that he will pay all due honour and deference to the Archbishop of Canterbury, and will respect and maintain the spiritual rights and privileges of the Church of England and of all Churches in communion with her.

367

1897
The Church and war

Encyclical Letter, *Lambeth Conference, 1897.*

There is nothing which more tends to promote general employment and consequently genuine comfort among the people than the maintenance of peace among the nations of mankind. But besides and above all considerations of material comfort stands the value of Peace itself as the great characteristic of the Kingdom of our Lord, the word which heralded His entrance into the world, the title which specially distinguishes Him from all earthly princes. There can be no question that the influence of the Christian Church can do more for this than any other influence that can be named. Without denying that there are just wars and that we cannot prevent their recurrence entirely, yet we are convinced that there are other and better ways of settling the quarrels of nations than by fighting. War is a horrible evil followed usually by consequences worse than itself. Arbitration in place of war saves the honour of the nations concerned and yet determines the questions at issue with completeness. War brutalises even while it gives opportunity for the finest heroism. Arbitration leaves behind it a generous sense of passion restrained and justice sought for. The Church of Christ can never have any doubt for which of the two modes of determining national quarrels it ought to strive.

368

1897
Continuation of Lambeth Conferences; the force of their Resolutions; the need for a Central Consultative Body

Resolutions 1–5, Lambeth Conference, 1897.

In this stocktaking exercise the third Lambeth Conference affirms the value of the Conferences and considers the needs which still have to be met.

1. That, recognising the advantages which have accrued to the Church from the meetings of the Lambeth Conferences, we are of

opinion that it is of great importance to the well-being of the Church that there should be from time to time meetings of the Bishops of the whole Anglican Communion for the consideration of questions that may arise affecting the Church of Christ.

2. That whereas the Lambeth Conferences have been called into existence by the invitation of the Archbishop of Canterbury, we desire that similar Conferences should be held, at intervals of about ten years, on the invitation of the Archbishop, if he be willing to give it.

3. That the Resolutions adopted by such Conferences should be formally communicated to the various National Churches, Provinces, and extra-Provincial Dioceses of the Anglican Communion for their consideration, and for such action as may seem to them desirable.

4. That the conditions of membership of the Lambeth Conferences, as described in the opening sentences of the Official Letter of 1878 and the Encyclical Latter of 1888, should remain unaltered.

5. That it is advisable that a consultative body should be formed to which resort may be had, if desired, by the National Churches, Provinces, and extra-Provincial Dioceses of the Anglican Communion either for information or for advice, and that the Archbishop of Canterbury be requested to take such steps as he may think most desirable for the creation of this consultative body.

369

1897
Provincial government and the regional primacy
Resolutions 6–10, Lambeth Conference, 1897.

This series of Resolutions stresses Anglican acceptance of the principle of regional primacy and underline some of the implications for the limitation of the jurisdiction of the Primate of Canterbury in other provinces. Cf. nos. 279, 530.

6. We desire to record our satisfaction at the progress of the acceptance of the principle of Provincial organisation since the date of its formal commendation to the Anglican Communion in the Official Letter of 1878. We would also express a hope that the

method of association into Provinces may be carried still further as circumstances may allow.

7. Recognising the almost universal custom in the Western Church of attaching the title of Archbishop to the rank of Metropolitan, we are of opinion that the revival and extension of this custom among ourselves is justifiable and desirable. It is advisable that the proposed adoption of such titles should be formally announced to the Bishops of the various Churches and Provinces of the Communion with a view to its general recognition.

8. We are of opinion that the Archiepiscopal or Primatial title may be taken from a city or from a territory, according to the discretion of the Province concerned.

9. Where it is intended that any Bishop-elect, not under the metropolitan jurisdiction of the See of Canterbury, should be consecrated in England under the Queen's Mandate, it is desirable, if it be possible, that he should not be expected to take an oath of personal obedience to the Archbishop of Canterbury, but rather should, before his Consecration, make a solemn declaration that he will pay all due honour and deference to the Archbishop of Canterbury, and will respect and maintain the spiritual rights and privileges of the Church of England, and of all Churches in communion with her. In this manner the interests of unity would be maintained without any infringement of the local liberties or jurisdiction.

10. If such Bishop-elect be designated to a See within any Primatial or Provincial Jurisdiction, it is desirable that he should at the Consecration take the customary Oath of Canonical Obedience to his own Primate or Metropolitan.

370

1897
Towards unity

Resolutions 34–36, Lambeth Conference , 1897.

'Visible unity' is here clearly seen as the goal for ecumenical endeavour. At this period there were strong hopes of a growing closeness between Anglicans and the Orthodox Churches.

34. That every opportunity be taken to emphasise the Divine purpose of visible unity amongst Christians, as a fact of revelation.

35. That this Conference urges the duty of special intercession for the unity of the Church in accordance with our Lord's own prayer.

36. That the Archbishops of Canterbury and York and the Bishop of London be requested to act as a Committee with power to add to their number, to confer personally or by correspondence with the Orthodox Eastern Patriarchs, the 'Holy Governing Synod' of the Church of Russia, and the chief authorities of the various Eastern Churches with a view to consider the possibility of securing a clearer understanding and of establishing closer relations between the Churches of the East and the Anglican Communion; and that under the direction of the said Committee arrangements be made for the translation of books and documents setting forth the relative positions of the various Churches, and also of such Catechisms and Forms of Service as may be helpful to mutual understanding.

371

1897
Infant baptism and the
instruction of children in the Faith

Encyclical Letter, *Lambeth Conference, 1897, and Resolution 48, Lambeth Conference, 1897.*

Ever since the general change to infant baptism in the West at the end of the fourth century it had normally been the case that the family remained in the same worshipping community until the child was old enough to make a personal confession of faith for itself at Confirmation. The Conference here faces the difficulty of ensuring that the infant receives instruction in the faith as he or she grows up, in an industrial society where families move frequently and may lose contact with their home Church.

We find that many of the Clergy, especially in the large towns of England, are troubled by doubts whether, in the present circumstances of life, especially where population is perpetually moving, infants ought to be baptized when there seems so little security for their due instruction. We desire to impress upon the

Clergy the need of taking all possible care to see that provision is made for the Christian training of the child, but that, unless in cases of grave and exceptional difficulty, the Baptism should not be deferred. We consider, further, that the baptismal promises of repentance, faith, and obedience should be made either privately or publicly by those who, having been baptized without those promises, are brought by our Clergy to Confirmation by the Bishop.

Resolution 48.
That in the opinion of this Conference it is of much importance that in all cases of Infant Baptism the clergyman should take all possible care to see that provision is made for the Christian training of the child, but that, unless in cases of grave and exceptional difficulty, the Baptism should not be deferred.

372

1902
Christian unity

N. Dimock, Christian Unity *(London, 1902), p. 5.*

'Church' is used in the plural in the early Christian period to refer to local churches, but always with a recognition that they are part of the one, holy, catholic and apostolic Church. Dimock here points to the anomalousness of speaking of 'Churches' in a denominational sense.

It is becoming a usual practice among many of the earth to speak of the various Christian denominations in our land as 'The Churches'. It is a manner of speech which can hardly fail to suggest some such inquiries as these: Is it according to the Scriptures of the New Testament, or is it by the teaching of the Scriptures according to the will of God, that there should be a variety of Churches, living side by side, in a state of separation from one another? Will a confederation of such bodies fully satisfy the Scriptural idea of Christian unity?

373

1902
Fundamentals

John Wordsworth (1843–1911), Bishop of Salisbury, The Bearing of the Study of Church History on some Problems of Home Reunion *(London, 1902) (Murtle Lecture, Aberdeen, 23 February 1902), pp. 10–2.*

The debate about what is 'necessary to salvation' or 'fundamental' was already a lively one in the late Middle Ages. It was in the minds of the framers of the Chicago-Lambeth Quadrilateral and continues to be important ecumenically as Christians come to a clearer view together both of their common faith and of those areas where there can be legitimate diversity. Cf. nos. 197, 213, 448, 461.

By 'fundamentals' I personally understand those truths and institutions which we can trace back to the first age of the Church, and on which all its after life is based... Why do we attach so much importance to primitive times? It is not merely because they come first, and therefore necessarily colour all that comes after, but because there was undoubtedly a more general outpouring of the Holy Spirit and a closer brotherhood of believers in the first 200 years of Christian history than in any other age.... The 'fundamentals' which we must primarily look to in every effort for Christian union [are the] Bible, Creed, Lord's Day, and sacraments. I venture to think that this is a much safer enumeration than that of Waterland and others like him... who start from some central idea, such as that of the Christian covenant, and consider what truths or institutions are necessary to support it.... In this list of fundamentals I have said nothing about the Church and the Ministry. This is not because I do not think them both in reality fundamentals, but because they are fundamental in a different sense. They are not so much concrete objects proposed for our acceptance, as necessary conditions of Christian life. The Church, as a society of believers, representing God to man, is presupposed in every one of the five points of primitive unity. The Ministry follows as the necessary instrument for keeping this life in its proper, regular and continuous course.

374

1908
Faith and contemporary thought

Encyclical Letter, *Lambeth Conference, 1908.*

The Lambeth Conference here reflects again on a subject of perennial concern in Christian thought: that of the relationship between 'science' or 'modern interpretation' and the maintenance of the unchanging truths of faith in the climate of each age (cf. nos. 193, 211, 244, 246, 280).

We turn first to the subject of our faith in relation to the thought of the present day. In humble reverence and unalterable devotion we bow before the mystery of the Trinity in Unity, revealed indeed once for all, but revealing to each generation and not least to our own, 'new depths of the Divine'. We bow before the mystery of God Incarnate in the Person of our Lord Jesus Christ, this, too, revealed once for all, but revealing to our times with novel clearness both God and man, and interpreting and confirming to us all that we have hoped or dreamed concerning union between them. We reaffirm the essential place of the historic facts stated by the Creeds in the structure of our faith. Many in our days have rashly denied the importance of these facts, but the ideas which these facts have in part generated and have always expressed cannot be dissociated from them. Without the historic Creeds the ideas would evaporate into unsubstantial vagueness... In the intellectual activity, the ferment of thought and the variety of opinion, which are characteristic of our day, we have in our holy faith not only a sure and steadfast anchor, but a centre of light which illumines the new truth and blends with the new light; for the new truth and new light are ultimately derived from the One Source of all truth and light.

375

1908
Moral responsibility: the Church and politics

Encyclical Letter, *Lambeth Conference, 1908.*

The Lambeth Conference here tries to lay down general principles of guidance for the Church in its dealings with political realities.

By the power of the truth which it carries and declares, the Church is constantly serving the cause of true progress. But it has a further duty to be watchfully responsive to the opportunities of service which the movements of civil society provide. The democratic movement of our century presents one of these opportunities. Underlying it are ideals of brotherhood, liberty, and mutual justice and help. In those ideals we recognize the working of our Lord's teaching as to the inestimable value of every human being in the sight of God, and His special thought for the weak and the oppressed. These are practical truths proclaimed by the ancient Prophets and enforced by our Lord with all the perfectness of His teaching and His life. We call upon the Church to consider how far and wherein it has departed from these truths. In so far as the democratic and industrial movement is animated by them and strives to procure for all, especially for the weaker, just treatment and a real opportunity of living a true human life, we appeal to all Christians to co-operate actively with it. Only so can they hope to commend to the movement the Spirit of our Lord Jesus Christ, which is at once its true stimulus and its true corrective.

376

1908
Service and the Church

Encyclical Letter, *Lambeth Conference, 1908.*

When the Lambeth Conference of 1908 asked itself 'What is the Church for?' in the contemporary world, it found an answer in terms of 'service'.

It was to be expected that the main trend and tenor of our deliberations would be taken, consciously or unconsciously, from that tendency of the Church's work, that conception of the Church's office, which is at the present time foremost in men's thoughts. By the word Church in this connection we mean the whole Society of Christian men throughout the world. We shall speak later of what belongs more distinctively to our own Communion. Different aspects of the Church and of its duty have been prominent in different epochs of Christian history; and according to this difference there has been a variation in the main current of men's interest and debate concerning the problems of the

Church's life: now one class of problems, now another, has seemed inevitable, absorbing, supremely important in all assemblies of Christian people. It is therefore a significant fact that, when we review the work of this Conference, and ask what aspect or idea of the Church has been predominant in our deliberations, we find that through them all, in the many fields over which they have travelled, there has been ever present the thought of the Church as ordained of God for the service of mankind....It may be well to note with regard to this thought, first, that it is at the very centre of the Church's character as declared by our Lord and Saviour Jesus Christ; and, secondly, that in our day men are realising it with increasing clearness and intensity.

377

1908
The ministry of healing

Encyclical Letter, *Lambeth Conference, 1908.*

Cf. nos. 46, 241, 577.

We have... had before us the subject of the unction of the sick with a view to their recovery, and have considered it in regard to its history and to its alleged origin in the precept of St. James (5. 14), and also in relation to the conditions prevailing in the Church at the present time. As the result of our investigation, we do not recommend the authorisation of the anointing of the sick as a rite of the Church. On the other hand, we do not wish to forbid all recourse to a practice which, as we are informed, has been carried out by many persons, both clerical and lay, within and without our Communion. We have thought good to advise that the parish priest, in dealing with any request made to him by a sick person who humbly and heartily desires such anointing, should seek the counsel of his bishop.

378

1908
Prayer Book revision

Resolutions 27–28, Lambeth Conference, 1908.

The Book of Common Prayer enshrines a body of doctrine as well as of liturgy. It has been seen as one of the 'foundation documents' of Anglicanism, as well as a means of maintaining a common worship which makes Anglicans feel at home with one another throughout the world. Its language is, however, inevitably sometimes unfamiliar and difficult for the modern reader. For the results of Prayer Book revision and liturgical development worldwide, see no. 337.

27. In any revision of the Book of Common Prayer which may hereafter be undertaken by competent authority the following principles should be held in view:–

  (*a*) The adaptation of rubrics in a large number of cases to present customs as generally accepted;

  (*b*) The omission of parts of the services to obviate repetition or redundancy;

  (*c*) The framing of additions to the present services in the way of enrichment;

  (*d*) The fuller provision of alternatives in our forms of public worship;

  (*e*) The provision for greater elasticity in public worship;

  (*f*) The change of words obscure or commonly misunderstood;

  (*g*) The revision of the Calendar and Tables prefixed to the Book of Common Prayer.

28. The Conference requests the Archbishop of Canterbury to take counsel with such persons as he may see fit to consult, with a view to the preparation of a Book containing special forms of service, which might be authorised by particular Bishops for use in their Dioceses, as far as they may consider it possible and desirable.

379

1908

Moral principles in economic life

Resolutions 48–50, Lambeth Conference, 1908.

Here the Lambeth Conference affirms the ancient and scriptural Christian principle of stewardship of property.

48. The Church should teach that the Christian who is an owner of property should recognize the governing principle that, like all our gifts, our powers and our time, property is a trust held for the benefit of the community, and its right use should be insisted upon as a religious duty.

49. The Conference urges upon members of the Church practical recognition of the moral responsibility involved in their investments...

50. The Conference holds that it is the duty of the Church to press upon Governments the wrong of sanctioning for the sake of revenue any forms of trade which involve the degradation or hinder the moral and physical progress of the races and peoples under their rule or influence.

380

1908

Drug abuse

Resolution 51, Lambeth Conference, 1908.

This is an early recognition of the international scale of the problem of drug-trafficking. Cf. nos. 350, 359 on alcohol abuse.

51. The Conference, regarding the non-medicinal use of opium as a grave physical and moral evil, welcomes all well-considered efforts to abate such use, particularly those of the Government and people of China, and also the proposal of the Government of the United States to arrange an International Commission on Opium. It thankfully recognizes the progressive reduction by the Indian Government of the area of poppy cultivation, but still appeals for all possible insistence on the affirmation of the House of Commons that the Indian opium traffic with China is morally indefensible. It

urges a stringent dealing with the opium vice in British Settlements, along with due precautions against the introduction of narcotic substitutes for opium. Finally, it calls upon all Christian people to pray for the effectual repression of the opium evil.

381

1908
A Central Consultative Body

Resolution 54, Lambeth Conference, 1908.

At this stage of its evolution, the notion of a Central Consultative Body for the Anglican Communion was of a body of bishops representative of the concerns of the then geographical distribution of Anglicans in the world. Cf. no. 395.

54. The existing Central Consultative Body shall be reconstructed on representative lines as follows: –

(*a*) It shall consist of the Archbishop of Canterbury (*ex officio*) and of representative Bishops appointed as follows: Province of Canterbury 2, Province of York 1, the Church of Ireland 1, the Episcopal Church of Scotland 1, the Protestant Episcopal Church in the United States of America 4, the Church of England in Canada 1, the Church of England in the Dioceses of Australia and Tasmania 1, the Church of the Province of New Zealand 1, the Province of the West Indies 1, the Church of the Province of South Africa 1, the Province of India and Ceylon 1, the Diocese of China and Korea and the Church of Japan 1, the missionary and other extra-provincial Bishops under the jurisdiction of the Archbishop of Canterbury 1. Total 18.

(*b*) The foregoing scheme of representation shall be open to revision from time to time by the Lambeth Conference.

(*c*) The mode of appointing these representative Bishops shall be left to the churches that appoint. A representative Bishop may be appointed for one year or for any number of years, and need not be a member of the body which appoints him...

(*d*) For the purpose of appointing the Bishop who is to represent the body of missionary and other extra-provincial Bishops under the jurisdiction of the Archbishop of Canterbury, each of those Bishops shall be requested by the Archbishop of Canterbury to nominate a Bishop to him. The list of Bishops so nominated shall be then sent to all the Bishops entitled to vote, and each of them shall, if he thinks fit to vote, send to the Archbishop the name of the one in that list for whom he votes. The largest number of votes shall carry the election.

382

1908

Religious Communities and Episcopal Jurisdiction

Resolution 57, Lambeth Conference, 1908.

This question is of considerable antiquity. Religious communities in the West had not always, even in late patristic times, been in all respects under the full and immediate jurisdiction of the local bishop, but had often been directly under the discipline of the Bishop of Rome. In many respects, by ancient tradition, they have been self-governing communities.

57. That the Archbishop of Canterbury be requested to transmit to every Diocesan Bishop in the Anglican Communion a copy of the Final Report of the Committee appointed by the Conference of 1897 to consider the relation of Religious Communities within the Church to the Episcopate, accompanying it with a request that it may be duly considered, and that each Province of the Anglican Communion will, if it consents to do so, send to him, through its Metropolitan, before July 31st, 1910, a statement of the judgement formed in that Province upon the subject dealt with in the Report.

383

1908

Christian unity

Resolution 58–59, Lambeth Conference, 1908.

The Lambeth Conferences have consistently called for unity. This text is important in its stress on visible unity in one future united Church.

58. This Conference reaffirms the resolution of the Conference of 1897 that 'Every opportunity should be taken to emphasise the

Divine purpose of visible unity amongst Christians as the fact of revelation.' It desires further to affirm that in all partial projects of reunion and intercommunion the final attainment of the divine purpose should be kept in view as our object; and that care should be taken to do what will advance the reunion of the whole of Christendom, and to abstain from doing anything that will retard or prevent it.

59. The Conference recognizes with thankfulness the manifold signs of the increase of the desire for unity among all Christian bodies; and with a deep sense of the call to follow the manifest guiding of the Holy Spirit, solemnly urges the duty of special intercession for the unity of the Church in accordance with our Lord's own prayer.

384

1919
Anglicans and Roman Catholics in Ireland

Report of the Conference of the Irish Fellowship, 1919, Irish Problems, *Irish Fellowship Papers, no. 1 (London, 1919), pp. 8–11, in* Irish Anglicanism, 1869–1969, *ed. M. Hurley (Dublin, 1970), pp. 213–4.*

To accept the bad old traditions that divide us from our fellow-Christians in Ireland is to sin. To acquiesce in a state of things we know to be wrong is sheer faithlessness. These were the convictions that came to us. And there came to us, too, an assurance that apathy and despondency in face of these conditions is not only wrong but unnecessary. We looked out into the world and saw men and women drawing together in the mission field to co-operate in a great common task, realising their unity of aim, planning and working and praying together... And we saw that in our own country, too, fellowship between those who differ can be achieved. The walls of ignorance, prejudice and suspicion that divide us and look so formidable collapse in the most amazing way when people make a determined effort to scramble over them. God's power to work miracles is not limited to India or China. No condition of things that falls short of the ideal should be regarded as fixed and unalterable. In Ireland to-day barriers are being broken down; a new spirit of co-operation is growing up. Social and philanthropic work is offering a meeting ground for those who differ in their religious and political associations, and intercourse is leading to real friendship. 'It is impossible to work with people without getting to like them'; 'People are really extraordinarily nice when you get to know them' — so spoke two of our Conference members. And one and another bore witness to the fact that where they had tried to get beneath the surface, to break down reserve and talk about the things they held most sacred with Roman Catholic friends, they had been met more than half way. It was an inspiration and an unutterable joy to know that there were some of our fellow-Christians of the Roman Church who were praying for us during those days of Conference, and to receive from among them this beautiful message: –'I am praying that the Holy Ghost will come and bring His Light and Love upon you in great abundance.' At our closing meeting there was a very real and general desire to express something of what we felt in a tangible way, and so we decided to send through the friend who had brought us the message the following greeting: 'The members of the Irish Fellowship, in Conference assembled, beg to send New Year greetings in Christ to their Roman Catholic brethren, and desire to declare their love to all who love our Lord Jesus Christ.' The following up of that message, the working out of its implications, is a sacred task to which each one of us is henceforth pledged.

385

1919
Ministry in the Church of God

Proposals for an approach towards unity, *Concordat prepared by members of the Protestant Episcopal Church and of the Congregational Churches in the United States of America, March 1919. (in* Documents bearing on the problem of Christian Unity and Fellowship, 1916–20 *(London, 1920), p. 17).*

Anglican ordination has always been, in intention, for ministry 'in the Church of God'. Cf. nos. 237, 238, 239.

The minister acts not merely as the representative of the particular congregation then present, but in a larger sense he represents the Church Universal; and his intention and meaning should be our Lord's intention and meaning as delivered to and held by the Catholic Church.

386

1920
The Church in Wales

Who are the Anglicans?, *ed. Charles Long, prepared for the Lambeth Conference, 1988 (Ohio, 1988), p. 60.*

Cf. nos. 407, 409, 522.

The Church of Wales was disestablished, i.e. became a separate Province on April 1, 1920. The first Archbishop was enthroned on June 1 of that year. The Church is governed by its Governing Body, a synod of bishops, clergy and laity which meets twice a year. Property is held and finances administered by the Representative Body.
[In 1975 the Church in Wales entered into a Covenant with three of the other main Churches in Wales to work and pray for the formation of one visible Church, but progress in implementing it has been slow.]

387

1920
Christian unity

An Appeal to all Christian People, *Lambeth Conference, 1920.*

In this important and influential statement the Lambeth Conference (with the Chicago-Lambeth Quadrilateral in mind) looks to a shared ordained ministry in a future united Church. It recognizes the authorization of the Holy Spirit in the ministries of non-episcopal communions. But it argues that the episcopate is a God-given instrument of unity and continuity which will enable God's people to meet in security in one Eucharist.

We believe that the visible unity of the Church will be found to involve the whole-hearted acceptance of: –

The Holy Scriptures, as the record of God's revelation of Himself to man, and as being the rule and ultimate standard of faith; and the Creed commonly called Nicene, as the sufficient statement of the Christian faith, and either it or the Apostles' Creed as the Baptismal confession of belief:

The divinely instituted sacraments of Baptism and the Holy Communion, as expressing for all the corporate life of the whole fellowship in and with Christ:

A ministry acknowledged by every part of the Church as possessing not only the inward call of the Spirit, but also the commission of Christ and the authority of the whole body.

VII. May we not reasonably claim that the Episcopate is the one means of providing such a ministry? It is not that we call in question for a moment the spiritual reality of the ministries of those Communions which do not possess the Episcopate. On the contrary, we thankfully acknowledge that these ministries have been manifestly blessed and owned by the Holy Spirit as effective means of grace. But we submit that considerations alike of history and of present experience justify the claim which we make on behalf of the Episcopate. Moreover, we would urge that it is now and will prove to be in the future the best instrument for maintaining the unity and continuity of the Church. But we greatly desire that the office of a Bishop should be everywhere exercised in a representative and constitutional manner, and more truly express all that ought to be involved in the life of the Christian Family in the title of Father-in-God. Nay more, we eagerly look forward to the day when through its acceptance in a united Church we may all share in that grace which is pledged to the members of the whole body in the apostolic rite of the laying-on of hands, and in the joy and fellowship of a Eucharist in which as one Family we may together, without any doubtfulness of mind, offer to the one Lord our worship and service.

388

1920
The Church of South India: a plan for local union

M.K. Kuriakose, History of Christianity in India: Source Materials *(Madras, 1982), p. 320, Joint Statement of the South India United Church and the Anglican Churches.*

Cf. nos. 401, 427, 432. This was one of the several preliminary attempts to work out a basis of union satisfactory to all parties. The sticking-points in such efforts to marry an episcopal with presbyterian and congregational systems of Church government have always been (a) the question of maintaining apostolic succession in ordinations to the satisfaction of all the participating Churches, and (b) the issue of the ministerial standing of existing ministers of each Church in the future united Church. Both are considered here.

1. We believe that the principle of the Historic Episcopate in a constitutional form is that which is more likely than any other to promote and preserve the unity of the Church; therefore, we accept it as a basis of union without raising other questions about episcopacy.
2. By Constitutional Episcopacy we mean:
    (a) that the Bishops shall be elected by representatives of the Province.
    (b) that the Bishops shall perform their duties constitutionally in accordance with such customs of the Church as shall be defined in a written constitution.
    (c) that the continuity with the Historic Episcopate will be effectively maintained, it being understood that no particular interpretation of the Historic Episcopate be demanded.
3. We are agreed that after union all future ordinations to the Presbyterate would be performed by the laying on of hands of the Bishops and Presbyters; and that all consecrations of Bishops would be performed by Bishops, not less than three taking part in each consecration.
4. By autonomy in the resultant Church we mean:−
    (a) that the Church in India ought to be independent of the State.
    (b) that the Church in India must be free from any control, legal or otherwise, of any Church or society outside India.
    (c) that, while the Church in India is free from such control, it would regulate its actions by the necessity of maintaining

fellowship with other branches of the Catholic Church with which we are now in communion.

With reference to the question of equality of the ministry, it was recorded that the South India United Church makes it a condition of union that its present ministers (Presbyters) shall after union be recognized as ministers (Presbyters) without re-ordination.

389

1920
The imperative necessity of unity

Encyclical Letter, *Lambeth Conference, 1920.*

The emphasis here is on the importance of putting right the anomaly which exists when the one Body of Christ is broken in its visible presence in the world; and on reassuring those who fear in a future united Church the loss of the distinctive characteristics of the life of the Church they know.

Men in all Communions began to think of the reunion of Christendom, not as a laudable ambition or a beautiful dream, but as an imperative necessity. Proposals and counter-proposals were made, some old, some new. Mutual recognition, organic union, federation, absorption, submission — these phrases indicate the variety of the programmes put forward. Some definite proposals came from the Mission Fields, where the urgency of the work of evangelization and the birth of national Churches alike demand a new fellowship.... The preparations for the World Conference on Faith and Order had not only drawn attention in all parts of the world to Christian unity, but had led to discussions in many quarters which brought to light unsuspected agreement between the leaders of different Communions. The great wind was blowing over the whole earth.... The unity which we seek exists. It is in God, Who is perfection of unity, the one Father, the one Lord, the one Spirit, Who gives life to the one Body. Again, the Body exists. It needs not to be made, nor to be remade, but to become organic and visible. Once more, the fellowship of the members of the one Body exists. It is the work of God, not of man. We have only to discover it, and to set free its activities....Terms of reunion must no longer be judged by the success with which they meet the claims and preserve the positions of two or more uniting Communions, but by their correspondence to the common ideal of the Church as God would have it to be. Again, in the past, negotiations for reunion have often started with the attempts to define the measure of uniformity which is essential. The impression has been given that nothing else matters. Now we see that those elements of truth about which differences have arisen are essential to the fullness of the witness of the whole Church. We have no need to belittle what is distinctive in our own interpretation of Christian life: we believe that it is something precious which we hold in trust for the common good. We desire that others should share in our heritage and our blessings, as we wish to share in theirs. It is not by reducing the different groups of Christians to uniformity, but by rightly using their diversity, that the Church can become all things to all men. So long as there is vital connexion with the Head, there is positive value in the differentiation of the members. But we are convinced that this ideal cannot be fulfilled if these groups are content to remain in separation from one another or to be joined together only in some vague federation. Their value for the fullness of Christian life, truth, and witness can only be realized if they are united in the fellowship of one visible society whose members are all bound together by the ties of a common faith, common sacraments, and a common ministry.

390

1920
Episcopal consultation

Encyclical Letter, *Lambeth Conference, 1920.*

This is included as an example of the spirit in which the 'Encyclical' or open pastoral letter has been sent out by the Lambeth Conferences, and as emphasising the pastoral role of the bishops who meet as their people's representatives at the Conference.

We who speak are bearers of the sacred commission of the Ministry given by our Lord through His Apostles to the Church. In His Name we desire to set forth before you the outcome of the grave deliberations to which, after solemn prayer and Eucharist, we have for five weeks devoted ourselves day by day. We take this opportunity of thanking from our hearts all those, both far and near, who have prayed God to give us His Spirit's present aid. We hope that the result of our work may bring encouragement and help to this great circle of intercessors, even in remote parts of the earth. Our deliberations were preceded by careful inquiry upon many sides into the matters about which we speak. In this Letter we propose to give a connected view of these matters, in the hope that it will make our Resolutions more intelligible, and lead some to study them, together with the Reports of our Committee on which they are based.

391

1920
Koinonia

Encyclical Letter, *Lambeth Conference, 1920.*

Each of the Lambeth Conferences has had a theme (cf. nos. 376, 441, 537). Here, in a Lambeth Conference with a special concern for unity, the theme is 'fellowship' or *koinonia*.

We find that one idea runs through all our work in this Conference, binding it together into a true unity. It is an idea prevalent and potent throughout the world today. It is the idea of fellowship... The foundation and ground of all fellowship is the undeflected will of God, renewing again and again its patient effort to possess, without destroying, the wills of men. And so He has called into being a fellowship of men, His Church, and sent His Holy Spirit to abide therein, that by the prevailing attraction of that one Spirit, He, the one God and Father of all, may win over the whole human family to that fellowship in Himself, by which alone it can attain to the fullness of life. This then is the object of the Church. In the prosecution of this object it must take account of every fellowship that exists among men, must seek to deepen and purify it, and, above all, to attach it to God. But in order to accomplish its object, the Church must itself be a pattern of fellowship. It is only by shewing the value and power of fellowship in itself that it can win the world to fellowship. The weakness of the Church in the world of to-day is not surprising when we consider how the bands of its own fellowship are loosened and broken.

392

1920
The authority of the Lambeth Conference

Encyclical Letter, *Lambeth Conference, 1920*.

The principles of provincial autonomy underlined by all the Lambeth Conferences are here balanced with the duty of the provinces to act with consideration for one another in mutual charity.

For half a century the Lambeth Conference has more and more served to focus the experience and counsels of our Communion. But it does not claim to exercise any powers of control or command. It stands for the far more spiritual and more Christian principle of loyalty to the fellowship. The Churches represented in it are indeed independent, but independent with the Christian freedom which recognizes the restraints of truth and love.

393

1920
The fellowship of the workplace

Encyclical Letter, *Lambeth Conference, 1920*.

The Conference here sounds a warning note about the habit of adopting adversarial attitudes in industrial relations, and points out that they have no place in Christian fellowship.

The relation of men one to another in industry or trade is another fellowship which God intended to exist and created to be good. Yet to-day we are confronted with a world-wide upheaval and embittered antagonism in social relations, the course of which none can foresee. We seem to be involved in an internecine conflict between capital and labour in which each aims at an exclusive supremacy. Any such supremacy would be inconsistent with the Christian ideal of fellowship. And the Church insists that, in its essential nature, industry is not a conflict, but a fellowship.... The message of Christianity in this matter is to make men see that here they can and must 'in love serve one another'. To all concerned, employer and employed, director and workman, investor of money and investor of brain or muscle — to all alike the Church must say: 'Put first your service to the community and your fellowship in that service. Do your work heartily, keenly, carefully as to God, because you are benefiting His children. Have good will, and expect others to have it. Rearrange your mutual relations, as men co-operating in fellowship, not competing in suspicion and hostility'. These are fundamental principles. Beyond them lies the whole region of practical application.

394

1920
The development of Provinces

Resolution 43, Lambeth Conference, 1920.

Notable here is the concern for the problem of missionary dioceses which must learn to stand on their own feet locally, both in ceasing to be dependent on the branch of the Anglican Communion from which the missionaries came, and in developing a working synodal system in which laity and clergy participate fully.

43.   Whereas it is undesirable that Dioceses should remain indefinitely in isolation or attached only to a distant Province, the gradual creation of new Provinces should be encouraged, and each newly founded Diocese should as soon as possible find its place as a constituent member in some neighbouring Province. The fact that Dioceses proposing to form a Province owe their origin to missions of different branches of the Anglican Communion need be no bar to such action.

(*a*)   In the opinion of the Conference four is the minimum number of Dioceses suitable to form a Province. No number should be considered too great to form a Province, so long as the Bishops and other representatives of the Diocese are able conveniently to meet for mutual consultation and for the transaction of provincial business.

(*b*)   In the initiation of any Province in the future, the organization which the Conference deems essential to provincial life is a House or College of Bishops to which the Metropolitans or the Presiding Bishops concerned have conveyed their authority for the consecration of Bishops. It is desirable that when a new Province is formed the Bishops of the constituent

Dioceses should transfer their allegiance to the Metropolitan of the Province or other authority constitutionally appointed to receive it, and thereafter all Bishops consecrated for the service of the Province should take the oath of canonical obedience to the Metropolitan or make a declaration of conformity to other authority before mentioned.

(c) In newly established Provinces arrangements should be made whereby the Province should have some distinct voice in the election of its Metropolitan.

(d) As to the *sedes* of the Metropolitan, customs vary and the decision must depend upon local circumstances.

(e) Until a missionary Diocese becomes largely self-supporting and is self-governed by a Synod the appointment of its Bishop should rest with the Province to which it is attached, after consultation with the Diocese and in such a way as the Province may decide.

(f) A newly constituted Synod of Bishops shall proceed as soon as possible to associate with itself in some official way the clergy and laity of the Province, provided that in the case of Provinces including Missionary Dioceses this procedure shall be subordinate to local circumstances. It is understood that each national and regional Church will determine its own constitutional and canonical enactments.

395

1920
A Central Consultative Body

Resolution 44, Lambeth Conference, 1920.

Cf. nos. 381, 480. Here we see a further step in the development of a Central Consultative Body for the Anglican Communion, with careful limitation of its powers.

44. In order to prevent misapprehension the Conference declares that the Consultative Body, created by the Lambeth Conference of 1897 and consolidated by the Conference of 1908, is a purely advisory Body. It is of the nature of a continuation Committee of the whole Conference and neither possesses nor claims any executive or administrative power. It is framed so as to represent

all branches of the Anglican Communion and it offers advice only when advice is asked for.

396

1920
The Diaconate and the ministry of women

Resolutions 46–54, Lambeth Conference, 1920.

The office of deaconess, important in the early Church, declined after the fourth century. It was revived in Germany, England and the USA in the nineteenth century. From 1861, deaconesses in the Church of England were appointed for life by the laying on of hands; but they were not ordained until the second half of the twentieth century, when some Anglican provinces have allowed them to become deacons. The principle that women should have an equal place with men in the Church's synodical decision-making is here (though not always) associated with their entry into the Church's special ministry.

46. Women should be admitted to those Councils of the Church to which laymen are admitted, and on equal terms. Diocesan, Provincial, or National Synods may decide when or how this principle is to be brought into effect.

47. The time has come when, in the interests of the Church at large, and in particular of the development of the Ministry of Women, the Diaconate of Women should be restored formally and canonically, and should be recognized throughout the Anglican Communion...

50. In every branch of the Anglican Communion there should be adopted a Form and Manner of Making of Deaconesses such as might fitly find a place in the Book of Common Prayer, containing in all cases provision for: –

(*a*) Prayer by the Bishop and the laying on of his hands;

(*b*) A formula giving authority to execute the Office of a Deaconess in the Church of God;

(*c*) The delivery of the New Testament by the Bishop to each candidate...

52. The following functions may be entrusted to the Deaconess, in addition to the ordinary duties which would naturally fall to her:–

(*a*) To prepare candidates for Baptism and Confirmation;

(*b*) To assist at the administration of Holy Baptism; and to be the administrant in cases of necessity in virtue of her office;

(*c*) To pray with and give counsel to such women as desire help in difficulties and perplexities;

(*d*) With the approval of the Bishop and of the Parish Priest, and under such conditions as shall from time to time be laid down by the Bishop:

(i) in Church to read Morning and Evening Prayer and the Litany, except such portions as are assigned to the Priest only;

(ii) in Church also to lead in prayer and, under licence of the Bishop, to instruct and exhort the Congregation...

53. Opportunity should be given to women as to men (duly qualified and approved by the Bishop) to speak in consecrated or unconsecrated buildings, and to lead in prayer, at other than the regular and appointed services of the Church. Such diocesan arrangements, both for men and for women, should wherever possible be subject to Provincial control and co-ordination.

54. The Conference recommends that careful inquiry should be made in the several branches of the Anglican Communion as to the position and recognition of women workers in the Church, the conditions of their employment, and the remuneration of those who receive salaries.

397

1927
Revising legal ties

The Indian Church Measure, 1927, 17 and 18 George V no. 1.

This Act of Parliament covers the legal as well as the ecclesiastical implications of the constitution of an autonomous Church in communion with the Church of England.

Whereas it is expedient that the legal union between the Church of England and the Church of England in India shall be dissolved... And whereas a petition to that effect has been presented to the Church Assembly by the General Council of the Church of England in India: And whereas the Secretary of State in the Council of India and the Governor-General of India in Council, and the Archbishop of Canterbury, and the bishops and duly appointed representatives of the clergy and laity of the Church of England in India in Council assembled, have approved the dissolution of such union... Upon the date of severance... the Metropolitan Bishop of the Indian Church shall not, in contemplation of the law, be subject to the general superintendence and revision of the Archbishop of Canterbury.

398

1930
Peace and war

Encyclical Letter, *The Lambeth Conference, 1930.*

The Christian must condemn war not merely because it is wasteful and ruinous, a cause of untold misery, but far more because it is contrary to the will of God. Peace is... something greater than a mere refusal to fight. Peace within the nation and among the nations depends on truth and justice. There cannot be peace unless we are trying to obey our Lord's command, 'Seek ye first the kingdom of God and His righteousness.' As citizens of that kingdom we are summoned to make war on injustice, falsehood and covetousness within ourselves and in the world around us. Evil social conditions — such as slums or unemployment – are causes of unrest because they are outward and visible signs of inward and spiritual wrong. We dare not acquiesce in them, for the remedy lies not only in the best means that economic science can devise, but also in the active witness and willing self-sacrifice of Christian people. Indeed we cannot be true witnesses to God's kingdom of peace, if we allow self-interest to be the ruling principle of any sphere of life. Neither industry nor commerce nor finance lie outside the borders of the kingdom of God, for at any point they touch human values and depend on human motives, and nothing human is alien to Him Who came that men might have life and have it abundantly. Only when we witness always and everywhere to His principles and rely upon His power, can we obtain from Him those gifts of truth and righteousness and love, of which peace is the perfect fruit.

399

1930
Race, nationality and the family of man

Encyclical Letter, *Lambeth Conference, 1930.*

Every family is a reflection of that great human family of which God is the Father, and of which the nations and races are the members. We who address you are ourselves representatives of that great family. For among the bishops here assembled there are representatives not only of the Western races but of the races of Japan, of China, of India and of Africa. We have found our brotherhood in Christ, and we are sure that only in His world-wide community can that brotherhood be securely established. No vague humanitarianism is enough. When men of different races and nations can say 'Our Father', believing in God who was made visible in Jesus Christ, then a unity begins to be felt which transcends the differences of colour and tradition.

400

1930
The Anglican Communion and wider unity

Encyclical Letter, *Lambeth Conference, 1930.*

This interim statement of an Anglican view of the relationship of Churches in fellowship touches on the problem of finding an 'organ' to express their unity. The rejection of 'any idea of a central authority' needs to be seen in the light of the story of the historical development of provincial autonomy and compared with nos. 381, 395, 480.

This Communion is a commonwealth of Churches without a central constitution: it is a federation without a federal government. It has come into existence without any deliberate policy, by the extension of the Churches of Great Britain and Ireland beyond the limits of these Islands. The extension has been of a double nature, and the Churches overseas bear its impress. Some of them are, primarily, Churches of the British people scattered throughout the world; others are, primarily, Churches of other peoples, planted by our Missions. Hitherto, they have all been Anglican, in the sense that they reflect the leading characteristics of the Church of England.

They teach — as she does — the Catholic Faith in its entirety and in the proportions in which it is set forth in the Book of Common Prayer. They refuse — as she does — to accept any statement, or practice, as of authority, which is not consistent with the Holy Scriptures and the understanding and practice of our religion as exhibited in the undivided Church. They are, in the idiom of our fathers, 'particular or national' Churches, and they repudiate any idea of a central authority, other than Councils of Bishops. They combine respect for antiquity with freedom in the pursuit of truth. They are both Catholic and Evangelical. This is still to-day a true description of the facts and ideals of the Anglican Communion. But these very ideals are working a change. Every Church of our Communion is endeavouring to do for the country where it exists the service which the Church of England has done for England — to represent the Christian religion and the Catholic Faith in a manner congenial to the people of the land, and to give scope to their genius in the development of Christian life and worship. As the Churches founded by our Missions in India, China, Japan or Africa, more and more fully achieve this purpose, they may, in many ways grow less and less like each other and to their Mother, and, in consequence, less and less Anglican, though no less true to Catholic faith and order. At the same time as we anticipate this progressive diversity within the unity of the Anglican Churches, we have before us a prospect of the restoration of communion with Churches which are, in no sense Anglican. Our negotiations with the Orthodox Church and the Old Catholics illustrate this possibility in one direction, and the creation of united Churches — such as that proposed in India – illustrates it in another. Thus beyond, but including, the federation of strictly Anglican Churches — which is now called the Anglican Communion — there may grow up a larger federation of much less homogeneous Churches, which will be in some measure in communion with the See of Canterbury. This federation, however, little centralized, would need some organ to express its unity. It is our belief that the Councils of the Bishops were in antiquity, and will be again, the appropriate organ, by which the unity of distant Churches can find expression without any derogation from their rightful autonomy. The Lambeth Conference with its strict adherence to purely advisory functions has been, perhaps, preparing our minds for participation in the Councils of a larger and more important community of Churches.

Every extension of this circle of visible fellowship would increase the power of the Church to witness to its Lord by its unity.

401

1930
The Church in South India:
the universal Church in local form

Encyclical Letter, *Lambeth Conference, 1930.*

The Church of South India, uniting Anglicans, Methodists, Congregationalists and Reformed was inaugurated in September 1947. For its basis of unity, see no. 427. For the 1948 Lambeth Conference's comments, see no. 432.

The Anglican Communion is a group of Churches bound together by very close ties of history and tradition, doctrine and practice. After the union in South India, Anglicans who will be included in the united Church will not give up the use of the Prayer Book or discard any of the doctrines held in the Anglican Churches. Yet the united Church in South India will not itself be an Anglican Church: it will be a distinct Province of the Universal Church. It will have a very real intercommunion with the Churches of the Anglican Communion, though for a time that intercommunion will be limited in certain directions by their rules. Its Bishops will be received as Bishops by these Churches. Its episcopally ordained ministers — a continually increasing number — will be entitled under the usual rules to administer the Communion in the Churches of the Anglican Communion. Its communicants will be entitled to communicate with the Churches of the Anglican Communion, except in cases forbidden by the rules of these Churches. On the other hand no right to minister in the Churches of that Communion will be acquired by those ministers who have not been episcopally ordained. The fact that the Church of South India will not be a member of the group of Churches called the Anglican Communion will inevitably impose on our brethren a temporary severance of close and treasured relationships, in council and synod, with their brethren in North India. But these are sacrifices which we believe they will make cheerfully in the hope of achieving a union between episcopal and non-episcopal churches such as has never yet been effected, and of building up a real and living Church in India. For our part we assure our brethren that they will never be disowned nor deserted by the Anglican Communion. It will preserve for them unimpaired their welcome to its love and fellowship, to its altars and its pulpits. For it will be looking forward to the day when their work will be rewarded and the unity of these Churches, not only in South India but in the whole of India, will be completed, and there will emerge a Province of Christ's Church, genuinely Catholic, loyal to all truth, within whose visible unity treasures of faith and order, nowhere in the Church at present combined, will be possessed in common, and the power of Christ will be manifest in a new richness. It was with unanimity and with profound sense of thankfulness that the Conference adopted the Resolutions relating to South India.

402

1930
The importance of public worship

Encyclical Letter, *Lambeth Conference, 1930.*

We recall our Church people and all who own the name of Christ to the privilege and duty which are theirs of expressing their faith and receiving pardon and renewal through joining with the brethren regularly in the public worship of the Church and especially in the Blessed Sacrament of the Holy Communion. The Church's chief duty is to love and worship God; and in that love and worship it gives its chief witness to the world. They should reflect what wrong they do to God, to others and to themselves if they grow slack in fulfilling, especially on Sunday, this clear and obvious duty. We whose privilege it is to lead others in worship are bound to make that worship as worthy as we can of Him to Whom it is offered, worthy in its spirit and its tone, worthy also in its range and scope, taking, as we ought, every opportunity that is ours of bringing all human concerns and interests within its ambit of praise and intercession. Worship unites us in a fellowship of adoration; and, when it is worthily offered, can become for us all a joy as well as a duty, and bring us that refreshment and encouragement for which thousands are really hungry, though they know not for what they hunger. *Sursum Corda*, 'Lift up your hearts' — such a call from God as we have ourselves heard is not easily expressed, least of all in such a Letter as this. Yet it was to this high theme that we in the Lambeth Conference were moved to direct our thoughts; and we commend to thoughtful people the Report of our first Committee.

403

1930
A call to the Ministry

Encyclical Letter, *Lambeth Conference, 1930.*

In the witness and the work of the Church as of every other community there is need of leadership. Our Lord Himself shows us the crucial importance of providing leaders by the care and patience with which He trained the twelve whom He chose out of the general company of His disciples 'that they might be with Him and that He might send them forth.' This ministry has been perpetuated from the first days until now. The need of the leadership which it gives is undiminished. The honour of that leadership still remains. We speak with knowledge gained in all parts of the world. We know that everywhere fields are white for the harvest. The Lord of the harvest calls for labourers that the harvest may be won. We who as Bishops of His Church have some title to speak in His Name, make now a strong appeal to young men, who accept Him as their Lord, to cherish the ambition of offering themselves in the Sacred ministry for the highest service to which human life can be dedicated. They will be ready to submit their ambitions to the judgement of the responsible authorities of the Church. If it seems right that they should be prepared for ordination to the ministry and they are unable with the means at their disposal to meet the cost of a training, demanded alike by the rising standards of education and by the honour of their service, we call upon the Church in all lands to regard it as a duty and privilege to provide that training for them. The leadership of women is needed as well as the leadership of men. We have sought in our Resolution to encourage in every way open to us the ministry of women. They have become free as never before in history to use in varied service to the community their distinctive gifts and ideals. We know that many of them desire to devote their lives to Him in Whose service is the perfect freedom. We would assure them of our determination to secure for them, as far as in us lies, a place of honour in the organized life of the Church. To this end we have reviewed and enlarged the work entrusted to the Order of Deaconesses. We believe that in that Order women of ability will find increasing scope for powers of leadership and witness. And we call upon clergy and people alike to welcome and to use to the full the ministry of women not only in the pastoral work of the Church but in its teaching and worship. We rejoice in the growth of religious communities within our own Communion as a sign of spiritual vitality, and as a source of spiritual strength to the whole body of the Church.

404

1930
Bible and Church

Resolution 1, Lambeth Conference, 1930.

1. We believe that the Christian Church is the repository and trustee of a Revelation of God given by Himself, which all members of the Church are bound to transmit to others, and that every member of the Church, both clerical and lay, is called to be a channel through which the Divine Life flows for the quickening of all mankind.

405

1930
The teaching office of the Church

Resolutions 6, 7, Lambeth Conference, 1930.

Resolution 7 here stresses the importance of the study of theology at the highest academic level. The relationship of the universities, with their independent scholars, to the teaching office of the Church has often been a vexed one since the Middle Ages; but they have been an invaluable resource ·in the Church's life.

6. ...There is need for the Church to renew and redirect its teaching office –

(*a*) By a fresh insistence upon the duty of thinking and learning as essential elements in the Christian life;

(*b*) By recalling the clergy to a fuller sense of their duty in the exercise of the *teaching office*. Of all their functions this is one of the most important. It demands, especially in these days, prayer and study, both individual and corporate, on the self-revelation of God in Jesus Christ and the manifestations of His Presence in the modern world;

(*c*) By the provision of similar opportunities for the laity;

(*d*) By a new emphasis upon the appeal to the mind as well as to the heart in the preaching of the Word as an element in Christian worship; and

(*e*) By providing both for the clergy and laity opportunities of Retreats and other well-tried methods for the deepening of the spiritual life through the growth of fellowship with God and man.

We especially desire to impress upon the younger clergy that the Church requires the service of men who will devote themselves to the study of theology in all its branches. The Church needs learning, as well as spiritual power and practical ability, in its clergy.

7. We welcome an increased readiness in many educational authorities to accept the influence and assistance of the Church in its teaching capacity, and we urge that every effort should be made throughout the Church to seek such opportunities and to use them with sympathy and discretion. As the intellectual meaning and content of the Christian doctrine of God cannot be fully apprehended without the aid of the highest human knowledge, it is essential that Christian theology should be studied and taught in Universities in contact with philosophy, science and criticism, and to that end that Faculties of Theology should be established in Universities wherever possible.

406

1931
Old Catholics and Anglicans: the Bonn Agreement

Growth in Agreement, ed. H. Meyer and L. Vischer (New York–Geneva 1984), p. 37.

The Old Catholics, who separated from Rome in the eighteenth and nineteenth centuries, regard themselves as having kept faith with the one Church which preceded the schism of 1054. Cf. no. 520 on Communion with North India, Pakistan and Bangladesh Churches.

1. Each Communion recognizes the catholicity and independence of the other and maintains its own.
2. Each Communion agrees to admit members of the other Communion to participate in the Sacraments.
3. Intercommunion[1] does not require from either Communion the acceptance of all doctrinal opinion, sacramental devotion, or liturgical practice characteristic of the other, but implies that each believes the other to hold all the essentials of the Christian Faith.

407

1935
Disestablishment and disendowment in Wales

Address of the Lord Archbishop of Wales, at the Church Congress, Bournemouth, 10 October 1935.

Cf. no. 409.

To 'establish' a thing means giving to it permanence or security; to 'disestablish' a thing means depriving it of permanence or security. Now, the State can only take away what it has given. When we say 'Parliament has disestablished the Church,' we mean that the State annuls those laws and customs affecting the Church which

---

[1]   It should be noted that the goal of most modern ecumenical agreement is simply 'communion', that is, union in the Church. The term 'intercommunion' is now avoided ecumenically, because, together with the placing of any adjecture such as 'full' before the word 'communion', it implies something less than the unity of Christians in one communion with their Lord.

fall within the purview of the State. Yet it is evident that such annulment cannot be absolute, for in that event the Church would be outlawed. There is not a religious body in this land, however loudly it protests its freedom from State control, that is really outside the law; the law conditions and protects its existence.... Here the Church in Wales was compelled to settle a prior problem. She was determined to do nothing which might savour of schism, or a breach of ecclesiastical order. Could the four Dioceses of Wales remain in the Province of Canterbury, so that the Convocation of Canterbury, acting as the Provincial Synod, could enact our ecclesiastical laws? But the Welsh Church Act extruded the bishops and clergy of the Church of Wales from the Convocation of Canterbury. The Convocation could not legislate for the Welsh Dioceses in the absence of the Welsh bishops and clergy; and the sessions of Convocation would be irregular and informal if thé Welsh bishops and clergy took part in them.... Thus the Province of Wales came into existence, and the Archbishop and Bishops of Wales, according to immemorial custom, were thenceforth the Provisional Synod of Wales, with its inherent authority to judge and to legislate.

It is well for churchmen to remember this original and inherent authority of the bishops. Customarily enveloped in conventions, it is unperceived, and is a latent force. But, in times of revolution, when customs and conventions are swept away, it emerges of right and dominates. The conventions which usually surround it spring from the common fellowship of bishops, clergy and laity in the Mystical Body of Christ, which, down the ages, has led them to mutual counsel, agreement and co-operation. In some such way the Canon Law of Christendom was composed. Throughout our work of reconstruction the bishops of Wales were animated by the intention to legislate in Council, and to delegate judicial functions as far as possible to legal experts. These general remarks will suffice as an introduction to our Constitution.

408

1936
Holiness

Evelyn Underhill, Worship *(London 1936), p. 77.*

Arising from its incarnational character, and indeed closely connected with it, is the fact that Christian worship is always directed towards the sanctification of life. All worship has a creative aim...; and here, the creative aim is that total transfiguration of the created order in which the incarnation of the Logos finds its goal. Christian worship, then, is to be judged by the degree to which it tends to Holiness; since this is the response to the pressure of the Holy which is asked of the Church and of the soul. The Christian is required to use the whole of his existence as sacramental material.

409

1937
The Constitution of the Church in Wales

C.A.H. Green, The Setting of the Constitution of the Church in Wales *(London, 1937).*

This discussion includes a statement on continuity in the life of a Church which undergoes a formal change in government. Cf. no. 407.

The Constitution of the Church in Wales ordained that 'The Governing Body shall at its creation accept the Articles, Doctrinal Statements... and... the Formularies of the Church of England as accepted by that Church and set forth in, or appended to, the Book of Common Prayer of the Church of England.' This section needs careful scrutiny and comment. First, what date is indicated by the phrase 'at its creation'? The Constitution of the Governing Body was created by the Convention held in Cardiff and ratified by it on the 5th of October, 1917, but the Governing Body itself was not then in existence. The earliest date on which the Governing Body as such could do anything was the date of the first Meeting, that is, the 8th of January, 1918. The Minutes of the Governing Body contain a record that, in fact, the Governing Body did, by formal resolution at its meeting on the 8th of January, 1918, 'accept the articles, doctrinal statements, etc.,' as required by the Constitution. Secondly, why was the Governing Body bound to accept Statements and Documents which it had not formulated itself? The reason is certain. Although the Governing Body was a new creature, the Church, whose organ it is, is not new. The Church, as a living organism, lives on from age to age, and in her growth spreads out on all sides through Time and Space. There was no breach in the life of the Church on the 31st of March, 1920; the Church is the same after as before Disestablishment, which only touched the surface of things. The living organism, bearing certain Articles, Doctrinal Statements and Formularies, carried them over with it into a new environment; and when the organism developed a special organ adapted to the new environment, it of course caused this organ to conform to its life. The Governing Body was such a new organ; it could not but take over the heritage bequeathed to it by the Convocation of Canterbury, defunct now so far as Wales and Monmouthshire are concerned. Thirdly, the Articles, the Doctrinal Statements, the Formularies, and the Book of Common Prayer, could not but be those of 'the Church of England' at the date on which the Governing Body came into real existence. This was inevitable if, as has been asserted, no breach in the continuous life of the Church was made by the Act of Disestablishment. But, it is to be noted, the 'acceptance' is limited to the date of the 'creation' of the Governing Body. The Church in Wales is not tied for ever to the past. The Constitution itself provides means whereby Articles drawn up by the English Convocation, and Doctrinal Statements and Formularies holding the synodical authority of the Church of England, can be altered from time to time if the Church in Wales so determines. The thirtieth section of the second chapter of the *Constitution* was not meant to be more than the base from which the Church of Wales would start out on a fresh career as guardian and witness of the Faith. Fourthly, where will the Articles, Doctrinal Statements and Formularies be found? They are those 'set forth in, or appended to, the Book of Common Prayer.' The best comment on these words is furnished by the First Schedule to Chapter VII. of the *Constitution*, by which a Clergyman is required to declare: 'I assent to the Thirty-Nine Articles of Religion, and to the Book of Common Prayer, and of ordering of Bishops, Priests and Deacons; I believe the doctrine as therein set forth to be agreeable to the Word of God.' This declaration makes explicit what is meant by the 'acceptance' of the Articles, Doctrinal Statements and Formularies as set forth in, or appended to, the Book of Common Prayer. The acceptance of this Standard of Christian thinking is made by the Governing Body in the name of the Laity as much as on behalf of the Clergy of the Church in Wales. There is not one standard for the Clergy and another standard for the Laity.

410

1937
Proposal for organic union with the Presbyterian Church in the USA

General Convention, 1937, Episcopal Church in the United States of America, A Communion of Communions, *1937.*

This resolution is of interest as an example of the exploration of the possibility of a union which will create a single united Church and not a federation of Churches (cf. no. 401).

Resolved, That the General Convention of the Protestant Episcopal Church in the United States of America, acting with full realization of the significance of its proposal, hereby invites the Presbyterian Church in the United States of America to join with it in accepting the following declaration: The two Churches one in the faith of the Lord Jesus Christ, the Incarnate Word of God, recognizing the Holy Scriptures as the supreme rule of faith, accepting the two Sacraments ordained by Christ, and believing that the visible unity of Christ's Church is the will of God, hereby formally declare their purpose to achieve organic union between their respective churches. Upon the basis of these agreements the two churches agree to take immediate steps toward the framing of plans whereby this end may be achieved.

411

1938
Ecumenical method

1922 Doctrine Commission, Doctrine in the Church of England
(1938), p. 24.

The Commission was set up in 1922 by the Archbishops of Canterbury and York. It included 'Anglo-Catholic', 'Evangelical' and 'Liberal' or 'Modernist' members and its brief was to arrive at a common statement with which all shades of Anglican opinion could agree. This passage describes a method used today in ecumenical conversations, of seeking to get behind the old controversial language to the common faith.

It must be the task of many generations to work out that synthesis of different apprehensions of the one revelation of God in Christ towards which our undertaking points. But we are persuaded that out of such a process of co-operative thought there may be fashioned at last a Christian theology more adequate than any that has preceded it. Certainly we have found that so soon as both parties to any controversy set themselves to find other expressions than those which have been traditional among them, they discover a far greater measure of substantial agreement than they had anticipated.

412

1938
An 'Anglican' theology?

1922 Doctrine Commission, Doctrine in the Church of England
(1938), p. 25.

Cf. no. 358.

There is not, and the majority of us do not desire that there should be, a system of distinctively Anglican Theology. The Anglican Churches have received and hold the faith of Catholic Christendom, but they have exhibited a rich variety in methods both of approach and of interpretation. They are the heirs of the Reformation as well as of Catholic tradition; and they hold together in a single fellowship of worship and witness those whose chief attachment is to each of these, and also those whose attitude to the distinctively Christian tradition is most deeply affected by the tradition of a free and liberal culture which is historically the bequest of the Greek spirit.[1]

413

1938
Bible and Church

1922 Doctrine Commission, Doctrine in the Church of England *(1938), p. 27.*

Two points are made here. The first is that Anglican faith cannot be separated from the faith of all Christians through the ages (cf. no. 412). Although we can speak of Anglican 'tradition' we cannot speak of a distinctively Anglican 'faith'. The second is that the witness of Scripture and the Church are intimately interconnected.

The faith and doctrine of Christianity are handed down to us in the context of a living fellowship. In its widest sense this fellowship is that of the Church Universal; to us as Anglicans the tradition is handed down through the Anglican Communion as part of Western Christendom. This involves for us two consequences. The first is that in interpreting our own tradition we must give attention to the background of the universal tradition of Christendom. The second is that in discussion of doctrine to-day we are bound to consider its historical sources and the authority which these should carry. The Christian religion is founded upon a specific revelation of God in history. To this revelation Scripture and the Church alike bear witness. But the Church has always claimed that its doctrine is based on Scripture. It is to Scripture, therefore, that we first turn in considering the sources and authority of Christian doctrine, though we proceed to offer also some observations upon the authority of the Church, and have appended further a brief note on Anglican formularies.

---

[1]   This is a reference to the 'modernists' or 'liberals'.

414

1938
Scripture

1922 Doctrine Commission, Doctrine in the Church of England
(1938), p. 28.

The Bible is here unequivocally given the central place in Christian witness.

From the Christian standpoint the Bible is unique, as being the inspired record of a unique revelation. It is the record of the special preparation for Christ, and of His direct impact upon men, through His Life, Death, and Resurrection. It sets before us that historical movement of Divine self-disclosure of which the Gospel is the crown.

415

1938
The authority of the Church in matters of faith: the *consensus fidelium*

1922 Doctrine Commission, Doctrine in the Church of England
(1938), p. 35.

The authority of the Church in the realm of doctrine arises from its commission to preach the Gospel to all the world, and the promises, accompanying that commission, that the Lord would always be with His disciples, and that the Holy Spirit would guide them into all truth. The Church's understanding of the Gospel is continually renewed by its experience of communion with God through Christ; and the authority of its doctrinal formulations ought always to be interpreted as resting, at least in part, upon the acceptance of these by the whole body of the faithful. This authority, in so far as it is derived from such a *consensus fidelium*,[1] rests upon the range and quality of the manifold experience which that consensus gathers up, and upon the witness which, alike in the devotional and other practice of Christians generally and in the doctrine of the theologians, it bears to the truth of the Gospel. The

---

[1] 'Consent, or consensus, of the faithful'

weight of the *consensus fidelium* does not depend on mere numbers or on the extension of a belief at any one time, but on continuance through the ages and to the extent to which the *consensus* is genuinely free.

416

1938
Teaching authority

1922 Doctrine Commission, Doctrine in the Church of England *(1938), p. 39.*

This text addresses the difficulty of ensuring that it is clear what is being taught as 'the mind of the Church' and what is the view of an individual teacher.

5. No individual can claim to receive the teacher's commission as a right, and the commission itself involves the obligation not to teach, as the doctrine of the Church, doctrine which is not in accordance with the Church's mind.
6. If any authorised teacher puts forward personal opinions which diverge (within the limits indicated above) from the traditional teaching of the Church, he should be careful to distinguish between such opinions and the normal teaching which he gives in the Church's name; and so far as possible such divergences should be so put forward as to avoid offending consciences.
7. In respect of the exercise of discipline within such limits as the above resolutions recognize, great regard should be paid to the need for securing a free consensus, as distinct from an enforced uniformity.

417

1938
Grace

1922 Doctrine Commission, Doctrine in the Church of England *(1938), pp. 52–3.*

The Commission here defines grace with the emphasis upon divine initiative and human need. It touches on two long-running controversies in the Church.

The first concerns the relationship between grace and the freedom of the human will, the second the 'means of grace' which are entrusted to the Church as the Holy Spirit works in its sacramental life.

Grace has... come to mean the will of God (which is also His love) regarded as active on behalf of and in man. It is not merely 'favour' or 'goodwill', but a 'power that worketh in us'.[1] Though the operations of grace have been distinguished for purposes of description and practical convenience, grace itself is one. For example, there is no distinction, except of mode, between 'prevenient' and 'co-operant' grace on the one hand, and 'sacramental' grace on the other. Grace is always prior to every good inclination of the human soul, both to that 'natural' goodness which persists despite the corruption of human nature through sin, and to that 'supernatural' goodness or sanctification which results from the work of the Holy Spirit in and through the Church. The operation of grace is not opposed to the freedom of the human will, since grace acts through the will and not externally to it. It is, indeed, only within the sphere of grace that true freedom is to be found. The word 'grace' has also been used to describe the effects of its operation in human character.[2] In this usage emphasis has customarily been laid upon the development in a man of a 'supernatural' righteousness. This conception is important, as witnessing to the distinctiveness of the Christian ideal and to the necessity of obtaining grace through Christ for the attainment of this ideal. This conception is independent of any particular view as to the way in which this grace is mediated.

418

1938
Sin

1922 Doctrine Commission, Doctrine in the Church of England *(1938), p. 57.*

In the teaching of Christ the primary emphasis is upon the positive nature of righteousness as being the expression of love to God and

---

[1]   Ephesians 3.20

[2]   Latin: *gratia: cf.* such phrases as 'graces of character'.

to man. Sin, therefore, becomes primarily a refusal of trust and of obedience on the part of His children toward a heavenly Father, or a failure of brotherly love. Sinfulness is ascribed both to individuals and to communities or classes. Sin lies in the disposition of the 'heart'. Its universality is assumed. It is to be noted that the commands of God are never arbitrary, but proceed from His righteousness and love, and that He always wills the highest good of His creatures.

419

1938
Atonement

1922 Doctrine Commission, Doctrine in the Church of England (1938), pp. 90–91.

The Commission here attempts the difficult task of drawing together in a brief statement the essence of centuries of Christian debate on why God became man and how his death redeemed us (cf. no. 162).

The preaching of the Cross is the proclamation of a fact far richer than any theory of Atonement. In the history of the Church very various theories have been held, and while affirming the fact of reconciliation to God through Christ, the Church as a whole has never formally accepted any particular explanation of that fact. Thus the doctrine of Atonement has not been defined in the same manner and degree as the doctrine of the Incarnation. But there are certain convictions which must control all Christian thinking on the Atonement. Fundamental to the Christian doctrine of the Atonement is the conviction that it is essentially the work of God, who in Christ reconciles mankind to Himself. In subordination to this primary truth of the Divine initiative Christian theology has also emphasised that which Jesus Christ in His Manhood wrought on bchalf of mankind towards God; but the Cross is first of all to be understood as a Divine Victory: God, in the Person of Jesus Christ, triumphs decisively over the forces of sin, death, and the devil. The doctrine of the Atonement is based on the reality of God's eternal and unchanging love. That love is more than benevolence. It is a holy love, and therefore always actively affirms itself both in condemning sin and also in striving to restore and to remake the sinner. Thus, on the one hand, God's love upholds the moral order of the universe, which is manifested both in the consequences attendant upon sin, including alienation from God and moral degeneration, and in the conviction of man's conscience that loss or unhappiness is due to him as a penalty for wrong-doing. The traditional phrase, 'the wrath of God', should be interpreted in the light of these considerations. On the other hand, God's love, by its own characteristic activity of redeeming sinners, completes and transcends the moral order thus manifested. This is the essence of the contrast between 'the law' and 'the Gospel'. The Cross is the supreme instrument of this redemptive activity of God. In it there is at once a revelation of the holiness of God and a real breaking of the power of sin. The sinner is enabled to repent and he can be freely forgiven.

420

1938
The visible Church

1922 Doctrine Commission, Doctrine in the Church of England *(1938), pp. 104–5.*

The 'visible' Church as instituted by Christ is identified here with the universal Church of the 'ever-expanding missionary brotherhood'. The Commission here seeks to counter the arguments of those who have seen it as manifested only in local communities of 'gathered believers'.

The life of the Church as visible and militant here in earth is expressed and manifested in the visible life of Christendom, the beginnings of which, as an historical phenomenon, go back to and spring from the redemptive work of the Lord Jesus Christ in His life upon earth. The New Testament traces back the beginnings of the organised life of the Church in this sense to the little company of disciples of Jesus, assembled together under the leadership of the Apostles who had been 'made' and 'sent out' by Him, upon whom the Spirit descended at Pentecost, who became the nucleus of an ever-expanding missionary brotherhood (admission to which was by Baptism, on the basis of repentance and faith in Jesus as the appointed Messiah and Redeemer), and of whom we read that they 'continued steadfastly in the apostle's teaching, and in the fellowship, and in the breaking of bread, and in the prayers'.[1]

421

1938
Christ's commission for ministry

1922 Doctrine Commission, Doctrine in the Church of England (1938), pp. 114–115.

This passage seeks to express the relationship between an ordained ministry and the whole people of God as it derives in continuity from Christ himself and the apostles.

The fundamental Christian Ministry is the Ministry of Christ. There is no Christian Priesthood or Ministry apart from his. His priestly and ministerial function is to reconcile the world to God in and through Himself, by His Incarnation and by His 'one sacrifice once offered', delivering men from the power of sin and death. The Church as the Body of Christ, sharing his life, has a ministerial function derived from that of Christ. In this function every member has his place and share according to his different capabilities and calling. The work of the Church is to bring all the various activities and relationships of men under the control of the Holy Spirit, and in this work each member has his part. The particular function of the official Ministry can only be rightly understood as seen against the background of this universal Ministry. The Church on the Day of Pentecost is set before us in the book of the Acts of the Apostles as a body of believers having within it, as its recognized focus of unity and organ of authority, the Apostolate, which owed its origin to the action of the Lord Himself. There was not first an Apostolate which gathered a body of believers about itself; nor was there a completely structureless collection of believers which gave authority to the apostles to speak and act on its behalf. To suppose that the organisation of the Church must have begun in one or other of these ways is to misconceive the

---

[1]   Acts 2.42

situation. From the first there was the fellowship of believers finding its unity in the Twelve. Thus the New Testament bears witness to the principle of a distinctive ministry, as an original element, but not the sole constitutive element, in the life of the Church. This fact is of great importance in any consideration of the relation which should subsist between the ministerial Body of Christ and the Ministry which is its organ for the performance of certain distinctive and characteristic acts. The Ministry, then, is to be regarded as an original and essential element in the Church. We must remember that in a historical process of growth the appearance of formality is often increased in retrospect, and we must beware of reading back into the earliest period the systematic organisation of later times. St. Paul was called to the Apostolate by a special revelation; James, the brother of the Lord, who presided over the Church in Jerusalem, was not one of the Twelve; the position of Barnabas does not fit easily into a clear-cut scheme. But a distinction corresponding to that drawn later between Clergy and Laity– κλῆρος and λαός– is there from the outset. In the same way, whether or not the succession of the Ministry as known from (at latest) the end of the second century can be traced through all its stages to the Apostles, yet the Ministry exists in succession to the original Apostolate. The Ministry does not exist apart from the Body, nor the Body apart from the Ministry. But Christ, in drawing men to Himself, unites them in a fellowship of which the Apostolate, which he appointed, and the Ministry, which is its successor, are the ministerial organs.

422

1938
Ministry and continuity

1922 Doctrine Commission, Doctrine in the Church of England *(1938), p. 119.*

Cf. no. 536 on the principle that ordained ministry should be in 'the Church of God', that is, in intention a ministry acting in the Universal Church, and thus a ministry of unity and continuity. See, too, nos. 343, 355 on the Chicago–Lambeth Quadrilateral.

It is of practical religious importance that the worship in which the individual believer takes part is the worship of the whole Church, and it is essential to the idea of the Ministry which leads that worship that it is an organ of the whole Church, not of a single group or congregation. Further, since it is a function of the Ministry thus to be a symbol and effective instrument of the unity of the Church, it is appropriate that it should be constituted by a rite of ordination having an agreed, universal, and traditional character. The ideal of the Church's Ministry requires that it be 'acknowledged by every part of the Church as possessing... the authority of the whole body.'[1] Such considerations make it clear why the Church has in fact preserved and set store by the continuity of the Ministry as, along with the Scriptures, Creeds, and Sacraments, a guarantee of its continuous identity. They also make it clear why, in our judgement, the acceptance of any Order of Ministry cannot be based on considerations of evangelistic effectiveness alone, apart from any regard for continuity and unity. The life of the Church is continuous from generation to generation; continuity of ministerial commission embodies in the sphere of Order the principle of Apostolicity in the sense of continuous mission from Christ and the Father.

423

1940
Constituent membership of the World Council of Churches

General Convention, 1940, Episcopal Church in the United States of America, A Communion of Communions, *1940.*

The World Council of Churches was not formally constituted until 1948, but the process of its formation was actively under way from 1937, as the Life and Work and the Faith and Order movements decided to merge at their respective Conferences at Oxford and Edinburgh.

---

[1]   'An Appeal to All Christian People', *Report of the Lambeth Conference,* 1920.

Whereas, These terms have been incorporated in the constitution drawn up and adopted at Utrecht in May, 1938, and

Whereas, The official invitation to become a constituent member of the World Council of Churches is now before this Convention, issued by the Committee of Fourteen appointed for this purpose by the Oxford and Edinburgh Conferences, therefore, be it

Resolved, That the General Convention of the Protestant Episcopal Church hereby accepts the invitation to become a constituent menber of the World Council of Churches; and further

Resolved, That the appointment of representatives from this Church to the Assembly of the World Council, should such appointment be necessary before the next General Convention, be made by the Presiding Bishop on nomination by the Commission on Faith and Order.

424

1940
Membership of a Federal Council of Churches

General Convention, 1940, Episcopal Church in the United States of America, A Communion of Communions, *1940*.

This represents an early stage of ecumenical rapprochement.

Resolved, That this Church hereby become a member of the Federal Council of the Churches of Christ in America, and that the National Council of this Church be and hereby is instructed to appoint such representatives as may be required to make that membership effective.

425

1942
The function of a cathedral

William Temple (1881–1944), written as Archbishop of Canterbury, Some Lambeth Letters, *ed. F.S. Temple (Oxford, 1963), p. 35.*

There is always a struggle between two leading conceptions of a Cathedral. One comes from the Monastic period and represents the Cathedral as a worshipping community where all the members of the Chapter should if possible be present at almost all the services... the other is that [of] the Cathedral as the central power station, so to speak, of the Diocese. Some large element of the former conception can be combined with it and indeed ought to be.

426

1944
The isolation of missionary bishops

William Temple (1881–1944), Archbishop of Canterbury, Some Lambeth Letters, ed. F.S. Temple (Oxford, 1963), p. 149.

Collegiality is of immense importance to the system of episcopal ministry. Here it is stressed that isolated missionary bishops need brotherly counsel and support too. Cf. no. 340.

The bishops of missionary dioceses attached to the Province of Canterbury are in an anomalous position. They belong to no bench of bishops and have to act very largely in isolation... I know that some of them would feel very much happier if they were linked in some corporate way with other bishops of their communion... until the time has come for the formation of separate provinces which would include their dioceses.

427

1947
The Church of South India: basis of Union

M.K. Kuriakose, History of Christianity in India: Source Materials *(Madras 1982), pp. 384–5,* Constitution of the Church of South India: Basis of Union, *13, 16.*

Cf. nos. 401, 432. The plan finally adopted made the following stipulations about ecclesiastical identity and ordained ministry:

The autonomy of the United Church:

13. The uniting Churches agree that the united Church should of right be free in all spiritual matters from the direction or interposition of any civil government. They further agree that the united Church must be an autonomous Church and free from any control, legal or otherwise, of any Church or Society external to itself. At the same time they remember that the united Church, on account of its origin and history, must have special relations with the Churches in the West through which it has come into existence, and they are confident that it will so regulate its acts as to maintain fellowship both with those Churches and with other branches of the Catholic Church with which the uniting Churches are now in communion. They also recognize that the united Church, as a part of the Church Universal, must give full weight to the pronouncements of bodies representative of the whole Church, and, in particular, would desire to take part in the deliberations and decisions of an Ecumenical Council, if such should in the mercy of God be some day called together...

The development of full unity in ministry and life within the United Church.

16. The uniting Churches agree, that it is their intention and expectation that eventually every minister exercising a permanent ministry in the united Church will be an episcopally ordained minister. For the thirty years succeeding the inauguration of the union, the ministers of any Church whose missions have founded the originally separate parts of the united Church may be received as ministers of the united Church... After this period of thirty years, the united Church must determine for itself whether it will continue to make any exceptions to the rule that its ministry is an episcopally ordained ministry, and generally under what conditions it will receive ministers from other Churches into its ministry...

428

1947–1970
United Churches: Churches formed by a union of Anglicans with Christians of other traditions

Who are the Anglicans?, ed. Charles Long, prepared for the Lambeth Conference, 1988 (Ohio, 1988), p. 75.

a. Church of South India (1947).
The Church of South India is the oldest United Church and the first to bring together Christians from Episcopal and non-Episcopal traditions. After 20 years of negotiation, the new Church was inaugurated on 27 September 1947 and brought together Christians from the Anglican, Methodist, Persbyterian, Congregationalist and Reformed traditions.
b. Church of North India.
The Church of North India was inaugurated in 1970 and is a union of six churches: The Anglican Church, the United Church of Northern India (Congregationalist and Presbyterian), the Methodist Church (British and Australian Conferences), the Council of Baptist Churches in Northern India, the Church of the Brethren in India, the Disciples of Christ. The Church of North India shares the same early history as that of the Church in South India.
c. The Church of Pakistan.
The Church of Pakistan was formed in 1970 as a Union between four churches: The Church of Pakistan (Anglican), the United Church of North India and Pakistan (Presbyterian), the United Methodist Church (American Methodist), the Lutheran Church of Pakistan.

429

1948
The extension of Anglicanism

J.W.C. Wand, The Anglican Communion *(Oxford, 1948), pp. 9ff.*

The extension of our Communion beyond the seas began as part of what Sir John Seeley described some sixty years ago in the book which made him famous, *The Expansion of England.* In its earlier stages it was not prompted by missionary zeal. Early in the seventeenth century Englishmen began to settle abroad as traders on the continent of Europe and in India, and as colonists in North America. (Newfoundland had been formally occupied by Sir Humphrey Gilbert as far back as 1573, but the whole island did not become British until the treaty of Utrecht in 1713.) Their motive was primarily economic, though religious, political and social considerations played a part. These commercial settlements, of which two of the most important in Europe were at Delft and Hamburg, were supplied with chaplains almost as a matter of course. But these chaplains were not in any sense missionaries. The East India Company was definitely opposed to any attempt to convert the natives, fearing that it would lead to disturbances. The position in America was somewhat different. A considerable proportion of the colonists had gone there in order to escape from the Church of England as represented by Laud and therefore preferred ministers of their own appointment to its clergy. Laud was at heart a successor of the politician-bishops of the fourteenth and fifteenth centuries. When he held the See of London he was also Lord Treasurer, which meant virtually Prime Minister, and instigated a scheme for extending the Church of England to every part of the world where the English government had, or might acquire, any interest. If it would be too much to say that he looked upon the Church primarily as a powerful instrument of national policy, he would certainly never have hesitated to use it for political purposes. At the same time he proposed to send a bishop to New England 'to keep the Puritans in order'. It may be assumed that the methods contemplated would not have been purely persuasive. In Laud's eyes a bishop who had no power to fine and imprison people who disregarded his godly admonitions would hardly have been a bishop in more than name. Circumstances made it impossible for either of these projects to be carried out. But they appear to have been the origin of the general jurisdiction over the colonies which came to be regarded as inherent in the See of London.

After the Restoration the Church began to take formal account of its responsibilities beyond the seas. In the Preface to the Prayer Book of 1662 it is pointed out that the new service for the Baptism of such as are of Riper Years 'may be always useful for the baptism of natives in our plantations and of others converted to the faith'. There was also a plan for the consecration of Dr. Alexander

Murray as Bishop in Virginia, and it is said that the letters patent making the appointment were actually prepared. But for some reason the scheme was allowed to lapse. Henry Compton, who was Bishop of London from 1675 to 1713, took a lively interest in American affairs and did all in his power to maintain a steady supply of clergy, but it was impossible that a jurisdiction exercised from a distance of three thousand miles through commissaries could be effective. It was by no means certain that letters written from one side of the Atlantic would ever reach their destination on the other. If they did arrive safely they were necessarily some months *en route*. An important step forward was taken when the *Society for Promoting Christian Knowledge* was founded in 1697 by Dr. Thomas Bray, who had won fame by the publication of a series of catechetical lectures. He was an enthusiast for religious education, and his original purpose was the distribution of Bibles and other good books amongst the poor in England. He soon extended his scheme to include lending libraries for America and paid a visit to Maryland as commissary for Bishop Compton. The *Society for the Propagation of the Gospel in Foreign Parts* was founded in 1701. The Archbishop of Canterbury has always been the President, so that it has always stood in a semi-official relation to the Church. Originally the Society was intended primarily for work among the colonists, but in 1710 it was decided that preference was to be given to 'the conversion of heathen and infidels'. In 1763 the Peace of Paris established England as an Imperial power. This led to a general quickening of interest in America and the question of a colonial episcopate was raised again. The need was obviously great and increasing, and it was equally obvious that the Jacobite sympathies of the clergy need no longer be taken seriously, if they existed. But the Crown was still reluctant to issue the customary letters patent and the Archbishops thought that they ought not to consecrate without them. If we are surprised at their attitude we must remember that at that time people thought in terms of law and institutions more than we do now. The events of 1688 were not very remote: there must have been still people living whose parents had remembered them. Moreover, the revolution of that year was not an isolated event. It was the last of a long series of struggles which had begun in the reign of King John, nearly five hundred years earlier, and had vindicated triumphantly the principle that the Law of England is not to be over-ridden or set aside by any person on any pretext for any purpose. It is not wonderful that the Archbishops thought that they must at any cost avoid any action the legality of which could be called in question. In 1783 Samuel Seabury, a native-born American, came to England seeking consecration. But although the independence of the American colonists had been recognized, the Archbishops still thought that they ought not to act without authorization from the Crown, and were unwilling to ask for what they believed would certainly be refused. If that should happen the position would be worse than ever.

Seabury is said to have contemplated approaching the bishops of Denmark, when it was pointed out to him that there were bishops whose Orders were not open to question nearer at hand, and that they could act without reference to the State because it had no official knowledge of their existence. He was consecrated as Bishop of Connecticut at Aberdeen by three Scottish bishops on 14 November 1784. It is believed that Martin Joseph Routh, subsequently President of Magdalen College, Oxford from 1791 to 1854, was to some extent responsible for this solution of the difficulty, though it is not known exactly what part he played. It is a matter for regret that the idea did not occur to anybody fifty, or even twenty, years earlier. On 4 February 1787 William White and Samuel Provost, both citizens of the new republic, were consecrated in the chapel of Lambeth Palace as Bishops of Pennsylvania and New York respectively. At the same time Charles Inglis, a British subject, formerly rector of Trinity Church, New York, was consecrated as Bishop of Nova Scotia. From that day to this our Communion has expanded steadily until it has become world wide.

430

1948
The basis of a General Synod (China)

Constitution and Canons of the Chung Hua Sheng Kung Hui together with the Preamble to the Constitution, 1948.

Preamble:

We, Bishops, Clergy, and Laity of the Holy Catholic Church, representing the various Dioceses and Missionary Districts established in China and Hongkong by the Church of England, the Protestant Episcopal Church in the United States of America, and the Church of England in Canada, accepting the Scriptures of the Old and New Testament, and believing them to contain all things necessary to salvation, and to be the ultimate standard of faith, professing the Faith, as summed up in the Nicene Creed and the Apostles' Creed, holding to the Doctrine which Christ our Lord commanded, and to the Sacraments of Baptism and the Lord's Supper which He Himself ordained, and accepting His Discipline, according to the Commandments of God, maintain the ministry of the Church which we have received through the Episcopate in the three orders of Bishops, Priests, and Deacons, which orders have been in Christ's Church from the time of the Apostles, being here assembled in Conference at Shanghai, on this twenty-sixth day of April, in the year of our Lord, one thousand nine hundred and twelve, hereby constitute a Synod which shall be called the General Synod of Chung Hua Sheng Kung Hui.

431

1948
Episcopal Ordination in a divided Church

Lambeth Conference, 1948, Committee Report on the Unity of the Church, appendix on the theory of 'supplemental ordination'.

Compare no. 401 on the Church of South India.

'It may be held that... the episcopate *ought* to be the ordaining organ of the whole Church. But though it once was, might become so again... in fact it is not so, since the whole of non-episcopal Christendom has separated itself from the bishops... The most we can say... for any ministries in the divided Church is that they carry a commission conferred by Christ in and through part of his body but not the whole'.

432

1948
Christian unity: The Church of South India

Encyclical Letter, *Lambeth Conference, 1948.*

Compare nos. 401, 431 on the problems of reconciling the ministries of the
united Churches in such a way that the new United Church remains in
communion with those Churches with which its member-Churches were
formerly themselves in Communion.

The Anglican Communion, as part of the Holy Catholic Church,
exists to proclaim the everlasting Gospel of our Lord Jesus Christ
to all the world and to be an instrument in the hand of God for the
fulfilment of His purpose. Deep divisions have long existed within
the Church itself, based in the main on divergent interpretations of
its faith and order; but, in spite of our divisions, we still know that
it is the will of Christ that we should seek to overcome our
separations and find again our true unity in Him. At every Lambeth
Conference this question of unity comes before us; and, at our
gathering this year, a great part of our time and thought has been
devoted to this subject. We have been made conscious yet again of
the hindrance to Christ's cause which springs from the fact that it
is a divided Church which ministers to a divided world. We have
heard with great thankfulness that in many parts of the world
separated Churches are making new ventures towards unity. Our
chief concern has been with the Church of South India, in which,
for the first time since the great division of Christendom at the
Reformation, an act of union has taken place in which episcopal
and non-episcopal traditions have been united. By that act four
dioceses of the Church of India, Burma, and Ceylon, speeded by
the consent and prayers of that Church, and encouraged by the
advice of the last Lambeth Conference, have joined with former
Methodists, Presbyterians, and Congregationalists in a more
comprehensive expression of the Universal Church. The Conference
gives thanks to God for the measure of unity thus locally achieved.
At the same time it records that some features of the Constitution
of the Church of South India give rise to uncertainty or grave
misgivings in the minds of many, and hopes that such action may
be taken as to lead to the day when the present measure of mutual
recognition and intercommunion may become full communion
between the Church of South India and the Churches of the
Anglican Communion. We have pledged ourselves to do all in our
power, by consultation, work, and prayer to bring about that end.

433

1948
Human freedom and responsibility
Encyclical Letter, *Lambeth Conference, 1948.*

God has given man responsibility. To exercise it, he must have freedom. The Christian Church therefore demands essential human rights for all, irrespective of race or colour. There are unhappily countries in the world to-day where such rights are denied. We are grateful for the work which is being done by the Commission of the United Nations on Human Rights. We pledge ourselves to work for the removal of injustice and oppression, and, in particular, to stand by those whose right to religious liberty is threatened.

434

1948
The doctrine of man and human rights
Resolutions 4–14, Lambeth Conference, 1948.

4. We fully share man's aspiration for fellowship in an ordered society and for freedom of individual achievement, but we assert that no view of man can be satisfactory which confines his interests and hopes to this world and to this life alone; such views belittle man and blind him to the greatness of his destiny.

5. The Conference believes that both the recognition of the responsibility of the individual to God and the development of his personality are gravely imperilled by any claim made either by the State or by any group within the State to control the whole of human life. Personality is developed in community, but the community must be one of free persons. The Christian must therefore judge every social system by its effect on human personality....

6. The Conference declares that all men, irrespective of race or colour, are equally the objects of God's love and are called to love and serve him. All men are made in His image; for all Christ died; and to all there is made the offer of eternal life. Every individual is therefore bound by duties toward God and towards other men, and has certain rights without the enjoyment of which he cannot freely

perform those duties. These rights should be declared by the Church, recognized by the State, and safeguarded by international law.

7. The Conference declares that among such rights are security of life and person; the right to work, to bring up a family, and to possess personal property; the right to freedom of speech, of discussion and association, and to accurate information; and to full freedom of religious life and practice, and that these rights belong to all men irrespective of race or colour....

9. The Conference re-affirms Resolution 25 of 1930 'That war as a method of settling international disputes is incompatible with the teaching and example of Our Lord Jesus Christ'.

10. The Conference affirms that it is the duty of governments to work for the general reduction and control of armaments of every kind and for their final elimination, except those which may be necessary for international police protection; but until such time as this is achieved, it recognizes that there are occasions when both nations and individuals are obliged to resort to war as the lesser of two evils.

11. The Conference urges that the use of atomic energy be brought under such effective international inspection and control as to prevent its use as a weapon of war.

12. The Conference appeals to all Christians to unite in working for the reconciliation of the nations which have been at war, and urges the allied nations to agree without delay upon treaties of peace with Germany and Japan, based on principles of justice.

13. The Conference, moved by the tragic plight of vast numbers of men and women who, owing to political conditions, have been exiled from their home country, and believing that there is room in which they may find new and permanent homes, urges the Governments of all countries represented in this Conference where such room can be found to take active steps for the admission of as many as possible of those men and women with their families as new settlers: and calls all Christian people within countries wherein they are permitted to settle to give them every help in their power.

14. The Conference urges the statesmen of the world together with their people to do their utmost to frame a world policy for the fuller development and a juster distribution of the world's economic resources, to meet the needs of men and women in all nations.

435

1948
Mutual recognition and reconciliation of ministry

Resolutions 56–58, Lambeth Conference, 1948.

Compare nos. 401, 431, 432 on the Church of South India.

56. The Conference calls upon all the Churches of the Anglican Communion to seek earnestly by prayer and by conference the fulfilment of the vision 'of a Church, genuinely Catholic, loyal to all truth, and gathering into its fellowship 'all who profess and call themselves Christians', within whose visible unity all the treasures of faith and order, bequeathed as a heritage by the past to the present, shall be possessed in common and made serviceable to the whole body of Christ'. It recognizes that 'within this unity Christian Communions now separated from one another would retain much that has long been distinctive in their methods of worship and service'. In the hope of setting forward the fulfilment of this vision, the Conference... records certain counsels and considerations which it believes should guide the Churches of our Communion in future approaches to reunion:

(*a*) The theological issues, especially those concerning the Church and the ministry, should be faced at the outset, and to this end the negotiating Churches should obtain the help of theologians in framing schemes for reunion or intercommunion.

(*b*) The unification of the ministry in a form satisfactory to all the bodies concerned, either at the inauguration of the union or as soon as possible thereafter, is likely to be a prerequisite to success in all future proposals for the reunion of the Churches.

(*c*) The integral connexion between the Church and the ministry should be safeguarded in all proposals for the achievement of intercommunion through the creation of a mutually recognized ministry.

(*d*) The goal in any steps towards a united Church within a given area should always be a Church with which the Anglican Churches could eventually be in full communion.

(*e*) Because the Anglican Communion is itself a treasured unity with a special vocation, a part of our Communion contemplating a step which would involve its withdrawal from the Anglican family of Churches should consult the Lambeth Conference or the Provinces and member Churches of this family of Churches before final commitment to such a course.

Schemes for organic union

57. The Conference has heard with satisfaction and hope of proposals for organic union in various areas, and, while calling the attention of those concerned in such schemes to the warnings contained in the Report of the Committee on Unity, believes that schemes of this type have undoubted advantages.

Schemes for the Provision of a Mutually Recognized Ministry

58. The Conference has heard with interest and sympathy of proposals for the provision of a mutually recognized ministry in advance of any explicit plans for organic union. In spite of the disadvantages attaching to such schemes, which are noted in the Report of the Committee on Unity, the Conference is not prepared to discourage further explorations along this line, if they are linked with provisions for the growing together of the Churches concerned and with the definite acceptance of organic union as the final goal.

436

1948
Baptism and Confirmation

Resolutions 101, 104, 105, 110, 111, 112, Lambeth Conference, 1948.

101. Believing that one and the same Spirit sustains and orders the life of the Church, the Conference emphasizes the essential unity and interdependence of the Ministry of the Word and the Ministry of the Sacraments....

104. While deprecating the hasty adoption of any policy which would lead to widespread exclusion of infants from Baptism, the Conference affirms that the service of infant Baptism pre-supposes that the infant will be brought up in the faith and practice of the Church, and reminds parents and guardians that they cannot be exempted from a major share in the responsibility for the Christian nurture and education of their children, and it therefore urges the clergy to put them in mind of this duty before their children are baptized and at other times as opportunity may be made.

105. The Conference calls attention to the rubric of the Prayer Book of 1662 that Baptism should normally be administered 'when

the most number of people come together' and after due notice, and recommends that the Sacrament should be administered more frequently in the regular services of the Church and that notice should be required....

110. The Conference recommends that care should be taken to see that before Confirmation all candidates are given definite instruction about repentance and about the means provided by God in His Church by which troubled consciences can obtain the assurance of His mercy and forgiveness, as set forth in the Exhortation in the Order of Holy Communion.

111. The Conference recommends that those who have been confirmed should from time to time be given opportunity, after due preparation, for the re-affirmation of vows and re-dedication.

112. The Conference acknowledges the faithful work which is done by the clergy generally in the preparation of candidates for Confirmation and recommends that the preparation of candidates for Confirmation should include, from their early years:

(*a*) Participation, with their family, in regular worship in church and at home;

(*b*) Group instruction in the Church's faith and practice;

(*c*) Training in fellowship and service through membership of a parochial society or group.

They should be led on to accept a rule of life comprising daily prayer and Bible reading, regular worship, and self-discipline, including almsgiving and personal service.

437

1948
Communion in both kinds

Resolution 117, Lambeth Conference, 1948.

Compare Article xxx of the Thirty-Nine Articles and no. 111.

117. The Conference affirms that the giving of Communion in both kinds is according to the example and precept of our Lord, was the practice of the whole Catholic Church for twelve centuries, has remained the practice of the Orthodox Churches, and has been universally upheld by the teaching and practice of the Anglican Communion since the Reformation.

438

1951
The Church of the Province of West Africa

Who are the Anglicans?, *ed. Charles Long, prepared for the Lambeth Conference, 1988 (Ohio, 1988), p. 31.*

The Province was founded in 1951, and at that time included the present Province of Nigeria (established 1979). Anglicans were found in Ghana as early as 1752. Work began in other countries of the Province early in the 19th century with the help of SPG[1] and, in Liberia, the Episcopal Church USA. Church growth has been slow to reach beyond the coastal areas of these countries and Christians remain a minority of the total population.

439

1955
Bringing a Province into being

The Constitution of the Church of England in Australia, as approved by General Synod at its meeting on Thursday, 6 October 1955, for submission to the Dioceses of Australia and Tasmania, Preface.

The question of a constitution to unite all the dioceses of the Church of England in Australia and Tasmania has occupied the attention of various synods and has been anxiously and carefully considered by constitution committees for a period of almost forty years. Several draft constitutions have been submitted to the dioceses, but none of them has found general acceptance. The present Constitution Committee had almost despaired of achieving success when the Archbishop of Canterbury visited this country. His Grace made an earnest appeal to the Church to continue its labours and offered most valuable suggestions as to the form which a draft constitution should take. Encouraged by His Grace's appeal and suggestions the Committee continued the task. The Committee, consisting of bishops of the Church and representatives drawn from various dioceses, included men of different outlook who for many

---

[1] The Society for the Propagation of the Gospel

years had studied problems of liturgiology and Christian doctrine within and without the Church of England. It is inevitable that there should be some conflict of opinion in such a company, but the Committee would place on record its appreciation of the spirit of brotherliness and goodwill that characterised its sessions. The aim of all was to make such concessions to differing opinions as would, while not endangering the vital doctrines of the Christian faith, embodied in the Catholic Creeds, and the principles of the Reformation, expressed in the formularies of the Church of England, embrace in a true spirit of comprehension those who were loyal members of the Church. The Committee has endeavoured, in the spirit of the framers of our liturgy, and of the revisers of the Book of Common Prayer in 1662, so to order those portions of the Constitution which relate to the doctrine and worship of the Church of England as 'to keep the mean between two extremes'; to make provision, on the one hand, for such reasonable alterations in our existing formularies as the circumstances of the time may demand; and, on the other, to exclude from such alteration anything that might 'strike at some established Doctrine, or laudable Practice of the Church of England.' The Committee has further endeavoured to provide means whereby the will of the Church might be suitably expressed without unduly curtailing the freedom of action at present enjoyed by the various dioceses. The resolution of problems associated with its effort was by no means easy, but the Committee entertains the hope that the genuine desire of all its members to understand and appreciate the position of those who do not wholly share their convictions on matters of ritual, ceremonial and discipline, will result in the framing of a constitution which will secure acceptance by the dioceses and weld the Church into closer bonds of union and concord as it addresses itself to the supreme task of leading men and women to a true and saving knowledge of our Lord and Saviour Jesus Christ. It commends the result of its labour to the goodwill of those whose interest it has sought to conserve, and prays that the Holy Spirit of God, Who is the Spirit of all wisdom, may so guide and control the deliberations thereupon, that this Church may make a right decision and thereby establish itself more firmly, and prove a light to men who seek the truth.

440

1958
Christian unity

Encyclical Letter, *Lambeth Conference, 1958.*

Cf. nos. 401, 431, 432 on South India.

The Church can be effective as an agent of Christ's reconciling power only in proportion as it is itself reconciled to God and is seeking reconciliation between its members. Every Lambeth Conference since 1878 has recognized this by its concern for the unity of the Body of Christ....

The world is often critical because we seem to move so slowly towards the goal of the visible unity of the whole Church of God. Yet we can thank God that the last ten years have shown so much progress, and we rejoice in the many signs of the strengthening of the fellowship of our Communion with Churches of other and different traditions. In our last Conference we could not make one unanimous recommendation with regard to the relations between our Churches and Provinces and the newly-united Church of South India. In the ten years that have passed, visits by delegations and individuals have dispelled misunderstandings, and we record with thankfulness that many of our Provinces have been able to establish a limited inter-communion with that Church on which the grace of God has been so abundantly and manifestly bestowed.

441

1958
Reconciliation and the Gospel

Encyclical Letter, *Lambeth Conference, 1958.*

Reconciliation was the theme of the 1958 Lambeth Conference.

At the heart of the Christian gospel is that thought of reconciliation which has been the keynote of our Conference. At the heart of the world's confusion is the failure of men to understand and accept the way God offers by which they may be reconciled to him. In such a situation it is the urgent duty of the Church to be the channel of Christ's reconciling power. We have tried to see all problems as problems of reconciliation, for the solution of which the spirit of renunciation and self-sacrifice is an essential condition. Tensions and differences there must be: they become creative when they are brought under the power and influence of God. When men, or groups, or nations find themselves in conflict because their opinions or their interests clash, though the flesh is weak the way is open for advance into a new and richer partnership. 'When any man is in Christ, there is a new creation'.

The word of reconciliation

We begin, as the faith of the Church must always begin, with the Bible, through which God has spoken his word of reconciliation. One of the distinguishing marks of our Anglican Communion is the supreme importance which is attached to the authority of the Bible in the formulation of doctrine. We give great prominence to the reading of the Bible in the services of the Church.

442

1958

Reconciliation and the Church's social responsibility

Encyclical Letter, *Lambeth Conference, 1958.*

To strengthen family life and to restore its unity where it is broken are essential parts of the ministry of reconciliation. To-day we can begin to see them not as problems of our own society alone, but as concerns of the whole human family: if one member suffers all must suffer, whether the one be a peasant in dire poverty through famine or a victim of too rapid industrialization. All are children of our Father: all are made in his image. The work of reconciliation must go forward.

443

1958
Prayer Book revision

Resolutions 73, 74, Lambeth Conference, 1958.

Cf. nos. 283, 337, 378, 389, 517, 550 and others on the question of liturgical revision.

Prayer Book Revision

73. The Conference welcomes the contemporary movement towards unanimity in doctrinal and liturgical matters by those of differing traditions in the Anglican Communion as a result of new knowledge gained from Biblical and liturgical studies, and is happy to know of parallel progress in this sphere by some Roman Catholic and Reformed theologians. ...

74. The Conference, recognizing the work of Prayer Book Revision being done in different parts of the Anglican Communion

(*a*) calls attention to those features in the Book of Common Prayer which are essential to the safeguarding of unity: i.e. the use of the Canonical Scriptures and the Creeds, Holy Baptism, Confirmation, Holy Communion, and the Ordinal;

(*b*) notes that there are other features in these books which are effective in maintaining the traditional doctrinal emphasis and ecclesiastical culture of Anglicanism and therefore should be preserved;

(*c*) and urges that a chief aim of Prayer Book Revision should be to further that recovery of the worship of the Primitive Church which was the aim of the compilers of the first Prayer Book of the Church of England.

444

1958
The Communion of Saints

Resolutions 77–9, Lambeth Conference, 1958.

The Commemoration of Saints and Heroes of the Christian Church in the Anglican Communion

77. The Conference holds that the purpose of a Kalendar is to increase our thankfulness to God and to strengthen our faith by

recalling regularly the great truths of the Gospel, the principal events in the life of our Lord, and the lives and examples of men and women who have borne pre-eminent witness to the power of the Holy Spirit, and are with us in the communion of saints.

78. The Conference considers that the power to revise or amend Kalendars should be exercised by the same authority as is required for the revision of the Book of Common Prayer within each several Church or Province, which authority may allow supplementary commemorations for local use in addition to the Kalendar at the request of a diocese.

79. The Conference is of opinion that the following principles should guide the selection of saints and heroes for commemoration:

(*a*)   In the case of spiritual saints, care should be taken to commemorate men or women in terms which are in strict accord with the facts made known in Holy Scripture.

(*b*)   In the case of other names, the Kalendar should be limited to those whose historical character and devotion are beyond doubt.

(*c*)   In the choice of new names economy should be observed and controversial names should not be inserted until they can be seen in the perspective of history.

(*d*)   The addition of new names should normally result from a widespread desire expressed in the region concerned over a reasonable period of time.

445

1958
The Church in an industrial age

Resolution 111, Lambeth Conference, 1958.

The Conference urges the Provinces of the Anglican Communion to give special study to the task, strategy, and ministry of the Church within industrial society, and by the use of bold and imaginative experiments to strengthen the impact of the Christian Faith upon the whole life and pattern of industry.

446

The family in contemporary society

Resolutions 112, 113, 116 and 121, Lambeth Conference, 1958.

Marriage

112. The Conference records its profound conviction that the idea of the human family is rooted in the *Godhead* and that consequently all problems of *sex relations*, the procreation of children, and the organization of family life must be related, consciously and directly, to the creative, redemptive, and sanctifying power of God.

113. The Conference affirms that marriage is a vocation to holiness, through which men and women may share in the love and creative purpose of God. The sins of self-indulgence and sensuality, born of selfishness and a refusal to accept marriage as a divine vocation, destroy its true nature and depth, and the right fullness and balance of the relationship between men and women. Christians need always to remember that sexual love is not an end in itself nor a means to self-gratification, and that self-discipline and restraint are essential conditions of the responsible freedom of marriage and family planning....

116. The Conference calls upon all Church people to have in mind that, since our Lord's ministry gave a new depth and significance to forgiveness, his Church and the families within it must be a forgiving society, and that there are no wrongs done by its members, one to another, that are unforgivable, or in which a costly forgiveness may not lead to repentance and, through repentance, to reconciliation and a new beginning in living together. The Conference believes that many tensions in marriage and family life are allowed to reach a breaking point because self-righteousness or a sense of injury takes priority of forgiveness, and that marital relations also break down because those involved do not in time take counsel with a wise advisor. It affirms that no husband or wife has the right to contemplate even legal separation until every opportunity of reconciliation and forgiveness has been exhausted....

121. The Conference commends, as an aid to better teaching about marriage and home life, the following summary of the marks of a Christian family. Such a family –

(*a*) Seeks to live by the teaching and example of Jesus Christ;

(*b*) Joins in the worship of the Almighty God on Sundays in church;

(*c*) Joins in common prayer and Bible reading, and Grace at meals;

(*d*) Is forgiving one to another, and accepts responsibility for one another;

(*e*) Shares together in common tasks and recreation;

(*f*) Uses abilities, time, and possessions responsibly in society;

(*g*) Is a good neighbour, hospitable to friend and stranger.

447

1959

Provinces and a future united Church (East Africa)

The Resolutions of the Dodoma Conference, 18–22 January 1959, Province of East Africa.

1 (11). That this Conference of delegates from the Dioceses of Mombasa, Zanzibar, Masai, Central Tanganyika and South-West Tanganyika requests the respective diocesan bishops to recommend to their synods (or governing bodies of the Church in their dioceses) that the assent of the Archbishop of Canterbury be sought to the immediate formation of a Province of the Church of East Africa consisting of the dioceses named.

2 (9). That the following Resolutions of the Conference of 1927 be re-enacted, namely:

'The Conference recognizes "that there are other ancient episcopal Communions in east and west, to whom ours is bound by many ties of common faith and tradition. On the other hand there are the great non-episcopal Communions, standing for rich elements of truth, liberty and life which might otherwise have been obscured or neglected. With them we are closely linked by many affinities, racial, historical and spiritual. We cherish the earnest hope that all these Communions, and our own, may be led by the Spirit into the unity of the Faith, and of the knowledge of the Son of God",'
and:

'The Conference earnestly recommends that the Province take every possible opportunity of action for the furtherance of the ideal of Reunion.'

3 (10). That while regarding the formation of the Province of the Anglican Church in East Africa as our immediate and primary responsibility in obedience to God, it is not our intention that this should in any way restrict discussions now taking place, or which may in future take place, between any diocese of the Province and other Christian bodies in East Africa directed towards a fuller Church union, provided always that such discussions are based on principles agreed by the Lambeth Conference and are conducted with the knowledge and approval of the Provincial Synod.

448

1959
Fundamentals (West Indies)

Constitution and Canons of the Church in the Province of the West Indies, 1959.

Declaration of Fundamental Principles
We, the Archbishop and Bishops of the Province of The West Indies, comprising the Dioceses of the Barbados, Jamaica, Antigua, Guiana, Nassau and the Bahamas, Trinidad and Tobago, The Windward Islands, and British Honduras, with the approval and consent of the Synods of the aforesaid Dioceses, declare that we receive and maintain the faith of Our Lord Jesus Christ as taught in the Holy Scriptures, held by the Primitive Church, summed up in the Creeds, and affirmed by the undisputed General Councils.

And we do further declare that we receive and maintain the Faith, Doctrine, Sacraments, and Discipline of the One Holy Catholic and Apostolic Church, according as the Church of England has received the same.

We receive The Book of Common Prayer, and the Ordering of Bishops, Priests and Deacons, as agreeable to the Word of God.

We disclaim for ourselves the right of altering any of the aforesaid Standards of Faith and Doctrine, provided that nothing herein contained shall prevent the Church in this Province, if it shall so determine, from accepting any alterations in the Formularies of the Church which may be adopted by the Church of England, or allowed by any General Synod, Council, Congress, or other Assembly of the Churches of the Anglican Communion, or from making at any time adaptations and abridgements of, and additions to, the Services of the Church, provided that all changes in or additions to the Services of the Church, made by the Church in this Province, shall be liable to revision by any General Synod of the Anglican Communion to which this Province shall be invited to send representatives.

449

1961
The Church of Uganda

Who are the Anglicans?, *ed. Charles Long, prepared for the Lambeth Conference, 1988 (Ohio, 1988), p. 15.*

Missionary work was begun in 1877 by the Church Missionary Society, responding to the explorer Stanley's call for missionaries after his visit to the court of Kabaka Mutesa in 1875. The Church grew rapidly, largely through the evangelization of Africans by other Africans, especially during the East Africa Revival; this began in 1927 and continues to be an influence today. The first Ugandan clergy were ordained in 1893 and the church became an independent Province in 1961. From the first the Church has produced its share of martyrs as well as evangelists and has suffered much in times of civil strife. The first Bishop, James Hannington, and his companions were murdered in 1886. Archbishop Janani Luwum was killed by the tyrant Idi Amin in 1977.

450

1961
History as a starting-point for conversation

General Convention of the Episcopal Church in the United States of America, A Communion of Communions, 1961.

In the discussion of the 'historic episcopate' of the Chicago–Lambeth Quadrilateral, it has often been emphasized that what is 'historic' is a 'fact'; that is, that it can be accepted without necessarily implying acceptance of any particular theory.

Resolved, that the Joint Commission on Approach to Unity be reminded of the various historic statements defining this Church's stand in the field of Christian Reunion beginning with the Chicago version of the Quadrilateral in 1886 and including several statements by successive Lambeth Conferences, particularly the Faith and Order Statement prepared by the Commission itself for the Lambeth Conference of 1948 and the General Convention of 1949; and that the Joint Commission on Approaches to Unity be, and it hereby is, instructed to make the historic position of this Church as defined in these several statements the framework for all Church unity conversations in which it shall be engaged.

451

1963
The Philippine Episcopal Church

Who are the Anglicans?, *ed. Charles Long, prepared for the Lambeth Conference, 1988 (Ohio, 1988), p. 50.*

As a Spanish colony since the 16th century, the Philippines became predominantly Roman Catholic. When the islands became an American colony in 1898, Bishop Charles Henry Brent of the USA established missionary work among the largely unevangelized tribespeople of Northern Luzon and among Muslim populations in the South. The missionary diocese of the Philippines was established in 1901. In 1971 and later the area was subdivided into four dioceses. The first Philippine bishop, E.G. Longid, was consecrated in 1963 and the church hopes to become an independent Province in 1989. Meanwhile it enjoys close working relationships with the Philippine Independent Church. All four dioceses are members of the General Convention of the Episcopal Church USA and part of Province 8 of that church.

452

1963
Mission and unity

H. Roberts, Anglican-Methodist Conversations *(London, 1963), pp. 12–3.*

It was largely as a result of the problem of confusion caused to new Christians in the missionary field that the ecumenical movement began in the late nineteenth century.

3. Our divisions have been and still are the source of great confusion in the Mission Field. The younger Churches are torn between a loyalty to parent Churches which are divided from each other and a determination to concentrate Christian forces in the face of the resurgence of non-Christian religions and a blatant materialism. It is not surprising that they have proved to be the pioneers in the quest of Christian unity, for the burden of division thrust upon them by the West is intolerable....
5. The need to concentrate Christian forces in this country is as urgent as it is overseas. Here as elsewhere the crucial conflict is not between the various historic Churches or between different schools of Christian thought but between a way of life that is centred in the revelation of God in Christ and a way of life that leaves God out of account altogether. To fail to discern the signs of times is to forfeit the claim and privilege of spiritual leadership. It is time the Churches realized where the battle for the Christian Gospel is joined. The things about which we differ as Churches are small compared with the things about which we agree over against the powerful onslaught made upon the Christian Faith and its values in modern society. The pressure of events is a pointer to duty for those who have eyes to see.

453

1963, revised 1967
Marriage

The Church of the Province of West Africa, Constitution. 1st edn. March 1963, rev. and repr. March 1967.

The regulations governing Christian marriage present special difficulties in societies where local practice permits polygamy or other variants.

Article I.

The Church believes that Marriage, by Divine institution, is a life-long and exclusive union and partnership between one man and one woman. Its law and regulations are based upon this belief.

Canon I.

(a) Solemnization of Holy Matrimony by the Rites of the Church is reserved to those who are baptized unless in the case of a marriage proposed between a baptized person and an unbaptized person, a dispensation granted by the bishop; ...

Canon II.

(a) Where two baptized persons are living together as man and wife, their union not having been solemnized by the Rites of the Church, the bishop may at his discretion give permission for one or both of the persons to be presented for Confirmation and/or admitted to Holy Communion; provided that the bishop shall first be satisfied *inter alia*, that the persons have been married under native customary law and that they are without other partners. Such permission, if given, shall not include the remaining privileges of Communicant status.

(b) Where two persons living together as man and wife under native customary law or any other generally accepted law and without other partners are admitted to Holy Baptism, their marriage is *ipso facto* raised to the status of Christian Marriage. The Church shall formally recognize this fact by bestowing upon it a form of blessing.

(c) A marriage contracted by non-Christians is not raised to the status of Christian Marriage by the baptism of one of the partners only. If after such baptism the unbaptized partner is unwilling to remain peacefully and without offence to God with the baptized partner without seeking to induce him/her to break any Christian Law or prevent the Baptism and Christian upbringing of the children, it is possible for the baptized partner to take advantage of the 'Privilegium Paulinum'.[1] If this course is desired application shall be made to the bishop, who shall satisfy himself by direct approach to the unbaptized partner that such unwillingness exists.

---

[1]   I Corinthians 7.12–16

If he be satisfied of it, the bishop may on the dissolution of the marriage permit the baptized partner to contract a new and Christian marriage. Until the former marriage is dissolved the baptized partner may follow his/her conscience in regard to cohabitation.

(d) Where local practice in regard to marriage is not repugnant to Christian Doctrine or Law, observance of such practice by two persons desiring to be married by the Rites of the Church shall not constitute a reason for refusing such Rites to them nor shall it be held in disrepute by the Church: provided that the priest who solemnizes the marriage shall be satisfied that both the persons are conversant with the principles of Christian Marriage and themselves intend that their marriage shall be monogamous and indissoluble. In case of any doubt as to whether any local practice is repugnant to Christian Doctrine or Law the ruling of the bishop shall be final.

(e) The inclusion of the English Law of Inheritance shall not of necessity be required as a condition of the solemnization of a marriage.

Nevertheless it is the duty of the husband to ensure that at his death adequate provision is made for his widow and children from his estate:...

Canon III.

(a) Unless under exceptional circumstances and with the direct permission of the bishop given in writing, no man living as a polygamist shall be admitted to Holy Baptism; a baptized person who becomes a polygamist shall not be admitted to Confirmation or Holy Communion.

(b) The wives of a polygamist may, subject to the provisions of Canon IV (e), be admitted to Holy Baptism and shall not be precluded from Confirmation and Holy Communion solely on account of such marital circumstances.

454

1964
The Episcopal Church, Province 9, Central America and adjacent areas

Who are the Anglicans?, *ed. Charles Long, prepared for the Lambeth Conference, 1988 (Ohio, 1988), p. 39.*

These former missionary districts of the Episcopal Church in the United States of America and parts of other Anglican missionary dioceses were formed into a regional Province of ECUSA in 1964. Although the Church in each country has its own history and distinctive features, they are all Spanish-speaking, most are of recent origin as separate dioceses, and most are built on the foundation of English speaking chaplaincies to expatriates or to immigrant workers from the West Indies and their descendants. The religious and cultural traditions of the region are overwhelmingly Roman Catholic, but Pentecostal and evangelical churches have grown rapidly in recent years. Mexico is an exception in that the Episcopal Church there has been indigenous from its beginnings as a nationalist secession from the Roman Catholic Church in 1857. The first Anglican bishop for Mexico was consecrated in 1879. Other dioceses with the dates of their foundation are: Panama 1920, Dominican Republic 1940, Colombia 1964, Ecuador 1970, El Salvador 1968, Guatemala 1968, Honduras 1968, Nicaragua 1968. While they are now full members of the General Convention of the Episcopal Church USA, it is expected that dioceses from the region will soon form an autonomous Spanish speaking Province of the Anglican Communion.

455

1964
A Synodical Stage of Reception

General Convention of the Episcopal Church in the United States of America, A Communion of Communions, *1964.*

On the World Council of Churches, see no. 423. This Synodical Resolution both approves this text and refers it for reception to the whole people of God in ECUSA; at the same time it affirms obedience to 'official' Anglican teaching defined as 'expressed' in Anglican 'formularies'. All these elements have a place in the continuing process of reception of new statements of faith: faithfulness to the past; conciliar recognition; and the consensus of the faithful.

Resolved, that subject to the official teaching of this Church as expressed in its own formularies, this Convention give its approval to the following two paragraphs adopted by the New Delhi Assembly of the World Council of Churches and commend them to the Church for use in ecumenical study and dialogue: We believe that the unity which is both God's will and his gift to his Church is being made visible as all in each place who are baptized into Jesus Christ and confess Him as Lord and Saviour are brought by the Holy Spirit into one fully committed fellowship, holding the one Apostolic Faith, preaching the one gospel, breaking the one bread, joining in common prayer, and having a corporate life reaching out to witness and service to all; and who at the same time are united with the whole Christian fellowship in all places and ages in such wise that ministry and members are accepted by all and that all can act and speak together as occasion requires for the tasks to which God calls his people. It is for such unity that we believe we must pray and work.

456

1965–80
The Church of Brazil

Who are the Anglicans?, ed. Charles Long, prepared for the Lambeth Conference, 1988 (Ohio, 1988), p. 33.

Christianity came to Brazil in the 16th century with the Portuguese conquest. There were Anglican chaplaincies to expatriates after 1810; separation of Church and State in 1889 allowed non-Roman Catholic missions and Anglican work was begun by two missionaries from the USA among Brazilians in two southern states, leading to the establishment of Southern Brazil as a missionary district of the American church in 1907. The Episcopal Church of Brazil became an autonomous Province in 1965, but counts its 'real birthday' as June 1, 1980, when it accepted full responsibility for self support. The Province is governed by a Provincial Synod, of two Houses, which meets every two years.

457

1965
Religious communities

Igreja Episcopal do Brasil Anglicana, Cânones Gerais IV, Canon 17.

Cânon 17 *Das Comunidades Religiosas*

Art. 1.º — Toda comunidade monástica, masculina ou feminina, que desejar o reconhecimento oficial da Igreja, deverá submeter sua Regra e Constituição ao Bispo da Diocese onde estiver situada sua casa matriz e onde for exercer seu ministério.

Parágrafo único — Nenhuma alteração da Regra da Constituição poderá ser feita sem aprovação prévia do Diocesano.

Art. 2.º — Deverá haver na referida Constituição um reconhecimento claro e definido da doutrina, disciplina e culto da Igreja Episcopal do Brasil, como autoridade suprema.

Art. 3.º — A referida Constituição e Regra deverá adaptarse, tanto quanto possível, à índole e às tradições culturais e religiosas do povo brasileiro.

Art. 4.º — Nenhuma Comunidade poderá estabelecer-se em uma outra Diocese desta Igreja, sem prévia permissão do Bispo de referida Diocese.

Art. 5.º — A Comunidade poderá eleger um Capelão, que deverá ser um Presbítero da Diocese em que estiver localizada. O Capelão será responsável perante o Bispo como qualquer outro clérigo.

Art. 6.º — Na ministração dos Sacramentos, deverá ser usado o Livro de Oração Comum sem quaisquer alterações, salvo se o Bispo Diocesano o permitir, conforme lhe faculta o mesmo Livro.

Art. 7.º — As propriedades de uma Comunidade serão sujeitas às mesmas prescrições canônicas que regem propriedades das paróquias e das Dioceses.

Art. 8.º – Os mmembros clericais de uma Comunidade estarão sujeitos a todos os Cânones que se referem ao clero da Igreja Episcopal do Brasil.

Art. 9.º — Uma Comunidade terá um Visitador, nomeado pelo Bispo da Diocese em que estiver localizada. São deveres do Visitador: a) fiscalizar a observância fiel da Constituição e da Regra da Comunidade;

b) receber e ouvir apelos da Comunidade ou de membros da mesma, quanto às transgressões da Regra;

c) promover o entrosamento da Comunidade com o plano geral de trabalho da Diocese. Parágrafo único — Nenhum membro pleno de uma comunidade poderá ser excluído sem direito de apelo ao Visitador, nem poderá ser dispensado dos seus votos sem a aprovação do mesmo.

Art. 10 –Não será permitido a um Bispo, que sucede a outro como autoridade eclesiástica de uma Diocese, cancelar a autorização dada pelo seu antecessor para o funcionamento de uma Comunidade, desde que as condições estabelecidas neste Cânon estejam sendo observadas.

Art. 11 — A Comunidade, que não observar as condições estabelecidas neste Cânon, poderá ter suas atividades canceladas pelo Bispo Diocesano.

The Anglican Episcopal Church of Brazil, General Canons [IV] Canon 17
Canon 17 — Religious Communities

Article 1. Every monastic community, male or female, which desires official recognition by the Church, must submit its Rule and Constitution to the Bishop of the Diocese where its house is located and where it will exert its ministry. The Rule and Constitution cannot be altered without previous approval of the Diocesan Bishop.

Article 2. The said Constitution must contain a clear and defined recognition of the doctrine, discipline and cult of the Episcopal Church of Brasil, as supreme authority.

Article 3. The said Constitution and Rule must be adapted, as far as possible, to the religious and cultural traditions of the Brazilian people.

Article 4. No community can establish itself in another Diocese of this Church without previous permission from the Bishop of the referred Diocese.

Article 5. The Community may elect a Chaplain, who must be a presbyter of the Diocese in which it is located. The Chaplain shall be responsible before the bishop as any other cleric.

Article 6. In the administration of the Sacraments, the Book of Common Prayer must be used with no alterations, unless allowed by the Bishop of the Diocese, as authorized by the same Book.

Article 7. The property of the Community will be subject to the same canonical prescriptions as govern the properties of the parishes and dioceses.

Article 8. The clerical members of a Community will be subject to all the canons which refer to the clergy of the Episcopal Church of Brazil.

Article 9. A Community will have a Visitor, appointed by the Bishop of the Diocese in which it is situated. The duties of the Visitor will be to –

(a) Supervise the faithful observation of the Constitution and Rule of the Community.

(b) Receive and listen to appeals of the Community or its members regarding transgression of the Rule.

(c) Promote the integration of the Community with the general working plan of the Diocese.

No full member of a Community can be excluded without a right to appeal to the Visitor, nor can he be dispensed without the Visitor's approval.

Article 10. A bishop who succeeds another as ecclesiastic authority of a Diocese will not be allowed to cancel the authorization given by his antecessor for the functioning of a Community, provided the conditions established in this Canon are being observed.

Article 11. The Community which does not observe the conditions established in this Canon may have its activities restricted by the Diocesan Bishop.

458

1965
The Episcopate

Constituição da Igreja Episcopal do Brasil, Capitulo VIII–X.

Capitulo VIII *Das dioceses*

Art. 21 — A área sob a jurisdição da Igreja Episcopal do Brasil está dividida em dioceses.

Art. 22 — Diocese é uma área eclesiástica reconhecida pelo Sínodo sob a jurisdição de um bispo.

Art. 23 — Em cada diocese há um concílio, presidido pelo bispo, composto dos clérigos e dos leigos representantes das paróquias, paròquias subvencionadas e missões.

Art. 24 — A diocese se rege pelos seus próprios cânones, respeitado o estatuído nesta Constituição e nos Cânones Gerais da Igreja.

Capitulo IX *Dos Conselhos Diocesanos*

Art. 25 — Em cada diocese há um Conselho Diocesano constituído segundo os cânones diocesanos. Êsse conselho exerce a autoridade eclesiástica na diocese sempre que não houver bispo canônicamente autorizado a exercê-la e nos casos previstos pelos Cânones Gerais. § único — A autoridade eclesiástica, nas dioceses que não preencham as condições do parágrafo 1°. do artigo 26 desta Constituição, é exercida, na falta do bispo, pelo Bispo Primaz ou por outro bispo por êste nomeado.

Capitulo X *Dos bispos*

Art. 26 — O bispo diocesano, o bispo coadjutor ou o bispo sufragâneo é eleito pelo concílio da diocese especialmente convocado para êsse fim sob a presidência do bispo diocesano ou, na falta dêste, de um bispo nomeado pelo Bispo Primaz.

§ primeiro — A diocese só pode eleger seu bispo quando tenha, no mínimo, três paróquias, quatro paróquias subvencionadas e sete presbíteros nela canônicamente residentes.

§ segundo — Nenhuma diocese pode proceder à eleição do bispo coadjutor ou sufragâneo sem o consentimento da Câmara dos Bispos.

Art. 27 — Criada nova diocese por desdobramento de outra, o bispo da diocese original escolhe a diocese de sua preferência, sendo o bispo da diocese restante eleito nos têrmos do artigo anterior.

§ único — No caso de a diocese que se desdobra possuir bispo coadjutor, êste se torna o bispo da diocese não escolhida pelo bispo diocesano.

Art. 28 — A eleição do bispo diocesano, bispo coadjutor ou bispo sufragâneo só se torna efetiva após ratificada pela maioria dos Conselhos Diocesanos e dos bispos em atividade.

Art. 29 — Os bispos de dioceses que não preencham as condições do parágrafo 1.º do artigo 26 desta Constituição são eleitos em sessão conjunta do Sínodo, em votação por ordens.

Art. 30 — O presbítero só pode ser sagrado bispo após atingir trinta anos de idade.

§ — Tomam parte na sagração ao episcopado pelo menos três bispos.

Art. 31 — É dever do bispo residir dentro dos limites de sua jurisdição e não se afastar dela por mais de três meses sem o consentimento, nos casos previstos pelos Cânones, do Conselho Diocesano ou do Bispo Primaz.

Art. 32 — O bispo não pode resignar sua jurisdição sem o consentimento da Câmara dos Bispos.

Art. 33 — Atingida a idade de sessenta anos, o bispo pode requerer sua aposentadoria, a qual será compulsória aos sessenta e oito anos.

Constitution of the Episcopal Church of Brazil Chapters VIII–X

Chapter VIII The Diocese

Article 21. The area under jurisdiction of the Episcopal Church of Brazil is divided into Dioceses.

Article 22. A Diocese is an ecclesiastical area recognized by the Synod under the jurisdiction of a bishop.

Article 23. In each Diocese there is a Council, presided over by the bishop, composed of the clergy and lay people representing the parishes, subvented parishes and missions.

Article 24. The Diocese governs itself by its own canons respecting the decrees in this Constitution and the General Canons of the Church.

Chapter IX Diocesan Councils

Article 25. In each Diocese there is a Diocesan Council constituted according to the Diocesan canons. This Council exerts the ecclesiastical authority in the Diocese whenever there is no bishop canonically authorized to exert it in the cases forseen by the General Canons. The ecclesiastical authority in the Dioceses which do not fulfill the conditions of the first paragraph of Art. 26 of this constitution is exerted in the absence of a bishop by the Primate bishop or by another bishop appointed by him.

Chapter X bishops

Article 26. The Diocesan Bishop, the Coadjutor Bishop or the Suffragan Bishop, is elected by the Council of the Diocese especially summoned for this end under the presidency of the Diocesan Bishop or, in his absence, of a bishop appointed by the Primate bishop.

1. A Diocese can elect a bishop only if it has at least three parishes, four subvented parishes and seven Presbyters canonically resident in it.

2. No Diocese can proceed to the election of a Coadjutor or Suffragan Bishop without the consent of the House of Bishops.

Article 27. If a new Diocese is created by duplication of another the Bishop of the original Diocese choses the Diocese of his preference, the Bishop of the remaining Diocese being elected as described in the preceding article. In the case of a duplicating Diocese which has a Coadjutor Bishop, he becomes Bishop of the Diocese not chosen by the Diocesan Bishop.

Article 28. The election of the Diocesan Bishop, Coadjutor Bishop or Suffragan Bishop is only effective after ratification by the majority of the Diocesan Councils and active bishops.

Article 29. The bishops of the Dioceses which do not fulfil the conditions of the first paragraph of Art. 26 of this Constitution are elected in a joint session of the Synod, the voting being by orders.

Article 30. The presbyters can be consecrated bishops only after 30 years of age. At least three bishops must take part in the consecration to the episcopate.

Article 31. It is the duty of the Bishop to reside within the limits of his jurisdiction and not to be absent from it for more than three months without consent of the Diocesan Council or of the Primate Bishop, as forseen by the Canons.

Article 32. The Bishop cannot resign his jurisdiction without the consent of the House of Bishops.

Article 33. Having reached the age of sixty, a bishop can request his retirement which will be compulsory at the age of sixty-eight.

459

1965
Fundamentals of Faith and Order (Korea)

Constitution and Canons of the Anglican Church in Korea, 1965.

Fundamental Declaration on Faith and Rites.

The Anglican Church in Korea holds communion with the Primatial and Archiepiscopal See of Canterbury, which gave it birth, and with all Churches belonging to the Council of the Church in South-East Asia in earnest anticipation of the day when the diversions of Christendom shall be done away and all the faithful again visibly united in one flock under one shepherd: Furthermore the Anglican Church in Korea; –

(1) Holds fast to the Doctrine of Christ as handed down by His Holy apostles and embodied in the Creeds of the Catholic Church — to wit 'the Nicene Creed, Athanasius's Creed, and that which is commonly called the Apostles' Creed':

(2) Holds fast to the Sacred Scriptures of the Old and New Testaments — to wit the thirty nine books of the former and the twenty seven of the latter commonly reckoned Canonical, –accepting them, when interpreted as far as may be in accordance with the universal and continuous tradition of the Holy Catholic Church, as the ultimate standard of faith and morals, and accepting also the other fourteen books (commonly called Apocrypha) as deuterocanonical and proper to be 'read for example of life and instruction of manners':

(3) Holds fast to the Sacraments ordained of Christ, believing them to be not only badges or tokens of Christian men's profession but effectual signs of grace and God's good will towards us, by the which He doth work invisibly in us; honouring in the first place and as generally necessary to salvation the two great Sacraments ordained, both as to matter and form, by Christ our Lord in the

Gospel, and typified by the Water and Blood which flowed from His pierced Side, that is to say Holy Baptism and the Holy Eucharist, and next to them, as suited to the needs of various states of life, those five commonly called Sacraments throughout Eastern and Western Christendom, that is to say, Confirmation, Penance, Orders, Matrimony, and Unction of the Sick:

And in the administration of the Sacraments as well as in the saying of the Divine Service and other public prayers, the Church and Diocese of which we are by Divine permission bishop and chief pastor holds to the prescriptions contained in, and the forms provided by, 'The Book of Common Prayer and Administration of the Sacraments and other Rites and Ceremonies of the Church according to the use of the Church of England, together with the Psalter or Psalms of David, pointed as they are to be sung or said in Churches; and the Form and Manner of making, ordaining and consecrating of Bishops, Priests and Deacons,' agreed upon by the Convocations of the clergy of both the provinces of Canterbury and York, in the year of our Lord one thousand six hundred and sixty two, except so far as variations from that use are authorized by the bishop of the Diocese in the lawful exercise of his *jus liturgicum*:[1]

(4) Holds fast to the Discipline of Christ, in accordance with the principles of which the Holy Catholic Church and its members have been governed since the days of the apostles...

460

1966
Missionary congregations

The Philippine Episcopal Church, Constitution and Canons of the Missionary District of the Philippines of the Protestant Episcopal Church in the United States of America, 1966.

Article 13.

Section 1. A Mission or congregation desirous of admission into union with the Convocation as a Parish shall present to the

---

[1] Authority in matters of liturgical form.

Ecclesiastical Authority for approval a certified copy of its Constitution and By-Laws in which it must be declared that such a Mission or congregation accedes to the Doctrine, Discipline and Worship, the Constitution and Canons of the Protestant Episcopal Church in the United States of America, and to the Constitution and Canons of this Missionary District.

Section 2: At least 2 months before the Annual Convocation such a Mission or congregation shall submit to the Ecclesiastical Authority written evidence, subscribed to by Wardens and Vestry, that it has been duly organized in terms of the approved Constitution for the space of one year; that during that time regular public services have been held, the Word of God duly proclaimed and the Sacraments faithfully ministered, and that the Mission or congregation is willing and capable of undertaking the responsibilities of parochial status. If the Ecclesiastical Authority does not approve of admissions to parochial status, the Ecclesiastical Authority shall submit in writing to the Convocation the reasons for such disapproval. The subject, with all documents pertaining thereto, shall be referred to a Special Committee of Convocation consisting of three Clerical and three Lay members for investigation and recommendation.

Section 3: A Parish duly admitted into union with Convocation shall not change its Constitution or By-Laws until the proposed changes shall have been submitted to the Ecclesiastical Authority for approval. If such changes fail of approval, the Parish may appeal to the Convocation whose action in the case shall be final.

Section 4: Whenever any Parish in union with Convocation shall neglect for three years in succession to make a Parochial Report, or... to employ a Clergyman as its Parish Minister, such Parish, with the consent of the Bishop and the Council of Advice, shall be regarded as having forfeited its connection with the Convocation, and shall no longer be entitled to representation in the same. The Bishop shall report such Parish to the Council of Advice, and also to the Convocation in his Annual Address.

Section 5: Any Parish presented by the Bishop and Council of Advice for violations of General Constitution or Canons of the Church, or the Constitution of Canons of the Missionary District, may be declared contumacious by a two-thirds vote of Convocation. The Bishop shall report any such Parish to the Convocation as occasion may require.

Section 6: But any Parish which has forfeited its right of representation may, upon its application, be readmitted into union with the Convocation by a vote of two-thirds of Convocation, such re-admission to take effect from and after the close of the session of the Convocation consenting thereto.

461

1966
Fundamentals (Singapore and Malaya)

Constitution of the Diocese of Singapore and Malaya, Synodical Government (1 November, 1966).

Synodical Government, Constitution of a Synod in the Diocese of Singapore and Malaya. Preface. Statement by the Archbishop of Canterbury on the Spiritual Background of the Diocesan Synod. ...The Diocese of Singapore and Malaya, for instance, has received through the Church of England what the Church received from the undivided Church and possesses in common with the whole Church of Christ. Is should be continually mindful of the greatness of that inheritance. It has received a membership in the Church which is Christ's body, and through it a knowledge of the revelation which God has made concerning Himself and concerning man, as well through His ancient people of Israel as by His only begotten Son, and through that new Israel, of which He is the eternal King. Through the Church, the Israel of God, it has received the Holy Scriptures of the Old and New Testaments, which record the giving of his progressive revelation. Similarly, it has received the Creeds which it repeats, and especially the Nicene Creed in which the whole Church professes its faith. It has received and reverently uses the two Sacraments of our Lord's institution, Baptism and the Holy Communion of His Body and Blood, and other sacred rites which His Church administers. It has received the Holy Orders of Bishops, Priests and Deacons, which have been in the Church since the days of the apostles. It has learned the doctrine and discipline of Christ what He taught men to believe and to do. It has learned to trust the Spirit Whom He promised to the Church for ever, and on the guidance of that Spirit it must rely as it endeavours to discern the needs of each successive generation, and to apply to them the truth and grace which are the gifts of Jesus Christ to His Church. The Diocesan Synod of Singapore and Malaya will deal rightly with its humble duties and local tasks, its few fellow-Christians and the many fellow-men as yet non-Christian around it, in proportion as it remembers the age-old and world-wide Body of Christ to which it belongs, and holds fast to its Divine Head under the influence of the Spirit Who bears witness to Him.

9
TOWARDS ONE COMMUNION
IN ONE CHURCH
1967–

462

1967
A plan for mission and service
The Church of Rwanda and Burundi, The fifth Provincial Assembly, Namirembe, 4–6 January, 1967. The Ten Year Plan, Draft.

II. Mission
'As the Father has sent me, even so I send you'.[1]

The Mission of the Church is always to proclaim the Gospel of salvation in Jesus Christ, in word and in deed. It is to witness to the forgiveness and new life which God offers to all men through the Cross of Jesus Christ. It is also to witness in intelligent and faithful action to His compassion, His reconciling love and His righteousness among all people. It is to bear witness to the grace and power of the new creation in every aspect of daily life. There are still 4 to 5 million people in our Province who have either not heard, or not begun to respond to, the good news of salvation in Jesus Christ. These must be a continuing burden upon us all, to say nothing of the millions in other areas of the world to whom we are sent as much as to the people within the geographical boundaries of the Province.

The Church which thinks only of itself and of its own members will die.

The question to ask at every step of every new proposal for action is 'In what way will this proposal advance the full mission of the Church?' ...

Proposal
It is proposed that the Church, with the advice and assistance of the Provincial Board of Mission,

---

[1]   John 20.21

(a) stimulate and encourage the whole Church to make detailed plans to take the Gospel into the whole of life throughout the Province; (b) accept specific responsibility for promoting the Gospel in areas *outside* the Province;
(c) train clergy and laity for the apostolate;
(d) work out practical arrangements for sending missionaries from one area of the Province to another, where the need is greatest, to be financed, if necessary, through Provincial sources.

III. Service to the Community
'The earth is the Lord's and all that therein is'.[2]
'I am among you as one who serves'.[3]

The whole world and the whole of life are under the Lordship of Jesus Christ. And the Church is called to bear witness to this fact in His way, as the compassionate servant.

463

1967
Local ecumenical progress
to be set in an international context

General Convention of the Episcopal Church in the United States of America, A Communion of Communions, *1967.*

Ecumenical progress locally always needs to be set in the context of the ecumenical movement worldwide, so that developments may keep pace, and nothing hinder the eventual achievement of a universal union.

Whereas, The conversations of the Joint Commission on Ecumenical Relations with the official representatives of the Roman Catholic Church have moved significantly toward theological understanding and common Christian witness; now, therefore, be it
Resolved, That this dialogue be strongly endorsed and that the Joint Commission be instructed to continue explorations toward theological agreement and effective working relationships with the Roman Catholic Church; and be it further

---

[2]   Psalm 24.1
[3]   Luke 22.27

Resolved, That the Joint Commission relate the conversations in the United States to the world-wide dialogue between the Roman Catholic Church and the Anglican Communion and include in its Report and recommendations to the next General Convention the developments from this wider consultation.

464

1967
Ecumenical study and prayer together

General Convention of the Episcopal Church in the United States of America, A Communion of Communions, *1967.*

Ecumenical study-groups involving people from different Communions working together locally are proving to be an indispensable tool for the growth of mutual understanding and the overcoming of old differences.

Resolved, That Church people in parishes and dioceses be and they hereby are encouraged to study the reports and documents of the Consultation on Church Union, together with such significant ecumenical developments as Vatican II, Anglican–Orthodox Relations, and other movements toward understanding, co-operation, and unity among God's people; that such studies be undertaken in concert with members of other Churches as much as possible, and that the Executive Council be and it hereby is authorized to provide designs and materials for such programs of study; and be it further
Resolved, That members of this Church be asked to keep the cause of Christian unity constantly in their hearts and minds and to make it the subject of daily intercession, both public and private.

465

1967
Statement on communion discipline

General Convention of the Episcopal Church in the United States of America, A Communion of Communions, *1967. Ecumenical Bulletin no. 26 (Nov.–Dec. 1977).*

The question of 'open communion' becomes a burning one in an age of ecumenical progress. Where Christians are working together locally it can seem natural to join in one another's Eucharists even before the divided Churches are united. The principle set out here is that to do so on any permanent basis is undesirable, because it obscures the imperative need for full organic unity, but that there should be the possibility of Eucharistic hospitality for individuals on occasion (cf. no. 477, Lambeth Conference, 1968, Resolution 46).

The Holy Communion must be seen in its proper context of the fellowship of committed Christians in the household of the Apostolic Faith, to which we are admitted by baptism. In the historic tradition which the Episcopal Church maintains and practices, the baptized member completes his baptismal initiation by personal profession of faith and loyalty, and so proceeds to the blessing of confirmation and participation in the Holy Eucharist.

In the historic Churches, Eastern and Western, the bishop, as the center of unity of the Christian family, is active in the whole process — authorizing the administration of baptism (usually by a priest, but sometimes by a deacon or a layman); confirming, either in person or (in some traditions) by delegation to a priest; ordaining the celebrant of the Eucharist, if he does not officiate at it himself.

The normative condition of the Church is union in one fellowship, at once of faith, sacramental practice, personal relations, and Church Order; and this is, therefore, the situation which the services and rules of the Prayer Book embody.

The anomalous situation of Christian division requires us to accept at the heart of our Christian experience the pain of its division which the present ecumenical renewal of the Church is beginning to overcome. Yet all who have been baptized in the Name of the Father, the Son, and Holy Spirit, have been made members of the Body of Christ.

Those who, in other Christian traditions than ours, have, by personal profession of faith and personal commitment affirmed their status as members of the Body, may, on occasion, be led by their Christian obedience to wish to receive Communion in our Church. We believe that such baptized persons may properly do so, where the discipline of their own Church permits, not only at special occasions of ecumenical gatherings specifically looking toward Church unity, but also in circumstances of individual spiritual need; and that this does not require any rubrical or canonical changes, since this Statement does not authorize what is commonly known as 'Open Communion.'

We hope that such recognition of the deep significance of our basic fellowship and baptism will help to speed the day when all the children of God will be able to join in fellowship around the Table of the Lord.

466

1967

A Church's identity

General Convention of the Episcopal Church in the United States of America, A Communion of Communions, 1967, Constitution, Preamble, Defining the Episcopal Church.

In a divided Church the separate Churches are obliged to define their positions and their relationships with one another in order to possess ecclesial 'identity'. This is only an interim necessity, as this text recognizes in its reference to the one, holy, catholic and apostolic Church.

The Protestant Episcopal Church in the United States of America, otherwise known as The Episcopal Church (which name is hereby recognized as also designating the Church), is a constituent member of the Anglican Communion, a Fellowship within the One, Holy, Catholic, and Apostolic Church, of those duly constituted Dioceses, Provinces, and regional Churches in communion with the See of Canterbury, upholding and propagating the historic Faith and Order as set forth in the Book of Common Prayer.

467

1967

The visible unity of the whole Christian Fellowship

General Convention of the Episcopal Church in the United States of America, A Communion of Communions, 1967.

Resolved, the House of Deputies concurring, That this General Convention affirm that the object of this Church's ecumenical policy is to press toward the visible unity of the whole Christian fellowship in the faith and truth of Jesus Christ, developing and sharing in its various dialogues and consultations in such a way that the goal be neither obscured nor compromised and each separate activity be a step toward the fullness of unity for which our Saviour prayed.

468

1968
A declaration of ecumenical intent

Declaration of Intent *of the Church of Ireland, the Methodist Church in Ireland and the Presbyterian Church in Ireland, in* Irish Anglicanism, 1869–1969, *ed. M. Hurley (Dublin, 1970), p. 77.*

We, the duly appointed representatives of the Church of Ireland, the Methodist Church in Ireland and the Presbyterian Church in Ireland, acknowledging our several Churches as being within the Church of God, and seeking to preserve the truths in our several traditions, affirm our intention to seek together that unity which is both God's will and His gift to His Church. It is our conviction that without this unity the fulfilment of Christ's mission to the world is being hindered. We make no claim to know the exact form which unity should take, or whether we shall attain to it. We are seeking no unity apart from the will of God, and we solemnly undertake to submit ourselves to what God will say to us together through His Word and through the witness of our several Churches. We recognize in so submitting ourselves that any such unity between our Churches will involve changes for us all. As we engage in these conversations, we will seek to discover how our Churches may do together at all levels those things which conviction does not require us to do separately. We know that our Churches will move to a deeper expression of unity only by growing together. We gladly acknowledge how great is the measure of our agreement on the common faith revealed in our earlier conversations. We recognize the need of mutual trust, involving sincerity on the part of each Church and the acceptance of the sincerity of others. We recognize the need of penitence for any prejudiced or uncharitable attitudes displayed by our representative Churches in the past. Above all we acknowledge the need of constant renewal by the Holy Spirit. As we seek together under the guidance of the Holy Spirit for the unity which Christ wills according to the Scriptures, we are not concerned for ourselves alone. We will welcome an approach to our Churches by any other Christian Church or Communion which wishes to join in the quest for this unity. We pray God that He will bless and direct our conversations and that He will use them for the enrichment of the whole Church of Christ.

469

1968
Christian unity

Message, *Lambeth Conference, 1968.*

Two points are worthy of note in this piece: the reference to 'doing together all that we can' (the 'Lund' principle of the World Council of Churches) and the recognition that Christians must act together in their service to the world so non-Christians will see clearly that they serve one Lord (cf. no. 477, Lambeth Conference, 1968, Resolution 44).

Unity
Christians cannot properly fulfil their ministry in a disunited Church. Even now, in spite of our divisions, it would be easier if whatever can be done together should be done together. We urge, therefore, that more attention be paid to local Councils of Churches; that all efforts to remedy social injustices, whether at national or local level, should be done ecumenically so that the world may plainly see that what is being done is being done not by this or that Christian denomination but by 'the Christians'. But even this is a poor substitute for a reunited Church, the one, holy, catholic, apostolic Church. Renewal demands unity.

470

1968
The ministry of the laity in the people of God

Message, *Lambeth Conference, 1968.*

The centrality of sacrificial service in all the Church's ministry was the theme of the 1968 Lambeth Conference. It is developed here in the context of the needs of the world.

Ministry

The role of the Church in the world is the role of her Lord: that of the suffering servant. To this theme of the servant Church we found ourselves returning again and again.... The test of every penny we spend, of every meeting we attend, and of every service we hold, is whether it makes it easier for Jesus to be seen as Lord and the Church as his servant. We call on the bishops and clergy to be vigilant against all temptations to worldliness and to strive to attain to that simplicity of living which is so evident in the life of our Lord. The ministry, the service, of the Church to the world is and must be discharged mainly by laity.... The ministry of the laity does not consist solely in the service to the Church or in the Church's worship. It also demands witnesses to the Christian gospel through word and deed in the world. The gospel is a proclamation of God's love for all men and of his will that all men should be one in the family of the children of God. It is, therefore, a gospel of reconciliation. In the home, at work, in industrial disputes, in the exercise of economic power whether as employers or employed, in the bitterly divisive issue of race, it is for the laity to bring to bear a Christian influence towards social justice, compassion, and peace.

In discharging their ministry in the world, the laity must be continuously renewed and strengthened by the assembling of themselves together in the house of God for corporate worship, to hear the word of God and to receive sacramental grace. The first duty of the ordained clergy is to make provision for this. The laity have a right to expect from the clergy help and teaching on the meaning of the Christian faith and on the practice of prayer. No less do they expect mutual encouragement and sympathy when facing the question of what Christians should do in a particular situation. They have a right to a proper share in the government of the Church.

471

1968
Ecology

Resolution 6, Lambeth Conference, 1968.

The Conference urges all Christians, in obedience to the doctrine of creation, to take all possible action to ensure man's responsible stewardship over nature: in particular in his relationship with animals, and with regard to the conservation of soil, and the prevention of the pollution of air, soil, and ocean.

472

1968
The Church and war

Resolutions 8, 9, 10, Lambeth Conference, 1968.

War

8. This Conference
(a) reaffirms the words of the Conference of 1930 that 'war as a method of settling international disputes is incompatible with the teaching and example of our Lord Jesus Christ'.
(b) states emphatically that it condemns the use of nuclear and bacteriological weapons.
(c) holds that it is the concern of the Church
    (i) to uphold and extend the right of conscientious objection to oppose persistently the claim that total war or the use of weapons however ruthless or indiscriminate can be justified by results....
(d) urges upon Christians the duty to support international action either through the United Nations or otherwise to settle disputes justly without recourse to war; to work towards the abolition of the competitive supply of armaments; and to develop adequate machinery for the keeping of a just and permanent peace.

Human Unity

9. The Conference affirms that human unity can only be achieved if all governments are willing to work towards a form of world government designed to serve the interests of all mankind.

Consultation regarding World Peace

10. The Conference invites the Archbishop of Canterbury on its behalf to consult with the Pope and the Ecumenical Patriarch and the Praesidium of the World Council of Churches on the possibility of approaching leaders of the other world religions with a view to convening a conference at which in concert they would speak in the interests of humanity on behalf of world peace.

473

1968
Christianity and other Faiths

Resolution 11, Lambeth Conference, 1968.

On Christian response to other faiths, cf. no. 364 and the passages on mission.

Christianity and other Faiths

11. It is the conviction of the Conference that, in their obedience to Christ's mission and command and in their obligation towards the contemporary world, the Christian Churches must endeavour such positive relationship to the different religions of men, and to the doubt and denial of faith, as will
(*a*) set forward the common unity of mankind and a common participation in its present history;
(*b*) encourage Christians to increasing co-operation with men of other faiths in the fields of economic, social, and moral action;
(*c*) call Christians not only to study other faiths in their own seriousness but also study unbelief in its real quality.

474

1968
Developing countries
Resolution 21, Lambeth Conference, 1968.

Developing countries

21. The Conference welcomes the deep concern about the economic and social frustration of developing countries expressed by the World Council of Churches at its recent Assembly in Uppsala. To produce decisive and wise action in this serious situation it recommends to the provinces of the Anglican Communion:

(*a*) the careful study of the issues of development including the new economic and political structures which it demands; and effective dissemination of knowledge about the issues to the Churches and to the public.

(*b*) that the efforts of the United Nations agencies to bring about world economic justice receive the active support and prayers of all the Churches.

(*c*) that they endorse the appeal of the World Council of Churches at Uppsala that the Churches should do their utmost to influence the governments of industrialized countries

(i) to increase annually the percentage of Gross National Product officially transferred as financial resources, exclusive of private investment, to developing countries,...

(ii) to conclude agreements stabilizing and supporting at an acceptable level the prices of vulnerable primary products and providing preferential access to developed markets for the manufactured products of developing countries.

(*d*) that they should urge their members to support more actively existing funds... to help meet some of the present emergencies in world poverty and hunger.

475

1968
The ministry of the laity

Resolutions 24–27, Lambeth Conference, 1968.

An increasingly clear recognition of the importance of the full participation of the whole *laos* or people of God in the Church's ministry is reflected here.

24. The Conference recommends that no major issue in the life of the Church should be decided without the full participation of the laity in discussion and in decision.

25. The Conference recommends that each Province or regional Church be asked to explore the theology of baptism and confirmation in relation to the need to commission the laity for their task in the world, and to experiment in this regard.

26. The Conference requests that information about experiments in lay training be made available to the whole of the Anglican Communion.

27. The Conference believes that there is an urgent need for increase in the quantity and quality of training available for laypeople for their task in the world.

476

1968
The Thirty-Nine Articles

Resolution 43, Lambeth Conference, 1968.

The limitations of the historical and cultural and even polemical context in which the Thirty-Nine Articles were produced is recognized here and difficulties in subscribing to them everywhere and by all ordained ministers allowed for. Cf. no. 488.

The Thirty-Nine Articles

43. The Conference accepts the main conclusion of the report of the Archbishop's Commission in Christian Doctrine entitled *Subscription and Assent to the Thirty-Nine Articles* (1968) and in furtherance of its recommendation suggests

(*a*) that each Church of our communion consider whether the Articles need be bound up with its Prayer Book;

(*b*) suggests to the Churches of the Anglican Communion that assent to the Thirty-Nine Articles be no longer required of ordinands;

(*c*) suggests that, when subscription is required to the Articles or other elements in the Anglican tradition, it should be required, and given, only in the context of a statement which gives the full range of our inheritance of faith and sets the Articles in their historical context.

477

1968
Practical steps towards Christian unity

Resolutions 44–6, 56–9, Lambeth Conference, 1968.

Renewal of unity

44. The Conference recommends that the following affirmations be referred to each Province for consideration, as means of furthering renewal in unity.

(*a*) We believe that each Bishop of the Anglican Communion should ask himself how seriously he takes the suggestion of the Lund Conference on Faith and Order that we should do together everything which conscience does not compel us to do separately. To do so... involves... the exploration of *responsible experiment* so that ecumenical work beyond the present limits of constitutional provision is encouraged to keep in touch with the common mind of the Church and not tempted to break away.

(*b*) We believe that prior attention in ecumenical life and action should be given to the local level, and point to local ecumenical action as the most direct way of bringing together the whole Christian community in any area.

(*c*) We believe that as ecumenical work develops in local, national, and regional areas the need becomes more apparent for an ecumenical forum on the widest possible scale. We therefore endorse the hope expressed at the Uppsala Assembly that 'the members of the World Council of Churches, committed to each other, should work for the time when a genuine universal council may once more speak for all Christians'. Our interim confessional and ecumenical organizations should be tested by their capacity to lead in this direction.

(*d*) We believe that areas in which little ecumenical activity is at present possible have a claim upon the encouragement and support of the more strongly established areas, which shold make provision of time and money to maintain fellowship with them.

Admission of non-Anglicans to Holy Communion

45. The Conference recommends that, in order to meet special pastoral needs of God's people, under the direction of the bishop Christians duly baptized in the name of the Holy Trinity and qualified to receive Holy Communion in their own Churches may be welcomed at the Lord's table in the Anglican Communion.

Anglicans Communicating in other than Anglican Churches

46. The Conference recommends that, while it is the general practice of the Church that Anglican communicants receive the Holy Communion at the hands of ordained ministers of their own Church or of Churches in communion herewith, nevertheless under the general direction of the bishop, to meet special pastoral needs, such communicants be free to attend the Eucharist in other Churches holding the apostolic faith as contained in the Scriptures and summarized in the Apostles' and Nicene Creeds, and as conscience dictates to receive the sacrament, when they know they are welcome to do so. (*For*, 351. *Against*, 75.)

The Orthodox Churches

56. The Conference warmly welcomes the proposed resumption of the pan-Orthodox and pan-Anglican discussions which began in 1931.

57. The Conference welcomes the proposals concerning Anglican relations with the Orthodox and Oriental (Orthodox) Churches, urging joint biblical study with Orthodox theologians and dialogue at the local level.

58. The Conference recommends the circulation to all Anglican provinces of the report of the delegation to Bucharest in 1935 and of the terms in which this report was accepted and endorsed by the Convocations of Canterbury and York 'as consonant with the Anglican formularies and a legitimate interpretation of the faith of the Church as held by the Anglican Communion'.

The Lutheran Churches

59. The Conference recommends the initiation of Anglican–Lutheran conversations on a worldwide basis as soon as possible.

478

1968
Collegiality and unity

Resolution 55, Lambeth Conference, 1968.

Collegiality implies equality and brotherhood in unity and rules out the 'absorption' of one Church by another. Cf. no. 479.

Collegiality

55. The Conference recommends that the principle of collegiality should be a guiding principle in the growth of the relationships between the provinces of the Anglican Communion and those Churches with which we are, or shall be, in full communion.

479

1968
General Episcopal Consultation

Resolution 65, Lambeth Conference, 1968.

Cf. no. 478 on collegiality.

65. The Conference recommends:
(*a*) that a General Episcopal Consultation (drawn from many countries) be held in the near future, and expresses the hope that the Archbishop of Canterbury will take the initiative in sending invitations primarily to those Churches which are in full or partial communion with the see of Canterbury or with the provinces of the Anglican Communion.
(*b*) that Regional Episcopal Consultations should be held on a wider basis of representation than that suggested at the General Episcopal Consultation, under such local auspices and arrangements as seem appropriate and helpful in each region.

480

1968
The Anglican Consultative Council

Resolution 69, Lambeth Conference, 1968.

69. The Conference accepts and endorses the appended proposals concerning the Anglican Consultative Council and its Constitution and submits them to the member Churches of the Anglican Communion for approval....

FUNCTIONS

1. To share information about developments in one or more provinces with the other parts of the communion and to serve as needed as an instrument of common action.
2. To advise on inter-Anglican, provincial, and diocesan relationships, including the division of provinces, the formation of new provinces and of regional councils, and the problems of extraprovincial dioceses.
3. To develop as far as possible agreed Anglican policies in the world mission of the Church and to encourage national and regional Churches to engage together in developing and implementing such policies by sharing their resources and manpower, money, and experience to the best advantage of all.
4. To keep before national and regional Churches the importance of the fullest possible Anglican collaboration with other Christian Churches.
5. To encourage and guide Anglican participation in the Ecumenical Movement and the ecumenical organizations; to co-operate with the World Council of Churches and the world confessional bodies on behalf of the Anglican Communion; and to make arrangements for the conduct of pan-Anglican conversations with the Roman Catholic Church, the Orthodox Churches, and other Churches.
6. To advise on matters arising out of national or regional church union negotiations or conversations and on subsequent relations with united Churches.
7. To advise on problems of inter-Anglican communication and to help in the dissemination of Anglican and ecumenical information.
8. To keep in review the needs that may arise for further study and, where necessary, to promote inquiry and research.

481

1968
Experience and understanding in Faith

Henry Chadwick, 'The "Finality" of the Christian Faith', Lambeth Essays in Faith, ed. the Archbishop of Canterbury (London, 1968), p. 30.

The doctrines of Scripture and the dogmas of ecclesiastical councils, while admittedly imperfect and inadequate as all human statements about God must necessarily be, are nevertheless not peripheral and secondary. Nor do they have the status of an abstract 'theory' that needs first to be taught and grasped so that it can then be expressed in practical Christian living. Although the work of fallible mortals, they are accepted, in faith, as formed with the assistance of the Holy Spirit, and are signposts pointing towards and safeguarding the inward mystery of the gospel, the divine Word himself. So our faith is in God, not in a Trinitarian dogma about God; yet the Trinitarian language of the Church Fathers may still be a valuable safeguard against one-sidedness and distortion and a positive pointer to the full richness of the Christian apprehension of divine love. This *via media*[1] has the merit of avoiding the apparent naïvety of the too simple 'translation' view and the rationalism of the notion that development consists in the strictly logical explication of truth 'implicit' in the deposit of faith. On the other hand, it seeks to avoid the incoherence of the illuminist view, where the notion of a private, incommunicable, wordless feeling is too individualistic and does not take sufficient account of the observable continuity in the actual transmission of Christian doctrine in the historical process.

---

[1]   'Middle way'

482

1969
Fundamentals (Province of Central Africa)

Church of the Province of Central Africa, Constitution and Canons, 1969, Fundamental Declarations.

I. The Church of the Province of Central Africa, hereafter called the Church of this Province, being in full Communion with the Church of England and with the Anglican Communion throughout the world, holds the Faith of Christ as taught in the Holy Scriptures, preached by the Apostles, summed up in the Creeds and confirmed by the undisputed General Councils of the Holy Catholic Church. With Faith as embodied in the Doctrine, Sacraments and Discipline of the Church we maintain according as the Church of England has received and taught the same in the Book of Common Prayer, and the the Ordering of Bishops, Priests and Deacons. We do also accept the principles of Worship set forth in the Book of Common Prayer. And we disclaim in this Province any right to depart from the standards of Faith and Order or the Principles of Worship set forth in the said formularies of the Church of England. Providing that nothing herein contained shall prevent this Province from accepting, if it shall so determine, any alterations in the formularies of the Church which may be adopted by the Church of England; or from making at any time such adaptations or abridgement of, or additions to the services of the Church as may, in its judgement, be required by the circumstances of this Province and shall be consistent with the spirit and teaching of the Book of Common Prayer.

II. The Church of this Province accepts the Archbishop of Canterbury as holding the first place among the Metropolitans of the Anglican Communion.

III. In conformity with Christian doctrine, the Church of this Province proclaims the equal value of all men before the righteous Love of God, and while careful to provide for the special needs of different peoples committed to its charge, allows no discrimination on grounds of racial difference only, in the membership and government of the Church.

IV. If any question arise in the Church of this Province concerning its adherence to the standards of Faith and Order or the principles of Worship herein set forth, or to the spirit and teaching of the

Book of Common Prayer, the Provincial Synod may refer the question to the Archbishop of Canterbury, together with the Anglican Consultative Council.

V. The Church of this Province has power to admit to membership of the Province and Diocese which may hereafter be formed whether within or beyond or partly within or partly beyond the bounds of the Dioceses of the Province existing at the time of its inauguration.

VI. If at any time (subject to the provision of these Declarations) the Church of this Province desires to be constitutionally joined with another Province or other Provinces of the Anglican Communion, nothing contained in these Declarations or this Constitution shall prevent this Province from accepting and subscribing such constitutional provisions concerning Faith, Order and Worship and Government as it may think fit to accept in order to achieve the proposed constitutional union.

VII. No alteration in these Fundamental Declarations may be made unless the proposed amendment, after having been provisionally approved by the Provincial Synod, has been approved by the Synod of each Diocese in the Province, and confirmed by the Provincial Synod by a two-thirds majority of those present, and has subsequently been endorsed by the Archbishop of Canterbury as not affecting the terms of Communion between the Church of this Province, the Church of England and the rest of the Anglican Communion.

483

1969
Some constitutional articles

The Province of the South West Indian Ocean, The Constitution, 1969 (Draft); the Articles of the Constitution, Articles 2–4.

Article 2: *Doctrine and Worship*

1. The Church of this Province, being in full Communion with the Church of England and with the Anglican Communion throughout the world, receives all the Canonical Scriptures of the Old and New Testaments as being the ultimate rule and standard of faith, given by inspiration of God, and containing all things necessary for salvation.

2. This Church holds the Faith of Christ as preached by the Apostles, summed up in the Creeds, and confirmed by the undisputed General Councils of the Holy Catholic Church.

3. It maintains this Faith as embodied in the Doctrine, Sacraments and Discipline of the Church as the Church of England has received and taught the same in the Book of Common Prayer and the Ordering of Bishops, Priests and Deacons. It accepts the principles of worship set forth in the Book of Common Prayer, and disclaims any right to depart from the standards of Faith and Order or the principles of Worship set forth in the said formularies of the Church of England.

4. The Church of this Province has power to accept, if it shall so determine through the Provincial Synod, any alterations in the Book of Common Prayer and the Ordinal aforesaid and any additional formulations of Doctrine and Discipline which may hereafter be adopted by the Church of England.

5. The Church of this Province may make and authorise such deviations from and additions and alternatives to the forms of service provided in the Book of Common Prayer and such new forms of service as may, in its judgement, be required to meet the needs of the Church in this Province and shall be consistent with the spirit and teaching of the said Book of Common Prayer.

6. In the interpretation of the aforesaid standards and formularies and in all questions of Faith, Doctrine, Discipline, and Worship, the Church of this Province is not bound by any decisions other than those of the ecclesiastical tribunals provided under the terms of this Constitution.

Article 3: *The Doctrine of Man*

In conformity with Christian doctrine, the Church of this Province proclaims that all men are of equal value and dignity in the sight of God, and, while careful to provide for the special needs of different people committed to its charge, allows no discrimination in the membership and government of the Church based solely on grounds of racial difference.

Article 4: *The Liturgy of the Church*

1. While the ultimate objective of the Province must be the achievement of a common liturgy for use throughout the Province, the following safeguard must be applied: No direction shall be

made by the Provincial Synod, or by a body authorised by it, for the revision of any existing Liturgy or service in any one Diocese, which has already received synodical authority in that Diocese, without the approval of the Synod of the Diocese concerned.

2. A Diocesan Bishop shall not authorise for use in his Diocese any alterations in a service approved by the Provincial Synod unless the body authorised by it for the purpose has approved the alteration as suitable in itself, as being required by the conditions of the Diocese, and as not introducing any difference of substance; and until a certificate to this effect shall have been submitted to the Provincial Synod and confirmed by it.

484

1969
The legal basis of a new Province
The Church of the Province of Tanzania, Constitution.

Preamble
In the Name of God the Father, God the Son and God the Holy Ghost, Amen.

Whereas it is in accordance with the ancient laws and usages of the Catholic Church that dioceses should be associated in provinces and whereas it is desired that a provincial union of the dioceses of Zanzibar and Tanga, Dar es Salaam, Masasi, Morogoro, South-West Tanganyika, Western Tanganyika, Victoria Nyanza and Central Tanganyika situated in the Province of East Africa should now be established as a new and separate Province with the title of The Church of the Province of Tanzania to the Glory of God, and for the furtherance of fellowship, comity and mutual support among them and for the strengthening of the Church in its work of witnessing in Tanzania to the redemption wrought for all in Christ and whereas the Diocesan Bishops of the dioceses of Zanzibar and Tanga, Dar es Salaam, Masasi. Morogoro, South-West Tanganyika, Western Tanganyika, Victoria Nyanza and Central Tanganyika have been authorised by their respective dioceses through their Diocesan Synods to consent and subscribe to the formation of a Province of Tanzania under the terms and provisions of the Constitution herein contained and have consented and subscribed and whereas the

Archbishop of Canterbury has in his capacity as Chairman of the Consultative Body of the Lambeth Conference signified his concurrence and satisfaction with the terms and provisions of the said Constitution and of the Canons herein contained and whereas the Archbishop of East Africa has signified his consent to the formation of the Province of Tanzania by the said dioceses now under his jurisdiction, subject to the terms and provisions contained in the said Constitution and Canons, and has directed that the said Province shall be constituted as from the date upon which the enthronement of the first Archbishop of the Province of Tanzania takes place.

Now we the Diocesan Bishops whose signatures are hereto subscribed do solemnly decree and declare that as from the date upon which the enthronement of the first Archbishop of the Province of Tanzania takes place the dioceses aforesaid are by our act and determination united in the Province of Tanzania with the intention that its organisation should be developed in accordance with the Constitution and Canons hereinafter contained as a Province of the Catholic Church in full Communion with the Church of England and with the Anglican Communion of Churches throughout the world.

485

1969

Common liturgical forms

Special General Convention, 1969, Episcopal Church in the United States of America, A Communion of Communions, *1969.*

Compare no. 331 on 'rites and ceremonies' and Article xxxiv of the Thirty-Nine Articles.

To seek agreement... in respect to those essential structures and basic formularies of sacramental and liturgical rites which are shared in common, whether deriving from the Holy Scriptures or from the universal traditions of the Church.

486

1969
The Church of England

Church of England Canons of 1969, Section A 1, Of the Church of England.

These Canons should be compared with those taken from the 1604 text, nos. 165ff.

The Church of England, established according to the laws of this realm under the Queen's Majesty, belongs to the true and apostolic Church of Christ; and, as our duty to the said Church of England requires, we do constitute and ordain that no member thereof shall be at liberty to maintain or hold the contrary.

487

1969
Secrecy of confession

Church of England Canons of 1969, Proviso to Canon 113 of the Code of 1603.

Cf. nos. 100, 186, 234, 268, 273, 496 and others on the Anglican tradition of confession and absolution.

Provided always, that if any man confess his secret and hidden sins to the Minister, for the unburdening of his conscience, and to receive spiritual consolation and ease of mind from him; we do not any way bind the said Minister by this our Constitution, but do straitly charge and admonish him, that he do not at any time reveal and make known to any person whatsoever any crime or offence so committed to his trust and secrecy (except they be such crimes as by the laws of this realm his own life may be called into question for concealing the same), under pain of irregularity.

488

1969
The Thirty-Nine Articles

Church of England Canons of 1969, A 2, Of the Thirty-Nine Articles of Religion.

It should be noted that this Canon does not insist upon subscription to the Articles as a condition of membership. Cf. no 476.

The Thirty-Nine Articles are agreeable to the Word of God and may be assented unto with a good conscience by all members of the Church of England.

489

1969
The Book of Common Prayer

Church of England Canons of 1969, A 3, Of the Book of Common Prayer.

It has been of some importance in Anglican history that the Book of Common Prayer and the Ordinal have been regarded as doctrinally as well as liturgically authoritative.

1. The doctrine contained in *The Book of Common Prayer and Administration of the Sacraments and other Rites and Ceremonies of the Church according to the Use of the Church of England* is agreeable to the Word of God.
2. The form of God's worship contained in the said Book, forasmuch as it is not repugnant to the Word of God, may be used by all members of the Church of England with a good conscience.

490

1969
The Church of England

Church of England Canons of 1969, A 4, Of the Form and Manner of Making, Ordaining, and Consecrating of Bishops, Priests, and Deacons.

Cf. Article xxiii of the Thirty-Nine Articles, which says that the ordained ministry must be 'lawfully called and sent... by men who have public authority given them'. The emphasis here is upon ensuring that competent authorities regulate the making of ministers and no one deems himself 'called' without the Church's due recognition of his calling. This element in ordination was stressed by reforming communities throughout sixteenth century Europe.

The Form and Manner of Making, Ordaining, and Consecrating of Bishops, Priests, and Deacons, annexed to the Book of Common Prayer and commonly known as the Ordinal, is not repugnant to the Word of God; and those who are so made, ordained, or consecrated Bishops, Priests, or Deacons, according to the said Ordinal, are lawfully made, ordained, or consecrated, and ought to be accounted, both by themselves and others, to be truly bishops, priests, or deacons.

491

1969
The Doctrine of the Church of England

The Church of England Canons of 1969, A 5, Of the doctrine of the Church of England.

The doctrine of the Church of England is grounded in the holy Scriptures, and in such teachings of the ancient Fathers and Councils of the Church as are agreeable to the said Scriptures. In particular such doctrine is to be found in the Thirty-Nine Articles of Religion, the Book of Common Prayer, and the Ordinal.

492

1969
Church Government

Church of England Canons of 1969, A 6, Of the government of the Church of England.

The Church is here declared to be governed 'by' those who bear office in it. Compare no. 493.

The government of the Church of England under the Queen's Majesty, by archbishops, bishops, deans, provosts, archdeacons, and the rest of the clergy and of the laity that bear office in the same, is not repugnant to the Word of God.

493

1969
Royal Supremacy

Church of England Canons of 1969, A 7, Of the Royal Supremacy.

Royal Supremacy has never laid claim to spiritual or sacramental, but only legal and certain jurisdictional, powers.

We acknowledge that the Queen's most excellent Majesty, acting according to the laws of the realm, is the highest power under God in this kingdom, and has supreme authority over all persons in all causes, as well ecclesiastical as civil.

494

1969
Healing schisms

Church of England Canons of 1969, A 8, Of Schisms.

Forasmuch as the Church of Christ has for a long time past been distressed by separations and schisms among Christian men, so that the unity for which our Lord prayed is impaired and the witness to his gospel is grievously hindered, it is the duty of the clergy and people to do their utmost not only to avoid occasions of strife but also to seek in penitence and brotherly charity to heal such divisions.

495

1969
Reception into the Church of England of adults from other communions

Church of England Canons of 1969, B 28, Of reception into the Church of England.

1. Any person desiring to be received into the Church of England, who has not been baptized or the validity of whose baptism can be held in question, shall be instructed and baptized or conditionally baptized, and such baptism, or conditional baptism, shall constitute the said person's reception into the Church of England.

2. If any such person has been baptized but not episcopally confirmed and desires to be formally admitted into the Church of England he shall, after appropriate instruction, be received by the rite of confirmation, or, if he be not yet ready to be presented for confirmation, he shall be received by the parish priest with appropriate prayers.

3. If any such person has been episcopally confirmed with unction or with the laying of hands he shall be instructed, and with the permission of the bishop, received into the Church of England according to the Form and Reception approved by Convocation, or with other appropriate prayers, and if any such person be a priest he shall be received into the said Church only by the bishop of the diocese or by the commissary of such bishop.

496

1969
Absolution

Church of England Canons of 1969, B 29, Of the ministry of absolution.

Cf. nos. 100, 186, 234, 268, 273 on confession, penance and absolution.

1. It is the duty of baptized persons at all times to the best of their understanding to examine their lives and conversations by the rule of God's commandments, and whereinsoever they perceive themselves to have offended by will, act, or omission, there to bewail their own sinfulness and to confess themselves to Almighty God with full purpose of amendment of life, that they may receive of him the forgiveness of sins which he has promised to all who turn to him with hearty repentance and true faith; acknowledging their sins and seeking forgiveness, especially in the General Confessions of the congregation and in the Absolutions pronounced by the priest in the services of the Church.

2. If there be any who by these means cannot quiet his own conscience, but requires further comfort or counsel, let him come to some discreet and learned minister of God's Word; that by the ministry of God's holy Word he may receive the benefit of absolution, together with ghostly counsel and advice, to the quieting of his conscience and avoiding of all scruple and doubtfulness.

3. In particular a sick person, if he feels his conscience troubled in any weighty matter, should make a special confession of his sins, that the priest may absolve him if he humbly and heartily desire it.

4. No priest shall exercise the ministry of absolution in any place without the permission of the minister having the cure of souls thereof, unless he is by law authorized to exercise his ministry in that place without being subject to the control of the minister having the general cure of souls of the parish or district in which it is situated: Provided always that, notwithstanding the foregoing provisions of this Canon, a priest may exercise the ministry of absolution anywhere in respect of any person who is in danger of death or if there is some urgent or weighty cause.

497

1969
Lay officers of the Church

Church of England Canons of 1969, E 1, Of churchwardens.

The churchwardens were, until Parochial Church Councils were set up in 1921, the only official representatives of the laity in English parishes. They have legal and financial responsibilities as well as disciplinary ones.

4. The churchwardens when admitted are officers of the Ordinary. They shall discharge such duties as are by law and custom assigned to them; thay shall be foremost in representing laity and in co-operating with the incumbent; they shall use their best endeavours by example and precept to encourage parishioners in the practice of true religion and to promote unity and peace among them. They shall also maintain order and decency in the church and churchyard, especially during the time of divine service.

5. In the churchwardens is vested the property in the plate, ornaments, and other movable goods of the church, and they shall keep an inventory thereof which they shall revise from time to time as occasion may require. On going out of office they shall duly deliver to their successors any goods of the church remaining in their hands together with the said inventory, which shall be checked by their successors.

498

1969
Lay officers of the Church

Church of England Canons of 1969, E 2, Of sidesmen or assistants to the churchwardens.

1. The sidesmen of the parish are by law elected by the annual parochial church meeting and the minister, provided that, if the annual meeting and the minister are unable to agree, one half of the sidesmen are elected by the annual meeting and one half are appointed by the minister...

3. It shall be the duty of the sidesmen to promote the cause of true religion in the parish and to assist the churchwardens in the

discharge of their duties in maintaining order and decency in the church and churchyard, especially during the time of divine service.

499

1969
Lay officers of the Church

Church of England Canons of 1969, E 4, Of readers.

1. Any lay person, whether man or woman, who is baptized and confirmed and who satisfies the bishop that he is a regular communicant of the Church of England, may be admitted by the bishop of the diocese to the office of reader in the Church and licensed by him to perform any duty or duties which may lawfully be performed by a reader according to the provisions of paragraph 2 of this Canon or which may from time to time be so determined by Act of Convocation.

2. It shall be lawful for a reader:

a to visit the sick, to read and pray with them, to teach in Sunday school and elsewhere, and generally to undertake such pastoral and educational work and to give such assistance to any minister as the bishop may direct;

b during the time for divine service to read Morning and Evening Prayer (save for the Absolution), to publish banns of marriage at Morning or Evening Prayer (on occasions on which a layman is permitted by the statute law so to do, and in accordance with the requirements of that law), to read the Word of God, to preach, to catechize the children, and to receive and present the offerings of the people; and give such further assistance as may be authorized under Canon B 12.

500

1969
Ecclesiastical Courts

Church of England Canons of 1969, G 1, Of Ecclesiastical Courts and Commissions.

This is included as an example of the kind of provision which needs to be made in every Province, first for the running of ecclesiastical courts as courts of law; and secondly to clarify their sphere of jurisdiction in relation to that of the secular authorities and in relation to a synod (which would be the proper place to consider a matter of doctrine, ritual or ceremonial).

The Ecclesiastical Courts which are or may be constituted in accordance with the provisions of the Ecclesiastical Jurisdiction Measure, 1963, are as follows:

1. For each diocese the court of the bishops thereof, called the Consistory Court of the diocese or, in the case of the diocese of Canterbury, the Commissary Court thereof, for the trial of offences against the laws ecclesiastical not involving matter of doctrine, ritual, or ceremonial and also of faculty and other causes provided in the Ecclesiastical Jurisdiction Measure.

2. For each of the Provinces of Canterbury and York
   a a court of the Archbishop (to be called in the case of the court of the Province of Canterbury the Arches Court of Canterbury, and, in the case of the court for the Province of York, the Chancery Court of York) having appellate jurisdiction[1] as provided in the Ecclesiastical Jurisdiction Measure.
   b Commissions appointed by the Upper House of the Convocation of the Province for the trial of a Bishop for an offence against the laws ecclesiastical, other than an offence involving matter of doctrine, ritual, or ceremonial.

3. For both the said provinces
   a a court called the Court of Ecclesiastical Causes Reserved for the trial of offences against the laws ecclesiastical involving doctrine, ritual, or ceremonial... The court also has appellate jurisdiction in... causes involving doctrine, ritual, or ceremonial.
   b Commissions appointed by the Upper House of the Convocation of both the said provinces for the trial of an Archbishop for an offence against the laws ecclesiastical, other than an offence involving matter of doctrine, ritual, or ceremonial.

4. There may be appointed by Her Majesty a Commission of Review, to review any finding of the Court of Ecclesiastical Causes Reserved or of any Commission of the Upper House of the

---

[1] that is, acting as a Court of Appeal

Convocation appointed for the trial of a Bishop or an Archbishop.
5. Her Majesty in Council has jurisdiction to hear appeals from the Court of Arches or the Chancery Court in... causes not involving matter of doctrine, ritual, or ceremonial.

501

1969
Ecclesiastical Courts

Church of England Canons of 1969, G 2, Of the Chancellor or Judge of a Consistory Court.

This provision reflects the ancient tradition that the diocesan court is the bishop's court, and so he must appoint the judges who act on his behalf.

1. The judge of the Consistory Court of a diocese is styled the chancellor of the diocese or, in the case of the diocese of Canterbury, the commissary general, and is appointed by the bishop of the diocese.

502

1969
Ecclesiastical Courts

Church of England Canons of 1969, G 3, Of the Judges of the Arches Court of Canterbury and the Chancery Court of York.

Cf. comment on Canon G 1 (no. 500).

1. The judges of the Arches Court of Canterbury and the Chancery Court of York respectively are five in number.
2. Of the judges of each of the said courts:
    a one, who is a judge of both courts (and, in respect of his jurisdiction in the Province of Canterbury, is styled Dean of the Arches and, in respect of his jurisdiction in the Province of York, is styled Auditor) is appointed by the Archbishops of Canterbury and York jointly with the approval of Her Majesty;
    b two are persons in holy orders appointed by the Prolocutor of the Lower House of the Convocation of the relevant Province;

c two are laymen appointed by the Chairman of the House of Laity after consultation with the Lord Chancellor and possessing such judicial experience as the Lord Chancellor thinks appropriate. ...

4. Before the Chairman of the House of Laity appoints a person to be a judge of either of the said courts, he must satisfy himself that that person is a communicant.

503

1969
Ecclesiastical Courts

Church of England Canons of 1969, G 4, Of Registrars.

Here the provision seeks to secure the appointment of persons with appropriate legal qualifications, and who are also communicating members of the Church of England, to serve the ecclesiastical courts.

1. The registrar of a Province and of the provincial court is appointed by the Archbishop of that Province, and the registrar of a diocese and its consistory court is appointed by the bishop of the diocese.

2. The qualifications of a person appointed to be such a registrar as aforesaid are that he should be a solicitor of the Supreme Court learned in the ecclesiastical laws and the laws of the realm; and the Archbishop or Bishop appointing him must satisfy himself that the said person is a communicant.

504

1969
Ecclesiastical Courts

Church of England Canons of 1969, G 5, Of Visitations.

The bishop's duty of 'visiting' his diocese is an ancient part of the ministry of oversight which makes him personally responsible for all the people who make up his diocesan flock in the parishes.

1. Every Archbishop, Bishop, and Archdeacon has the right to visit, at times and places limited by law or custom, the Province,

diocese, or archdeaconry committed to his charge, in a more solemn manner, and in such visitation to perform all such acts as by law and custom are assigned to his charge in that behalf for the edifying and well-governing of Christ's flock, that means may be taken thereby for the supply of such things as are lacking and the correction of such things as are amiss.

2. During the time of such visitation the jurisdiction of all inferior Ordinaries shall be suspended save in places which by law or custom are exempt.

505

1970
The Ordained Ministry (Tanzania)

The Church of the Province of Tanzania, The Constitution, 1970, Article 5.

Article 5: *The Ministry.*

1. The Church of this Province holds and teaches that from the apostles' times there have been these orders in Christ's Church: bishops, priests and deacons: and no man shall be accounted or taken to be a lawful bishop, priest, or deacon in the Council of this Province, or permitted to execute any of the said offices, except he be called, tried, examined, and admitted thereunto according to an ordinal approved in accordance with Article 2, or has had formerly episcopal consecration or ordination in some other church whose Orders are, at the time of the inauguration of the Province, recognized and accepted in accordance with the Constitution of any of the Dioceses of the Province, or shall thereafter be recognized and accepted by the Church of this Province.

2. Priests and deacons who have received authority to minister in any Diocese of the Province owe canonical obedience in all things lawful and honest to the Bishop of the same, and the bishops of the several Dioceses owe canonical obedience to the Archbishop of the Province and to the Constitution of the Province.

506

1970
Search for an ecumenical hymnal

General Convention of the Episcopal Church in the United States of America, A Communion of Communions, *1970.*

A hymnal, like a Prayer Book, is an expression of common faith and doctrinal agreement, and is therefore a valuable aid to unity when compiled ecumenically.

Resolved, That the Joint Commission on Church Music be empowered to seek the cooperation of other Christian bodies in the hope of the eventual production of an ecumenical hymnal.

507

1970
Church of the Province of Burma
Who are the Anglicans?, *ed. Charles Long, prepared for the Lambeth Conference, 1988 (Ohio, 1988), p. 47.*

Anglican chaplains from 1825, USPG missionaries 1859–1966. First diocese, Rangoon, established 1877; it continued as part of the Church of India, Pakistan, Burma and Ceylon until the India and Pakistan dioceses were incorporated in united churches. The church of the Province of Burma was inaugurated in 1970. In 1961 Buddhism was declared the State religion. In 1966 all foreign missionaries were forced to leave. On its own resources and under many difficulties the Church has continued steady growth.

508

1970
A Province's sense of identity

The Constitution, Canons and Rules of the Church of Burma, Preface.

The Anglican Church of Burma was in the past included in the Church of India, Pakistan, Burma and Ceylon, the administration of which was governed by a document known as the Constitution, Canons and Rules of that Church. In the years following the Second World War of 1939–45 and the coming of Independence to the four countries included in the said Church, it became increasingly difficult for the Church of Burma effectively to participate in the life and affairs of the Province and to take its proper part in its councils.

After long and careful consideration it was therefore agreed by the General Council of the Church of India, Pakistan, Burma and Ceylon that the Church of Burma should be allowed to give effect to its expressed desire, first, to become a separate Province within the Church of India, Pakistan, Burma and Ceylon, and then as a second step, to sever its juridical connection with that Church in order to become an autonomous Province within the family of Churches known as the Anglican Communion. The legislation necessary to give effect to these plans was embodied in an Enactment which passed its first reading in the General Council of January 1968 and its second reading in January 1970, the voting on both occasions being unanimous. In order, however, that the emerging autonomous Church of Burma should preserve its spiritual identity and continuity, it was mutually agreed that in drawing up its Constitution it should include in that document sufficient and significant portions of the Constitution, Canons and Rules of the Church of India, Pakistan, Burma and Ceylon. This has been done by incorporating in the... Constitution, Canons and Rules of the Church of Burma, in addition to other sections of less importance,... the parts of the earlier Constitution which are of basic significance: –

Relation to the Catholic Church

1. The Church of Burma is a part of the one Holy Catholic and Apostolic Church, the body of Christ, which He is building up out of all generations and races of men. We are what we are as a Church and as members of the Church by reason of what we have received from Him through and in the Holy Catholic Church.

Founded on God's Revelation of Himself

2. We have received from God a revelation about Himself. That revelation was made as a gradual self-disclosure. It was begun in many parts and manners, when God revealed Himself to a chosen people, as the Old Testament records, by prophets and lawgivers. It

was completed and imparted to all the world, when, as the New Testament records, He revealed Himself in His eternal Son, who took our nature upon Him. 'God so loved the world that He gave His only begotten Son, that whosoever believeth on Him should not perish but have everlasting life'. Jesus Christ was so born, so lived, so died, so rose again from the dead that He draws all men unto Him, and, having ascended into Heaven, He ever liveth to make intercession for them. By Him we are ever being drawn to clearer knowledge and deeper love of the unseen God, who first loved us.

The Revelation of the Inner Nature of God

3. We have received the revelation that God is one and from the words of the Son of God we have learned to know, within the unity of the Godhead, the Father, the Son and the Spirit, whom following the tradition of the Western Church, we call the three Persons of the Trinity. Thus we acknowledge the glory of the eternal Trinity and in the power of the Divine Majesty we worship the unity.

The Benefits of the Incarnation towards Men

4. We have received the benefits of the coming of the Son of God upon earth and of the atonement which He wrought, in that through Him we have received the adoption of sons, the remission of our sins, and incorporation into His Body, the Church wherein we are being saved by grace unto life eternal. With all our forefathers in the faith, we glory in nothing save in the Cross of our Lord Jesus Christ, and we praise Him for our redemption in His blood, and the risen life which He has given us to share.

The Church and the Communion of saints

5. We have received and accept with gladness a place and portion in the Church, which we acknowledge to have been made, not by any human plan or agreement, but by the will of Jesus Christ, who founded it upon His Apostles and Prophets, giving command to go forth into all the world and to make disciples of all nations. By which will and command of Christ our Lord, there has been gathered together through baptism into one body an innumerable company of men and women, with whom, whether they be departed the life or are yet in the flesh, we are in communion through Him who is the Head.

The Spirit of Truth

6. We have received the benefits of the indwelling of the Holy Spirit in the Church guiding it from age to age into all truth. We have received His witness in the canonical Scriptures of the Old and New Testaments, and recognize those Scriptures as living oracles of God, and as of supreme authority in all matters concerning the salvation of man.... We have inherited and gratefully used the sound doctrines which the undivided Church upheld and explained in accordance with the same Holy Scriptures, and particularly that statement of the common faith of the Church, usually called the Nicene Creed, which we most firmly believe and in our common worship thankfully recite. We have inherited also from later ages much that godly men, with the same Spirit in their hearts and the same Scriptures before their eyes, learned and delivered, as the needs of such generation and country required. We believe that the same Spirit is with us now, guiding us according to our needs.

The Church the Household of Grace

7. We have received and ever use with gladness all the gifts of grace bestowed upon us in the Church. Thus we receive the Sacraments of Baptism and the Supper of the Lord, as our Saviour commanded and as His Apostles expounded them. In these two Sacraments God granted to us fellowship with Himself and enables us through that fellowship with Him to have fellowship one with another. We receive the laying on of hands, both upon all these who have been baptized, that by the inward working of the Holy Spirit they may be strengthened to live the Christian life, and also upon the special ministers of the New Covenant, that each may minister in his office by the power of the same spirit. We receive the message of forgiveness which our Lord Jesus left authority to His Church to give to all sinners who truly repent and believe in Him. We receive the godly practice of prayer for the healing of soul and body, accompanied, according to apostolic custom, by the laying on of hands upon the sick or anointing with oil, at the same time accepting and using the skill and knowledge which in later days God has given to medical science, with all gratitude to the Giver. We receive the due order of the Church as of a body having many members and those members each his own office. And in particular we receive the three orders of the ministry, bishops,

priests and deacons, in their offices, as they have come down to us from the primitive Church and have continued to this day. We have received the sanctification of all human life by the incarnation of the Son of God, and with it an increasing sense of the sacredness of all honourable states of life and callings among men, and particularly that regard for the sacredness of marriage, which our Lord taught to His Church and His Church has ever fostered by its teaching and laws. We receive all these things as from the Lord the Spirit, and it is our will reverently to use and faithfully to maintain them under that guidance which we continually pray Him to give.

509

1970
Church of the Province of Kenya

Who are the Anglicans?, ed. Charles Long, prepared for the Lambeth Conference, 1988 (Ohio, 1988), p. 21.

Anglican work began in 1844 with the arrival of the first Church Missionary Society missionary at Mombasa. Rapid growth began later in the 19th century, with the first African ordinations in 1885 and a mass movement of conversions starting in 1910. The Diocese of Mombasa was established in 1927. The first two Kenyan bishops were consecrated in 1955. Besides Church Missionary Society, the Bible Churchman's Missionary Society played and important role. The church became part of the new Province of East Africa established in 1960. In 1970 the Province was divided into separate Provinces of Kenya and Tanzania.

510

1970
Church of the Province of Tanzania

Who are the Anglicans?, ed. Charles Long, prepared for the Lambeth Conference, 1988 (Ohio, 1988), p. 29.

The Province was founded in 1970 from the former Church of the Province of East Africa with nine dioceses. There are two traditions of Anglicanism, those brought by the former Universities Mission to Central Africa and by the Church Missionary Society. UMCA began work in 1863, in Zanzibar. Church Missionary Society work spread from what is now Kenya, beginning in 1886. The Province is governed by the Provincial Synod which meets every three years.

511

1970
The Church in Sri Lanka

Who are the Anglicans?, *ed. Charles Long, prepared for the Lambeth Conference, 1988 (Ohio, 1988), p. 49.*

Until 1970 part of the Church of India, Pakistan, Burma and Ceylon. First Anglican services in 1796. Church Missionary Society missionaries from 1818. The two dioceses have planned to become part of a united Church of Sri Lanka, a plan frustrated thus far by legal problems and civil strife. They continue as extra-provincial dioceses under the Archbishop of Canterbury.

512

1970
The Church of North India: local union

M.K. Kuriakose, History of Christianity in India: Source Materials *(Madras 1982), pp. 419–22.*

The Church of North India was inaugurated on 29th November 1970. Its constitution was similar to that of the Church of South India with certain features of the Sri Lanka scheme included. Its most distinctive feature was the unification of the ministries of the uniting churches by the procedure described here. Bishop D.M. Kennedy gives the following eye-witness account of the inauguration. 'Work in Progress: The CNI History, III', *Indian Church History Review*, vol. VII, no. 1 (June 1973), pp. 20–4.

All who witnessed the Unification Rite — so much discussed and argued over in the long drawn-out period of negotiation — were able to note its true significance. It included an unequivocal affirmation by *all* the representative ministers, non-Anglican as well as Anglican,... of their willingness to receive *from God* whatever 'of Christ's grace, commission and authority' *He* might wish to give to each. A prayer with the same 'intention' was followed by a silent laying-on of hands on groups of ministers coming forward together, not on a denominational but on a regional basis; and in a marvellous reverent stillness the Service moved on to the sharing in the Bread and Wine and to the triumphant recessional hymn, 'Glorious things of thee are spoken, Zion, city of our God'. We marched now, not in our denominational groups, but as one body under one banner, of the Church of North India.

513

1971
A Constitution (Japan)

Constitution and Canons for the Government of the Nippon Sei Ko Kai as amended by General Synod, 1971.

Constitution

Article 1:
The Nippon Sei Ko Kai shall be a Province represented by the Primate and consisting of a number of Dioceses administered by Bishops. Each Diocese shall include a number of Parishes administered by Priests.
Article 2:
In each Parish there shall be a stated place of worship in which the Priest appointed by the Bishop regularly conducts Common Prayer, administers the Sacraments, and performs other Rites and Ceremonies of the Church with the participation of the Laity.
Article 3:
In Common Prayer, in the administration of the Sacraments, and in the conduct of other Rites and Ceremonies of the Church, the Book of Common Prayer According to the Use of the Nippon Sei Ko Kai shall be used. Forms of prayers for special occasions must be authorized or approved by the Diocesan Bishop.

Article 4:

A Bishop shall receive his office, after completion of the established canonical procedure, through Consecration at the hands of at least three Bishops.

Article 5:

A Priest or a Deacon shall receive his office, after completion of the established canonical procedure, by ordination at the hands of a Bishop.

Article 6:

A layman is a person who has become a member of the Holy Catholic Church by Baptism. The Laity shall adhere to the doctrine and discipline of the Church under the pastoral care of the Diocesan Bishop and Priest, shall receive the Sacraments, and shall contribute to the peace and progress of the Church.

Article 7:

The House of Bishops shall be constituted of Bishops in active service and shall uphold the heritage of the faith of the Church.

Article 8:

In the Nippon Sei Ko Kai there shall be a General Synod, consisting of the Diocesan Bishop, and of Clerical and Lay Delegates. The General Synod, between its sessions, shall be represented by the Board of Executives.

Article 9:

The General Synod shall have authority over:

    1.Matters relating to the peace, progress and unity of the Nippon Sei Ko Kai;

    2.Matters relating to domestic and foreign mission work;

    3.Amendments to the Constitution and Canons; and the revision of the Book of Common Prayer;

    4.The establishment and alteration of Diocesan boundaries.

Article 10:

In each Diocese there shall be a Synod convened by the Diocesan Bishop, consisting of the Clergy in active service and Lay Delegates. Between sessions a Standing Committee shall assist the Bishop and participate in Diocesan administration.

Article 11:

In each Parish there shall be a Vestry representing the Laity, which shall be organized under the Priest who is the Rector.

Article 12:

The Constitution shall be implemented by the Canons.

Article 13:
Amendments of the Constitution and revisions of the Book of Common Prayer which have received the approval of a regular General Synod shall be adopted, if confirmed by the next regular General Synod by a vote of at least two-thirds of the Delegates present.

514

1971
Province, Diocese and the Episcopal Order

The Time is Now; Anglican Consultative Council, First Meeting, 1971 (London, 1971), Resolutions 21, 22, 24, pp. 32–3.

21. *Creating and Dividing Provinces*

Although there is no official definition of a Province of the Anglican Communion, it can be described as the smallest complete unit of the Anglican Church because it exists under a College of bishops — each of whom with his clergy and laity is autonomous within a diocese. A college requires to be more than a trio of bishops and is severely limited if it consists of less than four diocesan bishops. A Province must have some common constitution, its geographical and political area must allow good communications, and, however much it transcends linguistic, national, or cultural boundaries, its peoples must have a community of concern which can unite them in a community of worship. In the light of this outline, the Council makes the following recommendations:

(a) It is expected that a new Province should normally contain at least four dioceses.

(b) It must be ensured that the remaining area of the former Province is not unduly weakened in finance, personnel, or institutions.

(c) The proposed Province must have financial stability, adequate leadership, proper administration, and accessibility to and from each diocese.

(d) There must be the good will of the existing Province in order not to create difficulties of disunity after division.

(e) Before the creation of a new Province there should be consultation with the Anglican Consultative Council or its Standing Committee for guidance and advice, especially in regard to the form of constitution most appropriate.

22. *Criteria for the Size of a Diocese*

The people of God who make up a diocese may come from diverse communities but should come from a natural area in which they live individual and corporate lives. The bishop, under God, is in a special way responsible with them and his clergy for the faith, teaching, unity, mission, and worship of that area, commonly called a diocese. Thus he represents the whole Church in and to his diocese, and his diocese in and to the councils of the Churches. He should also foster close relationships with other Churches and as far as possible with other faiths. The Council therefore suggests that the following are the criteria for the size of a diocese in which the bishop may exercise his *episkope*[1] properly:

(a) It should be of a size to enable those living in it to feel they belong to a witnessing fellowship.

(b) It should be large enough for it to be seen as the Church uniting people of different activities, backgrounds, and cultures.

(c) It should be large enough to engage the bishop fully and small enough for him to have a sufficiently intimate knowledge of his clergy and people.

(d) It should have sufficient measure of financial and administrative independence and not be so small as to be unable to organize and plan its work effectively.

(e) Its boundaries should coincide as far as possible with those of the community and therefore dioceses will vary in size.

Where a diocese or region is too large for one bishop, either in population or in geographical extent, the Council believes that consideration might be given to the possibility of sustaining a diocese by means of a college of bishops. When such a pattern is followed, this Council would emphasize the importance of each area of a diocese having a bishop whom it would regard as its own.

---

[1]   Oversight

24. *Status for Bishops Who No Longer Hold Jurisdiction*

Having received a request from the USA for advice on the status and ministry of bishops who no longer hold jurisdiction, the Council recommends that:

(a) all bishops, even those who do not hold jurisdiction, are in the episcopal order, and each Province should be encouraged to make use of their gifts and experience for episcopal and pastoral purposes;

(b) bishops who have been forced out of their dioceses, or who have resigned to make way for an indigenous successor, should be regarded with special concern by member Churches with a view to assuring their retention within the bonds of fellowship;

(c) not by right, but only by invitation, would each such bishop attend or vote in the councils of the Church;

(d) each Province should decide for itself whether any particular bishop, other than a diocesan, should be considered as having jurisdiction.

515

1971
The Church of Bangladesh

Who are the Anglicans?, ed, Charles Long, prepared for the Lambeth Conference, 1988 (Ohio, 1988), p. 78.

Bangladesh was previously East Pakistan. It was part of the State of Pakistan partitioned from India in 1947 to form a separate Muslim state. After civil war between East and West Pakistan, which ended in 1971, East Pakistan became an independent state, Bangladesh. Before independence the Diocese of Dhaka was one of the dioceses of the Church of Pakistan and its early history is that of the Church of Pakistan. Today the Church has just one diocese and is a minority church in a minority religion.

516

1972
The dignity and rights of man

The Church of the Province of Uganda, Rwanda, Burundi and Boga-Zaïre, Provincial Constitution 1972, Article 3.

Article 3: *On the dignity and rights of man*

In conformity with the established Christian doctrine, the Church of this Province shall proclaim and hold that all men have equal value, rights and dignity in the sight of God, and, while mindful to provide for the special needs of different people committed to its charge, shall not allow discrimination in the membership and government of the Church solely on the grounds of colour, race or tribe.

517

1972
Doctrine and worship

The Church of the Province of Uganda, Rwanda, Burundi and Boga-Zaïre, Provincial Constitution 1972, Article 2.

Article 2 — *On Doctrine and Worship*

(a) The Church of Uganda, Rwanda, Burundi and Boga-Zaïre being in full Communion with the Church of England and with the Anglican Communion throughout the world, receives the Canonical Scriptures of the Old and New Testaments as being the ultimate rule and standard of faith, given by inspiration of God, and containing all things necessary for salvation.

(b) This Church holds the Faith of Christ as preached by the Apostles, summed up in the Creeds and confirmed by the undisputed General Councils of the Holy Catholic Church.

(c) It maintains its faith as embodied in the Doctrine, Sacraments and Discipline of the Church as they have been received by the Church of England and set forth in the Book of Common Prayer and the Ordinal and in the Articles of Religion commonly called the Thirty-Nine Articles. It accepts the principles of worship set forth in the Book of Common Prayer and disclaims any right to depart from the standards of Faith and Order or the principles of Worship set forth in the said formularies of the Church of England.

(d) No direction shall be made by the Provincial Assembly for the revision of any Prayer Book or Ordinal in use in a Diocese at the time of the inauguration of the Province without the approval of the Diocese concerned.

(e) The Church of Uganda, Rwanda, Burundi and Boga-Zaïre has power to accept, if it shall so determine through the Provincial Assembly, any alterations in the Book of Common Prayer and the Ordinal aforesaid and any additional formulations of Doctrine and Discipline which may hereafter be adopted by the Church of England or any other Church within the Anglican Communion.

(f) The Church of Uganda, Rwanda, Burundi and Boga-Zaïre through its Provincial Assembly may make and authorise such deviations from and additions or alternatives to the forms of service provided in the Book of Common Prayer and such new forms of service as may, in its judgement, be required to meet the needs of the Church of Uganda, Rwanda, Burundi and Boga-Zaïre and are consistent with the spirit and teaching of the said Book of Common Prayer.

(g) If questions of interpretation arise concerning Faith, Doctrine, Discipline and Worship, they shall be decided according to the provisions of this Constitution.

(h) The Diocesan Bishop shall have power to make such changes in the services provided for Public Worship and to authorise such special services in addition to those provided in the Book of Common Prayer as may in his judgement be desirable to meet the pastoral needs of his people, provided that such services do not depart from the doctrine of the Church of Uganda, Rwanda, Burundi and Boga-Zaïre.

(i) The jurisdiction to determine any matter concerning Faith, Doctrine and Worship is hereby vested in the House of Bishops constituted in accordance with this Constitution.

(j) If in the House of Bishops doubt or dispute arises concerning a matter of Faith, Doctrine or Worship which cannot be resolved with general unanimity the House may, or if two members of that House require in writing, shall, refer the question to the Anglican Consultative Council.

(k) The expression 'Anglican Consultative Council' includes any body, persons or person for the time being performing the appropriate functions of such Council, whether by delegation, or substitution, and which is or are approved for the purpose by the Provincial Assembly.

(1) The Provincial Assembly shall be constituted in accordance with the provisions of Article 5 hereof.

518

1973
Fundamentals (Melanesia)

The Constitution of the Church of the Province of Melanesia, Articles 1–2.

The Constitution of the Church of the Province of Melanesia (commonly called the Church of Melanesia).

The Diocese of Melanesia, formerly an Associated Missionary Diocese of the Church of the Province of New Zealand, has now withdrawn from that Province with the permission of General Synod of the Church of the Province of New Zealand.

At a Diocesan Conference held in Honiara, British Solomon Islands, on the 7th day of January in the year of our Lord 1973, the bishops and representatives of the other clergy and laity of the Diocese agreed to the setting up of a Province of Melanesia and a Constitution for this Province. Now, therefore, the bishops, clergy and laity assembled in Diocesan Conference accept as the Constitution of the Province of Melanesia the following: –

Article 1. *Foundations of Faith*

The following are the foundations of faith and practice which are acceptable by the Province of Melanesia. We accept and teach the faith of our Lord Jesus Christ and the teachings, sacraments and discipline of the One Holy Catholic and Apostolic Church as the Anglican Communion has received them. We accept the following as standards setting forth this faith and these teachings, sacraments and discipline: –

    1. The Holy Scriptures of the Old and New Testaments.

    2. The Catholic Creeds.

We also give honour to the teachings of the early Church, especially the decisions of those General Councils of the Church as are accepted by the Eastern and Western Church.

The Holy Scriptures are accepted as the final rule and standard of faith, given by inspiration of God and containing all things necessary to salvation. The Church of this Province has no right to alter or depart from these standards, but has the right to make alterations in its form of worship and discipline, so long as these are agreeable to Holy Scripture and the other standards of faith as the Anglican Communion has received them.

Article 2. *The Teaching of the Church*

In explaining the meaning of the standards of Faith, Teaching, Sacraments and Discipline accepted in Article 1 and in dealing with all questions on these matters and those of worship, the Church of the Province is not bound by any decisions except those of its own Church Courts provided in this Constitution.

519

1973
Church of the Province of the Indian Ocean

Who are the Anglicans?, ed. Charles Long, prepared for the Lambeth Conference, 1988 (Ohio, 1988), p. 19.

The Province of the Indian Ocean was founded in 1973. Prior to that the Seychelles and Mauritius formed one bishopric. Madagascar also had one bishop. The Anglican mission was first established in Mauritius in 1810 after the British captured the island from the French. From Mauritius, missionaries were sent out to the three islands. The Province is governed by a provincial synod which meets every four years. Between sessions a Standing Committee of Synod runs the diocese. The Archbishop is elected for a term of five years which is renewable.

520

1973
Communion with North India, Pakistan, and Bangladesh Churches

General Convention of the Episcopal Church in the United States of America, A Communion of Communions, *1973.*

Each Anglican Province has to agree communion with the United Churches. Here ECUSA extends its invitation to United Churches of the Indian Sub-Continent (cf. no. 432 on South India and no. 406, Old Catholics and Anglicans: the Bonn Agreement).

Resolved, That the Episcopal Church invite the Church of North India, the Church of Pakistan, and the Church of Bangladesh (Diocese of Dacca) to enter into full communion with it, on the principles of the 1931 Bonn Concordat; namely,

(a)   Each Church recognizes the catholicity and independence of the other, and maintains its own.

(b)   Each Church agrees to admit members of the other to participate in the sacraments.

(c)   Full communion[1] does not require from either Church the acceptance of all doctrinal opinions, sacramental devotion, or liturgical practice characteristic of the other, but implies that each believes the other to hold all the essentials of the Christian faith.

521

1974
Episcopal Church of the Sudan

Who are the Anglicans?, *ed. Charles Long, prepared for the Lambeth Conference, 1988 (Ohio, 1988), p. 27.*

Although the Church Missionary Society began work in Omdurman in 1899, in an overwhelming Muslim population, Christianity spread more rapidly among black Africans of the southern region. Until 1974 the Sudan was a single diocese under the Archbishop in Jerusalem. In 1974 it was divided into four dioceses, each under a

---

[1]   'Intercommunion' in the 1931 text. Cf. no. 588.

Sudanese bishop, and became an independent Province. The Church has suffered much in the last generation from almost continual civil and religious strife between north and south and from a constant flow of refugees in and out of the country.

522

1975
Covenants of unity

The covenant between the Church in Wales, the Methodist Church in Wales, the Presbyterian Church in Wales, the United Reformed Church (later joined by others).

The terms of the Covenant mean that the Church in Wales recognizes that its Covenant partners share with it in the same mission to the people of Wales,... within the Church of God, and that consequently the grace of God, through ministry and sacraments, is truly at work within all the Churches. Cf. nos. 386, 407, 409.

Confessing our faith in Jesus Christ as Lord and Saviour, and renewing our will to serve his mission in the world, our several churches have been brought into a new relationship with one another. Together we give thanks for all we have in common. Together we repent the sin of perpetuating our division. Together we make known our understanding of the obedience to which we are called:

1. (a) We recognize in one another the same faith in the gospel of Jesus Christ found in Holy Scripture, which the creeds of the ancient Church and other historic confessions are intended to safeguard. We recognize in one another the same desire to hold this faith in its fullness.

   (b) We intend so to act, speak, and serve together in obedience to the gospel that we may learn more of its fullness and make it known to others in contemporary terms and by credible witness.

2. (a) We recognize in one another the same awareness of God's calling to serve his gracious purpose for all mankind, with particular responsibility for this land and people.

   (b) We intend to work together for justice and peace at home and abroad, and for the spiritual and material well-being and personal freedom of all people.

3. (a) We recognize one another as within the one Church of Jesus Christ, pledged to serve His Kingdom, and sharing in the unity of the Spirit.

(b) We intend by the help of the same Spirit to overcome the divisions which impair our witness, impede God's mission, and obscure the gospel of man's salvation, and to manifest that unity which is in accordance with Christ's will.

4. (a) We recognize the members of all our churches as members of Christ in virtue of their common baptism and common calling to participate in the ministry of the whole Church.

(b) We intend to seek that form of common life which will enable each member to use the gifts bestowed upon him in the service of Christ's Kingdom.

5. (a) We recognize the ordained ministries of all our churches as true ministries of the word and sacraments, through which God's love is proclaimed, his grace mediated, and his Fatherly care exercised.

(b) We intend to seek an agreed pattern of ordained ministry which will serve the gospel in unity, manifest its continuity throughout the ages, and be accepted as far as may be by the Church throughout the world.

6. (a) We recognize in one another patterns of worship and sacramental life, marks of holiness and zeal, which are manifestly gifts of Christ.

(b) We intend to listen to one another and to study together the witness and practice of our various traditions, in order that the riches entrusted to us in separation may be preserved for the united Church which we seek.

7. (a) We recognize in one another the same concern for the good government of the Church for the fulfilment of its mission.

(b) We intend to seek a mode of Church government which will preserve the positive values for which each has stood, so that the common mind of the Church may be formed and carried into action through constitutional organs of corporate decision at every level of responsibility.

We do not yet know the form union will take. We approach our task with openness to the Spirit. We believe that God will guide his Church into ways of truth and peace, correcting, strengthening, and renewing it in accordance with the mind of Christ. We therefore urge all our members to accept one another in the Holy Spirit as Jesus Christ accepts us, and to avail themselves of every opportunity to grow together through common prayer and worship in mutual understanding and love so that in every place they may be renewed together for mission.

Accordingly we enter now into the solemn Covenant before God and with one another, to work and pray in common obedience to our Lord Jesus Christ, in order that by the Holy Spirit we may be brought into one visible Church to serve together in mission to the glory of God the Father.

523

1975
Church of the Province of Melanesia

Who are the Anglicans?, ed. Charles Long, prepared for the Lambeth Conference, 1988 (Ohio, 1988), p. 69.

The Anglican presence in Melanesia dates from 1849 when George Selwyn, first Bishop of New Zealand, toured the islands and brought back some young Melanesians to his school in Auckland. John Patteson became the first Bishop of Melanesia in 1861 and was murdered ten years later, probably as a result of blackbirding activities. The first Mission in Melanesia Headquarters was on Norfolk Island. Permanent stations were set up in Melanesia in the 1880s. The Melanesian Brotherhood was founded in 1925. The autonomous Province was founded in 1975.

524

1976
Enlarging or shrinking a Province (Papua New Guinea)

The Anglican Church of Papua New Guinea, Province of Papua New Guinea, Provincial Constitution, Article 1.

Article I, ...
b. The Provincial Council shall have power to admit to the Province any other Anglican Diocese that shall wish to join it; to

join the Province with other Anglican Dioceses or Provinces to form a new Province or Provinces; to divide the Province so as to form two or more new Provinces; to seek to enter a united or uniting Church; to transfer areas from one Diocese to another; to divide a Diocese into two or more Dioceses; to combine two or more Dioceses into one; to take areas from two or more Dioceses to form a new Diocese.

c. Any Diocese may leave the Province if its Diocesan Synod has asked for this at two successive meetings, at intervals of not less than a year, and if the Provincial Council is satisfied that: –

    1. The reasons stated are adequate.

    2. The departing Diocese will remain in fellowship with the Anglican Communion or with some Church that will commune with it.

d. If the Diocesan Synods and Provincial Council agree, the Province may enter into associations with other Provinces, Dioceses and Churches.

525

1976
Fundamentals (The Sudan)

The Constitution of the Province of the Episcopal Church of the Sudan.

Declarations of the Episcopal Church of the Sudan,
Article 2

(a) The Province of the Episcopal Church of the Sudan, being in full communion with the Anglican Communion throughout the world, holds the Faith of Christ as taught in Holy Scriptures, preached by the Apostles, summed up in the Creed and confirmed by the undisputed General Councils of the Holy Catholic Church. Which Faith as embodied in the Doctrine, Sacraments, and Discipline of the Church, it maintains according as the Church of England has received and taught the same in the Book of Common Prayer, and the Ordering of Bishops, Priests and Deacons. Provided that nothing herein contained shall prevent this Province from accepting, if it shall so determine, any alterations in the formularies of the Church which may be adopted by the Church of England; or from making at any time such adaptations of, or additions to, the services of the Church as may, in its judgement, be required by the circumstances of this Province and shall be consistent with the spirit and teaching of the Book of Common Prayer.

(b) The Province of the Episcopal Church of the Sudan accepts the Archbishop of Canterbury as holding the first place among the Metropolitans of the Anglican Communion.

(c) In conformity with Christian doctrine, the Province of the Episcopal Church of the Sudan proclaims the equal value of all men before the righteous love of God, and while careful to provide for the special needs of different people, committed to its charge, allows no discrimination on grounds of racial difference only, in the membership and government of the Church.

(d) If any question arises in the Province of the Episcopal Church of the Sudan concerning its adherence to the standards of Faith and Order of the principles of Worship herein set forth, or to the spirit and teaching of the Book of Common Prayer, the General Synod may refer the question to the Archbishop of Canterbury, together with the Secretary General of the Anglican Consultative Council, for advice.

526

1976
Toward a mutual recognition of members

General Convention of the Episcopal Church in the United States of America, in A Communion of Communions, *1976.*

Resolved, that this 65th General Convention receive with gratitude the document transmitted to it by the Consultation on Church Union entitled 'Toward a Mutual Recognition of Members: An Affirmation', welcoming the agreement as representing the traditional Anglican teaching that 'The Church is the Body of which Jesus Christ is the Head and all baptized persons are the members'.

527

1976
Communion with the Church of South India

General Convention of the Episcopal Church in the United States of America, in A Communion of Communions, *1976.*

Cf. no. 520 on North India, Pakistan and Bangladesh.

Resolved, that this Church enter into communion with the Church of South India and instructs the Secretary of Convention to communicate this action to the proper authorities in the Church of South India.

528

1976
Conversations with Baptists

General Convention of the Episcopal Church in the United States of America, in A Communion of Communions, *1976.*

Resolved, that the Joint Commission on Ecumenical Relations establish ongoing conversations with the several Baptist associations, churches and conventions through those agencies which are appropriate in order to create a better understanding and communication, and to foster where possible, local cooperation in ministry.

529

1976
Authority in the Church

First Anglican-Roman Catholic International Commission, Authority in the Church *(Venice, 1976), 1–3.*

1. The confession of Christ as Lord is the heart of the Christian faith. To him God has given all authority in heaven and on earth. As Lord of the Church he bestows the Holy Spirit to create a communion of men with God and with one another. To bring this

koinonia to perfection is God's eternal purpose. The Church exists to serve the fulfilment of this purpose when God will be all in all.
2. Through the gift of the Spirit the apostolic community came to recognize in the words and deeds of Jesus the saving activity of God and their mission to proclaim to all men the good news of salvation. Therefore they preached Jesus through whom God has spoken finally to men. Assisted by the Holy Spirit they transmitted what they had heard and seen of the life and words of Jesus and their interpretation of his redemptive work. Consequently the inspired documents in which this is related came to be accepted by the Church as a normative record of the authentic foundation of the faith. To these the Church has recourse for the inspiration of its life and mission; to these the Church refers its teaching and practice. Through these written words the authority of the Word of God is conveyed. Entrusted with these documents, the Christian community is enabled by the Holy Spirit to live out the gospel and so to be led into all truth. It is therefore given the capacity to assess its faith and life and to speak to the world in the name of Christ. Shared commitment and belief create a common mind in determining how the gospel should be interpreted and obeyed. By reference to this common faith each person tests the truth of his own belief.
3. The Spirit of the risen Lord, who indwells the Christian community, continues to maintain the people of God in obedience to the Father's will. He safeguards their faithfulness to the revelation of Jesus Christ and equips them for their mission in the world. By this action of the Holy Spirit the authority of the Lord is active in the Church. Through incorporation into Christ and obedience to him Christians are made open to one another and assume mutual obligations. Since the Lordship of Christ is universal, the community also bears a responsibility towards all mankind, which demands participation in all that promotes the good of society and responsiveness to every form of human need. The common life in the body of Christ equips the community and each of its members with what they need to fulfil this responsibility: they are enabled so to live that the authority of Christ will be mediated through them. This is Christian authority: when Christians so act and speak, men perceive the authoritative word of Christ.

530

1976
Primacy

First   Anglican–Roman   Catholic   International   Commission,
Authority in the Church *(Venice, 1976), 21.*

See 279, 369, 606 on primacy.

21. If primacy is to be a genuine expression of *episcope* it will
foster the *koinonia* by helping the bishops in their task of apostolic
leadership both in their local church and in the Church universal.
Primacy fulfils its purpose by helping the churches to listen to one
another, to grow in love and unity, and to strive together towards
the fullness of Christian life and witness; it respects and promotes
Christian freedom and spontaneity; it does not seek uniformity
where diversity is legitimate, or centralize administration to the
detriment of local churches.
A primate exercises his ministry not in isolation but in collegial
association with his brother bishops. His intervention in the affairs
of a local church should not be made in such a way as to usurp the
responsibility of its bishop.

531

1976
The Episcopal Church in Jerusalem and the Middle East

Who are the Anglicans?, *ed. Charles Long, prepared for the
Lambeth Conference, 1988 (Ohio, 1988), p. 65.*

The Jerusalem Bishopric was founded in 1841 and became an
Archbishopric in 1957. Its primary mission was to form links of
friendship with the ancient churches of the area and to provide
chaplaincy service to expatriate communities. There was also a
slow but steady growth of missionary work among Palestinian
Christians and various non-Christian populations, supported by
Church Missionary Society and other missionary societies. The
Province was founded in 1976, as part of a general reorganization
of Anglican work in four dioceses, linked together for mutual

support and to further the indigenization of the church. It is governed by a Central Synod under a President Bishop who is elected for a five-year term.

532

1977
Doctrine, worship and the rights of man

The Anglican Church of Papua New Guinea, Province of Papua New Guinea, Provincial Constitution, Article 2–3.

II. *Doctrine and Worship*

We accept and teach the faith of our Lord Jesus Christ and the teachings, sacramants and discipline of the One, Holy, Catholic and Apostolic Church as the Anglican Communion has received them. We accept the following as standards setting forth this faith and these teachings, sacraments and discipline:

a. The Holy Scriptures of the Old and New Testaments as containing all things necessary to Salvation and as being the rule and final standard of faith.

b. The teaching and practice of the early Church including the decisions of the first four General Councils.

c. The Apostles' Creed as the baptismal Symbol; and the Nicene Creed as the sufficient statement of Christian Faith.

d. The principles of worship as set out in the Book of Common Prayer. However, the Anglican Church of Papua New Guinea claims the right to make alterations in its form of worship so long as they are consistent with the spirit and teaching of the Book of Common Prayer.

III. *The Dignity and Rights of Man*

The Anglican Church of Papua New Guinea declares that all people are of equal value in the sight of God and will take care to provide for the needs of all people committed to its charge and allows no discrimination in the membership and government of the Church solely on the grounds of race or tribe.

533

1977
Fundamentals (Nigeria)

Draft Constitution of the Church of the Province of Nigeria, Fundamental Declarations.

I. (a) The Church of the Province of Nigeria, hereafter called the Church of this Province, being in full communion with the See of Canterbury and with all dioceses, provinces and regional churches which are in full communion with the See of Canterbury, holds and maintains the Faith, Doctrine, Sacraments and Discipline of the Church of Christ as the Lord hath commanded in His Holy Word, and as the same are received and taught by the Church of England in the Book of Common Prayer and the Ordinal of the year 1662 and in the Thirty-Nine Articles of Religion.

(b) The Church of this Province has power to accept, if it shall so determine, any alterations in the aforementioned formularies which may hereafter be adopted by the Church of England.

(c) The Church of this Province has power so to order its discipline as to banish and drive away all erroneous and strange doctrines which are contrary to God's word as understood and interpreted in the aforementioned formularies.

(d) In the interpretation of the aforementioned standards and formularies and in all questions of Faith, Doctrine and Discipline, the Church of this Province is not bound by any decisions other than those of its own ecclesiastical tribunals.

II. (a) The Church of this Province holds as its standard of worship and authorizes for general use the Book of Common Prayer of the Church of England.

(b) The Church of this Province has power to make and authorize such deviations from the additions or alternatives to the forms of service provided in the said book and such new forms of service as may be required to meet the needs of this Province and are neither contrary to the doctrinal standards named in Declaration I nor indicative of any departure from them.

534

1977
The Anglican Church of Papua New Guinea

Who are the Anglicans?, *ed. Charles Long, prepared for the Lambeth Conference, 1988 (Ohio, 1988), p. 73.*

The Anglican Church came to Papua New Guinea with the arrival of Fathers Albert Maclaren and Copeland King in 1891, near Dogura. In 1898 Papua New Guinea was organized as a missionary diocese of the Church in Australia. The first Papuan priest, Fr. Peter Rautamara, was ordained in 1914, and in 1960 the first indigenous bishop (George Ambo) was consecrated. The Province was founded on February 27, 1977. It is governed by a Provincial Council and House of Bishops which meets once a year.

535

1978
Preparing for Holy Communion

Exhortation, The Church of England in Australia, An Australian Prayer Book, *Buchanan, p. 209.*

This is modelled on the Exhortation in the *Book of Common Prayer.*

It is intended, on [...day] next, to administer to all who shall be devoutly disposed, the most comforting sacrament of the body and blood of Christ, to be received by them in remembrance of his meritorious cross and passion, by which alone we obtain remission of our sins, and are made partakers of the kingdom of heaven. We must thank our heavenly Father that he has given his Son our Saviour Jesus Christ, not only to die for us, but also to be our spiritual food and sustenance in that holy sacrament. This is so divine and strengthening a thing to those who receive it worthily, and so dangerous to those who presume to receive it unworthily, that it is my duty to exhort you, in the meantime, to consider the dignity of that holy mystery and the peril of the unworthy receiving of it, so that you may come holy and clean to such a heavenly feast. The way to prepare yourselves is to examine your lives by the rule of God's commandments, and wherever you see you have offended in will, word, or action, there to repent and confess your sin to God, with full purpose of amendment of life. And if you think that you have injured not only God but also your neighbour, then you must ask his forgiveness as well, and make good, to the full extent of your ability, any injury or wrong that he has suffered at your hands. You must likewise forgive others who have injured you, if you desire God to forgive your offences. For if you receive the Holy Communion without God's forgiveness, you only increase the judgement under which you already stand. So then, should any of you be a blasphemer of God, a hinderer of his word, an adulterer, or be in malice, or envy, or in any other serious offence, repent of your sin, or else do not come to that holy table...

And since no one should come to the Lord's table without a full trust in God's mercy and a quiet conscience, if there is any of you who cannot quieten his conscience by these means, but needs further help or counsel, let him come to me, or to some other discreet and learned minister of God's word, and open his grief, that by the ministry of God's holy Word he may receive the benefit of absolution, together with spiritual counsel and advice, and so be quietened in his conscience, and resolve all scruples and doubts.

536

1978
Ordination and ministry in the Church of God

Henry Chadwick, Episcopacy in the New Testament and early Church, *address to the Lambeth Conference, 1978.*

Cf. no. 422.

The ancient Church understands ordination as more than a local authorisation limited to the local community where the ordination has taken place. The orders of episcopate, presbyterate, and diaconate are universally extended orders; that is to say, a presbyter ordained at Corinth needs only a letter of recommendation by his own bishop to be accepted, without reordination, in, say, Rome or Ephesus, and allowed to officiate there with the agreement of the local bishop. The priesthood in which he shares belongs to the universal Church and at his ordination other presbyters join the bishop in the laying on of hands. A newly elected bishop, chosen by his flock, is duly entrusted with the charism of episcopal office by other bishops, who represent, therefore, this universal recognition. This is in line with the New Testament records in which all those commissioned to exercise pastoral oversight are appointed by those who themselves have previously received such a commission. Nevertheless, the ancient Church had a deep sense of the intimate bond between a bishop and his own flock. He is, or ought to feel himself, married to his church.

537

1978
The Church's responsibility in society

Resolution 1.5, Lambeth Conference, 1978.

'Stewardship' is a Christian responsibility taken seriously in the New Testament and the early Church and central to the ancient ministry of deacons.

1.5... We must direct our efforts to the achievement of a kind of society where the economy is not based on waste, but stewardship, not on consumerism but on conservation, one concerned not only with work but with the right use of leisure. We may need to contemplate a paradox — an increasing use of appropriate technology, while returning, where possible, to many of the values of pre-industrial society.

538

1978
Human rights

Resolution 3, Lambeth Conference, 1978.

The Conference regards the matter of human rights and dignity as of capital and universal importance. We send forth the following message as expressing our convictions in Christ for the human family world-wide. We deplore and condemn the evils of racism and tribalism, economic exploitation and social injustice, torture, detention without trial and the taking of human lives as contrary to the teaching and example of our Lord in the Gospel. Man is made in the image of God and must not be exploited. In many parts of the world these evils are so rampant that they deter the development of a humane society.

539

1978
The Church and war

Resolution 5, Lambeth Conference, 1978.

5. [Christians are] to take with the utmost seriousness the question which the teaching of Jesus places against violence in human relationships and the use of armed force by those who would follow him, and the example of redemptive love which the Cross holds before all people.

540

1978
The companionship of prayer

Resolution 6, Lambeth Conference, 1978.

6. Since prayer, both corporate and personal, is central to the Christian life, and therefore essential in the renewal of the Church, the fulfilling of the Christian mission, and the search for justice and peace, the Conference gives thanks for all who are endeavouring to increase and strengthen the companionship of prayer throughout the world, and joins in calling the whole Christian community to share personal prayer daily and corporate services of prayer on regular and special occasions. We also invite all who desire and labour for justice and peace in this world to join with us each day in a moment of prayerful recollection of the needs for a just peace among all people.

541

1978
The Holy Spirit in the Church

Resolution 7, Lambeth Conference, 1978.

This Resolution seeks to maintain the balance between 'charism' and 'order', that is, between the ordered corporate life of the Church and the imperative to remain open to the free movement of the Holy Spirit.

3. We rejoice at the prompting of God's Spirit within the many expressions of ecumenicity among Christians, for the new forms of Christian communal life springing up and for Christian witness on behalf of world peace and the affirmation of freedom and human dignity.

4....

a. We all should share fully and faithfully in the balanced corporate and sacramental life of the local parish church. Informal services of prayer and praise need this enrichment in the same way as the sacramental life needs the enrichment of informal prayer and praise.

b. We all should ensure that reading and meditation of the Bible be part of the normal life of the parish and be accompanied by appropriate study of scholarly background material so that the Scripture is understood in its proper context. Those who search to understand the scholarly background material in their reading of the Bible should ensure that they do so under the guidance of the Holy Spirit, so that the Scripture is understood in its proper context.

c. We all should search out ways to identify with those who suffer and are poor, and be involved personally in efforts to bring them justice, liberation, healing, and new life in Christ.

542

1978
Provincial autonomy and authority in the Anglican Communion

Resolution 11, Lambeth Conference, 1978.

This Resolution reflects some disquiet over any exercise of provincial autonomy in matters which concern the whole Anglican Communion and which is not undertaken with prior consultation and catholic intention. Cf. no. 587 from the 1988 Conference.

The Conference advises member Churches not to take action regarding issues which are of concern to the whole Anglican Communion without consultation with a Lambeth Conference or with the episcopate through the Primates' Committee, and requests the primates to initiate a study of the nature of authority within the Anglican Communion.

543

1978
Episcopal ministry

Resolutions 18, 19, Lambeth Conference, 1978.

18. *Public ministry of the bishop*

The Conference affirms that a bishop is called to be one with the apostles in proclaiming Christ's resurrection and interpreting the Gospel, and to testify to Christ's sovereignty as Lord of lords and King of kings. In order to do this effectively, he will give major attention to his public ministry. Reflecting the ministry of the prophets, he will have a concern for the well-being of the whole community (especially of those at a disadvantage) not primarily for the advantage or protection of the Church community. The bishop should be ready to be present in secular situations, to give time to the necessary study, to find skilled advisers and to take sides publicly if necessary (in ecumenical partnership if at all possible) about issues which concern justice, mercy, and truth. Members of the Church should be prepared to see that the bishop is supported in such a ministry.

19. *Training for bishops*

The Conference asks each member Church to provide training for bishops after election in order more adequately to prepare them for their office, and to provide opportunities for continuing education.

544

1978
The ministry of women

Resolutions 20, 21, 22, Lambeth Conference, 1978.

Compare Resolution 11 above (no. 542) and no. 587 from the 1988 Conference. The ordination of women raises unprecedented difficulties, with which the 1978 Lambeth Conference is grappling here, in connection with the maintenance of mutual recognition of ministry within the Anglican Communion.

20. *Women in the diaconate*

The Conference recommends, in accordance with resolution 32 (c) of the Lambeth Conference of 1968, those member Churches which do not at present ordain women as deacons now to consider making the necessary legal and liturgical changes to enable them to do so, instead of admitting them to a separate order of deaconesses.

21. *Women in the priesthood*

1. The Conference notes that since the last Lambeth Conference in 1968, the diocese of Hong Kong, the Anglican Church of Canada, the Episcopal Church in the United States of America, and the Church of the Province of New Zealand have admitted women to the presbyterate, and that eight other member Churches of the Anglican Communion have now either agreed or approved in principle or stated that there are either no fundamental or no theological objections to the ordination of women to the historic threefold ministry of the Church. We also note that other of its member Churches have not yet made a decision on the matter. Others again have clearly stated that they do hold fundamental objections to the ordination of women to the historic threefold ministry of the Church....

3. The Conference also recognizes

a) the autonomy of each of its member Churches, acknowledging the legal right of each Church to make its own decision about the appropriateness of admitting women to Holy Orders;

b) that such provincial action in this matter has consequences of the utmost significance for the Anglican Communion as a whole.

4. The Conference affirms its commitment to the preservation of unity within and between all member Churches of the Anglican Communion. 5. The Conference therefore
   a) encourages all member Churches of the Anglican Communion to continue in communion with one another, notwithstanding the admission of women (whether at present or in the future) to the ordained ministry of some member Churches;
   b) in circumstances in which the issue of the ordination of women has caused, or may cause, problems of conscience, urges that every action possible be taken to ensure that all baptized members of the Church continue to be in communion with their bishop and that every opportunity be given for all members to work together in the mission of the Church irrespective of their convictions regarding this issue;...

8. This conference urges that further discussion about the ordination of women be held within a wider consideration of theological issues of ministry and priesthood....

22. *Women in the episcopate*

While recognizing that a member Church of the Anglican Communion may wish to consecrate a woman to the episcopate,[1] and accepting that such member Church must act in accordance with its own constitution, the Conference recommends that no decision to consecrate be taken without consultation with the episcopate through the primates and overwhelming support in any member Church and in the diocese concerned, lest the bishop's office should become a cause of disunity instead of a focus of unity.

545

1978
Ecumenical relations

Resolution 28, Lambeth Conference, 1978.

Compare nos. 589ff. for examples of Resolutions made by the 1988 Conference forwarding these hopes.

---

[1] This has now taken place. See no. 603.

28. *Ecumenical relationships*

The Conference:

1. re-affirms the readiness of the Anglican Communion as already expressed in resolution 44 (c) of the Lambeth Conference of 1968 (with reference to the Uppsala Assembly of the World Council of Churches), to 'work for the time when a genuinely universal council may once more speak for all Christians';

2. acknowledges the pressing need stated by the Nairobi Assembly of the WCC[1] that we should develop more truly sustained and sustaining relationships among the Churches, as we look towards the time when we can enjoy full conciliar fellowship (see *Breaking Barriers: Nairobi 1975*, p. 60);

3. encourages the member Churches of the Anglican Communion to pursue with perseverance and hopefulness the search for full communion and mutual recognition of ministries between themselves and other World Confessional Families and the Methodist and Baptist Churches both internationally and locally, on the basis of the Lambeth Quadrilateral and the counsel offered by successive meetings of the Anglican Consultative Council;

4. calls on member Churches of the Anglican Communion to review their commitment to ecumenical structure as well as bilateral conversations at various levels with a view to strengthening the common advance by all Churches to the goal of visible unity.

546

1979
Some constitutional articles (Kenya)

The Church of the Province of Kenya, Constitution as revised at 26 November, 1979, Articles 2–3.

Article II — *On Doctrine and Worship*

(a) The Church of this Province, being in full communion with the Anglican Churches throughout the World, receives all the

---

[1]   World Council of Churches.

Canonical Scriptures of the Old and New Testaments, given by inspiration of God, as containing all things necessary for salvation and as being the ultimate rule and standard of faith and life of the Church.

(b) This Church holds the Faith of Christ as preached by the Apostles, summed up in the Apostles' Creed, and confirmed by the first Four General Councils of the Holy Catholic Church.

(c) The Church of this Province, being a wholly autonomous and self-governing part of the Body of Christ, affirms its right to draw up its own formularies of faith, and to set forth in terms that it considers suitable to the present day and to the needs of the peoples of this Province, the Faith which this church holds; and also to determine those forms of liturgical worship by which it judges that its peoples can best be edified and led into maturity of Christian life and expression, and in which God will be glorified.

(d) Until such time as these formularies can be drawn up and accepted, and the liturgical life of the Church of this Province can be established on its own foundations, the Church of this Province is content to declare its acceptance of the Doctrine, Sacraments and Discipline of the Church as these are set forth in the Book of Common Prayer of 1662 and in the Form of Ordering Bishops, Priests and Deacons attached to the same Book. It accepts the Principles of Worship set forth in that Book as consonant with the Gospel of Christ, and as the source from which Anglican Christians in East Africa have long been nurtured. By this declaration it affirms its continuity with its own past, and its fellowship with all the other Churches of the Anglican tradition.

(e) On the one hand, the Church of this Province does not interpret this declaration as implying any limitation on its right and duty to discover for itself the truth as it is in Jesus, and to express that truth in life and in liturgy. On the other hand, the Church of this Province disclaims any wish or intention to depart from the standards of Faith and Order so nobly set forth in these venerable documents of the Church.

(f) The Church of this Province may make and authorise such deviations from and additions or alternatives to the forms of service provided in the said Book of Common Prayer and such new forms of Service as may, in its judgement, be required to meet the needs of the Church in this Province and shall be consistent with the spirit and teaching of the said Book of Common Prayer.

(g) In the interpretation of the aforementioned standards and formularies and in all questions of Faith, Doctrine, Discipline, and Worship, the Church of this Province is not bound by any decisions other than those of the Provincial Synod.

(h) If an issue of great importance has been raised in the field of Faith and Order and the Provincial Synod has been unable to reach agreement on the matter and to find an acceptable solution, the Archbishop shall, at the request of the Provincial Synod communicate the problem and the issues raised to the Anglican Consultative Council or such other body as the Provincial Synod may select for advice. On receipt of such advice the Archbishop shall commit all the relevant documents to a commission, which may be the Provincial Tribunal for the hearing of Appeals or a commission especially appointed, with instructions to draw up a report. On receiving the report, the Bishop of the Province shall draw up a statement for presentation to the Provincial Synod at its next meeting. If the Provincial Synod accept the statement, this shall become part of the law and practice of the Province. If the Provincial Synod fails to reach agreement, no further action shall be taken. In either case the decision of the Provincial Synod shall be final.

(i) The absence from the foregoing sections of this Article of any reference to the Thirty-Nine Articles shall not preclude the Synod of any Diocese including reference to that document in its own Diocesan Constitution and from requiring subscription to it in the oaths and declarations made at the ordination or licensing of its clergy.

Article III — *On the Value and Dignity of Man*

The Church of this Province proclaims that all men are of equal value and dignity in the sight of God, and, while careful to provide for the special needs of different people committed to its charge, allows no discrimination in the membership and government of the Church based on grounds of racial difference.

547

1979
Eucharistic prayer

The Eucharistic Liturgy of the Episcopal Church in the United States of America, Eucharistic Prayer A, Buchanan, p. 143.

Holy and gracious Father: In your infinite love you made us for yourself; and, when we had fallen into sin and become subject to evil and death, you, in your mercy, sent Jesus Christ, your only eternal Son, to share our human nature, to live and die as one of us, to reconcile us to you, the God and Father of all. He stretched out his arms upon the cross, and offered himself, in obedience to your will, a perfect sacrifice for the whole world.

At the following words concerning the bread, the Celebrant is to hold it, or lay a hand upon it; and at the words concerning the cup, to hold or place a hand upon the cup and any other vessel containing wine to be consecrated.

On the night he was handed over to suffering and death, our Lord Jesus Christ took bread; and when he had given thanks to you, he broke it, and gave it to his disciples, and said, 'Take, eat: This is my Body, which is given for you. Do this for the remembrance of me.' After supper he took the cup of wine; and when he had given thanks, he gave it to them, and said, 'Drink this, all of you: This is my Blood of the new Covenant, which is shed for you and for many for the forgiveness of sins. Whenever you drink it, do this for the remembrance of me.' Therefore we proclaim the mystery of faith:

Christ has died.
Christ is risen.
Christ will come again.

We celebrate the memorial of our redemption, O Father, in this sacrifice of praise and thanksgiving. Recalling his death, resurrection, and ascension, we offer you these gifts. Sanctify them by your Holy Spirit to be for your people the Body and Blood of your Son, the holy food and drink of new and unending life in him. Sanctify us also that we may faithfully receive this holy Sacrament, and serve you in unity, constancy, and peace; and at the last day bring us with all your saints into the joy of your eternal kingdom. All this we ask through your Son Jesus Christ. By him, and with him, and in him, in the unity of the Holy Spirit all honour and glory is yours, Almighty Father, now and for ever. *Amen.*

548

1979
Racism

The governing body of the Church in Wales; a Report on racism by the advisory commission on Church and Society (1979), p. 7.

While racial prejudice arises from lack of self knowledge, and from historical experience, and is essentially psychological, racist beliefs, while having a psychological function and basis, are essentially ideological; they are analogous to heresies rather than to individual moral faults. They contradict the biblical doctrine of man and flout the second great commandment. In this connection we would single out particularly any suggestion that races can be ranked in any order of human worth. We would also maintain that the suggestion that differences in racial behaviour or culture result from genetic differences between races is unreasonable and unlikely to be true. The Church has a duty to condemn such suggestions or beliefs which will have adverse consequences for our behaviour towards our fellow men. They not only feed on racial prejudice in individuals; they help to generate it. They are, in the strict sense of the word, pernicious.

549

1979
Church in the Province of Nigeria

Who are the Anglicans?, ed. Charles Long, prepared for the Lambeth Conference, 1988 (Ohio, 1988), p. 23.

The first Anglicans in what is now Nigeria were freed slaves from Sierra Leone. In the 1840s the Church Missionary Society followed and soon established extensive educational and evangelistic work. The first African bishop was consecrated in 1864. Anglicans are now found in every part of the country and are the largest Christian body after the Roman Catholics. The Province was established in 1979, by division from the Province of West Africa (1951).

550

1980
Intercession at the Eucharist

The Eucharistic Liturgy of the Province of the West Indies, Prayers, Form E, Buchanan, pp. 163–5.

Leader: Let us pray for the fellowship of the Church of Christ, and for all God's creatures.
With all who confess the name of Jesus, as Lord and Saviour, we offer our prayers and praises, in Spirit and in truth. Father in Heaven,
All: Hear our prayer.

Leader: With Jesus Christ, our Great High priest, who ever lives to intercede for us, we uphold all ministers of God's Word and Sacraments, that they may fulfill their high calling in the Faith. Father in Heaven,
All: Hear our prayer.

Leader: We pray for the unfailing guidance of the Holy Spirit on those who are called to interpret and expound the will of the Lord to others. Father in Heaven,
All: Hear our prayer.

Leader: We pray for the organizations, within the fellowship of the Body of Christ, that their work may edify the people of God, and bear faithful witness to the Gospel. Father in Heaven,
All: Hear our prayer.

Leader: We pray for all persons who do not share our confession of faith, that with courage, truth and love we may work together with them, and promote the common good. Father in Heaven,
All: Hear our prayer.

Leader: For the leaders of our country, and all who make decisions on our behalf, that they may be filled with the fruit of the Spirit, to direct our affairs in righteousness and peace. Father in Heaven,
All: Hear our prayer.

Leader: For our Judges, Magistrates and all who administer justice, that in all things they may seek to do your will, and to promote the rights and freedom of your people. Father in Heaven,
All: Hear our prayer.

Leader: In our schools, and in all other places of learning, may true knowledge, sound wisdom, and godly discipline ever be found. Father in Heaven,
All: Hear our prayer.

Leader: To the poor, the hungry, the unemployed, the persecuted immigrants, and the victims of racial oppression, may God in Christ help us all to bring relief and just protection. Father in Heaven,
All: Hear our prayer.

Leader: To all who suffer now from pain and disease, from human discomfort and misery, may God in Christ bring healing and joy, for the renewal of their faith. Father in Heaven,
All: Hear our prayer.

Leader: That we may use aright the fullness of the Earth, that our pursuits in science, and the advancement of our skills, may ever be in the service of that true humanity, which is created in the image of God. Father in Heaven,
All: Hear our prayer.

Leader: That we may never become slaves of money, or of the lust for power, but may rather strive for victory through the power of love. Father in Heaven,
All: Hear our prayer.

Leader: That with all who belong to the communion of saints, both living and departed, we may ever rejoice in the blessed assurance of that hope, which has been won for us in Christ, Father in Heaven,
All: Receive these our prayers in the name of your dear Son, even Jesus Christ our Lord. Amen.

551

1980
Changing the liturgy

The Alternative Service Book of the Church of England, 1980, Preface.

This Alternative Service Book is the product of many years' development of patterns of worship tried out in the churches. Cf. examples from other Churches of the Communion in this volume.

The Church of England has traditionally sought to maintain a balance between the old and the new. For the first time since the Act of Uniformity this balance in public worship is now officially expressed in two books, rather than in one. The Alternative Service Book (1980), as its name implies, is intended to supplement the Book of Common Prayer, not to supersede it. The addition of a date to its title may serve as a reminder that revision and adaptation of the Church's worship are continuous processes, and that any liturgy, no matter how timeless its qualities, also belongs to a particular period and culture. It is a remarkable fact that for over three hundred years and despite all attempts at revision, the Book of Common Prayer has remained the acknowledged norm for public worship in the Church of England, as well as a model and inspiration for worship throughout most of the Anglican Communion. Rapid social and intellectual changes, however, together with a world-wide reawakening of interest in liturgy, have made it desirable that new understandings of worship should find expression in new forms and styles. Christians have become readier to accept that, even within a single Church, unity need no longer be seen to entail strict uniformity of practice. The provision of alternative services is to be welcomed as an enrichment of the Church's life rather than as a threat to its integrity. As long ago as 1906 a Royal Commission reported that 'the law of public worship in the Church of England is too narrow for the religious life of the present generation'. Three-quarters of a century later it can be said with even greater certainty that the gospel of the living Christ is too rich in content, and the spiritual needs of his people are too diverse, for a single form of worship to suffice. There are few parts of the Church which have not been affected by the recent phase of liturgical revision. The Church of England set up its own Liturgical Commission in 1955, and subsequently authorized new services for experimental use under the Prayer Book (Alternative and Other Services) Measure, 1965. Since then the Commission has prepared revised forms, sometimes as many as three distinct series, for almost every aspect of the Church's worship. Those which are judged to be most generally useful are here gathered together in a single book. Its publication marks a pause in a programme of liturgical business which has occupied, first the Convocations and the House of Laity, and latterly the General Synod, for more than fifteen years. This new book of services is the first fully authorized alternative to the Book of Common Prayer. Under the terms of the Worship and Doctrine Measure, 1974, from which such services now derive their legal status, the Book of Common Prayer retains its authority as a doctrinal standard. According to Canon A5, 'The doctrine of the Church of England is grounded in the holy Scriptures, and in such teachings of the ancient Fathers and Councils of the Church as are agreeable to the said Scriptures. In particular such doctrine is to be found in the Thirty-Nine Articles of Religion, the Book of Common Prayer, and the Ordinal.' New forms of worship do not erode the historical foundations of the Church's faith, nor render respect for them any less appropriate than it was before.

Nevertheless, Christians are formed by the way in which they pray, and the way they choose to pray expresses what they are. Hence those who seek to know the mind of the Church of England in the last quarter of the twentieth century will find it in this book as certainly as in those earlier formulations. Few books can have had their origin in so much, and such detailed, public debate. With the exception of the Psalter and the readings at the Holy Communion, the wording of every part of the book has been subject to repeated scrutiny by the General Synod. But words, even agreed words, are only the beginning of worship. Those who use them do well to recognize their transience and imperfection; to treat them as a ladder, not a goal; to acknowledge their power in shaping faith and kindling devotion, without claiming that they are fully adequate to the task. Only the grace of God can make up what is lacking in the faltering words of men. It is in reliance on such grace that this book is offered to the Church, in the hope that God's people may find in it a means in our day to worship him with honest minds and thankful hearts.

552

1980
The Apostles' Creed

The Alternative Service Book of the Church of England, 1980.

This is the text of the Apostles' Creed as used in Morning and Evening Prayer.

I believe in God, the Father almighty, creator of heaven and earth. I believe in Jesus Christ, his only Son, our Lord. He was conceived by the power of the Holy Spirit and born of the Virgin Mary. He suffered under Pontius Pilate, was crucified, died, and was buried. He descended to the dead. On the third day he rose again. He ascended into heaven, and is seated at the right hand of the Father. He will come again to judge the living and the dead.
I believe in the Holy Spirit, the holy catholic Church, the communion of saints, the forgiveness of sins, the resurrection of the body, and the life everlasting. Amen.

553

1980
A Eucharistic Prayer for use with the sick

The Alternative Service Book of the Church of England, 1980.

The need for brevity at the sick-bed gives us a distilled version of the liturgical essentials in this order of service. The intention is to avoid where possible the reservation of the sacrament after the parish Eucharist to be taken later to the sick, by actually celebrating the Eucharist with the sick person and friends or relatives.

President: The Lord be with you *or* The Lord is here.
All: And also with you. *or* His Spirit is with us.

President: Lift up your hearts.
All: We lift them to the Lord.

President: Let us give thanks to the Lord our God.
All: It is right to give him thanks and praise.

President: It is indeed right, it is our duty and our joy, to give you thanks, holy Father, through Jesus Christ our Lord. Through him you have created us in your image; through him you have freed us from sin and death; through him you have made us your own people by the gift of the Holy Spirit. Hear us, Father, through Christ your Son our Lord and grant that by the power of your Holy Spirit these gifts of bread and wine may be to us his body and his blood;

Who in the same night that he was betrayed, took bread and gave you thanks; he broke it and gave it to his disciples, saying, Take, eat; this is my body which is given for you; do this in remembrance of me. In the same way, after supper he took the cup and gave you thanks; he gave it to them, saying, Drink this, all of you; this is my blood of the new covenant, which is shed for you and for many for the forgiveness of sins. Do this, as often as you drink it, in remembrance of me. Therefore, Father, proclaiming his saving death and resurrection and looking for his coming in glory, we celebrate with this bread and this cup his one perfect sacrifice. Accept through him, our great high priest, this our sacrifice of thanks and praise, and grant that we who eat this bread and drink this cup may be renewed by your Spirit and grow into his likeness; Through Jesus Christ our Lord, by whom, and with whom, and in whom, all honour and glory be yours, Father, now and for ever. *Amen.*

554

1980
Conditional baptism

Alternative Service Book of the Church of England, 1980.

This provision allows for baptism in cases of uncertainty, without there being any suggestion of rebaptism. Cf. nos. 495 and 605.

If it is not certain that a person was baptized with water in the name of the Father, and the Son, and of the Holy Spirit, then the usual service of baptism is used, but the form of words at the baptism... shall be

N, if you have not already been baptized, I baptize you in the name of the Father, and of the Son, and of the Holy Spirit. Amen.

555

1980
The Church of the Province of Burundi, Rwanda and Zaïre

Who are the Anglicans?, ed. Charles Long, Prepared for the Lambeth Conference, 1988 (Ohio, 1988), p. 13.

This Church was formed as a result of the division of the former Province of Uganda, Rwandi, Burundi and Boga-Zaire in 1980. The first Archbishop was Bezaleri Ndahura. The three countries making up the Province are French-speaking. All were formerly ruled by Belgium and the majority of the citizens are Roman Catholic. Anglican work in Rwanda was founded by Church Missionary Society medical missionaries from Uganda in 1924. A Ugandan evangelist, Apolo Kivebulayo, at the turn of the century crossed snow capped mountains to preach to the people of the Ituri rain forests in Boga-Zaire. The Province is governed by a Synod which meets every four years and by a Standing Committee and House of Bishops which meet twice yearly.

556

1980
Marriage

The Alternative Service Book of the Church of England, 1980.

The bride and bridegroom stand before the priest, and the priest says

We have come together in the presence of God, to witness the marriage of *N* and *N*, to ask his blessing on them, and to share in their joy. Our Lord Jesus Christ was himself a guest at a wedding in Cana of Galilee, and through his Spirit he is with us now. The Scriptures teach us that marriage is a gift of God in creation and a means of his grace, a holy mystery in which man and woman become one flesh. It is God's purpose that, as husband and wife give themselves to each other in love throughout their lives, they shall be united in that love as Christ is united with his Church. Marriage is given, that husband and wife may comfort and help each other, living faithfully together in need and in plenty, in sorrow and in joy. It is given, that with delight and tenderness they may know each other in love, and through the joy of their bodily union, may strengthen the union of their hearts and lives. It is given, that they may have children and be blessed in caring for them and bringing them up in accordance with God's will, to his praise and glory. In marriage husband and wife belong to one another, and they begin a new life together in the community. It is a way of life that all should honour, and it must not be undertaken carelessly, lightly, or selfishly, but reverently, responsibly, and after serious thought. This is the way of life, created and hallowed by God, that *N* and *N* are now to begin. They will each give their consent to the other; they will join hands and exchange solemn vows, and in token of this they will give and receive a ring. Therefore, on this their wedding day we pray with them, that, strengthened and guided by God, they may fulfil his purpose for the whole of their earthly life together.

557

1981
Maori bishopric

Considerations arising out of the setting up of a Maori bishopric in the Province of New Zealand, *Southern African Anglican Theological Commission, 1981.*

This text raises the important question, increasingly urgent in the modern world, of the need to ensure provision of episcopal oversight appropriate to local cultural needs and the issue of the conflict which may arise between such needs and the territorial integrity of the diocese with its bishop.

From time to time oversight has been provided within the Anglican communion for certain language or racial groups, where the boundaries of the oversight overlapped with the normal diocesan or parochial areas. Examples of this are the Anglican chaplaincies in Europe including the Diocese of Gibraltar, the proposal for a bishop for the Order of Ethiopia in South Africa, and the newly-formed diocese of Aotearoa in New Zealand.

The questions that need to be posed in relation to these developments are the following:

1. Has this oversight been provided for pastoral and practical reasons (e.g. language, population distribution etc.)?

2. Have reasons from the world's agenda pressurised the church into separate areas of oversight (e.g. questions of resurgent nationalism, political pressures, cultural exclusivism)?

3. Have all normal methods of oversight been fully explored?

4. Finally, have Paul's words in Ephesians 2.11ff. been fully accepted by the communities concerned?

558

1982
Pastoral care and the ministry of the laity

'Go... and make disciples',[1] *The Report of the Commission for a Plan of Advance for the Diocese of Colombo of the Church of Ceylon, published by the Diocese of Colombo, Church of Ceylon (1982), pp. 29–31.*

III C. Pastoral Care and Evangelism

1. The Parish

1. The Parish is the basic pastoral unit of the Diocese. One of its primary concerns now appears to be to help the prayer life of its members through corporate worship. But there is a great and widespread need for wider pastoral care in perhaps all our parishes, according to the responses received to our enquiries concerning Pastoral needs. There is a serious challenge here both to the clergy and to the laity cooperating with each other for, under the Good Shepherd, all his disciples both clergy and laity are called to be under-shepherds helping each other through mutual pastoral care in home, church, place of work and wherever else there is pastoral need e.g. in politics and business. Few seem to be aware that there is a great need for pastoral care specially in these latter fields.

2. Perhaps there is also a fresh understanding needed of what a parish is and a new conceptual framework for a parish must be found not as a group of persons who are members of a congregation, paying subscriptions and attending church services, but rather as persons-in-communion in a particular neighbourhood belonging to the Family of God and the Body of Christ. Such a parish will be a fellowship — with a spirit and message from those

---

[1]   Matthew 28.19

who are within to those who are without, even if some within the area belong to other churches or to no church at all. Considering this there has to be a new vision and new understanding of the structure of parish life with a basic sense of mission involved in the very concept of a parish which today many parishes seem to lack.

3. In a parish which is such a missionary fellowship, faith in Christ and the love for Christ and for all people should dominate not only all its services but all its programmes. The members of such a parish would be constantly concerned with their quality of life and their relationships one with another rather than with mere attendance at church services and participation in church projects, collecting funds, paying subscriptions and voting or being voted in for office.

4. Therefore one of the primary concerns of pastoral care, understood as a joint responsibility of both clergy and people and specially of the people who are the church's officers, council and committee members, is both to promote relevant and meaningful forms of worship in their richness and variety and to preserve the essential fellowship of the congregation (without which worship becomes superficial and hypocritical). A question that should be asked in every parish is how friendly the ordinary worshipper is to the stranger who might come into a service of worship and how he is helped to be 'at home' in the church...

2. The Role of the Parish Clergy

1. In planning the Church's work for advance, renewal and reform we trust that the clergy will fulfil their important and wider role of leadership in such a manner as to promote active lay participation in pastoral care in every parish. It is a widespread conviction that clergy should avoid the temptation to dominate in the things they do in parish life and should function more as guides and enablers, so as to stimulate a better understanding of the Christian gospel with discussion and action undertaken by the congregation. A priest cannot undertake alone the many and varied services concerned with the welfare and development of all those in a parish, be they Christians or not. But he certainly has a responsibility to create an awareness among the laity of the need for such services and stimulate them to fulfil an active role in the formulation and implementation of the manifold projects and programmes which should be a natural part of the life of every parish.

559

1982
The 'Filioque Clause'

The South African Provincial Synod (1982).

The clause 'and the Son' added to the Creed in the West, but not in the East, was the main cause of the schism of 1054, which has never been healed. It is now beginning to be omitted by Western Churches for reasons 1 and 2 stated here.

The South African Provincial Synod (1982) passed the following resolution: That this Synod, noting developments within the Anglican and Roman Catholic Communions since 1979, agrees to the principle that the Nicene Creed should be recited omitting the Filioque clause for the following reasons:

1. that in this form it is a right statement of the Christian faith concerning the eternal relationships within the Godhead;

2. that we see this as a gesture of love and reconciliation towards our brothers in the Eastern Church;

3. that this is a concession to the inadequacy of language and the difficulty of accurate translation into the various South African languages.

Synod therefore requests the Archbishop of Cape Town to forward this resolution to the Secretary-General of the Anglican Consultative Council and requests the South African Anglican Theological Commission to prepare material so that the issue may be discussed and understood in the dioceses of the Province.

560

1982
The Episcopal Church in the United States of America

The Constitution of the Episcopal Church in the United States of America, originally adopted 1789 and subsequently amended.

We include here a series of extracts on bishops because of the topicality at the time of going to press of ECUSA's decision to consecrate its first woman bishop and the ensuing debate about alternative patterns of episcopal oversight (such as the use of 'Episcopal Visitors' to provide pastoral care for those who cannot accept the ministry of a woman bishop or of priests ordained by her). See in particular Article II.3 here.

Constitution of ECUSA, Article I.

Sect. 1. There shall be a General Convention of this Church, consisting of the House of Bishops and the House of Deputies, which Houses shall sit and deliberate separately; and in all deliberations freedom of debate shall be allowed. Either House may originate and propose legislation, and all acts of the Convention shall be adopted and be authenticated by both Houses.

Sect. 2. Each Bishop of this Church having jurisdiction, every Bishop Coadjutor, every Suffragan Bishop, every Assistant Bishop, and every bishop who by reason of advanced age or bodily infirmity, or who, under an election to an office created by the General Convention, or for reasons of mission strategy determined by action of the General Convention or the House of Bishops, has resigned his jurisdiction, shall have a seat and a vote in the House of Bishops. A majority of all bishops entitled to vote, exclusive of bishops who have resigned their jurisdiction or positions, shall be necessary to constitute a quorum for the transaction of business.

Sect. 3. At the General Convention next before the expiration of the term of office of the Presiding Bishop, it shall elect the Presiding Bishop of the Church. The House of Bishops shall choose one of the bishops of this Church to be the Presiding Bishop of the Church by a vote of majority of all bishops, excluding retired bishops not present, except that whenever two-thirds of the House of Bishops are present a majority vote shall suffice, such choice being subject to confirmation by the House of Deputies. His term and tenure of office and duties and particulars of his election not inconsistent with the preceding provisions shall be prescribed by the Canons of the General Convention.

Sect. 4. The Church in each Diocese which has been admitted to union with the General Convention shall be entitled to representation in the House of Deputies by not more than four Presbyters or deacons, canonically resident in the Diocese, and not more than four Lay Persons, communicants of this Church, in good standing in the Diocese but not necessarily domiciled in the Diocese; but the General Convention by Canon may reduce the representation to not fewer than two Deputies in each order. Each Diocese shall prescribe the manner in which the Deputies shall be chosen.

The Church in each Missionary Diocese beyond the territory of the United States of America, which shall have been established by the House of Bishops or by the Constitution, and the Convocation of the American Churches in Europe, shall each be entitled to representation in the House of Deputies equal to that of other Dioceses, subject to all the qualifications, and with all of the rights, of Deputies, except as otherwise provided in this Constitution. Each such Missionary Diocese, and the Convocation of the American Churches in Europe, shall prescribe the manner in which its Deputies shall be chosen.

To constitute a quorum for the transaction of business, the Clerical order shall be represented by at least one Deputy in each of a majority of the Dioceses entitles to representation, and the Lay order shall likewise be represented by at least one Deputy in each of a majority of the Dioceses entitled to representation.

On any question, the vote of a majority of Deputies present shall suffice, unless otherwise ordered by this Constitution; or, in cases not specifically provided for by the Constitution, by Canons requiring more than a majority; or unless the Clerical or the Lay representation from three or more Dioceses require that the vote be taken by orders. In all cases of a vote by orders, the two orders shall vote separately, each Diocese having one vote in the Clerical order and one vote in the Lay order; and the concurrence of the votes of the two orders shall be necessary to constitute a vote of the House. No action of either order shall pass in the affirmative unless it receives the majority of all votes cast, and unless the sum of all the affirmative votes shall exceed the sum of other votes by at least one whole vote.

Article II.

Sect. 1. In every Diocese the Bishop or the Bishop Coadjutor shall be chosen agreeably to rules prescribed by the Convention of that Diocese. Bishops of Missionary Dioceses shall be chosen in accordance with the Canons of the General Convention...

Sect. 3. A bishop shall confine the exercise of his office to his own Diocese, unless he shall have been requested to perform episcopal acts in another Diocese by the Ecclesiastical Authority thereof, or unless he shall have been authorized by the House of Bishops, or by the Presiding Bishop by its direction, to act temporarily in case of need within any territory not yet organized into Dioceses of this Church.

Sect. 4. It shall be lawful for a Diocese, with consent of the Bishop of that Diocese, to elect one or more Suffragan Bishops, without right of succession, and with seat and vote in the House of Bishops. A Suffragan Bishop shall be consecrated and hold office under such conditions and limitations other than those provided in this Article as may be provided by Canons of the General Convention. He shall be eligible as Bishop or Bishop Coadjutor of a Diocese, or as a Suffragan in another Diocese, or may be elected by the House of Bishops as a Bishop of a Missionary Diocese...

Sect. 6. A bishop may not resign his jurisdiction without the consent of the House of Bishops.

Sect. 8. A bishop exercising jurisdiction as the Ordinary, or as the Bishop Coadjutor, of a Diocese or Missionary Diocese, may be elected as Bishop, Bishop Coadjutor, or Suffragan Bishop, of another Diocese, or may be elected by the House of Bishops as a Bishop of a Missionary Diocese; *Provided*, that he shall have served no less than five years in his present jurisdiction; and *Provided always*, that before acceptance of such election he shall tender to the House of Bishops his resignation of his jurisdiction in the Diocese in which he is then serving, subject to the required consents of the bishops and Standing Committees of the Church, and also, if he be a Bishop Coadjutor, the right of succession therein, and such resignation, and renunciation of the right of succession in the case of a Bishop Coadjutor, shall be consented to by the House of Bishops.

561

1982
The mutual recognition of Baptism

Baptism, Eucharist and Ministry: Report of the Faith and Order Commission, *World Council of Churches (Lima, 1982), Baptism, 15–16.*

15. Churches are increasingly recognizing one another's baptism as the one baptism into Christ when Jesus Christ has been confessed as Lord by the candidate or, in the case of infant baptism, when confession has been made by the church (parents, guardians,

godparents and congregation) and affirmed later by personal faith and commitment. Mutual recognition of baptism is acknowledged as an important sign and means of expressing the baptismal unity given in Christ. Wherever possible, mutual recognition should be expressed explicitly by the churches.

16. In order to overcome their differences, believer baptists and those who practice infant baptism should reconsider certain aspects of their practices. The first may seek to express more visibly the fact that children are placed under the protection of God's grace. The latter must guard themselves against the practice of apparently indiscriminate baptism and take more seriously their responsibility for the nurture of baptized children to mature commitment to Christ.

562

1982
The mutual recognition of ordained Ministries

Baptism, Eucharist and Ministry: Report of the Faith and Order Commission, *World Council of Churches (Lima, 1982), Ministry, 51–5.*

51. In order to advance toward the mutual recognition of ministries, deliberate efforts are required. All churches need to examine the forms of ordained ministry and the degree to which the churches are faithful to its original intentions. Churches must be prepared to renew their understanding and their practice of the ordained ministry.

52. Among the issues that need to be worked on as Churches move towards mutual recognition of ministries, that of apostolic succession is of particular importance. Churches in ecumenical conversations can recognize their respective ordained ministries if they are mutually assured of their intention to transmit the ministry of Word and sacrament in continuity with apostolic times. The act of transmission should be performed in accordance with the apostolic tradition, which includes the invocation of the Spirit and the laying on of hands.

53. In order to achieve mutual recognition, different steps are required of different churches. For example:

a) Churches which have preserved their episcopal succession are asked to recognize both the apostolic content of the ordained ministry which exists in churches which have not maintained such succession and also the existence in these churches of a ministry of *episkopé* in various forms.

b) Churches without the episcopal succession, and living in faithful continuity with the apostolic faith and mission, have a ministry of Word and sacrament, as is evident from the belief, practice and life of those churches. These churches are asked to realize that the continuity with the Church of the apostles finds profound expression in the successive laying on of hands by bishops and that, though they may not lack the continuity of the apostolic tradition, this sign will strengthen and deepen that continuity. They may need to recover the sign of the episcopal succession.

54. Some churches ordain both men and women, others ordain only men. Differences on this issue raise obstacles to the mutual recognition of ministries. But those obstacles must not be regarded as substantive hindrance for further efforts towards mutual recognition. Openness to each other holds the possibility that the Spirit may well speak to one Church through the insights of another. Ecumenical consideration, therefore, should encourage, not restrain, the facing of this question.

55. The mutual recognition of Churches and their ministries implies decision by the appropriate authorities and a liturgical act from which point unity would be publicly manifest. Several forms of such public act have been proposed: mutual laying on of hands, eucharistic concelebration, solemn worship without a particular rite of recognition, the reading of a text of union during the course of a celebration. No one liturgical form would be absolutely required, but in any case it would be necessary to proclaim the accomplishment of mutual recognition publicly. The common celebration of the Eucharist would certainly be the place for such an act.

563

1982
Principles of liturgical revision

Introduction to the Scottish Liturgy, 1982.

This text emphasizes the interdependence of liturgy and theology of which Anglican tradition has always been conscious. Cf. no. 569 for the ecumenical dimension of this understanding.

We believe that the proper starting point for liturgical revision lies in theology. A theological analysis of the nature of the service, when conducted in the light of the tradition of the Church universal, should indicate clearly enough those elements that are essential to a particular service and should therefore in no way be tampered with, and those that are optional and therefore subject to constructive change at any given time. Once we have identified the essential constituent elements of the service, we can look again to the tradition of the Church to offer an appropriate framework in which to organise them. Having identified both what we want to say and the order in which we are to say it, we can then proceed to search for a structural model which may enable expressive words, actions, gestures and postures to be given equal and balanced weight.

The next step should be to identify the most suitable variable elements and to see how they should best be placed within the newly thought-out structure. It is at this point, and at this point alone that liturgy may be allowed to become, like politics, the science of the possible. No effort should be spared in making sure that within the limits of our ability the final product is a thing of spontaneous and balanced beauty. The language must be as evocative as we can make it. The vertical and horizontal dimensions must be carefully matched. Local knowledge should guide the individual congregations in choosing variables suitable to the time and the occasion, and in matching periods of silence with carefully selected music and parts said by the priest with parts said by the congregation. Above all, the basic structure of the service should remain clear throughout. No amount of embellishments, however cherished, must be allowed to obscure this.

564

1983
The Inauguration of the
Province of the Southern Cone of America
(Iglesia Anglicana del Cono Sur de América)

Report of the inauguration in Estandarte Cristão, *Journal of the Episcopal Church of Brazil (May, 1983).*

La Iglesia Anglicana del Cono Sur de América, la provincia número 27 de la Comunión Anglicana, quedó inaugurada aquí en la Catedral de San Juan Bautista el 30 de abril con un solemne culto eucarístico. La nueva provincia, que comprende las diócesis de Argentina, Norte Argentino, Paraguay, Chile y Perú y Bolivia, se constituye para 'hacer efectiva la consulta, coordinación, colaboración y servicio entre sus Diócesis'. En el oficio inaugural al que concurrieron maś de 400 personas, los obispos diocesanos de las cinco jurisdicciones anglicanas dieron su consentimiento para la formación de la nueva provincia y prometieron fortalecer y desarrollar los vínculos provinciales. La autoridad metropolítica de estas diócesis antes residía en el Arzobispo de Cantórbery, pero ésta fue transferida al Consejo Anglicano Sud Americano (CASA) en 1974. Desde entonces las diócesis han funcionado como 'Provincia en fromación'. CASA continuará como organización de contacto entre la nueva provincia y la Iglesia Episcopal de Brasil. En el sermón inaugural, el Revmo. Omar Ortiz, obispo asistente de Paraguay, recordó los pioneros y mártires que por más de 150 años sembraron la semilla del Evangelio. 'Elevamos alabanzas y gratitud al Padre por la fidelidad de los hombres y mujeres de Dios que nos han precedido', dijo Ortiz. En especial recordó al Capitán de la Marina Británica Allen Gardiner que junto con sus seis acompañantes pereció en la Tierra del Fuego en 1851. Una nota emocionante del culto inaugural fue el oir las lecturas de las Escrituras y las oraciones de intercesión en mataco, toba-pilaga, guaraní, lengua y mapudongo, idiomas delas comunidades indígenas en las que la Iglesia Anglicana ha trabajado por muchos años. El Obispo David Sheppard de Liverpool, ostentó la representacion del Arzobispo de Cantórbery. Entre los invitados especiales se encontraban el Cardenal Arzobispo de Buenos Aires, Juan Aramburu; el obispo metodista y presidente del Consejo Latinoamericano de Iglesias, Federico Pagura y otros clérigos luteranos, ortodoxos y evangélicos. La inauguración de esta provincia estaba señalada para el año pasado pero tuvo que ser pospuesta debido al conflicto armado argentino-británico sobre las islas Malvinas (Falklands).

Por esa razón s etemió que ciudadanos ingleses que debián asistir a la inauguración no pudieran hacerlo por falta de visas pero a última hora todas las visas fueron concedidas. La inauguración tuvo lugar durante cinco días de conferencias en los que los 93 delegados e invitados de otras partes del mundo discutieron el rol de la Iglesia en el mundo de hoy, la identidad anglicana, los cambios litúrgicos y la educación teológica ministerial.

Ronald Maitland, arcediano de Córdoba, presentó un trabajo en el que delineó a grandes razgos las principales características de la obra anglicana en el Cono Sur. 'Somos una iglesia pequeña, dispareja, con influencias foráneas, inmadura, insegura y dependiente', dijo Maitland. Añadió que como cristianos, los anglicanos no deben vivir de ilusiones sino de realidades y que a pesar de estas características la nueva provincia debe ser un instrumento de unificatión en medio de la diversidad existente. Señaló que en los años futuros la provincia debe hacer énfasis en lo positivo, delinear une estrategia global y reafirmar su catolicidad en una región tan fragmentada como es el Cono Sur. El Dr. Arnoldo Canclini, bautista argentino, pronunció una conferencia en la que señaló importantes momentos históricos de la presencia anglicana en América del Sur y la contribución que hombres como William C. Morris hicieron en medio del pueblo. Canclini terminó diciendo que los anglicanos no deben vivir del recuerdo de pioneros y mártires sino que deben 'hacer historia' aún más gloriosa que la de sus antepasados.

El Obispo David Sheppard de Liverpool, dio una conferencia sobre la ciudad y el Evangelio en la que dijo que la Iglesia está llamada por Cristo a estar al lado de los pobres y oprimidos. Señaló que la iglesia tiene que ser santa, católica y apostólica si quiere ser fiel a su misión histórica. 'Cristo mostró una opción preferencial por los pobres y nosotros debemos seguir se ejemplo', dijo Sheppard. Durante los días de convivencia se celebraron varios talleres que discutieron temas de interés común. (Véanse sus recomendaciones más adelante.) El primer sínodo de la Provincia del Cono Sur de América fue constituido el día de la inauguración, en el cual se ratificó la constitución y cánones que regirán la provincia, y también se ratificó el Consejo Ejecutivo electo. El Pbispo David Leake, del Norte Argentino, fue aclamado como Obispo Primado de la nueva provincia. En sus comentarios finales dijo: –Necesitamos acentuar la educatión teológica. Estudiar mejo el aspecto sacramental del ministerio ordenado y el ministerio de los laicos. Necesitamos una institución teológica residencial. – Estamos en la última etapa de tener obispos extranjeros, necesitamos más obispos nacionales. – Necesitamos estar más conscientes de lo que significan los derechos humanos. La Biblia está llena de referencias sobre este tema. – Necesitamos un anglicanismo latino. Necesitamos ser misioneros. Dios quiera que pronto podamos enviar nuestros propios misioneros a otras tierras. – Tenemos que trabajar con los jóvenes. El 90 por ciento de los habitantes de nuestros países tienen menos de 22 años.

— Tenemos que tener más comunicación con el resto de la Comunión Anglicana y con otros hermanos cristianos. Necesitamos un boletín internacional en castellano que nos informe y nos inspire del trabajo que en nombre de Dios se hace en otras partes del mundo. – Necesitamos que nuestras reuniones sean verdaderos encuentros de compañerismo y crecimiento espiritual. Necesitamos animarnos en la obra a que Dios nos ha llamado. La oración debe ser siempre un recurso indispensable. – Necesitamos llevar a la práctica todas las buenas ideas que aquí hemos discutido. Muy bonito estar todos juntos pero ahora tenemos que regresar a la realidad del mundo del dolor, del desempleo, de la injusticia y de la cárcel. Que el Señor nos dé su gracia para que le seamos fieles y llevemos esta obra adelante para su honra y gloria. Que la Provincia del Cono Sur sea un instrumento eficaz para la extensión de su Reino.

The Anglican Church of the Southern Cone of America, Province no. 27 of the Anglican Community, was inaugurated here in the Cathedral of St John the Baptist on 30 April with a solemn Eucharist. The new Province, comprising the dioceses of Argentina, North Argentina, Paraguay, Chile and Peru and Bolivia, is constituted in order to 'make possible consultation, co-ordination, collaboration and service among the dioceses'. At the inaugural service, at which more than 400 people were present, the diocesan bishops of the five Anglican districts gave their consent to the formation of a new Province and promised to strengthen and develop provincial links. The Metropolitan authority of these dioceses previously resided in the Archbishop of Canterbury, but this was transferred to the Anglican Council of South America (CASA) in 1974. Since then the dioceses have functioned as a 'Province in process of formation'. CASA will continue to exist as a link organization between the new Province and the Episcopal Church of Brazil. In his inaugural sermon, the Very Rev. Omar Ortiz, assistant Bishop of Paraguay, remembered the pioneers and martyrs who for more than a hundred and fifty years sowed the seed of the Gospel. 'We praise and thank the Father for the faithfulness of God's men and women who have preceded us,' said Ortiz. He especially remembered the British Naval Captain Allen Gardiner who, together with six companions, perished in Tierra del Fuego in 1851. A moving feature of the inaugural service was to hear readings from the Scriptures and prayers for intercession in Mataco, Toba-pilaga, Guarani and Mapudongo, the languages of the indigenous communities amongst which the Anglican Church has worked for many years. Bishop David Sheppard was present representing the Archbishop of Canterbury. Amongst the special guests were: the Cardinal Archbishop of Buenos Aires, Juan Aramburu; the Methodist Bishop and President of the Latin-American Council of Churches, Federico Pagura, and other Lutheran, Orthodox and Evangelical churchmen. The inauguration of this Province was originally planned for last year, but it had to be postponed on account of the armed conflict over the Falkland Islands.

For this reason it was feared that British subjects who ought to have been present at the inauguration would not be able to come for lack of visas, but at the last moment all the visas wre granted.

The inauguration was held over five days of lectures in which the 93 delegates and guests from other parts of the world discussed the role of the Church in the modern world, Anglican identity, liturgical changes and theological training for the ministry.

Ronald Maitland, Archdeacon of Córdoba, gave a talk in which he defined in broad outline the main characteristics of the work of the Anglican community in the Southern Cone. 'We are a small church,' he said, 'disparate and containing outside influences, immature, unsure of ourselves and dependent.' He added that, as Christians, Anglicans should not live in their dreams but in reality, and that despite this description of it, the new Province should be an instrument for unification in the midst of existing diversity. He said that in future years the Province should lay emphasis on the positive side of things, work out an all-embracing strategy and reaffirm its catholic qualities in this highly fragmented region which makes up the Southern Cone.

Dr Arnoldo Canclini, an Argentine Baptist, gave a lecture in which he referred to important moments in the history of the Anglican presence in South America and the contribution that men like William C. Morris made among people. Canclini ended by saying that Anglicans should not live on the memory of pioneers and martyrs, but that they should themselves make 'history' which would be even more admirable than that of their predecessors.

Bishop David Sheppard gave a lecture on the city and the Gospel, in which he said that the Church is called by Christ to be with the poor and the oppressed. He said that the Church has to be holy, catholic and apostolic if it wishes to be faithful to its historic mission. 'Christ showed a preference for the poor, and we must follow his example,' said Sheppard.

During the time we were together several workshops were held, at which topics of common interest were discussed... The first Synod of the Province of the Southern Cone of America was constituted on the day of the inauguration at which the constitution and canons that will govern the Province were ratified, and the Executive Council elect was also ratified. Bishop David Leake, from North Argentina, was elected Primate Bishop of .the new Province by acclamation. In his final comments he said: – We need to put strong emphasis on theological training. We must study more deeply the sacramental side of the ordained ministry and the lay ministry. We need a residential theological college. – We are now in the final phase of the time of foreign bishops; we need more native-born bishops. – We have to be more aware of what is meant by human rights. The Bible is full of references to this matter. – We need a Latin-American form of Anglicanism. We need missionaries. May God grant that we may soon be able to send our own missionaries into other lands. – We have to work with young people. 90% of the inhabitants of our countries are less than 22 years old.

We must have more communication with the rest of the Anglican Community and with other Christian brothers and sisters. We need an international bulletin in the Spanish language to keep us up-to-date and to inspire us by the example of the work done in God's name in other parts of the world. – Our meetings have to be true meetings of companionship and spiritual growth. We must take courage in the work to which God has called us. Prayer should always be our indispensable resort. – We need to put into practice all the fine ideas we have discussed here. It is all very nice to be here all together, but now we have to return to the reality of the world of pain, of unemployment, of injustice and of the prison. May the Lord give us his Grace to make us faithful to him and carry forward this work for his honour and glory. May the Province of the Southern Cone be an effective instrument for the spread of his Kingdom.

565

1983
Intercession at the Eucharist

The Anglican Province of Papua and New Guinea, Buchanan, p. 239.

The priest or one or more of the people shall offer the Prayers of the Church.

Reader: Let us pray:
Almighty God, you have taught us to give thanks for all people;
we thank you for... Father we thank you
People: Through Jesus Christ our Lord.

Reader: You have promised to hear the prayers of those who ask
in faith, we pray for all our brothers and sisters in Christ
throughout the world... and that your whole Church may grow in
unity and love; Lord, in your mercy
People: Hear our prayer.

Reader: For this Province of Papua New Guinea, especially for the
work of the Church in...; Lord, in your mercy
People: Hear our prayer.

Reader: For... our bishop(s); for all our priests and deacons; For
Evangelists, Church Councillors and other lay workers; For the
Brothers and Sisters of Religious Communities; For the members
of this congregation; Lord, in your mercy
People: Hear our prayer.

Reader: For those who have lost you, that they may find you
again; For those who have rejected you, that they may repent;
For unbelievers, that they may come to know the truth in Christ;
Lord, in your mercy
People: Hear our prayer.

Reader: For peace and justice throughout the world; For the
leaders of all nations, especially for our Queen Elizabeth; and her
deputy here... our Governor General. For our nation, Papua New
Guinea; For those in authority... For this place... and for all who
live here; Lord, in your mercy
People: Hear our prayer.

Reader: For our homes, and for all parents and children; For
teachers, and all who lead others by their words, writings and
actions; For students that they may know wisdom and truth; Lord,
in your mercy
People: Hear our prayer.

Reader: For all men and women in their daily work; For our food
and crops, that they may grow well; For the businesses and
industries of our nation; For all who travel by land, sea and air;
Lord, in your mercy
People: Hear our prayer.

Reader: That you may give healing and comfort to those who are sick or suffering... sorrowful or needy... worried or frightened... and that you may bless all who serve them...; Lord, in your mercy
People: Hear our prayer.

Reader: For our ancestors, for our fathers in the faith, and for all Christian people who have died... that they may have your light and peace; Lord, in your mercy
People: Hear our prayer.

Reader: For ourselves that we may follow the holy saints and martyrs... in being good soldiers and servants of Christ, and that we may have a holy and happy death, rest in paradise, and share in your glory.
People: Grant these prayers of ours, merciful Father, for the sake of your Son, our Saviour, Jesus Christ. Amen.

566

1983
Intercession at the Eucharist

The Eucharistic Liturgy of the Province of West Africa, Second Litany, Buchanan, pp. 184–5.

Let us pray.
For the peace that is from above and for the salvation of our souls; let us pray to the Lord.
All: Lord, have mercy.

Celebrant: For the welfare of God's people; for the unity of the Church, and for love to live together as brethren and to reveal God's glory in the world; let us pray to the Lord.
All: Lord, have mercy.

Celebrant: For our bishops, priests and deacons, especially N. our Archbishop and N. our bishop; that with a good heart and a pure conscience they may fulfil their ministry; let us pray to the Lord.
All: Lord, have mercy.

Celebrant: For our rulers and all in authority in our land; that they may govern us according to the will of God; let us pray to the Lord.
All: Lord, have mercy.

Celebrant: For the sick, the suffering, the sorrowful, the dying; let us pray to the Lord.
All: Lord, have mercy.

Celebrant: For the poor, the hungry, orphans and widows and those who suffer persecution for their faith; let us pray to the Lord.
All: Lord, have mercy.

Celebrant: For ourselves and all who confess the name of Christ; that we may show forth the excellence of Him who called us out of darkness into His marvellous light; let us pray to the Lord.
All: Lord, have mercy.

Celebrant: For all who have served God here and now rest in the sleep of peace, and for the faithful witness of the saints in every age; that with them we may enter into the fullness of His unending joy; let us pray to the Lord.
All: Lord, graciously have mercy. Amen.

Celebrant: Almighty and eternal God, the fountain of all wisdom, who know our needs before we ask, and our ignorance in making our requests before you; have compassion on our weakness; may it please you to give us, because of the blood of your Son Jesus Christ, those things, which because of our blindness we cannot ask, and because of our unworthiness we dare not ask; through the same Jesus Christ our Lord and Saviour.
All: Amen.

567

1983
Baptism

A guide produced by the South African Anglican Theological Commission, *September, 1983*.

Cf. no. 495 on the question of re-baptism.

Should a person, having received 're-baptism', wish nonetheless to remain a member of the Anglican Church, pastoral guidance will need to be given with a view to helping such a person find the right way forward. He may be moved to repentance and renunciation of the 'second baptism' as a mistake. He may come to understand the 'second baptism' in purely symbolic terms as an outward expression of his new found faith and not as a denial of his prior baptism. The purpose behind such pastoral guidance would not be to exercise a harsh and unsympathetic discipline, but instead to seek clarity of understanding and to help the person concerned to see the seriousness of his first and only baptism, together with all that has flowed from it in further spiritual growth and experience.

Some have asked whether the Church of the Province of South Africa could not itself allow for immersion in water as a symbolic action, for those who may wish to give expression to their new-found faith in this way. The reason why this cannot be allowed is that such an action is in great danger of being confused with baptism itself. The Church would prefer to see new-found faith in Christ and life in the Spirit expressing itself in testimony and good works, in reaffirmation of baptismal vows (as at the Easter vigil), in sacramental confession and in frequent participation in the Eucharist. Pastoral guidance should be given in helping the faithful into these directions of spiritual growth, rather than into an unnecessary and questionable experience of immersion in water which invariably looks like a new baptism. It is far better to build on what is already there than to give an impression that what is already there is irrelevant. This is particularly true of the foundation event of baptism in the life and pilgrimage of a Christian.

568

1984
The Election of a Bishop (Bermuda)

Constitution of the Synod of the Anglican Church of Bermuda, 1984.

Methods of choosing bishops have varied a great deal in the history of the Church. But the selected candidate has normally been consecrated by a Metropolitan and at least two other bishops, for a specific pastoral charge.

15. (a) When the office of bishop falls vacant the Archbishop of Canterbury in his Appellate Jurisdiction shall issue a mandate requiring that a special session of the Synod shall be summoned within one month by the Commissary, or if there be no Commissary by the Archdeacon, or if there be no Archdeacon by the senior incumbent, to appoint a Committee of six persons, to be known as the Vacancy in See Committee, to prepare a list of names for the consideration of the Synod;

(b) the Vacancy in See Committee shall consist of three clergymen to be appointed by the House of Clergy and three laymen to be appointed by the House of Laity;

(c) the Vacancy in See Committee shall appoint its own Chairman, who shall be a member of the Committee;

(d) the Vacancy in See Committee shall receive information concerning all those who are nominated to it, and prepare a statement setting forth the age, training and experience and other relevant information of each candidate and shall bring such information regarding all the proposed candidates before the Synod;

(e) each candidate shall be proposed and seconded in writing by a member of the Synod. The written permission of each candidate must be submitted to the Vacancy in See Committee;

(f) within two months of the meeting called to set up the Vacancy in See Committee a further meeting of the Synod shall be called for the election of the bishop by the Commissary, or failing him by the Archdeacon, or failing him by the senior incumbent;

(g) two weeks before such meeting the Vacancy in See Committee shall send to each member of the Synod a confidential statement setting out the names and qualifications of those who have been nominated as is provided in (d) above;

(h) at the meeting of the Synod called to elect the bishop each proposed name shall be formally proposed and seconded, and no speeches shall be permitted;

(i) only those candidates who have been nominated through the Vacancy in See Committee shall be considered;

(j) no election for filling the vacancy in the bishopric of the Diocese shall be valid unless not less than half of all the members of the House of Clergy and not less than half of the members of the House of Laity be present, nor unless a majority of not less than two thirds of each House present and voting shall vote in favour of any one candidate;

(k) the name of each of the proposed candidates shall be placed before the Synod, and each member of Synod shall be entitled to vote for one candidate only;

(l) the vote shall be by secret ballot. The Chairman shall appoint tellers;

(m) the name of the priest so elected shall be communicated to the Archbishop of Canterbury, who may approve or disapprove his election and if necessary give directions for his consecration;

(n) if no candidate has received sufficient votes for election the Synod shall meet again in Special Synod, when the procedure shall be as at the first session;

(o) if at the second session no candidate has received sufficient votes for election the Synod shall meet again in a Special Synod, when the procedure shall be as at the first session;

(p) if at the third session no candidate has received sufficient votes for election the choice of a bishop shall be made by the Archbishop of Canterbury.

16. The bishop may at any time resign his office, and shall retire on reaching the age of seventy years.

569

1984
Faith and worship

Anglican–Orthodox Dialogue, The Dublin Agreed Statement *(1984), 53.*

Cf. no. 563.

Faith and worship are inseparable. Dogmas are not abstract ideas existing in and for themselves, but revealed and saving truths and realities, intended to bring mankind into communion with God. Through the liturgical life of the Church creation comes to share in this saving reality. Thus in worship the Church becomes what she really is: body, fellowship, communion in Christ. She maintains the true faith and is maintained in the true faith by the action and work of the Holy Spirit.

570

1984
The Communion of saints

Anglican–Orthodox Dialogue, The Dublin Agreed Statement
(1984), 67.

Those who believe and are baptized form one body in Christ, and
are members one of another, united by the Holy Spirit. Within the
Body each member suffers and rejoices with the others, and in
each member the Holy Spirit intercedes for the whole. These
relationships are changed but not broken by death, 'He is not God
of the dead, but of the living' (Matthew 22.32), for all live in and
to him. This is the meaning of the communion of saints.

571

1984
Prayers for the dead

Anglican–Orthodox Dialogue, The Dublin Agreed Statement
(1984), 73–4.

Prayers for the departed are therefore to be seen.... as an
expression of mutual love and solidarity in Christ: 'we pray for
them because we still hold them in our love' (Catechism of the
Episcopal Church, USA). The prayers of the saints on our behalf
are likewise to be understood as an expression of mutual love and
shared life in the Holy Spirit.

572

1984
The origin of ministry in the Church

God's Reign and Our Unity: The Report of the Anglican-Reformed
International Commission *(1984), 74–6.*

The company gathered behind closed doors on that first Easter evening[1] was the Church in embryo.... The same company gathered in that shuttered room was also the ministry in embryo. Those who were there commissioned and anointed were sent to call others to be with Jesus and, in their turn, to be sent. The disciples are to 'make disciples of all nations'[2] As they have heard and obeyed the call of Jesus, 'Follow me', so they in turn are to call others, and these others are, in their turn, both to 'be with Jesus' and to 'be sent' in the service of God's Kingdom. Thus from the very beginning there is a pattern of ministerial leadership in the life of the Church. It is to the whole Church that the commission is given, but the Church was never an unstructured aggregate of individual believers out of which a ministerial structure had to develop. On the contrary there was from the beginning a pattern of calling and following. The first disciples are both the first followers and the first apostles sent to call others to follow. And this calling is always to a double relationship with Jesus: to be with him and to be sent.

573

1984
The diaconate

The Scottish Ordinal, 1984.

The presentation of the Candidate

The candidate is presented by a deacon or presbyter and a lay person of the diocese.

Presenter: Reverend Father in God, we present to you N. He is commended by those in this Church who know him and by those who have taught and prepared him. We therefore ask you to ordain him to serve in the order of deacons.

Response of the bishop. All sit except the candidate

Bishop: The Church is the People of God, the Body of Christ and the dwelling of the Holy Spirit. It is built upon the foundation of

---

[1]   John 20.19ff.
[2]   Matthew 28.19

the apostles and prophets. Jesus Christ himself being the chief corner stone. In baptism every disciple is called to make Jesus known as Saviour and Lord and to share his work in renewing the world. Some by ordination are given particular tasks. A deacon shares with the bishop and his presbyters in the ministry of word and sacrament and in works of love. In a distinctive way the deacon is a sign of that humility which marks all service offered in the name of Christ. He bears witness to his Lord who laid aside all claims of dignity, assumed the nature of a slave and accepted death on a cross. In the name of the Church, he is to care for those in need, serving God and his creation after the pattern of Christ our Master. To fulfil such a task is not in human power but depends upon the grace of God who alone can give us that mind which was in Christ Jesus through whom we now pray.

Silent prayer

574

1984

Rules for the celebration of the Eucharist

Eucharistic Liturgy of the Anglican Church of Canada, Buchanan, pp. 93–4.

1. The holy table is spread with a clean (white) cloth during the celebration.
2. The celebration of the Eucharist is the work of the whole People of God. However, throughout this rite the term 'celebrant' is used to describe the bishop or priest who presides at the Eucharist.
3. As chief liturgical officer it is the bishop's prerogative to preside at the Lord's table and to preach the Gospel.
4. It is appropriate that other priests who may be present stand with the celebrant at the altar during the eucharistic prayer, and join in the breaking of the bread and in the ministration of communion.
5. It is the function of a deacon to read the Gospel and to make ready the table for the celebration, preparing and placing upon it the bread and cup of wine. The deacon may also lead the Prayers of the People.

6. Lay persons should normally be assigned the readings which precede the Gospel, and may lead the Prayers of the People. When authority is given by the bishop, they may also assist in the ministration of communion.

7. It is desirable that the readings be read from a lectern or pulpit, and that the Gospel be read from the same lectern or pulpit, or in the midst of the congregation. It is desirable that the readings and Gospel be read from a book or books of appropriate size and dignity.

8. The leader of the Prayers of the People should use creativity and discretion in the planning of the intercessions and thanksgivings, and scope should be provided for members of the congregation to add their own petitions. The suggested forms are examples; these may be modified as local customs and needs require. The use of silence in the intercessions is optional.

9. If there is no communion, all that is appointed through the Prayers of the People may be said. (If it is desired to include a confession of sin, the service begins with the Penitential Order.) A hymn or anthem may then be sung, and the offerings of the people received. The service may then be concluded with the Lord's Prayer, and with either the Grace or a blessing, or with the exchange of the Peace. In the absence of a priest, all that is described above, except for the absolution and blessing, may be said by a deacon or, if there is no deacon, by an authorized lay person.

10. When a certain posture is particularly appropriate, it is indicated. For the rest of the service local custom may be established and followed. The Great Thanksgiving is a single prayer, the unity of which may be obscured by changes of posture in the course of it.

11. During the Great Thanksgiving it is desirable that there be only one chalice on the altar and, if need be, a flagon, decanter, jug or suitable container of wine from which additional chalices may be filled after the breaking of the bread.

12. Care should be taken at the time of the preparation of the gifts to place on the holy table sufficient bread and wine for the communion of the people so that supplementary consecration is unnecessary. However, if the consecrated bread or wine does not suffice for the number of communicants, the celebrant consecrates more of either or both, by saying: We thank you, heavenly Father,

for your saving love, and we pray you to bless and sanctify this bread (wine) with your Word and Holy Spirit, that it also may be the sacrament of the precious body (blood) of your Son, our Lord Jesus Christ. Amen.

13. Opportunity is always to be given to every communicant to receive the consecrated bread and wine separately.

14. Communion should be given at each celebration of the Eucharist from bread and wine consecrated at that liturgy.

15. Any remaining consecrated bread and wine (unless reserved for the communion of persons not present) is consumed at the end of the distribution or immediately after the service. This is appropriately done at the credence table or in the sacristy.

575

1985
Our need for forgiveness

The Church of the Province of New Zealand, Buchanan, p. 257.

Happy are those whose sins are forgiven, whose wrongs are pardoned. I will confess my sins to the Lord, I will not conceal my wrongdoings.

Silence

God forgives and heals us.
We need your healing, merciful God: give us true repentance. Some sins are plain to us; some escape us, some we cannot face. Forgive us; set us free to hear your word to us; set us free to serve you.

The presiding priest says

God forgives you; forgive others; forgive yourself.

Pause

Through Christ, God has put away your sin: approach your God in peace.

576

1985
Canonisation

Comment by the South African Anglican Theological Commission on 'Canonisation'. For the Synod of Bishops, April 1985.

The question at issue here is what is meant by recognizing a person as a 'saint' and on what authority such recognition may rest.

2. We believe that Episcopal Synod is the proper body to promulgate the formal recognition of a person as a saint.

1. We believe that a lapse of many years will be necessary before a true perspective may be gained in the consideration of any particular case.

2. Episcopal Synod would need to draw up guidelines for the critical investigation of cases that might arise.

3. Episcopal Synod would need to set up a special commission to examine each case.

4. In the event that a person should then be formally recognized as a 'saint', Episcopal Synod should arrange for a solemn Act of Thanksgiving and Rejoicing to be made during which the formal Act of Promulgation would take place. The date of the festival day and degree of liturgical observance shold also be promulgated.

5. This Act of Thanksgiving and Rejoicing in which the life of God's servant would be set out for the veneration and encouragement of the faithful should be presided over by the Archbishop or by the Bishop of the diocese in which the saint lived.

6. The Liturgical Committee should be requested to make provision for such a service.

3. We believe the calendar should distinguish with greater clarity between those regarded by the Province as 'saints' and those whose names may merely be commemorated although they have never been canonised. Liturgical provision should also be made for this distinction. Consideration should be given to the restoration of Red Letter Days, Black Letter Days and commemorations as in the South African Prayer Book.

577

1985
The minister of holy unction

Comment by the South African Anglican Theological Commission on the Minister of Holy Unction. For the Synod of Bishops, April 1985.

See nos. 46, 241, 377. Note the pastoral emphasis here.

1. *Historical*

The only two references to anointing for healing in the New Testament are Mark 6.13 and James 5.14ff. The former reference doubtless reflects regular practice in the first century even though the reference in Mark is to the Twelve (v. 7). The reference in James supports this understanding of unction as a regular way of conferring healing on the sick, and the elders (hoi presbuteroi) are probably to be seen as [the] official ministers....

2. *Canonical*

The *South African Prayer Book* rubrics (pp. 460ff.) clearly indicate that the minister of unction is the priest. Similarly Canon B 37.3 of the Church of England allows only a priest to administer unction with oil 'consecrated by the bishop of the diocese or otherwise by the priest himself'. This reflects the practice of most Anglican Provinces and of the Orthodox and Roman Catholic Churches. A rubric, however, of the Episcopal Church of the U.S.A. states 'In cases of necessity, a deacon or lay person may perform the anointing, using oil blessed by a bishop or priest'. To adopt a similar practice in the CPSA would therefore in no way endanger the unity of the Anglican Communion, nor is it likely to have any effect on relations with the Roman Catholic Church, where the healing ministry of the Church is also a matter of concern, though one should note that Vatican II *Sacrosanctum Concilium* nn. 73–5 still thinks of the sacrament as being for those 'in danger of death'.

3. *Theological*

The restrictions placed on rites concerned with the healing of the sick stem from the desire of the Church to avoid superstitious practices, so that actions and prayers are firmly linked to the whole life and worship of the Church. Thus from the beginning there was a tendency to associate unction with the Eucharist. Caesarius, talking of various means used by the sick to find healing, says 'How much better... it would be that they should run to the Church and receive the Body and Blood of Christ and should in faith anoint themselves and the members of their household with consecrated oil'...

The important point seems to be that the rite should be administered in the name of the Church. For this reason, in other contexts, the bishop or priest has regularly been the minister of absolution and the president of the Eucharist, since in his person he represents the whole church. If acts of healing performed in the name of Christ are to be seen as acts of Christ in and through his Church, it follows that the Church must define the limits within which ministers or members of the Church may carry out their healing ministry. All such ministry, whether it consists of prayer or the laying on of hands or unction, must be firmly linked to the life of the whole Body of Christ. For this reason the healing ministry generally, and unction in particular, has frequently been associated with the Eucharist in which the faith of the Church is expressed.

It does not seem theologically necessary that the minister of unction should always be a priest, though the priest as the ordained representative of Christ in his Church would be the most fitting minister. The essential factor is that those who carry out a healing ministry should be duly authorised by the bishop. For the same reason the oil which is used should be consecrated by the bishop, or at least by the priest.[1] The healing ministry of the Church bears important witness to the concern of the Lord for the whole person, for his bodily health as well as for his spiritual growth, and there by shows too the Church's concern for the political and social structures in which life is lived.

4. *Some suggested pastoral guidelines*

A. The rite of laying on of hands should be seen in a more flexible form than is found in the *South African Prayer Book*. There are many occasions where laymen should be encouraged, under the guidance and direction of the parish priest, to lay hands on the sick and pray for healing, either in healing services or in homes or hospitals. Where possible, others should join in prayer with the one who lays hands on the sick person. No doubt there will be occasions calling for greater solemnity when the priest

---

[1]   On the proper ministers, cf. no. 46.

should be the minister, and the form of service should then follow the lines of the present *South African Prayer Book* rite. Often, though not necessarily, the laying on of hands would be associated with the Eucharist.

The laying on of hands is normally the most suitable rite for repeated ministration to the same sick person.

B. Unction is a more solemn matter.

    i. It should normally be associated with the laying on of hands, and, where convenient, with the Eucharist.

    ii. The oil used should be natural vegetable oil (preferably olive oil) consecrated by the bishop.

    iii. In cases of necessity the oil may be blessed by a priest.

    iv. Unction should always be associated with a call to penitence and may be preceded by a confession of sin.

    v. Normally the priest is the proper minister of unction.

    vi. In view of the importance of the healing ministry and of the limited number of priests, bishops should:

        a. As a general practice authorise deacons to administer unction.

        b. License lay-ministers, on the nomination of the priest-in-charge, to administer unction.

In both these cases the ministration of unction, as all other aspects of the healing ministry, should be undertaken under the direction of the priest-in-charge.

    vii. Teaching should regularly be given on the healing ministry to all members of the Church, and to lay-ministers in particular. The parish priest should ensure that lay-ministers and deacons in the parish understand the theology of the healing ministry of the Church.

    viii. When the minister of unction is a priest a form of absolution should be included in the rite.

    ix. In cases of exceptional pastoral need unblessed oil may be used. In such cases the parish priest should be informed as soon as possible.

    x. Normally unction is not repeated in the course of the same illness.

C. In view of the various ways in which it is recommended that unction be administered and in view of the growth in number and forms of healing services, new liturgical forms should be drawn up, indicating what is required to be included and what might be regarded as optional.

578

1986
The objectives of a Province

Constitution and Canons of the Anglican Church of the Southern Cone of America, Article 5.

Art. 5. Main Objectives:
The Province is formed:

5.1 To strengthen and develop the Church of Jesus Christ and, at the same time, to be a visible expression of the Anglican Communion within its jurisdiction.

5.2 To provide an effective means of consultation, coordination, cooperation and service among the Dioceses in the spirit of the interdependence in the Body of Christ and in such a way as may be conducive to the general advancement of the Church in the Province.

5.3 To continue and develop relationships with other parts of the Anglican Communion, especially in Latin America.

5.4 To encourage and guide ecumenical relationships between the Churches of the Anglican Communion and other Christian Churches established within the continent and outside it.

5.5 To represent and to appoint representatives of the Province to the Anglican Consultative Council and to other organizations as required.

5.6 To bring about the creation of other structures that facilitate the development of the Church.

5.7 To exercise the metropolitan function enumerated in the Canons.

579

1986
Conscientious objection to military service

A Pastoral Letter to Parents from the Bishops of the Church of the Province of Southern Africa, 1986.

We, the Bishops of the Church of the Province of Southern Africa, are very conscious of the distress and perplexity of members of our Church, black and white, whose children are caught up in the turmoil of our times. There are those whose sons are called upon to serve in the South African Defence Force. Others have children who have left the country, either to avoid such service, or to wait until a better order is found for the land. There are others whose children have left in order to take part in 'the armed struggle'. All these, parents and children, are beloved members of God's family, to whom we are concerned to minister in the love of Christ. In a normal society a Defence Force may be considered to have a legitimate place in order to protect against foreign aggression or malicious insurrection. In most civilised societies some persons find such military service unacceptable in conscience. These are usually termed pacifists or conscientious objectors and provision is made for reasonable alternative service. Christian tradition acknowledges that it is right to allow people to follow conscience even where a majority believes that conscience to be in error. The pain and perplexity in South Africa arise from the fact that in the eyes of the majority of the governed, the Government lacks legitimacy. The socio-political and economic system which has been established is seen to be unjust and oppressive. In their experience black people, and especially youth, have increasingly come to realise the human damage caused by the systematic denial of proper education to them. The legal restraints upon their participation in the 'free enterprise' system and the generally unequal life opportunities available to them have come to be seen as hostile and provocative. For these reasons the South African Defence Force is seen as defending an unjust order. In a normal society stability and order are capable of restoration, but in an unjust one police or military action is perceived as oppressive and so fuels the cycle of violence. Many young people (with or without support from their parents) are therefore in Christian conscience seeking other options for serving their country than the South African Defence Force. We condemn violence from whatever source. The Church upholds the sanctity of human life. Jesus said: 'Love your enemies and pray for those who persecute you.'[1] State sponsored brutality and brutal reaction to it are both intolerable. Bombings, necklacings, shootings, sjambokkings, teargassing and torture are all horrible. We must recognize that until the inhumanity of injustice is removed, such inhumane things will continue.

---

[1]   Matthew 5.44

By use of the Defence Force in the townships, South African is turned against South African. On the border too it is not a foreign enemy who invades. The pain is still more intense for Namibians, who see the presence of the South African Defence Force as a mark of illegal occupation. Fellow Christians face each other across the guns. Some believe that the SADF is defending South Africa against communism. We condemn communism as godless and materialistic because of its devaluation of the worth and God-given dignity of each person. We believe the proper defence against communism is the propagation of the Gospel of our Lord Jesus Christ within a just society. Communism has rarely flourished where society has been justly ordered.

We call on you, the people of God, of every race and background, to come together and find each other as sisters and brothers in Christ. Understandable white fears, fuelled by guilt and propaganda, can be greatly eased by encountering the warmth and humanity of the black community expressed in *ubuntu* (humaneness, compassion, sharing, togetherness and reverence for human life). Blacks gripped by fury need to be recalled to these very roots. In view of this, the Church has to be concerned for people with varied needs and differing attitudes conscientiously held.

The Church seeks to minister with understanding and sympathy to:
1. Those who agonise over their Christian responsibility in the face of military call-up.
2. Those who decide to serve in the SADF.
3. Those who in Christian conscience seek other ways of national service, or who refuse to serve at all.
4. Children who have left the country.
5. Those affected by the experience of military service, imprisonment or exile.
6. The parents of all these groups, who sometimes cannot understand their children's decisions or who may be unable to trace their whereabouts.
7. All those who are confused and damaged by the present turmoil.

This search to minister to all these different groups presents many complex problems, in spite of which the Church tries to do all that it can to provide adequate pastoral care for its members. We pray for you, and ask you to hold together in the love of Christ even where there are grave differences in thinking about the way forward into that peace and justice which we all seek by the grace of Christ our only Saviour.

580

1986
Justification and sanctification

Salvation and the Church, Second Anglican-Roman Catholic International Commission, Llandaff, 1986 (London, 1987).

The Llandaff text seeks to state an agreed position on a topic deeply divisive in the sixteenth century debates over justification by faith. For the sixteenth century Anglican view, see Articles x–xiv of the Thirty-Nine Articles and cf. nos. 122, 123, 133, 136, 150, 214.

15. Justification and sanctification are two aspects of the same divine act.[1] This does not mean that justification is a reward for faith or works: rather, when God promises the removal of our condemnation and gives us a new standing before him, this justification is indissolubly linked with his sanctifying recreation of us in grace. This transformation is being worked out in the course of our pilgrimage, despite the imperfections and ambiguities of our lives. God's grace effects what he declares: his creative word imparts what it imputes. By pronouncing us righteous, God also makes us righteous. He imparts a righteousness which is his and becomes ours.

581

1986
The role of faith in salvation

Salvation and the Church, *Second Anglican-Roman Catholic International Commission, Llandaff, 1986 (London, 1987).*

Cf. Articles x–xiv of the Thirty-Nine Articles and nos. 122, 123, 133, 136, 150, 214.

---

[1]   I Corinthians 6.11

9. When we confess that Jesus Christ is Lord, we praise and glorify God the Father, whose purpose for creation and salvation is realised in the Son, whom he sent to redeem us and to prepare a people for himself by the indwelling of the Holy Spirit. This wholly unmerited love of God for his creatures is expressed in the language of grace, which embraces not only the once for all death and resurrection of Christ, but also God's continuing work on our behalf. The Holy Spirit makes the fruits of Christ's sacrifice actual within the Church through Word and Sacrament: our sins are forgiven, we are enabled to respond to God's love, and we are conformed to the image of Christ. The human response to God's initiative is itself a gift of grace, and is at the same time a truly human, personal response. It is through grace that God's new creation is realised. Salvation is the gift of grace; it is by faith that it is appropriated.

10. The gracious action of God in Christ is revealed to us in the Gospel. The Gospel, by proclaiming Christ's definitive atoning work, the gift and pledge of the Holy Spirit to every believer, and the certainty of God's promise of eternal life, calls Christians to faith in the mercy of God and brings them assurance of salvation. It is God's gracious will that we, as his children, called through the Gospel and sharing in the means of grace, should be confident that the gift of eternal life is assured to each of us. Our response to this gift must come from our whole being. Faith, therefore, not only includes an assent to the truth of the Gospel but also involves commitment of our will to God in repentance and obedience to his call; otherwise faith is dead.[1] Living faith is inseparable from love, issues in good works, and grows deeper in the course of a life of holiness. Christian assurance does not in any way remove from Christians the responsibility of working out their salvation with fear and trembling.[2]

---

[1]   James 2.17
[2]   Philippians 2.12–13

582

1986

Christian obedience and unjust law

Province of South Africa, Statement entitled Christian Obedience and Unjust Law: *revisions suggested to a statement entitled* Civil Disobedience, *from the Board of the Provincial Department of Justice and Reconciliation, with a view to the sending of a pastoral letter from the bishops (1986) (Letter subsequently published).*

We... commend the following guidelines to Christians who believe that their witness to the truth of the Gospel and obedience to God may demand disobedience to the law of the land:

1. Law is essential to the ordering of human society, and so must be respected.
2. All such witness must be undertaken only after serious prayer and thought.
3. A decision to act should normally be taken individually only after consultation with other Christians, especially the Church Council.
4. The law may be disobeyed only by those who are prepared to suffer the consequence of their actions.
5. Respect for the due process of law must be maintained.
6. Only with a clear appreciation of what is involved, and with love towards all who think differently, may the law be disobeyed.
7. All who contemplate breaking the law in Christian witness must carefully examine their conscience with regard to their motives, and avoid any desire for personal martyrdom.
8. Aims and objectives must be carefully defined. Possible alternative ways by which the same objectives may be lawfully attained must be considered.
9. All participants in such actions must be fully informed about the objectives, the plan and the discipline of non-violent action and the possible consequences.
10. As far as possible, a public explanation for this kind of witness should be given.
11. The individual's conscience must be respected. People may not be coerced or manipulated into any act against their will.
12. Great care must be taken to avoid violence and injury to bystanders and to other non-participants.

583

1986
The way forward in mission

An account of the Partners in Mission Consulation, 20–2, August 1986 Dodoma, Tanzania.

On the 'smallest complete unit' of Church life, see no. 514. These notes list some of the priorities for cooperative work in mission.

Provincial Priorities for 1987–1991

Preamble:

'In the Anglican Communion, the Province is an essential part of the life of the Church. It is the basic unit of Church life, being the smallest unit to reproduce itself. A diocese may choose a bishop, but it cannot consecrate him. The Anglican Church expresses itself in Provincial terms. This however is not a legalistic relationship, but one willingly entered into by dioceses. This is how we express the interdependence of the body of Christ.'

I. *Evangelism/Education*

1. *Christian Education for Laity*
    (a) Consolidation of Bible Schools and standardization of syllabi.
    (b) More consideration be given to the training of women in both the Bible Schools and Theological Colleges.
    (c) To provide qualified teachers.
    (d) To encourage students to study for Provincial Certificate.
    (e) Provincial support to students' groups.

2. *Selection and Training for Ordained Ministers*

    (a) Involvement of Church members in selecting candidates for ministry.
    (b) Entrance qualification to Theological Colleges be Form IV level.
    (c) Planning towards degree level studies at Theological Colleges be started, including the expansion of staff, libraries and accommodation.
    (d) Regular refresher courses and remedial studies for clergy, and specialist training for chaplains.
    (e) Encourage opportunities for graduate and post-graduate studies.

3. *Alternative Methods of Training*

Co-ordination and flexibility of all training methods be improved: e.g. Cassette ministry, Bible Schools, TEE Programme, and Theological Colleges.

II. *Stewardship and Development*

1. Development of resources for evangelism, e.g. manpower, equipment, etc.
2. Projects for development of local resources leading to self-reliance, e.g. agriculture, livestock, etc.
3. Development of the Provincial Secretariat to enable evaluation of diocesan development and sharing of resources between dioceses. Priority was given to the post of a Development Officer.
4. To expand the Role of Prayer within the Province, and exchange of resources of personnel for Mission outside the Province.

Structures and Decision-Making

1. Deliberate and conscious cross-fertilization of the two traditions of Churchmanship by Bishops, Clergy, Laity and Theological Colleges.
2. Intensifying transparency between dioceses within the Province; between the Province and Partners; and between Partners.
3. Development of Communication tools — e.g. radio call, Diocesan Newsletters, sharing of resources between diocesan groupings.
4. Personnel needs at Provincial Secretariat:
    (a) Analysis of need and financial implications;
    (b) Regular performance review; and
    (c) Standardization of Provincial Terms and Conditions of Service.
5. Strengthening of the Decision-Making process in the Province:
    (a) Collegiality of bishops at Provincial level;
    (b) Bishop of Synod;
    (c) Clergy in Parochial Councils;
    (d) Church involvement at all levels; and
    (e) Mutual accountability in all levels of leadership.

6. In the formation of new dioceses, the following issues have to be addressed:
   (a) Viability analysis;
   (b) Distribution of resources;
   (c) Provincial support in the formative years.

IV. *The Church in the World*

1. Encourage Partner Churches in educating the peoples and governments of the richer countries concerning the effects of the present unequal trade system.
2. The Church at home and overseas should make a stronger stand against the world-wide problem of corruption in all possible ways.
3. (a) To co-operate with Government plans for Primary Health Care and also Hospital Extension when needed; and
   (b) Greater effort for Church involvement in secondary education.
4. To encourage dialogue and co-operation with other Christian traditions.
5. To endeavour to share the Gospel with non-Christians with love and concern.

584

1987
Anglicans and history (West Indies)

Leslie Lett, Faith and Life: A Handbook for Anglicans *(Barbados, 1987), Introduction.*

Anglicans need to remember that, as part of the Catholic Church, our history goes back to New Testament times. Our history includes the sacrifice of countless martyrs who died that we today could have the Word and Sacraments. Our faith has been tested and strengthened over a long history of persecution and suffering; it has given courage to ordinary men and women to face their everyday lives with true Christian joy and confidence, and it has given courage to them to face death in the powerful hope of the resurrection.

585

1987
The truths we share

The Niagara Report: Report of the Anglican–Lutheran Consultation on Episcope *(1987), 61–71.*

A basis of common faith is set out here as an essential element in the union of Churches.

61. We accept the authority of the canonical Scriptures of the Old and New Testaments. We read the Scriptures liturgically in the course of the Church's year.[1]

62. We accept the Niceno–Constantinopolitan and Apostles' Creeds and confess the basic Trinitarian and Christological Dogmas to which these creeds testify. That is, we believe that Jesus of Nazareth is true God and true Man, and that God is authentically identified as Father, Son and Holy Spirit.[2]

63. Anglicans and Lutherans use very similar orders of service for the Eucharist, for the Prayer Offices, for the administration of Baptism, for the rites of Marriage, Burial, and Confession and Absolution. We acknowledge in the liturgy both a celebration of salvation through Christ and a significant factor in forming the *consensus fidelium*. We have many hymns, canticles, and collects in common.[3]

64. We believe that Baptism with water in the name of the Triune God unites the one baptized with the death and resurrection of Jesus Christ, initiates into the One, Holy, Catholic and Apostolic Church, and confers the gracious gift of new life.[4]

65. We believe that the Body and Blood of Christ are truly present, distributed and received under the forms of bread and wine in the Lord's Supper. We also believe that the grace of divine forgiveness

---

[1]   *Lutheran–Episcopal Dialogue II* (= LED II), 1980, pp. 30–1; *Pullach Report*, 17–22

[2]   LED II, p. 38; *Pullach Report*, 23–25

[3]   *Helsinki Report*, 29–31

[4]   *Helsinki Report*, 22–25

offered in the sacrament is received with the thankful offering of ourselves for God's service.[5]

66. We believe and proclaim the gospel, that in Jesus Christ God loves and redeems the world. We 'share a common understanding of God's justifying grace, i.e. that we are accounted righteous and are made righteous before God only by grace through faith because of the merits of our Lord and Saviour Jesus Christ, and not on account of our works or merit. Both our traditions affirm that justification leads and must lead to "good works"; authentic faith issues in love'.[6]

67. Anglicans and Lutherans believe that the Church is not the creation of individual believers, but that it is constituted and sustained by the triune God through God's saving action in word and sacraments. We believe that the Church is sent into the world as sign, instrument and foretaste of the kingdom of God. But we also recognize that the Church stands in constant need of reform and renewal.[7]

68. We believe that all members of the Church are called to participate in its apostolic mission. They are therefore given various ministries by the Holy Spirit. Within the community of the Church the ordained ministry exists to serve the ministry of the whole people of God. We hold the ordained ministry of word and sacrament to be a gift of God to his Church and therefore an office of divine institution.[8]

69. We believe that a ministry of pastoral oversight (*episcope*), exercised in personal, collegial and communal ways, is necessary to witness to and safeguard the unity and apostolicity of the Church.[9]

70. We share a common hope in the final consummation of the Kingdom of God and believe that we are compelled to work for the establishment of justice and peace. The obligations of the Kingdom are to govern our life in the Church and our concern for the world. 'The Christian faith is that God has made peace through

---

[5] LED·II, pp 25–29; *Helsinki Report*, 26–28.

[6] *Helsinki Report*, 20; cf. LED II, pp. 22–23

[7] *Helsinki Report*, 44–51

[8] *Helsinki Report*, 32–42

[9] *Pullach Report*, 79

Jesus 'by blood of his cross'[10] so establishing the one valid centre for the unity of the whole human family'.[11]

71. Because of all that we share, we concur with the conclusion of the Anglican–Lutheran European Regional Commission: 'There are no longer any serious obstacles on the way towards the establishment of full communion between our two Churches'. We 'acknowledge each other as true Churches of Christ preaching the same gospel, possessing a common apostolic ministry, and celebrating authentic sacraments'.[12]

586

1988
Daily prayer

Daily Prayer, Scottish Episcopal Church, 1988, Introduction.

The simple forms of morning and evening prayer given here are designed to encourage attentive prayer, either by groups or by individuals. The words are few, and are meant to be repeated slowly, quietly and reflectively, so that they may become part of us and may give voice to our own prayer.

Our prayer becomes the prayer of Christ's people: Christ's people's prayer becomes our prayer.

Ample opportunity should be taken for silence. Silence allows Christ's words to touch and to mingle with the thoughts of our hearts. It has always been the Christian custom to pray with Christ at the beginning and the end of each day: The morning is the time of his resurrection: as the new light breaks we pray to be made new in him. The evening is the time of his descent from the cross: as the sun sets we pray to find our final rest in him. Even if we are insulated from the natural rhythm of dawn and dusk, as many these days are by patterns of work and family life, let our prayer fit the hymn:

'With thee began, with thee shall end the day'

---

[10] Colossians 1.20
[11] Anglican–Reformed International Commission 1984: *God's Reign and Our Unity*, 18 and 43; cf. *Pullach Report*, 59.
[12] *Helsinki Report*, 62–63

as a sign that we seek to place all that we are, all that we say, and all that we do within the unending praise of the God and Father or our Lord Jesus Christ. The structure of these simple forms is as follows:

I. A short invocation — calling upon God (in the morning from Psalm 51, in the evening from Psalm 70). Gloria — praise of the God who through Jesus invites us to worship him as Father, Son, and Holy Spirit.

II. A psalm, followed by a short reading from Scripture. (These vary according to the season.)

III. A canticle (in the morning *Benedictus*, in the evening *Magnificat*). Short prayers, including the Lord's Prayer.

This structure is a very ancient one and has therefore been tested through long Christian experience. It is offered here in simple form in the hope that it may encourage all who use it to 'keep on praying and not to lose heart'.

587

1988

The ordination or consecration of women to the Episcopate and the unity of the Anglican Communion

Resolution 1, Lambeth Conference, 1988.

This Conference resolves:

1. That each Province respect the decision and attitudes of other Provinces in the ordination or consecration of women to the episcopate, without such respect necessarily indicating acceptance of the principles involved, maintaining the highest possible degree of communion with the Provinces which differ.

2. That bishops exercise courtesy and maintain communications with bishops who may differ, and with any woman bishop, ensuring an open dialogue in the Church to whatever extent communion is impaired.

3. That the Archbishop of Canterbury, in consultation with the Primates, appoints a commission:

(a) to provide for an examination of the relationships between Provinces of the Anglican communion and ensure that the process of reception includes continuing consultation with other Churches as well;

(b) to monitor and encourage the process of consultation within the Communion and to offer further pastoral guidelines.

4. That in any Province where reconciliation on these issues is necessary, any diocesan bishop facing this problem be encouraged to seek continuing dialogue with, and make pastoral provision for, those clergy and congregations whose opinions differ from those of the bishop, in order to maintain the unity of the diocese.

5. Recognizes the serious hurt which would result from the questioning by some of the validity of the episcopal acts of a woman bishop, and likewise the hurt experienced by those whose conscience would be offended by the ordination of a woman to the episcopate. The Church needs to exercise sensitivity, patience and pastoral care towards all concerned.

588

1988

Ecumenical and inter-Church relations: Churches in full Communion with Anglican Churches

Who are the Anglicans?, ed. Charles Long, prepared for the Lambeth Conference, 1988 (Ohio, 1988), p. 79.

'Full Communion' here implies the retention of the ecclesial distinctness of the Churches involved. It falls short of organic union in one Church. Cf. nos. 406, 520.

A majority of Anglican Provinces have ratified agreements of full communion with

1. The Church of South India
2. The Church of North India
3. The Church of Pakistan
4. The Church of Bangladesh
5. The Old Catholic Churches, Union of Utrecht
6. The Philippine Independent Church
7. The Mar Thoma Syrian Church of Malabar, India

The Old Catholic Churches of Europe and North America, with 443,000 members, were separated from the Roman Catholic Church at various times and for various reasons during the 18th and 19th centuries. They maintained the historic episcopate and many other elements of Catholic faith and order. In 1889 the Dutch, German and Swiss Old Catholic Churches united in a common profession of faith, the Declaration of Utrecht. The largest branch of the church, the Polish National Catholic Church, grew out of an ethnic dispute in the Roman Catholic Church in America in 1890. The Bonn Agreement between Old Catholics and the Church of England in 1931 established full communion with the Church of England and was soon ratified by other Anglican Churches. Each national Church is governed by its own Synod of bishops, priests and laity. The Archbishop of Utrecht is Primate and Chairman of the International Old Catholic bishops' Conference but only has jurisdictional power in his own diocese. The Philippine Independent Church was established in 1902 by leaders of the popular revolution against Spain in 1896, which sought among other things religious emancipation and a national identity for Filipino Christians. Today it claims 4,000,000 members in 28 dioceses, with 50 bishops, 600 priests and 2,600 organized congregations. It sought and received consecration of bishops in the apostolic succession from the Episcopal Church USA in 1961. Subsequently full communion was established with the Episcopal Church and other Anglican Provinces. Through a concordat it cooperates closely with the much smaller Philippine Episcopal Church and, since the 1950s, clergy of the two churches have been trained together at St Andrew's Seminary in Manila. The Mar Thoma Church traces its history through the Syrian Orthodox Church of Malabar, to the planting of Christianity in India by St Thomas the apostle. The Mar Thoma Church is now in full communion with the united churches of India and with most of the Anglican Communion. It includes an estimated 350,000 members in 5 dioceses and 640 congregations.

589

1988
Anglican–Oriental Orthodox relations

Resolution 5, Lambeth Conference, 1988.

Cf. no 56.

This Conference:

1. Warmly welcomes the renewal and development of relationships between the Anglican Communion and the Armenian Apostolic, Coptic Orthodox, Ethiopian Orthodox, Syrian Orthodox and Indian Orthodox Churches.

2. Warmly welcomes the renewal of relationships between the Anglican Communion and the Holy Apostolic Catholic Assyrian Church of the East.

3. Particularly welcomes the presence of more Observers from these Churches than at any previous Lambeth Conference, thus regaining the momentum of the Conferences of 1908 and 1920.

4. Notes with satisfaction the visits to these Churches made before and since the WCC Assembly at Vancouver in 1983 by bishop Henry Hill, the meeting of the Anglican–Oriental Orthodox Forum held at St Albans in 1985 and the subsequent publication of the symposium *Light from the East*, as well as the meetings between the Archbishop of Canterbury and the Patriarchs of these Churches, including that with Pope Shenouda III in 1987 resulting in their Joint Declaration.

5. Affirms our friendship with these two families of Churches, and recognizes the severe difficulties and challenges faced by them through war and persecution, through the growth of secularism and militant atheism, and also recognizes the challenge presented by the interface with Islam.

6. Recognizes that we are present together in many parts of the world, and offers our hopes for the development of friendship, fellowship and support wherever we find ourselves side by side.

7. Values greatly the rich contribution that these Churches have made to the spirituality of the Church as a whole throughout the centuries.

8. Affirms and supports the work of the Anglican–Oriental Orthodox Forum, and commits itself to the task of the forum in developing areas of possible co-operation, particularly:

(a) The development of dialogue on matters of common theological interest and concern.

(b) The establishment of theological scholarships mainly for postgraduate study for students who have completed their basic training in their own institutions and the possibility that some Anglican students spend some time in Oriental Orthodox theological institutions and monasteries as part of their regular training for the ministry.

(c) The hope that theological seminaries of the Oriental Orthodox Churches can be assisted, especially in the building up of libraries, in the supply of new books, and in subscriptions to scholarly journals, with journals and magazines published by the Churches of the two Communions being exchanged on a more systematic basis.

(d) The need for regional co-ordinating bodies for promoting understanding and co-operation among the Churches especially in the USA and Canada, in the Middle East, in Australia and New Zealand, and in the United Kingdom.

9. Desires that in view of the importance of Anglo-Oriental Orthodox relations, the Anglican Consultative Council enter into consultation with the relevant Oriental Orthodox authorities with a view to the Forum being upgraded to a formally recognized Commission.

590

1988
Anglican–Roman Catholic relations

Resolution 8, Lambeth Conference 1988.

This Conference:

1. Recognizes the Agreed Statements of ARCIC I on *Eucharistic Doctrine, ministry and ordination*, and their *Elucidations*, as consonant in substance with the faith of Anglicans, and believes that this agreement offers a sufficient basis for taking the next step forward towards the reconciliation of our Churches grounded in agreement in faith.

2. Welcomes the assurance that, within an understanding of the Church as communion, ARCIC II is to explore further the particular issues of the reconciliation of ministries; the ordination

of women; moral questions; and continuing questions of authority, including the relation of Scripture to the Church's developing Tradition and the role of the laity in decision-making within the Church.

3. Welcomes *Authority in the Church (I and II)* together with the *Elucidation*, as a firm basis for the direction and agenda of the continuing dialogue on authority and wishes to encourage ARCIC II to continue to explore the basis in Scripture and Tradition of the concept of a universal primacy, in conjunction with collegiality, as an instrument of unity, the character of such a primacy in practice, and to draw upon the experience of other Christian Churches in exercising primacy, collegiality and conciliarity.

4. In welcoming the fact that the ordination of women is to form part of the agenda of ARCIC II, recognizes the serious responsibility this places upon us to weigh the possible implications of action on this matter for the unity of the Anglican Communion and for the universal Church.

5. Warmly welcomes the first Report of ARCIC II, *Salvation and the Church* (1987), as a timely and significant contribution to the understanding of the Churches' doctrine of salvation and commends this Agreed Statement about the heart of Christian faith to the Provinces for study and reflection.

Explanatory Note: This Conference has received the official responses to the *Final Report* of the Anglican–Roman Catholic International Commission (ARCIC I) from the member Provinces of the Anglican Communion. We note the considerable measure of consensus and convergence which the *Agreed Statements* represent. We wish to record our grateful thanks to Almighty God for the very significant advances in understanding and unity thereby expressed.

In considering the *Final report*, the Conference bore two questions in mind:

(i) Are the *Agreed Statements* consonant with Anglican faith?
(ii) If so, do they enable us to take further steps forward?

Eucharistic Doctrine

The Provinces gave a clear 'yes' to the statement on *Eucharistic Doctrine*.

Comments have been made that the style and language used in the statement are inappropriate for certain cultures. Some Provinces asked for clarification about the meaning of *anamnesis* and bread and wine 'becoming' the body and blood of Christ. But no Province rejected the Statement and many were extremely positive. While we recognize that there are hurts to be healed and doubts to be overcome, we encourage Anglicans to look forward with the new hope which the Holy Spirit is giving to the Church as we move away from past mistrust, division and polarisation. While we respect continuing anxieties of some Anglicans in the area of 'sacrifice' and 'presence', they do not appear to reflect the common mind of the Provincial responses, in which it was generally felt that the *Elucidation* of *Eucharistic Doctrine* was a helpful clarification and reassurance. Both are areas of 'mystery' which ultimately defy definition. But the Agreed Statement on the Eucharist *sufficiently* expresses Anglican understanding.

Ministry and ordination

Again, the Provinces gave a clear 'yes' to the Statement on *ministry and ordination*. The language and style have, however, been a difficulty for some Provinces, especially in the Far East. Wider representation has also been called for from Africa. Though this has now been partially remedied in ARCIC II, there is still currently no representation from Latin America, a subcontinent with very large Roman Catholic populations. An ambivalent reply came from one Province, which has traditionally experienced a difficult relationship with the Roman Catholic Church. This seems to reflect the need for developing deeper links of trust and friendship as ecumenical dialogue goes forward. While some Provinces asked for a clarification of 'priesthood' the majority believed this had been dealt with sufficiently — together with the doctrine of the Eucharist — to give grounds for hope for a fresh appraisal of each other's ministries and thus to further the reconciliation of ministries and growth towards full communion.

Authority in the Church

The Responses from the Provinces to the two Statements on *Authority in the Church* were generally positive.
Questions were, however, raised about a number of matters, especially primacy, jurisdiction and infallibility, collegiality, and the role of the laity. Nevertheless, it was generally felt that *Authority in the Church* (I and II), together with the *Elucidation*,

give us real grounds for believing that fuller agreement can be reached, and that they set out helpfully the direction and agenda of the way forward.

591

1988
Recognition of saints

Resolution 60, Lambeth Conference, 1988.

Cf. no. 576.

This Conference:
1. Welcomes the proposal by Africa Region that the Anglican Communion should recognize men and women who have lived godly lives as saints by including them in the calendars of the Churches for remembrance; and
2. Recommends that the Anglican Consultative Council discusses this matter and advises the Provinces on the procedure to follow in recognition of such saints.

592

1988
Europe

Who are the Anglicans?, ed. Charles Long, prepared for the Lambeth Conference, 1988 (Ohio, 1988), p. 63.

The Diocese in Europe (Gibraltar); Province of Canterbury. The diocese is responsible for the Church of England chaplaincies and organized congregations throughout the whole of continental Europe, from Norway to Russia, Greece to the Azores and including Turkey and Morocco. The Cathedral is in Gibraltar, with Pro-Cathedrals also in Malta and Brussels. The diocese was organized in its present form in 1980. From 1841 the Bishop of Gibraltar had been in charge of the same territory under the Bishop of London.

The Convocation of American Churches in Europe consists of six congregations in Western Europe, including a Pro-Cathedral in Paris, under the jurisdiction of the Presiding Bishop of the Episcopal Church USA and administered by a bishop appointed by him. The American bishop cooperates closely with the Bishop of Gibraltar in Europe and with the American Suffragan for the Armed Forces.

Lusitanian Church (The Portuguese Episcopal Church) since 1980 an extra-provincial diocese under the Archbishop of Canterbury. This small church was first organized in 1880 by a group of dissident Roman Catholic priests and laymen, with the help of the Episcopal Bishop of Mexico and with the intention of becoming part of the Anglican Communion. Subsequently, episcopal supervision, confirmations and ordinations were provided by a Council of Bishops from the Church of Ireland. The first Portuguese bishop was consecrated in 1958. In the 1960s full communion was established with the Episcopal Church USA, Ireland, England and other Anglican Provinces. In 1980, the diocese became a full member of the Anglican Communion. There are an estimated 850 members in 12 congregations, served by 2 bishops and 10 other clergy. The Spanish Reformed Episcopal Church, since 1980 an extra-provincial diocese under the Archbishop of Canterbury, has had a history similar to that of the Lusitanian Church, with its beginnings among former Roman Catholics in the 19th century and a long period of informal relations with certain bishops of the Church of Ireland. After its organization as a diocese and the consecration of its first bishop, the church entered into full communion in 1963 and into full membership in 1980 with the Anglican Communion. It has an estimated 1,200 members in 15 congregations served by 14 clergy. It sponsors, with other Evangelical bodies, a seminary in Madrid and has growing cooperation with the English speaking Anglican community in Spain of nearly 12,000 members, attached to the Diocese of Gibraltar in Europe.

593

1988
Extra-Provincial Dioceses

Who are the Anglicans?, ed. *Charles Henry Long, prepared for the Lambeth Conference, 1988 (Ohio, 1988), p. 45.*

Bermuda: Extra-provincial to Canterbury. Bermuda was first colonized by Anglicans from Great Britain in 1609 and within a few years 9 parishes were established, each with its own church. Until 1813 the church was under the Bishop of London, then, until 1917, under the Bishop of Newfoundland. Since 1925 it has been under the direct jurisdiction of the Archbishop of Canterbury. There are today 25,000 members (42% of the population) in 17 congregations. Two thirds of the population are Black, 98% are Christian. After the Anglican Church, the major churches are Protestant (26%) and Roman Catholic (18%). Cuba: Under the Spanish Empire, Cuba became Roman Catholic. The Spanish-American War of 1898 opened the country to the work of other churches. It became a missionary district of the Episcopal Church USA in 1901. Cuba received its first missionary bishop in 1904, its first Cuban bishop in 1961. Since 1966 Cuba has been an autonomous diocese under a metropolitan council made up of the primates of the West Indies and Canada and the president of Province 9, USA. An estimated 3,000 active members (many having emigrated to the USA) in 42 parishes served by 13 clergy, make up 0.1% of the population. Costa Rica: Extra-provincial diocese, related to Province 9, USA, 5,000 members, 14 clergy in a predominantly Roman Catholic population estimated at 2,286,000. Anglican contacts and occasional services from 1837. Under Bishop of Belize (British Honduras) from 1896. Under Episcopal Church USA since 1947. J.A. Ramos of Cuba elected first Hispanic Bishop of Costa Rica in 1968; the diocese became independent soon after. Puerto Rico: Extra-provincial diocese related to Province 9, USA. First missions established among West Indian migrant workers by the Bishop of Antigua in the 1860s. Following the Spanish-American War the island became an American dependency, and in 1901, a domestic missionary district of the Episcopal Church. Election of the first Puerto Rican bishop in 1964. Partly as a result of local agitation for either statehood or independence, the diocese sought and obtained autonomy from the

American church, but continues to work as closely as possible with that church and with the Spanish speaking Anglican neighbours. The island is 92% Roman Catholic. 15,000 Anglicans in 40 parishes served by 49 clergy, make up 0.4% of the population. Venezuela: Extra-provincial diocese of Province 9, USA. Chaplaincies for English speaking residents since 1830s. In the 1960s Canadian Anglicans started missionary work and Venezuela in 1976 became a diocese in the Province of the West Indies. Spanish speaking congregations were begun and in 1981 the first Venezuelan priest was ordained. In 1982 the diocese was transferred to the 9th Province of the Episcopal Church with extra-provincial status. There are approximately 1,000 Anglicans in 8 parishes served by 11 clergy.

594

1988
Human rights for those of homosexual orientation
Resolution 64, Lambeth Conference 1988.

This Conference:
1. Reaffirms the statement of the Lambeth Conference of 1978 on homosexuality, recognising the continuing need in the next decade for 'deep and dispassionate study of the question of homosexuality, which would take seriously both the teaching of Scripture and the results of scientific and medical research'.
2. Urges such study and reflection to take account of biological, genetic and psychological research being undertaken by other agencies, and the socio-cultural factors that lead to the different attitudes in the Provinces of our Communion.
3. Calls each Province to reassess, in the light of such study and because of our concern for human rights, its care and attitude towards persons of homosexual orientation.

595

1988
Homosexuality

A Statement of the Bench of bishops of the Church of Wales (1988).

We all need to be reminded of St Paul's words: 'All have sinned and fall short of the glory of God'.[1]

Sexual morality is only one aspect of personal moral integrity; personal moral integrity is only a part of a wider social moral order on which depends the well-being of the world. We are all of us caught up in a sinfulness which ranges from the pride and envy in the individual heart to racial conflict and the injustices of the international economic system. 'All have sinned': none of us is without fault. It ill befits any person to condemn another, particularly when we don't have to walk in the other's shoes. Rather, the Gospel calls us all to repentance, to support and up-build one another within the Body of Christ, and offers to each one of us forgiveness and healing according to our particular need.

596

1988
The way forward

Church in the Province of the West Indies: A statement on The Way Forward *by the House of Bishops.*

As a Province we have been searching for several years for a clearer understanding of what God is calling us to do. I believe that it is only as this understanding is owned by all concerned that we will be able to respond faithfully.

What is our new understanding? Indeed can we say that it is 'new' or is that understanding that which we have inherited, and as a result have been trying to put new wine in old bottles?

Certainly the Caribbean of the 70s is not the Caribbean of the late 80s and the chances are, it will not be the Caribbean of the 21st century. The Gospel imperatives are not the same when most

---

[1]   Romans 3.23

of us became bishops, and this is even more true when we were beginning as deacons in the Church of God. It even appears today, that the Gospel imperatives are more in conflict than ever before.

The world, and even the Church as institution, calls us to be successful. Yet our mandate has always been to the faithful, and the tendency in this regard often prevents us form losing our life for Christ's sake and the Gospel's, as the conservative forces rise to confront us from many a quarter.

There are threats to our survival as 'Church', and we are often drawn to adopt plans and policies in response to our instincts to 'protect'. Or in our desire to be successful, or to appear so, we rush into a situation which confirms Vidal Naipaul's observation that we are 'mimic men'.

In the economy of God we have been given many gifts and opportunities, and these lie in the very part of the world which is the locus for his mission and amongst the people we are called to serve his name. The question that we must constantly face is: How can we utilize the resources God has given us in the best possible ways for the furtherance of his mission in this area?

One of the greatest deterrents to the advance of the Gospel is the feeling of isolation. Therefore the Province must put in place, as a matter of priority, facilities for a closer relationship among the people of the Province for mutual support and strengthening in the faith. At the moment such a relationship is confined to the House of Bishops, and even so, the quality of the meetings needs to be improved. Their potential should be maximized and this can be accomplished, though not without imagination and commitment.

A view of our Caribbean situation today offers many opportunities for witnessing, caring, acting and growing. Unfortunately, such action seems to be confined to times of national disasters.

> Many of our people are unconscious of or do not know that many of their brothers and sisters are ill-fed, ill-housed, exploited, afraid.

> Many still live without the reality of the knowledge, love and redeeming power of Jesus Christ.

> The elderly are not only becoming more numerous, but more neglected, and spiralling inflation increases their poverty and robs their future of any hope.

The youth hang around street corners, stand-pipes, 'yards', often learning to become lawbreakers and falling prey to substance abuse as jobs are non-existent and they have ceased to have hope in 'the system'.

Decision makers are quite un-influenced for the most part by Christian teachings.

In the technological arena where life and death issues are dealt with, no longer are these understood as being in the hands of God.

Clergy and Laity alike, in large measure, are not excited about what mission is all about, and their concerns are often confined to balancing the budget.

This is not to say that this is the total picture. All of us can point to places, people and situations where the love of God is clearly manifested, and where redemption has taken place, bringing new life. But I have listed these to suggest that we need to develop mechanisms and strategies *together* that will help us to address these concerns more effectively, especially when we stand in the stream of catholic theology and practice, as well as being inheritors of the tradition of being the Church of and for the nation.

While the Province is by no means a picture of uniformity, comprising as it does of a number of different nations, varying social and economic patterns, differing political hues, nevertheless we need to be open to the possibilities of doing new things in new ways and not slip into the easy groove of 'our situation is different' and close the door to the transfer of insights, resources and solutions to problems.

It seems to me that in light of the need to be more open to the Holy Spirit and to each other, that we will need time to permit this to happen, and not only at the level of the House of Bishops.

It is a matter for concern that it is only at Partnership-in-Mission Consultations, that 'hard evidence' is produced from each diocese (and this is done at varying levels of success and openness). Once the consultation has ended, the material is put on the shelf. Thus a resource for joint participation is not maximised.

We need therefore, to be more faithful in what can be a source for strengthening our common life as well as trust in one another. We seem to infer by our treatment of the material, that our analyses are for our overseas partners and not primarily for ourselves as we engage in Partnership-in-Mission.

The way forward is not easy, for the faithful carrying out of our personal and corporate ministry in today's world is full of many unknowns. After all, this particular challenge has never been attempted before, given the personnel and the context in which we live. We will need to discuss, and move from disagreement to agreement and even back again, but we must try to succeed at being faithful and obedient to God. At times, we shall no doubt feel that the choices are too difficult, fraught with too many dangers, even too costly. Perhaps the rewards may be too few and too insignificant, but we must not let our vision be dimmed still less permit our faith in the risen Christ to be swamped by fear. In his name therefore, let us Go Forward.

Submitted for discussion, House of Bishops' meeting, Nassau, November 1988.

❖ Clive Trinidad & Tobago

597

1988
A new liturgy for Sri Lanka
(A Revision of the 1938 Ceylon Liturgy)
Bishop of Colombo, Letter to the editors, October 1989.

In 1927, fifty-four priests of the Church of Ceylon petitioned the then bishop, Mark Carpenter-Garnier, asking for a Liturgy to suit local needs. The result was the Ceylon Liturgy, experimentally authorised in March 1933 and generally sanctioned for alternate use in Sri Lanka on 1st March 1938. The Liturgical Committee said at that time 'We have aimed at preparing an Order of Service simple in character, liturgically correct, doctrinally sound, and satisfying our devotional instincts... We have freely borrowed from Eastern and Western sources...' 'Fifty years have passed since then and there has been much liturgical research and experimentation in the World Church, both Anglican and otherwise. The intention of the present Church of Ceylon Liturgical Commission during the last 20 years has been no different to their predecessors in the thirties, but in the process of the concept of indigenization promoted by bishops De Mel and De Soysa and Wickremasinghe, the revision of the 1938 Ceylon Liturgy had progressed from a stage of 'Adaptation' to one of 'Incarnation' as in Africa. That is to say that whilst the appeals to antiquity, flexibility and congregational involvement have been the dominant feature in the new revision, there is a strong emphasis on the worship of the Cosmic Christ, and a concern for a truly Sri Lankan way of worship — an expression of the socio-cultural and national aspirations of a newly emergent nation in a contemporary style of language. The intention of the compilers has been the provision of an authentic and original Liturgy in the context of today's Sri Lanka, allowing much variation and flexibility but keeping to a uniform sequential pattern in a contemporary style of language, so that there will be an end to the liturgical chaos now prevalent in Sunday Worship in Sri Lanka'. This revised Liturgy — now named 'A Liturgy for Sri Lanka 1988, the Holy Eucharist or the Lord's Supper' – caters to the needs and aspirations of the small Anglican Community in the Independent Republic of Sri Lanka in relating worship to our particular cultural context. It also encourages a greater participation of the people and their closer identification with what takes place in the Service. His Grace the Metropolitan and the Bishops of Colombo and Kurunegala have authorised the supplementary use of this Liturgy for experimental use in the Church of Ceylon in accordance with Canon 7 (a) of Chapter 23 of the Provincial Constitution.

598

1988
The (Anglican) Council of Churches of East Asia

Who are the Anglicans?, ed. Charles Long, prepared for the Lambeth Conference, 1988 (Ohio, 1988), p. 46.

Pending the establishment of new Provinces, the Council serves as a link between the churches and dioceses in Burma (5 dioceses), the Philippines (4 dioceses), Korea (3 dioceses), Hong Kong and Macao, Kuching (Borneo), Sabah, Singapore, Taiwan and West Malaysia. Burma is an independent Province, Taiwan and the Philippine Episcopal Church are part of Province 8, USA, and the rest are extra-provincial dioceses under the Archbishop of

Canterbury. The Philippine Independent Church and the Anglican Church of Australia are also members of the Council. The Episcopal Church in Korea: Founded by USPG missionaries within the last century, the Church now includes an estimated 53,000 members in 3 dioceses and more than 70 congregations, all presently in South Korea. It is a minority church in a traditionally Buddhist country with a rapidly growing Christian population of many denominations, mainly Presbyterian and Methodist. Roman Catholics also claim 1,400,000 members or about 4% of the population. Hong Kong and Macao, established in 1843, once included most of South China, within the Anglican Church in China (Chung Hua Sheng Kung Hui). The diocese was subdivided during and after World War II. More than 50 clergy minister to 29,000 members. The diocese has maintained a large system of schools and social service centers and has supplied many leaders to Chinese communities in other countries. Taiwan. Before World War II there were congregations of Japanese Anglicans on the island. Work was begun again in 1949 under the Bishop of Hawaii in response to the need for pastoral care of Chinese Anglicans who had left the mainland. It became an independent diocese in 1965 and now has 23 clergy and more than 1,000 members.

Singapore. Anglican chaplaincy from 1826. Society for the Propagation of the Gospel missionaries from 1856. Diocese was founded in 1909. It has served as a centre for theological training and for evangelism among Malaysian and other peoples of the region. West Malaysia (1970) and Kuching and Sabah (1962) in North Borneo, were established to strengthen the work of evangelism in predominantly Muslim areas and among adherents of indigenous religions. Sabah, for example, now includes 15,000 Anglicans in 19 parishes with 21 clergy.

599

1988
The way forward in Brazil

The Episcopal Church of Brazil, Confelider 88, statement of meeting of the bishops, with sixty priests (60% of the whole body) and about eighty lay persons in Porto Alegre in October 1988.

Presentation:

In general terms, the document of Confelider shows with great emphasis the weak or negative aspects of the Episcopal Church of Brazil. The Church, meeting together in Porto Alegre was ready to face courageously her weaknesses and mistakes looking for solutions and proposals. This should be understood as a sign of maturity of the Church. The relationship between the questions raised and the proposals and recommendations, indicates the possibility of vitalizing the Church, pointing with conviction to the real reason for commemorating the 100 years of the Episcopal Church of Brazil....

Important questions such as social problems of the cities and rural communities were included; nevertheless, there was a notable absence of a clear and objective position of the Episcopal Church of Brazil in favour of suffering people and the necessity of the Church to place evangelization as its essential task. Even though pessimism was predominant there was hope and the desire that this hope not be frustrated by authoritarianism. The group studies showed up some of the urgent necessities of the Episcopal Church of Brazil in relation to its missionary task; the valuing of the ministry of all Christians, the strengthening of local communities, solid teaching, work through specific areas of pastoral concern which lead to a commitment in action in society.

Mission:

1. There is a necessity in the Episcopal Church of Brazil to awaken the laity to assume with the clergy the whole gamut of ministry, so that there is not a concentration of these ministries only in the clergy. Evangelization is principally the work of all and can not be accomplished by the clergy alone. Only in this way will our missionary action be relevant....

3. We live on a continent marked by the presence of the poor, marginalized by our socio-economic and political model. Brazil is a country with a population predominated by youth. In this context and understanding the practice already in some dioceses is to find space and official recognition for lay ministry that can respond to specific areas of pastoral concern (poor pregnant women, youth, people without land, minorities and others).

4. The Church is absent in the effective work in our small communities, since prayer alone is not enough, it is necessary to roll up our sleeves and to go forth in service.

5. Considering the institutions that the Episcopal Church of Brazil has, it should be stressed that many of them were created without Church involvement and planning. Therefore, these do not have an educational and social action policy which express the guide-lines of the Episcopal Church of Brazil for her activities.

6. These institutions, at times, show themselves to be far from reality; it is important and necessary to have people prepared to direct them, incorporating the communities in the process of development of the same.

Recommendations:

1. Capacitate or train the non-stipendiary lay worker to develop his ministry in the local community.

2. To educate the new generations of clergy theologically to exercise their ministry with the people and not for the people (paternalistic model).

3. Each local community stimulate and support financially the formation of the laity that wish to develop specific ministries.

4. To organize and stimulate new forms of communities (urban and rural community centres).

5. Liturgy is an activity for 24 hours a day because it cannot stop at the door of the Church. As a means of liturgical renewal, we suggest that each parish have a liturgical team.

600

1989
A Province takes stock

Church of the Province of Central Africa, from the Provincial Secretary.

The Church of the Province of Central Africa was founded in 1955. It comprises ten dioceses in four countries, viz; Botswana, Malawi, Zambia and Zimbabwe, covering a total area of 718,940 square miles. There are over half a million (590,000) Anglicans in the Province. The Diocese of Botswana was formed in 1972. Previously it had been divided into two, the Southern part belonging to the Diocese of Kimberley and Kuruman (Church of the Province of Southern Africa) and the northern part belonging to the diocese of Matebeleland (Church of the Province of Central

Africa). The first Bishop was the Rt. Revd. Shannon Mallory, who resigned in 1978. The present Bishop, Dr. Khotso W.P. Makhulu was elected in 1979 and is also the Archbishop and Metropolitan of the Province of Central Africa. Dr. Robert Runcie, the first Archbishop of Canterbury to visit the country since Independence in 1966, in a Sermon preached at a Pontifical Eucharist said; 'A young Church in a young country full of young people. That is the Anglican Church in Botswana.... I pray that you trust God who calls you to do great things for him'.[1] The young Church is faced with an acute shortage of priests and one of its major concerns is to promote vocations and develop training for the ministry. Other concerns are in Stewardship and Evangelism.

The country was until recently, one of the twenty poorest Nations in the World. This has however, changed after the discovery of diamonds and other minerals. It can now boast of having one of the fastest growing economies in the world, and among the richest in Africa. Malawi is mainly an agricultural country. It has two Dioceses headed by the Rt. Revd. Benson N. Aipa, Bishop of Southern Malawi, and the Rt. Revd. N. Nyanja, Bishop of Lake Malawi. The Pioneers of these Dioceses were William Johnson and Charles Johnson. The latter died 12 years after their arrival in 1882. For 46 years, William Johnson worked from Likoma Island on Lake Nyasa, establishing Missions and spreading the gospel. The Church in Malawi is growing at a rapid pace, and there are plans to establish a suffragan see at Mzuzu in the Diocese of Lake Malawi. As part of its mission the church is involved in assisting refugees from Mozambique. Zambia comprises three Dioceses, Lusaka, Central Zambia and Northern Zambia. The bishops are Stephen Mumba, Clement Shaba and Bernard Malango, respectively. Southern Zambia was divided into three Dioceses in 1970. However, the new Dioceses' bishopric Endowment Fund was inadequately endowed. The Dioceses are still trying to build up their bishopric Endowment Fund. Much of the work of the three Dioceses is co-ordinated by the Zambia Anglican Council. It also oversees the work of Inter-diocesan Institutions such as St Francis Hospital, Katete, and St John's Seminary at Kitwe.

The history of the Church in Zimbabwe dates back to 1811 when Bishop Knight Bruce of Bloemfontein journeyed to create the

---

[1]   Archbishop of Canterbury's Sermon at Pontifical Eucharist, Cathedral of the Holy Cross, Botswana; 4 June, 1989.

Diocese of Mashonaland. The Diocese of Matebeleland was formed in 1953. In 1981 the Diocese of Manicaland and the Lundi were created. Provincial Synod in 1986 approved a motion to change the name of the Diocese of Mashonaland to Harare. A recent development among the four Dioceses is the proposed establishment of an inter-Diocesan College to be based in Harare for the training of clergy. The Province is making preparations towards holding a Partners in Mission Consultation in the near future.

601

1989
An Archbishop's charge to the Provincial Synod

Church of the Province of Central Africa, September 1989 — Harare Zimbabwe.

My brothers and sisters in our Lord Jesus Christ. I welcome you to this session of Provincial Synod.... We are living in a complex world, one that is dominated by powerful image builders, trendsetters and outright propagandists. They all serve their causes, whether it be selling a new product, person, ideology or lobbying for a campaign. These are the realities of our times and we can no longer live as innocents, gullible enough to swallow any old thing. Our calling as Christians demands that we live as witnesses in a divided world. Come, let us learn the gospel imperatives which will guide us through the maze of conflicting values and interests. It will no longer do simply to take sides because you have been sold a point of view on a divisive issue. The integrity of the household of God and the basic clarity about what is right or wrong must come to be reflected in our decision making.... May we rediscover the ability of speaking the truth in love out of reverence for Christ.... Pray for the church at this challenging time, that the ensuing decade will provide for us an opportunity for proclamation and service, transformation and fidelity to the glory of the triune God.

602

1989

Church union in Sri Lanka

Bishop of Colombo, letter to the Editors, October 1989.

The origin of Church Union in Sri Lanka could be traced as far back as 1934 when the first Conference of Church Leaders in Sri Lanka (then Ceylon) was held to discuss the problems relating to Church Union. The invitation to the Churches in Ceylon to explore the possibility of opening negotiations for Church Union was issued by the Ceylon Provincial Synod of the Methodist Church in February 1940 and, with the acceptance of the invitation by the Churches, there was set up in November 1940 the Joint Committee on Church Union. By 1946 the Negotiating Committee produced an Interim Report. To be very brief, by 1955 the Third Revised Edition of the Scheme was issued. By 1970 all the Diocesan Councils in the Province of India, Pakistan, Burma and Ceylon reported in favour of the Scheme and the General Council gave the Scheme its final approval, adopted it as a sufficient basis of union, and gave permission to the Dioceses of Colombo and Kurunegala to enter the Church of Lanka. In 1971 the Colombo Diocesan Council resolved to enter into union on the basis of this Scheme, provided that all the other negotiating Churches decide to enter the Scheme of Union simultaneously. In 1975 the Colombo Diocesan Council approved a draft bill to be presented to the national legislature. After nearly 38 years of negotiations, Church Union was to become a reality. Advent 1972 was fixed for the inauguration of the United Church. However, the United Church did not materialise due to litigation. The subject of Church Union had thereafter been relegated to the background for some years in each of our denominations. However, under God, this subject has been revived once more by each and every denomination, as well as by the National Christian Council, and thus the Heads of the various denominations met and made various decisions. The Heads of the various denominations are convinced that we have no message to give to our nation in its hour of crisis, unless we ourselves have experienced the healing, reconciling power of Christ within our own body. We recall to mind the words of the famous German pagan philosopher, Nietzsche, who said once 'Show me that you are redeemed, and then I will believe in your Redeemer'.

The people of our country may well say to the denominations 'Show us that you are united, and we will think in terms of a United Sri Lanka'. It thus behoves the various denominations to ponder seriously on our dividedness and to realise how ineffective we are to speak the word to our nation in this hour of crisis. Secondly, our dividedness makes us weak and ineffective in the proclamation of the Gospel. In a world of escalating costs and falling interests, the denominations are frittering away the limited resources given to us in the mercy of God by attempting to maintain our several Churches in a single area for the well being of a few Christian people. This is a criminal waste of resources given to us by God, to whom we are accountable. Our dividedness will, therefore, result in our death; or at least in our ineffectiveness as a Christian Community. It has been said that 'God can do much more with a mature minority than with an immature majority'. When we become one in Christ, we may still be a minority in our land, but we will be a mature minority whom God can use mightily. Thirdly, it is the Will of God that we be one in Him. We all know this to be the truth, enshrined in Scripture. Yet we do not live by it. It is the earnest expectation of the Heads of our several denominations that we begin to take meaningful steps towards this Unity in Christ. In the Diocese of Colombo I have appointed a Church Union Select Committee to study and advise me on steps to be taken. Every effort is being made to get the study of the Scheme to percolate down to the members of the pew. We are willing to be used by God in any way He chooses towards the consummation of the hope expressed by Our Lord 'That they all may be one'. We request you, dear reader, to uphold us in your prayers.

With Christian greetings.

603

1989
The first woman bishop in the Anglican Communion

Letter from the Presiding Bishop of the Episcopal Church in the United States of America, 8 February, 1989.

Greetings in our Lord Jesus Christ. As I noted in my letter to you of September 27th, the Revd. Barbara C. Harris has been elected

Bishop-Suffragan of the Diocese of Massachusetts. The required canonical process following her election has now been fulfilled, in that the election has been consented to by the majority of Diocesan Standing Committees and bishops having jurisdiction. I will ordain her to the episcopate on February 11th in Boston. I ask your prayers for the Bishop-elect, for the Diocese of Massachusetts and its Bishop, the Rt. Revd. David E. Johnson, and for The Episcopal Church and Anglican Communion. For twelve years, our Church has experienced the gifts of women in the priesthood. It is our hope, prayer, and clear expectation that we will have a similar experience with women in the episcopate. We believe that the incorporation of women in the catholic episcopate and priesthood as the Anglican Communion has received it, enhances the wholeness and the mission of the Church. I pray that their inclusion will come to be seen as a gift to the Church catholic and a contribution toward a deeper understanding of holy orders. The Episcopal Church seeks to maintain and develop the highest possible degree of communion with partner Churches. We have taken every reasonable step. Within our own Church we have sought pastoral provisions for those who cannot accept women in the episcopate. Within the Anglican Communion the Archbishop of Canterbury has appointed a commission[1] to prepare guidelines to enable Provinces which differ in this issue to live together in one Communion. Ecumenically we have consulted with the several partner churches through official dialogues. We rejoice in the growth of communion in recent years with Orthodox, Roman Catholic, Lutheran, and Protestant Churches. Yet the road to Christian unity is not a straight line. The question of women's ordination, in the form in which it is put today, is a new one, and is still in an early stage of reflection and discussion among the churches. Given the complexity of the process which must take place, discussion will be difficult and lengthy. An essential part of the process will be the experience of a more active participation by women in the life and mission of the Christian community. Our ecumenical dialogues will be driven to a deeper theological seriousness as a result of the ordination of women to the episcopate. In dialogues with Churches that maintain the historic

---

[1]　The Eames Commission

episcopate we should concentrate on the serious theological reasons for opening the historic episcopate to women. In dialogues with Churches that do not claim to have the historic episcopate we should show how teaching about the catholic episcopate is compatible with the ordination of women. At this moment, our action brings rejoicing to some and anguish to others. The Lambeth Conference spoke directly to this situation when it resolved, 'The Church needs to exercise sensitivity, patience and pastoral care toward all concerned.' We remember too, that within the holy catholic and apostolic Church some suffer pain because women are excluded from the episcopate and priesthood, and others suffer pain because they see ordination of women as a violation of God's will. I ask that we enter into one another's pain so that the fellowship of suffering may become, together with the fellowship of rejoicing, a sign of our deeper communion and a witness to the healing of the nations. Faithfully yours in Christ,

✠ Edmond L. Browning, President Bishop

604

1989
The Prayer Book

An Anglican Prayer Book, 1989, Church of the Province of Southern Africa.

Preface

The two Offices of Morning and Evening Prayer in their present form evolved from Cranmer's forms in the sixteenth century Book of Common Prayer, and behind that from the Offices used in monasteries from as early as the fourth century A.D. But from the very beginning the Church had its times of prayer, whether for groups of Christians or for individual disciples. In this it followed the example of our Lord, who himself grew up within the Jewish tradition of prayer. We read in the Acts of the Apostles that the disciples came together at the third hour;[1] Peter went up on the

---

[1]   Acts 2.1–15

housetop to pray at the sixth hour;[2] Peter and John went to the temple at the ninth hour;[3] and late at night Paul and Silas were praying and singing God's praises.[4] Behind their practice lies what our Lord did.[5] His times of prayer to his Father gave his life a foundation of prayer, so that it may be said that his whole life was one of prayer. When we use these Offices we share in a form of prayer which is similar to that used by Christians throughout the world, and in very varied situations. They are used for large, corporate gatherings, often for a Sunday service when the Eucharist is not celebrated. They are used by religious communities, by small groups of Christians meeting together and by individuals on their own. Among these are the clergy, whose joyful obligation it is to pray with these Offices twice a day; for some of them the Eucharist takes the place of one of the Offices. There are also many lay Christians for whom the Offices are a means of bringing order to their prayer and to their life. By praying with these Offices, the individual Christian shares in the prayer of the whole Church, and so in the prayer of Christ. When we use these Offices of Morning and Evening Prayer, we are, first of all, offering worship, praise and thanksgiving to God the Holy Trinity, and at many points in these services we come back to this expression of our love for God. In the holy Scriptures we receive the word of God, meditating on it in all its variety, as it challenges, nourishes, and always reminds us of our Lord Jesus Christ, the Word made flesh. One of the principal parts of the Offices is the saying of the Psalms, the songs of God's people which tell of his action in the history of salvation. Even though they belong to the Old Testament and contain some difficult sections, they bring us back again and again to the infinite variety of God's relationship with his creatures. Christ himself knew the Psalms well and made them his own. As we use them we identify with him in his life of prayer. Throughout these Offices we seek God's face. We acknowledge our need for his grace and guidance on our earthly pilgrimage. The Offices feed our personal prayers, and they strengthen our participation in the holy Eucharist. Morning and Evening Prayer should be seen as the

---

2   Acts 10.9

3   Acts 3.1

4   Acts 16.25

5   Luke 3.21–22; 6.12; 11.1; Matthew 14.19 and 23; Mark 1.35; etc.

prayer of the Church for the whole world, both when we are praying specifically for others and in all the activities which make up the Offices. In this way the Church is sharing in the eternal prayer of Christ to his Father in the Spirit on behalf of this disordered and needy world. When the Church prays it is united with Christ who is the Way to the Father, and it is the Holy Spirit who prays in us, by helping us in our weakness[6] and enabling us to cry 'Abba, Father'.[7] So when we pray, corporately or individually, we share in the life of God the Holy Trinity, and we express our very nature as the community of the Church, and as human beings created in God's image. When God created the world, he brought order out of chaos, and the ordered prayer life of the Christian community should be a small reflection of the order which is God's purpose for the world.

605

1989
Conditional and emergency baptism

The Church in the Province of the West Indies, Liturgical Texts.

Cf. nos. 495, 554.

If there is a reasonable doubt that a person has been baptized with water, 'In the name of the Father, and of the Son, and of the Holy Spirit,' the person is baptized in the usual manner, but this form of words is used.

If you are not already baptized, N, I baptize you in the name of the Father, and of the Son, and of the Holy Spirit.

AMEN

Emergency baptism

In case of emergency, any person present may administer baptism according to the following form.

Using the given name of the one to be baptized (if known), pour water on him or her, saying:

---

6   Romans 8.26
7   Romans 8.15

I baptize you in the name of the Father, and of the Son, and of the Holy Spirit.

AMEN.

The Lord's Prayer is then said.
Other prayers, such as the following, may be added.

Heavenly Father, we thank you that by water and the Holy Spirit you have bestowed upon this your servant the forgiveness of sin and have raised him/her to the new life of grace. Strengthen him/her, O Lord, with your presence, enfold him/her in the arms of your mercy, and keep him/her safe for ever.
AMEN

The person who administers emergency baptism should inform the priest of the appropriate parish, so that the baptism may be properly registered.
If the baptized person recovers, the baptism shall be recognized at a public celebration of the sacrament. The person baptized under emergency conditions and his or her sponsors shall take part in all parts of the baptismal liturgy, except for the baptism in water itself.

606

1989
Universal Primacy

The Archbishop of Canterbury's address to the General Synod of the Church of England, November 1989, on his visit to the Pope in September–October 1989.

Cf. nos. 279, 369, 530.

We also touched on my words about an 'ecumenical primacy' for the Universal Church. This is a new thing for the Pope to consider. It was also raised during his recent visit to Scandinavia by the Lutheran bishops. He was fascinated that other Christians should be looking to the Bishop of Rome for his ecumenical leadership. It must be for ARCIC[1] to continue to explore how future unity can best be served by what I call the recovery of an earlier Primacy. I was looking for a Primacy to serve mission and unity.

---

[1]   The Anglican-Roman Catholic International Commission

AFTERWORD
ARCHBISHOP OF CANTERBURY 1991–

One of the aims of *The Anglican Tradition* is to show the coherence of Anglicanism with mainstream Christianity and the 'catholicity' of its faith.

As the millennium draws to a close, with all its opportunities for sharing faith, we as Anglicans need to reaffirm our commitment to this historic deposit of faith and perhaps to rediscover the richness of our tradition. I believe that as we do so, we shall be aware of a growing convergence in God's truth with other Christians as we together seek to explore with gratitude that 'Faith once delivered to the saints'.

✣ George Carey
Archbishop of Canterbury, 1991–

October 1990.

INDEX OF SCRIPTURAL REFERENCES

Numbers refer to documents

GENERAL INDEX

Numbers refer to documents